6

7

8

9

6. Woman dancer of Bali, Indonesia
7. Hill country farmer of Java, Indonesia
8. Cantonese man from south China coast
9. Korean man of southern Korea in old costume
10. Japanese woman of southern Japan in modified
    native dress

10

ASIA

EAST by SOUTH

ASIA
EAST by SOUTH
A Cultural Geography

J. E. SPENCER
Professor of Geography
University of California
Los Angeles

JOHN WILEY & SONS, INC.
NEW YORK   LONDON

To

CHARLES A. SPENCER

who excited in his small son a perennial curiosity
about people and places

JONATHAN A. GARST

who motivated a critical questioning
of man and the earth

CARL O. SAUER

who pointed up a philosophy of
human culture and environment

Preface

This volume is concerned with cultural geography in its widest interpretation, but perhaps it ought to be labeled a preliminary study. Since man and culture always operate in a particular setting, an orientation to the physical environment is necessary. I have presented such an orientation in the opening chapters, and it naturally is both selective and somewhat subjective, since it tries to cover a large subject briefly. The physical environment having been dealt with, attention will range widely over many of the elements of the cultural environment. This, also, is selective and necessarily less complete than many will desire. Though incomplete in many respects, I have tried to bear in mind, in writing this study, that, if the geographic interpretation of man and nature in the Orient is going to be useful both to the student of geography and to his non-geographer colleagues, it must range beyond matters of crop distribution, settlement forms, and the lines of transport.

Most of the materials with which the cultural geographer must deal are tangible data concerning material culture which can be applied to questions of regional distribution and analysis of the current landscape. Beyond this, however, there are important but less tangible bodies of data that are important to an understanding of the ways of man in the landscape. However one may feel able to limit himself to tangible topics in writing of the geography of selected portions of North America, the cultural geographer cannot shirk dealing with many of these intangible subjects in writing of the Orient. There can be no finite limit placed upon the variety of data with which the regional cultural geographer must deal in his effort to depict the operation of man in his chosen landscape. Regional cultural geography is the outcome of culture groups living in, and doing things to, a particular portion of the earth. It seems to me that it is up to the cultural geographer not only to describe that particular landscape, but to describe the processes by which it came to be in the shape that it is today.

This volume is a contribution to a more complete understanding of the Orient. It has many faults, and my own list already is long, though I have just completed the last chapter. There is much obscured ground in the cultural geography of the Orient. In some important allied fields, scholars have not yet completed or agreed upon a common statement of the basic facts. In some countries there are better data than in others. At times I have but imperfectly achieved my own aims. My personal contact with the lands of the Orient is uneven and less complete than it should be for a task of this sort. It was with humility that the task was commenced some fifteen years ago, a humility that has steadily increased as the questions "where?", "what?", "who?", "how?", and "why?" kept recurring, only to remain often unanswered. I have felt unable to deal with all of Asia, and I know that many matters are dealt with almost casually. Respect for the purchaser's pocketbook, and my own limited knowledge, both are to blame for the inadequacies of the volume.

There are many who share in the growth of this book. Students in my classes over some years have repeatedly asked questions that provoked some of the content, and some of my seminar students have shared in the evolution of ideas. My wife, Kathryn, and daughter, Patricia, have helped in too many ways to list. Richard A. Newsham helped solve the early problem of maps. William L. Thomas, Jr., contributed the physiographic diagrams, and Don Wilbur drew all other maps. Walter Glazer provided the end-paper sketches. Marianne Blount performed numerous chores, and Fred Neurath managed the typing and proof reading of the manuscript. Karl J. Pelzer critically read the whole manuscript, some of it twice, made a host of excellent suggestions, and helped me to avoid numerous errors, but he cannot be held accountable for the imperfections that remain. The University of California repeatedly assisted with research grants, and the Institute of Pacific Relations was instrumental in enabling me to study the Philippines at first hand. The people of China paid my salary as a civil servant for some years, and the U. S. Army ordered me hither and yon, sometimes over territory I had not seen before. None of these helpful people and agencies are responsible, of course, for the errors and shortcomings of the volume.

J. E. SPENCER

Department of Geography
University of California
Los Angeles, California
May, 1954

Contents

Contents

PART 3: FOR USE IN REFERENCE

Introductory: On the Geography of Asia

The southern and eastern portions of Asia often are placed together under the terms the Orient or the East, and are placed in contrast to the Occident or the West. There is a unity of human life here that sets the territory apart from Siberia and from southwestern Asia. The relations of the one lie chiefly with eastern Europe, and those of the other lie chiefly with Arabia and the eastern Mediterranean. It is with these lands and peoples of the Orient that this volume is concerned.

HOE CULTURE AS A SYSTEM

There are more farmers in the Orient than in the rest of the world combined. Agriculture is the most widespread occupational activity of all human callings in the East. And the terraced ricefield with reflections flashing from its liquid surface is the most distinctive picture of the Orient. Among the most easily observed characteristics of southern and eastern Asia are its native agricultural systems. These patterns of agriculture have often been described under the general term hoe culture or garden culture. Fundamentally hoe culture is an agriculture of small fields, of much detailed hand labor on the part of the cultivator, of relatively few mechanical aids to cultivation, and of relatively small numbers of draft animals per farm unit. It was at one time primarily a subsistence agriculture, concerned with food supply and only in minor proportions interested in a product for sale in a commercial market. Rice is its primary food crop, giving way to some other food plant only when water supply fails, soils will not allow rice cultivation, or local climatic factors other than precipitation make rice impossible. It is a crop of flooded fields, the only great crop so grown. This predominance of flooded fields causes the rest of the agricultural pattern to be fitted rather closely to the landscape and the planting season in order to secure a harvest.

As a crop of small field units rice produces a distinctive landscape which varies considerably in appearance in the course of the year. Where rice, itself, is not the backbone of the crop series throughout the Orient one still finds the basic features of hoe culture, though in a few regions variations have been introduced in recent centuries. That hoe culture is at least partially independent of rice is clear from the fact that rice has not always been cultivated everywhere throughout the realm. Detailed hand labor, with the very simplest of tools, and close-knit social organization are more diagnostic of oriental agriculture than is any one crop. Small fields have long been effective in forestalling the evolution of mechanical aids to cultivation. And the very detail with which cultivation is carried on reaches out beyond agriculture into many other features of the several cultures to make its print upon oriental civilization.

Around the mainland margins of the Orient the contrast between sedentary garden culture and the culture of the pastoral nomad naturally is very great. The location of the Tibetan Plateau limits the zone of contact between the pastoral nomad and the garden cultivator. Such a zone is best exemplified in Mongolia where the fixed Chinese dwelling, the cultivated field, the slow-moving cart or wheelbarrow, and the tall sorghum known as kaoliang push against the movable felt yurt home, the grass turf, the mobile horseman, and the flocks of animals. This contrast has long been expressed in conflict, with one or another of the two patterns of landscape use on the offensive against the other through the historic barbarian invasions of China or the ruthless push of the Chinese colonist into the grazing lands of Mongolia. The contrast again shows up in Baluchistan and parts of northwest India.

The contrast between hoe culture and the mechanized agriculture of the Occident as shown in the United States may be measured in many ways. The beautiful panorama of small terraced fields reflecting in their thin water cover the clouds piled up on the horizon is a world far removed from the American rolling prairie wheat field in which one can sight a harvester swath for miles across a single field. The grain elevator on the midwestern plains past which thunders a freight train made up of refrigerator cars carrying green vegetables from California cannot be matched anywhere in the Orient. Nor can the Szechwanese professional porter, balancing two baskets of green vegetables or hand-winnowed grain from his shoulder pole, and shuffling five miles to the nearest village, be matched in our own realm.

Another contrast that must be made is that of native hoe culture as against the modern tropical plantation. The latter has been transferred to the Orient within the last two centuries. It now exists side by side with native cultivation, and it depends markedly on a voluminous labor force working with relatively few tools. The plantation, however, is an impersonal corporate thing, shipping both its crop and its profit out of the Orient to fatten the economy and the purse of the Occident. As such it, too, has had a strong impact on the Orient, not always for the worse. Far removed from hoe culture in certain of its expressions it nevertheless has helped maintain hoe culture as the agricultural system of the native population.

Lastly, this intense cultivation of the soil has long promoted a higher concentration of population than most other systems of agriculture. Once effectively organized, its very nature required a larger population to operate it well, which in turn made it more able to support a dense population. This circle of operation has had its checks and balances, just as it has had its extra stimulation from time to time. In simple comparisons, however, this region of hoe culture has become the most populous portion of the earth. But hoe culture has now about reached its maximum limits of support, and many regions no longer are able to feed themselves.

ON EUROPE, ASIA, AND EURASIA

What are the regional limits of hoe culture in this part of the world? Hoe culture obviously is not peculiar to the Orient alone, but in Asia there are regional limits. To answer this we must first examine the arrangement of divisions on the earth's largest land mass. For many decades it has been the custom to divide the world into a fixed number of continents. Occasionally there was some doubt whether Australia should be given continental status or termed an island. Seldom, however, was even a thought given to questioning the right of Europe to be termed a continent. As the center of "the known world" and the home of "the great explorers" Europe naturally rated a place among the premier land masses, even though Europe is but a series of peninsulas on the continent of Eurasia. At the same time the larger half of the great land mass also had to be termed a separate continent. Geographers, in making up statements about places and peoples, normally have maintained this terminology, even though recently some have declared that such a division has no validity. The organization of occidental public instruction, from the grade school to the university, has favored the maintenance of the single arbitrary line of demarcation across the largest continent on our globe. From the European end it has made some sense in the past, but from the Asiatic viewpoint, the very bulk of the territory has prevented effective presentation and instruction alike.

In my experience the conventional continent of Asia is valid neither as a continent nor as a unit of geographic presentation. Few human beings, certainly not including the writer, are able in one lifetime to learn sufficient about the vast area and the widely diversified cultures to justify covering the whole territory within the covers of a single volume. Included are nearly one third of the total land mass of our globe and over one half the human inhabitants of our earth. Those two facts alone are sufficient to warrant making an effort to find some basis for further limiting the scope of a single volume in the field of geography.

Occasionally a simple climatic division of Eurasia has been made, three segments resulting. These are the dry lands of southwest and central Asia, the cool humid lands of north and northwest Eurasia, and the hot humid lands of south and eastern Asia. The factor of climate as such is hardly a justified criterion, but it does happen to agree with one set of broad cultural units, a fact which lends some validity to the choice. Were one making this selection as of seventeenth-century historical geography it could work very well, except that Siberia might well go by default. In the twentieth century the world has changed sufficiently to suggest another approach to the problem, that of cultural-economic realms. Western Europe has moved in one direction, culturally, to tie itself to many outlying portions of the globe, while Slavic Europe has moved in another, more completely occupying the great land area of northern Eurasia. The Soviet realm, of this generation, can form as convenient and full-sized a unit of study for the geographer as for the political economist. The portion of Asia variably called the East, the Orient, Monsoon Asia, and other similar terms, long has been a significant realm from several points of judgment. One must grant, at the outset, that there is no completely satisfactory way to divide up portions of the world for detailed study. A threefold division of the one great continent of Eurasia provides a practical plan for handling most of the regions, cultures, economic and political statistics out of which the student generally must build his own organized interpretation of the patterns of our earth.

It is with three convictions that this volume has set for itself the limits of Monsoon Asia. First, that area does hang together decently, whether from the criteria of geomorphology, climate, folk psychology, culture history, or modern political economy. Second, the area does not include much territory or many peoples that belong predominantly in another zone or realm. Third and perhaps most important of all, it is the largest possible portion of Eurasia with which I feel in any degree capable of dealing in my lifetime. If no other justification stands scrutiny, this last must bear the full burden.

THE ORIENT AND THE OCCIDENT

In occidental literature there has been no common agreement regarding the use of the several terms: East, Far East, Middle East, Orient, Malaysia, Indonesia, Monsoon Asia, and others. With some the Orient begins at the Strait of Gibraltar if one faces the African shore. With others only those lands fronting on the Pacific are the Orient. To some India is in the Far East; to others it is the last unit of the Middle East. Monsoon Asia is a term employed by many to refer to the territory from northwestern India around the seashores to the islands north of Japan, but excluding Tibet and Chinese Turkestan. The countries that make up this great section of the earth have many things in common and should have one recognized term to cover them. To coin, here, a new term would only further complicate the problem. Therefore, in this volume the two terms Monsoon Asia and Orient will be used as synonyms to refer to any portion of the whole realm being discussed.

To further define terms clearly: Far East will apply to those lands fronting on the Pacific Ocean, i.e., excluding Burma, India, Tibet, and Central Asia. Southern Asia will be used for mainland southeast Asia: Malaya, Indochina, Thailand, Burma, and India. The general term the East will be used only for a most general poetic contrast with the West. Malaysia will refer to Malaya and the main portion of the Indies west of New Guinea; Indonesia and Indies will be synonyms pertaining to all the islands south of the Philippines, and not just to the Dutch territories. The latter will be specifically designated either the Dutch Indies or the Republic of Indonesia. The name Indochina is satisfactory when applied to one country only, but it is confusing when also applied to the southeastern peninsula of the mainland, and will not be so used. Purely for convenience one new term is thrust upon the reader: Burmo-Malaya will refer to the peninsular mainland comprising Burma, Thailand, Indochina, and British Malaya.

The contrast between the oriental and occidental worlds is not as profound as implied in the usually quoted first line of Kipling's famous poem "The Ballad of the East and West." Nevertheless, there is a very real difference in psychology, in outlook, in national aspirations, and in the judgment of group happiness between the several cultures of the Orient and those of the Occident. It is a commonplace to say that the West, particularly the Anglo-American West, rushes at life with a speed that is nowhere matched in the Orient. The slower tempo of the oriental, however, is projected into much more than his failure to rush from a committee meeting to a bridge luncheon to a pink tea party on a precise timing schedule. Fewer and simpler amusements and diversions are needed to fill a life, and there is no worry as to how to fill the random idle hour. The average expectancy of life is less, and the restless concern with the eternal will-o'-the-wisp progress is notably lacking. Tolerance, whether it be of transport, of his fellows' accomplishments, or of the tendencies to reform old institutions of society is characteristic of the Orient. It is customary to think of the Orient as the unchanging land of mysticism, of strange customs, of queerly devious psychology which cannot possibly be fathomed by an occidental, a custom often quite overdone. A long list of these differences could be compiled to indicate the numerous ways in which some one of the oriental peoples differs from some one of the occidental peoples.

It is necessary to point out that one cannot speak of the Orient as though it were an area of completely homogeneous culture in which every individual is like every other. Even as the Occident recognizes differences in temperament between Englishmen, Frenchmen, Germans, and Americans, so in the Orient one must recognize that the Indian, the Burmese, the Japanese, and the Filipino occupy separate positions within the larger thing called oriental culture. Further one must recognize that cultures change and that what may have been true of any oriental a century ago may well have been altered by the impact of time and alien cultures. It is not all clear how great is going to be the change in group culture or group psychology in any single country within the next century, or just what the direction of change will be, but changes are inevitable. Perhaps in one country there may be some rather fundamental changes coming about at present whereas in another the changes will be but superficial. Perhaps in a third country the acceptance of new customs, new tools, and new goods will expand the existing culture in very marked fashion without fundamentally altering the oriental psychology of her people. Whatever these changes may add up to, there is no section of the Orient that has not been affected by four and a half centuries of contact with the Occident, even as every section of the Occident has in some way been affected by that same contact with the Orient. Whatever comparison may be made of oriental and occidental, there can be no question that the Orient is undergoing some change with respect to what the several peoples expect of life. In some countries this is a relatively peaceful process, whereas in others it has been, and will continue to be, a militant and violent process that will continue until the ends are won. Unfortunately in some countries there is no unanimity of opinion on just what the ends may be. It is not enough to describe the Orient as it was yesterday or is today. If we are at all concerned with our own future we must have concern with where the Orient is going tomorrow.

THE QUESTION OF ISOLATION

It has been the occidental fashion in dealing with the eastern portion of the Eurasian continent to make much of the point of isolation of those far corners in trying to explain why the mystic Orient is as it is. This seems only half an issue, for, if the orientals were so long isolated from the western end of the great continent, perhaps it is the West that was isolated overlong from the East. The fact is that for most of the early period of human history the two ends of the continent, comprising quite separate culture realms, knew almost nothing about each other. It does not follow that either end of the continent lived in isolation. It will be the burden of later chapters to indicate how much cross contact there actually was, and it must suffice at this point to state categorically that none of the countries and none of the cultures of the Orient evolved in isolation. Most of the several regions were not only in frequent contact with each other but also had contacts with the lands of central and western Asia and with the islands of the Pacific and Indian Oceans, outside the zone of the Orient itself.

The environmental setting of India may appear isolated from Scandinavia, just as Italy would seem to be in an isolated position with regard to China, or as Malaya can be said to be isolated from Kamchatka. Certainly the Eurasian continent does consist of an enormous solid core around which are arranged a series of peninsulas, island arcs, and coastal seas. And it may well be that man has moved into certain of these peninsular portions from a centrally located Garden of Eden like traffic along a one-way street. This can be indicated for the western as well as the eastern penin-sulas. But as the increasing volume of prehistoric and historical records are continually read with more accuracy and understanding there seems less and less possibility of proving the thesis of isolation for any selected peninsula or island arc. The more the record piles up, the longer the period of, and the greater the volume of, contacts appear to have been in almost all cases. Sometimes this contact amounted to a regular volume trade in economic goods, like that which exported timber from India to Babylonian Ur by sea about 500 B.C. Sometimes it amounted to the never-ending invasion of the permanently settled agricultural country by a variety of militant pastoral peoples. At other times it consisted in the dispatching to India of selected Chinese scholars interested in the study of religion, philosophy, religious architecture, and matters of art. Certainly, there was a tremendous mixing of peoples that slowly went on throughout the whole Orient. Even more important than this mixing of blood streams were the cultural transfer and exchange that was constantly going on in one or another direction.

It is not a negation of the above statement to admit that not the whole of each regional environment participated equally in the mixing of man and his cultures. Certain negative zones in many of the countries served as lands of refuge to the oppressed, zones in which there was a degree of stagnation, of decadence, even of retrogression. And there were some islands at which not all wandering groups of visitors touched, so that some of them remained in the Stone Age until after the day of contact with the occidental. On the other hand, the reader need not be surprised that in certain positive zones the sheer volume of historical contact is so bewilderingly great that it is hard to get the story simplified sufficiently.

Beyond the simple matter of chance isolation or refuge in a negative and unattractive hill country there is the rather more complicated question of cultural hibernation. By this is meant the arbitrary decision on the part of a people that it wanted no contact with the outside world. The Occident has been both startled and annoyed to find that there were cultures that thought themselves sufficient, which felt that there could be no real worth in dealings with the West. In some cases the statement undoubtedly should read "no *more* dealings with the Occident after having witnessed some exhibitions of their customs," about which more will be said in a later chapter. Regardless of whether the Occident is itself partly responsible for the cases of hibernation, the very retreat from the world into a period of cultural hermitage produces a type of isolation. The repercussions from this kind of isolation were greater by far than the effects of simple distant environmental location.

THE SPECIFIC OBJECTIVE

The aim of this volume is to present a reasonable statement of the appearance of the several landscapes of the oriental realm, what goes on in them, how their peoples developed particular patterns of culture, and how these peoples happened to achieve their present positions in the world at large. This involves a composite geographical presentation, though primary emphasis is placed upon the cultural aspects.

In the organization of the volume there are two major subdivisions. The first section deals with certain topics systematically, covering the whole of the Orient in the sweep of each chapter. This section makes an effort to paint on a broad canvas the systematic framework of the oriental realm, including both its physical and cultural structural members. It lacks many pertinent details as presently written—because of limitations both of knowledge and of space.

The second section of the book is an attempt to deal with the evolution of group cultures according to the broad regional molds in which they have developed. In each of these units there is an attempt to evaluate the landscape for differing societies, to present the growth of culture in that landscape, to consider the factors making for progress or decadence, and to discuss the problems of modernization and the future world for each people. Along with this will be presented a survey of present-day agriculture, economic resources, trade, and industry. Both in the first and in the second sections statistical material is held to a minimum in an effort to improve the presentation of the broad picture. In recognition of the real need for comparable data of measurement for all the Orient, a separate final chapter is given over to the presenting of such statistical data as are available. It is hoped that putting all of this, concisely, into one single section will make it more usable, and prevent the futile, random search through many a volume for facts that are never given twice in like manner and seldom completely.

Systematic Geography

Geomorphology and the Bare Landscape

ASIA AS A LAND MASS

The continent of Asia is at once the largest, the most complicated, and the least thoroughly described of the land masses that make up our conventional list of continents. Any statement concerning the structure and surface of Asia must either leave many blanks or spread the brushwork of language, map, and diagram across great blocks of territory with some degree of error. And yet, for all the gaps in knowledge, a simple statement of the basic structure of the continent can be set down, and most of its surface can be described in fairly satisfactory terms.

The western Arctic fringe of Asia is an extension of the great lowland of northern Europe. Southward and eastward from this Siberian Plain is a broad zone of ancient rocks that early in geologic time were folded, faulted, and intruded, not once, but several times. The worn roots of mountain ranges, plateaus, massifs, and other structural units today form a rugged and complicated area which serves as the headward zone for most of the Arctic-flowing rivers of Siberia. This zone occupies much of central and southern Siberia. Southward lie a number of major structural basins and truncated plateau surfaces covering hundreds of thousands of square miles in the dry heart of Asia. The partially eroded roots of mountain ranges separate the several commonly recognized divisions, Russian Turkestan, the Tarim Basin, Dzungaria, and the Mongolian Plateaus. These basins are nuclear masses of the most ancient land units, surrounded and enveloped in the early mountain-building episodes. Some of the ranges still reach a considerable elevation, and some of the basins are deeply filled, though one of the world's lowest continental depressions below sea level occurs almost in the center of the continent. Most of the structural building and deformation took place a long time ago, with repeated but minor happenings occurring in more recent geologic time along the same general lines as previously. One more step southward brings one up onto the Roof of the World in the great Tibetan Plateaus, a structural product of more recent geologic time. This zone consists of a series of high, enclosed basins, set apart by mountain ranges that primarily trend east-west. The Tibetan area is a part of the long Alpine Chain that reaches from Spain across Eurasia. Tremendous folding, faulting, and overthrusting were involved here as in Europe, and the approximate record is just beginning to be understood.

The eastern mainland of Asia is made up of a variety of units that range in age from Pre-Cambrian shields to Recent mountain arcs and recently foundered blocks. The several units cross and re-cross each other in a complex pattern in east Siberia, Manchuria, and China, and are in part eastward projections of elements previously described. The southern mainland of Asia consists of old blocks of deformed strata and Recent sedimentary basins lying next to or sandwiched into the Tertiary Alpine Chain which swings across Tibet and curves down the backbone of Burmo-Malaya. Lastly, set off the mainland coast are several series of islands, from the Indies to the Kuriles, set on structural arcs of varying radius. Most of them are the products of Tertiary and Pleistocene geologic time in their present outlines, though most have older basement foundations. All the arcs are the result of the movement which has wrinkled up the edges of the several stable blocks of the earth's crust that join along the western margins of the Pacific Ocean. It is likely that certain mainland structural lines are related to the island arc lines in origin. Some of the principal oceanic deeps lie alongside several of the island arcs, whereas but shallow continental shelf waters separate other arcs. These latter waters form a string of coastal seas which have been as significant to eastern Asia as the several seas separating the peninsulas of Europe.

GLACIATION AND RECENT MOUNTAIN BUILDING

In tracing the patterns of glacial action during the Ice Age most attention has been focused on North America and northwestern Europe. Only slowly is it becoming accepted that fairly large portions of the Asiatic highlands were affected by one or more of the cool pluvial periods that caused the accumulation of ice sheets. A considerable amount of detailed study and even re-examination of certain regions are needed with this problem in mind. The main mass of the young Tibetan Highland probably was not widely glaciated because of its aridity, and only the margins exposed to rain-bearing winds suffered glaciation. Similarly only certain highland portions of central Asia and Siberia were glaciated. It is likely that ice was a significant factor in sculpturing some of the mountain zones of China, though much of the evidence has been mutilated subsequently. The higher mountainous cores of Japan, Formosa, Borneo, and New Guinea, at least, show evidence of glaciation. More important than the erosion of hard rock surfaces by ice are the erosional and depositional effects of water and wind around the glaciated margins. Scattered throughout the Orient are a complicated series of terraces, benches, and shelves. Some are the normal erosional forms produced by running water or by marine planation in periods of high sea level. Karst landscapes of varying degrees of maturity are widely scattered but probably related to pluvial periods. Other forms are depositional: shallow sea sediments or lake deposits now exposed; normal valley fill; glacial deposits of various kinds; and aeolian deposits ranging from fossil dunes to thick beds of loess. Loess, particularly, is now known far beyond its classical location in the highlands of northwest China. Until about 1940 these varied marks upon the landscape were being studied separately, but correlation of many of these minor landforms seems possible.

Important in this further study will have to be the events transpiring outside the range of glaciation but during the periods of ice advance. It is likely that the lands nearest the tropics had a relatively warm and moist climate even during pluvial periods of ice accumulation on the cool northern highlands. However, there must have been changes in climatic regimes for southern lands during the ice ages that had as much effect upon those landscapes as Himalayan glaciers had upon the landscape of northern India. And, in the expansion and contraction of the several climatic regimes during the ice ages, many minor landscape forms and soil types were produced that now are out of place under current conditions. Even plant and animal distributions are occasionally out of place as remnants or as invaders beyond their expected zones. It may even be that some of the curious and anomalous distributions of human beings are thus to be explained.

A significant item is the fluctuation in the shore line of eastern Asia. The depression of sea level during the last advance of the ice was on the order of 220–240 feet. This would empty the Gulf of Pohai, much of the Yellow Sea, and much of the coastal shelf separating the Indies from the mainland of southeastern Asia. During previous ice advances lowering of sea level as much as 330 feet occurred, further increasing the land area of eastern Asia.

A troublesome variable in this situation is the way in which whole mountain ranges have grown up during late Tertiary and Pleistocene time. Between the advance of the first and the last ice sheets in the western Himalaya the Pir Panjal range in the Lesser Himalaya grew sufficiently so that it cut off rain-bearing winds and thus locally altered the effects of glaciation. The Indies, except for Borneo, might almost be called modern islands, in that they owe their primary build to Pleistocene structural arching accompanied by extrusive volcanism of ash, tuff, and flow-basalt, and their outlines to the rise of sea level in the postglacial period.

THE PATTERNS OF MONSOON ASIA

To shorten the focus from a view of all of Asia to an examination of the physical patterns of Monsoon Asia, one discovers that most of the variety of geomorphic structure that characterizes the larger physical framework is still present. For convenience a somewhat imaginative set of figures is sketched to indicate the general patterns into which the structure and landscapes of Monsoon Asia fall. There is no more than a superficial resemblance between the continental margins and these imaginative figures, but they will serve as the skeleton upon which to build a detailed discussion of the geomorphology and surface landscapes of the several broad regions. There are four such sketch patterns. On the south is the Indian Triangle, including the territory from Tibet to the island of Ceylon. On the southeast is the Burmo-Malayan Fan which takes in the mainland countries of Burma, Thailand, Indochina, and Malaya. On the east is the Chinese Checkerboard ranging from south China to northern Manchuria, with its roots deeply buried in central Asia. Off coast lie the Island Arcs, reaching from Sumatra and New Guinea on the south to the Kuriles and Sakhalin on the north.

THE INDIAN TRIANGLE

If one could observe the whole of the Indian Triangle from the crest of Mount Everest, on top of the main Himalayan Range, it would be seen that it consists of four distinct parts. To the north lie range after range marking the high segments of the Tibetan Plateau.

THE TIBETAN PLATEAU

The body of the plateau lies above 15,000 feet, fenced on the south by the Trans-Himalayan ranges and on the north by the Kunlun Shan, Altyn Tagh, and Nan Shan. Narrow and highest toward the western end, the great spiked ridges spread to the north and

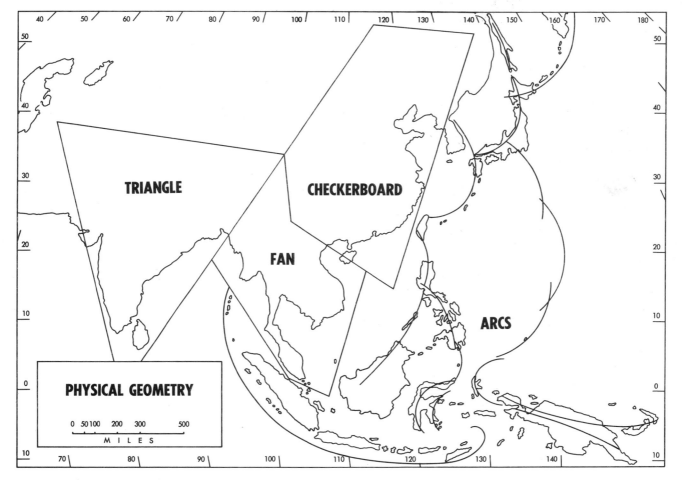

Fig. 1. The physical geometry of the oriental world indicates four major physical units, which are described in the first two chapters.

Alongside and underfoot are the tremendous curving ranges of the Himalaya. From its abrupt facing onto the low country to the south this crest zone is termed the Mountain Wall. Conforming closely to the Himalayan line is the great subsiding trough of the North Indian Plain, a 300,000-square-mile basin gradually being filled with the materials excavated from the Himalayan ranges and southern fringe of the Tibetan Plateau. Beyond the great plain rises gradually the fourth unit, the old and much worn surface of Peninsular India, about a million square miles of territory forming one of the world's great, ancient massifs.

south as they run eastward. There are many of these ranges, and they fill the whole plateau with ragged alpine topography carved in bold outlines. There are innumerable basins between the ranges, most of them longer east-west than north-south, and variably filled with rock debris from the near-by ranges. Many of the basins contain permanent lakes varying in size from small marsh-ponds to large bodies of water which fluctuate in size from time to time. There are many great alluvial piedmonts surrounding individual basins, and in parts of the plateau denudation and filling has broadened the passes into open saddles affording comparatively easy access from basin to basin. There are few real rivers in the heart of the plateau, though not all the basins are internal drainage units. Passes between basins often lie above 17,000 feet.

The section that best fits the above description is known as the Chang Tang, which is the main body of the plateau. In area the region measures nearly

are fewer filled basins with open saddles, fewer lakes and internal drainage units, but entrenched streams, greater relief, more exposure of the rock flanks of ranges, many marks of glaciation, and a steadily deepening pattern of earth sculpture on a tremendous scale.

A portion of southern Tibet also is trenched by great rivers that have prevented the building of high, filled

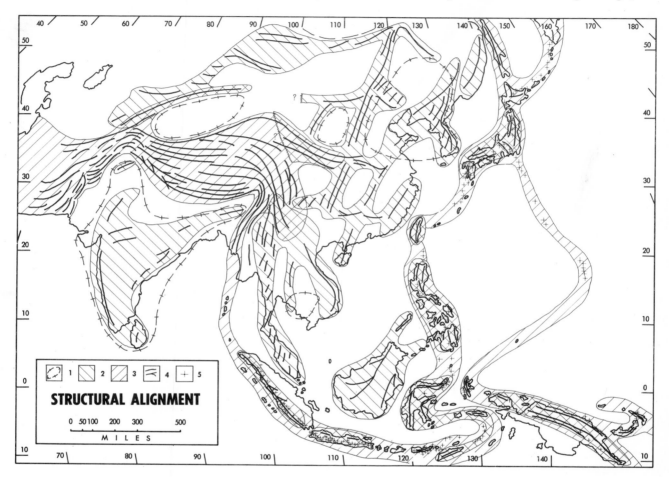

Fig. 2. Patterns of structural alignment: (1) ancient nuclear land units; (2) areas of old mountain building; (3) areas of young mountain building; (4) representative placement of present mountain ranges; (5) volcanos recently active.

400,000 square miles, being about 1,500 miles long and having a maximum width of about 400 miles.

Set somewhat lower than the Chang Tang in the northeastern corner of Tibet is a large, irregular basin area partially divided by subordinate branches off the Altyn Tagh and the Nan Shan ranges to the north. The Tsaidam is the largest single basin unit of Tibet, some 400 by 100 miles in rough measure.

South of the Tsaidam the east-west trend of the Tibetan ranges swings gradually southward, and the whole of eastern Tibet has been trenched by the headwaters of the great rivers of eastern Asia, the Huang, the Yangtze, the Mekong, and the Salween. Here there

basins. Two major Indian rivers, the Brahmaputra and the Indus, have circled the east and west ends of the Himalaya to drain a long and narrow strip of southern Tibet. The primary alignment of the drainage net is with the structural patterns of the plateau, with the deepest gorges placed where streams cut across ranges.

At the narrow western end of the plateau is the Pamir Knot. Here elevations generally are somewhat lower than in the Chang Tang or Southern Tibet, but the ranges are closer together, the interrange basins are almost lacking, and stream dissection has deeply carved the outer edges of the highland. This is the spot at which the main Himalaya of the south, the enormous

Karakorum of central western Tibet, the Tien Shan and Kunlun ranges from central Asia, and the Hindu Kush and Sulaiman ranges of Afghanistan intersect in a confused and complicated highland knot.

THE MOUNTAIN WALL

For over 1,500 miles the Himalaya stand out above the alluvial plains of northern India. In the west the

portion of Tertiary time. Others are complex bodies of folded and overthrust rocks of varying ages, involving repeated mountain building operations throughout the Tertiary and Pleistocene epochs. All the ranges appear to be set on arcs of circles of varying radius, their convex faces toward the North Indian Plain. Most ranges have multiple structures with variable rates of curvature, and with bifurcations at points of curvature change. There appears to be some continuity clear

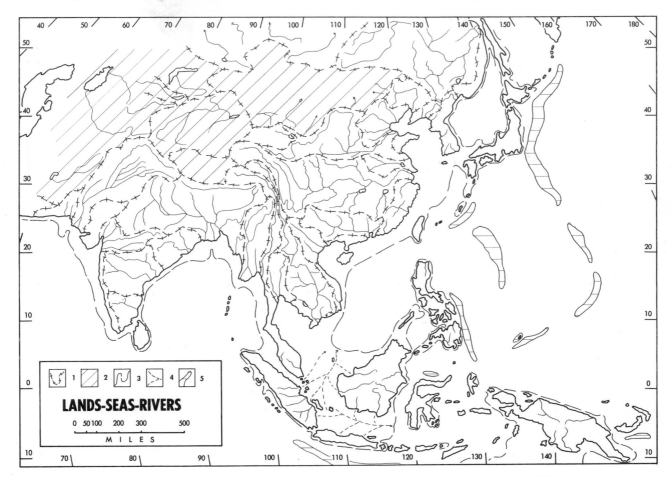

Fig. 3. Asiatic drainage patterns: (1) divides between major drainage systems; (2) regions of interior drainage; (3) encloses coastal shelf at 100 fathoms; (4) river channels of old Sunda Land; (5) oceanic deeps.

several ranges of eastern Afghanistan and Baluchistan form a descending highland wall irregularly framing the North Indian Plain for nearly 800 miles. On the east the ancient rock mass of the Assam Plateau lies in front of a curving range system that projects southward along the Burma-India border country and, for nearly 500 miles, limits the North Indian Plain on the east.

In morphologic structure there is considerable variety in the many ranges that ring northern India. Some are simple folded mountain ranges formed during one

around the Mountain Wall rather than mere orographic juxtaposition of three unrelated sets of mountain ranges. Mountain building has continued until very recent geologic time, and today an active earthquake zone blankets the inner side of the Mountain Wall.

The physiographic patterns of the Mountain Wall show great variety also. Though not exceptional in height the ranges of the northwestern and western border zone have been affected primarily by the dry-land processes of denudation. Seasonal streams, steep-walled canyons, precipitous gorges, alluvial fans, much bare rock exposure, and considerable aeolian erosion and deposition are elements in the formation of the present landscapes.   In the Himalaya, on the other hand, there has been considerable glacial activity, and U-shaped valleys, hanging valleys, cirques, and the spectacular angular lines of ice work on hard rock are to

processes operate much as in the Himalaya to produce a deeply dissected landscape.

THE HIMALAYA RANGES.   The Himalaya are sometimes divided into four units from east to west, the Assam, Nepal, Kumaon, and Punjab sectors, on the basis of the penetration across the main range by the

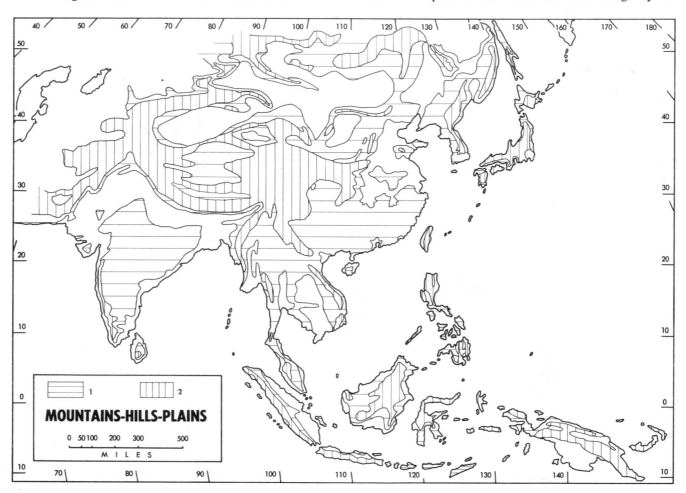

Fig. 4.   Patterns of surface configuration.   Blank areas are plains and smoother-surfaced lands: (1) hill lands and rough surfaces; (2) mountain lands and steep surfaces.

be seen.   At lower altitudes the depositional products of mountain glaciation are intermixed with voluminous amounts of landslide debris that periodically block stream channels, causing temporary lakes and subsequent serious flooding downstream.   Most of the rivers of the Himalaya are youngish streams with precipitous upper courses and deep and often tremendous gorges where they cut across mountain ranges.   Deep, flat-floored valleys alternate with narrow gorges until the streams finally come out upon the North Indian Plain to entirely change their behavior in the flat lands.   In the Burmese border ranges glaciation is very evident in the northernmost sector.   Farther south the humid-land

headwaters of the Tista, Kali, and Sutlej rivers.   These are not the only streams to penetrate the ranges, however, and it is somewhat more satisfactory to describe the Himalaya as three series of parallel mountain ranges with longitudinal valleys, set abruptly above the North Indian Plain.   On an average the breadth of the zone is between 150 and 200 miles, somewhat wider in the west and narrower in the east.   The highest elevations are in the central eastern sector.   The western fourth of the zone is much less dissected than other parts and the water parting correlates closely with the main crest, whereas in the central and eastern sections headward stream cutting has pushed the water parting

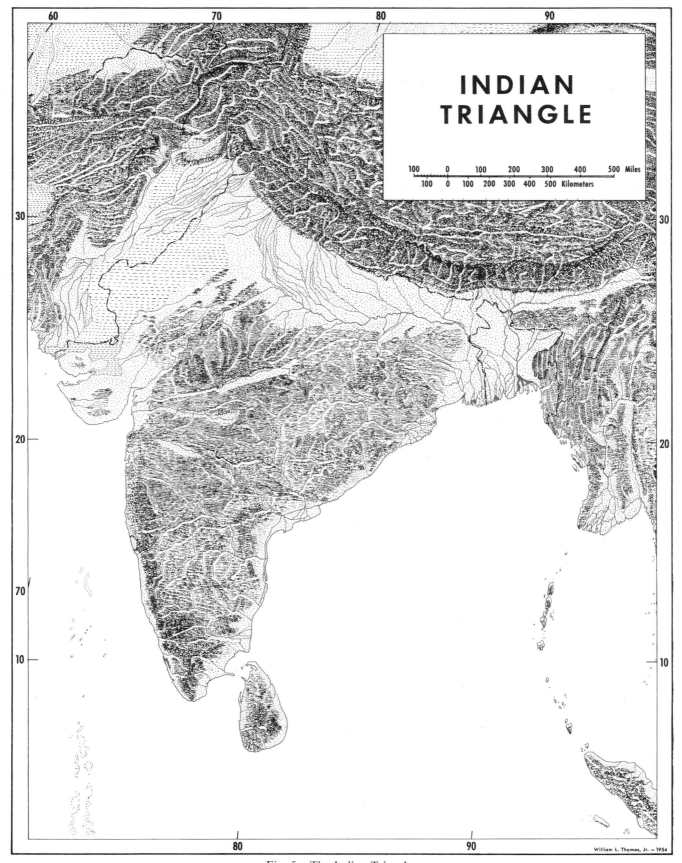

Fig. 5. The Indian Triangle.

15

Fig. 6. The Burmo-Malayan Fan.

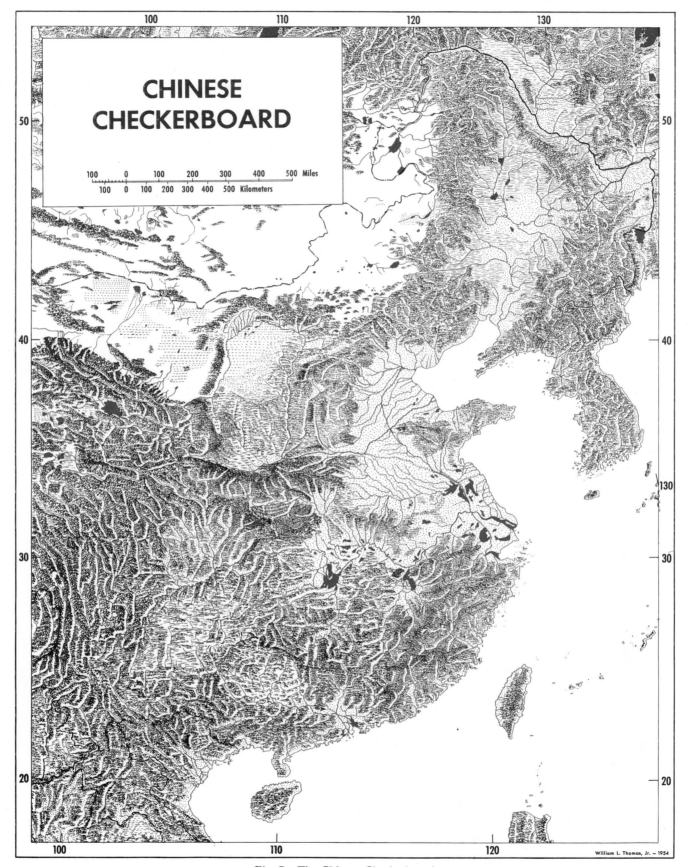

CHINESE CHECKERBOARD

100   0   100   200   300   400   500 Miles
100   0   100   200   300   400   500 Kilometers

William L. Thomas, Jr. – 1954

Fig. 7. The Chinese Checkerboard.

17

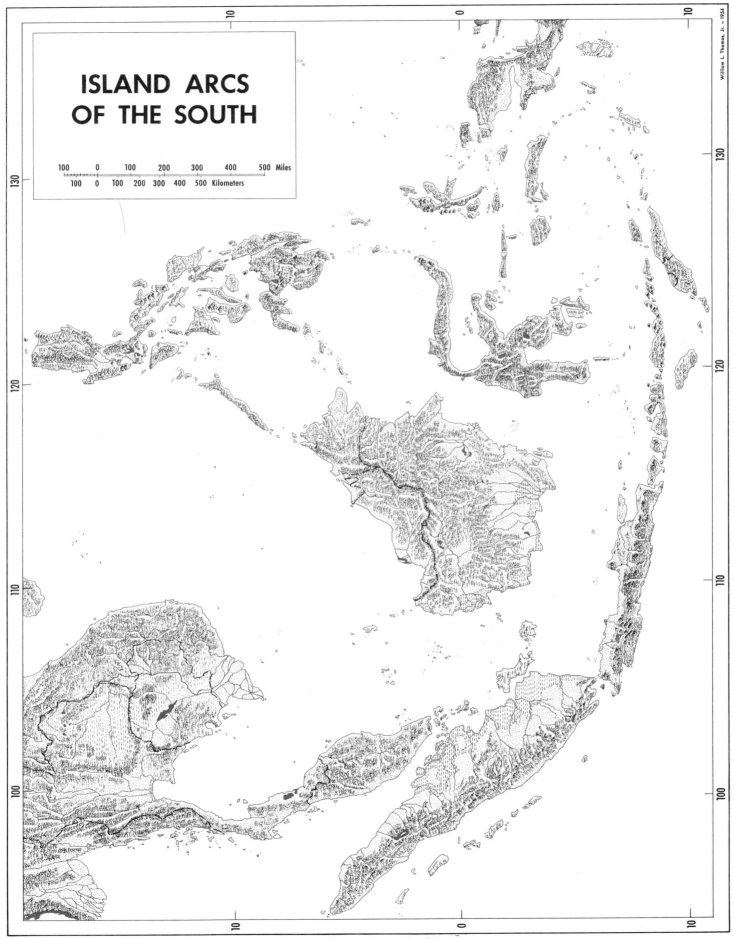

Fig. 8.   The Southern Island Arcs.

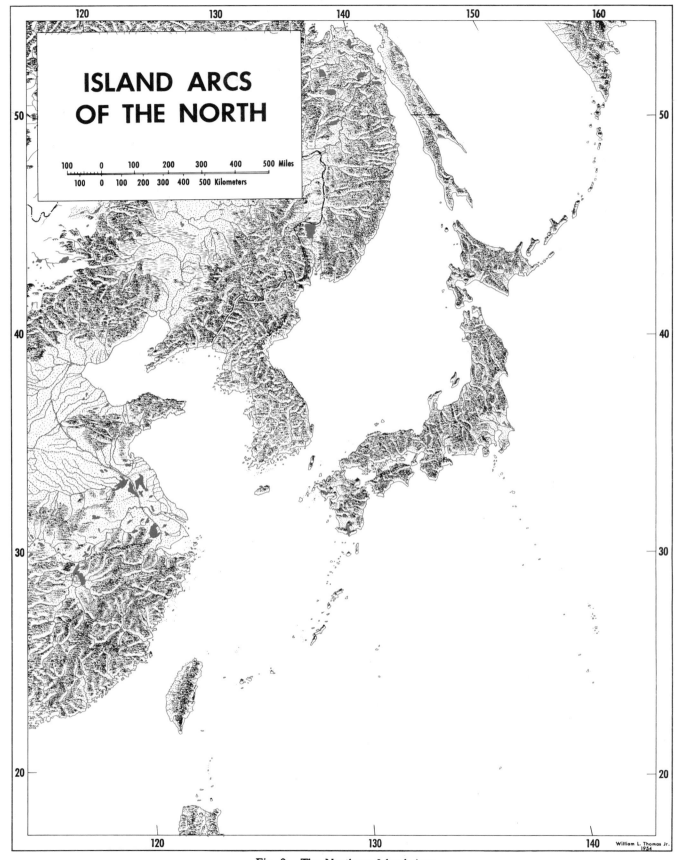

ISLAND ARCS OF THE NORTH

| 100 | 0 | 100 | 200 | 300 | 400 | 500 Miles |

| 100 | 0 | 100 | 200 | 300 | 400 | 500 Kilometers |

William L. Thomas Jr.
1954

Fig. 9. The Northern Island Arcs.

19

back of the main crest line some fifty miles and has cut many deep canyons into the frontal section of the ranges. A cross-sectional view of the Himalaya, south to north, shows the three following divisions.

Outer Himalaya. Set just above the alluvial plains at elevations of 2,500 to 4,000 feet is the Outer Himalaya, also known as the Siwalik Hills. This is a foothill zone, composed of Tertiary river-borne sediments similar to but older than those forming the North Indian Plain. In the west this foothill zone is perhaps 30 miles wide and well developed, gradually thinning out eastward until, in Assam, it is rather inconspicuous. Behind the foothills are open valleys running longitudinally and draining into the large streams that have cut deeply into the main range.

Lesser Himalaya. Above the foothill strip is an intricate system of ranges known as the Lesser Himalaya. Some fifty miles wide on the average it also narrows from west to east and gradually becomes less important. Elevations seldom reach above 15,000 feet. It is composed of granites and other crystalline rocks, some ancient sedimentaries, and metamorphosed strata. Deeply dissected by many streams, it consists of bifurcations off the main Himalayan ranges which gradually shift in direction to become parallel ranges forming a continuous line. Both within and behind the Lesser Himalaya are more longitudinal valleys. These vary considerably in elevation, but are set a step above those of the Outer Himalaya, and sometimes contain small lakes.

Great Himalaya. Towering above the lesser ranges is the Great Himalaya, with a perpetual snow line and a great many peaks above 20,000 feet. The range system composed of granites and other resistant rocks contains bold and striking relief. There are numerous bifurcations north and south at points of curvature shift, and several outstanding peaks are set just south of the main line of the range system. Of the eighteen Asiatic peaks positively identified as standing above 26,000 feet, twelve are in the main Himalayan range, one in the west, and all the others in Nepal, where the Mount Everest and Kanchenjunga clusters of peaks are situated. In the west the main crest sits far back from the North Indian Plain, but toward the east the lesser units of the Mountain Wall thin out and the high peaks stand close above the plains. There are hundreds of passes and avenues through the Himalaya, many of no current significance because they do not lead to any real objective. In the west the routes of travel must cross at true passes over the main Himalayan crest, but in the east most travel has always followed the shoulders of the many deep stream channels

through the main range, seeking out the lowest water partings available behind the high peaks.

THE WESTERN BORDER RANGES. Apparently turning the corner in northwest India and swinging southward into Afghanistan is a part of the Himalayan structure pattern. Of concern here are only the easternmost limbs of the mountain systems, which spread as they extend south and west their convex faces toward India. Nowhere is the Afghan or Baluch zone built to such a height as those in the Himalaya. The southward ranges fall off in height toward the Gulf of Arabia, from elevations of some 13,000 feet in Afghanistan to around 7,000 in central Baluchistan, running down to the Makran coast as rugged but low hill ranges. In the north, set just inside and across the elbow bend, lies the flat-topped Salt Range, rising sharply out of the plain but sloping back toward the elbow bend and cut by the Indus River. The Salt Range is a complex faulted region of old sediments.

West of the Salt Range the Sulaiman system rises above the Indus plain as relatively simple folded ranges composed of Tertiary rocks. Beyond it lie other similar ranges with alluvial valleys leading southwest to the Seistan Basin, but the drainage of much of the arid Sulaiman is southward and back to the Indus. After a 400-mile stretch the Sulaiman curves and merges into the next arc line to the west. The simple folded Tertiary Kirthar ranges continue toward the Arabian Gulf, most of them curving westward along the coast. Drainage of the area is toward the Gulf by individual small stream basins that cut through the coastal hill ranges.

The western border mountain systems have served far less well than the northern systems to isolate India. The western border is passable at many points, through passes across the crest lines and by entrenched streams which cut behind the main ranges toward more westerly water partings. Many passes are located at elevations which made animal or foot travel much more practicable in the past than the rough and arid landscape would seem to suggest to the modern traveler. Khyber Pass, in the north, is under 4,000 feet, the Gomal Pass, behind the Sulaiman Range, is under 3,000 feet, and the Bolan Pass through the northern Kirthar is under 6,000 feet. Along the Makran coast travelers can remain close to sea level. Many other passes less well known in modern times at similar elevations long have facilitated movement between India, Iran, and Russian Turkestan.

THE EASTERN BORDER RANGES. Set out in front of the Burma border is the oblong mass of the Assam Plateau, reaching a top elevation of 6,400 feet. This region really belongs to the ancient massif of Peninsular India, for it is composed of the same kind of rock and has the same structure. It is deeply dissected and is slowly being cut into three remnant portions. By its position the Brahmaputra cannot take the simple course to the sea followed by the Indus, but must traverse the long, narrow Assam Valley around the obstruction. The Assam Plateau also obscures the front of the long, sweeping arc of the several ranges of the Arakan Yoma-Lushai Hills-Patkai Hills that separate Burma from India and become the island-strewn west coast of Burma fronting on the Bay of Bengal. The eastern border ranges are placed convex to the North Indian Plain. They are composed of Tertiary rocks and, apparently, have a fairly simple general structure pattern. They are markedly parallel in alignment. This dissected and jungle-covered wilderness was one of the least studied portions of the Orient before the Burma campaigns of World War II.

Elevations at the great bend of the Alpine Chain are somewhat higher in the northeast than in northwest India. The structural knot is not so tight or narrow, and the great rivers draining Eastern Tibet have dug very deep trenches. Consequently there are but few really passable avenues from the upper Brahmaputra across to China, to Thailand, or to Indochina. Movement into or out of India in this quarter faces far more difficult travel than in the northwest, and the barrier protection to the North Indian Plain here is almost as complete as along the Tibetan zone itself.

THE NORTH INDIAN PLAIN

When the Tertiary era of mountain building began, a shallow and retreating arm of the sea lay between the new and growing upland to the north and the old massif to the south. South of the trough the Assam Plateau was connected with the rest of Peninsular India so that the trough was very much elongated and open only at the western end. Into this region the streams draining the slowly growing Himalayan ranges piled their sediments. Later those first strata were folded into the Outer Himalayan foothill strip, as both heavy sedimentation and mountain-building pressures continued. At some period a 150-mile strip of the northern end of the massif foundered, opening a gap to the sea between the present Assam Plateau and the Rajmahal Hills. Coupled with major readjustments in surface drainage for all of southern Tibet, the opening of this gap gradually led to a reversal of direction for a considerable number of streams that now are parts of the Ganges River system.

During and after the close of the glacial era the narrow central section, near modern Delhi, was built to a higher level, further separating the drainage of the Ganges and Indus river systems. Since Neolithic time a number of channels near this water parting have been abandoned or have continuously shifted their courses. Abandoned oxbows, natural levees, terrace levels, bluffs cut into older alluvium, silted-up distributaries, changes in regional centering of seasonal floods, widely braided and island-filled channels all attest the fact that local changes in surface are being produced everywhere in the North Indian Plain.

Today there is an enormous alluvial plain covering nearly 300,000 square miles. Its simple proportions are impressive. It is nearly 1,800 miles air-line distance from the Kirthar ranges on the west to the head of the Brahmaputra Valley in Assam, about 800 miles from the Himalayan front in northwest India to the Indus Delta margin. Generally the width of the plain is between 120 and 200 miles. The Indus Delta has a seafront width of 120 miles, the narrow Delhi Gap is but 85 miles, the Ganges Delta seafront is 300 miles wide. The valley of the Brahmaputra, however, is seldom over 50 miles wide throughout its 500-mile-long section behind the Assam Plateau. Most of the plain lies below 500 feet in elevation, and the Delhi Gap just tops 700 feet as the highest point between Indus and Ganges drainage. Local relief is very slight and the open plains landscape is a monotonous one to a slow traveler. Its margins along the Mountain Wall are somewhat higher, and fairly smooth in alignment, with only minor irregularities. Most of the line of contact with Peninsular India, on the other hand, is marked by deep embayments of alluvium and protruding spurs of hard rock in the process of burial under the alluvial fill. In Rajputana this contact zone contains the Thar Desert, a slowly expanding area of alternating sand and subdued bare-rock surfaces. Much of the western Rajputana rock basement has been almost base-leveled. South of the Thar lies the Great Rann of Cutch, in which the line of demarcation between plain and peninsula becomes even more difficult. A few bare-rock hills are the remnants of a period of marine planation of the corner of Peninsular India around which sedimentation from Rajputana and the Indus has taken place to bring the surface almost to sea level. In the winter the area is an enormous, dusty, salty, and desolate surface. During the summer the monsoon winds blow sea water into its lowest-lying sections and blow salt, sand, and silt off the higher portions back into the Thar Desert.

The Indus portion of the plain is served by one great river, the Indus itself, and five major tributaries that make up the Punjab's "five rivers," the Sutlej, Beas, Ravi, Chenab, and Jhelum, which carry more water than the Indus. The alluvial deposition of the Indus and its tributaries has built the upper Punjab to a higher level than other Himalayan piedmont margins of the plain. The water sources are primarily the Himalayan highland rains and snows, fed the year round but with a peak period of flood in April and May in normal years. Time was when the Indus could be navigated clear up to the Salt Range gorge, but modern irrigation systems that feed millions of acres take too much water out of the rivers.

The Ganges system is a combination of nine or ten principal tributaries, most of which have their sources in the Himalayan front and, like the Indus system, are fed by seasonal snow melt and summer monsoon rain. With a rainier drainage basin the Ganges carries a larger volume of water than the Indus, but enormous irrigation canals seriously reduce the regular flow, and the river no longer carries significant shipping. The Ganges floodplain is flatter than that of the Indus, with a greater amount of meandering and seasonal flooding.

The Brahmaputra with fewer large tributaries than the other two major streams drains a larger and rainier catchment basin, loses little water by irrigation, and has a much narrower floodplain for alluvial deposition. Its channel therefore carries more water, and it appears a much greater river, navigable for some 800 miles by river steamers, barges, and launches.

The three river systems bring to the two great deltas a total of not far from 3,000,000 tons of sediment per day. Both deltas are growing steadily, particularly the larger Ganges Delta, which has been changing rather markedly in recent centuries. The western and eastern distributaries have silted up, annual flooding has changed its patterns, the Ganges has shifted eastward, the Brahmaputra westward, and the tidal Sundarbans have grown outward considerably.

PENINSULAR INDIA

The foundations of Peninsular India consist of Pre-Cambrian igneous and metamorphic rocks. Over a little more than half of the peninsula this ancient basement lies directly below the surface. Very early structural deformation created a number of linear patterns varying from northeast-southwest to north-south, which today show up in different physical features. A random scattering of Paleozoic and Cenozoic fresh-water sediments are distributed over the whole area, but there were only minor periods of small-scale marine deposition. Preceding and accompanying the earliest building of the Tertiary Alpine Chain was a long period in which innumerable thin layers of basalt poured from fissures in the underlying basement rock. These beds variably total a few hundred to several thousand feet

in thickness and mostly lie in horizontal position. They now total some 200,000 square miles in area, perhaps a third less than the maximum coverage once attained. On the northwest the basalt extends clear to the coast, but the inland margins have been cut back until much of the previously covered basement structure is exposed again.

Considerably before Tertiary time the peninsular block was given its basic structural position, a tilt slightly north of east, a position never basically altered. Accompanying the building of the Alpine Chain were a variety of strains and stresses that have affected the northern margins of the peninsula. Later in the Tertiary minor fluctuations of the block occurred, with respect to sea level, for there are numerous evidences of changes in shore line on both east and west coasts.

The east-west water parting, in the peninsula, is amazingly near the west coast everywhere except in the northwestern sector, where three streams were able to excavate long, narrow trenches along fault or fracture lines to push the drainage divide more than halfway across the peninsula. Otherwise, all the long streams flow toward the east, with the tilt of the block. Along the east coast several streams have both falls and rapids in their headwater sections, with steep gradients and narrow valleys in this zone. Once out of the highland headwater zone, relief is rather subdued, though it may be considerable. Most streams are shallow and have graded courses, with well-developed floodplains, along their lower sections. Every stream has a delta, built proportionately to its basin area and flow. Numerous clumps of remnant hills and many monadnocks and inselbergs are distributed over much of the peninsula. The Eastern Ghats lie inland from the coast and are a discontinuous line of hills in the south, but increasing both in bulk and elevation toward the north.

All the streams of the west coast, with the three northern exceptions, are short and precipitous in grade, with falls near their heads and rapids in their lower courses. Catchment basins are very small in all the streams, and the sediment load is small. Dependent upon the precipitation total, increasing from north to south, each stream may handle a much larger flow than the catchment area would indicate. None has very deeply notched the steep-fronted west coast, so that there are remarkably few gaps across the divide. From the sea the Western Ghats appear as a steep-fronted mountain range, with elevations just above and below 5,000 feet from the north well down the peninsula. Toward the southern end elevations gradually rise and reach a maximum in the Cardamom Hills at 8,840 feet. Just north of the Cardamom Hills lies the Palghat Gap, a saddle pass only 800 feet in height, the only real pass anywhere in the Western Ghats. Though none of the west coast streams has cut the face of the Ghats very deeply, they do not form a smooth, high line. Their front is irregular throughout, with occasional remnant foothill patches and a number of deep embayments, which noticeably enlarge the narrow coastal strip.

Peninsular India does not easily divide into regional units, but the following notes on separate areas are helpful in attempting to describe the differing landscapes.

THE ARAVALLI-SATPURA HILL RANGES. In the northwest the worn-down edges of the ancient massif disappear under sand dunes and alluvium along an irregular and shifting line. Bare-rock exposures vary from almost flat and featureless surfaces to rugged hills of bole and craggy relief. The maximum elevations approach or exceed 5,000 feet. Structure often is locally complex in the north, with a variety of ancient rocks exposed at the surface; to the south the basalt flows mask the surface but have been carved into a varied relief. Marine planation gives the Kathiawar Peninsula a smoother, more worn-down surface. The strike of the Aravalli Range is northeast-southwest, that of the Vindhya Range is east northeast-west southwest, whereas the Satpura Range is lined up almost east-west. None of the ranges is single, but each is a multiple expression of ancient deformation of the peninsular block. Draining this area are the three long streams flowing to the west coast, occupying structural breaks, the Tapti, the Narbada, and the Mahi. Drainage of the whole area is split between Gulf of Arabia and Indus and Ganges systems.

THE DECCAN PLATEAUS. South of the Tapti River the main mass of the basalt forms a large tableland or low plateau from 1,000 to 2,000 feet, often known as the Bombay Deccan. On the west it reaches to the crest of the Ghats; its eastern margins are rather strongly dissected by the Godavari River system. The tableland itself bears only shallow stream valleys, and much more noticeable in the landscape are the terraced mesas and rollings plains formed by the many horizontal layers of basalt. Slopes connect many of these varying levels, rather than vertical cliffs as might be suggested by its basalt composition. To the south the elevation generally increases to above 2,000 feet as one passes out of the basalt region and into the red soil of the Deccan Plateau proper. The southern portion is above 3,000 feet. Here the Western Ghats form a high barrier margin, whereas on the east and south the plateau is quite deeply trenched by several stream systems.

THE NILGIRI-PALNI PLATEAUS. The high southern end of the peninsula is not all ragged mountain crest,

for two small plateaus are set rather abruptly above the surrounding lowlands. The steepness of the plateau margins and the height involved seem quite out of keeping with the description of Peninsular India as an old, worn-down plateau. The Nilgiri Hills cover some 700 square miles of area with open basins and highland swales at about 6,500 feet and rocky ridges and rounded domes rising above 8,000 feet. Across the Palghat Gap lies the Palni Hills spur, offset from the Cardamom Hills. The Palni Hills cover somewhat more than 500 square miles, and elevations range from about 7,000 to 8,200 feet. The Cardamom Hills, further south, have been so deeply dissected that no plateau surface remains. There are a number of peaks above 8,000 feet. This highland area presents a very different landscape from that of the lower lands of the south.

THE WEST COAST. Below the steep front of the Western Ghats the lowland strip varies in width from 5 to 70 miles. Almost everywhere along the ocean shore the southwest summer monsoon has piled up a sand dune strip and keeps it annually agitated and changing in detail of pattern. In the north the monsoon is less effective than in the south, and here the rivers, aided by tidal sweep, keep their channels open to the sea. As one goes southward along the coast one finds the rivers less and less able to maintain direct channels to the sea, until, in southern India along the Malabar coast, there is a permanent inland lagoon that runs for many miles behind the dunes and is broken only at intervals. Behind this dune zone is a flat lowland strip. In the north this is a wide bench of marine planation, with but slight alluvial cover, whereas to the south a larger amount of alluvium is frequently distributed over the lowland strip behind the lagoons. The long coast, therefore, changes gradually in appearance from the flat, dry, bare, and barren north to the moist, tropical jungle-lagoon south. Good harbors are few in number along the coast, the natural harbor of Bombay being the only large one.

THE EAST COAST. The east coast of India is in strong contrast to the west coast. Here, first of all, the Eastern Ghats form but a disconnected line of hills lying well back from the shore line. The delta lands are relatively large, and closely spaced, with distributaries usually reaching the sea. Between the deltas and the Ghats there is an emerged coastal plain of varying width. Rivers have deep embayments of valley lowland along them. Along part of the coast sand spits and dune strips have created a marsh or lagoon strip behind them, but this usually is in the zone between stream deltas. The lowland is widest in the far south and narrowest between the Godaviri and Mahanadi rivers, where the Eastern Ghats are nearest the coast and at their maximum in height and relief.

THE CHOTA NAGPUR UPLAND. In the northeast corner of the peninsular area is a ragged zone of hill country with several small inset plateaus. Much of the area is about 2,000 feet in height, with the marginal river channels below that and the occasional clumps of highland reaching up to 4,500 feet. The drainage is radially outward, mostly shared by the Mahanadi and the Ganges systems. Considerable deformation of this northern portion of the peninsula has occurred, and it is here that the coal and iron beds are located in structural depressions filled with sedimentary rocks. No easy route allows access through, across, or around this rugged upland.

CEYLON. The island of Ceylon is an offset unit of the peninsular mainland. The high point of the island is an 8,800-foot peak well toward the south, off center from a location that would give a symmetrical pattern to relief and surface. Around and north of this high point are set a number of small plateaus, shoulders, steps, and platforms. Below these features is a zone of rolling hill country, narrow around the south and extending well north along the island. Surrounding the whole is the coastal plain, narrower and with variable local relief in the south, broader and flat toward the north. The whole hilly and highland center is composed of ancient gneisses, whereas the coastal plain has an alluvial cover, replaced in the north by marine limestones. A shallow synclinal structure is aligned north-south along the main axis of the island. Drainage naturally is radial, in a series of streams that always are short, steeply pitched in their upper courses and smoothly graded in their lower sections. Much of the eastern coast is cliffed; parts of the west coast have a sand dune and lagoon fringe.

THE BURMO-MALAYAN FAN

From a lesser peak than Everest in the southeastern corner of Tibet our observer now could look down to the south and see before him the whole of the Burmo-Malayan Fan. Its primary alignment is from north to south, and near his feet would be the base of the fan, with its ribs close together, high above the narrow veins. The ribs are the mountain ranges, the veins are the deep trenches of the master rivers of southeastern Asia. On the right a rib curves off to the west and south as the previously mentioned Arakan Yoma. Far to the south are the Andaman-Nicobar Islands in the line of the Arakan. The central ribs extend fairly straight, and the primary one stretches out for a long distance until, at the neck of the Malay Peninsula, its

pieces are offset to the left as the Alpine Chain tightens its arc toward the Indies. The eastern ribs flare to the left, the largest one swinging in an S-curve around Indochina.

As the ribs decrease in elevation southward and run into the sea the veins widen out and become broad valleys with deltas at their far ends. Set into the pattern of the fan are branching ribs and veins. Also inset are several old blocks of strata that partly upset the neat construction of the fan. These are ancient massifs which now occupy positions as low platforms or higher plateaus. Physically the whole zone is quite similar in structure pattern though it is variable in the age of its strata and in the date of mountain building. The two western ribs belong to the Tertiary Alpine Chain, and their uplift separated the old North Indian Trough from the Irrawaddy Trough. The Shan Plateau and all the fan to the east of it are the results of an older mountain-building era, though it is likely that all were somewhat affected by the events of the Tertiary period.

Historically this large area has come to be recognized as the four political units of Burma, Thailand, Indochina, and British Malaya. Since there are no easily drawn regional subdivisions that facilitate discussion, most written accounts tend to follow political lines even when dealing with the natural landscape. The following pages attempt a systematic description by major physical features, regardless of prevailing political boundaries.

THE MOUNTAIN RANGES

At about 28° N. lat. the bend of the Alpine Chain structure is at its narrowest. Here, in an air-line distance of some 30-odd miles, one can cross from the river trench of the Yangtze to that of the Irrawaddy. A total of 100 miles brings one to a tributary of the Brahmaputra. Within this latter distance are squeezed the folded structures that spread out southward to become many of the ranges of southeastern Asia. Here in the north the heights are just the dissected, knife-like interstream divides between the great trenches. Their elevations reach nearly 18,000 feet at the elbow bend, and they carry a perpetual snow cover.

South of the tight bend the ranges spread out rapidly and send off branches. For a distance of 200 to 300 miles the mountains occupy much more space than the river canyons. Elevations decrease rather rapidly both on the ranges and in the river trenches. This is the zone over which the famous "Hump" flights were made during World War II, from Assam to China. One jumbled range after another fills the whole landscape, with steep slopes leading down to V-shaped drainage channels. By about 24° N. lat. the spread of the ranges is very wide. They now are clearly differentiated, one from another, and must be individually considered.

The Burmese side of the Arakan Yoma is a series of fairly simple Tertiary folded mountains containing numerous faults. Intricate relief and a highly developed drainage net make the country some of the most difficult in Asia to traverse. East of the Chindwin River lies a simpler edition of the border ranges, known as the Kumon Bum in the north and the Pegu Yoma in the south where it fades out to a range of hills in the alluvial lowland. East of the Irrawaddy a long narrow divide, in the north, shades into the Shan Plateau, to be discussed later. Between the Salween and the Menam runs the peninsular spinal column. It is not one continuous ridge line but, as a series of elongated blocks placed *en echelon,* it maintains its place as the central water parting clear through the Malay Peninsula to Singapore. The core of all blocks is Cretaceous granite intruded into already folded and faulted flank formations of Paleozoic limestones and sandstones. Elevations vary considerably, with individual sections rising to 8,800 feet on the Yunnan border, over 7,300 feet in Tenasserim, about 3,700 feet in the Kra Isthmus zone, and nearly 7,200 feet in Central Malaya. There are many passes and gaps through the ranges, located fairly high in the north but becoming low-level openings in Tenasserim and Malaya.

East of the Mekong River, range structure ties into the alignment of the Sino-Tibetan border ranges, about which more will be said later. Southward from the great bend these ranges decrease quite rapidly in elevation, northern Laos reaching only somewhat over 9,000 feet and no point in the southern section reaching 8,000 feet. The main mass of highland sweeps southward in a double curve, S-shaped, known as the Annamite Cordillera. It is rather massive in build in the north, but thins out south of Laos to become quite asymmetrical in form. Its steep face is close to the South China Sea throughout most of its length, and its longer slope is toward the Mekong. In the north, inset between individual ranges, is the irregular plateau of Tran Ninh; to the south smaller plateau remnants are found in the upland zone. There are no good routes across the northern highland, but in the narrow, central section several passes lie below 1,300 feet, and a number of reasonably good routes lead across the southern uplands.

For some hundreds of miles the Annamite Cordillera parallels the Indochina coast, falling abruptly away and leaving but a narrow fringe of lowland between the mountains and the sea. It is a rather irregular coast, with many open bays and anchorages, a few islands offshore, and many sections in which the shore is cliffed. Many small streams pitch down out of the highlands in short, independent courses, that have built little delta patches and thin alluvial floodplains. A last, spreading rib of the fan is the short member north of the Songhoi River, running into the sea along the Chinese border of Indochina. It is much lower in elevation with a number of good gaps across it that facilitate movement between south China and the Tonking lowland. Both this and the Annamite Cordillera are composed of ancient crystalline rocks overlain with marine limestones, the whole considerably folded and faulted.

RIVER VALLEYS AND DELTAS

Like the ranges, most of the valleys of the great peninsula run from north to south. All the present broad delta-mouthed valleys occupy subsiding troughs left over from a previous era of mountain building. The streams that feed the great valleys have their headwaters on the Tibetan Plateau. Unlike many other river systems elsewhere the central, upper portions of their drainage basins are not extended catchment areas with many small tributaries feeding larger ones until the master stream is reached. Each river is individually framed with a double ring of mountains to isolate its valley from that of every other river. No two river valleys are precisely alike but, the Salween excepted, all the great valleys are rather similar in their physical development.

In the west the Irrawaddy, Chindwin, and Sittang rivers jointly have filled the remaining section of the old trough. The Irrawaddy has moved its course considerably as Tertiary mountain building took place. The Irrawaddy system is shorter than either the Salween or the Mekong, but its lowlands are more extensive. Some 800 miles long, the lowland is divided into a number of sectors by rocky gorges. The Irrawaddy drains most of the Shan Plateau and the eastern units of the Arakan Yoma. Its delta is a rapidly growing one, 150 miles long by 120 miles broad at the seafront. A total lowland area of some 40,000 square miles is included in the Irrawaddy basin.

The Salween is so restricted that it has very few tributaries of any kind and has built no appreciable delta at its mouth. It flows in a long structural trench dug deeper by the river itself, flowing right through the tight base of the fan structure sketched above. Its water volume does not change so markedly from season to season as that of the other streams, for its lowland catchment basin is both small and sheltered from the rainy winds of both monsoons. There is almost no flat land along its channel, there are many gorges and sections of rapids, the river is not navigable, and its canyon leads to no objective. It is probably one of the least useful streams among the great rivers of the world.

The Menam Chao Phraya is the shortest of the great rivers of southeastern Asia, draining a rather compact basin. Its lowland area totals about 26,000 square miles, being some 300 miles long by 75 to 100 miles wide. It has been filling in the upper end of another old gulf of the sea, but has not yet finished its task so that its delta resembles an estuary fill.

The Mekong is the most irregular of the rivers of this area. Its course, at present, detours around several of the primary regional blocks of southeastern Asia. From northern Thailand to the sea it has a variably developed floodplain, with minor floodplains along a number of tributaries draining the Korat Plateau and the Cambodian Saucer. Tributaries with steeper gradients drain the west slope of the Annamite Cordillera. The Mekong is the largest river in southeastern Asia, with a tremendous flow of water. It has built an irregular delta some 75 by 100 miles in dimensions.

The smallest of the big rivers is the Song Hoi or the Red River. This stream drains a long narrow structural trench that is aligned very suggestively in an extension of the Yangtze River of China, which originally flowed out to the sea by this line. The lowland is little more than a subsiding embayment fitted into the structural framework of eastern Asia at a point of change in pattern. A true delta, some 60 by 100 miles in dimensions, has been built in this embayment.

THE INSET BLOCKS

Three large separate blocks of old strata today form significant exceptions to the description of the Burmo-Malayan Peninsula as a series of mountain ranges with intervening alluvial troughs. Each of these reacted to the enveloping mountain building in a slightly different way.

THE SHAN PLATEAU. The dimensions of the plateau are about 250 miles long by 75 miles wide, nearly 20,000 square miles of area. The Salween River's structural trench lies on one side of it, and a fault scarp zone fronts the Irrawaddy lowland on the west. At present its pattern is that of a folded and faulted block, uplifted as a unit. It is composed of sedimentary rocks containing deep intrusive masses of crystalline rock. It probably was elevated to about its present position early in the Tertiary as a part of the developments along the Alpine Chain. Today, though it still retains most of its highland features, it is fairly deeply dissected and is by no means a perfect definition of a plateau. In ele-

vation it ranges between about 2,800 and 5,000 feet. As a rugged upland block it has little flat land for agriculture and presents few really favorable sites for concentrations of population.

THE KORAT PLATFORM. The region frequently labeled the Korat Plateau is really a rather low platform set a few hundred feet above the floodplains of the Menam and Mekong rivers. Structurally the platform is composed of horizontal Triassic red sandstones which are slightly uptilted around the southern and western margins. This platform rim is a peculiar, narrow zone of strongly folded and faulted older strata much dissected into a rugged line of hills separating the platform from the Menam Plain, and directing the surface drainage eastward to the Mekong. A stream net is lightly entrenched in the surface of the platform, which has a general elevation of about 500 feet in its central section, rising gradually to nearly 2,000 feet near the south and western rim of hills. Toward the margins of the platform are occasional mesas and patches of hills standing a few hundred feet above the general level. The platform has an area of nearly 60,000 square miles, and its dimensions roughly approximate a square, nearly 250 miles on a side.

THE CAMBODIAN SAUCER. Set below the level of the Korat Platform and just above sea level is the broad and shallow Cambodian Saucer. Fronting on the Gulf of Siam is a small patch of hill country almost connected to the rim of the Korat Plateau. The oval-shaped saucer lies between these hills and the southern end of the Annamite Cordillera, with the Mekong flowing, now, across the eastern sector. The bottom of the saucer is occupied by a large fresh-water lake, Tonle Sap, whose dimensions vary with the precipitation cycle. Much of the surface of the saucer today is covered with alluvial sediments, but it appears to be another block of old strata that reacted independently to the last era of mountain building. There are a number of hard-rock hill patches standing above the lowland level. In total area the Cambodian Saucer approximates 45,000 square miles.

THE MALAY PENINSULA

The peninsula is here considered to be the whole elongated region from the head of the Gulf of Siam to Singapore, a section some 900 miles long. The Kra Isthmus, the narrowest zone, is about 40 miles wide, but shallow navigable estuaries and streams on either coast are less than 20 miles apart, with a drainage divide less than 500 feet in height in a number of places. Here the mountain ranges are in strictly linear pattern, with but a slight offset *en echelon,* though they do not form a continuous high crest. Farther south in British Malaya more range blocks occur together in parallel formation over a wider span so that the peninsula spreads out to a maximum width of about 200 miles. The islands of Banka and Billiton are the terminal pieces of the long system. Throughout the peninsular region occur limestones and quartzites, along with minor amounts of other sedimentary rocks into which the Cretaceous granites were intruded. The sedimentary rocks most often show up around the flanks of ranges as low foothills set above the alluvial plains. In some places, however, the limestones have developed into strong karst landscapes with spectacular relief resulting, as in northwestern Malaya. Normally the granite range cores stand boldly above the lesser relief pattern of the lowlands. Many peaks in Malaya are more than 5,000 feet, and a few are more than 7,000. In Malaya granites are exposed over about half of the surface area.

Short streams drain limited areas both to east and west. The peninsular divide generally is nearer to the west coast than to the east coast. Many of the streams flow northward or southward, taking their orientation from the alignment of the structural blocks. This is particularly noticeable in Malaya, where the drainage net is clearly developed on the *en echelon* framework. In Malaya streams are longer than in the isthmus region, but they still are shallow, have unequal catchment basins, and are without significant deltas. Much of the lowland is not flat but molded in subdued relief; it slopes gently toward the sea along both coasts. Marine terrace levels around the alluvial coast are the expression of changing ice-age sea level. The alluvial cover on the Malayan west coast gradually deepens from the inland ranges toward the present shore line, where it locally exceeds 450 feet in thickness and extends downward below present-day sea level. Where hard, solid rock occurs numerous monadnocks and inselbergs may occur above the lowland, or rocky islands may be found in the strip offshore. The alluvial cover of the northern portion of the peninsula is restricted to isolated small patches or to stringy, narrow shore-line strips. It increases in thickness and breadth southward. The coastal plain ranges from 20 to 40 miles in width along the Malayan west coat, but on the east coast it rarely exceeds 20 miles. The alluvial cover is widely spread in much of the interior peninsula also, located at various levels. About one sixth of Malaya is surfaced by this alluvial cover. The foothills surrounding the mountain blocks grade off into the alluvial plains with no easy line of demarcation. Particularly in Malaya a considerable area of poorly drained flat lowland lies between the foothills and the coast. Though there are many islands along the central peninsular coast, there are few good harbors anywhere. The west coast of Malaya tends to be a shallow, muddy coast. The whole east coast of the peninsula suffers from the wind and sea during the Northeast Monsoon: the surf is high then, sand bars are built across river mouths, and sand dune strips are piled up along the shore. At the other season a broad and hard beach strand frequently is exposed.

THE ANDAMAN-NICOBAR LINE

A distance of some 750 miles separates Burma and the northwestern corner of Sumatra. Scattered over about 600 miles are the 225 islands making up the Andaman and Nicobar Islands. The former group numbers over 200 bits of land and totals some 2,500 square miles. The latter totals about 20 islands and measures some 635 square miles in area. About a half dozen are sizeable islands, the rest being mere rocky islets. The line of the two groups forms an arc roughly parallel to the peninsular coast, smoothly indicating the extension of the Alpine Chain from Burma around to Sumatra. Most of the islets are, of course, only the rocky exposed tops of buried mountains. The larger islands are irregular in shore line, steep sloped and rugged in surface, with minute patches of flattened lowland.

The Chinese Checkerboard

China consists of a large number of hilly, plateau-like or mountainous masses surrounding a variety of lowland units. Each section is placed at a different level, and no two accord with any one definition of basin, plain, plateau, hill, or mountain. The peculiar placement of units, the odd patterns of drainage systems, and the irregular blanketing of parts of the whole by wind-blown dust combine to defy any neat, simple, or concise description of the complex landscape of China. Unless recourse is taken to some systematic, and perhaps arbitrary, simplification, only a very considerable confusion can result in the mind of the reader. If only a mild confusion results from the following pages, therefore, the present attempt should be considered reasonably successful. This effort approaches the problem from the point of view of the structural skeleton of China rather than from that of a running account of its hills and basins.

The basic pattern of China, Korea, Manchuria, and eastern Mongolia is that of a lopsided and irregular checkerboard in which mountain systems are the separating lines and subsiding blocks and basins are the squares inside the lines. Few of the lines are straight or perfectly parallel, and none of them meet at right angles, so that none of the blocks are rectangles.

The primary structural lines appear to be four strips of hard rock running northeast-southwest as discontinuous lines. The most easterly form the south China coast between Canton and Shanghai; the most westerly marks the line of the Huang River in west Shensi. Second, there appear to be four east-west lines, set several hundred miles apart. This set is a somewhat schematic matter, admittedly. The most southerly is a vague line today, expressed as the Nanling Shan of South China; the most northerly is the Kentai Shan just south of the Siberian border. A third set of lines is a series of north-south ranges that form the borderlands of Chinese Tibet and carry on their eastern flanks the plateaus of south-west China. Placed irregularly between the three systems of lines are the subsiding basins that today show up as lowlands and sections of the coastal seas.

On this framework the physical history of China has been built in repeated and successive geologic eras. Some of these lines go back into the Pre-Cambrian, but were quiescent elements part of the time. Others have been the scene of significant happenings in every major tectonic period. At intersections of lines subordinate branchings and oblique forms have developed, to complicate the description and understanding of the present landscape. Very generally speaking, eastern China is lowest, and each line to the westward is set at a higher level until one comes out on the Plateau of Mongolia or rises into the highlands of Chinese Tibet.

THE TIBETAN BORDER RANGES

South of the Kunlun-Tsinling line there is a wide zone of the Tibetan borderland that has not been fully canvassed as to its physical relations to the Tibetan highland patterns. From east to west this strip is perhaps 300 miles wide, and it is 450–500 miles long. On the south these border ranges tie into the range alignments at the base of the Burmo-Malayan Fan. On the north, against the Tsinling, the ranges bend westward to fit into the general Tibetan alignment. A few peaks atop the higher borderland ranges rival the second-rank mountains of the main Himalayan range. Minya Gonka is the only one whose elevation is fixed with even tentative accuracy, at 24,891 feet, but there are a number of others close to 20,000 feet, and snow-covered crests run for hundreds of miles. This is a zone of deep river canyons and gorges excavated along structural lines. Primary alignment is very old and is basically north-south. In late Jurassic or very early Tertiary, prior to the main Alpine Chain orogeny, western Kweichow, Yunnan, westernmost Szechwan and

Hsikang were folded and faulted in a two-dimensional field whose primary orogenic lines ran north-south, but across which ran several important east-west lines such as that framing the southern flank of the Szechwan Basin. In this primary north-south trend lies the connection with the main ranges of the Burmo-Malayan Fan.

Mid-Tertiary orogeny of this border zone involved much differential uplift and probable overthrusting of a large order as the Himalayan ranges were erected to the west. The eastern part of this old structural field is the Yunnan Plateau and its associated Kweichow Plateau; the western part forms the massive Tibetan foreland. Tectonic movements and adjustments have continued into Recent geologic time, and the western section still is an active earthquake belt. Late glacial stream erosion has markedly deepened the upper courses of the major rivers. A number of isolated ranges, high but open basins, and minor inset plateaus occur as products of differential uplift and faulting. Glaciation has had a considerable share in shaping the present landscape, and there are U-shaped valleys and a wide variety of glacial and alluvial deposits on terraces, platforms and shoulders. There is little flat land, however, and much bare-rock surface.

THE ANCIENT MASSIFS

Along three definite zones the ancient bedrock of eastern Asia shows up. In all three there are Pre-Cambrian igneous and metamorphic rocks, with later granitic intrusions. Each zone is from 50 to 125 miles in width. All three have been variably affected by faulting, fracturing, and folding, most of which is developed lengthwise along the zones. All now are discontinuous strips, owing to the foundering of sections of each massif at a late geologic date. The three zones are separated by synclinal troughs. This pattern is one that goes back into early geologic time and has frequently been recurrent. The alignment is also somewhat similar to that of Burmo-Malaya and may have shared with it some of the earlier mountain-building history.

THE FUKIEN MASSIF. The easternmost line, forming a sea border to the Chinese mainland, extends from the Canton lowland to the Pootoo Islands in one sweep. Internal structural lines run northeast-southwest through the massif, though there are minor cross faults. The seaward side of the China section now is a submerged coast, with numerous islands, bays, inlets, estuaries, and cliffed coastal sections. Present-day topography is developed across the structural grain, with a water parting toward the western margin of the old massif. Most of the streams have cut separate and independent channels

to the coast, with their tributaries set into structural weaknesses longitudinally. Stream gradients are rather steep, and gorged and open sections alternate along the main streams. None of the streams is very large, their sediment loads are light, alluvial floodplains are small and narrow, and there is but little alluvial filling of the estuary which is the normal stream mouth. Each end of the massif has a stream entrenched along the structural line, and some of the highest, western portions beyond the water parting drain northward into the Poyang Lake division of the Yangtze Basin. Elevations along the crest zone average 3,500–4,500 feet, with a few strips over 5,000 feet. The whole massif is a rugged zone of hard rock and fairly strong relief, turning its back on mainland China and oriented to the seacoast along its separate valleys.

THE SHANTUNG-LIAOTUNG MASSIF. The second positive segment of the northeast-southwest set of lines extends from south China through the Shantung and Liaotung peninsulas. A shallow reverse curve then carries the massif into the highlands of eastern Manchuria. There are many fault and fracture zones which both run the length of the segment and cut across it at various angles. This causes the margins of the several pieces to be lower and to be set with blocks of old strata enclosing younger sediments. The northern end is more massive and less distorted, but also less well studied. In Shantung and Liaotung rounded and domed granite landscapes are cut in bold outlines and fairly strong relief. Elevations vary considerably from north to south, and just exceed 5,000 feet in Kiangsi where Kuling Shan stands abruptly above the lowland plain. West Shantung also just exceeds 5,000 feet in China's most sacred mountain, Tai Shan, but east Shantung is considerably lower. West Shantung has many embayments of alluvium around its ragged margin as part of the North China Plain, but in eastern Shantung these become cliff-lined bays, harbors, and inlets of the Yellow Sea. The Liaotung Peninsula, on its seaward side, is very like the corresponding section of Shantung. Northward in the Manchurian Highlands the zone grows broader, elevations are greater, and various segments become separate mountain ranges. Along the Korean border elevations reach a maximum of 9,000 feet where the ancient rocks are capped with much later extrusive igneous rock.

South of Kuling Shan, toward southern China, the massif runs underground and continues only as the somewhat uplifted water parting between Kiangsi and Hunan provinces to the intersection with the Nanling Shan. Across this lies a suggestive but subdued line of hills which points toward Hainan Island. The latter stands right on the line of the massif, but too little is known to make this affiliation more than a suggestion. Hainan appears to have a central highland core and a roughly radial drainage pattern. The central highland reaches about 5,000 feet, but is deeply dissected, and there is an irregular belt of spurs and river plains between the highland core and the coast. Parts of the coast now are very subdued in relief, and there are a number of wide alluvial coastal plains. If Hainan is a piece of the old massif, its island position has permitted denudation to sculpture its surface deeply to produce a landscape somewhat different from that found in the northern sectors.

THE TAIHANG-HSINGAN MASSIF. This third line suggests itself as one of the master lines of eastern Asia. It would appear to extend from northern Indochina clear to the Siberian border in a multiple curve as the third ancient massif. It has a monoclinal structure, with an eastern tilt, that sets the country to the west some 3,000 to 6,000 feet above the basins to the east. The southern half is fairly well buried under the marine limestones of the Kweichow and Yunnan plateaus, but the structural expression correlates with the physiographic one. The typical granite topography does not appear until north of the Huang River where the Taihang Shan fronts the North China Plain. From this point northward the third segment is continuous. In Shansi the Taihang is only one of the ranges that make up the massif segment, for faults, fractures, and overthrust zones have split it up considerably and separated its pieces. The roots of the separate ranges are similar in composition, but there are many sections of younger sediments distributed over the province that yield different topography.

As the ranges of Shansi trend northward their orographic expression is confused, in southern Jehol, by the intersection of one of the east-west lines, to be mentioned later. In northern Jehol northeast-southwest hill ranges fill much of the area between the main massif and the Gulf of Pohai. These gradually subside northward, merging into the denudational surface of the Manchurian Plain. To the west the Hsingan ranges carry the monoclinal massif pattern northward toward the Siberian border, where the Amur River skirts its tapering ridges on the north.

Everywhere strong relief and rugged topography are common. From the eastern basins the massif often appears a high and rugged mountain front with but few good passes through it. From the west, however, it is much less formidable, since the plateaus are set well above the basins. Crest elevations range between 8,000 and 9,000 feet in the Taihang, between 4,000 and 5,500 feet in the north and in the south. General elevations in the mountain country are less than these

figures, and there are some deep river canyons and structural breaks in the massif line.

THE ALA SHAN LINE. Approximately parallel to and some 250 miles west of the Taihang-Hsingan Massif runs the short line of the Ala Shan, a series of ranges marking the westernmost northeast-southwest structural line. The mountains are the upfolded and fractured edges of sedimentary strata and the faulted and intruded igneous core. Little field work has been done in this region, but the Ala Shan appears to be the highest of the northeast-southwest members. Rather than a broad massif the ancient core here is but a narrow mountain upland. At its junctions with the Tsinling and the Yin Shan are curving offset ranges. These are much more pronounced in the north, against the Yin Shan, where the curving lines give the mountains a semblance of continuity. Since the physical displacement involved is not great, the Ala Shan is not a high mountain range standing above the plateau level. Rather it is a rough, ragged, and dissected series of desert hill and mountain ranges. Its crests reach elevations of over 8,000 feet, but stand out above the surrounding plateaus no more than 3,000 feet at most. South of the Tsinling the line of the Ala Shan is replaced by the much greater ranges of Chinese Tibet. North of the Yin Shan in Mongolia there appears to be no surface continuation of the line.

THE EAST-WEST TECTONIC LINES

Opposed to the alignment of the ancient massif segments are four east-west tectonic zones that help cut China into separate blocks. These appear possibly younger than the massifs and are somewhat narrower in their physical proportions. All have their roots deep in central Asia. Three of the four do not present, today, great mountain ranges along their lines since they have not been active in recent geologic time, their last products being somewhat worn down at present. The fourth zone, however, has been a line of considerable Tertiary and Pleistocene activity and is one of the most significant physical lines in all China. Wherever an east-west line intersects a massif line there is structural complication and orographic confusion. Wherever an east-west tectonic line crosses a massif line, curved or offset units result as the extension of the tectonic line. Several different kinds of pressure have been exerted on the earth's crust which, particularly at intersections, has produced variable branchings, cross connections, and oblique mountain ranges. Much denudation and, in some cases, further tectonic distortion have made the complete analysis of the resulting pattern very difficult. Eastern Asia has not yet been adequately studied to allow the unraveling of all component threads of crustal development.

THE KENTAI SHAN. Near the northern border of Outer Mongolia runs the Kentai Shan in a trend that is largely east-west though there are major deflections in the line. To the east, as it approaches the Hsingan member of the western massif, its ranges appear to swing northward. East of the Hsingan is a southward curving group of ranges known as the Little Hsingan, that terminates against the next massif to the east. These two sets of ranges are complementary parts of an east-west tectonic line whose clean trend is affected by the mass of the older massif. This portion of Asia is too little studied to allow more than a suggestive comment. However, the mountain ranges of this line do form a margin to the Chinese checkerboard on the north, setting a northern limit alike to the Mongolian Plateaus and the Manchurian Plain.

THE YIN SHAN. On the southern side of the Mongolian Plateaus the line known as the Yin Shan has a trend very similar to that of the Kentai Shan farther north. Across northern Shensi, just above the Yellow River, its ranges trend roughly east-west. But as its members come up against the Taihang-Hsingan Massif they bend northward very much as do the ranges of the northern line. East of the massif there is a suggestion of a similar southward curving orographic trend, comparable to that of the Little Hsingan, but it shortly terminates in the Gulf of Pohai. The intersection of the two zones appears to be a rather complicated one, with various curving offsets not yet fully mapped. Throughout the whole line of the Yin Shan there is folding and simple faulting of strata. In addition a considerable amount of overthrust faulting has produced some sharp contrasts in local landscapes.

In the west the lines of the Yin Shan system run out into the dry open spaces of the southern Gobi country and seem more structural roots than upstanding highlands. Orographically the Ala Shan and the Yin Shan show some continuity. Eastward across Shensi and Shansi the ranges begin to gather bulk, greater height, and stronger relief. Near and on both sides of the Taihang-Hsingan Massif dissection has so effectively jumbled the present topography that it is difficult to pick out predominant lines. The intersection makes passage outward from the North China Plain difficult, both into Manchuria and into Inner Mongolia. It is significant that the best passes occur close to the intersection. Though this is not a rainy landscape today, an intricate stream net has been cut into the rugged mountain country, giving a maximum percentage of steep slopes and a minimum total of flat or open lands.

THE TSINLING SYSTEM. A very different mountain complex is the Tsinling Shan. Northeastern Tibet is not well known, but it would appear that the Tsinling is an extension of the Kunlun system of northern Tibet. It has been a zone of major tectonic activity as late as mid-Pleistocene, has a very complicated structure, and stands up as tall and precipitous ranges along its western sector. Leaving Tibet it consists of two slightly divergent segments, the Tsinling Shan proper on the north and the Tapa Shan on the south. The two segments extend as far as the intersection with the Taihang-Hsingan Massif, but beyond this only a single contorted line continues. In the west strong Tertiary and Pleistocene earth movements complement similar movements in the north-south border ranges of Chinese Tibet. Simple faults and complicated overthrusts of considerable proportions are part of this development.

The Tsinling emerges from Tibet with elevations of over 16,000 feet and a north face that is among the world's great fault scarp zones. Elevations taper gradually toward the intersection with the Taihang-Hsingan Massif. The southern segment, the Tapa Shan, is less rugged and high than the Tsinling proper, and its southern flanks have been deeply laid open by Yangtze River tributaries. The Han River, draining the zone between the two segments, has cut upland valleys both north and south. Although the natural orientation of the Han Valley is eastward, there are enough passes at practical elevations to enable movement across the Tsinling even in its highest sector.

In the intersection of the Tsinling with the Taihang-Hsingan Massif there are some branchings in Honan, known as the Funiu Shan. Southward contortions of the main line of the Tsinling close off the eastward extension of the Tapa Shan and turn the Han River southward toward the Yangtze. East of the intersection just mentioned the Tsinling displays little evidence of recent tectonic activity. Consequently relief and elevations decrease so that the general level is between 2,000 and 3,000 feet. Though there are no great or sheer scarp zones, relief is very rugged and dissection seems nearly complete, so that travel across the line is almost as difficult as in the western zone unless the pass routes are followed. Near the Taihang-Hsingan intersection occurs the lowest gap across the whole of the Tsinling, a level route under 1,500 feet, known as the Nanyang Gap. To the east there are a number of low passes none of which, however, is so easy to traverse as the Nanyang Gap. Southeastward the Tsinling line continues under several names as a tapering range of rugged hills. About where it again should have intersected a massif segment the trend of the hills shifts northward, and it dies out as low and tapering spurs and inselbergs in the edges of the North China Plain.

THE NANLING SHAN. The most southerly of the east-west lines is hard to trace structurally and ill preserved physically. It is a line of older activity than that which built the border ranges of Chinese Tibet and elevated the Yunnan Plateau. The Nanling shows no correspondence with the western segment of the Tsinling, but only with its central and eastern end. In the west the Nanling line is buried under the Yunnan Plateau and to the east is a recurved line which swings northward along the southern flank of the Fukien-Korean Massif. The south China water parting between the Yangtze River system and the rivers of Kwangtung and Kwangsi provinces lies just north of 25° N. lat. Dissection has proceeded very far in the western section, where only the remnants of karst landscapes exist, producing spectacular scenic effects and a low-level, canalized route through the hills, known as the Hsiang-Kuei Gap. Eastward karst features decrease as the country rock changes from limestone to older, less soluble sediments. General elevations increase eastward also until the oblique curves of the Nanling join the Fukien Massif, where elevations above 5,000 feet are common. Passes through the hills are common and practical for land travel along the whole length of the Nanling, those to the east being true passes and not low-level gaps as in the west. This is a hilly country with almost a maximum of dissection outside the karst landscapes, an intricate drainage net, and very little flat land in the hill lands themselves.

THE SYNCLINAL BASINS

On either side of each massif segment is an elongated synclinal trough, divided into sections. The several troughs did not react alike, any more than did sections of any one trough. The Yellow Sea now does cover parts of both, massif and trough, and the China Sea covers the synclinal area between the Fukien Massif and the nearest junction of Island Arcs in Formosa. Some of the trough sections, however, did not founder completely but remain as subsiding basins of varying amounts of movement. In some basins alluvial sedimentation has kept their bottoms above sea level, just as it has elevated a few foundered sections above sea level as deltas. Several sectors show synclinal structure but only very shallow physical basins, whereas in one or two sectors not even synclinal structure developed in the appropriate location. Thus there are no two checkerboard squares exactly alike.

THE MANCHURIAN PLAIN. The amount of recent subsidence of the northern section of the central trough is only moderate and has not been continuous. The present surface of the Manchurian Plain is the result of denudation rather than deposition, and is divided between the two river systems, the Sungari on the north and the Liao on the south. The water parting between the two systems is a gradual one, not noticeable in the landscape so that the basin retains its unity. The margins of the plain, both east and west, are irregular, as there are embayments along tributary streams draining the massifs on either side. Much of the plain has an elevation of 400–700 feet, and the surface is a gently rolling one, with stream channels rather lightly entrenched in most places. In the north the intersection of the Little Hsingan with the Shantung-Manchurian Massif is not a tight one, and the Sungari River has developed a wide gap through to the Amur River. This is the only real gap in the whole northern rim of the basin. In the south the breadth of the lowland is restricted by the eastward projection of the Yin Shan line and the thickening of the uplands around its intersection with the Taihang-Hsingan Massif.

THE NORTH CHINA PLAIN. The North China Plain is the filled area of both trough and massif segments between the Yin Shan and Tsinling lines east of the Taihang-Hsingan Massif. The Huang River was principally responsible for the large northern sector, the Yangtze River for a small southern sector, with the smaller Hwai River giving assistance in the central southern area. Early in the sedimentation process Shantung was an island in the Yellow Sea, but such was the volume of materials available that the whole of the narrow trough was filled, the island half surrounded, and over one third of the original water area filled in. Innumerable shifts north and south of the former island have kept both sections progressing approximately alike at a present rate of about a mile a century. Many small streams come into the present plain but, like even the larger Hwai River, their sedimentation effects are minor and obscure compared to the effects of the Huang. These subordinate streams cause many floods, however, for they cannot maintain their channels to the sea against the Huang, and their waters become ponded behind the natural levees, alluvial fills, and torrential flood deposits of the larger stream. There is a surface uniformity about the North China Plain that gives it a considerable monotony as a landscape. There are minor differences in relief and surface forms, but almost more important than these are the differences in soils and water supply conditions. The plain slopes gradually eastward from an elevation of almost 500 feet against the Taihang and Funiu ranges. The Huang flows above the plain most of the distance to the sea, on a mud ridge built of its own sediments, and the task of keeping the river on the ridge is a difficult and a recurrent one. Throughout parts of the southern plain inselbergs stand out as bare rock, and long low swells of hard rock at the surface indicate marine planation before the filling of the sector above sea level.

POYANG LAKE PLAIN. South of the Yangtze River and between the Fukien and the Shantung massifs is a portion of the eastern trough that forms a separate synclinal basin with a lake in its bottom. This is one of the smaller basin units occupying a square on the checkerboard. Poyang Lake varies with river and flood level, between 20 by 65 miles in winter low water and 30 by 90 miles in summer flood periods. Into it drain a series of streams, the largest of which flow from the south. The southern lake margins have been filled above average summer level, and the streams themselves have developed floodplains. The lake has become steadily smaller during historic time but the rate of filling is much less than in the North China Plain. Subsidence may be continuing, slowly, to maintain the permanent water body, for the floor of the lake is just below sea level. The margins of the basin are quite irregular, being full of lowland embayments and protruding hill spurs consequent upon a long-continued active denudation.

TUNGTING LAKE PLAIN. This is the next basin west, beyond the Shantung-Manchurian Massif. The synclinal basin covers northern Hunan and south central Hupeh across the channel of the Yangtze River. Historically the Chinese name for Hunan and Hupeh was "liang hu," meaning "the two lake provinces," and within historic time alluvial sedimentation has considerably reduced the area of permanent water surface. The northern section has been more completely filled than the southern, which now contains the only large body of water, Tungting Lake. The big lake varies from 20 by 60 miles in winter to 50 by 80 miles in summer, but there are numerous small lakes in the central and northern part of the basin. Tungting Lake itself is being filled by summer flood waters of the Yangtze River which escape the normal channel through overflow cutoffs, in peak periods of upper river floods, into the northwestern margins of the lake area.

Large rivers enter the plain both from north and south, and river floodplains reach far back along several streams. The central portion of the basin in summer is a watery marsh maze, with small lakes, old river channels, canalized channels, natural levees, and major and minor dike lines forming an almost indecipherable pattern. Because more sediment is available in this western basin than around Poyang Lake, more filling has been done and the land level is higher than that of the eastern basin. The basin margins are as irregular as those of the Poyang Basin but the chief embayments are deeper.

THE RED BASIN. Set a step above the two main trough lines is a western trough which contains only one obvious synclinal basin. Central Szechwan was a Cretaceous-Tertiary lake basin partially filled with buff, red, and purple sandstones and shales. The Red Basin consists of the lowland heart of Szechwan Province and is ringed by hills and mountains belonging to the positive elements in the checkerboard. The basin now is drained by the upper Yangtze River system which has cut a mighty series of gorges into the surrounding mountain landscapes on all sides to maintain the drainage of central China. Inside the basin the Yangtze and its tributaries have lightly etched the floor of the basin with an intricate stream network. The intensity of elaboration of this stream pattern is difficult to visualize, but there probably are few spots on the globe that surpass it. It is this region which contributes the color and the largest share of the sediment volume to the Yangtze River with which the lake basins and the delta to the east now are being filled. The floor of the basin is less than 900 feet in elevation, but its outer margins reach 1,500 to 1,800 feet. A number of minor late Tertiary structural ridges run northeast-southwest across the basin to give it local subdivisions. One of these, in the northwest corner of the basin, fences off the only flat territory in all Szechwan. The Chengtu Plain is an enormous, flat alluvial piedmont built behind a protective ridge, and is a local area of real contrast to the rest of the Red Basin.

MINOR SYNCLINAL BASINS. Of a number of remaining squares on the checkerboard none is a synclinal basin in the obvious physical sense, but brief comments about some of them will help fill out the description of China.

The Shensi Basin. Between the Tsinling and Yin Shan lines and between the Taihang-Hsingan and Ala Shan massifs is the structural basin of Shensi. During later geologic time this has not been a subsiding basin, so that its classification is geologic. Having been also an arid region for much of recent time no stream system has turned it into a denudational lowland as in the case of the Manchurian Plain. On the contrary, during part of Recent time it has been an area of accumulation, of loess in the southern section, and of dune sand in the northern section. Even more recently tributaries of the Wei and Huang rivers have been rapidly eating into the loess cover and have turned much of eastern Shensi into a desiccated badland of strong relief.

The East Mongolian Basin. Between the Yin Shan and the Kentai Shan, west of the Taihang-Hsingan

Massif, the open plateau surfaces of eastern Mongolia show several gentle, local synclinal units. Being also an arid region no water volume ever accumulated sufficient to cut across one of the bounding limits to drain the area. Much of the Mongolian Plateaus to the west seem to consist of alternate swells and hollows of structural nature.

The Yangtze Estuary. At the southern end of the North China Plain is a small subsiding zone just inside the Fukien Massif line. This is now the filled estuary mouth of the Yangtze River, aided by other small streams. Not all the zone has been filled in so far, as Hangchow Bay is a part of the subsident zone. It is not entirely clear what is the relation of this part of the trough to the larger portion listed as the Poyang Basin.

The Canton Lowland. The little submerged unit at the collective mouth of the three river systems of Kwangtung is also a minor synclinal unit along the eastern trough line, for it clearly is not a true delta in the usual definition. South of the Nanling Shan and southwest of the Fukien Massif, it would occupy a square of the checkerboard that runs out to sea. The three rivers have filled a considerable area of lowland that still has inselbergs sticking up through the plain. Offshore lie numerous islands that still are beyond reach of the fill.

The Kwangsi Platform. Central western Kwangsi is another checkerboard square in which no obvious synclinal structure can be noted, though geologic field work is by no means complete. The Kwangsi Platform lies below the uplifted Yunnan Plateau, just as the Manchurian Plain lies below the uplifted Mongolian Plateau. Here, however, the positive lines on east and south are only weak ones which fail to provide a positive physiographic framework. The Hsi River has developed a drainage net that includes the southern slopes of the Nanling Shan and the edges of the Kweichow and Yunnan plateaus. The landscape of the platform is shallow and open, with wide floodplains and deep waterways which have not yet developed many meanders.

THE SOUTHWESTERN PLATEAUS

Previously it was suggested that, except for the Red Basin, the territory west of the Taihang-Hsingan Massif is an elevated plateau region. Where the north-south ranges of Chinese Tibet approach and impinge upon the massif in southwest China the normal upland was lifted even higher. Here were produced two distinctive landscapes, the Yunnan Plateau on the west and the lower Kweichow Plateau on the northeast.

THE YUNNAN PLATEAU. The plateau consists of alternating basins, mountain ranges, and broad rolling highlands. The general elevation is above 6,000 feet, with mountain ranges standing above the broad highlands. Most of the ranges are oriented north-south, but there are some transverse elements, as suggested on an earlier page. In the south they reach about 9,000 feet, increasing toward the north to elevations around 16,000 feet. The Yunnan Plateau then shades north and west into the ranges of Chinese Tibet with still higher elevations. The basins vary in size from units of a few square miles to districts over 1,000 square miles in area. Normally the basins are bounded on at least one side by a fault scarp, and usually they possess a permanent lake. Many of the isolated ranges, some of the basins, and most of the lakes are the products of very late Tertiary and Pleistocene mountain building, and today the western section is still an earthquake zone. Glacial features show up in the west, and toward the east incipient karst features appear, with numerous small basins. This karst landscape increases in degree of maturity as one moves down onto the Kwangsi Platform.

The plateau is deeply trenched by streams on all margins. The Yangtze cuts a long and tremendous gorge in making its way eastward across the northern end. On the west the Mekong and Salween trenches bound the plateau, with minor Mekong tributary gorges on the west and southwest. On the south the Song Hoi of Indochina has deeply cut into the body of the plateau; on the east the Hsi River and its tributaries have cut some enormous canyons and trenches. Much of this deep erosion is thought to be early Pleistocene interglacial in age.

THE KWEICHOW PLATEAU. The southern ramparts of the Red Basin of Szechwan and the western uplands above the southern Tungting Lake Basin form the Kweichow Plateau. Except for its western margins, joining the Yunnan Plateau, it is a poor example of the physiographic species: plateau. It consists of strongly folded and faulted marine limestones for the most part, so that much of its surface is divided into separate structural basin units. Its primary structural alignment is northeast-southwest, but there are many local variant lines. Its southern and southeastern margins are strongly affected by karst developments so that many ragged and streamless basins with spectacular highland rims dominate the landscape. To the north and east streams have cut gorges and canyons deep into its front. It is difficult country through which to travel by any means of transport. Extensive deforestation and soil erosion have added to its rough and barren appearance. A rugged, rocky landscape of strong local relief and irregular local landscapes, it is one of the poorest sections of China.

THE DRAINAGE PATTERN

The somewhat confusing patterns of the checkerboard break down into a rather simple set of drainage divisions or stream systems. Those squares lying in the Mongolian Plateaus obviously are internal drainage units of their own, by patterns not well mapped. The Manchurian Plain is the only basin unit with two independent drainage systems. All the squares of the checkerboard between the Yin Shan and the Tsinling Shan proper belong to the Huang River system. The rather curious course of the main stream itself derives from the fact that as the separate steps between the sea and the Tibetan Plateau were elevated steadily higher in the building of Tibet the river adapted itself to changing conditions. Every major change in the course of the stream after leaving Tibet is now dictated by some part of either massif members or tectonic lines.

The Yangtze River system now drains all the region between the Tsinling and the Nanling lines, divided into several separate divisions corresponding to the synclinal basin patterns. The stream originates in eastern Tibet, swings southward along the ranges of Chinese Tibet and formerly flowed into the Gulf of Tonking. Tectonic earth movements promoted stream capture of the Tibetan stream by a headwater tributary of the Yangtze.

Between the divergent Funiu Shan and Hwaiyang-Shan sections of the eastern Tsinling system there was room for a small river drainage basin, and here the Hwai River elaborated a normal basin. As the Huang built up its own delta, however, it appropriated the Hwai Basin upon occasion, a performance repeated several times within the historic period. Eventually the Hwai River has been boxed off from the sea by the depositional action of the Huang and the Yangtze.

Fukien, as suggested previously, drains to the coast in its own separate pattern of short streams, forming a whole series of separate, small drainage basins.

South of the Nanling Shan there are three rivers that join in the Canton Lowland, the Tung, the Pei, and the Hsi, the East, North, and West rivers. The Tung and the Pei drain the southern end of the Fukien Massif and the southern slopes of the Nanling Shan. The Hsi drains the main territory south of the Nanling Shan, the Kwangsi Platform, and the edges of the Kweichow and Yunnan plateaus. It has sunk a shallow but distinct basin so that a line of low hills separates it from the narrow seaward slope of the littoral.

LOESS AND THE LOESS UPLANDS

The structural patterns of China have been partially disguised during winter windstorms by the blanket of yellow dust they have blown out of inner Asia. This fine yellow dust is known as loess, and there are a number of unsolved problems around its origin and movement. Whatever the final answers may be, it does cover much of north China today, and is an important factor in the landscape. Settling as a layer of variable thickness over most of north China it covered up much of the landscape produced by denudation during late Tertiary and early Pleistocene time. The higher and steeper surfaces either never received or quickly lost their dust blanket to keep protruding through the soft and smooth new landscape as inselbergs and remnant mountains. Also some of the more important Huang River tributaries kept their own basins nearly free of the dust blanket and today are relatively deeply set into the loess landscape as elongated strips of quite different nature. In the central area of western Shansi, northwestern Honan, and southern Shensi the dust blanket became several hundred feet thick in the deeper hollows and protected spots. All around the margins the blanket gradually thins out. Depositional dust storms heavy enough to darken the sky were part of the late Pleistocene seasonal weather pattern almost everywhere in China north of the Tsinling Shan. Very little dust is being added to north China today, though considerable local redistribution does take place by means of winter windstorms. A large amount of re-sorting by stream action has occurred almost everywhere in northern China. In any one local area the loess is uniformly fine in texture, shows only slight differences from bottom to top, stands in vertical columns or walls when cut or eroded, absorbs water like a sponge and returns it to the surface in the same way, is easily cultivated, and is everlastingly rich as a farm soil without the addition of fertilizer. The addition of a loess cover to almost any landscape in the world would improve it, from the standpoint of its agricultural resource. To the hard and ancient rocks of the Taihang-Hsingan Massif loess soils prove a tremendous contrast.

On the other hand, the cessation of loess deposition has allowed denudation free action all over north China. The very softness of loess has made it very easily eroded by the work of water and wind. With a given expression of energy the forces of denudation can produce a rougher landscape with a higher relief component in loess than in almost any other landscape material. Consequently much of the loess landscape has changed greatly within the historic period and now parts of it are a rough and dissected badland region difficult to cultivate or to travel through. The material removed by water has largely been redeposited in some portion of the North China Plain, an incidental factor in building an extremely rich delta landscape.

In blanketing the underlying landscape and in providing a new surface of variable thickness and distribution, loess deposition has given the geographer an added problem. The pattern of deposition did not fit the regional patterns of the older landscape. One may ask the question whether the surficial unity of the loess uplands is greater and more significant than the underlying structural patterns and remnant features of the older landscape, particularly when they show through as clearly as in north China. There can be no easy answer to this question, and there is no agreement among geographers.

GLACIATION IN THE CHINESE LANDSCAPE

Only since the early 1930's has it been recognized that glaciation was a factor in developing the upland physiography of a part of China. Though only an incomplete survey has been made so far it would appear that mountain glaciation and the seasonal action of ice and snow fields have left their prints fairly widely over China in glacial cirques, U-shaped valleys, serrated ridges, and a variety of morainic deposits ranging from beds of scratched boulders to thick mantles of glacial debris. Much of the evidence has been mutilated by consequent denudation or, in the lower areas, concealed by cultivation effects. Zones of glaciation now are being mapped in most of the uplands of central and western China, as well as in Formosa. Particularly along the Tibetan foreland is glaciation important in the present landscape. The problem of north China's loess is connected with the history of glaciation in eastern Asia, since much of the earlier bottom layers of loess appear to have water-borne clays, sands, and silts mixed with them.

THE KOREAN PENINSULA

Off on the northeast corner of the checkerboard the east Asian coast is close to a junction with the long loops of the Island Arcs, and here crustal blocks did not perform quite as they did elsewhere. Most of Korea is sometimes considered to have been part of an ancient north China massif, whereas south Korea has been considered an extension of the Fukien Massif. The Korean Peninsula, though showing definite relation to the northeast-southwest massif alignment, does not today exhibit the clearly alternate massif and synclinal pattern that marks China. There are no evidences of the east-west lines. On the other hand, along the southeast coast appear features that belong to the Island Arcs. In the simplest analysis Korea can be

divided into three separate structural units, each involving several subdivisions of an order too detailed for individual consideration here. We may note, in passing, that the 38th parallel, chosen to divide northern and southern Korea at the end of World War II, has no relation to any physical feature of the Korean landscape.

NORTHERN KOREA. Closely aligned with the northern sector of the Shantung-Manchurian Massif northern Korea has an underlying ancient rock complex that is faulted and tilted to present a steep eastern scarp zone and a gentler slope westward to the Gulf of Pohai. Along the northern border early Pleistocene extrusions of basalt built inland sections to elevations averaging above 6,000 feet, culminating in higher volcanic peaks. Consequent dissection, with further faulting, has created a rugged landscape of high relief, confused local patterns, and very small patches of land level enough to permit easy cropping. Along the northeast coast there is a narrow dissected coastal bench set above sea level and between fault scarps. It is a strip of hard-rock outcrops standing in bluffed headlands along the coast, with intervening bits of alluvial lowland built by steep, short streams. On the west, in contrast, there is a wide belt of country which tapers from the high interior to the Gulf of Pohai in a descending scale of relief. Much of this was once a synclinal trough but later was strongly compressed in folded and faulted structures on a northeast-southwest trend. The present landscape is cut into the folded and faulted surface. Toward the volcanic highland relief is strong and streams are deeply entrenched. Nearer the coast relief becomes subdued and the landscape open, with wide floodplain strips along rivers. The littoral is a zone of alluvium and low spurs protruding seaward, with an outer strip of shallow water sediments and marine-planed flats alternately washed by high tide waters and exposed as muddy flats at low water. Tide ranges reach nearly 40 feet at maximum in some of the inner embayments.

SOUTHERN KOREA. A large portion of southern Korea is a block nearly 300 miles long, bounded on the north and east by major fault scarps and tilted southwestward during Tertiary time. Though a massif during much of geologic time, the block was broken by internal fault and fold zones, so that parts of the region reacted somewhat independently. The primary alignments are northeast-southwest, both structurally and orographically. Since there are different rock strata involved the whole massif is not uniformly dissected and landscaped. The Diamond Mountains are perhaps the most spectacularly sculptured. The backbone is close to the east coast, and reaches elevations well above

6,000 feet. Off this main ridge line numerous spurs run southwestward, gradually decreasing in elevation until, as peninsulas, they dip into the sea with island peaks in line beyond them. On the northern west coast there are fewer of these protruding spurs and the littoral resembles that of northern Korea, but along the southwest and south this indented and cliffed coast is highly developed.

The drainage of the southern block is less simply arranged than that of the northern, and the pattern of stream dissection has added to the complexity of the physiography by cutting across the structure. Three primary streams have cut valley systems into the block, drain most of the territory, and have floodplains along their lower courses. These streams drain to different corners, northwest, southwest, and southeast, leaving a central highland zone which effectively separates the lowland units of southern Korea.

THE EASTERN COAST. Below the high scarps of the backbone of southern Korea lies a very narrow, curved bench that is the east coast of Korea. It reaches from the northern end of the block to the south end of the Korean Peninsula, widening out somewhat in the last 100 miles. The coastal bench is a narrow section between major faults which are the northern ends of one of the lines of the Island Arcs. Therefore, this is a junction between continental and Pacific Margin structural elements. This rocky bench has short, steep streams spaced along it, each with a minuscule alluvial formation at the coast. There are few good passes along the central reach of the coast to connect this narrow land with the main bulk of the peninsula.

THE ISLAND ARCS

Three of the primary crustal segments of the earth meet in south and eastern Asia. Separating each of the three run the lines of Tertiary-Pleistocene orogeny in a variety of folding, faulting, overthrusting, uplift, volcanism, and earthquake spasms. These major lines are rather old geologically and have repeatedly been the scene of continued section. On the mainland this mountain building is expressed as the high, curving Alpine Chain. Beyond the mainland these same curving arcs are expressed as chains of islands. There are nearly a dozen separate arcs with varying lengths and rates of curvature. Some have but a single main axis and no branches, but others show multiple lines and a variety of branching spurs. Almost all the Asiatic arcs are convex toward the Pacific Basin. A few are pitched rather high above present sea level; others are set lower and expose only their mountain tops as small islands. Many contain much more mass than shows above the

sea. Along several are the deepest of the world's marine trenches, and the physical separation of mountain peak and trough bottom is greater in a number of cases than that along the main Himalayan range.

Some of the island arcs are Tertiary in origin, but most of the large ones are much older, for some of the same pressures were applied in earlier geologic times. It is likely that some pattern of land has long been a part of the contact zone between the Pacific, Indian, and Asiatic crustal segments. Whether these were the whole continents sometimes inferred as the source of present continental sediments or whether some of them were but island chains is difficult to answer. Almost every present island chain shows a volume of simple or metamorphosed sedimentary rock. In addition some of the chains show considerable old intrusive granitic rocks. Some of these old cores have very complex structures. Late Tertiary and Pleistocene mountain building appeared to express itself in arcs set along two master lines, an Asiatic and a Pacific line. Both master lines are double lines. The first is an extension of the Alpine Chain of western Burma around through Sumatra, Java, and Timor. Then commences a series of sharp curves which carry the line north and west through Ceram, north again through Celebes and into the Philippines. Passing on to Formosa the line then loops back through the Ryukyu chain into Japan. From northern Japan divergent arcs approach the mainland of northeastern Asia. The second master line is one out of the south Pacific into and through New Guinea. Its northern projection is more speculative as a continuous line. Swinging northward at the Moluccas it loops back through Palau, the Marianas, and the Bonins to join the other master line in central Japan. The near contact of the two lines in the Indies is at the common junction of all three crustal segments, and is more complex than the line marking the meeting of any two of the segments.

Volcano building is the only form of vulcanism that has been active in the Pleistocene and Recent periods. In the Asiatic master arc only the inner line shows volcanos from Sumatra to the Philippines; elsewhere volcanos are more scattered. There are hundreds of old craters, but the active volcanos number in the vicinity of two hundred, over half of which are to be found in the Indies.

Along the Asiatic master arc there are a number of individual arcs. The ends of some of them seem to intersect or cross, and at each point of crossing is found a rather massive island buttress. Formosa, Kyushu, and Hokkaido are certainly such intersections, and several small arcs meet in Honshu. Luzon and Mindanao are less clear cases of such arc meeting. North of

Mindanao the largest islands are the buttress points of the arcs.

In southeastern Asia the present arrangement of land and sea, and the number and configuration of individual islands, is a matter of Pleistocene geologic time. During the Pleistocene sea level was such that Sumatra, Java, Borneo, and Malaya were connected in one great land mass sometimes called Sunda Land. Present island streams are but the headwaters of much larger rivers. In reverse, the present single island of Mindanao was at one time (pre-Pleistocene) separated by shallow waters into about five islands. Throughout the whole of the Island Arcs this kind of fluctuation of land and sea has gone on ever since early Tertiary time.

An added complication is the Tertiary, Pleistocene, and Recent coral reef building. Like the whole south Pacific a great many of the islands south of Okinawa are fringed by active coral reefs. Some of the smaller islands are really thin layers of accumulated sediment resting on coral reef foundations. Coral reefs are found along many coastal sections of large islands, and here they are but a small part of the structural basement. Throughout the Indies there are many raised coral reefs, some now resting as high as 3,000 feet above sea level. Coral does not seem to be present along many of the volcanic coasts, owing to the steady outwash of sediments. Recent submergences of a small order characterize at least the Sunda Shelf region, and aggradation marks most coral reef islands. Along the main Island Arcs here discussed coral reefs are but a minor aspect of the physical history of the larger islands, are important parts of many of the smaller islands, but nowhere play the role common to them in the open Pacific Ocean.

THE INDIES

Most of the hundreds of islands that compose the groups known as the Indies are set along both master arc lines. In the Indies at least both master arcs are double lines, so that there are either two rows of islands or two structural axes. In the open parts of the arcs island contours are relatively simple, but in the sharply curved junction zone there have resulted some peculiarly shaped mountain ranges. In the Indies also, structure of a part of the continental shelf makes chain arrangement less obvious than in such groups as the Kuriles or the Ryukyus. Borneo and certain lesser islands were not actually a part of the most recent mountain building. Some of the islands are large and complex blocks; others are just the tops of volcanos built above present sea level. Among the hundreds of islands and islets there is a great and real variety of landscapes, varying from the smooth lowland marsh fringes

to the high mountain scarps and boiling volcanic cauldrons.

SUMATRA. Third largest in size, 163,000 square miles, Sumatra is set on the western lobe of the inner arc with a northwest-southeast trend, with the equator running almost through its center. Its west coast is steep and cliffed most of the way, with a very narrow lowland fringe, since the axis of the volcanic line runs close to the coast. On the east side of the line folded and faulted spurs branch off toward the coast, tapering gradually until they run under the wide alluvial zone which, itself, ends in a broad strip of tidal marsh and mangrove swamp. The volcanos are perched atop the sedimentary core of the highland and reach elevations of 11,000 and 12,000 feet.

JAVA. Java is only the fifth largest of the islands of the Indies, with a total of about 48,000 square miles. It is set on the same inner arc line as Sumatra, with a similar structural pattern. The main highland axis is nearest the south coast, and there are offset spurs, branches, and minor fold axes running along the north side of the island. Its south coast is a narrow fringe only, cliffed and rugged. The north side of the island is variable in relief, from hill patches to alluvial plains. An alluvial plain stretches along much of the littoral, backed by a rolling to hilly zone. Through the central highland runs the volcanic zone, with craters at many different elevations, the highest being above 11,000 feet. Few good harbors on the south coast, in contrast to a number on the north coast, help orient the island northward.

CELEBES. With an area of 73,000 square miles Celebes is a group of peninsulas representing the folded and volcanic tops of the two main axes of the Asiatic master arc at one of the points of tightest curvature. It is mostly hilly to mountainous upland, with elevations above 5,000 feet along the spine of every peninsular unit of the island. Narrow lowland strips and little lowland embayments cut by short streams surround the island, along with narrow marine terraces.

NEW GUINEA. The largest island of the Indies totals about 304,000 square miles and is the main land mass on the Pacific master arc line. It shows a double axis pattern, one mountain fold line running parallel with the north coast and close to it, the other forming the inland mountain core. The northern range of hills has but few spots above 5,000 feet, but the central range has several peaks above 16,000 feet and is one of the world's great mountain ranges, extending through the island for a distance of over 1,000 miles. South of the central range a broad, subsiding lowland slopes gradually off to the sea. Peninsular extensions project east and west at both ends of the island, along the main axis. Until World War II this was one of the least known parts of the world, and there still remain sections in which simple exploration still must be done.

BORNEO. Borneo is the second largest island of the Indies, with an area of approximately 287,000 square miles. Lying on the Asiatic crustal segment, Borneo is inside the Asiatic master arc. There seem to be at least two Tertiary structural lines that trend northeast-southwest and intersect the Asiatic master arc in the Philippines. Orographically, a central spinal column runs from the northwest corner of the island, where the granite mass of Mount Kinibalu stands over 13,000 feet in height, down the center of the island. Spurs branch off both southeast and southwest, and there are many peaks scattered over the island above 7,000 feet in height. A radial drainage pattern has developed, with numerous streams. Some are short and steep, but others have cut deep lowland embayments with subdued hill lands and wide floodplains. A coastal plain extends along most of the shore line, though several spurs branching off the highland run clear into the sea as hilly uplands. This is another of the world's unexplored remainders, for little is known about the highland core.

MINOR ISLANDS. There are hundreds of small islands and islets scattered along the arc lines and lying on the crustal shelf. Some of these islands are in clusters; others are single islands in a close-order chain. Many of the large islands have a scattering of small islets around their shores. Off Sumatra's west coast the Asiatic outer arc line parallels the inner and is marked by several clusters totaling about 60 islands. One of the most important of the small island groups is the Moluccas, some 40 islands totaling about 30,000 square miles. This is a group on the Pacific arc line at its sharpest turn, where Halmahera repeats the peculiar pattern found in Celebes. On the Asiatic coastal shelf, between the Asiatic master arc and the mainlands are many small islands, worn down mountains, hills, and irregular remnants, now separated from each other by shallow water. A small shift of the crustal segment or of sea level would tremendously enlarge the land area here and tie the region together again. Repeated shifts of this sort must have happened since the Pleistocene period began.

PHILIPPINES

Over 7,000 separate pieces of land above sea level make up the Philippine Islands, with a total coastline of over 14,000 miles. Only 9 are more than 1,000 square miles in area, and only about 460 are larger than 1 square mile each. The largest is Luzon, almost 41,000 square miles in area; the only other large island is Mindanao, covering some 37,000 square miles. Thus, except for these two, the islands are just the crests of a series of submerged mountain ranges. Except for the Sulu Sea most of the waters separating islands are shallow, and a relatively small downward shift of sea level would nearly triple the total land area.

The structural ranges forming the skeleton of the island system are numerous but fairly simple in their arrangement. The oldest lines are those proceeding northward from east Borneo, through the Sulu Archipelago into western Mindanao, Negros, and Cebu, and from west Borneo through Palawan into Luzon. Around the ends of these sweep the later lines of the Asiatic master arc in a multiple series of ridges. Most of the structural lines have variable kinks in them which denudation has deepened, so that now the ridge crests describe a quite variable series of paths. Most of the islands have a simple north-south alignment, being longer in this dimension than in the east-west. Mindanao is almost an exception, being a series of north-south units tied together above sea level. Most of the islands also consist of but a single mountain range and its foothill spurs. Both Mindanao and Luzon differ in this respect. Beyond Luzon the arc tapers off toward Formosa, with only a few small mountain tops to mark it.

Many of the mountain cores are composed of igneous rocks, both intrusive and extrusive. Around their foothill belts frequently occur Tertiary sediments capped by Recent stream deposited alluvium. These Tertiary beds often are warped by Recent uplift and cut into considerable relief by radial stream patterns. Many spurs of hills project clear to the coasts and end in cliffed fronts on narrow beach strips. Between them small streams have cut valleys which sometimes disregard structure. Around most islands there are bits, patches, and larger tracts of alluvial land in estuaries, delta fills, and seafront alluvial plains. Many islands from Cebu southward contain patches or long reefs of coral limestone uplifted above sea level.

The highest elevations in the islands are volcanic peaks, a number of which exceed 7,000 feet. There are at present above a dozen active volcanos, but there are several dozen dead craters with truncated tops, indicating that explosive volcanism has been active since the close of the Tertiary period. There are few sheet flows of lava, most igneous materials being basaltic ash, pumice, tuff, and similar debris. These cones are mostly set along critical fault or fracture zones, some above highlands and others on the flat lowlands. There are numerous active fault lines running longitudinally through the islands. Associated with these active lines is the long Mindanao Trough, which has a recorded depth of over 35,000 feet just east of the northern point of Mindanao Island.

MINDANAO. This southern island is a series of peninsulas topped by mountain ranges, joined together by plateaus and lowland strips. There are four north-south range systems spaced across the island, with one east-west volcanic cross line. Extinct volcanos are scattered along the range systems, and ash, tuff, and some sheet basalt have built up the Lanao and Bukidnon sectors, along the cross line, as rolling plateaus at roughly 2,000 feet elevation, capped by high volcanic peaks. Every range has several peaks of more than 5,000 feet, and a few of more than 8,000 feet. The slightly truncated crater of Mount Apo, 9,610 feet in height, in the southeastern part of the island, is the highest point in the Philippines. Bays and gulfs reach into the lowlands between the peninsular range systems. There are three extensive alluvial lowlands, the Agusan, Davao, and Cotabato valleys. The first two are set between the two eastern range systems, opening northward and southward, whereas the Cotabato Valley opens westward in the southern part of the island. Both the Agusan and Cotabato valleys are only slightly above sea level and contain extensive marshlands. Elsewhere there are but narrow and discontinuous fringing lowlands along the coast.

LUZON. Toward the northern end of the Philippines Luzon consists of an elongated and joined set of peninsulas set *en echelon* and on a somewhat variable alignment. Numerous bays and gulfs occupy the sections between the ranges, and a very slight subsidence would turn Luzon into a number of islands. Several of the southern peninsulas are only rough to hilly areas with tall volcanos perched upon them, so that there is a significant amount of sedimentary and alluvial lowland of but slight relief. The central section is a lowland floored by volcanic tuff and shallow alluvial fill, all very close to sea level except for scattered volcanic cones. Manila Bay and the large lake, Laguna de Bay, are the remains of the shallow Tertiary sea which covered most of central Luzon. North of Manila Bay a broad lowland stretches northward, ending in another embayment, Lingayen Gulf. This lowland drains both to north and to south, and is the most important plain in the Philippines, placed between mountainous east and west coasts. In northern Luzon the highlands are more massive. Particularly in the northwest relief is strong, elevations are above 5,000 feet with peaks above 8,000 feet, and topography is rough and deeply dissected. A lower, narrower range of mountains parallels the east coast rather closely. Between the two

highlands lies the long Cagayan Valley, with its river meandering northward over a wide floodplain.

FORMOSA AND THE RYUKYU CHAIN

Formosa is the buttress upon which the Philippine arc is suspended in the north. Similarly it is the southern anchor island for the Ryukyu chain which stretches northward some 900 miles to Japan. Formosa itself may well not be an integral part of either island arc, whose lines hinge on the east coast, as though they ended against the steep eastern scarp of the island. It is a rugged and high-backed island, longer north-south than east-west, with its axial line closer to the east coast than the west. Its maximum elevations are over 14,000 feet, and Pleistocene glaciation has marked the crests. It presents a steep, faulted eastern face above a cliffed and narrow coast. The west coast is a wide foothill zone of subdued relief. Small stream basins and a series of gravel-covered terraces are set behind foothill strips reaching to the coast. Floodplains broaden out along the lower courses of these streams, and the littoral itself is a wide and flat coastal belt of alternating tidal marsh, low rocky projections, and moving sand deposits.

The Ryukyu chain consists of some 55 islets, totaling just under 1,000 square miles. There are several clusters of islands, grouped by the Japanese into three groups. Only the northern islands show Recent evidence of volcanism. The others are rocky masses of Paleozoic to Tertiary sediments, metamorphosed rocks, and intrusives. Most of the islands have rather a strong relief, with rocky shores and only minute bits of arable land. A few are relatively flat, low islands of simple relief pattern.

The Ryukyu arc line appears to project beyond its northern buttress in Kyushu along the east coast of southern Korea. The two small islands of Tsushima, lying between southern Japan and the Korean coast, appear suggestively related to this arc line.*

THE JAPANESE ARCS

From a quick glance at a large map the Japanese islands seem just another wide-swinging arc on the

---

* Most customary in the interpretation of the structure pattern is the suggestion that southern Korea is part of a shorter, tighter arc connecting Korea and southwestern Honshu, sharply convex toward the Pacific. The present interpretation sees no conflict in the existence of such a minor arc. It would be strange if the intersections of some of the arcs did not involve some of the same offset shear forms that accompany the intersections of the northeast-southwest massifs and east-west tectonic zones in China.

Asiatic master line. From southwest Kyushu to northern Hokkaido are some 1,100 miles along the curve. It would be better, however, to think of the Japanese islands as an arc system, recognizing that it is composed of elements of several shorter arcs and minor curved forms. As farther south along the Asiatic master arc, here and there is a double structural line through Japan, customarily known as the Inner and Outer zones. The Gifu Node and the Fossa Magna of central southern Honshu are, respectively, the complex junction of minor arcs of the Japanese system and the junction of the Pacific master line with the Asiatic master line. This double zone of structural and orographic confusion separates the Inner and Outer zones into northern and southern sectors. Four primary morphologic zones are recognized in Japan, namely, the Southwest Inner Zone, the Southwest Outer Zone, the Northwest Inner Zone, and the Northwest Outer Zone. Kyushu, the southern buttress-node, lies in both Inner and Outer zones, as does Hokkaido, the northern buttress of the Japanese arc system.

The amount of mountain building involved in this arc system is tremendous, for the near-by Tuscarora Deep almost equals the Mindanao Deep off the Philippine arc, and the tops of the Japanese Alps exceed 10,000 feet. This activity must have been initiated prior to the Tertiary, but a great deal of uplift took place during the late Tertiary and the early Pleistocene. At many relatively high points in the islands are the fairly clear marks of old denudational surfaces, indicating earlier subdued relief, glaciation, and possibly peneplanation. The Japanese islands have undoubtedly suffered the greatest amount of faulting of any of the Island Arcs, and that this intense fracturing process is not yet completed is seen in the 1,500 earthquakes per year that affect Japan today and in the many raised and drowned shore lines. Accompanying the block faulting has been the process of volcanism, by which some 500 volcanic cones have been built in the islands. Though cones and craters are found widely distributed over Japan, they are concentrated in several sectors. The northern and southern buttress islands, Kyushu and Hokkaido, have many cones along the line of contact with the Ryukyu and Kurile arcs. Similarly the junction of the Pacific arc, along the Fossa Magna, is marked by a series of cones, including Mount Fuji, the highest point in Japan (12,461 feet) and the most revered Japanese mountain. Not including the volcanos in the Ryukyus, Kuriles, and Bonins, over 40 craters in Japan have been active within historic time.

In the composition of its rocks there is represented in Japan material from every geologic era and almost every lithic variety, with igneous intrusive and extrusive rocks making up something over a third of the total surface. So completely cut into separate and differently placed blocks is the land mass that there is little regional continuity of rock type. Many local and acute changes in type and hardness of country rock are normal.

The combination of rather complex structure, a voluminous block faulting, a rapid and strong mountain building, and an extremely varied lithic composition have promoted an extremely complicated pattern of denudational processes that, since the Pleistocene, have produced an intricate physical landscape. This island landscape is dominated by high elevations, central highland blocks, strong relief, steep slopes, fault scarp cliffs, volcanic peaks, and strongly dissected uplands. Almost completely excluded are large unit areas of low relief, extensive coastal plains, valley floodplains, sizeable deltas, and the like. The stream network is a highly developed one, notwithstanding the fact that the two longest rivers are only some 225 miles long, and each drains basins of about 5,000 square miles only. On many heights the preservation of subdued and truncated ancient surfaces and the rounded knob forms of granites contrast strongly with the highly dissected uplands. In the latter angular forms, both of faulting and of normal but rapid denudation, predominate, so that the landscape is usually made up of steep slopes and sharp lines. Even the alluvial lowlands have suffered recent uplift and are dissected. Most such lowlands are divided between an older, upper remnant surface and a lower, flatter zone separated by angular bluffs and steep slopes.

The detail of this landscape makes generalized description difficult. The 146,000 square miles of Japan proper, a little less than the State of California, have been divided into 196 physiographic districts with the accompanying remark that the list was ". . . merely a broad outline, incomplete in many respects, which will serve as a guide for more detailed study in the geomorphology and general geography of the Island Empire." * The Kwanto Plain, Japan's largest alluvial lowland, contains only about 5,000 square miles and, itself, contains several subdivisions of different characteristics and utility. In all Japan there are nearly 3,000 separate islands, though perhaps only about 450 of them are more than isolated rocks. The coastline is even longer and more intricate than that of the Philippines. The central and northwest coast is relatively smooth and in agreement with basic structure. Elsewhere the coast is extremely irregular. Southern Japan generally, and southwest

* R. B. Hall and A. Watanabe, "Landforms of Japan," *Papers of the Mich. Acad. of Sci., Arts and Letters*, vol. 18, 1932, p. 207.

Japan in particular, have undergone a tremendously varied physical history that is rather plainly exhibited along its varied and island-studded coast.

THE MORPHOLOGIC REGIONS. Since there are differences in the Japanese area that do not accord with the occurrence of land areas in islands, brief comment is needed upon the morphologic units of the Japanese arc system.

The Outer Southwest Zone (The Shikoku Arc). One of the cleanest lines in Japan is the long fault scarp zone, placed concave to the Pacific in contrast to most arc lines, that overlooks the Inland Sea and cuts through the islands of Kyushu, Shikoku, and southeast Honshu. This whole sector is fairly uniform in its structural and geologic patterns. Except at the Ryukyu arc intersection there are no volcanos, and there is but little early intrusive granite exposed at the surface. In Shikoku Island there are two parallel fault scarp zones, with a line of fault valleys between. Local downwarping of portions of the zone has submerged three sections, giving two broad gaps into the Inland Sea and one deep embayment into the Honshu coast. Elevations gradually decrease toward the southwest. There are numerous marine terraces expressive of recent local uplift. Also indicating recent uplift, most of the rivers are entrenched in meander patterns in their valleys and show very little floodplain area at present. Flat-topped remnants of earlier subdued landscape forms are few in this part of Japan. Normal erosion has been strongly operative and has produced a landscape that is nearly mature, strongly dissected, and consists of steep slopes and rather high local relief.

The Inner Southwest Zone (Tsushima Arc). Southwest Honshu and northern Kyushu is the region of Japan in which block faulting has been most highly developed. There are many kinds of block units, but uplifted horst blocks and down-dropped graben blocks are most common. Fault scarps run in several directions, but there is a maximum trend that would suggest a probable arc line convex to the Pacific, opposing the Shikoku Arc, and related to or offset from the larger Ryukyu Arc. This is a zone in which intrusive granites are very common and, to the Japanese geomorphologists, granite and block faulting go together. There is a general decrease in elevation westward from the Fossa Magna into Kyushu, where the volcanic peaks stand well above the older landscape. Many crest areas preserve remnants of an older subdued landscape surface, and granites produce rounded and knobby outcrops. The many fault valleys and down-dropped blocks have been partly filled to produce basins, lowlands, or surfaces of low relief. The Inland Sea is an irregular submerged section between the two opposing arcs. The

Kyushu end of this zone was lowered less than the northern end and, by virtue of its volcanic cover, closes off the Inland Sea. The submerged shore line is the most common shore form in this sector. There are few plains areas of any extent, but numerous small patches are found at varying elevations. Mostly a rugged and hilly landscape, the region has been strongly dissected and consists mostly of steep slopes.

The Outer Northeast Zone (Eastern Honshu Arc). The Tsushima Arc ends just south of Fossa Magna in a confused highland mass known as the Gifu Node. The Fossa Magna itself is a downfaulted trough partly filled with volcanic material which marks the junction of the Pacific and Asiatic master arcs. It forms a barricade right across the island of Honshu for, to the north, is another bunched highland mass almost as high and as formidable as the Gifu Node to the south. Away to the north this highland separates out into linear mountain ranges with intervening valleys. These are set on a single broad arc pattern known as the Honshu Arc. The distinctions between outer and inner sectors are less clear than south of the Fossa Magna.

The Outer Zone of the Northeast includes the easternmost mountain ranges of Honshu and the central north-south ranges of Hokkaido. There are four mountain units involved. These have cores of old metamorphosed sediments and intrusive granites, are uplifted as separate block units, with both folded and faulted marginal basin elements. The highland crests show remnants of old erosional surfaces, somewhat deformed and warped during uplift. In general this is a region of rugged terrain, of hard rocks and steep slopes. Within the mountain block units themselves there is but little flat land, though lowland sediments have been built across the marginal roots of the ranges from the structural valleys west of the ranges. In Hokkaido east of the central range line, the junction of the Kurile Arc has built a line of volcanic cones with marginal alluvial-ash slopes which replaces the erosional landscape found elsewhere. Whether this is one complex arc or whether it is the orographic grouping of several arc units is still a matter of conjecture.

The Inner Northeast Zone (Northwestern Honshu Arc). This sector is made up of two roughly parallel range systems and the three related basin strips. The central mountain system of northern Honshu, the eastern of the two ranges here considered, is the drainage divide for the island. It is a high massive folded range system, with intrusive granite roots, a Tertiary sedimentary cover capped by a number of volcanic craters and some lava flows, particularly in its southern half. The western range system is less formidable and continuous, having been breached and cut away in a number of places by streams. It is also structurally a folded range system. The Inner Zone of the Northeast has a minimum of faulting in rather parallel linear patterns which do not break the country up into the many separate blocks found further south.

The two inland basin strips are structural basins set on linear pattern. The eastern strip has been filled so that its parts slope directly off toward the sea, around or past the mountains of the east coast. The central series of basins now drains out to the westward, each through a stream that cuts across the western range system. There are nine such basins, set off from each other by transverse ridges connecting the two mountain systems. The western lowland fringe along the Sea of Japan is a narrow one, with embayments along the streams that cut across the western range system. The whole zone is an area of strong relief contrasts, of steep slopes, of angular patterns, of little flat land, but of beautiful scenery.

THE PRIMARY UNITS. In addition to the above, brief comments on individual islands and the Inland Sea are needed to form a picture of the island empire of Japan.

Kyushu. This southern island of under 14,000 square miles forms the buttress of the Ryukyu Arc and the Japanese arc system. It is made up of three kinds of landscapes, rather jumbled together. The southern half of the island belongs to the massive faulted Shikoku Arc; the northern half is related to the block-faulted landscape of the Tsushima Arc. Widely distributed over the island are the volcanic surfaces, volcanos, craters, and hot springs that mark the junction of the separate arcs. The more massive uplands are blocks of old hard rock, strongly dissected and steep sloped. A number of short streams penetrate the central highlands rather deeply, and little patches of lowland are scattered around the coast. Northwest Kyushu is a varied assortment of small block peninsulas, downfaulted lowlands and gulfs, volcanic uplands, and a very irregular shore line.

Shikoku. The smallest of the main group of islands, Shikoku totals only a little under 7,000 square miles in area. Its main mass forms the highest section of the upfaulted Shikoku Arc. Overlooking the Inland Sea is a long highland ending in a fault scarp zone. Below this is an irregular sector that is part of the Inland Sea structurally but that remained above present sea level as part of the island. At the western end the primary fault scarp stands high above the Inland Sea directly. Behind this major fault zone minor faults have been opened into linear fault valleys. The southern peninsulas are lined with a succession of marine terraces ending in wave-cut cliffs at the present sea margin. The main block of the island tilts southward,

so that the two peninsulas taper off into the sea. The whole island is a rugged upland region with very little flat lands or true lowlands.

Honshu. This is the chief island of Japan, measuring about 88,000 square miles. Within its relatively small area it combines a tremendous variety of landscapes. Elongated north-south, it is some 825 by 160 miles in major dimensions. Its northern and southern extremities are quite dissimilar, though many of these differences are related to climate and vegetation, rather than to inherent differences in the landforms themselves. Southwestern Honshu is a region of small fault blocks, a submerged coast on the Inland Sea side, and a fringe of minor islands, small bays, and inlets. It is markedly oriented to the Inland Sea. Small patches of lowland are scattered here and there, at the heads of bays and in fault valleys. Northward toward the Fossa Magna elevations increase, the island thickens in width and becomes more massive in its proportion. The Fossa Magna itself makes a strong mark across the island, with its faulted lowland and tall volcanic peaks. Just north and east of this transverse barricade lies the Kwanto Plain, the largest alluvial lowland in Japan. Northward the island is a series of linear mountain ranges and intervening river basins, having no common orientation except outward from the central highland line toward the sea. This rugged northern landscape the Japanese have found difficult to utilize in their preferred manner.

Hokkaido. The odd-shaped island of Hokkaido measures about 260 miles from north to south and a little more on the east-west axis, to total under 30,000 square miles. Its shape derives from the fact that it is the buttress junction of three arcs. Its southwestern fish-tailed peninsula is related to the structural pattern of the inner side of the Honshu Arc. The main backbone of the island is a north-south linear range system connected with the Sakhalin Arc, producing the northern and southern peninsulas. The eastern peninsula is formed by a line of volcanic peaks at the end of the Kurile Arc. Thus, each arc is related to a highland sector. The three do not meet at a common center, however, and the marginal sections are occupied by structural lowlands and alluvial-ash piedmonts. The higher parts of these sloping margins are rather strongly dissected today, whereas the bottoms are low-lying marshy tracts. Around the island are many gravel-surfaced marine terraces, set at a number of different levels. But a small proportion of Hokkaido is amenable to agricultural use, comprising a landscape of a kind the Japanese do not thoroughly appreciate. That one of the largest alluvial lowlands of all Japan is located in Hokkaido is an unfortunate circumstance.

This is the Ishikari Plain, of southwest Hokkaido, totaling about 850 square miles.

The Inland Sea. Nearly 250 miles long and varying in width from about 5 to 50 miles, the Inland Sea of Japan occupies the lower portions of a number of downfaulted blocks, which lie along the margins of the Tsushima Arc. The upper parts of the several blocks are represented by the hundreds of islets and small peninsulas of the three large islands that surround the sea. Rather than a negative unit of the island empire, and merely the space between the large islands, the Inland Sea is a very vital region and is one of the more significant parts of Japan. Though its distinctive character is partly derived from its climate, the Inland Sea shores and islands might be termed the "typical Japanese landscape." There are five sections of relatively open water, representing the blocks now most deeply submerged. Depths everywhere are quite shallow, and a shift of sea level of no more than 150 feet would again expose almost the whole of the severely dissected zone now covered by water. The many islets are arranged in roughly parallel structural lines. Many of them are but steep rocky peaks; others are of larger size and are of irregular shape and surface. Some have miniature deltas and alluvial fills situated at protected spots, with exposed headlands surrounded by marine benches and cliffs. Strong tidal currents move through the Inland Sea, sweeping out channels and locally forming a serious navigational hazard.

THE SAKHALIN ARC

Offset eastward 100 miles from the Honshu Arc of northern Japan lies the Sakhalin Arc, extending from the south coast of Hokkaido through the northern end of Sakhalin Island. Some 900 miles long, this arc swings close to the Asiatic mainland before terminating in the Sea of Okhotsk. It describes a shallower curve than do most of the other arcs along the Asiatic master line. Two large islands make up the arc, the southern buttress island of Hokkaido and Sakhalin itself.

SAKHALIN. The island is some 600 miles long by perhaps 50 miles wide throughout most of its extent. It consists of two folded and faulted mountain systems with an intervening structural lowland. The eastern member is composed of Paleozoic sedimentary and metamorphic rocks, rugged in outline but of locally subdued relief. It is at its highest in central Sakhalin, where elevations exceed 6,000 feet. A disconnected segment of this member forms a small peninsula at the southeastern corner of the island. The western member is a late Tertiary structural unit running the whole length of the island, broadening out toward the northern end and decreasing in elevation. Maximum elevations are less high in the western ranges than in the eastern system, but relief is locally stronger and the degree of dissection in many places is greater, since the country rock here is younger and somewhat softer. The structural depression extends from the upper east coast southward between the two range systems to Taraika Bay. It now is covered with an alluvial fill from both highland areas. The structural depression is continued at the southern end of the island, a lowland lying across the small peninsular section of the eastern range system. Elsewhere flat lowlands are but thin strips of alluvial material piled up along the coast.

THE KURILE ARC

The last northern island arc on the Asiatic system stretches for some 750 miles between mainland Kamchatka and the buttress island of Hokkaido. The Kamchatka Peninsula itself appears to be set on this same Asiatic arc line but to be an arc set concave to the Pacific, its northern end being in alignment with the structural trend of northeastern Siberia. Kamchatka at its broadest appears to be the junction zone of the two arcs which, being reversed in curvature, give the peninsula a wide spread in its central region.

The 32 islands in the Kurile group total somewhat over 6,000 square miles. The largest island is Etorofu, toward the southern end of the chain, with an area of about 1,000 square miles. Primarily the rugged and steep-sloped tops of mountains, the chain contains a number of active volcanos, the tallest of which exceeds 7,000 feet. No significant areas of flat land or of lowland occur on any of the islands, steep shore lines often dropping right into the sea. On some of the larger southern islands there are minute patches of alluvial fill at stream mouths, and a few wave-cut benches. The Kuriles are the least populated and the least significant of the island arcs, though their position gives them a value in the military strategy of the northern Pacific Ocean.

Climatology and Sensible Climate

The "monsoon" of Monsoon Asia was the first intricate aspect of regional climatology to bother man mentally, well over 2,000 years ago. Between the mouth of the Red Sea and the Solomon Islands the northern and southern hemispheres are not even faintly symmetrical in the distribution of land and sea, and atmospheric phenomena do not behave as elsewhere around the globe. There still is a serious shortage of data, and its summarization is very uneven. The region has often been studied piecemeal rather than as a whole. And in this large climatic realm there are very real differences between the climates of the Malabar Coast of India, the north coast of Java, the Red Basin of China, and the island of Hokkaido in north Japan. That there is a common rainy period and seasonal agreement in air movements does not make these diverse climates amenable to inclusion in one simple classification. Satisfactory generalizations will come only in the future, formulated on the basis of data pertaining to the area. The following pages discuss the topic from the subjective viewpoint of sensible climate rather than from that of impersonal objectivity.

TEMPERATURE PATTERNS

Maps of actual temperatures for the respective seasons indicate several important features. It is notable that much of the total lowland area has no really cold weather, though every country has some cool territory. The southern lands all possess highlands, mountain ranges or peaks that project above the hot lowlands. In the southern zone temperature variations are vertical rather than horizontal. On the other hand, in spite of the fact that the northernmost lands are really part and parcel of the Orient by cultural inclusion, they really have long and severe winters with short growing seasons. And in the northern zone horizontal temperature gradients are marked both regionally and seasonally.

Japan's temperature map reveals that only a small portion of the island empire has the subtropical weather that supports the bamboo groves and paper houses of the popular picture of Japan. The thermal contrast between the southward-facing portion of Japan and the northern regions is sharp and strong, with consequent variation in the length of the growing season.

While the eastern Yangtze Valley country has real winter weather, Szechwan then is a subtropical enclave comparable to southern Asia. In summer the whole of the Yangtze Basin is extremely hot and sticky, with but few breaks in the monotonous heat. Yunnan and Kweichow form a transitional zone rather comparable to tropical highlands in their mild but even-tempered conditions. China's thermal contrast in summer, from north to south, is relatively slight, but in east China it is notably strong in winter, central and south China having the coolest winters for their latitudes of any part of the world. This is related to the strong outblowing winter monsoon winds. The difference in the length of the growing seasons from Hainan Island to northern Manchuria is great.

India, Burma, Thailand, and Indochina are notable for a peculiar seasonal division of the year into three periods rather than two or four as is customary in so much of the world. This is produced by the cooling effect of the onset of the summer monsoon period, and by the peculiarities of monsoonal air movement. It is significant that northwestern India has a hot zone quite separate from the central Asiatic high-temperature center. This seems to serve as a local attraction to the Indian sector of the summer monsoon air drift. Across northern India and Burma there is an all-year sharp temperature gradient, lying roughly along the Himalayan mountain wall.

Generalized maps cannot possibly show the vertical thermal gradations of the island arc zone, in which many mountain-crest localities have relatively cool

weather the year around.   Southern India and southern
Burmo-Malaya share with the Indies and Philippines
this characteristic to a considerable degree.   The great
river trenches of northern Burmo-Malaya show some
extreme contrasts from range divides to canyon bottoms.

monsoon starts as a dry wind, but in various sectors it
absorbs considerable water vapor as it crosses coastal
seas to become a rain provider to several coastal and
island regions.   In the north velocities are much greater
than in the south where the movement is but a gentle

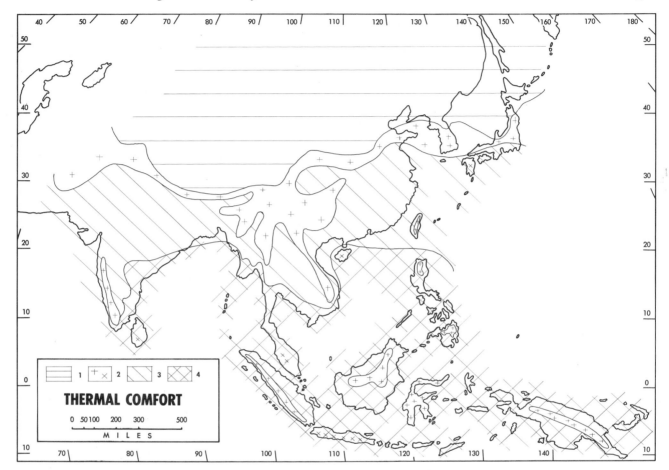

Fig. 10.   Zones of thermal comfort: (1) cold or windy winters; (2) reasonable conditions all year; (3) hot and muggy summers;
(4) lowlands hot and muggy all year, uplands comfortable.

THE MONSOON AS A CLIMATIC AGENT

The old Arabic word monsoon applied to a season
of the year, and hence to the wind that prevailed during
the period.   Modern English usage has applied it also
to the precipitation regime.   The prevailing pattern of
air movement for south and eastern Asia is a double
one.   During the northern winter generally southward
and eastward air movements occur, with local directional divergences according to location and with variable length of the season.   In the north these winds
fortify the prevailing westerlies; in the south they complement the northeast trades.   In the Indies the monsoonal effect is obscured by the patterns of the northeast
trades and by local land and sea breezes.   The winter

drift.   In the north, also, the winter monsoon is a cold
wind; in the south its coolness is but relative.   Lastly,
the northern winter monsoon often begins with a sudden cold windstorm, an unheard-of happening in the
south.

During the northern summer, on the other hand, the
prevailing air drift is from some southerly direction, its
precise compass reading and period of duration again
depending upon location.   In this season the southern
regions experience stronger winds than the northern,
which may have but fitful and gentle breezes.   The summer monsoon "bursts" upon India, but comes gradually
to China.   The summer air drift is relatively a warm
wind and, until it reaches inland localities, is a moist
wind.   Sumatra and British Malaya do not show a well-

developed summer monsoon drift, and in the central and eastern Indies local variations in air movements are marked. The Philippines are affected by the major air mass movements drifting toward China and northern Asia.

Both seasonal movements are comparatively shallow, surface layers of air, not often extending above 10,000

tinental and central Pacific Ocean pressure structures. The dates of cessation and reversal in direction of the two air drifts are not equally timed in all sectors; they vary considerably from region to region.

Both air drifts possess irregularities of a large order in timing, in distribution, and in volume of moisture carried. The seasonal air drifts themselves possess no

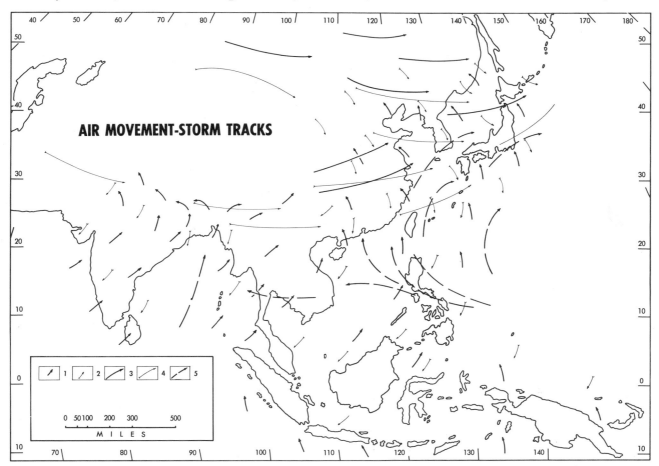

Fig. 11. Seasonal air movement and storm tracks: (1) summer monsoon air drift; (2) winter monsoon air drift; (3) summer cyclonic storm tracks; (4) winter cyclonic storm tracks; (5) typhoon tracks.

feet. Two exceptions to this are the India-Burma sector of the summer southwest monsoon and Manchurian-Japan sector of the winter northwest monsoon, both of which appear to be somewhat thicker. Particularly the northern end of the summer monsoon drift and the southern end of the winter monsoon drift appear to be shallow layers. The monsoon air movements seem to respond to seasonal shifts in continental heating and cooling, but there are many unknown and variable factors. Neither monsoon drift is a steady current, but each possesses somewhat variable pulsation tendencies. In the south the field of motion is across the equator; in the east it appears to lie between the northern con-

inherent mechanisms for precipitation production or other weather manifestations, but the changes that take place in the inward or outward sweeping air masses determine the weather and precipitation of the Orient. As suggested below there are a number of different storm mechanisms and control factors that operate variably throughout the Orient to produce its variable weather.

The Tibetan highland, with its southeastern projection, appears to separate the mainland Orient into two primary sectors, there being some intermixture along the coastal fringe and in the Island Arcs. The southern sector primarily exhibits tropical weather and climate, with only a minimum of extratropical phenomena during the winters or at high elevations. The northern sector exhibits rather emphatic extratropical phenomena during much of the year, though some of the basins and blocks of the Chinese checkerboard show rather anomalous winter conditions and southernmost China is almost tropical the year around. The Island Arcs from the Philippines southward belong to the southern sector.

If both monsoon air drifts are considered as regional displacement of air masses, the eastern sector receives large amounts of Polar Siberian (Ps) air during the period of the winter monsoon to carry cold winter weather across all of Korea and Japan and as far south as the Fukien hill country in eastern China. Protected by the Tsinling Shan and the Tibetan Plateau, western China and the whole of the southern sector are not normally and directly affected by cold Polar air masses. Some cool Polar air does penetrate Thailand, Indochina, and the Philippines occasionally. The southern sector during the winter receives returning Tropical air masses (Tropical Indian and Tropical Pacific, Ti and Tp) which have become cooler, drier, and, in the eastern sector certainly, mixed with some Polar air in the seasonal interchange. In summer the first northward advance of the monsoon involves warm and moist Tropical air from the Indian Ocean and the South Pacific (Ti and Tp), and it is likely that this is followed by Equatorial Marine (Em) air masses during the main period of the summer monsoon. Southwest China appears, along with all of northern Burmo-Malaya, to receive considerable Tropical Indian air, and it is likely that south China's summer weather is produced by a seasonally variable mixture of Tropical Indian, South Pacific, and Equatorial Marine air. For the Indies the situation is complicated by a position across the equator, by highly complex local conditions of land and sea, and by southern-hemisphere air movement over Australia. Since the whole region is out of reach of purely Polar air masses from either side, only mixtures of Equatorial, Tropical, and Polar air are involved. The multiplicity of islands of varying sizes and shapes interjects the land and sea breeze into weather and climate in a very positive way. There appear to be many situations in which the land or sea breeze may cancel the normally prevailing monsoon air drift, to make local air movement the dominant factor in local weather and climate, even though the two-way monsoon drift does provide a major, seasonal exchange of air masses from one side of the equator to the other.

The action of the monsoons in response to primary pressure gradients, therefore, seems to be that of very generally circulating the surface atmosphere on a broad scale, thereby seasonally providing alternating winds and volumes of moisture over the whole of the Orient which storm mechanisms fashion into a variety of local weather patterns. For centuries traders from Arabia to Japan have sailed by the monsoon's alternating drifts, and farmers have prayed for its regularity of arrival and dependability of precipitation.

MECHANICS OF WEATHER CHANGE

Most simply stated there are four different mechanisms that produce weather changes and precipitation throughout the Orient. The cyclonic storm is the most widespread of the four, the others being the convectional thundershower, the typhoon, and what may be termed the "orographic squeeze." Each has its area of maximum significance, though in many localities all four either may combine or remain completely inactive. The accompanying map of seasonal air movement and storm tracks indicates the areas affected by moving air phenomena.

Cyclonic storms are of two types, the weak-gradient tropical low and the cyclic extratropical storm moving in the westerly wind belt. Little is yet known of the former's origins and paths of movement, but it would seem that local, non-continuous wave disturbances develop along the shifting intertropical fronts, providing local weather variations. The extratropical cyclone moving eastward frequents a series of paths from northern India in the winter to the all-year Siberian route. In these zones it is a significant factor in fluctuating weather, naturally being more effective in the more northerly sectors. East China and the Yellow Sea receive about 85 storms per year, spring being the most active period. Storm diameters are smaller than those of United States storms, and the action usually is somewhat less vigorous.

The southernmost of the cyclonic paths runs across the North Indian Plain and into southwest China, south of Tibet, during the winter, regeneration sometimes taking place by the time the storm reaches China. Storms crossing north India often are not noticeable in daily weather, owing to the absence of the strong intervening cold wave of Polar air. The probable origin of the China-born storms lies in the zonal fronts that separate the several air masses over China much of the year. The most recognizable front shifts south of the Indies during the northern winter, gradually shifting northward over China, Korea, and the Japan Sea in the spring with the thrust of the summer monsoon. On the Indian side of this front few cyclonic storms seem to form, but over China local instabilities along the front during middle and late spring cause small storms that move out across east China and southern Japan. These storms produce the rains known in the Far East as the "plum rains," which provide the water for rice planting and the early summer crop growth. The main frontal zone usually shifts northward in summer to become less active, retreating southward in late August and September. Over central China autumn storms originate similarly to those of the spring period. Stagnation of a frontal disturbance over some part of China regularly produces one of the disastrous floods that have filled Chinese history. Also, the failure of the frontal zones to produce storms over an interval results in an undue sweep of warm air and the damaging drought that seems almost as common as the flood.

Other winter cyclonic storms reach the Far East after crossing Siberia, swinging down into northern China or Manchuria and out across Japan and Korea. They produce little more than windstorms over China, but over Korea and particularly Japan they cause rain and snow. Intervening anticyclones bring cold waves and accompanying dust storms to northern China but not often do they fully succeed in crossing the Tsinling system to harshly freeze central and south China.

The summer convectional thundershower is rather common almost everywhere in the Orient. It often precedes the dramatic summer rainy season in India and Burmo-Malaya, in the Indies appearing the year around, and in China being associated with the monotonous and sticky heat of the summer. Japan has amazingly few thundershowers, whereas Formosa, the Gulf of Tonking, and Bengal are centers of this type of storm. Data are inadequate, but it would appear that those islands of the Indies nearest the equator receive the largest number of thundershowers, with Java recording well over 300 per year. As a source of precipitation the thundershower is fully as important as the cyclonic storm. In many sections thundershowers both precede and follow the main monsoon rainy season. Though the meteorological records often do not enumerate separate thundershowers during the main rainy seasons, they certainly occur. In my own personal experience Chungking averages more than 16 thundershowers per year, and the contrast between official records for Chungking and western Java must lie partly in unequal criteria for tabulation. Not all thundershowers are convectional in origin, for convergence of major or local regional air masses and the passage of cyclonic fronts sometimes provoke them.

The typhoon, known in American literature as the hurricane, and in India as the cyclone, has two zones of occurrence, the Indian Ocean and the western Pacific Ocean from the southern Philippines northward to Japan. In both regions the storms are destructive to shipping, to agriculture, and to shore installations. Some of the Bay of Bengal storms do not reach full hurricane intensity but climatically serve the same purpose. Late summer is the peak period of occurrence, but in the western Pacific the season is rather a long one, extending from May to January. Aside from its locally destructive aspect, the typhoon is important as a precipitation producer for many miles on either side of its path. Eastern India, Burma, Indochina, most of the Philippines, the southeastern coast of China, and southern Japan are the regions receiving significant amounts of moisture from this source. The typhoon thus is an important late summer and early autumn weather agent. Pacific Ocean storms move westward and Indian Ocean storms move mainly northward, both sets recurving to the north and east into the patterns of movement normal to the extratropical cyclones. A good many Pacific Ocean typhoons fail to curve northward along the China coast, sweeping somewhat southward and across Burmo-Malaya. Some of these continue intact into the Bay of Bengal, where they regenerate and swing northward and eastward into eastern India and north Burma. Storms that pass along the China coast provoke rainfall as far inland as 500 miles. In Japan typhoons passing close to the south coast attract masses of cold northern air, upon occasion, to cool much of Japan unduly, and to contribute to autumn rainfall. The Philippines also receive cool spells and some autumn rainfall from October to December from this same source.

The term "orographic squeeze" involves more than the simple matter of air blowing over a mountain. Often there appears to be horizontal convergence of air masses, along oblique obstructions or in funnel-like lowland embayments, which may be more important than the vertical lift over the obstruction. In many instances horizontal and vertical elements are intermixed and rather complicated. Under this heading, for lack of clear interpretation, may be included some of the results of the weak tropical lows. The "squeeze" mechanism is very widely operative in the southern sector, and is significant, though less important, in the northern sector also. The west coast of India, the eastern Himalayan front, the Burma coast, the Indochina coast, and many localities in the Indies and Philippines have steep mountain fronts obstructing with spectacular results the movement of relatively strong monsoon winds. Horizontal convergence is a significant factor in producing rainfall over northern India during the peak summer period. There is a tremendous and continued thrust of air into the Bengal Delta, against the Himalayan front, forcing major air currents to wheel leftward up the Ganges Valley and rightward up the

valley of the Brahmaputra.   On the west coast of northern Japan the squeeze play on cold winter air produces
extremely heavy falls of snow.

MOISTURE AND ITS DISTRIBUTION

In spite of the fact that the Orient is a humid landscape with perennial lowland floods, and with a large

and in rain-shadow position for winter cyclonic moisture.   The Island Arcs all have their local rain shadows
and peculiar characteristics in one or another season
of air drift.   Only in northwest India and central Asia
is this rain-shadow effect strong enough to produce true
desert.   Elsewhere the moisture shortage is a relative
situation.

The second important factor contributing to regional

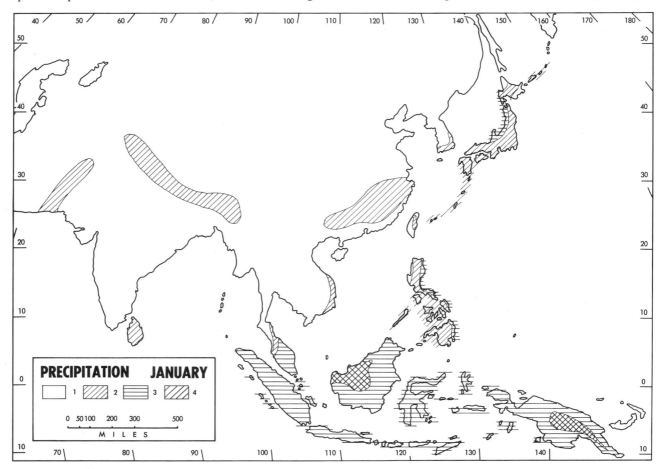

Fig. 12.   Precipitation in January: (1) blank areas have under 2 inches; (2) 2–4 inches; (3) 4–16 inches; (4) over 16 inches.

amount of water visible in the landscape much of the
year, a number of regions with serious rainfall shortages belie such a description.   The first factor in this
regional shortage is the rain-shadow position of many
of the lowland basins and river valleys.   The several
lowland veins of the Burmo-Malayan fan are in rain-
shadow position during both summer and winter wind
drifts.   Of these central Burma is most seriously affected.   The central peninsula of India is in rain-
shadow position during the summer monsoon and out
of position to receive either monsoon or cyclonic rains
in winter.   Both northwest China and northwest India
are out of position for the summer monsoon rainfall

shortage of moisture is the enormous variability of the
monsoon air drift and the irregular operation of its
several storm mechanisms.   This variability is both in
timing and in annual total.   Though native folk calen-
dars and almanacs throughout the Orient long have had
set dates for the commencement of their respective
rainy seasons, vagaries in actual commencement are
common.   Delays often are times of elaborate prayer
and penance rituals.   Flood and drought in the same
summer are not unheard of.   Variation in total often
exceeds 100 per cent, though in the humid sectors this
usually goes unnoticed.   Average variability becomes
critical on the dry margins particularly, in peninsular

India, in central Burma, in northwestern India and the border country, and in north and northwest China. Some of the islands of the Indies east of Java receive too little moisture. Elsewhere shortage of moisture through variability is less frequent, though in individual years it may cause serious economic and social repercussions. The accompanying map of rainfall variabil-

flood descends during the 6 months of the summer monsoon. The southwest coast of India, the eastern Himalayan front, the Arakan Yoma-Assam Plateau line, the coast of lower Burma, and the Indochina coast are the outstanding regions of excess rainfall.

It has been mentioned that the Orient primarily receives its moisture during the summer growing season,

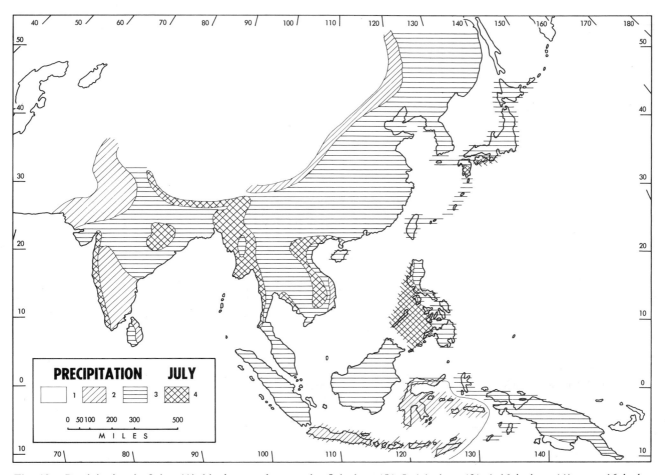

Fig. 13. Precipitation in July: (1) blank areas have under 2 inches; (2) 2–4 inches; (3) 4–16 inches; (4) over 16 inches.

ity suggests those areas in which variability is particularly serious.

And as there are zones with too little moisture, so are there areas with possibly too much rainfall. There are several mountain walls lying directly in the path of one of the monsoon drifts over which several storm mechanisms combine to raise the total precipitation to spectacular figures. Cherrapunji at an elevation of 4,300 feet in the Assam Plateau of northeastern India, directly in the path of the summer monsoon sweep, holds the precipitation record, with 431 inches per year, 905 inches being the maximum for any one year. This is over 35 feet for the average and just over 75 feet for the record annual fall, and the majority of this

this being a factor in its productive agriculture. Most of this summer rainfall comes as heavy downpours. The onset of the rains often finds the earth dry and parched, but after the first few days the balance is excess moisture even in a rice-growing land and runs off the soaked mountains and ponded slopes to pile up torrential floods in the lowland valleys. Comparison of the two seasonal precipitation maps indicates that some areas receive a considerable part of their total moisture as winter rain or snow. In northern lowland India and the upland mountain wall, and from central China northward, winter moisture primarily is cyclonic in origin, is apt to come in smaller volumes per time period and is less destructive than the summer rain torrents. In the upper Himalayas or in northern situations there are considerable falls of snow, which in northwestern Japan often exceeds 6 feet in depth.

In those areas near the equator there is, of course, no winter or summer distinction of wind or rainfall seasons in the ordinary sense. In the Indies particularly

An aspect of moisture of great subjective importance is the humidity pattern. It is the moist heat of the Orient, particularly, which makes it uncomfortable and unhealthy for the white man. And for the native too though there has been less said about this phase of the problem. Examination of data for Rangoon and

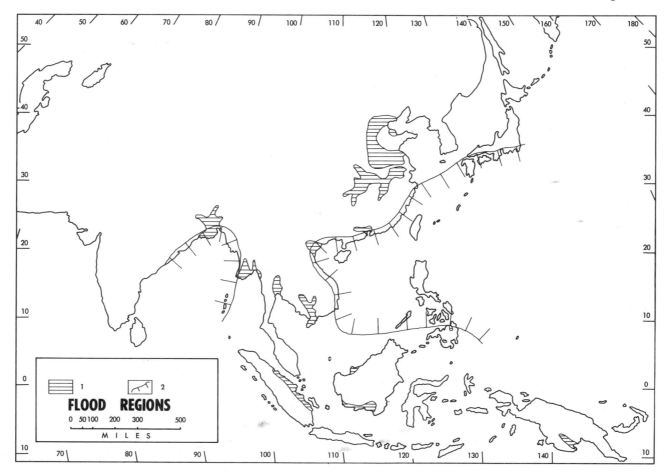

Fig. 14. Regions subject to flood: (1) major areas, subject to seasonal flooding by rainfall runoff; (2) zone of sudden floods and storm damage caused by typhoons.

the two seasonal sets of winds affect different local areas of small dimensions, resulting in a mosaic of differently timed and patterned rainfall regimes. Except for parts of the Philippines and for eastern Java and near-by islands, the island areas do not experience long dry seasons or moisture shortages.

Since the monsoon air drift is comparatively shallow the elevation of maximum rainfall is not very great. In India at least this level is not far from 4,000 feet, and above 5,000 feet rainfall totals decrease steadily, so that the highest mountain ranges do not receive abnormally heavy precipitation totals. Where cyclonic effects are added proportionately larger amounts of moisture are received at elevations higher than 5,000 feet.

Tokyo, cities chosen at random, makes clear the seasonal discomfort of the climate.

TABLE 1

SELECTED CLIMATIC DATA FOR RANGOON, BURMA

Period	Mean Temp.	Mean Maxima	Mean Minima	Relative Humidity, %	Precip., in.	Rainy Days	Cloud Cover
January	77	89	65	70	0.21	0.3	1.1
March	84	96	71	68	0.32	0.6	1.2
May	84	92	77	83	11.98	14.0	5.9
July	81	85	76	93	21.42	25.0	8.7
September	81	86	76	92	15.27	20.0	7.2
November	80	88	73	83	2.79	0.3	2.9
Annual	81	89	73	82	99.03	122.0	4.5

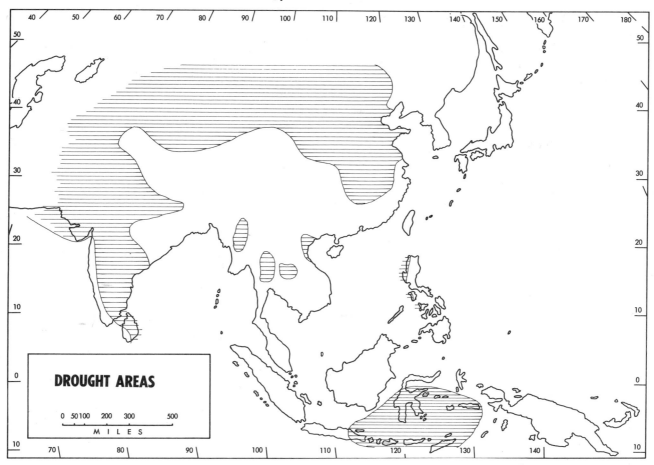

Fig. 15. Regions subject to drought. Lined areas are the major zones of seasonal drought damaging to agriculture.

TABLE 2

HOURLY CLIMATIC DATA FOR TOKYO, JAPAN

For the Month of January

Period	Relative Humidity, %	Mean Temp.	Mean Cloudiness	Precipitation
1 AM	71	33.8	3.8	0.09
6 AM	73	31.5	4.3	0.10
2 PM	50	45.2	4.5	0.09
9 PM	68	36.3	3.7	0.13
Monthly mean	64	37.4	4.2	Total 2.42

For the Month of July

Period	Relative Humidity, %	Mean Temp.	Mean Cloudiness	Precipitation
1 AM	92	72.1	6.8	0.26
6 AM	92	75.7	8.3	0.28
2 PM	69	81.9	7.4	0.04
9 PM	87	74.3	6.3	0.28
Monthly mean	82	76.0	7.5	Total 5.01

The table for Rangoon uses mean monthly data. Hourly humidity data for Tokyo are more suggestive of one phase of the problem.

These two tables indicate that the summer humidities do build up to a rather high point. In Rangoon during the summer it rains heavily almost every day and, although temperatures are somewhat lower, this is offset by the increased humidity. Examination of the Tokyo data shows that the night hours have the highest humidities at all seasons. The inability to sleep soundly at night is a critical item in climatic discomfort. "I would not mind the days so much, if I could just sleep at night" is a wail that is uttered by both white man and native, undoubtedly related to the daily curve of humidity, as well as to the daily temperature curve.

VARIETIES OF WEATHER

Selecting a residence in terms of weather alone, I would pick New Delhi, north India, from early November to late March, spend April and May in Kashmir in northwest India, stay in western Kweichow or Yunnan in southwest China from June until midSeptember, and pass the remaining weeks on an island in the Inland Sea of Japan. This would provide steady sunshine with warm days, cool nights, comfortably low humidities and a few interesting thundershowers. Other people may have different climatic preferences. Since few people

CLIMATIC REGIONS

Most climatic classifications now in use are formulated upon simply devised vegetative or uncritical weather-seasonal criteria. Such schemes, variably adjusted to fit conditions in Europe or the Americas, do not lend themselves to adequate climatic differentiation

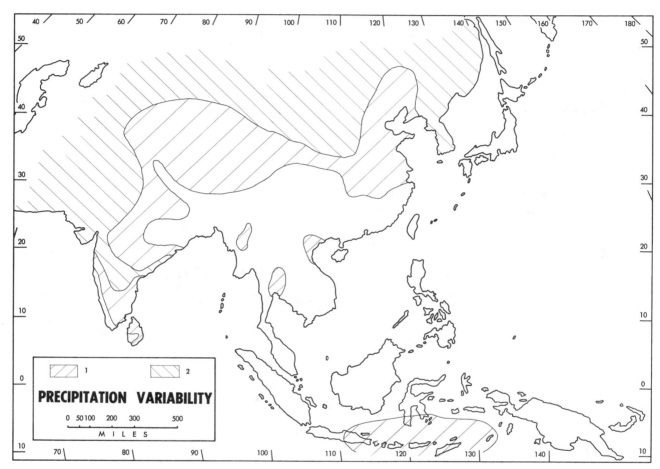

Fig. 16. Variability of precipitation: (1) zones of moderate variability occasionally damaging to agriculture; (2) zones of great variability often damaging to agriculture. Blank areas possess no dangerous variability during most years.

can arrange life so neatly there is abundant climatic discomfort for both native and white man during much of the year everywhere in the Orient. Figure 10 suggests the regional patterns of temperature conditions for the Orient.

The following summaries outline the sequence of weather and illustrate the climatic data for a number of different climatic regions. On each chart the continuous line presents temperature by the monthly mean, and the dashed line indicates relative humidity by the monthly mean. No attempt has been made to describe all regions or every pattern of weather.

of the several monsoon regions of eastern Asia. Vegetative reaction to climatic elements is rather complex and is involved with a variety of geologic, soil, and cultural effects. Ordinary annual weather patterns shaping human comfort are produced by seasonal air mass movements and storm mechanisms. Climatology has not yet produced a satisfactory empirical set of formulae applying equally well to all parts of the world. Climatologists in Japan, China, and India have studied their home areas with little attention to the over-all application of their regional systems. For any large region, such as China, it is fairly easy to describe subjectively five or six different major kinds of climate. It is difficult, however, to arrange a simple classification for such a region that is objectively accurate and that will permit the drawing of faultless boundary lines. The ac-companying maps present several different approaches to the problem, no one of which appears fully satisfactory.

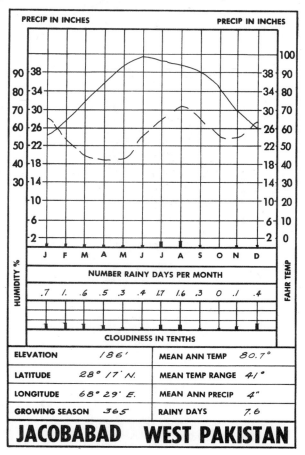

ELEVATION	186'	MEAN ANN TEMP	80.7°
LATITUDE	28° 17' N.	MEAN TEMP RANGE	41°
LONGITUDE	68° 29' E.	MEAN ANN PRECIP	4"
GROWING SEASON	365	RAINY DAYS	7.6

JACOBABAD   WEST PAKISTAN

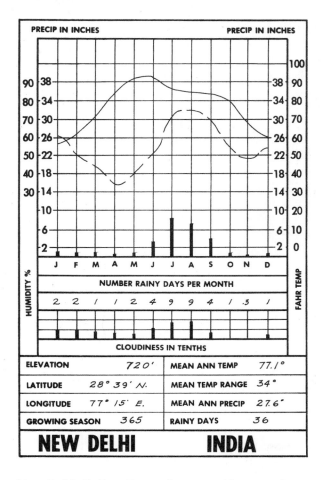

ELEVATION	720'	MEAN ANN TEMP	77.1°
LATITUDE	28° 39' N.	MEAN TEMP RANGE	34°
LONGITUDE	77° 15' E.	MEAN ANN PRECIP	27.6"
GROWING SEASON	365	RAINY DAYS	36

NEW DELHI   INDIA

Jacobabad, West Pakistan. November through March, warm, sunny days with crisp nights barely above freezing. Most clouds of year in short spells from shallow cyclonic storms, with light, variable breezes, but rare rainfall. April through June, increasing heat with June hottest month of year, absolute maximum 127°. Very few clouds, minimum humidity, rainfall rare, wind shifted to southeast. July and August very hot, maximum humidity, more than one rainy day per month, with nearly half the year's total rain from thundershowers from southeast winds related to summer monsoon. September and October, decreasing heat. Almost never rains in October.

New Delhi, India. Dry and sunny with warm days and crisp nights just above freezing from late October through March. Occasional cloudy spell and drizzly rain of cyclonic origin. Increasing temperature in April, seasonal maximums over 110° in May, with thundershowers in May and early June. Monsoon frontal rains with thundershowers begin in late June. Humidity, uncomfortably high in main rainy season. Irregular rains through early September. Cooler, drier, and sunnier during late September and October.

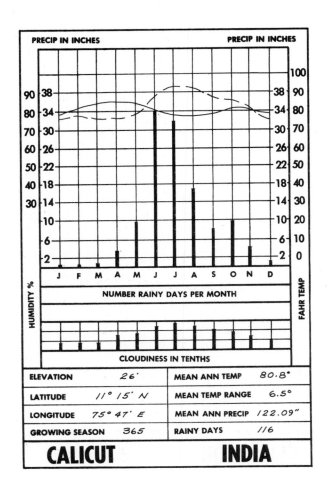

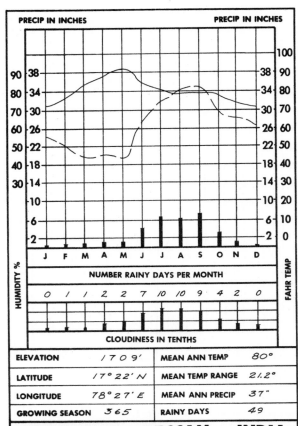

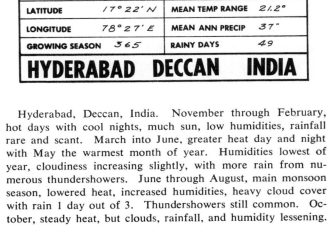

Calicut, India. December through March, hot days with mild nights; during March, the heat increasing. Much sun, moderate humidities, slight rainfall. April into June, highest temperatures of year both day and night, increased clouds and rainfall, but humidities remain moderate. June through August, decreased temperatures but very high humidities with heavy cloud cover and heavy rain almost every day after sudden break of monsoon. September through November, steady heat, decreasing rainfall, lower humidities, and fewer clouds. Winds are somewhat irregular all year, with land and sea breeze offsetting heat all year.

Hyderabad, Deccan, India. November through February, hot days with cool nights, much sun, low humidities, rainfall rare and scant. March into June, greater heat day and night with May the warmest month of year. Humidities lowest of year, cloudiness increasing slightly, with more rain from numerous thundershowers. June through August, main monsoon season, lowered heat, increased humidities, heavy cloud cover with rain 1 day out of 3. Thundershowers still common. October, steady heat, but clouds, rainfall, and humidity lessening.

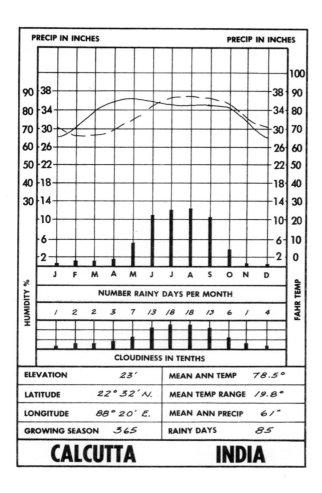

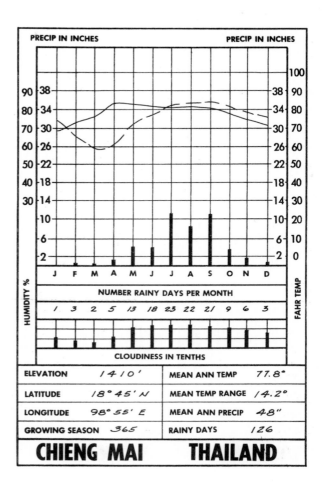

Calcutta, India. November through March, dry and sunny, warm days and very mild nights, minimums around 50°. Humidity fairly high. April becomes sultry as heat and humidity increase. May thundershowers precede southwest monsoon break in late June. Maximum temperatures decline with rains, but stickiness increases and cloud cover is heavy. Main rains abate late September, with short showers, sultry weather, and more sun during October.

Chiengmai, Thailand. December through February, warm days and mild nights, light cloud cover, moderate humidities, scant rain. March begins warming up; humidity and cloud cover are at minimum for year. April and May, warmest months of year, humidities higher, cloud cover and rainfall increasing, particularly in late May. June through September, steady heat, high humidity, heavy cloud cover, but only moderate rainfall, occurring almost every day. Rain, cloud, and humidity often at maximum in September. October and November, a slow transition period, with heat and humidity lessening, cloud cover thinning, and rain slacking off.

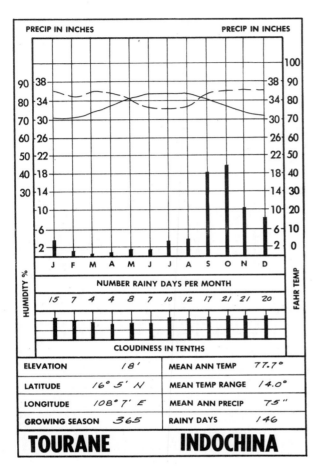

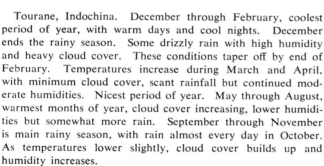

ELEVATION	18'	MEAN ANN TEMP	77.7°
LATITUDE	16° 5' N	MEAN TEMP RANGE	14.0°
LONGITUDE	108° 7' E	MEAN ANN PRECIP	75"
GROWING SEASON	365	RAINY DAYS	146

TOURANE   INDOCHINA

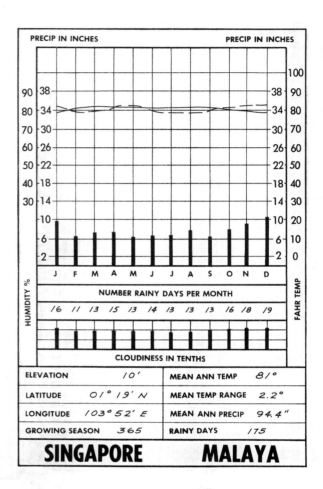

ELEVATION	10'	MEAN ANN TEMP	81°
LATITUDE	01° 19' N	MEAN TEMP RANGE	2.2°
LONGITUDE	103° 52' E	MEAN ANN PRECIP	94.4"
GROWING SEASON	365	RAINY DAYS	175

SINGAPORE   MALAYA

Tourane, Indochina. December through February, coolest period of year, with warm days and cool nights. December ends the rainy season. Some drizzly rain with high humidity and heavy cloud cover. These conditions taper off by end of February. Temperatures increase during March and April, with minimum cloud cover, scant rainfall but continued moderate humidities. Nicest period of year. May through August, warmest months of year, cloud cover increasing, lower humidities but somewhat more rain. September through November is main rainy season, with rain almost every day in October. As temperatures lower slightly, cloud cover builds up and humidity increases.

Singapore, Malaya. Typical equatorial station, with very slight temperature range which produces no seasonal rhythm. Diurnal changes of temperature, humidity, cloudiness, and rainfall are of greater human importance than annual ones. Cloud cover is moderately high all year, with daily cycle of clear sky, cloud, thundershower, and heavy rain, such days interspersed with spells of cloudy, sultry weather.

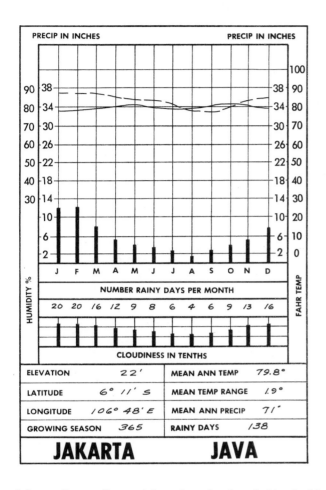

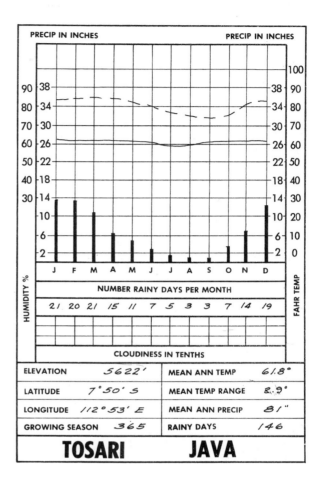

Jakarta, Java. Equatorial station showing feeble double maxima and minima of temperature which are less important to human comfort than diurnal changes. Jakarta is on a windward shore during retreating winter monsoon, when daily sea breezes, trade winds, and monsoon effects combine to give least good weather of year. Heavy winds, high cloud cover, high humidities, and torrents of thundershower rainfall on 2 out of 3 days during January and February. During season of northern summer monsoon, north shore of Java is in relative rain-shadow position. Light cloud, moderate humidities, comparatively little rainfall, which is climaxed in August with only 4 rainy days. This is least uncomfortable season of year.

Tosari, Java. Highland station showing equatorial temperature curve with very slight annual range. Temperatures low enough for comfort. This record is typical of many hill stations throughout the southern Orient. Period of maximum rain, December to March, is period of minimum cloud cover. Humidity varies with precipitation curve. High humidities not uncomfortable in lower temperatures.

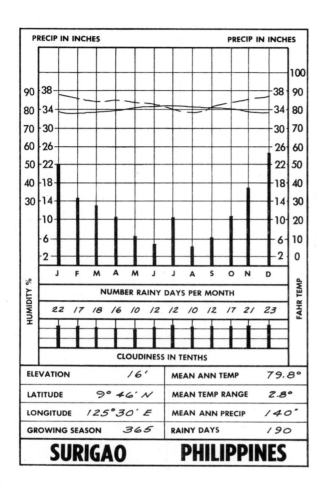

ELEVATION	16'	MEAN ANN TEMP	79.8°
LATITUDE	9° 46' N	MEAN TEMP RANGE	2.8°
LONGITUDE	125° 30' E	MEAN ANN PRECIP	140"
GROWING SEASON	365	RAINY DAYS	190

SURIGAO   PHILIPPINES

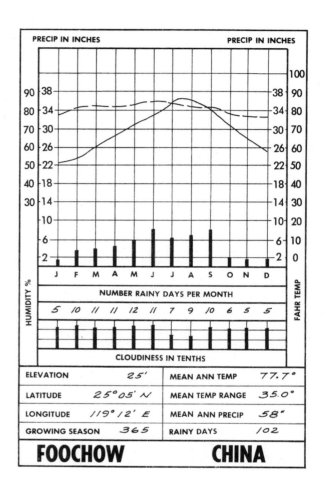

ELEVATION	25'	MEAN ANN TEMP	77.7°
LATITUDE	25° 05' N	MEAN TEMP RANGE	35.0°
LONGITUDE	119° 12' E	MEAN ANN PRECIP	58"
GROWING SEASON	365	RAINY DAYS	102

FOOCHOW   CHINA

Surigao, Philippine Islands.   November into April, coolest period, main rains from convergence storms of trades and retreating monsoon, with maximum cloud and humidity.   Late April and May, warmer, less rain and cloud, but humidity remains high.   June into September, minimum rain and humidity, but warmest period with more cloud. Late September and October, increasing rain and humidity, slightly decreasing heat.

Foochow, China.   December into March, cool to mild nights and warm days, mild cyclonic weather, and small amount of rain, with heavy cloud and least sticky weather of year.   Late March into May, increasing heat, humidity, and rain from local thundershower and weak cyclonic effects.   June through September, hot and sticky though maximums rarely top 100°.   Thundershower and southeast monsoon rains, but fewest clouds of year.   July through September, main typhoon season, may bring heavy rainfall.   October and November, lowered heat and rain, sultriness slowly abating with increasing cyclonic weather.

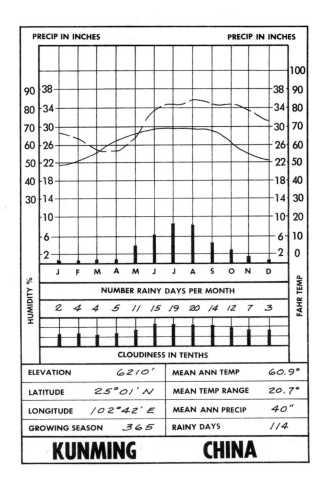

ELEVATION	6210'	MEAN ANN TEMP	60.9°
LATITUDE	25°01' N	MEAN TEMP RANGE	20.7°
LONGITUDE	102°42' E	MEAN ANN PRECIP	40"
GROWING SEASON	365	RAINY DAYS	114

KUNMING   CHINA

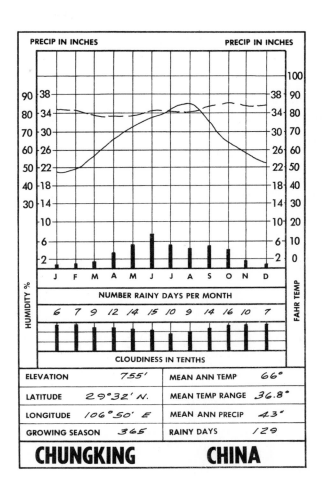

ELEVATION	755'	MEAN ANN TEMP	66°
LATITUDE	29°32' N.	MEAN TEMP RANGE	36.8°
LONGITUDE	106°50' E	MEAN ANN PRECIP	43"
GROWING SEASON	365	RAINY DAYS	129

CHUNGKING   CHINA

Kunming, China. November into March, cool nights and warm days, some clouds, a little light cyclonic rain, some raw weather. Late March into May, warmer, but cool nights, increasing cloud, increased cyclonic rain. June through September, warm days and mild nights, heavy thundershower rains, much cloudy weather, maximum humidity but rarely oppressive. October is more sunny, cooler, and drier.

Chungking, China. November through mid-March, heavy overcast sky, sun rarely seen, high humidity and mist, days and nights cool and often raw. Frost on higher hills. Late March through May, weak cyclonic effects, warmer, a little more sun. drizzly rains in some volume, lowest humidities of year, best weather. June through August, maximum temperatures around 100°, small daily range, thundershower rains, sticky monotonous weather even though maximum sun and humidity not at highest. In September heat lessens, but humidity increases. Cloud cover builds up in October with cooler weather, some cyclonic rains.

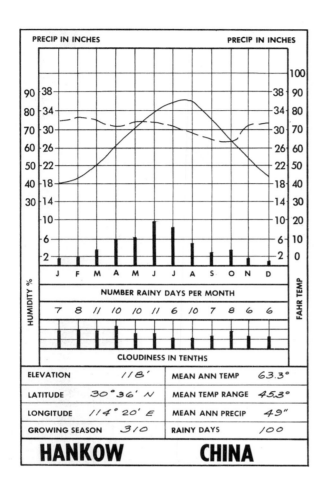

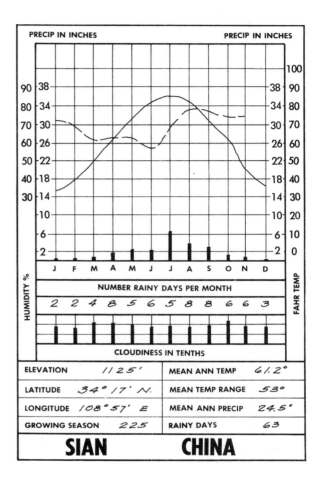

Hankow, China. December to mid-March, cool to raw days, cool to cold nights, frequent frost, cyclonic weather, rather cloudy, light rains, and some quick-melting snow. April and May, transitions of warming days and mild nights, cyclonic weather, more rain. June through August, monotonous sticky heat day and night, thundershower and frontal rains with much sun. September breaks heat gradually, rain slackens. October and November, cooler, cloudier, more cyclonic weather.

Sian, China. November into March, very cold nights and cold to mild days with fairly clear weather, northwest winds, cyclonic changes, small snowfall. Late March through May, warming weather, abating northwest winds, considerable cloud, cyclonic effects with moderate rain in good years. June through August, very hot days, warm nights, slightly more sun, irregular thundershowers, unpredictable rainfall on few days per month. September and October, cooler, cyclonic changes and northwest winds commencing. Humidity seldom bothersome at any time of year.

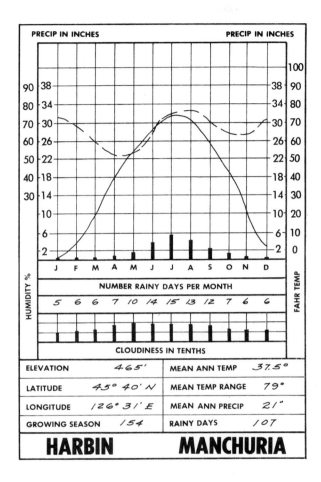

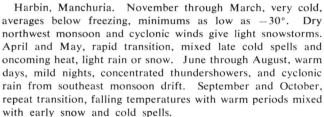

ELEVATION	465'	MEAN ANN TEMP	37.5°
LATITUDE	45° 40' N	MEAN TEMP RANGE	79°
LONGITUDE	126° 31' E	MEAN ANN PRECIP	21"
GROWING SEASON	154	RAINY DAYS	107

HARBIN   MANCHURIA

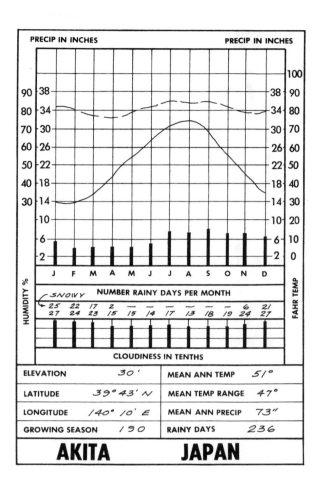

ELEVATION	30'	MEAN ANN TEMP	51°
LATITUDE	39° 43' N	MEAN TEMP RANGE	47°
LONGITUDE	140° 10' E	MEAN ANN PRECIP	73"
GROWING SEASON	190	RAINY DAYS	236

AKITA   JAPAN

Harbin, Manchuria. November through March, very cold, averages below freezing, minimums as low as −30°. Dry northwest monsoon and cyclonic winds give light snowstorms. April and May, rapid transition, mixed late cold spells and oncoming heat, light rain or snow. June through August, warm days, mild nights, concentrated thundershowers, and cyclonic rain from southeast monsoon drift. September and October, repeat transition, falling temperatures with warm periods mixed with early snow and cold spells.

Akita, Japan. Late December into March, cold, freezing averages, cyclonic weather with strong northwest monsoon, rain almost every day. Heavy snow on about 90 days during 6 months. Most winter days very cloudy, humidity high, weather damp and raw. April and May, rapid intermonsoon transition, abated northwest monsoon, cyclonic weather and rainfall, somewhat more sun. June into September, warm days and mild nights, sultry, high humidity, and variable cloud cover. Cyclonic effects mixed with light southeast monsoon, heaviest rainfall of year, on fewest days. Late September and October, autumn intermonsoon transition, cyclonic weather, possible early cold spells. November into December show returning northwest monsoon, more clouds, increasing rainy weather, lowering temperatures, snow, and raw conditions. Fog is scant on this coast compared with frequency on east coast of northern Honshu.

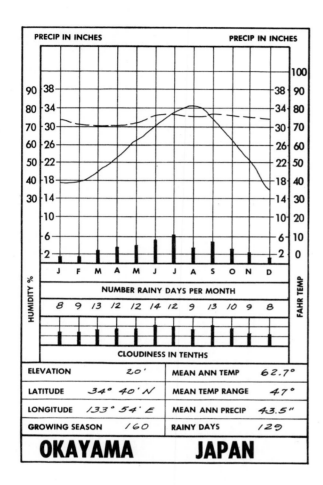

ELEVATION	20'	MEAN ANN TEMP	62.7°
LATITUDE	34° 40' N	MEAN TEMP RANGE	47°
LONGITUDE	133° 54' E	MEAN ANN PRECIP	43.5"
GROWING SEASON	160	RAINY DAYS	129

OKAYAMA   JAPAN

Okayama, Japan. December through February, mild sunny days and cool to frosty nights, intermixed cloudy and rainy weather, cyclonic storms, and moderate northwest monsoon winds. Light snow on few winter days. March through May, warmer weather, more clouds, more cyclonic rain on more days, northwest monsoon abated. June through September, very warm days and mild nights, considerable sun, rainy but less so than other parts of Japan, occasionally uncomfortable afternoon humidities, but effective land and sea breezes and prevailing southeast monsoon. August and September, typhoon rains, little cyclonic weather. October and November, less heat, most sun of year, moderate rainfall, increased cyclonic changes, and, during November, return of the northwest monsoon. October into December, very pleasant weather.

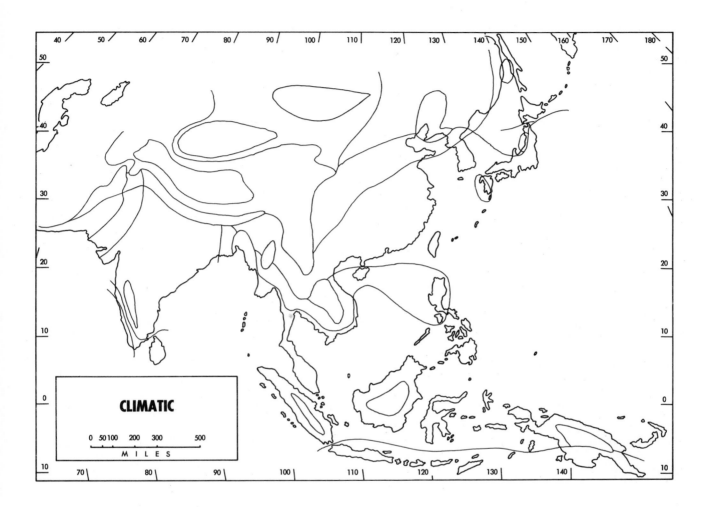

Fig. 17. Thornthwaite's climatic boundaries.

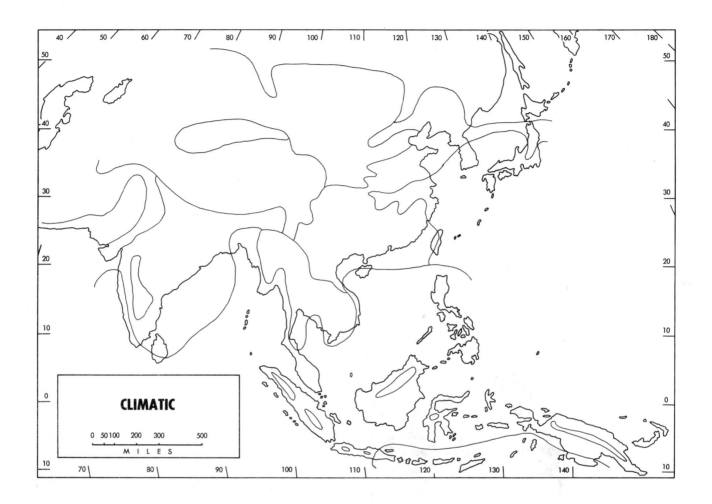

Fig. 18. Köppen's climatic boundaries, **modified** after Cressey, and *Goode's Atlas.*

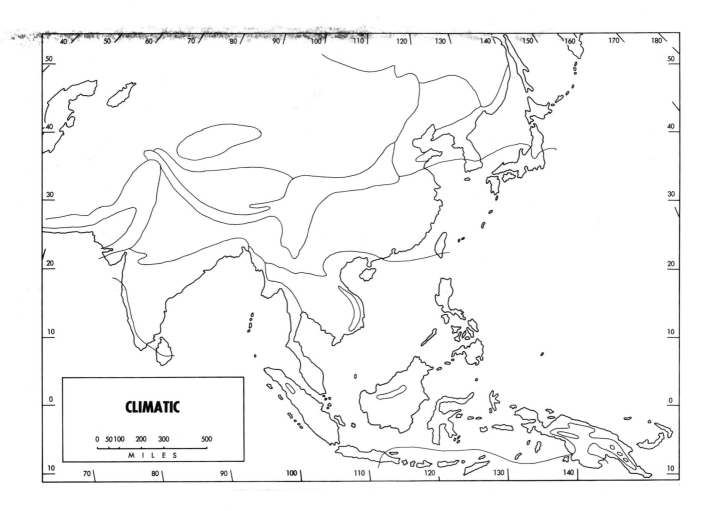

Fig. 19. Climatic boundaries, after Russell and Kniffen.

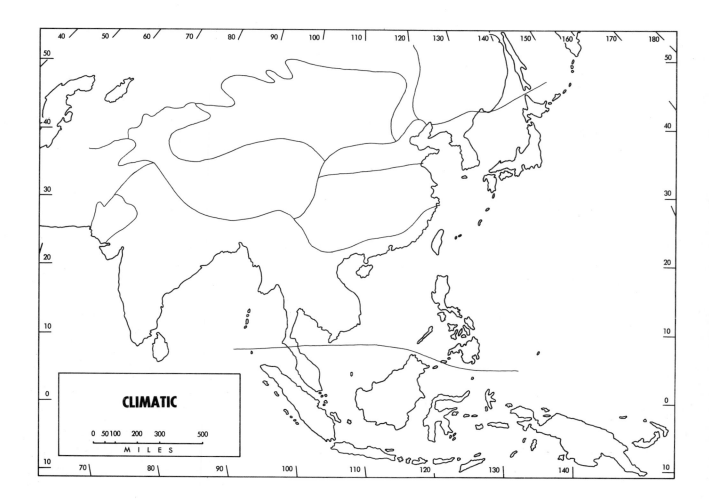

Fig. 20. Climatic boundaries, after Stamp.

Mineral Geography

THE ORIGINS OF MINERAL USE

No country in the Orient holds a record for originating metal technology; both India and China developed high skills in fabrication of metals at an early time. The origins of metal technology seem to lie in the ancient Near East, from which region China and India were early to learn the techniques. Certainly not all the Orient learned the use of minerals with equal speed and facility. Peoples on some islands of the Indies have remained in the Stone Age until modern time. In some cases the use of iron pressed close upon the spread of bronze.

India was not the original center of iron technology, but its manganese alloy iron ores allowed a very early production of superior steel long before the use of alloys was consciously developed. India was probably an early source of what became known to the West as "Damascus steel." The use of iron and ability to produce it must have been carried into southeastern Asia by Indian trader colonists. It is likely that iron did not become at all common in China until a few centuries B.C. The Chinese soon became expert at iron casting but never developed a really high proficiency at working steel. On the other hand, the Chinese early and thoroughly mastered the handling of bronze and with it created a variety of utilitarian products that in the modern era rank among the world's finest art goods. It is not certain how bronze penetrated southeastern Asia and the Island Arcs, but it preceded iron by some centuries in most areas.

Since nothing similar to a modern geological survey was ever carried out, the sources of common minerals only gradually became widely known. A number of sources of copper were widely scattered, and some trade developed in the raw metal and its products. Iron ores are scattered so widely that probably nothing more than local trade ever developed in iron ores and their simple products. Steel, on the other hand, was a very different commodity, and Indian steel circulated over much of the ancient world in small amounts. Tin was a trade specialty of the Malay Peninsula as a whole, though gradually tin ores were mined from Banka to Yunnan.

Mercury, cinnabar, salt, sulphur, and saltpeter were also minerals enjoying a certain trade movement. Their use in China and India was a very early development, and the use of salt and sulphur was extremely widespread and appeared almost as early as any kind of trade. Jewel stones of various kinds were quarried, traded, and used from early Stone Age time in every populated region, though gradually certain areas became famous for particular stones. The precious metals and stones of the Orient naturally attracted more spectacular attention than tin, copper, or salt, and were the subject of many stories and tales that grew into fabulous legends. Gold, gathered widely in the earlier eras, is another mineral of very early interest. The earliest gold was alluvial, picked up in some of the rivers of most countries. Slowly it became a mine product in a number of areas.

The collecting of alluvial gold, collecting of jewel and semiprecious stones, and gradually the quarrying of each of these probably were a spontaneous activity at an early time widely over the Orient. Mining as a developed kind of quarrying seems to have had its origin somewhere west of the true Orient. It would seem that real mining was an activity learned by most Orientals after they had already become interested in gold and decorative stones. Copper, bronze, iron, lead, zinc, silver, tin, and perhaps some other minerals had their first conscious use in some part of the Near East. The knowledge of use, ore mining, and metal smelting spread eastward toward India, through Central Asia into China, and gradually beyond these two regions. Some of the mixtures of ores and metals may have developed in some part of the Orient, but others appear introduced at a rather late date. In comparison to the production of bronze, brass is quite recent in use and manufacture in China. Coal was first used consciously in north China, and mica may well be an Indian introduction, but the real mining of both is late in appearance.

DISTRIBUTION OF MINERALS

Considered in terms of simple unit area the Orient almost has its share of the world's economic minerals. In proportion to population, however, the Orient has far less than its share; in addition there is an uneven distribution of the separate minerals among the countries of the realm. Adequacy of supply is a variable situation, dependent upon the use to which a given society may put its minerals. In the judgment of an agrarian society, whose primary agriculture is complemented by handicraft industry, China or Thailand might be said to be adequately supplied with iron ore. However, modern industrial judgment records that China is in a fair position only and that Thailand is badly off. It would be impossible in Thailand to mine millions of tons of iron ore even for one year, unless there are resources not now known. The Japanese shortages began to be evident only when Japan launched upon her campaign of modern industrialization of her economy. Surveys are everywhere incomplete, except possibly in Japan, and many new minerals and larger reserves may be widely present but still unknown. At least Japan owned her own minerals, and their exploitation was of her own choosing. But in every country of the Orient, to some extent, production has been controlled and profits extracted by some distant exploiting corporation or country. The petroleum of the Indies or the iron ores of Korea have been of little value to the population of either country in the past generation. The accompanying table shows the political control of important minerals. Judgment has been made in terms of the needs of a peaceful economy only. Maps showing the locations of mineral production will be found in each regional chapter.

SOURCES OF POWER

China and India, as the two largest units of the Orient, possess the largest potential volumes of industrial power. China stands fourth among the countries of the world in coal resources. Coal resources are well scattered and varied in quality, though the best reserves are concentrated in Shansi and Shensi. Coal is mined in every province of China proper, and the annual total in the past slightly exceeded 30,000,000 tons, only

about half of which was put to work in industry. Some mines are modern in equipment, but many are operated in the crudest possible manner with exceedingly bad labor practices. The annual production figure is increasing slowly.

India's coal reserves are small compared to those of China, but sufficient for a reasonable period, unless production increases tremendously in the near future. The coal is not of the best quality and is not well distributed, the Chota Nagpur hill country having most of the reserves. Production figures are slightly lower than those of China, but most of the coal mined is used in transport or in industry. Pakistan possesses little coal and is highly dependent upon India for the operation of her rail system and her relatively small industrial program. Japan has been the leading oriental producer of coal during this century, her annual figure having exceeded 45,000,000 tons after about 1930. Coal is widely distributed throughout Japan, but it is low in quality for industrial use and reserves are comparatively small for a country with industrial ambition. Korea has fair reserves of coal that, mined for her own use only, will answer most needs for a long period. In the last generation Japan mined Korean coal for the good of Japan only. Northern Indochina has considerable hard coal, with a significant annual export, but not much good soft coal. The other countries of the Orient have only very small amounts of fair to poor coal. It is mined in every country in small amounts, but only in the Indies and Malaya is it a significant addition to available power.

The Indies stand third among world petroleum producers, but only modest reserves are known, though much surveying remains unfinished. Sumatra, Borneo, and Java are the leading productive islands, but New Guinea will one day appear in the list. A wide range of oils is included in the 70,000,000-barrel annual production average. Occidental corporations produce, control, and export oil from the Indies, this being the Orient's major source of petroleum products. Burma is the only other significant producer of petroleum, from fields northwest of Rangoon in the folded mountain country. Burmese oil, like that of the Indies, is today produced, controlled, and exported to eastern markets by occidental corporations. Natural seeps have been producing oil under very crude native methods for centuries.

Both China proper and India now produce small amounts of petroleum, but the prospects for the future in China do not look favorable owing to faulty geological structure. Shensi now produces all of China's oil, and Assam yields India's total. Sinkiang's good petroleum prospects may cause this distant border re-

TABLE 3

Occurrence of Mineral Deposits

	Paki-stan	India	Burma	Thailand	Indo-china	Malaya	Indies	Philip-pine Islands	China	Korea	Japan
Power Sources											
Hard coal		+			++				+++	+	✓
Coking coal		+							++	+	✓
Steam coal		++							+++	+	+
Low-grade coal	✓	+	✓	✓	✓	+	✓	✓	++	+	+
Petroleum	✓	✓	++				+++		✓		✓
Oil shale		+		+					++	+	✓
Water power	+	+++	+	+	+	+	++	+	++	++	++
Monazite		++									
Industrial Metals											
Iron Ore	✓	+++	✓	✓	+	++	+	++	+	+	✓
Manganese	✓	+++			+	++	+	++	+++		✓
Tungsten			++	++	+				+++	+	
Chromium		+			+			+++			+
Nickel		+	✓				++		✓	+	✓
Vanadium											✓
Molybdenum				+					✓	+	✓
Antimony					+				++		✓
Lead			++	✓	+			✓	+	+	✓
Zinc			++		+			✓	+	+	✓
Aluminum ores	✓	++	+			++	+++		++	+	
Copper	+	✓	++					++	✓	✓	+
Tin			+	++	+	+++	+++		++		✓
Precious Metals											
Gold	✓	+	✓		+		+	++	+	+	+
Silver			✓				+	++	✓	+	✓
Platinum			✓					✓			✓
Non-Metals											
Phosphates		✓			+		✓		✓		✓
Nitrates	+	+							+		
Sulphur	+	+					++	+	+		++
Salt	+	++	+	++	+	✓	+	+	++	+	✓
Gypsum	+	+							+		✓
Mercury									++	✓	✓
Graphite		++							✓	++	✓
Mica		+++							✓		✓

+++ Outstanding resource.
 ++ Surplus beyond domestic need.
  + Adequate for present use.
  ✓ Present but insufficient.
blank No commercial resource.

gion to become a strategic issue before China can reap any advantage therefrom. It is possible that Szechwan and Shensi will prove productive, to China's benefit. Pakistan began her separate political career lacking petroleum resources of proved worth, but there are possibilities of future discoveries of resources in both Pakistan and India, around the fringes of the northern mountain wall. Northern Japan is a very small petroleum producer, without prospect of larger yields. Sakhalin's modest petroleum production has been returned to Russian control after a period of Japanese exploitation. No other country appears certain to possess petroleum resources, although Philippine expectations may materialize. A fair volume of oil shale and very soft coal gives China a source of petroleum products once the industrial procedures are mastered and in operation. Japan, Korea, India, and Thailand have small amounts of oil shale, but these do not merit optimism as regards adequate petroleum.

The Orient as a whole possesses a hydroelectric potential estimated as well above that of North America or Europe. Of the total India-Pakistan holds nearly 40 per cent, China just over 20, the Indies nearly 15, Japan about 7, and Indochina 6 per cent. Each other country has a significant though smaller power potential based on water. Much of the 103,000,000 horsepower estimated as available 95 per cent of the time in the Orient will be rather costly to develop, requiring both money and engineering from the outside world. It will be a long time before much of the potential is actually available in many countries. In the present developed volume of water power innumerable simple water wheels are operating in every country, which are used for the grinding of grain and similar operations. In terms of developed hydroelectric power available for industrial use, Japan with her 7 per cent of the total potential possesses over 75 per cent of the developed power, with over 6,000,000 horsepower. The Japanese empire, during the Sino-Japanese War, had a developed total of about 8,000,000 horsepower, most of this extra power being located in Korea. The total developed hydroelectric power of the Orient is less than 9,000,000 horsepower, India and Java being the only spots outside the former Japanese empire with any developed power.

Monazite, a thorium-producing mineral, has become more than a minor product with the growth of atomic energy research. For many years the southwest coast of peninsular India and the west coast of Ceylon have produced monazite and related minerals. Used in the normal preatomic industrial processes, a small tonnage satisfied the world's needs. No other part of the Orient

is known to produce more than sample amounts of any atomic energy mineral.

INDUSTRIAL METALS

For the metals group China, Korea, and Indochina are the best off, according to modern industrial needs. Each has a wide variety of metals in respectable quantities. China does not have large reserves of copper or of good iron ore, and this will eventually prove a handicap. Formosan copper has moved away from China since the Japanese began its production. China is short in some of the ferroalloys but possesses exportable surpluses of others. More complete geological surveys may yet turn up deposits of needed metals to widen more fully the present respectable basis for an industrial program. Korea's metal minerals are now fairly well known through Japanese survey and exploitation and exist in adequate proportion to her needs in rather a wide range. Indochina has in Tonking a considerable mineral storehouse, but mismanagement and stock-floating operations have prevented an even and effective development.

Japan possesses a wide range of the metals in quantities adequate for a modest, peacetime industrial program producing for home markets. Even so a shortage of iron ore would still exist. The upsurge of her modern industrial growth revealed that Japan is short in the large volumes and basic reserves of many metals so needed by a militant industrial export economy. India was in moderately good position under rule as a single country with shortages in lead, zinc, and some of the ferroalloys. Under a divided pattern of government the shortages of Pakistan are rather great, whereas those of India are not so marked.

The other countries of the Orient are but imperfectly known geologically, and the story changes with each decade. Present-known metals distribution is irregular, and quantities vary widely. Malaya has one of the smallest ranges of minerals of any region, yet one of the most active mining programs, centered on tin. Only the Japanese, prior to World War II, were interested in the Malayan deposit of manganese, bauxite, and iron ore, where they operated concession mines along the southeast coast. In comparative terms Thailand perhaps is the most poorly endowed, tin being her only really productive metal. In the famous Bawdwin mines Burma possessed a rich mineralized area that had been worked by the Chinese for centuries before the British began exploitation. World War II inflicted serious damage upon the mines, but redevelopment of operations producing lead, zinc, and by-product copper, silver, and cobalt is proceeding and the resource remains of value. In the Philippines surveys have found rich deposits of iron, manganese, and chromite ores, to add to the copper resources. It is possible that other industrial metals will also be located to make the islands relatively well supplied with the metals of the modern world. Additional geologic surveys throughout the Orient undoubtedly will change the scoreboard of resources available in the future.

NON-METALLIC MINERALS

In this group India, China, and Korea are in the best relative positions, with Japan again short a number of critical items. Southeastern Asia has an irregular distribution of these items, more significant for its abscences and shortages than for its valued resources. Perhaps most serious is the shortage of adequate fertilizer minerals. Though it is true that the nitrates and phosphates can be synthetically produced, this can be done only in industrial countries with a large hydroelectric supply, and the countries which most need the fertilizer are in no position to produce their own synthetically. Indochina possesses the only known phosphate rock resources. Large deposits of such minerals as graphite and mica provide India and Korea with export surpluses.

PRECIOUS METALS AND STONES

The varying value placed upon the several precious stones is a distinguishing feature between oriental culture groups. Rubies, sapphires, diamonds, and pearls long have been the most prized precious stones in India, and this pattern is variably shared by those parts of southeastern Asia, and the Island Arcs that were culturally affected by India. The Chinese realm, on the other hand, has always put the highest value on the jades. Pearls, diamonds, sapphires, turquoise, beryl, amber, crystal quartz, and other stones are esteemed but none rank with jade. The precious stones, among different peoples, carry a religious significance, a more noticeable feature of the Indian realm than the Chinese.

Over the centuries there have been various sources of pearls scattered around the coast of India, along the southern coast of China, the Sulu Archipelago, and in parts of Japan. Diamonds have long come from Borneo and peninsular India. Rubies and sapphires are products both of the Burmese Shan Plateau and of Ceylon. Lesser stones are very widely scattered. There are many kinds of jade, ranging in color from cream to brilliant green, and fashions have changed repeatedly. The sources of jade are as scattered as its variety. The Tsinling Mountains, in southern Shensi, are one of the most accessible sources, currently providing one of the modern green jades. Regions as distant as Lake Baikal in southern Siberia, the highlands of Russian Turkestan, the border ranges of northern Tibet, and the hill country of North Burma have been tapped again and again for varying grades and color shades of nephrite, jadeite, and related stones that pass as jade or its counterfeits.

Gold occurs rather widely throughout the Orient in varying amounts. Peninsular India, Sumatra, and Borneo have been the historically fabulous sources, but it is possible that the best deposits have been worked out, for a lessened production over recent centuries has not lived up to the fabulous legends. Korea and the Philippines are significant modern additions to the list of producing regions. Indochina, western China, Formosa, and Japan are small producers. Silver occurs less widely than gold, and often is a by-product of other mining. Burma, the Indies, Korea, and the Philippines are the notable contemporary sources. India and China, the world's primary long-time buyers of silver, produce almost none. A little platinum is produced in the Indies, in Burma, and in Japan as a by-product of gold and silver mining.

Everywhere throughout the Orient are active and abandoned quarries and mine workings from which precious stones and metals have long been taken. Some of the sources were already mythical when the Portuguese first tried to trace the home of oriental riches. Others have been worked out in recent centuries; some continue to yield their precious wares today at a steady rate. Some countries, such as Korea and the Philippines, have become major producers of gold only in recent decades, despite a long history as minor sources.

Soils, Plants, and Plant Cultures

Climate, man, birds and animals, soils, and plants form a complex of interacting agents that spread a variety of plant covers over the earth which are used, altered, rearranged and shaped into many regional patterns. Climate often is the primary regional factor. But soil frequently counters climate to increase, vary, or lessen the plant complex. Both birds and animals are important agents of distribution and change. Plants, through genetic evolution, adaptiveness, and ability to compete with each other are themselves significant agents in the vegetation of a region. Most capable of altering the plant complex of any area, however, is man, who cuts, burns, weeds, plants, and abandons areas in the course of time. This chapter is a tentative survey of selected phases of this large complex.

PROBLEMS IN SOILS

Soil technologists in the tropics today find that they have produced more questions than answers. This is the result of a half century of modern work in soils, done mostly outside the tropics. Most generalizations about midlatitude soils seem at least partly untrue when applied to the tropics or subtropics. The larger part of the Orient today possesses tropical and subtropical climatic regimes, and a large share of the soils fall into groups not well studied and classified. China proper is the one major section of the Orient in which real progress has been made in modern soil studies, though the task is far from complete. The Philippines are being studied systematically though here the task is only begun. On Java the Dutch have made penetrating studies of local soils. In India and in Japan the study of soils remained overlong in the hands of hard-rock geologists, but recently a new start has been made in each country. Some of the best work has been

done in Thailand, but no complete survey has been made.

In earlier studies it was assumed that two fundamental soil-forming processes operate in the humid zones of the earth, podzolization in the cool wet regions and laterization in the hot wet regions. Too simply stated, the first was thought to remove the soluble salts, iron, and aluminum compounds from the surface horizons, leaving a gray silica residue. The second was believed to begin by removing the soluble salts, and transferring the iron and aluminum compounds to the subsoil, but to conclude by removal of silicates and the restoration of iron and aluminum compounds near the surface horizons with the clays accumulating just under them, producing red to mottled red and gray soils.

More recently podzolization has been found active well into the tropics, and advanced laterization is admitted as restricted to certain situations wherein alternate wetting and drying regularly take place. Very porous surface soils in the tropics frequently seem to become podzolized, but some ricefield soils are also similarly affected. Where black soils once were thought to be confined to midlatitude grassland dry margins, and their formation understood, they now are recognized within the tropics without, as yet, a satisfactory explanation of their origin and development. Better understanding of the upward and downward seasonal movement of ground water and the position of the water table appears essential to further progress in understanding tropical soils. Better knowledge of Tertiary and Pleistocene climatic variations is needed to fathom the history of soil formation.

It seems to me that the standard theory of soil formation needs considerable alteration. Leaching is the basic process affecting surface horizons of soils all over the world, operating similarly but at different rates under different climatic regimes. Soil formation normally is a slow process, and in many parts of the world what are termed mature soils cannot be the product of strictly contemporary climates. What are taken for mature soils may well be fossil soils, arrested in some stage of development under previously operative climatic regimes, and now only slightly affected by contemporary climates. Such soils may also be lower horizons of fossil soils stripped of their earlier higher horizons. Failure to recognize this history may well have led to the conclusion that tropical soils are affected by processes different from those operating in higher latitudes. The very heavy, deep, red soils of parts of the tropics, found in areas of tectonic stability, may well be such fossil types, primarily produced by climates other than those prevailing in these areas today. The absence of such heavy red soils, and the absence of the mature laterites, in such structurally young areas as Java and most of the Philippines seem to point to this conclusion.

Perhaps the two most common misjudgments that the Occident has made about soils of the tropics concern their fabulous richness and their complete lack of organic matter. Many tropical and subtropical soils are very deep, but not often are lowland tropical soils really rich soils with a long productive life. Tropical soils supporting a real plant cover do have organic materials in their surface horizons. The speed of decomposition never permits a deep layer of unrotted humus to collect on the surface. As long as a heavy plant cover remains undisturbed the plant association, working with solar energy and moisture, is able to feed into the soil dead organic material to maintain a supply of soluble elements and to support soil bacteria, both of fundamental value in the growth process.

A long period is required for the plant cover to build itself up to heavy forest even where precipitation is adequate. But, when the plant cover is removed, the slim reserve of soluble plant foods is removed from tropical soils far more rapidly than is true in midlatitude soils. Within a few years a soil that supported a 200-foot multilayered tropical rainforest may be so exhausted that it will support only the poorest of scrubby plants. The tropics are dotted with the marks of nature's and man's removal actions and nature's slow recovery programs.

On some of the islands of the Indies and the southern Philippines, volcanism periodically provides a new layer of unweathered soil material. Where basic rather than acidic volcanic extrusives are provided young and immature soils are extremely productive. Here the very speed of weathering and the rate of soil formation are counter to all midlatitude experience. Such volcanism provides a reshuffling of soil horizons and a renewal of fertility of extreme importance.

Most tropical soils are some shade of red or black. The oxidation of iron compounds provides a color stain that frequently is dominant over other coloring elements. The origin of the black coloring is not well understood. However, under situations in which relations of ground water, precipitation, vegetation, denudation, aggradation, and weathering processes are altered locally, a wide variety of colors may exist, from black to buff, brown, and light gray. Redness of color does not always denote lateritic soils. Many red and yellow soils of the tropics and subtropics are soils in some immature or arrested stage of development. Considerable attention has been given to laterite and the term often has been misused. In lowland situations of long stability of major causal factors, with a relatively high water table, seasonal wetting and drying, the lateritic process has sometimes proceeded to maturity, producing crusted layers properly termed laterite. This probably is a fossil product, however, and not one forming today. Mature laterite is scattered widely throughout the southern Orient, but does not bulk very large in square-mile total. Such products are worthless as agricultural soils and usually support only a scant native plant cover. Laterite varies considerably in chemical formula and physical characteristics. Sometimes it has provided building stone; at other times its high iron content has permitted its use as iron ore. Bauxite ores at or near the surface appear related to the formation of mature laterite.

Occidentals often have closely related soil quality to workability. European agriculture in upper latitudes has been accustomed to use considerable cultivation in its cropping practice and, therefore, to regard easy workability as a good soil characteristic. The soil chemist suggests that under cold to warm temperatures stirring the soil is a useful act. Cultivation on the dry margins, to save moisture, has furthered the soil-stirring idea. Heavy clay soils usually have not been regarded as good soils, owing to low workability and the low content of soluble salts. In the tropics under permanently high temperatures too great stirring of the soil promotes too rapid chemical and bacterial reaction, resulting in loss of plant foods. Heavy clays in the tropics give surprising yields when properly handled.

A very important question in areas long inhabited concerns the cultural effect of man upon the soil. The repeated piling of canal mud on a Chinese terrace dug from a hill to make a field in which rice has grown for a thousand years results in a soil quite unequal to that which nature would have provided on that hillside had it remained undisturbed. Though much of the loessial soils of northwest China have suffered very great erosion, even to the production of rough badlands, soil type and quality have not greatly changed, owing to the peculiarities of loess. Centuries of overuse have lowered the quality of soils in many parts of India without changing the soil type.

Where Chinese practice has obtained for any period soils usually are fairly productive. The continuous use of human wastes, garbage, and green manures maintains a relatively high ratio of nitrogens, potashes, phosphates, and other needed soluble elements to compare with the best in occidental fertilization practice. The limits in these techniques have been the supplies of available materials. Rather closely related to the human factor is the action of termites in many parts of the tropics. The building of mounds of subsoil above the water table where aeration can oxidize chemical elements and speed up soil formation is significant in a number of countries. Termites appear to operate everywhere from southern Japan and the Yangtze Valley southward in the lowlands. The use of old termite mounds for garden planting is frequent in several parts of the Orient. The long-range effect of termites on soil formation is little understood at the present time.

The conclusion is almost inescapable that in the long run the handling of a tropical soil is more important than its innate physical characteristics, chemical content, and color. In particular, soil color is noticeable to the traveler and helps distinguish one regional landscape from another, but it often seems to mean little as to productivity. Where nature developed and maintained a heavy forest man can do the same or can maintain productive crop plantings. Poor soils can be built up to high productivity in a very few decades by careful handling and feeding. Few tropical soil bodies cannot be quickly impoverished by one-way exploitive use within a short span of years. More detailed soil study is imperative, to learn ways and means of properly handling various soils. And the Orient must avoid numerous pitfalls in its modernization of agriculture, lest it find retrogression the result rather than progress.

DISTRIBUTION OF SOIL GROUPS

The individual oriental farmer judges his own land as better or poorer than that of a neighbor in the next village. From the farmer's point of view almost every region possesses rich and poor soils. The student of regions concludes that every country has a share of naturally richer and poorer soils. In the Orient, at least, the soils of no one country condemn it to poverty or guarantee it most of the wealth. Man's manipulation of soils, by groups, types or individual fields, can and does supplement or nullify this particular natural resource in his landscape, and certainly management of some soil groups is easier and cheaper than that of others. Though no objectively accurate picture is possible, it seems worth trying to summarize the distribution of the major soil groups, as they have been mapped to 1950, in the accepted patterns of describing and mapping soils.

Figure 21 and Fig. 22 and Table 4 present a classification and distribution as far as possible at this time. Seventeen major groups have been chosen to represent the hundreds of individual soil types to be found between Ceylon and Hokkaido. The major groups have been divided into two standard American categories, the pedocals or calcium-bearing soils and the pedalfers or aluminum- and iron-bearing soils, the letters "cal," "al," "fe" standing for the three distinctive elements. In simple terms this division separates the basic soils from the acid soils.

The division into acid and basic soils is sound agriculturally. The degree of soil acidity is subject to marked changes within short distances, for many factors enter into promoting this characteristic, and no simple map of this sort can be completely accurate. Therefore, the accompanying map is a very simple regional generalization. Some crops prefer soils that are definitely basic, among them being wheat, some of the sorghums and millets, most of the oil seeds, cotton, and numerous vegetable crops. Others prefer definitely acid soils, among these being rice, tea, and the oil palm. Maize, some of the millets, tobacco, the coconut palm, coffee, many of the tree fruits, and many vegetables prefer neutral to slightly acid soils. Many domesticated plants have a rather wide range of tolerance and can be grown on many different types of soils without the strong penalty of reduced yields.

In every region with an old and well-established agriculture the farmer long since has worked out the soil preferences and tolerances of the common crops. Many plant varieties have developed to allow the farmer to take advantage of soil and moisture conditions of a particular sort. In this way there have come to be over ten thousand varieties of rice, many of which are grown only on particular soils and in certain water depths. Where new crops have come into a region there often must be an experimental period before the regional and locational preferences and tolerances of a plant can be discovered.

Podzols are held to be primarily soils of midlatitude cooler climates. Slightly to moderately podzolized soils occur mainly in middle lower latitudes, but reach well into the tropics, both on the lowlands and at higher elevations. The midlatitude black earths, chernozems, are

tered. Thus the Philippines and many islands of the Indies show red soils but no laterite. Mature, crusted laterite is found in rather small patches in the south Indian peninsula, in Ceylon, in eastern India, and parts of lower Burma, quite widely in lowland Thailand, in

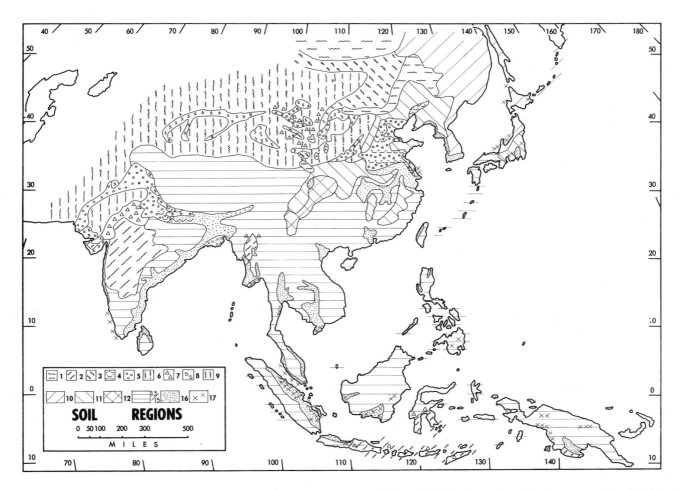

Fig. 21. Soil regions: *Group A, Pedocal Soils:* (1) chernozem group; (2) tropical black earths; (3) chestnut earths; (4) lakeland soils; (5) alluvial soils; (6) loessial soils; (7) non-saline arid-land soils; (8) saline soils; (9) skeletal desert and mountain soils; *Group B, Pedalfer Soils:* (10) podzolic group; (11) Shantung brown soils; (12) purple-red soils; (13) podzolized red earths; (14) podzolized skeletal mountain soils; (15) lateritic red earths; (16) alluvial soils; (17) peat, muck, and marsh soils.

not equivalent to tropical black earths in a number of important attributes. Both crack and shrink when dry, expand and bulge when wet, and are what is known as "self-cultivating." Both are among the most naturally productive and long lived of the world's soils.

Lateritic soils are mainly restricted to the tropics and subtropics. The distribution of laterite and lateritic soils agrees fairly well with zones of tectonic stability. Peninsular India and much of the lowland of Thailand, and Indochina, as well as the lowlands on the older more stable Indies show patches of laterite. Younger and immature red earths are much more widely scat-

Malaya and in some of the more stable Indian islands. In many areas benches and terraces are topped by fossil laterite caps, owing to a local lowering of base level and the water table.

Many long-cultivated surfaces located within what are termed lateritic soil regions have become podzolized. The most interesting and economically significant of these podzolized red earths are the rice-paddy soils. Rice and such subsidiary aquatic crops as taro, nipa palm, the water chestnut, and lotus require soil-handling techniques that are not matched elsewhere in the world. In some areas these rice-paddy soils will not yield well when planted to other crops during winter periods. Many fields under rice in summer therefore lie idle during the winter.

Alluvial soils are subject to sharp local distinctions hard to map but significant to village farmers. In India a distinction is made between the older, somewhat leached, and less productive alluvium known as *bhan-*

3,000 years. Elsewhere the practice of shifting horticulture has been going on since man first domesticated plants. Almost everywhere the lowlands are pockmarked with the destructive effects of burning and girdling the forest to permit cropping for a year or two. This often has resulted in soil depletion, followed by soil erosion and a somewhat erratic replacement of the

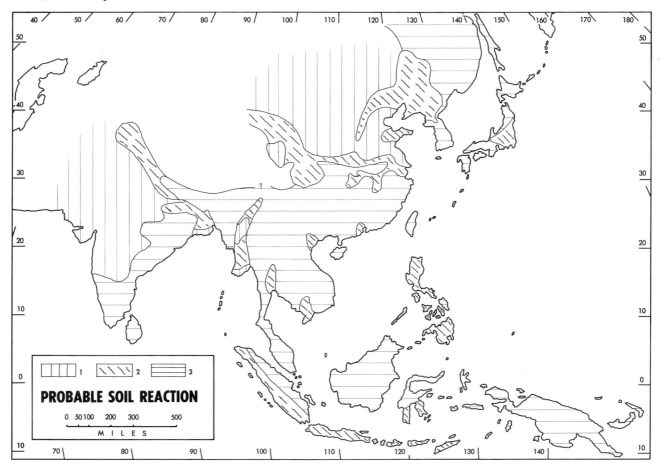

Fig. 22. Regions of probable soil reaction: (1) soils generally having alkaline reaction; (2) soils neutral to slightly acid in reaction; (3) soils generally acid in reaction.

gar, and the lower-lying, younger, floodplain alluvium known as *khadar.* Locally in many delta floodplains distinctions are made between those lands frequently flooded and replenished and lands currently well diked or lying far from flood distributaries. Decreasing land values, lower yields, emigration, and the decay of rural society often go with the latter lands.

NATURAL VEGETATION

In a large share of the Orient today there is no such thing as natural vegetation. In many regions man has been cutting and replanting landscapes for more than

plant cover. Within recent centuries this type of cropping has been carried clear to the tops of mountains, and has reworked the most favored sites repeatedly. The map on page 80 presents a simple conception of very early patterns of plant cover without any attempt to designate regional genera or species dominance.

Nature's replacement of a break in the vegetative formation takes time and some kind of plant succession. In warm, moist regions plants rapidly fill in any "vacuum" created by a clearing. If these first entrants are helpful "nurse-plants," a succession may proceed rapidly, with an early replenishment of soil fertility. If they are monopolistic, they may inhibit a succession

TABLE 4

SOILS GROUPS AND THEIR DISTRIBUTION

A. Pedocals	*Zone of Occurrence*
1. Chernozem group	NW China, Inner Mongolia, Manchuria.
2. Tropical black earths	Central India, Central Burma, lowland patches in middle eastern Indies
3. Chestnut earths	NW China, Inner Mongolia, Manchuria
4. Lakeland soils group	North China Plain, Upper Ganges Valley

5. Alluvial soils group
   a. Younger flood plain soils
   b. Older bench and terrace soils
	Both subgroups scattered in North China, Manchuria, central Asian Outer Zone, N and NW India

6. Loessial soils group	NW China, SW Manchuria, southern Inner Mongolia, NW India

7. Non-saline arid land soils group
   a. Brown soils
   b. Sandy light-colored soils
	NW China and central Asian Outer Zone; NW India; patches in middle eastern Indies; Central Burma

8. Saline soils group *a.* Desert saline soils	NW China and central Asian Outer Zone; NW India and NW Frontier
b. Coastal saline soils	Widely scattered; North China and NW India have significant areas

9. Skeletal desert soils group
   a. Sand-dune types
   b. Piedmont sands and gravels
   c. Upland rocky soils
	NW China and central Asian Outer Zone; NW India and NW Frontier

B. Pedalfers	*Zone of Occurrence*
10. Podzolic soils group	Lowlands of N Japan, Korea, N and E Manchuria
11. Slightly podzolic brown soils group	S Manchuria, N China; hill country of S China; highlands of Indochina; NW India; highland patches of tropics not shown on map
12. Slightly podzolic purple-red soils group	West and SW China

13. Podzolized red earths
   a. Older red earths
   b. Younger yellow earths
	From central China southward on lowlands into India and Indies in particular localities

c. Rice-paddy soils	Found in lowland valleys and terraces where rice has been long cultivated

14. Podzolized skeletal mountain soils group
   a. Northern colder
   b. Tropical version
	Widely scattered from S Japan and central China southward on uplands at increasing elevations into tropics

15. Lateritic red earths *a.* Immature red earths	Widely scattered in southern zone on lowlands; fossil red earths on lower uplands
b. Mature laterite	Scattered areas of peninsular India, Thailand, Indochina, and the Indies

16. Alluvial soils group
   a. Lateritic older bench alluvium
   b. Floodplain soils
   c. Fresh delta soils
	N Japan and Central China southward through southeastern Asia and Indies, and around to India, Deccan and N and NW India being exempted

17. Peat, muck, and marsh group
   a. Midlatitude peat and moor
   b. Tropical marsh swamp
	Scattered patches in Philippines, Indies, Malaya, and Indian peninsular coast

and retard restoration of soils. Retrogressive succession in vegetation and soils often occurs where man destructively uses fire and other forces. It is difficult to know how many species earlier made up the native flora of China or Java, but a well-based estimate suggests reduction by over half. In the Philippines, about 59 per cent of which is forested, casual observation might suggest little serious cultural tampering with plant life or the soil. However, there is little old or mature forest left, and many species of useful plants are almost extinct, though human pressure on the Philippines has been less than in many other parts of the Orient. Where man has used a large part of the landscape only those plants maintain themselves that are tolerant in respect to semicultural treatment, soil fertility, conditions of light, "nurse-plant" assistance, and later surroundings.

In some parts of the Orient cultural influence has increased the coverage of tall grasses, particularly where such influence has been accompanied by fire and shifting horticulture. In other areas bamboo jungle replaces grass on such disturbed surfaces. Eventually succession replaces the grasses and bamboos with other plant associations, provided man does not continue burning. The replacement program is slow, and much land is rendered non-productive in the early stages of the sequence.

Man fosters many trees and shrubs selected out of the early plant formations which ordinarily are not termed domesticated plants. Most of the forests, jungles, parklands, scrublands, and open grasslands of the Orient today are secondary growths. In many areas these plant ranges have been managed well and in others very poorly indeed. About 1520 Krsnadeva Raya, the Emperor of the south Indian state of Vijayanagar and an active political theorist, said in connection with peace preservation: "Increase the forests that are near your frontier fortress and destroy all those that are in the middle of your territory. Then alone will you not have trouble from robbers." *

* T. V. Mahalingam, *Administrative and Social Life under Vijayanagar,* Madras, 1940, pp. 155–56.

Altitude, affecting temperatures, and moisture are the chief environmental factors determining plant life in the tropics and subtropics. The so-called frost line, a function of altitude, is important. It is found at varying elevations in different areas, of course, but above it grow mountain associations, below it those of the lowlands.

DISTRIBUTION OF NATURAL VEGETATION

May we accept the judgment that "native" vegetation is any plant growth not arranged by field patterns and not seasonally cultivated? The map on page 81 pre-

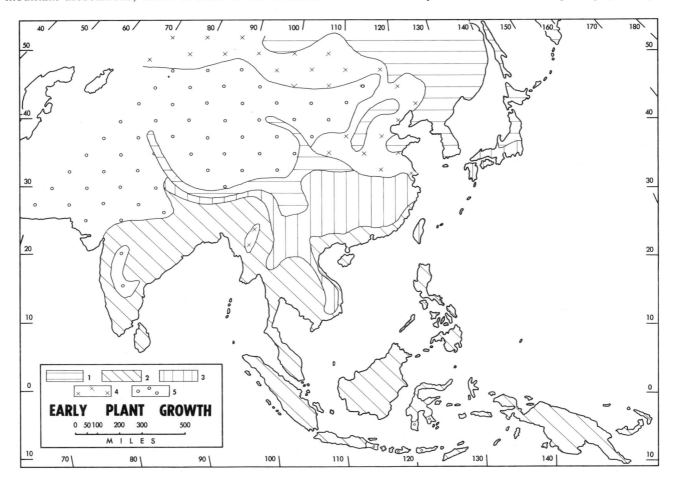

Fig. 23. Probable early natural vegetation: (1) midlatitude slow-growth forests; (2) tropical rapid-growth forests, jungles, and parklands; (3) subtropical rapid-growth forests, jungles, and parklands; (4) open parklands; (5) open scrub-shrub-grasslands.

About 2,500 feet is commonly a significant elevation equatorward of south China and Luzon, with the critical temperature somewhere between 60 and 70° F. Of importance also are exposure, geology, and soils. An annual rainfall, in monsoonal distribution, of about 40 inches ordinarily separates the thorny scrublands of southern Asia from the monsoon forests, and 80 inches ordinarily divides the monsoon forest and the evergreen rainforest, but this is not always true. There are good rainforests supported in favored sites on 60 inches of moisture, poor monsoon forests on poor, rocky soils receiving well over 100 inches, and poor scrub covering very moist but highly laterized soils.

sents regional patterns of plant life on the somewhat arbitrary principle that the landscape of the Orient today is one largely dominated by man. Only the broader patterns can be indicated on a map of this scale, and innumerable patches of fields, forests, or grasslands are omitted. Areas predominantly forested are indicated as such whether natural or cultural. Cultivated landscapes include many much-used, non-cultivated plants. These range from the wild fruits gathered from jungle growth around village clearings and marketed in the cities to the firewood twigs and branches annually stripped from trees growing on ricefield margins, and the tool wood, firewood, and general-use poor lumber cut from the field margin thickets of many areas of dry field crop areas.

Students have worked on different principles and varying scales in every country of the Orient in describing plant associations. This has immensely increased the broad descriptive task and has motivated the present

ited, is to be found almost everywhere, but there is little that can support life for man or the higher animals.

Next it is possible to block out those arid-land margins and high, cold localities that only occasionally permit tree growth. Parts of central Asia, the Mongolias, non-mountainous north China and southern Manchuria

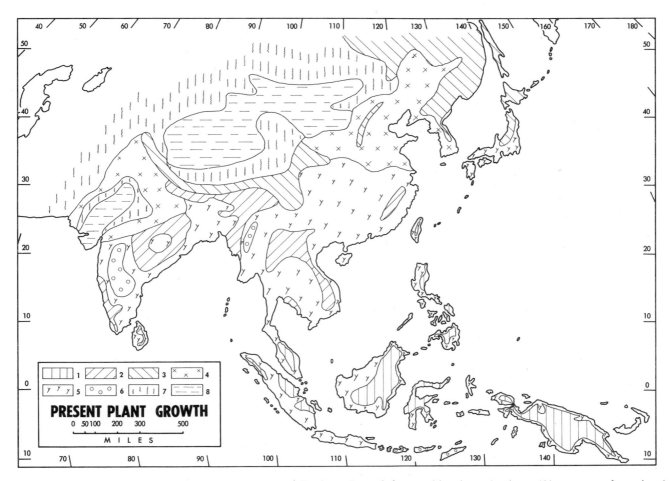

Fig. 24.   Present varieties of plant growth: *A, Forested Regions:* (1) rainforest with minor clearings; (2) monsoon forest-jungle with numerous clearings; (3) midlatitude forest with numerous clearings; *B, Cultivated Landscapes:* (4) parklands with planted and tolerated trees of slow growth and sparse volume; (5) restrained jungle-forest, frequently reasserting itself, with rapid growth and abundant volume; (6) restrained scrub parklands, tree growth cultural, rapid growth but scant volume; *C, Scrub and Grassland Ranges:* (7) mountain and riverbank forests but with tree growth elsewhere only in oases; *D, Natural Barrens:* (8) dry, cold, rocky, sandy ranges having sparse wild growth of shrubs and grasses, tree growth only in oases or at higher elevations.

simplified approach.   Easiest to block out are the naturally barren areas.   Lowland sectors of central Asia and the Mongolias, including some parts of northwest China, much of the Tibetan highland, and some of lowland northwest India fall in this category.   Causal factors are extreme drought, strong denudation leaving but bare-rock expanses, sand-dune accumulation, and sheer alpine cold.   Locally unusual water supply, protected situations, and other favorable agencies promote vigorous plant oases.   Some form of plant life, however limited

the lower fringes of the Tibetan highland, some surfaces of the Yunnan Plateau in southwest China, limited parts of northwest India, and a few localities of the central Indies belong in this group.   In this zone gallery forests naturally occur along streams and in deep clefts in the highlands.   Favored situations promote scrub and thorn forest.   The normal open-country plant cover is grasses and a variety of shrubs.   In the arid lands where man has used his ability to lend protection and provide extra water, trees, shrubs, and flowering plants create cultural oases. These are subject to historic shifts of location and to periodic growth and abandonment with the fortunes of sedentary settlement in a landscape that normally requires mobility on the part of man. Plant species are limited, and seldom does the added planting amount to more than rows, clumps, or clusters around settlements. However, where large-scale irrigation projects are developed, as in the Indian Punjab, the added vegetation often is sufficient to alter the appearance of the arid landscape.

In well-populated areas seldom is wild plant growth allowed to interfere with economic and cultural activities of farming, grazing, cutting cheap timber, or exploiting particular plants. These predominantly cultural landscapes range from the dry margins to the wettest of the tropical rainforests. They naturally exhibit a wide range of trees, shrubs, grasses, flowering plants, epiphytes, and parasites. What the farmer calls weeds are today a constant problem. In some areas the plant cover reclaims its own if man's diligence and group ability declines, as indicated in the forest cover of Cambodia, when, in 1859, the French first stumbled upon the ruins of the twelfth-century Khmer capitol of Angkor. There are many possibilities of subdividing such regions, but for simplicity's sake the accompanying map has but three such subunits. This culturally dominant zone varies in relative size in each country. In India it is today a large share, in the Indies outside of Java a small one. In some countries it is sandwiched in between hill and dale, mountain and swamp, with the result that wild growth may appear dominant. In others, with great expanses of flat and open country, wild growth is scant and restricted to odd corners or to such chosen spots as temple gardens.

Scanning what remains, the country dominantly forested, one finds it in bits and pieces that do not fit easily into any simple causal pattern. There are sound historical reasons for many forested spots, good climatic reasons, reasons of physiography, and reasons of physical isolation to account for the remaining forests of the Orient. In some regions that remainder is fast disappearing, and in others the area under managed permanent forest is increasing in total, though with changes taking place in location. The Indian plan to return some 50,000,000 acres of culturally bruised land to permanent wild growth will change the landscape of parts of India. In the forested zone, too, the variety of species is great in the sweep from the arid margins to the tropical rainforest.

Economically valuable timber trees, wild fruits, and oil- and gum-producing plants vary from region to region. With a number of unknowns and inequalities in the mapping of forest distributions, the accompanying map does not attempt detailed representation of forest regions.

FLORAS AND PLANT DOMESTICATIONS

Plant explorers and botanists have long prowled through parts of the Orient, hunting for useful crop and decorative plants and filling out the taxonomic record, though this is far from complete on both counts. Far too little attention has been given to the economic plants in the systematic study of floras, and we know comparatively little about the whole range of economic plants. Many of them are extremely old in use, there have been many transfers from one region to another, and there are hundreds of varieties of many of them, some quite localized and others very widely distributed.

Though too little is known of precise regional patterns of the several floras of the Orient, it is possible to make some useful crude generalizations. In the northeastern part of the Orient there is a northern coniferous-broadleaf forest flora that resembles that of eastern Anglo-America in species, autumn coloration, and distribution. This covers Manchuria, northern Japan, Korea, and the upland parts of northern China. It has a high economic utility to modern man, but it provided not many sources of plant foods to early man. In northwest China and Mongolia is a grassland-shrub flora of relatively few species. Much of North China, the region of loess deposition, may never have been heavily covered with plant growth, the lowlands sharing the floral characteristics of inner Asia, and the uplands sharing the northern forest flora. Central China possesses a numerous flora of wide variety and species. The Tibetan high country possesses a distinctive flora of its own, sparse in species, in variety, and in utility. The mountain and valley country of southwestern China, the Tibetan border, northern Burma, Thailand, and Indochina is one of the most varied of all, and one of the richest, for it combines elements of other regional floras with a large number of endemic species. An India-Burma flora belonging to the moist lowlands is a significant member of the floral picture, one with a wide range of species and a high degree of value both in early times and to modern man. A Malaysian flora related to the old Sundaland shelf zone, existent prior to the last major shift of sea levels, has contributed many thousands of species, probably more than any other zone. A Papualand flora, corresponding to the Sundaland flora, evolved with a center on New Guinea, and spread predominantly southeastward.

Although there have been no sharp boundaries successfully drawn around each of the suggested floral centers, owing to their large amount of intergrading, earlier practice, using Wallace's Line, sharply divided the Asiatic floras from those of Australasia. This now proves to be an inadequate boundary in respect to plants, though it is useful in relation to animals and will be discussed in the next chapter. Rather than to draw sharp zones of demarcation between source regions, it is better to recognize that there are horizontal and altitudinal climatic zones throughout the Orient and that floras of different derivation and climatic preference overlap each other at different elevations or occur in disjunct distributions in satisfactory climatic regions, provided there has existed an avenue of plant migration. Thus, southern bamboos and flowering subtropicals live in lowland, southern Japan, and a northern coniferous-broadleaf association occupies upland and northern Japan. Himalayan temperate mountain and alpine plants are at home in upland Sumatra, and Central Asian species are at home in northwestern India and northwestern China. The wealth of plant species found in the region from central China south and west to the middle Himalayas is a result of the mixing together of several regional floras, combining both endemic and immigrant species from many different sources.

Multiplicity of species alone does not signify a flora highly useful to man in the most general sense, in view of all the levels of human culture. The 5,000 species of orchids at home in the Indies, or the 3,000 species of timber trees of the Philippines were far less important to early man than smaller numbers of plants that provided varieties of products that he could use. There obviously were regional differences in the usability of plants in the whole of the Old World in the past, and man slowly came to recognize these differences. Certain regions can be picked out as centers of economically useful plants, and it is around these that the history of domestication of crop plants in this part of the world hinges.

It is a curious thing that, with so much movement within the Orient, so many items should have remained restricted to certain regions. Examination suggests that the natural distribution of wild plants sometimes did include distant areas, but unrelated human cultures did not make the same choices. Perhaps the outstanding example of this is tea, the wild shrub scattered from north India into central China. People in south China did, and the Indians did not, domesticate the plant and learn to drink tea, a trait all Chinese eventually acquired. In breaking the Chinese monopoly on tea in the midnineteenth century the British brought Chinese tea plants to India, later to find the wild relatives growing in the very area to which they took the importations.

Within the Orient there perhaps are four centers of significance in the domestication of plants. These are north central China, south China-Tonking, the moist lowlands of southeastern Asia (one kind of region but in several pieces today), and eastern India-Burma. Related plant centers are southwestern Asia and Abyssinia, lying just outside the Orient but in close contact with it.

From these several centers both India and China eventually drew almost all the commonly used Old World plants. Some transfers took place so early that the plants appear native to far areas. Rarely has a century gone by, since the historic era began, without the coming of some new plant to China. Almost all the economically significant crop plants of the Philippines are cultural importations during the long period of human occupation. Localities such as southern Thailand, which lies far from the plant centers outside the Orient and which possesses a limited range of climate and soils, never accumulated the great wealth of domesticated plant life that is possessed by China or India. Thai agriculture remains that basically developed with the plants from the southern oriental domestication centers. In those countries with a wide range of climate, soils, and opportunity, agriculture has become a very complex matter, shifting somewhat over the centuries as new plants come to compete with the older ones. Modern plant breeders and agricultural missionaries have done much to broaden the economic botany of most regions in a short period.

To mention the basic items briefly, wheat, some of the pulses, a range of vegetables, grapes, melons, some of the stone fruits, and a variety of other fruits and nuts, all came from southwestern Asia into India and China. Except for some of the vegetables none of these products has successfully been utilized throughout the whole of the Orient. The accompanying map suggests the limits of cultivation for selected exemplary items. On the other side, the coconut and a number of other palms, the yams, the taros, and a host of tropical fruits such as the jackfruit, breadfruit, mangosteen, and durian were domesticated somewhere in the mainland-island fringe of southeastern Asia. Many of the tropical fruits still grow wild also. From the original centers many of these plants spread outward in all directions, some going far outside the Orient even in the pre-Columbian period. Within the Orient various of them spread to the approximate climatic margins of growth, or to the cultural limits of acceptance, in India, China, or Japan. South China-Tonking contributed most of the citrus fruits, most of the bananas, tea, such fruits as the lichee and longan, many of the Chinese cabbages, perhaps some of the soybeans, and the mulberries. The northcentral China center contributed the persimmon, some of the pears, the apricot, some of the peaches, some of the millets, soybeans, and a variety of vegetables and lesser fruits. The eastern Indian areas provided rice, sugar cane, some sorghums, some of the millets, and some of the subtropical fruits such as the mango and some bananas.

seventeenth centuries. To almost every country of the Orient, except Korea and Japan, the sixteenth and seventeenth centuries were important in this respect. Not mentioned above is the nineteenth century during which scientific plant introduction and plant breeding has been a lesser or major part of the economy of every country in the world. Many new strains of older

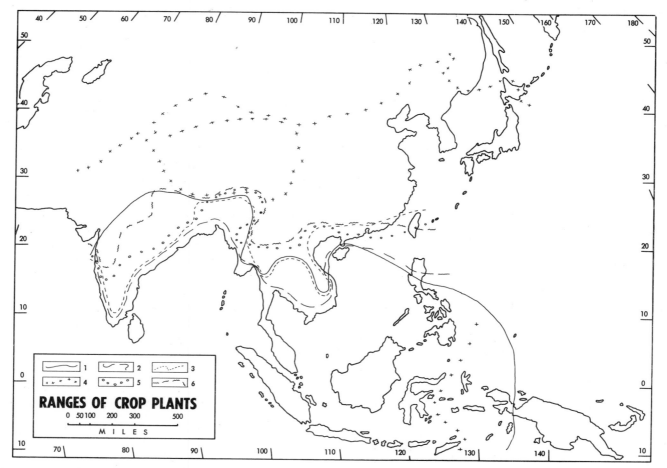

Fig. 25. Ranges of oriental crop plants: (1) northern-eastern limit of the mango; (2) northern limit of the coconut; (3) northern limit of the fruiting banana; (4) northern-eastern limit of rice; (5) southern limit of wheat; (6) southern limit of the peach.

Cotton came to India from northeast Africa so early as to seem at home there. *Acacia arabica* also seems a very early introduction into northwest India as a wood-supplying tree. Coffee, on the other hand, came surprisingly late.

Plant transfers took place steadily, though there were peak and slack periods in the exchange. Periods of importance in Indian agriculture were the second millennium B.C., the several centuries preceding the onset of the Christian era, and the sixteenth and seventeenth centuries. In China very significant periods were the four centuries from 200 B.C. to A.D. 200, the eighth and ninth, the thirteenth, and the sixteenth and

plants have been moved about, overlooked items have been developed, old breeds improved. The whole of the Orient has been combed by the plant explorers, searching for useful and decorative plants. In this process many economic plants of value to the Orient and Occident alike have been turned up. The task is far from complete, and the effects will continue to be felt for a considerable period.

THE PRACTICE OF AGRICULTURE

One thesis holds that plant domestication and crop growing began in the moist tropical lands which abound in species of plants directly of use to early man. This thesis suggests that fishing peoples, perhaps well provided with a food supply, began the first specific working with plants and plant products in net and trap making, and that they discovered the many gums, poisons and spices that are so frequent in the tropics. Tubers, roots, and rhizomes, gathered both for food and for body paints and other dyes, came within their working patterns and gradually came to be the first specific crop items in a simple agriculture that depended upon vegetative reproduction of live plant material. Seed agriculture and other cropping practices, in this thesis, are held to be later developments. It follows that digging-stick subsistence crop growing would constitute possibly the oldest agricultural system, that more complex systems of subsistence agriculture would be later in evolution, and that systems of agriculture concerned with surpluses, trade, and commercial practices would evolve last of all.

Much uncertainty concerning the whole complicated matter of plant domestication, centers of domestication, Old World-New World transfers, and the evolution of agricutural systems still exists. But it is clear that a digging-stick agriculture originally concerned primarily with roots, tubers, and rhizomes lies at the bottom of agriculture in the Orient. This still shows up among the simpler cultures in many parts of the moist tropical regions, but it is today at its peak in the eastern Indies where the taros, yams, and other root and tuber crops have provided the staple bases of food economy. This early primitive digging-stick culture gradually increased in crop variety and practice, evolving into tropical shifting agriculture.

Tropical shifting agriculture now has a number of regional names, *caingin* in the Philippines, *ladang* in the Indies, *tam rai* in Thailand, *taung ya* in Burma, *jhum* in northeastern India, *chena* in Ceylon, and *milpa* in the American tropics. Also, in English there are many near synonyms. The commonest of these are: migratory agriculture, digging-stick agriculture, transient agriculture, shifting cultivation, slash-and-burn cultivation, and fire-field agriculture. Jungle gardening and simple hoe culture are other common terms that sometimes are applied, but these two patterns may also be followed by sedentary peoples. Essentially it involves making a clearing by girdling, felling, or topping the tall forest canopy, slashing the lower layers and burning as much as possible to let light down to the ground, give free space, and fertilize the soil. With no cultivation seeds, roots, and tubers are placed in holes made by simple digging sticks or hoes. The rankest weeds are kept out and the fields watched against theft and damage until the harvest can be skimmed. Seldom is a given plot cropped more than three times, when the process is repeated on a new site located near by or at some distance, for the weeds become too rank, soil quality decreases, and yields decrease. Upland rice today is the crop most frequently grown on such fields west of Celebes and south of China, though yams, taro, bananas, and various vegetables are also important. Outside the tropics a related shifting agriculture is often used in China, Manchuria, and Korea on steep mountain slopes, where a variety of crops adapted to upland culture is planted.

It is wrong to consider either version of this kind of farming only as an elementary one thought up by primitive people but always abandoned by a society that has become advanced, stabilized, and sedentary. Such agriculture, when not under pressure, is really a long-range soil and crop rotation system, the wild plant growth of jungle and forest alternating with planted crops. When not under pressure such cultivation seldom totally ruins soils or permanently destroys the plant association. For a light population able to shift widely over jungle and forest ranges such a system could be permanently productive even though settlements were permanent. As such it was practiced over a large share of the Orient for many centuries. However, where a large population built up, the frequency of "rotation" increased, and the extractive drain upon the reproducing jungle or forest became great; a landscape could not bear up permanently. Suggestions have been made that the Khmers of Cambodia and some early south Indian and Ceylon peoples used shifting culture until they so overworked the available landscapes as to induce soil exhaustion and diminishing agricultural returns, producing decaying societies ripe for the militant raids of expanding neighbors.

The facts are that under pressure of sheer need for land in many parts of the Orient contemporary farmers have pushed shifting agriculture, both in and outside the tropics, clear to the tops of mountain ranges in a desperate effort to maintain an existence. Modern governments discourage such agriculture because it makes census and taxation difficult, destroys timber, interferes with lowland water supplies, and induces violent soil erosion when carried out on too steep slopes or slopes that are cleared too thoroughly and too frequently. Under population increases and the growth of foreign trade economy pressures and stresses are accumulating all over the Orient today. Despite government discouragement shifting agriculture will continue to persist in many parts of the Orient among varied elements in the whole population.

The agricultural landscapes of the Orient are chiefly man-made landscapes, many topographic features being rearranged to
of time.   These four views show the considerable variety in detail that results around the common element, the wet-ricefield
two *lower* photographs are lowland landscapes of central Luzon, Philippines, and they illustrate the simple tools and group
tion Bureau.   Other photos are

fit patterns of occupance. They involve concerted human labor in large amounts, working with simple tools over long periods
landscape. *Upper left* is a lowland landscape from Java, and *upper right* is a lowland landscape from western China. The
labor systems that are characteristic of so much of the Orient. (Javanese photo, courtesy of Republic of Indonesia Informa-
from the author's collection.)

Outside the moist tropical regions shifting cultivation and digging-stick culture in early times would support but few people, particularly in regions of unpredictable rainfall. Here also the plants susceptible to vegetative reproduction are few, and seed agriculture becomes dominant. In central and northwest India, and in north and northwest China, another system of agriculture gradually matured. This gradually became a hoe culture working on permanent fields to till the soil periodically to permit the planting of seed crops. Both in India and China the chief elements of this hoe culture began with small village societies, closely knit and productive of cooperative labor. The earliest seed crops are not certainly known but the millets, sorghums, legumes, oil seeds which could also be grown as green vegetables, and some minor crops were important. Eventually wheat and rice entered this pattern, and so did a number of the shrubs and trees producing fruits and nuts. Many of these crop plants originated outside the Orient but they became adapted to the cooler and drier margins long before the historic period began.

The origin of wet-field rice culture, today the mainstay of much of the Orient, is somewhat puzzling. It may have begun as a dry-field crop, or it may have commenced as a simple swamp and marsh culture. Wild rices are widely scattered in the Orient, though their taxonomy and use history are poorly known. But eventually rice did enter into the patterns of shifting cultivation on the one hand, and became the central crop of an intensive wet-field culture on the other. Whatever the origin, wet-rice agriculture evolved into a specific system through the development of terrace building, field leveling, plant selection, water control, seed bed and transplanting, puddling of soils by wading men and animals, and plowing, harrowing, and other techniques of soil preparation. Such items as the plow seem to have come into the Orient from the area of western Asia, but the water buffalo obviously is a product of southeastern Asia.

Though the origins of the separate items of the complex of wet-field rice culture cannot be pinned down, the complex is a product of moist southeastern Asia. But within the Orient it is obvious that rice culture, and the auxiliary crops that go with it, has been a spreading and expanding pattern of agriculture throughout much of historic time. Even as late as the arrival of the European, rice was not the dominant food crop on Java, and rice has not spread throughout the Indies even today. Many mainland culture groups do not yet grow rice, though their environment would permit it. Modern statistics suggest that rice culture has spread very greatly in the last century, so that one can even describe the agriculture of Thailand today as dominated by rice. The expansion of rice growing has faced not only cultural inertia among many peoples but also climatic limits. North China never can make of rice its chief crop, since the supply of water is limited and upland rice does less well than several other crops available to the Chinese.

Though wet-field rice culture differs in some respects from the dry-field agriculture of the drier margins of the Orient, they are both part of the intensive agriculture of the Orient that is almost a garden hoe culture. Small fields, a large volume of hand labor, simple tools, and the minimum use of draft animals and animal-powered tools go with it. High production per acre is found in many areas where farmers have been efficient, but the productivity of much oriental agriculture is lower than is often assumed. And its man-hour total of labor per acre is extremely high for many crops and in many regions. The sheer pressure of men upon the land in regions where 3,000 people are supported per square mile of cultivated land has forced an intensification uncommon in other parts of the earth.

Dooryard plantings of fruit trees of many kinds are common throughout the Orient, particularly in southeastern Asia. There commonly is little order to these plantings, from the European viewpoint, but in fact there often is an excellent ecologic balance among the plantings, which require little steady maintenance effort. Many such plantings are almost wild plantings today, but they constitute a significant share of native agricultural production. Only in a few parts of the Orient are the fruits grown in regular single-crop orchards, and most of these are relatively recent in origin.

In many parts of the Orient today simple digging-stick root culture, a more varied shifting cultivation, intensive wet-field rice culture, vegetable and fruit culture are carried on side by side, sometimes even by subunits of the same culture group. But there are few large regions in which agriculture is as productive as it needs to be to support the resident populations. Many areas no longer provide their own food supplies, and, expressed in political units, only Burma, Thailand, and Indochina produce surpluses of food supplies that have been the main object of oriental agriculture in the past. A peaceful Korea, not disturbed by war, could be added to this list.

Though commercial production of selected agricultural commodities is very old in the different parts of the Orient, such commercial production in the past always was a minor factor in regional agriculture.

The modern period has brought change to agriculture in most parts of the Orient, owing to the influence of the occidental and his interest in cheap crop commodities for sale in markets outside the Orient. This commercialization has introduced a new element into traditional small-farmer agriculture, and also has introduced a new system of agriculture, the plantation. The new element has been the cash crop production of a wide range of commodities in volumes far beyond the needs of the producing region. First were the spices of the Indies, followed by silk and tea in China. Gradually a number of crops have been added to the list, some traditional in the Orient, such as sugar, soybeans, jute, abaca, and coconut, and some are new crops introduced from abroad or moved to new regions, such as rubber, tea in India and Ceylon, maize, coffee, and palm oil. The introduction of the plantation system into southeastern Asia was a profitable thing for the occidental, for it utilized abundant cheap labor producing its own food supply. But this grafting of commercial export agriculture onto traditional agriculture has helped to upset the economy of almost every region and every country in the Orient. It has resulted in the Orient's becoming a source of cheap commodities competing for world markets and taking space from subsistence production to the extent that few regions now feed themselves. It is no wonder that throughout the Orient today there is a strong urge toward industrialization.

Forest cropping, through reforestation programs, has not yet developed into a specific form of agricultural practice in the Orient. Forest management, of a sort, is very old in several countries but, on a modern commercial basis, is just beginning to develop. The area and opportunity for profitable forest economy are ample, and indications are that it is on the way. In some areas this can be through private initiative; in others it will involve long-range government programs, with conservation of soil, water, and land as primary objects and forest products secondary.

In any one country the land utilization pattern today is a complex of most of the above. Upon many areas the pressure of man, foreign trade, and dollar profits rests but lightly. In some areas it is easy to provide the things that local society demands of every person, and the landscape reflects this lightness of pressure. New Guinea is such a region for, in eastern New Guinea, the Iron Age only now is replacing the Stone Age. But in North China or the Punjab of India the pressures have been heavy and the landscape shows them clearly. Unequal landscapes, however, do not react in the same way to human pressures. The fresh and fertile island of Java, about 49,000 square miles in area, bears the impact of over 50,000,000 Javanese more easily than does the hard rock "island" of upland Shantung, about 28,000 square miles in area, bear the pressures of perhaps 15,000,000 Chinese.

Marine Life and Animals in Oriental Economy

The oriental world is often described as a realm having a vegetable economy, whereas both marine and animal life have significantly entered into the total economy and culture. Marine life is here meant to include both fresh- and salt-water fish, mollusks, crustaceans, corals, and other aquatic life forms. Animal life includes both the higher animals, the rodents, the fowls, and the reptiles, domesticated and wild, large and small. In many areas fish forms the second most important source of food, and at least one of the animals is a significant food source in every part of the Orient. None of these forms of life has been adequately studied throughout the Orient in terms of its economic significance, and at this stage of our knowledge a completely effective presentation cannot be made. This chapter can serve only as a preliminary statement of the subject.

ANIMAL GEOGRAPHY

The area discussed in this volume falls into three of the five major faunal zones of the earth, the Holarctic, the Oriental, and the Australian. The eastern Asian portion of the Holarctic zone usually is termed the Palearctic. Between the Oriental and the Palearctic zones no definitive boundary can be drawn, owing to the long-continued land continuity along the eastern fringe of Asia. This continuity, coupled with major Pleistocene shifts in environmental conditions, has led to a great amount of intermixing of animal forms between the north and south of Asia. The most appropriate line of division separates Japan and the Ryukyu Islands, crossing inland and along the Tsinling Mountains to the higher Tibetan foothill country. It then sweeps southward, zigzagging into the deep valleys and outward around the higher ranges until it turns westward along the Himalayan front. The lesser Himalayan front range forms the boundary clear across into Kashmir.

On the west the Oriental zone intergrades into the Ethiopian life zone of Africa, for a number of African fauna have penetrated northwestern India. On the other corner rather clear boundaries between life zones exist in the Indies, separating the Oriental from the Australian zone. This often is known as Wallace's Line, after the great nineteenth-century naturalist Alfred Wallace. This line first was drawn north-south across the Indies between Bali and Lombok, Borneo and Celebes, Mindanao and Celebes. Various modifications have been suggested, such as shifting its northern end westward to run between Palawan and Mindoro and between Formosa and the Batanes Islands. Another line has been drawn between Australia and Timor, between Tenimber and Aroe, between New Guinea and Ceram, between New Guinea and Halmahera. This is known as Weber's Line, after Max Weber, another great naturalist.

Wallace's Line is usually taken as limiting primary eastward penetration of the large complex of Oriental life forms, and Weber's Line as the limit of primary westward penetration of the Australian life complex. The several groups of islands lying between Wallace's Line and Weber's Line now are often termed Wallacea, for they form a transition zone in which some of the Oriental and Australian life forms intergrade. Even so, the division between zones is far more discernible than that between the Oriental and the Palearctic zones. The accompanying map of the distributional ranges of oriental animals shows both Wallace's Line and Weber's Line.

A few Palearctic forms have not naturally occupied the Oriental region within Recent time, such as the horse, the moose, or the yak. Conversely, some Oriental forms have not occupied any portion of the Palearctic within Recent time, such as the rhinoceros, the tapir, the apes, and the slow lorises. In contrast, the great majority of animal forms are widely distributed throughout both zones, though this is not commonly recognized. The cats, tigers, lynxes, wolves, foxes, bears, dogs, weasels, otters, martens, badgers, pigs, shrews, rats, mice, hares, rabbits, squirrels, antelopes, deer, goats, sheep, and cattle, all are to be found in both zones. Species differentiation has occurred, cer-

In earlier times, late Pleistocene and early Recent, through the land continuity of eastern Asia and the variation in climatic-floristic environments, the intergrading of fauna was of even greater degree than at present. Over sixty animal groups transgress the limits of Palearctic and Oriental life zones as these are

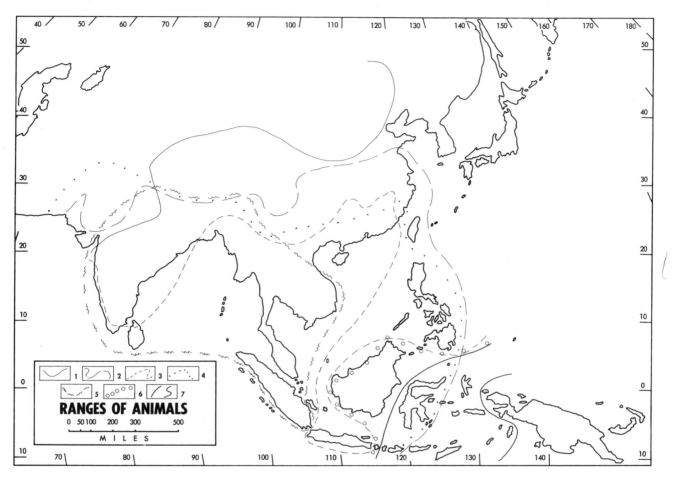

Fig. 26. Ranges of oriental animals: (1) inward limit of camel in the Orient; (2) outward limit of water buffalo in the Orient; (3) inward limit of sheep in the Orient; (4) outward limit of zebu cattle in the Orient; (5) limit of the Indian elephant; (6) eastern limit of the horse; (7) encloses Wallacea. The original Wallace's Line is on the west, with the modified Weber's Line on the east.

tainly, and today it is true that there are northern and southern species of each of the above animals, which now are acclimated to particular local environments. For example, the polar bear *Thalassarctos maritimus* never ranges south of the Amur River, and the Malayan bear *Helarctos malayanos* never ranges far north of upper Burma; the Siberian roe deer *Capreolus capreolus pygargus* never runs south of the Tsinling Mountains, and the Indian muntjak *Muntiacus muntjak vaginalis* never runs north of central Yunnan; our common cattle *Bos taurus* of their own accord remain in the north and the zebu *Bos indicus* keep to the south.

presently delimited, representing remnants of earlier patterns of zoning. A large number of animals ranged from Burma and South China into southern Siberia along the mainland, and others may have spread along the Island Arcs nearest the mainland, from Malaysia to Japan. Thus the tiger *Panthera tigris* is considered a northern form which earlier was at home in southern Siberia and North China. Slowly the tiger migrated southward through China, into Burmo-Malaya, and finally into India. Its present range is from Manchuria to southern India to Java in a series of discontinuous local environments. In Manchuria the tiger still depends upon wild pigs for food to a considerable extent, and shows a distribution similar to that of the Holarctic pig *Sus scrofa*. Elsewhere, its own subsistence patterns have varied somewhat and, as more forest and jungle have been turned into settled farmland, the tiger often has had to raid man's domestic animals or to prey upon man himself, thus becoming a dangerous pest. Also the civets are a northern group now widely spread throughout the Holarctic and Oriental zones.

On the west a number of Ethiopian life forms have relatively recently invaded India. The lion *Panthera leo* is a late arrival from Africa who never penetrates beyond the Narbada River, and some of the antelopes of African origin are restricted to northwest India.

Within the Oriental zone certain animal groups seem to have become regionally acclimated at an early date in India and the mainland portion of southeastern Asia and were early migrants into what today forms the western portion of the Indies. Thus the macaque monkeys, squirrels, palm civets, deer, buffaloes, pigs, and others, as early migrants, are more widely spread in the islands of the western Indies than are some of the later animal groups of the Oriental region. Some of the early migrants even crossed Wallace's Line and perhaps acted to prevent the northward and westward migration of the Australian animals. Thus Weber's Line is a better single line demarcation than is Wallace's Line. Other major groups, such as the apes, leaf monkeys, cats, weasels, bears, zebu cattle, rhinoceroses, and elephants were later migrants toward the southeast and did not become established in the far corners of the old mainland before the last major changes in sea level. These later migrants are not therefore well represented in the island fringe of the western Indies, none of them of their own accord crossed Wallace's Line, and many did not even reach Java and Borneo. Among the reptiles the Asiatic poisonous snakes all stop short of New Guinea, and the New Guinea group do not occur west of Weber's Line. New Guinea has many lizards, large and small, not found to the west. The marine turtles are at home in the western Indies and along coastal edges of the mainland of southeastern Asia, as far north as Hongkong but were not limited by the patterns of land and sea.

Within the Oriental region itself, therefore, there exist a number of regional concentrations of animal groups which serve to allow delineation of several subdivisions of the Oriental zone. Between the drier and more moist parts of India, between the Himalayan mountain country and the lowland, between Burma and India, between Burmo-Malaya and the western Indies, between Burmo-Malaya and southern China it would be possible to draw regional boundaries significant in animal distributions. Similar subdivisions could be delineated within the Palearctic zone, separating Tibet, the dry interior of Asia, North China and Manchuria, southern Siberia, and the northern ends of the Island Arcs. A factor in regional distribution lies in the fact that the heavier, canopied forests carry smaller animal populations than jungles, secondary forests, and grassland margins.

Within the Australian life zone there live seven groups and roughly four hundred species of mammals. Some, such as the bats, seals, and sea cows, are not unique to Australia or the eastern Indies, since their powers of mobility made it possible for them to cross barriers insurmountable to other forms. The dogs were introduced by man. Two special Australian forms are the marsupials and monotremes, ancient animals not now found elsewhere in the world. The Australian rodents are all members of the Muridae or rat family, and not all of them are truly unique to Australia. Many of these animal groups are found only in parts of the life zone; others are scattered throughout, clear up to Weber's Line. Of the marsupials, some of the smaller species of wallaby are found throughout New Guinea and related islands, as well as in Australia itself. The rat bandicoots, living on insects, worms, and beetles, are widely spread from New Guinea south and east. The koala is restricted to ranges supplying eucalyptus plant foods and, therefore, is seldom found in New Guinea. Of the monotremes, the platypus does not occur in New Guinea, but the echidna, or spiny anteater, is widely spread over the island. It is obvious, therefore, that here, too, one can draw regional subdivisions of significance. New Guinea and its related islands form a subregion of importance to this study.

In very real degree there is also a regional concentration of bird life in various parts of Asia. Many species are distributed on the broad zonal outlines suggested above, though others are not limited by such regional bounds and are found in many other parts of the world in identical or related species. Some birds are but seasonal in any one country, like many of the ducks which winter in India or Indochina and summer in Soviet Siberia. Along the Island Arcs some seasonal bird occupations also occur with summer ranges both northward to Hokkaido and southward to New Zealand, winter ranges lying in the Indies and the Philippines. On the other hand, many species present in lowland India, Burma, or Thailand during the winter merely shift northward and upward into the near-by mountain country for the summers. A few species, like some of the pheasants and jungle fowls, are permanent residents of restricted jungle and forest environments of southeastern Asia. Others prefer rocky coastal sites from western peninsular India to Celebes, like those chosen by the sea-swiftlet, *Collocalia fuciphaga,* and related species, which produce the edible bird's nests so prized by the Chinese. Several of the multicolored birds of New Guinea have been economically significant for their feathers, and the cassowary bird has been important as a source of food, sinew, bone, and feathers. All the New Guinea birds have restricted territorial ranges.

ANIMAL DOMESTICATION

Our concepts concerning wild animals useful or dangerous to man, and the relations between them and man that led to domestication need much more examination before we can account for the phenomena of domestication and properly orient its regional development. It has been a commonplace to think of the dog as the first domesticated animal, but the reasoning accounting for the achievement, its motivations, its regional relationships, and its significance has not been well marshaled. Next in line has been the commonplace of the domestication of the Holarctic cattle *Bos taurus* as the first economically useful animal. The evidence for this as the first of our useful animals, similarly, has not been well pieced together. I cannot pretend, therefore, to present a completely articulated story of animal domestication, but it seems very doubtful if *Bos taurus* was the first useful animal on the list. We need to know much more of the problems of taming animals, of the significance of pets in early cultures, of the habits of many wild animals such as the scavengers, herbivores, and the cats, and of the development of religious sacredness attaching to various animals before we can explain the whole phenomenon of domestication.

Many peoples have long tamed various of the deer, and yet the reindeer seems to be the only deer domesticated, a late accomplishment. Simple taming does not seem the chief tool in domestication. Among many primitive cultures it is not uncommon for women able to nurse their own offspring to suckle the young of small animals such as the dogs, pigs, goats, and sheep. Was this an important element in taming and domestication? I cannot conceive of this practice with such large animals as cattle, buffalo, the donkey, or the elephant. An ancient sacredness of the pig has been all but obliterated under the late spread of the tabu upon the pig as an unclean animal. Our modern love for the dog as a pet has colored our thinking about his usefulness as a source of food to early man, and our

reaction to that use among some of the less complex human groups today is one of abhorrence. Americans now suffer under the partial tabu upon horsemeat. Could pets be eaten if they first were made sacred and used as items of sacrifice?

There is evidence that both the dog and the pig, as small jungle scavengers around campsites, were tamed and domesticated very early in southeastern Asia, but the technique of domestication is not at all clear. There is some evidence that these two animals, as pets, useful, or sacred animals, spread out of southeastern Asia in all directions both with early movements of man, and as animals were passed from group to group. The tabus upon the eating of both do not generally relate to early times in southeastern Asia, but were later developed elsewhere by peoples of different cultures. It seems possible that southeastern Asian techniques in taming and domestication of both of these animals started the process, and that techniques perhaps elsewhere already partly applied to local animals finally succeeded in domesticating other animals as the techniques matured.

Within the oriental life zone domestication seems to have succeeded with a significant number of life forms. In addition to the dog and pig, cattle of the zebu strain, *Bos indicus,* the water buffalo, *Bos bubalus,* and the elephant were domesticated. These latter events I would assign to a slightly later time in India-Burma. The domestication of the water buffalo is complicated by variant forms, such as *Bos sundaicus* of the Indies and *Bos frontalis* of Indochina, which may have been later domestications of related forms of the buffalo. The zebu seems related to the open and drier plant ranges of central to northwest India, the water buffalo to the wet lowland littoral, and the elephant to the grass-jungle-forest ranges of the moist lowlands. As yet we know little of how the fowls were brought into the picture, but there were a number of them disciplined to handling by man in the oriental zone. The duck, the goose, the peacock, the pheasant, and the chicken, all were domesticated in this large region. Taming of certain other animals, perhaps constituting a first step in domestication, also is found here, but there is an uncertain line between the taming of individuals and domestication of a species line. The performing Himalayan bears, the monkeys, the apes, the mongooses, and questionably the handling of even the dangerous cobra come within this framework.

In the process of hunting animals for food, for leather, for sinew, or for ivory and bone, many animals must have been restricted to much smaller ranges than they occupied in their wild state within Recent time. The elephant once ranged in central China, but has not lived there wild within historic time. The true wild water buffalo is thought by some authorities to be totally extinct, though many have gone wild again, and related animals are still found in scattered remnant locations. We cannot at this time specify how significant taming and domestication of certain animals was to some people, as opposed to rejection of taming and domestication of the same animals by other people. It is likely that the variable interest of culture groups in certain animals significantly enters the question of distribution today. Though the elephant motif in Chinese art is strong, the Chinese do not seem to care for the live animal. And the elephant in Borneo seems a matter of rather recent cultural introduction to the northwestern portion of the island.

Outside the Oriental region a number of significant domestications must be placed. There is evidence that the goat and the sheep came first out of the rougher hill country, the goat seemingly related to western central Asia and the sheep possibly to Afghanistan or near-by areas. Through a combination of domestication of, and the interbreeding by, various wild sheep, a number of different types finally appeared. Such are the hairy highland sheep, the open-range soft-wool sheep, the fat-tailed sheep, and the fat-buttocked sheep, and necessarily a wide range of local environments must have been finally involved. The yak of modern Tibet seems to have originated in southern Siberia as a domesticated animal among northern peoples, with its restriction to Tibet coming fairly late. Our modern cattle *Bos taurus* is a late form, domestication having begun perhaps with *Bos namadicus* and *Bos brachycepheros* among Indo-European and proto-Tibetan peoples somewhere on open grassland ranges of central Asia. The domestication of early cattle may well have had much to do with the onset of the Neolithic phase of culture in that its overlay upon early crop growing brought the rapid rise of levels of culture in southwestern central Asia. The whole question of milking is involved here, along with the dairying complex. Young children often drink directly from goats and sheep among people keeping them, and the use of milk possibly began with the first goat and sheep peoples. Its later extension is both varied and complex, full of tabu and acceptance.

The origins of horse culture lie north of the great mountain ranges of central Asia. This involved several kinds of horses, several Turkish peoples, and portions of western and central Asia. The camel involves at least the two forms, single- and double-humped camels, a variety of peoples, and territory ranging from southwestern Asia to North Africa. The donkey seems to relate to this same range of territory but is mixed up with the early history of half domestication of the onager.

All of these Holarctic animals came slowly and in succession into the area of concern to this volume. Two approaches are involved: through the mountain wall of northwestern India and through the Kansu Corridor into North China. Each form has penetrated to the limit of its physiological ability, but none has been able to compete with the domestications of the Oriental zone in utility to man except on the drier and cooler margins.

All the Holarctic animals mentioned may have lived over such distributional ranges that they could have entered the Oriental zone in their wild states, had they chosen to do so. For all except the hardiest of the sheep and goats, and also the yak, this would have meant crossing the northwest mountain wall of India or approaching eastern Asia through the Gobi Desert. The three animals just mentioned are probably the only ones which naturally could have crossed the Tibetan highlands into the Oriental zone. There is evidence that some of the goats and sheep did intergrade the Oriental region through northwest India and northwest China-Manchuria. It is unlikely that any other of the now-domesticated animals from the Holarctic zone did willingly migrate into the Oriental zone in their wild states. Each of them has been taken by man throughout the zone, but not one of the Holarctic forms is truly at home deep in the Oriental zone. Except on the drier, cooler margins, all downbreed rapidly, losing size, stamina, and utility. Thus the horse in Yunnan often is but half as large as the central Asian pony, and the sheep of the lower Indian peninsula are poor animals, both for meat and for wool. Of all the Holarctic domestications perhaps the goat is the best able to survive, in what today must be a selected strain which no longer could survive in its original homeland.

Conversely two of the Oriental zone domestications do not live easily far outside their own types of environments. The water buffalo does not do well either in cold climates or in totally dry ones. Away from the wet littoral he must be provided with bathing pools in which to cool himself frequently. The zebu cattle do better than the water buffalo but they do not adapt well to regions with really cold winters unless they are interbred with cattle of northern origin. The accompanying map depicts current distributional limits for selected animals native to the Holarctic and Oriental life realms, but it should be noted that these limits are cultural ones, in part, set by man rather than by the animals concerned.

ANIMAL ECONOMIES

In south and eastern Asia both domesticated and wild animals play significant roles in regional economy. Except where religious tabus against the taking of life have historically become effective, all levels of culture indulge in hunting wild animals, both for sport and for economic gain. This has ranged from the earlier, organized, great autumn hunts of the Mongols and Manchus, which combined military field maneuvers with sport and the securing of food, to the daily food hunting of primitive groups. The very abundance of wild animal and bird life in most parts of the realm is astonishing. Wild duck, partridge, or other game birds are often obtainable in markets almost all over China, and venison often is a preferred food in many areas. By the winter's end many a village in the lower Indus Valley possesses a large pile of duck feathers—testimony to the frequency of migrant wild duck in the seasonal food economy of the local villagers.

Different culture levels, of course, have their own techniques of hunting, vary in the animals or birds which are their objective, and also vary in their utilization of the proceeds of hunting. Many of the simpler peoples, using simple techniques, hunt small game and birds, eat animals that higher cultures no longer value, or use the products in ways long since discarded by higher cultures. The spear, blowgun, bow and arrow, the snare, pitfall, antique firearm, and modern rifle all are used by one people or another, plus many other hunting techniques. The proceeds of hunting among many groups form important additions to their material economy.

Except upon the inner Asian margins of the Orient pastoralism in the normal sense is missing from the Orient. In earlier times in northwest India and north China-Manchuria it was practiced by peoples who, as pastoralists, invaded these two margins of the Orient. Invaders successful in gaining a foothold in either margin always concluded by slowly giving up their pastoral economy for the more sedentary calling of agriculture, though they seldom completely gave up their attachment to animal economy. This carryover of animal economy in northwest India and north China-Manchuria introduced the Holarctic domestications into the edges of the Orient. With the animals as such came significant additions to the cultures and economies of the Orient. The horse, camel, and donkey changed transport and supplied draft power in agriculture. They entered into military tactics, art motifs, and the field of clothing. Since many of the later invaders were not just simple pastoralists but were also crop cultivators, they were instrumental in introducing the plow and other agricultural tools. Perhaps in this way dairying was introduced to India, but the Chinese rejected dairying, for some reason not easily explained.

It is not yet clear just how far transport and draft agricultural application had been developed within the ancient Orient, using the zebu and the water buffalo. The peculiar usage to which elephants can be put seem entirely native to the Orient, but they are not closely related to the economic usage of the other animals.

Gradually the Holarctic domestications became spread very widely throughout the Orient, within their physiologic limits, and today Holarctic cattle, zebu cattle, the water buffalo, and the horse make up the population of large animals of such an area as Java or the Philippines. Slowly a distinct division of labor has come to be assigned to the several animals in many areas. In the Philippines today, for example, horses pull passenger carts, are ridden, and perform at race courses; both zebu and Holarctic male cattle pull sleds and two-wheeled cargo carts, and cows serve a small dairy purpose; water buffalo chiefly are used to cultivate ricefields, but occasionally they pull sleds or carts, and sometimes stamp out grain on the threshing floors.

All the domesticated animals of both life zones are important sources of food supply to the many culture groups of the Orient. In early times there were no tabus against the use of any animal as food. The dog and the pig were eaten by many groups, but common use of the dog as food has been kept only by some of the simpler peoples who do not yet use the large animals as food sources. The use of the dog for food by the Chinese was common until recent centuries. Animals were bred particularly for food and fed on special diets, in which grain foods predominated. Beyond the food problem, almost every people in the Orient makes use of leather in clothing or equipment. A considerable amount of bone is utilized in the making of tools, charms, and curios. There are few tabus against the use of leather, sinew, bone, feathers, or shells. There are almost no tabus against the use of sheep wool, goat hair, yak wool, or camel hair. Both in the unprocessed forms of leather garments with the wool or hair still attached and in the finished forms of woven textiles, the products are widely used around the cooler edges of the Orient and penetrate considerable distances. There are, of course, regional patterns of significance in this use of animals.

In Manchuria and Korea neither the zebu cattle nor the water buffalo do well, owing to the cold winter conditions and, therefore, are not significantly represented in the animal population. The pig, a more adaptable animal, is common in both areas. The Holarctic animals, cattle, sheep, goats, and horses, are relatively numerous in Manchuria and, both as meat and commercial products, play a significant role in regional economy. Cattle and horses perform most of the Manchurian local transport and draft labor in a somewhat interchangeable role. Cattle and pigs are the only numerous animals in Korea, cattle having to serve as all-purpose animals. Though cattle never have been present in adequate numbers in the modern era, the Koreans take good care of them and strongly appreciate their value. Japan perhaps makes less use of animals than any other portion of the Orient. The landforms of Japan do not favor animal husbandry, and the natural browse is poor. Cold winter climates keep out the animals from the Oriental life region, and the hot summers of central to southern Japan do not favor those of the Holarctic zone. Holarctic cattle and horses are the only numerous large animals. The Japanese never have learned how best to use any domestic animal. Fish has taken the place of meat, and the Chinese were not the people to teach the Japanese dairying. Cattle and horses today are fairly common for transport and draft purposes, but less than half the farm families of Japan have one of either animal. Pigs are only slowly becoming more common; chickens are widely scattered in small numbers. Interestingly enough the rabbit, an animal well adapted to small land holdings, since 1940 has increased in numbers markedly in Japan.

The Chinese everywhere eat all the animals that they can raise. In the north this means almost the whole range of domesticated animals, excepting the zebu cattle, the water buffalo, and the elephant. In the northwest Moslem Chinese do not favor eating the pig. In Szechwan and western China generally the goat is more numerous, in relative terms, and supplies a considerable meat volume, plus a volume of skins. In South China the Holarctic cattle, goats, and sheep disappear, zebu, water buffalo, and the pig becoming dominant. Though cattle, camels, horses, and water buffalo are used in transport and for draft purposes, there are not enough animals for those purposes. Chickens and ducks all over China are depended upon for food to a considerable extent. Statistically, the animal population per capita is relatively low and, therefore, the per capita consumption of meat is low. Were the pressures upon land for food crop growing less severe, however, the Chinese would use larger amounts of animal foods.

In India today it is only the Moslems and the pagan groups that make use of animal foods. This is a historical matter, however, for very early India had no tabus against any animal. The tabus against the killing of animal life have grown steadily and slowly, start-

ing with the cow and the pig, until today strict Hindus will not kill domestic animals or even the dangerous wild forms of life, such as the tiger, the cobra, or other lesser pests. This has meant, among Hindus and in predominantly Hindu areas, that the hunting of wild game has died out and that animal economy has become modified. Tabus upon the use of milk products and upon eggs have not developed among Hindus, so that chickens are numerous almost everywhere, and the dairying industry of India rivals that of northwestern Europe or the United States. Among Moslems there is only the tabu on the pig, with no other strictures operative today, so that in predominantly Moslem regions animal economy is well developed and comprehensive.

Neither have there developed tabus against the use of animals as power sources in India. Therefore, all possible animals are used in transport and as draft animals, to turn grinding mills, pump water, cultivate the fields, and do other miscellaneous chores. Whereas the tabus rest very strongly upon the upper castes of Hindus, and to an extent control animal economy for the whole Hindu population, the lower castes and outcastes are much less bound by these strictures. Lower-caste Hindus often seem to have no scruples about the raising of animals and fowls or about selling them to Moslems who perform the slaughtering and processing of meat products, hides and skins, and other by-products.

As the Indian tabus against killing developed modification resulted in the animal population, both domestic and wild. There is an abundance of wild life in most parts of the country, the species varying with local environments, so that parts of India today remain paradises for the hunter and collector. India today is one of the chief exporters of wild animals, snakes, and birds. Monkeys, elephants, tigers, and a variety of birds are most in demand, the monkey export amounting to thousands of animals per year. As the pig lost favor as a food source, his lack of utility in other ways caused him to become unimportant in numbers, particularly since in more recent centuries he could not be sold to the Moslem. Sheep today are common everywhere except on the peninsular west coast and from Bengal eastward; goats are common almost all over India. The camel has a limited climatic range in India and is chiefly confined to the northwest. The few horses, mules, and donkeys are chiefly for riding or cart pulling in the northwest and in the central northern peninsula. Holarctic cattle, as separate breeds, are not now common but undoubtedly have historically interbred with the zebu varieties fairly deeply into India. This mixed cattle population, with the rise of the tabu on killing cattle, has steadily increased until today in India alone it numbers in excess of 150,000,000. The water buffalo no longer is restricted to moist areas but is to be found everywhere except in the strongly arid parts of northwest India, and today in India reaches a total of about 50,000,000 animals.

With the rise of tabus on the killing of animals, control over domestic livestock has lessened in respect to their personal freedom and their breeding. Therefore, most of the Indian domestic animal population today is relatively low grade. Certain local regions have used care in breeding cattle or water buffalo to give regional inequality to the value of the stock. Today there are perhaps fifty regional varieties of cattle, some of which are of high quality for draft purposes, food purposes, or dairy use. Around some of the large urban centers modern breeding of water buffalo for dairy stock has reached a fairly high plane. In the modern Indian dairy industry water buffalo form the best dairy stock, producing more milk and higher ratios of butterfat than do zebu cattle. The per capita consumption cannot be effectively expressed for all India, for either meat or dairy products, because of the regional and religious differences. Meat consumption is very low, and, although the milk products consumption total also is low as compared with the United States, the total is higher than that of any other oriental country.

Southeastern Asian animal economy is more restricted than that of north China or northeast India. Many of the Holarctic animals are not adaptable to the region climatically, nor do they do well upon the browse available. Horses, sheep, and goats are present only in small numbers and are relatively modern in origin. On the drier Lesser Sunda Islands horses do fairly well, and Flores is a local horse-breeding center. Zebu cattle are found in considerable numbers, but even they are not numerous east of Celebes, the scarcity being largely a historical matter of non-introduction and non-familiarity on the part of local populations. The water buffalo becomes the most important animal in local economy in the southeastern mainland countries and in the western Indies and Philippines, but it becomes very scarce in the middle Indies and is rare in New Guinea and related islands. This again is a historical matter rather than an environmental one. The pig comes back into its own in these lands and in many areas is the only useful domestic animal familiar to many of the simpler population. The Moslem tabu on the pig is operative to some degree in Malaya and the western Indies but is less effective than it is in India or the Near East. Burma, Thailand, and parts of Indochina have a nominal tabu against the killing of animals among the Buddhist peoples, derived from India, but nowhere is the tabu as strong as it is in India.

In regions such as the Philippines where the Spanish and Americans have tried to increase the population and range of domestic animals, most of the common ones are to be found. This is true of Sumatra and Java also, but not of the eastern Indies. The chicken, however, and the duck, to a lesser extent, are widely distributed and steadily depended upon. Until man establishes the proper living conditions and sources of animal foods, the domestic animal population of southeastern Asia and the island zone will remain relatively low, the role in economy will be small, and the material economy will be restricted as compared to that in most other parts of the world. Only the water buffalo, the pig, and the chicken seem well able to inhabit this area in large numbers, but since it is their home environment they do well in the matter of survival.

In summary it must be pointed out that, whereas the use of domestic animals for draft and transport purposes is fairly well developed in most parts of the Orient, the use of both domestic and wild animals in food economy adds far less to the dietary of most oriental peoples than is true in the Occident. The average consumption of meat in China probably does not exceed 30 pounds per person per year from all sources, excluding fish products, against the figure of close to 140 pounds in the United States. The figure for India is probably comparable among the Moslems, but well below that total among all other Indian peoples. Probably the Filipinos eat as much meat as any other oriental people, but even here the figure is little over 30 pounds per person per year. The use of eggs from several types of fowls is fairly high in parts of China and in the Philippines, but elsewhere it probably is below that of much of the Occident today.

The use of dairy products is most highly developed among the Hindu peoples of India, and the annual total of dairy products compares with that of the United States. The per capita consumption, however, is considerably lower than that of the United States by virtue of greater division among a far larger number of consumers. Elsewhere in the Orient the per capita consumption of dairy products is very low indeed. Neither the meat consumption nor the use of eggs and dairy products will be raised very high in the near future, owing to the widespread tabus and the already existent severe pressure of men upon the land. A general exception to these remarks, of course, is involved with respect to the pastoral peoples of the inner Asian frontiers of the Orient.

THE GEOGRAPHY OF AQUATIC LIFE

The salt and fresh waters fringing the southern and eastern Asiatic coasts, both at sea and on land contain a tremendous variety of aquatic life. The water territory probably possesses the richest fishery resource in the world, both as to species and to economically useful volume. The value of the salt waters of northeastern Asia is now recognized, since modern Japanese fishery yields are so heavy, but the resource of southern Asia is still questioned because a neat body of statistics to demonstrate it is lacking. It has been standard practice to speak of small fish populations in tropical waters, but in the Orient, at least, I believe this to be a fictional conclusion unsupported by fact.

Over half the world's marine fish are shore fish, and these are the important food fish. Their distribution and numbers depend partly upon the volume of food available to them and partly upon their preference for certain aquatic environments. The food volume depends upon the nutritive value of the waters, the light available, and the temperature conditions of the waters. Though water temperatures that are too high operate to decrease the water storage of food supply, shallow waters are more productive of food than are deep waters, and the light factor in low latitudes is more productive of food than in high latitudes. The aquatic environments of southeastern Asia include a great deal of shallow, brackish to fresh-water swamp and marsh lands that form an inviting and productive home to many kinds of fish. The shallow, warm shore waters of southeastern Asia present one set of conditions making for large fish populations; the shallow, cool waters of northeastern Asia present another set of conditions also making for large fish populations of different species. In southern waters there are over 2,000 species of fish, against over 1,000 species in the waters off Japan. Other forms of aquatic life are far more numerous in southern than northern waters. Statistically I cannot produce figures from southern waters as to numbers of fish, but I believe the populations to be large, to be important in past economies, and to be potentially significant to future economies.

A general uniformity in aquatic life of fresh waters, coastal, and near-coastal waters, from the Arabian Sea around to the South China Sea, suggests a single major tropical zone of aquatic life, usually termed the Indo-West Pacific region. The salt-water margins of this great region taper off to the Hawaiian Islands. This Indo-Pacific area contains more families and genera of fish, crustaceans, and mollusks than are found elsewhere. In part this wealth of forms relates to the common history of drainage of the old Sundaland shelf, long a part of the Asiatic continent.

Northern salt waters, such as the Sea of Japan and the Sea of Okhotsk, possess a uniformity of their own, to suggest a second zone, which often includes the whole North Pacific region. The waters of the eastern Indies and Australia show a fair degree of uniformity that separates them into a third regional unit, the Australian region. Factors in this unit are the scarcity of fresh-water aquatic forms to be found east of Wallace's Line and the localization of many life forms in and around the eastern Indies.

Over and above these regional patterns of aquatic life, of course, are some features common to all tropical salt waters of the earth. Coral growth is common everywhere in southern Asia, under the right conditions, and extends as far north as Formosa and the southern Ryukyu Islands. With corals go certain fish, crabs, and other minor life forms. Related species of many forms, such as the herrings, the oysters, and the mackerels, seem to inhabit all three zones. Other forms, such as the giant crabs of far northern waters, or the giant mollusks of Indian waters, seem to inhabit a single zone only. Environmental conditions control localized distributions within any one zone. Though oysters live in all three zones, they are not to be found everywhere, owing to locally unsuitable environments, and pearl oysters are to be found only in a few scattered environments of particularly suitable nature. Some forms, such as the tunas, some of the sharks, and some of the sardines, are pelagic, migratory rovers, and their distributions and ecologies are dependent upon oceanic conditions rather than upon conditions of the coastal shelves. The catfishes are a very old group with southern origins and areal relations. The fresh-water carps and carp-like fishes are younger and, in origin, are related to China. Though the carps now are distributed to the edges of Africa and into the Indies they do not reach Australia, and few of the catfishes are to be found in Australia.

In respect both to marine and fresh-water life forms this triple zoning results from basic differences in geographic environments. Northern waters are cool to cold and produce and store large amounts of food materials for all forms of aquatic life. Here are stimulated distinctive rhythms of reproduction, long life cycles, long-range migration patterns, and particular ecologic conditions that affect the aquatic populations. Japanese waters, particularly, undergo variations in temperature from year to year as the major Asiatic warm and cold currents fluctuate in volume and in relative location. Many species of fish are extremely sensitive to temperature ranges and, in some years, simply do not appear in Japanese waters.

Southern waters also possess environmental continuity, but of a different sort. The close connections of the western Indies with the mainland of southern and southeastern Asia, and the continuity of coastal waters throughout this large region, contribute to a common history of aquatic life. Here life cycles are often shorter, and reproductive patterns are often related to estuarine conditions. Different but even more voluminous patterns of food production support more aquatic life than can be supported by northern waters. Migration habits seem of shorter range, and quite different sets of ecologic relations exist among far more species. When rivers flood the flat lowlands, inland penetration of many kinds of aquatic life takes place. Spawning often occurs away from stream channels, and the natural planting of fish covers wide areas, which contain ample food supplies. Many of the fish species native to this region possess auxiliary breathing equipment that enables them to live under poor water conditions. Some species can even estivate in mud at the bottom of shallow ponds and drying flood surfaces.

The separation of the eastern Indies and Australia is a matter of geologic history, and voluminous biologic and botanical research testifies to the relative completeness of the separation. East and south of this zone of separation occurs another set of coastal marine and fresh-water environments, with their own patterns of reproduction, migration, life rhythms, and regional ecologies.

Shifts of sea level consequent upon glaciation, deglaciation, and mountain building have markedly altered the areas of land and of coastal seas during the Pleistocene geologic time. These changes have rearranged the fresh-water river systems, coastal seas, and ocean currents of most parts of southern and eastern Asia. Changes in marine climate and physical changes in aquatic environments have altered species distributions and ecologic conditions within local regions. The paleontologic and archaeologic record clearly indicates that early Asiatic man in any one area had available slightly different life forms from those that are present in the same waters today.

Such changes produced in fresh-water and marine environments caused shifts, from time to time, in the dividing lines between life regions, but it seems likely that the triple division is one of long standing. Wallace's Line was first thought to be a definite boundary, whereas today the separation between Asiatic and Australian life regions is recognized to be transitional. This separation is, of course, far more noticeable in fresh-water life forms than it is in those of salt water.

No such demarcation can be placed upon the map to distinguish between the northern and southern regions, either fresh or marine. At sea Formosa lies close to a possible zone of division, and in fresh water the dividing zone seems to lie close to the drainage divide that separates China from Indochina. Naturally, within the major regions a number of secondary regional distinctions doubtless exist, but our knowledge does not permit a full elaboration of these detailed patterns.

THE PRACTICE OF FISHING

Everywhere around these coasts man has long used marine products, both for food and for other purposes. Early man probably considered fish merely as aquatic animals requiring only a specific application of general hunting techniques. His methods of exploiting marine products, and his yields, have increased in variety with the passage of time. As the most recent deglaciation progressed, raising sea level and flooding large areas of lowlands throughout the world, the members of close-in shore fish increased markedly in waters accessible to man. This permitted an increase in fishing as an economic activity, and it is in this relatively recent period that fishing tools and techniques, and dependence upon aquatic food, became really important. No part of the world was more benefited in this respect than southeastern Asia, and no people developed further the practice of fishing than did those peoples around the littoral of the present southeastern Asia. Fresh water has long been well utilized everywhere in the Orient. Fishing of shore waters is old and often is well developed, though today yields could be greatly increased by improved equipment and a better knowledge of marine resources. Pelagic fishing seldom has been highly developed in oriental waters, and only the Japanese have efficiently exploited this zone of marine resources. Elsewhere fishermen have many ingenious pelagic fishing methods which enable them to catch large fish, but their simple resources do not permit a highly productive fishery yield. Deep-sea fishing has been but scantily practiced in the Orient, and again only the Japanese do much of it. Even Japanese pelagic and deep-sea fishing is quite recent in appearance.

Perhaps earliest and easiest of fishing methods was the beachcomber technique of the strand line, most productive on those rocky shores marked by a distinct tidal range. Here shell fish, crustaceans, seaweeds, and small fish can be acquired for food, and various other usable products can be picked up. This can be a simple system of gathering, and, since it can be repeated with every tidal cycle, it has a permanent aspect that does not require great mobility. At an early date it may even have inhibited progress by being too amply productive of food supplies—simple food problems here were too easily solved.

Gradually man has supplemented the natural productiveness of the strand line, however, by walling off small catchment ponds or corrals and by building a variety of fish traps. The shores of many parts of the Orient are lined by these devices, particularly those flat shores containing no natural barricades and those lacking marked tidal ranges. Today in Japan, particularly, one can see the coastal folk follow each ebb tide, gathering in the harvest in what must be an age-old technique. And southeastern Asia, particularly Malaysia, shows a high density of coastal fish traps of many sorts. They often are ingeniously built, artistically patterned, and possess considerable regional specialization in design. These marine traps also include small hand-set underwater traps of a number of types. Traps in general are used for many kinds of fish, and also for crabs, lobsters, prawns, and other crustaceans.

A second major group of procedures employed by coastal fishermen involves spears, hooks, and nets. From the water's edge these tools have but limited application, however, and some device for getting man out beyond wading depth was a necessary early complement. This need led to a great variety of floats, rafts, and boats. Each of these separate subgroups of fishing tools has considerable variety, for each involves an ancient technique, long practiced and well developed in many areas.

Spearing of fish is an old and primitive technique that still is widely used in the Orient, from the Laccadive Islands to New Guinea to Japan. It is chiefly a remnant technique today, used for subsistence fishing mostly, but also indulged in as a recreational activity. Variants of it involve torches and night fishing, goggles and underwater work, floats, harpoons and, on the southern west coast of India, even the blowgun. Hook-and-line fishing is employed in a wide variety of ways, but today it is chiefly significant for boat fishing in shore and pelagic waters. One sees rod-and-line fishermen in almost all parts of the Orient, working with equipment so simple as to horrify an expert American dry-fly caster.

Small circular hand casting nets are used in every part of the Orient, with regional specialization in materials, form, and method of use, depending on water depth, the product sought, and the skill of the populace. Fish, shrimp, prawns, and lobsters are obtained by means of nets. Most parts of the Orient have developed large and more complex types of nets, used with boats, catamarans, or rafts. Today many kinds of nets are used, requiring from one to a dozen boats and crews of from two to thirty men. Specialization in the use of a given type of net and concentration upon particular kinds of fish are frequent, and varied systems of division of labor, sharing of the catch, and marketing have developed. In detail these often depend on local fishing conditions, but they are also related to social systems and to factors in the over-all economy of a local region.

Not all peoples are equally good net fishermen. The southern west coast of India, the Bengal delta lands, British Malaya, the north coast of Java, the Philippines, the northern Kwangtung-Fukien coast of China, the Shantung Peninsula of China, the southwestern coast of Korea, and the Inland Sea coasts of Japan are sections in which fishing skills and equipment are notable today and the annual catch of fish is large.

Trawling, a modern, advanced system of net-and-line fishing, today is found in all parts of the Orient, but the Japanese are the only fishermen to make effective use of it so far. Since 1900 they have progressively spread their range of power-boat fishing from their own waters northward into the North Pacific, southward through the South China Sea, and out into the open South Pacific. Out of almost every major port elsewhere in the Orient move a few modern power boats to fish near-by shore waters, but no country in the Orient other than Japan has really developed modern scientific and powered fishing methods.

It is in the estuarine and fresh-water zone that some of the most distinctive fishing methods appear. The Orient undoubtedly presents the richest complex of estuarine and fresh-water fishing methods of any part of the world. The lowland river valleys of southeastern Asia present unusual conditions, both as to physical environment and as to types of fish. Part of this peculiarity pertains to the variety of plant life that surrounds these lowlands. Early man, working with a wealth of plants, searching for textile fibers and edible products, long ago discovered that many plants contain strong poisons. In these procedures he discovered that these poisons temporarily stupefied fish and caused them to float to the water surface where they were easily caught. The process works less well in salt water than in brackish or fresh water. It gradually became a common method of fishing among peoples in river valleys who could not apply the beachcomber techniques of the tidal strand line. Moist southern India to Borneo and Sumatra probably were the original center of this technique in the Old World, but it spread west to the Red Sea and north to Japan. It still is common in the more moist parts of southeastern Asia where the poisons are available, but it is decreasing in favor of better methods developed at later dates. A related modern technique is the use of explosives, but this is discouraged as a destructive process that kills fish of all ages, many of whom are too small for use.

Bengal perhaps is the center around which are clustered more varieties of catching fish with traps than in any other part of the world. The Bengali has devised a trap for every possible type of fish and every circumstance of water from the shallowest of ricefield covers to the deep waters of the Ganges estuary. From India out into the Indies runs this multiple pattern of fresh-water fish traps, slowly decreasing in number. The Bengali is serious about his fishing as an aid to his material economy, but he also loves to fish for the fun of fishing, perhaps more so than any other oriental people. His lines, hooks, and rods may be ever so simple, but it is in the finesse of the multiple compounds used as bait that he discloses his true relationship to Izaak Walton.

Throughout southern Asia, when the water in tanks, ponds, and isolated channels becomes low it is common to hold fish drives. Women and children gather about a spot where the drive is to end, while a crew of men goes into the shallow water at a distance, wading and threshing about, but gradually working toward the selected spot. Small nets, turbans, sarongs, baskets, and other implements come into play when a volume of fish have been cornered, everyone getting into the water in a scramble to scoop up the fish before they can disperse.

When the tanks, ponds, and old river channels sometimes dry out so that there is only mud in the bottom, it is common to dig fish out of the mud with spades and similar tools. Many of the species of the Oriental life region, as mentioned previously, estivate in the mud at the bottoms of ponds, where they can survive a considerable dry spell.

China shows less multiplicity of tools and techniques for the catching of fresh-water fish than does Bengal, though the devices are both numerous and ingenious. One of the most common and widespread methods is the counterbalanced dip net, rigged on bamboo poles and mounted either on a medium-sized fishing boat or on a river bank.

Allied to the nets, lines, and traps that catch fish are the boats, catamarans, and floats that often assist in the operation either in fresh or salt water. It cannot be stated flatly that the evolution of boats is tied to fishing, and yet a great many of the regional styles of boats, building methods, and sailing techniques certainly have long related to the practice of fishing.

There appear to be at least five separate boat-building complexes in the Orient, all amenable to influence by the fishermen. The west coast of India, with the coasts of Arabia, seem to share one tradition, and the end of peninsular India and Ceylon share another. There is the inland-waterway, dug-out canoe tradition, originating in the lowlands of southeastern Asia, but now distributed from south India to the Philippines and into Oceania. Third is the complex tradition of the outrigger canoe, for sea-going purposes, now scattered from Madagascar to Hawaii, touching Ceylon, Malaya, the Philippines, and the Indies. The Indies now form the center of the outrigger techniques, but this is a secondary development. It is not certain whether the Indonesian boat-building tradition is a separate one, or one derived from India. In eastern waters there is the separate North China junk tradition with its fresh- and salt-water variants. This Chinese tradition may have derived in part from Korean boat builders, but it spread to Japan and southward along the coast, recently affecting local boat styles as far south as Singapore. The inland water boats of China show more variety in design than do those of any other part of the world.

Behind all these, possibly, are the still older reed, raft-like boats often termed balsas from the Spanish-American name. There are suggestions of carryover of this ancient tradition into later ones, as in the boat of the Tenasserim sea gypsy, whose boat possesses a wooden keel and reed-built sides. There well may be other and still older boating complexes in the prehistory of the Orient that enabled man to learn marine fishing and helped to execute early island hopping in intervals of high sea levels which divided southeastern Asia.

Behind the individual boat-building techniques also is the catamaran, still used in south Indian waters. This involves several shaped logs leashed together into a wet, boat-like sea-going raft. It is used by many groups for several purposes in shore waters, and may have been very widely dispersed in earlier time. Today the catamaran usually is worked in pairs of two, leashed together and equipped with a lateen sail.

More directly related to fishing practices are the various kinds of floats used by fishermen. These begin with the simple block of wood used by the lower Ganges River fisherman who, equipped with a small net and a creel, floats downstream with the current, scooping up fish as he goes. He may carry his block back upstream to repeat his operation. They include the large pottery jars upon which the Indus River fishermen squat while handling a net, and the raft-like assemblage of pottery jars used in large Bengal tanks and ponds. They also include the large wooden tubs used by the canal and pond fishermen of China and other ingenious devices used in several local areas.

In any one area undoubtedly a succession of fishing methods has been applied by successive generations, but there is little comparative data on the subject. In the Philippines, for example, it is thought that the spear, bow and arrow, and poisons are among the oldest of fishing methods. Fish corrals or stone dams across beach embayments and tidal inlets were a later method, in turn followed by various types of traps. Last to come into use were the variety of hand nets and the larger nets involving the use of boats in the pre-Spanish period. Pond culture is also pre-Spanish. Recent techniques are trawling and dynamiting. The efficiency of fishing practice varies with the diversity of methods in use in any one region.

Fishing practice in the Orient has one other aspect, that of pisciculture. By this is meant the planting of spawn or fingerlings in controlled waters and the later harvesting of fish and other aquatic products. The raising of carp and carp-like fishes began in South China possibly before 1000 B.C., and variants of old Chinese practices have spread throughout the Orient. In most of the areas that grow wet rice, fish are introduced into ricefields. For the most part Chinese fish-farming practices today are those of hundreds of years ago, and the best methods now used are relatively recent developments in newer areas, though South China productive yields per acre still are the highest in the world.

In China small controlled lakes, canals, and ponds all are used for raising fish. Several kinds of fish are often raised in the same waters, their different diets and feeding habits making for greater efficiency. An estimated 400,000 acres in central and South China are devoted to such farming. In addition to half a dozen kinds of fish, a variety of mollusks and crustaceans are produced in these same waters.

Javanese fish farming has reached a rather mature status. Permanent ponds are laid out, regular feedings and controls over water movement, breeding, and marketing turn this kind of fishing into a developed type of land use. As coastal ponds gradually become desalted they are turned into ricefields, and new fish ponds are built on the seaward margin. For these coastal fish farms spawn of the bandeng, *Chanos chanos,* are taken in shallow coastal waters and placed in controlled ponds. The bandeng, a vegetarian fish well adapted to pond culture, weighs from 3 to 10 pounds when marketed. In the interior hill country fish farms, the gurami is grown, an Osphromenidae, which is native to the area from Burma to Borneo.

This fish is an air breather, having an air chamber just above the gill cavity, so that large numbers of gurami can be grown in restricted waters. Elsewhere in the Indies fish farming is not so well developed as in Java but today is spreading gradually along many coastal strips, and the acreage of fish farms is well over 300,000 acres for the Indies. Thailand and Indochina have expanding patterns of fish farming, and Malaya is just beginning the practice though in none of the three is there a large development as yet. The Philippines in 1951 had about 200,000 acres in salt-water fish ponds, with steady annual additions to the area and a potential of about 1,200,000 acres suitable for fish farming. The chief fish raised is the same salt-water fish used in Java, *Chanos chanos,* here called bangos.

The Koreans have done a certain amount of fish farming, though not so much as the landscape of the west coast would permit. Japan has a small but significant variety of water farming, producing the widest range of products of any oriental country. Pond raising of carp began only about 1800, and planting of fish in ricefields began to be extensive only about 1850. Currently about 30,000 acres of ponds and reservoirs are used for raising fish of several types. A variety of seaweeds are grown in coastal ponds, and a significant pearl industry along the central east coast of Honshu depends upon culture methods that amount to farming.

Fishing, in the larger sense, also seeks such other aquatic products as shells, pearls, coral, seaweed, whales, turtle eggs, shark fins, and a variety of minor products. India is probably the area with the largest interest in shell, though the southern waters of the Philippine Archipelago produce a significant shell volume. From Kathiawar around to Madras a shallow-water mollusk, *Turbinella pyrum Linn,* is gathered at low tide for a variety of uses. Large specimens of the shell termed conch are sacred religious items in Hindu India, but the shell has a variety of secular uses also in the field of jewelry and personal adornment. This fishery, begun long before the Christian era, is gradually losing its importance today. Various types of mollusks have shells that have long interested man; they range from marine green snails and those producing mother of pearl to that used for windowpane making in the Philippines and the wide variety of cowry shells used for decoration and as a medium of exchange in earlier periods. Pearl diving is an old fishing pattern in the Indian Ocean, which well could be the region in which the pearl became more important than the oyster in fishery work. The Gulf of Mannar, between Ceylon and India, is one of the oldest pearl fishing banks. Local shifts in area and annual irregularity of production are marked in these waters, and may be typical of most pearl oyster banks in the Orient. Along the west coast of India good pearling banks are found only near Karachi in the northwest. The Tenasserim coast of Burma, south of Mergui, is a minor source of pearls. Some pearls come from the Sulu Archipelago, which has a very old record of production. Some of the shore waters of Borneo yielded seed pearls to the Japanese in the 1930's. Japan also has old pearling waters. The modern Japanese production of cultured pearls is the first well-known effort to increase the yield of this natural fishery. Elsewhere in the Orient in modern times it has been tried in a small but never successful manner.

Never an important phase of fisheries has been the gathering of, and diving for, coral around a number of islands in the southwestern Pacific. Nice black coral comes out of the Sulu Archipelago, and other types of coral are sought in other areas. Similarly seaweed is sought in a minor way in many parts of the Orient. Japan is the only region in which seaweed harvesting has become at all significant, supplementing the total Japanese food supply, though in many parts of the Orient a few people go after selected seaweeds. Whaling, as a purposeful part of fisheries, seems to have been practiced only in the northern Orient, where the aboriginal Ainu of the Japanese islands did some whale hunting with poisoned harpoons. The Japanese long have been whalers, having learned from the Ainu, and the attention paid to this form of fishery has increased during modern times, as the Japanese have developed and copied some of the more efficient whaling methods.

Turtle egg harvesting, an applied hunting-fishing pattern, is widely practiced in the western Indies, with Borneo as a center. Shark fishing, earlier for fins and a few wanted bits, is an old fishery wherever peoples have been in touch with the Chinese, and today the demand for fish liver oil has enlarged shark fishing. Edible bird's nests collected around several rocky coasts of southeastern Asia, the mucin-like product of the sea swiftlet, are not fishery products as such, but primarily are gathered by fishermen as a side-line activity. Various minor phases of the fishery industries are locally practiced in several parts of the Orient.

ORIENTAL FISHING ECONOMIES

The approximately 3,500,000 full-time fishermen in the Orient use in the vicinity of 1,000,000 boats, plus an **uncounted** volume of fishing equipment, and produce in the vicinity of 9,500,000 tons of edible aquatic products per year. Many millions more are part-time fishermen, but their catch cannot be tabulated. The total product ranges from fish little larger than minnows to huge fish 8 feet long, from little shrimp to big whales, from turtle eggs to edible mollusks and edible seaweeds. This volume of products forms a most important secondary food pattern in the dietary of the Orient. Since the consumption of meat and other proteins is extremely low in many parts of the realm, the per capita consumption of fish products is relatively more important than in many other parts of the world.

The Japanese probably eat more aquatic products than any other oriental people, with an annual figure of over 100 pounds per person, against a figure of about 6 pounds for the United States. Probably second stand the Filipinos, who consume about 40 pounds per person per year, including the fish imported from abroad. British Malayan consumption of fish per year is just under 40 pounds per capita. Effective data for other oriental countries are not available, but some suggestions may be made. Korean fish consumption perhaps is close to 12 pounds per capita per year, Chinese use about 7 pounds per person per year, and Indochina uses perhaps 15 pounds per person per year. The figure for Thailand is somewhat higher, perhaps 25 pounds per person per year, the annual per capita figure for the Indies may stand at about 12 pounds, the Burmese figure is not more than 7 pounds, and India stands at the bottom with an annual per capita figure of about 4 pounds per year.

These simple averages, of course, do not adequately express the role of aquatic products in the whole economy or in the dietary customs of the several countries. Almost all coastal people today have fish products available to them, but the peoples in the interior portions of many countries have no such opportunity, owing to the absence of fresh-water aquatic products and to inadequate transport facilities for marine products. All parts of Japan can procure adequate volumes of fish products in one form or another, whereas in far western China fish products in any form are rare and so high priced that only a few well-to-do people may consume them often. Even between the coasts of the larger Philippine Islands and the island interiors fish consumption drops from perhaps 125 pounds of fresh sea food per capita per year to 15 pounds of cured or tinned fish per year. In both western China and the Philippine Islands interiors this modern scarcity of local aquatic products is in part a matter of exhaustion of local resources almost to extinction, in part a lack of conditions in the natural environment for replenishment of aquatic resources, and in part a lack of transport and trade facilities.

In contrast to this scarcity of aquatic products in western China or interior Mindanao is the situation of Thailand, western Indochina, and central China, in which great rivers with open courses provide easy access far inland for many forms of aquatic life. The fresh-water fisheries of the upper Mekong River are of economic significance to local Thai and Indochina populations, and the fisheries of Hupeh and Hunan play a considerable role in the food economies of those two Chinese provinces. The fisheries of the Tonle Sap of Cambodia produce a huge and widely consumed volume of produce. The widespread distribution of overflow river channels, reservoirs, and ponds throughout the more moist parts of India is a factor in the widespread local distribution of aquatic products to a large number of people, even though the total supply of fish products in interior India today is not great enough to permit a large per capita consumption.

The coastlines and large river banks of the whole of the Orient total a tremendous mileage in the vicinity of 60,000 miles, serving to place a large share of the population fairly close to some water body productive of useful aquatic life. The concept "useful" has a far wider application throughout most of the Orient than in the United States, owing to the severe pressure of man upon the environment. Around coasts, along river banks, in areas of seasonal and permanent water bodies, and even throughout the rice landscape of the more moist parts of the Orient live millions of people of many culture levels, primarily employed with agriculture or other callings who augment their food supplies when they can by using some of the hundreds of tools for obtaining aquatic products. No statistical data indicate accurately either this total population or the value of their product.

In the northern portion of the Orient the problems of handling aquatic products are relatively simple much of the year, as temperature conditions are not such as to make them spoil rapidly. In Japan, of course, where conditions are relatively good, the best facilities have been developed for long-term handling of fish products, namely the canning industries. Elsewhere throughout the Orient it is only in purely local situations or in the big cities that much of the aquatic product can be delivered to the consumer in the fresh state. In local situations in which the fisherman or his neighbors often are the chief consumers most fish products can be used fresh, since a time interval of only a few hours normally elapses between the catching and the consuming. Around the big city fish markets served by power boats, and with refrigeration available, a large volume of fish is delivered to urban consumers as fresh products. In southern waters producing a number of fish with auxiliary breathing apparatus the problem of keeping fish alive is not difficult, and so here, also, fresh fish delivery is actually fairly extensive at considerable distances from sources of the catch. It would take elaborate refrigeration and transport equipment to provide fresh fish products to a large share of consumers of the Orient.

A large share of the fish consumed in the whole southern half of the Orient must be preserved in some manner. Salting and sun drying are the commonest techniques, with local variations, and smoking is often practiced in many areas. The smaller fish may be strung on reeds and sticks, as on the Tenasserim coast of Burma, or most fish may be salted and packed in baskets as in Malaya. Many of the fish caught off the coasts of China do not can well and are normally salt-cured. Different kinds of aquatic products are handled in different ways. The sea slugs known as bêche-de-mer, produced along the west coast of Borneo, and the shark fins widely produced are usually sun-dried but not salted for export to southern China. The native peoples of Burma and Thailand usually mix small fish, shrimp, and prawns together and prepare them as fish paste, whereas the Chinese fishermen in these waters boil the shrimp and prawns and then dry them for export sale. Indian fishermen normally dry and salt the surplus that cannot be disposed of as fresh fish, and the Indians do not use much fish paste. From Burma and Ceylon around to the Philippines and well out into the Indies, on the other hand, partly fermented and spiced fish paste, made from many different aquatic products, is an extremely common method of preservation for the surplus catch. Particularly the Burmese, Thai, Annamese, Javanese, and the Cambodians are partial to the somewhat odorous fish paste as a part of their daily menu.

Trade in fish products within the various portions of eastern and southern Asia is fairly considerable. Java no longer provides her own supply and imports fish pastes and cured fish from Indochina, Thailand, and various islands of the outer Indies. Borneo is an exporter of several types of aquatic products, ranging from salt-cured fish, pearl shell, and agar-agar to bêche-de-mer, shark fins, turtle eggs, and edible bird nests, many of the exports going to China. Indian fishing ports export local specialty products to Malaya to be consumed by Indian plantation labor. A large volume of fish passing through Singapore moves in many directions within the oriental trade realm. Practically every country lists a variety of aquatic products both in its imports and exports, though for Indonesia, the Philippines, and China the imports greatly outweigh the exports. Korea throughout the period of Japanese control exported a large volume of sea produce to Japan, and aquatic products have been one of the large Japanese exports for decades.

In most parts of the Orient fishing is properly termed subsistence fishing. Much of this is carried on by full-time fishermen who barter small surpluses for their other economic needs, but much of it is spare-time or slack-season endeavor by family members not otherwise employed. Around the major cities and seaports in all parts of the Orient the fishery industry has become something of a commercial activity. In southeastern Asia and western Indies there is considerable small-scale commercial fishing, in which the Chinese are important, either as fishermen directly, as processors of surplus, or as wholesalers and traders. Prior to World War II Japanese commercial fishermen, with power boats, improved equipment, and even small canneries had spread throughout much of southeastern Asia. In Borneo there were three Japanese canneries in operation, but there is a question whether this was a legitimate economic operation or a screen for strategic intelligence activities. Undoubtedly such fish canning could be made to pay its own way as an economic development in most areas.

In some areas shell gathering and related phases of the fishery industry are full-time occupations, but many of these also are auxiliary occupations. The pearl diving of the Gulf of Mannar in southern India is a short-season auxiliary activity that brings participants from a rather wide area. Ricefield fishing is strictly seasonal, as are many of the special kinds of fishing, such as drives, mud digging, and pool fishing that go on during the dry seasons. The fishermen of the east coast of Malaya do almost no fishing from November to March, during the height of the winter monsoon storm conditions along this rough coast; the fishermen of the central west coast of India do no boat fishing in shore waters between June and late September. In Ceylon professional fishermen shift from the south and west coasts during the summer monsoon to the north and east coasts, shifting back again during the winter monsoon. In the far north Japanese and Russian salmon operations are confined to the short season when the fish migrate to spawning grounds.

In contrast to the seasonality of many direct fisheries is the regularity of some of the coastal fishing by large marine traps on quiet shores and that of controlled-pond fish culture where it has become maturely developed. Many of the estuarine and fresh-water fisheries, and those of protected coastal bays, also continue the year around. Power-boat fishing around urban centers has developed a year-round pattern to accommodate its modern commercial pattern. Pond culture in China, Thailand, Java, and the Philippines now supplies an appreciable share of local markets. That of the Philippines, for example, produced in 1951 about 60,000,000 pounds of fish, approximately 12 per cent of the total island production. South China pond culture locally produces up to 4,000 pounds of fish per acre on a regular cycle of annual harvesting.

The occupation of fishing, for the full-time professional fishermen of the Orient, with their simple equipment, basic techniques, and limited markets does not produce a high standard of living. The failure of fish to appear in regular waters, the occasional bad weather, the loss of boats, nets, traps, or other equipment during storms or accidents, the occasional glut of fish that overwhelms a market pattern unprepared to cope with large surpluses, and the other random difficulties that beset the small fisherman without capital funds, all make for fairly small returns and many financial hazards during the year. Financial returns range from $50 to $300 per fisherman per year for a large number of the full-time fishermen. A part-time fisherman may merely add fish for a few meals during the year.

One remaining item of significance is the acceptance of edible aquatic products as food by the peoples of the Orient. Religious scruples of the higher sects of Buddhists and Hindus prohibit any but a vegetarian diet, thus ruling out all fish and related aquatic foods. A fair generalization may be that over 80 per cent of all Indians may freely consume fish and related food products. In Ceylon fish curing has probably been the second most important economic activity for centuries and practically all classes of native Singhalese and more recent immigrants consume fish. Though Burmese priests technically decry fishing, all ranks of Burmese eat fishery products. The limits upon fish consumption, therefore, are less those of religious scruples than availability of supply. This points toward the fact that improvement of fishery techniques in all parts of the Orient is one of the acceptable methods of improving the dietary and food economy. Much can be done in almost all parts of the Orient to improve the yield of fishery products.

The Geography of Health and Disease

China and India are often thought of as lands in which every edible object is covered with countless harmful germs. The whole Orient, like central Africa, often brings to mind the frightening names of serious epidemic diseases like cholera and typhus, or such disfiguring ailments as leprosy and the innumerable skin infections. With these exaggerated descriptions often goes the passing judgment that the occidentals are chiefly in danger, whereas the "natives" are immune to the trials of the environment. But sometimes, as in my own family, it is said: "The children were born in the Orient, so they take these things more easily." And then statistical tabulations show that millions of "natives" die every year of preventible diseases, to add to the belief that life is cheap in the Orient. Slowly and gradually the medical world is learning about both the threats to health in the Orient and the means of preserving and lengthening human life. It is occidental medicine, in the hands both of occidental and oriental doctors, that is achieving this result. Slowly it is appearing true that, in the Orient, all men are subject to the laws of health and disease when they lead the same kinds of lives. At the same time oriental and occidental peoples do differ in their resistances or susceptibilities to different ailments. It is much too early to try to record a definitive story of this topic, but the general outline may be indicated.

THE ROLE OF CLIMATE

Since occidentals first arrived in the East the causes of ill health in the Orient have been laid at many doors. Decaying fish left by floods and high tides, foul air blowing off swamps, queer habits of human beings, disturbances of the harmonics of nature, despoiling of temples and shrines, and climate are but the commonest. Of all the causes that can be compiled, climate has been the most maligned. Every-

thing in the way of human discomfort and ailment has been at one time or another laid at its door. Certainly there is discomfort in the moist heat of a long Yangtze Valley summer, or the year-long, unvarying heat of lowland Malaya. Assuredly such climatic conditions favor the growth of bacteria, good and bad. However, it is not true that climate alone, any more than habits of eating, drinking, and clothing, causes all ailments. Nor does climate make it impossible for any one group, oriental or occidental, to live in the tropics or elsewhere in the Orient. There still are all too few data on life expectancy, the incidence of various diseases and the causes of death to permit flat statements upon this whole subject.

Varying degrees of healthfulness, however, are associated with different landscapes of the Orient. For example, the heavy cloud cover that hangs over the Szechwan Basin of western China maintains winter-long temperatures between about 33 and 45° F. With a high relative humidity and poor domestic heating arrangements, the millions of Szechwanese inhabiting the Basin suffer a high incidence of winter-long chronic colds. Better economic ability and changed cultural practices could, of course, eliminate the seasonal epidemic of colds, but the climatic factor certainly is operative. Throughout the Orient the lower foothill margins seem the least healthful zone. South of about 35° N. lat. the zone between some 2,000 feet and 5,000 to 6,000 feet seems, on the century-long experience of the hill stations and mountain resorts, to be the healthful one both for the oriental and the occidental. Man has been slow to learn of, and to utilize, this vertical zoning, and, so far, only the well-to-do can take advantage of it. Assuredly there is a climatic factor tied up in this zonal inequality.

With respect to many of the communicable diseases, Japan, before 1937, was the healthiest part of the Orient whereas, in some respects, Tibet ranked ahead of all other oriental lands. Many false generalizations are circulated concerning these matters. The tendency, also, is to make generalizations about the virility of cultures in relation to the climatic factor, but in the long histories of the various oriental peoples proof can be found both for and against any specific generalization. Too many other factors have been operative to permit climate alone to be held responsible for the level of culture in the Orient.

THE ENVIRONMENT OF DISEASE

Many causes can be advanced for the rise and fall in epidemic waves of the various severe diseases that afflict the Orient. The causes of these outbreaks are not always known, and many may lie in natural environmental conditions not yet understood by the medical world. To a considerable extent, however, the environment of disease in the Orient is a cultural one, vested in human traits, institutions, and customs. It long has been an accepted notion that the Chinese use of night soil as garden plot fertilizer contaminates all produce grown thereon, though recently real doubt has been cast on the idea, and it certainly is an unproved theory. The Japanese habit of eating large amounts of raw fish induces a wide variety of intestinal ailments. The Philippine Catholic custom of juveniles kissing the hand of elders upon all occasions of meeting seems partly responsible for the rapid spread of tuberculosis. The Indian custom of periodic and massed religious pilgrimages induced recurrent epidemics of cholera until British medical services isolated endemic centers and instituted mass preventive inoculations. The very widespread oriental custom of family communal gathering, eating, and praying with and over a sick member often operates to spread the afflicting disease. Unsanitary habits of bathing and sleeping in many parts of the Orient account for many widespread skin diseases and ailments carried by lice and similar pests. Under normal conditions these and other localized customs may well be offset by others. Thus the very old Chinese customs of drinking hot tea and eating chiefly hot food fresh from the stove serve in normal times to prevent widespread sickness from diseases carried by germs on raw vegetables and fruits. However, in times of flood, famine, or civil and military unrest Chinese general living and food habits break down under pressure, so that epidemics of many kinds become widespread and take tremendous tolls.

In the oriental failure to understand, or the casual disregard for, the means of spreading diseases, the need for isolation of infectious diseases, the need for household cleanliness and for the clean handling of food products lies the explanation of much of the high incidence of disease in the Orient. In earlier centuries, when total populations were smaller, and crowded housing and close association in large cities was less than it is today, this misunderstanding produced fewer deaths from preventible causes. Preventive medicine has made great strides in many lines, but in others lack of understanding, excessive crowding in poor housing, and neglect have greatly expanded certain ailments. Affiliated with these contributory causes is the perpetuation of ancient medical beliefs. Though many of them have proved perfectly sound in the light of modern knowledge, many others are worthless as today practiced and only worsen the total health situation.

The oriental ricefield sometimes is held to be one of the chief breeding grounds for the malaria mosquito. Undoubtedly many malaria-carrying mosquitoes do breed in ricefields, but recent research makes it clear that there are a great many species of malaria-carrying mosquitoes, breeding under all kinds of conditions, and that in most cases ricefield mosquitoes are only innocent pests. Every oriental country has its own specific environment in which malaria flourishes, so that no one cure will operate for the whole region.

Increasing relative and downright poverty of the lower segment of society, coupled with the growing custom of using refined foods, in a number of countries today has induced many ailments of malnutrition, which in turn increase susceptibilities to other ailments. Difficult circumstances during the war years, 1937–1946, increased such conditions very greatly. The widespread and excessive use of opium in varied sectors of the Orient during the last three generations also has contributed to the serious problems of health.

The sheer abundance of flies, mosquitoes, fleas and lice particularly, plus the added presence of sand flies, mites, ticks, leeches, and many kinds of parasites in different localities form a great problem. The simple housing of most of the Orient makes the exclusion of these pests very difficult. A large number of them are the primary or intermediary carriers for serious diseases; others, like the bedbug, are but haunting and distasteful pests. As in the Occident no agency, government or private, attempted their elimination in earlier centuries. The size of the job has been beyond the abilities of the small modern health services, particularly where public consciousness and cooperation is not yet fully aroused.

One rather interesting feature, and distinct blessing, is that, although the mosquitoes that carry yellow fever in Africa are very widely distributed throughout the Orient, no yellow fever has so far been reported.

THE CHIEF DISEASES AND THEIR DISTRIBUTION

Certain of the diseases of the Orient are very general in their distribution. Others are more limited in their affliction, being caused by particular local situations and customs, or being limited by organized medical services and natural environmental factors. The following discussion merely attempts to suggest the outline of conditions surrounding the more important of the oriental diseases. On accompanying maps are presented distributions for selected diseases only.

Widely Distributed Major Diseases

Considering the whole Orient it is probable that malaria is the most serious ailment. Of the many specific types of malaria discussion here will generalize these under the one name. It is one of the most widely distributed diseases, in the regional sense and, owing to the method by which it is spread, often has a higher incidence among the general population than does any other disease. In many regions practically the whole population suffers, and it is particularly hard on children. Statistics suggest that over 100,000,000 cases occur every year in India, more than 20,000,000 per year in the Indies, and at least that many in China. Its chief result is not death directly, but a lethargic and weakened population which falls prey to secondary diseases. Nevertheless, incomplete medical statistics point to the probability that about 4,000,000 orientals die every year of malaria alone, in normal years. When widespread unsettled conditions obtain, this figure may be doubled. The accompaning map depicts the very general variation in seriousness of the disease.

Since there is no single species of vector, there is not just one set of breeding conditions or one method of eliminating malaria. In northern Borneo as the jungle is cut off and the lands are put into ricefields malaria recedes with the jungle, for here the vector is a jungle-breeding mosquito. In British Malaya, however, cutting off the jungle only induces the invasion of a new malaria vector, breeding in fresh running waters under quite different conditions. In upper Bengal and Assam, after much land was cleared and cultivated, partial relief from malaria carried by mosquitoes breeding in sunny running streams was provided by planting shade trees along the streams.

Throughout the moist portions of the Orient today malaria is worst along the rough foothill tracts that normally remain in jungle growth and forest. Below, on those flat plains that long ago became well cleared and populated, malaria seldom has strikingly high in-cidences today though mosquitoes are numerous and annoying. Above the foothills, at an elevation of roughly 2,000 feet, mosquitoes disappear and malaria dies out. The foothill zones surrounding old settled plains remain constant and serious malaria threats. In the colonial spread of population in southeastern Asia, the Philippines and the Indies, the foothill jungle-forest fringes often threaten the success of settlement by causing extremely high incidences of several kinds of malaria, some of them having high mortality rates. This foothill health hazard may account for the failure of the Annamese to colonize the empty hill country behind the narrow and over-crowded coastal plain of Indochina. The large amount of jungle and forest growth in southern China, the moist areas of India and throughout moist southeastern Asia, both on the lowlands, and in the foothill zone just above the lowlands, make for an almost permanently endemic zone of malarial diseases. Recurrent abandonment of once settled tracts through historic change has renewed these conditions in areas once relatively free of such diseases. Thus eastern and northern Ceylon today has a serious malaria problem in areas once healthy and heavily populated.

Despite modern medicine no truly adequate, cheap, and easily administered curative or preventive drug has become available to date for all the population of the Orient. Currently various new synthetic wonder drugs are being hailed as permanent cures. Relatively efficient permanent reduction in malarial incidence may occur in selected localities, but complete success in the Orient still is questionable. Mosquitoes may become adapted to these drugs just as other insect life elsewhere has failed to become extinct under the application of modern scientific discoveries. The preventive problem has barely been tackled. There is reason to doubt that, in a region of very moist climates, of permanent forest and jungle, any full preventive procedure ever can be devised and adapted to the physical and cultural local environments now present. The mosquito net seems to be a permanent piece of housekeeping equipment among those peoples southward of central China who aspire to even relative freedom from malaria. The somewhat harsh conclusion therefore presents itself that severe malaria is going to be with the Orient a long time.

Tuberculosis is today an extremely serious disease almost everywhere in the Orient, and in some regions it is more serious than malaria. The causes for its rise are complex and not well understood. Very little is being done against its spread, except in a few selected regions and on a very small scale. Excessive crowding in cities and towns, malnutrition, and changed food and clothing habits are perhaps the more important reasons.

Each of these will continue operative in the future. Whereas the well-to-do may secure treatment today, the huge poverty-stricken section of oriental society cannot afford the rest cure that is the best prescription the medical world can give at present. With a mortality rate from five to ten times as great as that of tuberculosis areas. Lack of proper control over domestic water sources and over sewage disposal is a chief contributing cause, and proper control in these matters is very scattered and spotty throughout the Orient.

Typhus is a term for several diseases carried by fleas, lice, and a variety of mites. Too little notice of it was

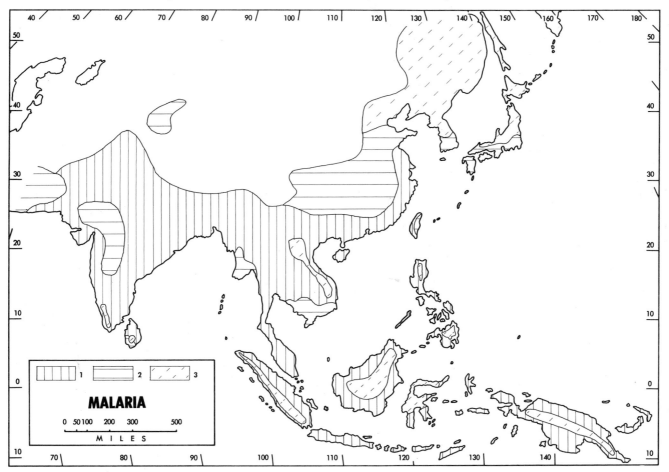

Fig. 27. Distribution of malaria: (1) incidence of pandemic proportions except in local highlands and local lowlands long fully settled; (2) incidence normally of moderate proportions except for local highlands; (3) incidence normally of minor proportions. Blank areas are affected only spasmodically.

in the United States, and with perhaps 100,000,000 people afflicted to some degree, the problem is becoming steadily more serious.

The several types of dysentery, grouped together, form another serious threat to the health and life of the whole Orient. The several varieties are endemic almost everywhere, so that the disruption of normal living conditions ordinarily means an epidemic. Ordinarily the rainy seasons of the year increase the number of cases in some areas, though in regions with prolonged dry seasons and water shortages the dry season may be the worst period of the year. Usually the dysenteries are more serious in crowded urban regions than in rural

taken in much of the Orient until perhaps 1930, but the incidence is much greater than the sporadic records would indicate. Its vector in Manchuria, North China, Korea, and much of India is a louse, whereas in most of the rest of the mainland it is a flea. On the mainland borders of southeastern Asia and in those parts of the islands where heavy grass is important in the present vegetation cover mite-borne typhus is found, although little was known of it until World War II. In the years of peace, preceding 1937, typhus had been widely endemic but seldom epidemic. During the war years North China and Manchuria suffered severe epidemics, and outbreaks of "scrub typhus," the mite-borne variety, occurred among military forces and civilians throughout southeastern Asia. Under the best clinical conditions mortality is not high, but under neglected wartime conditions it often ran above 20 per cent.

Often associated with typhus in epidemic conditions is relapsing fever, also a louse-carried ailment widely

seems something cyclic in the virility of epidemics of cholera, and in such years a high mortality results. Its treatment under organized conditions reduces the mortality greatly, and preventive measures applied regionally can reduce its threat. The unsettled conditions of many recent years in the Orient, and the inability of undermanned and ill-equipped bureaus dealing with

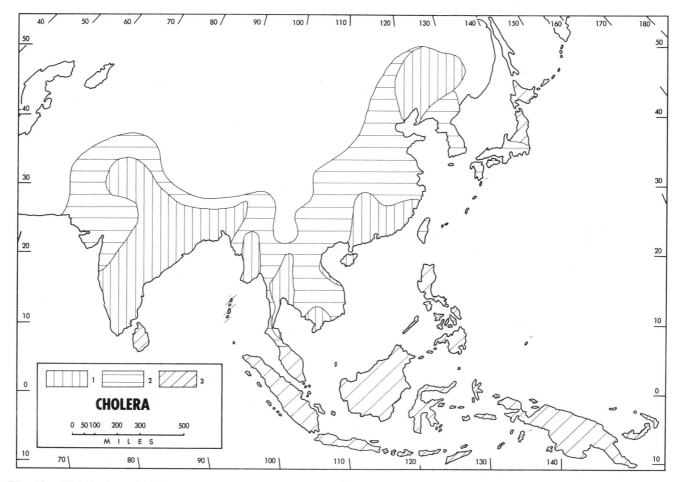

Fig. 28. Distribution of cholera: endemic centers suffering frequent epidemics; (2) areas of low normal incidence but occasional epidemics; (3) areas of sporadic occurrence and rare local epidemics.

distributed over the Asiatic mainland. In China relapsing fever is much more common in the south, where typhus is apt to be lighter. The kind of conditions that promote epidemics of typhus also stimulates relapsing fever.

Cholera is one of those oriental diseases best known in the Occident. It is very widely endemic though medical control in most of the island regions has reduced it to an unimportant position. Cholera ordinarily is a late summer disease that flashes up from its endemic centers in rapidly and widely spreading epidemics when unsettled conditions prevail in a major region. There

large populations have rendered its complete control and eradication impossible. China and India have been the two worst regions; the island zone has been relatively free since 1930. Organized British measures have reduced the impact of epidemics in India but have not cleared up the endemic centers. The accompanying map displays the broad regional spread of cholera.

Plague is another oriental disease rather fatalistically accepted by many orientals but greatly feared by the modern Occident. Most of the Orient except western China, Tibet, and Central Asia are variably affected by plague. The south coast of China, central India, and a number of small areas in the Burmo-Malayan peninsula are endemic centers for plague and suffer almost annual attacks. Its regional distribution is shown on an accompanying map. From South China, in the last century, it has spread clear into Manchuria and now seems rather deeply intrenched in inland Fukien and in Manchuria. Annual epidemics, varying in intensity, trated. Mosquitoes are the vectors in both cases. Mortality rates are not high, but both cause rather prolonged periods of ill health. The area from south China and central India through the Indies is the chief zone of occurrence. Dengue fever is a disease which often afflicts occidentals newly arrived in areas in which the disease is prevalent.

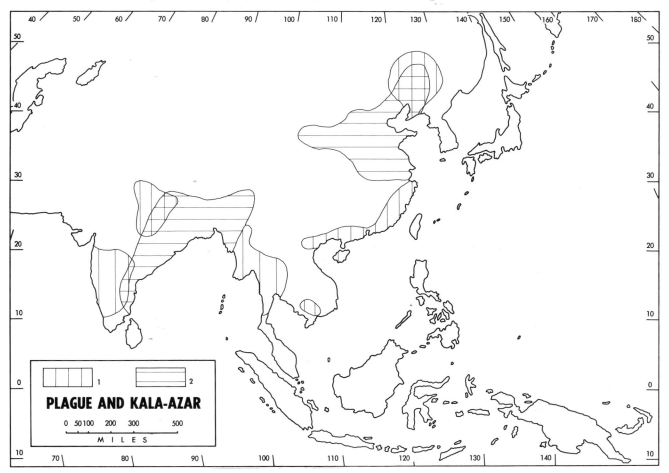

Fig. 29. Centers of plague and kala-azar: (1) endemic homes and chief regions afflicted by plague; (2) regions of incidence of kala-azar.

have been rather common in local areas in many parts of the mainland Orient. Extensive efforts by organized medical services were making considerable headway when the war stopped the work in 1937. Korea, Japan, and Formosa, under organized Japanese efforts, have held control over the disease, and no epidemic situations have developed in the last several decades. Similarly the Philippines and British Malaya have not suffered outbreaks since 1925. The Indies house a number of small endemic regions, but no serious outbreak has occurred in some decades.

Dengue fever and blackwater fever are two relatives of malaria that are widely spread but locally concen-

Under the general term filariasis are a number of types of worm infections for which some of the mosquitoes are the vectors. These diseases affect a rather narrow band of country from southern Korea and southern Japan clear around to the Red Sea and across to the north coast of Australia. Occidentals, with ordinary care, seldom are affected, but sporadic epidemics and localized endemic situations occur very widely.

Yaws is a disease which affects the native peoples from the east coast of India and Hainan Island through New Guinea. The occidental seldom is bothered by the ailment. In considerable part a malnutritional ailment, it is also a disease prevalent in areas short of water supply. It is rather easily cleared up by medical treatment, though it will return unless the mode of living is improved. It has a rather low mortality, but it permits secondary infection and is uncomfortable and unsightly. It is not epidemic in the ordinary sense, though in some localized areas its incidence may run as high as 90 per cent of the population.

Widely Distributed Minor Diseases

A number of diseases prevalent in the Orient are considered differently there from in the Occident. Typhoid fever, smallpox, measles, and similar diseases all are widespread, but not often do they reach large epidemic proportions. Mortality rates in local areas occasionally are high, but the over-all effect of each ailment is far less than for some of those already mentioned. For the occidental the oriental strains of some of these diseases often seem more virulent than those of his homeland, and precautions are mandatory.

Pneumonia and influenza are paid rather scant heed by the populace and the medical profession alike, but they occur in large numbers with rather serious results. Spring and autumn seasons, and the onset of the rainy season with its moist and cooler air, produce cyclic ups and downs in incidence.

Leprosy is a disease very casually accepted in the Orient, without segregation, except where occidental colonial control has motivated it. The Philippines and British Malaya have most completely put segregation into effect. Almost the whole of the Orient is affected, but South China and the central peninsular portion of India seem to be the chief centers. An estimated 2,500,000 individuals are afflicted in the whole of the Orient.

Serious eye ailments caused by trachoma, smallpox, and venereal diseases, afflict perhaps 40,000,000 orientals. Again China and India are the areas worst affected. Apathy and carelessness are the two worst cultural factors in the situation. The end result of complete blindness and physical incapacitation affects perhaps 5,000,000 people in the whole of the Orient.

Venereal diseases are very widespread everywhere in the Orient, with less concern over the final implications than in parts of the Occident today. Prostitution is more widely prevalent, and, among many societies and cultural groups, sexual promiscuity is rather common, promoting the scattering of all five types of venereal disease. Very few statistics are available in this field.

Skin infections, such as impetigo, scabies, and the several tinea infections, also are extremely common in almost every part of the Orient. Normal peaceful conditions permit a population to exercise some control over many of these ailments, despite the warm and moist climate prevailing over much of the Orient. Unsettled conditions and extreme poverty rapidly increase skin infections. In many local areas a large share of the population seems to be affected. To the traveler parts of central and north China seem to have the highest incidence of skin ailments of any part of the Orient, but this may well not prove true when statistics become available.

Regionally Confined Diseases

A number of ailments are confined by environmental conditions to particular regions of the Orient. One of the most serious of them is kala-azar, an ailment carried by a sand fly. It occurs from the north side of the Yangtze Valley into Manchuria in China and from Madras into Assam in India. It is active during the summer, becoming locally epidemic. More active in rural than urban areas, it chiefly affects children and younger adults. Without proper medical care the disease has a rather high mortality. Its regional distribution is shown in Fig. 29.

The central and lower Yangtze Valley is the chief home of a rather serious disease common among farming populations who frequent the many creeks and canals in fishing and farming operations. A snail living in the creeks and canals is the intermediary carrier for schistosomiasis. The China coast southward toward Canton and some minor areas in interior South China also are affected.

Perhaps more properly listed under skin ailments is copra itch, common to the coconut-producing regions from Ceylon around to the Philippines.

Southern Korea and the main Japanese islands are peculiarly afflicted by a large series of parasites carried by fish. The custom of eating raw fish is largely responsible for this particular group of intestinal worms and other parasites.

Central western Yunnan, the Yunnan-Tibetan border, and northern Laos form a large region afflicted with goiter. This region consumes salt produced from local springs and wells, deficient in iodine, and is isolated from contact with the seacoast towns through which either sea salt or fish products can come in adequate quantities. North Borneo contains another small region in which goiter affliction is common. A few other minor regions are also affected.

A great many special regional diseases of significance affect particular territories of the Orient about which little is commonly known. Many missionary, private, and public health doctors have learned something of how to cope with them, but a large amount of exploratory and comparative medical work will be required to deal adequately with the mass of these diseases.

PROBLEMS OF MALNUTRITION AND FAMINE

Beri-beri is often thought of as a disease affecting occidentals on shipboard during the seventeenth to early nineteenth centuries. It is a disease of malnutrition caused by the lack of a well-rounded diet and the lack of fresh vitamin-rich foods. Several of these malnutritional diseases have affected various parts of the world in recent centuries. It is not commonly known, however, that beri-beri and related diseases provoked by dietary deficiencies are extremely common throughout the Orient today. They have been increasing in seriousness within the last century and today are particularly common in the towns and cities of most parts of the Orient. There are a number of contributing causes, some of which are environmental but most of which are economic or cultural.

Not much is yet known concerning the comparative nutritional value of given foods grown on varying types of soils. It is common to assume a standard caloric value for rice, oranges, or carrots regardless of the variety or parent field. Vitamin and mineral content, as well as nutritional worth, are assumed as equivalent everywhere. Common consideration regards only quantity per acre as changing with different soils or cultural practices. Almost no oriental data of an objective sort are so far available in this field, but there can be little question that the overworked and the depleted soils of parts of India must not only produce low yields per acre but foods lower in quality than those young and rich soils of parts of Java or the culturally fortified soils of much of China. What may be the role of climate, soil, water, and other environmental factors in nutrition and general health is yet speculative, but certain it is that there are regional differences in this matter in an area as large and as variably used as the Orient. A considerable share of modern oriental malnutrition may derive from a misunderstood and overworked physical environment.

The economic factor of modern regional poverty of many oriental areas is a large factor contributing to widespread malnutrition. A majority of orientals today are simply too poor to be able to purchase foods adequate to maintain themselves in reasonable health. The prosperous and the rich can afford a sufficiently wide variety of diet to maintain a high level of health, but too many millions of people in all parts of the Orient must restrict their diets to what they can grow or purchase, and the variety of food types too often is very narrow and restricted to the cheaper, basic carbohydrates. Simple poverty often prohibits even an adequate volume of food consumption as well as a limited range.

But it is on cultural practices that much of the blame must rest for modern malnutritional diseases. Just as the West has shifted from whole-grain wheat breads to impoverished white-flour breads with the rise of industrial wheat milling, so much of the Orient shifted from whole rice to polished rice. In the Orient highly milled wheat is increasing in use, and gradually many other kinds of refined foods are coming into volume consumption. These practices first showed up in port cities frequented by occidental traders, missionaries, and orientals returned from abroad with new habits in diet. They have gradually spread to other cities, towns, and rural hinterlands and are part and parcel of the process of westernization commonly held as marking the progress of the Orient. And malnutrition has followed closely behind, so that beri-beri and similar diseases are an inevitable result. They affect chiefly the middle classes and the urban poor, who have accepted the milled rice, white flour, and refined foods but neither know as yet how to supplement diets nor can afford the expensive extracts made from rice milling.

Thus the cities and towns of the Orient are the centers of extensive nutritional ailments that weaken and starve millions of people. And as these practices have spread into rural hinterlands they have affected whole populations of many regions of the Orient. Small-scale attacks on the problem, such as the fortification of milled rice in parts of the Philippines, have made tremendous changes in the health and well being of regional populations, but much remains to be done to repair the impact of changed cultural practices of the last century and a half.

HOSPITALS, MEDICAL PERSONNEL, AND PUBLIC HEALTH SERVICES

Throughout the whole Orient medical services are scarce and completely inadequate to deal with the problems of the huge population. In selected cities the number of hospital beds, doctors, nurses, dentists, and technicians stands not far below the levels prevalent in the better-served parts of the Occident. In general, however, these per capita services for the rural countryside, the small towns, and the isolated hinterlands are almost hopelessly low compared to the needs. In India only about three fourths of the cities over 50,000 population have piped water systems with proper medical control, and very few smaller settlements are so served. In China the proportion thus served is even lower than in India. In the Philippines, on the other hand, most towns, even small ones, have piped systems that provide safe, clean water. India has some 7,000 hospitals with a total of nearly 100,000 beds, about one thirtieth of the bed space available in the United States, per capita. India has but 1 qualified doctor to about 6,500 people and 1 dentist to some 300,000 people, whereas the Philippines has 1 doctor to about 4,000 people and one dentist to some 7,500 people. In the Republic of Indonesia there is but 1 modern-trained doctor for every 60,000 people. Increasing output of medical personnel generally is gradually improving conditions in many areas, but these tend first to be centralized in urbanized regions and frequently they are far from endemic homes and epidemic centers. As trained personnel do become available the wider extension of public health services continues. Every country has medical schools and national and local public health services of some sort.

In general, Japan has medical services which prevent epidemics in many of the diseases rampant elsewhere, though many others go almost untreated. The Philippines have perhaps the best all-round medical services of any part of the Orient. In part the credit may lie with the United States, but, on the other hand, the Filipinos seem attracted to medicine as a profession and make good practitioners in all its phases. Both in British Malaya and in the Indies rather effective work had been done in certain lines, before 1942, but the whole health program must start over again. Both China and India, however, presented problems almost too large for solution in a period of a few decades. The hill country of northern Indochina, northern Thailand, northern Burma, and southwestern China comprised a back-country almost completely neglected by medical services before 1937, but containing seriously threatening endemic and epidemic conditions dangerous to all surrounding territories.

There is a tremendous well of indifference, ignorance, adherence to traditional behavior, and acceptance of traditional medical procedures that makes the problem of the medical pioneer a hard one. Refusal of the patient to follow directions, and the inability of medical workers to enforce known procedures, is a story told all over the Orient.

The Peoples and Their Languages

WHERE IS THE GARDEN OF EDEN?

Regardless of just where in the Old World one located the Garden of Eden, it would probably be within reach of some part of the Orient. It has become quite evident that early man wandered very widely indeed, and there probably are few, if any, sizable areas of land outside Antarctica through which early man did not pass many times. Sometimes these migrations left certain localities quite empty, whereas at other times groups of people remained to occupy a landscape for a period. Thus the island group, known as the Moluccas, or the Malabar coast of India, must have been discovered many times before the Portuguese and Spaniards started the modern search for the fabulous Spice Islands. But if man went just about everywhere in his early wanderings, certain regions, at least, have been continuously occupied during most of the period of human existence. It appears that, despite some recurrent immigration from outside, modern east Asian man is a lineal descendant of earliest east Asian man.

Whether or not the human races had a multiple origin, several regions have served as population incubators to spill out the human beings that have populated much of the earth since middle Paleolithic time. Apparently three major regions helped in populating the lands of the Orient. An east African locality seems the most probable source of the Negrito and other members of the Negroid family of races. Southwestern Asia contributed the strains lumped together under the heading of the Caucasoid family of races. Central eastern to northeastern Asia served as the home region for the units making up the Mongoloid family of races. It seems reasonable that the Negroid and Caucasoid incubators were the earliest to start spreading their broods, and that the Mongoloid races are somewhat younger.

Since 1600 certain regions have been producing large surpluses of people that probably exceed any incubator broods of the earlier past for sheer numbers. Thus the populating of Manchuria by millions of surplus Chinese from Chahar, Hopei, and Shantung since 1900 is a contemporary expression of a racial incubator. Kwangtung has sent a smaller modern wave of Chinese into Indochina, Thailand, Malaya, the Philippines, and the Indies that may eventually have important results in terms of race mixture. Indian migration to Burma and Malaya is yet another example, less liable to race mixture owing to the labor-contract terms and restricted freedoms involved. The Dutch tried for years to start a Javanese exodus to the Outer Territories, without real success. Equally the Japanese have failed in colonizing the Asiatic mainland.

RACE MIXTURE AND MOVEMENT

The suggestion of primary centers of human types does not preclude both later mixing and the evolution of special local strains, as groups from the several centers have wandered widely, crossed paths, become swallowed up, produced new types, or stagnated in particular localities. This varied result must always have been the consequence of the peripatetic nature of human beings. Extreme mixing is the only explanation of the modern Japanese or the Indian, and wide wandering the only answer to the Philippine Negrito and the Ainu of Japan.

As the early and late products of any one incubator certainly varied, the end product of race mixture also has varied. Such local variants as the Chinese Moslems of Kansu and the Anglo-Indian are expressions of the process. It is almost impossible to tell just how much of what racial elements have gone into the blend that is the contemporary Javanese. Most

Javanese mixing occurred in the protohistoric era, and the rapid growth of population within the last 500 years has produced a hybrid strain that runs fairly true to type. The Chinese, Indian, Arabic, and Dutch additions to Java in the last 5 centuries are substantially small in proportionate volume and have not materially altered the Javanese subrace, though they have produced some radical local variants.

Stray columns of proto-Negroid and proto-Caucasoid peoples penetrated southeastern Asia and Australasia. The earliest mixtures of these strains must have occurred at a very early date. Over most of southeastern Asia went the Negrito, to be a factor in the makeup of almost every people south of China. Today there remains only a remnant of each on the Andaman Islands, in southwestern Indochina, and in the Malay Peninsula, a few thousands in the Philippines, and an unknown number in New Guinea. As a lowland-valley forest people by preference, they have had but little of the right kind of country into which to retreat before invaders and have melted away over the centuries, except in New Guinea to which fewer peoples came later. In New Guinea and near-by eastern islands, in the interiors, survival of mixed Negroid strains, such as the Papuans, is much more complete than in the western islands of the Indies. The Philippines show little evidence of the earliest Caucasoid peoples, but considerably more of the Negrito.

On the mainland of southeastern Asia, it is difficult to recognize and label more than a small residual effect of the earliest Negroid or Caucasoid peoples, with a little more Negrito influence, but unquestionably all three elements are present in the racial understructure of the region. Here proto-Mongoloid and Mongoloid stocks predominate.

It is difficult to suggest just how and by what means race movement through today's island world occurred. It is not at all clear for how long the present distribution of land and sea has been fixed. The main oceanic deeps lie outside the Island Arcs, and most of the present coastal seas are very shallow. Man certainly was exploring the land world before the final close of the Glacial Epoch, and the diffusion and mixing of the earliest groups of contemporary men probably began before the contemporary landscape was cut up into islands by the rising and widening of the seascape to its present extent.

It seems fair to suggest that in India the mixture of proto-Negroid and proto-Caucasoid was not at all uniform, yielding a northern variant with lighter colored skins and a southern one, more nearly black. The primary zones of Negroid and Caucasoid expansion lay not eastward into India but within Africa and toward Europe, respectively. Later Caucasoid additions to India have been insufficient to lighten skin coloring and dominate the racial blend in eastern and southern India. Southeastern Asia received directly only small numbers of later Caucasoid and later Negroid races. Instead hybrid peoples from different parts of India moved eastward during the Christian era in sufficiently strong numbers to contribute significantly to the blood stream of the western Indies, southern Burma, southern Thailand, and southern Indochina. A few centuries after the Christian era began, this Indian movement slackened off markedly, to be resumed again at later dates. Within India itself the prevailing trend of human movement has been southward and eastward ever since the last big Caucasoid immigration began in the third millennium B.C. This sometimes led to the deep penetration and isolating of certain racial groups as in the Nilgiri Hills, but in general it served to foster slow intermixture. There have been a few countermovements of peoples, the most notable of which is probably the emigration from India toward Europe of the Gypsy strain from the northwestern peninsular region about 1,000 years ago.

Out of the Mongoloid race incubator has come a succession of peoples as variable as those from the Negroid or Caucasoid hearths. The earliest waves probably spread in all directions, but found the easiest zone of movement in eastern mainland Asia. Into the Philippines, southeastern Asia, and the western Indies moved the early proto-Mongoloid groups to share the region with representatives of the early Negroid and Caucasoid races. Some of these peoples spread out further eastward into the South Pacific. The amount of true mixing may be questioned, but certainly there was some. The western Indies produced a countermovement of mixed peoples who are often termed proto-Malay. They are sometimes also labeled Indonesian "A" and Indonesian "B," respectively. The line of this movement was locally into Malaya, but also it trended northward along the coast and through the Island Arcs, reaching to southern Japan and touching most of the coast and all the islands between Sumatra and Honshu. Some areas received successive waves of these people; northern coastal embayments and islands were reached less often. The other direction of proto-Malay and Malay movement, eastward into the Pacific, is of less interest in this study.

On the eastern Asiatic mainland the Mongoloid races were dominant and spread continuously southward in waves that carried them throughout Indochina, Thailand, and Burma, though not until modern times have they again moved into the Indies. Negroid, Caucasoid, and Malay blends of peoples have merged into the spreading Mongoloid races or remained as islands of isolation around the coastal fringe of southeastern Asia. This locally has noticeably altered the modern racial type, but nowhere did it stem the southward drift of Mongoloid peoples. In some cases only the barest of

Already beyond them were the Ainu, usually thought of as a mixture of proto-Mongoloid and proto-Caucasoid or Caucasoid-like people who had taken an unusual migration path to become lost in the enveloping Mongoloid realm and develop into a special physical

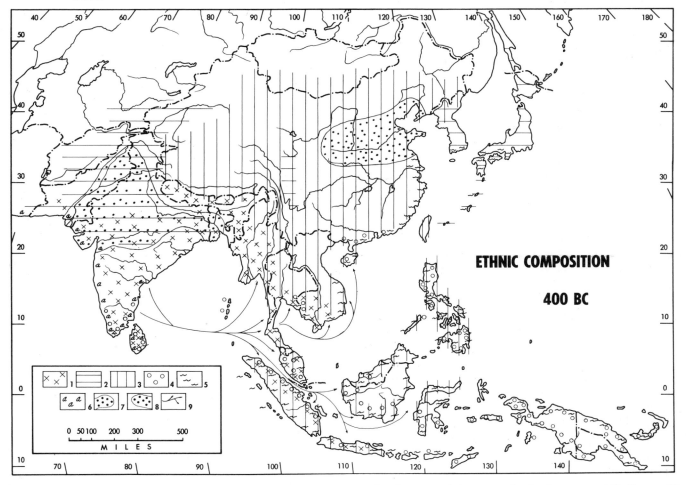

ETHNIC COMPOSITION

400 BC

Fig. 30. Patterns of ethnic contact, about 400 B.C.: (1) remnants of unknown racial groups of mixed ancestry; (2) Caucasoid peoples of variable origin and time of arrival; (3) Mongoloid peoples of variable origin and time of arrival; (4) Negroid peoples of variable origin and time of arrival, now variably intermixed with earlier arrivals; (5) proto-Malay and Malay peoples of variable time of arrival; (6) Arab-Mediterranean port and coastal residents; (7) encloses Indian culture hearth; (8) encloses Chinese culture hearth; (9) "Indian" colonial contacts.

traces remain, in the vague stories of myths and legends, and the random curly hair and facial features which point to some kind of Negroid people in southernmost China at some early date.

The Mongols proper may well be the youngest strain of the Mongoloid race, occupying a home somewhere near the racial incubator location. Into eastern Manchuria and Korea at an early date had gone waves of proto-Mongoloid and Mongoloid peoples to become somewhat blended and probably mixed with some non-Mongoloids as the source for the modern Koreans.

type. The least that can be said is that the stocky, olive-skinned, curly-haired, brown- to hazel-eyed Ainu, growing heavy beards and much body hair, resemble no other Mongoloid people. At one time they seem to have ranged from the southern Ryukyu Islands to Hokkaido, with some influence as far south as Luzon in the Philippines. They have entered strongly into the makeup of the modern Japanese and probably also the Koreans. There seem to be several racial elements intermixed but not synthesized in the modern Japanese, so that there are several kinds of "typical Japanese."

In addition to Ainu there seem to be proto-Malay, early Mongoloid, and later Korean hybrids, but no satisfactory analysis of Japanese racial origins has yet been made.   Northward spread a number of Mongoloid groups into Siberia and beyond, out of the scope of this volume.

similar escape was possible.   In particular the Chota Nagpur hill region of northeast peninsular India and the Indian and Chinese Tibetan borderlands have served the earlier races of men in the struggle to maintain themselves.   On the Chinese side of Tibet there may well be remnants of Caucasoid migration groups.   The

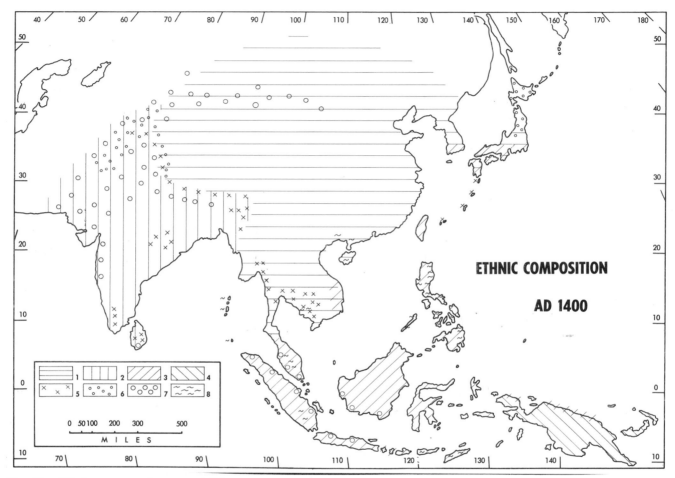

Fig. 31.   Ethnic patterns about A.D. 1400: (1) Mongoloid mixed stocks; (2) Indian mixed stocks; (3) Malay mixed stocks; (4) Papuan mixed stocks; (5) mixed remnants of uncertain origin; (6) old Caucasoid Ainu remnants; (7) recent Caucasoid immigrants; (8) Negrito remnant peoples.

Everywhere in the Orient are marks indicating that the broad movements just suggested have not resulted in full racial synthesis and that they still are not completed.   That some Negrito exist in quite pure form in the Philippines is ample proof of the failure of synthesis, just as their impurity in Malaya and also in the Philippines points to mixture.   Throughout the Island Arcs there are numerous spots of refuge that housed some fairly pure racial strains and allowed them to escape some part of the blending process.   On the mainland several rough hill land regions served both as homes of refuge and as lines of infiltration by which

invasions of barbarians into China throughout the Christian era and the coming of the Moslems to India in the last 1,000 years are major items in the process. In the coming of the Europeans since the discoveries, the mass migrations of Chinese during the Sino-Japanese War, and the mass transfers of Moslem and Hindu Indians upon the division of India are seen important recent episodes in the further mixing of races in the Orient.

In regional summary one may describe the modern racial patterns of eastern Asia in the following terms. No political state in the Orient is populated by a single race, every country containing a multiple mixture. Caucasoid stocks entered directly into this mixture in every country, early or late. Negroid stocks have been direct contributors everywhere except in Tibet, north China, Manchuria, Korea, and Japan. Mongoloid stocks have contributed directly to every region except New Guinea and India south of the Himalayan mountain wall and a portion of northwest India.

Notwithstanding the extreme mixture of primary racial stocks, simple generalizations may be made. Pakistan is chiefly composed of Caucasoid stocks, both in east and west sectors. North India is largely Caucasoid, whereas southern India is very mixed in composition. Burma and Thailand are populated by early Mongoloid stocks over an early base of mixed peoples. Indochina contains a regionally variable mixture of Mongoloid stocks, varying from very early to recent, merged into a mixture of early peoples. Malaya is almost equally composed of Malays and Chinese, both being mixed Mongoloid stocks. The western Indies are mostly Malay, but eastward the Negroid element increases, and there enters a wide variety of mixture. The Philippines is populated by peoples mostly Malay in origin, but with considerable early Negroid and other mixed elements, and with a considerable addition of modern Chinese elements. China is chiefly Mongoloid, but this involves very early and rather recent types. And in the south it includes some Negrito, and in the northwest some Caucasoid. Korea is a very diverse mixture of early Caucasoid and Mongoloid, with considerable late Mongoloid addition. Japan often has been considered predominantly Malay, but this seems unlikely. More probable is a variety of early to middle Mongoloids drawn from different parts of the mainland, composing the larger source of the modern Japanese. Into this variety were absorbed the proto-Caucasoid Ainu and a steady increment from Korea, this latter itself a composite population. Obviously these simple generalizations are gross generalizations, but they are as valid as any one-or-two sentence answers can be to the question: "What are the peoples of the United States?" Two maps of ethnic patterns (pp. 117-118) help to define regional patterns and to suggest changes in the period before the arrival of the occidental. These maps are more suggestive than factual, since little work has been done in historical anthropology in the Orient.

THE PATTERNS OF LANGUAGE

Language often may bear no relationship to race, a fact to which many third-generation Americans can bear strong witness. The language map of the Orient today is a complicated mosaic of nearly a thousand languages and their dialects. To some degree this map exhibits facts in the movement and mixture of races, but there are borrowed languages among peoples who have lost their own original speech. Also there has been marked change in the structure and vocabulary of certain languages whose users have moved into new environments and rubbed shoulders with older, unrelated inhabitants. Certain language families or dialects appear dominant in usage and gain speakers by the spread of speech; others are recessive and gradually are replaced. The Indo-European languages of northern India are gaining ground against the Dravidian family of languages of southern India, and the northern dialect of Chinese is gaining ground against other Chinese dialects. Negrito remnants of southeastern Asia, except the Andamanese, have lost their own mother tongue and borrow the language of their neighbors.

Anthropologists and linguists often have tried to arrange the world's languages schematically into family groups by classifying them in various ways. For the Orient there has so far been no real agreement in these matters and the student of another discipline finds himself caught up in a quarrel over whether this or that tongue really belongs to one or another speech family. Admittedly it is a perplexing problem, for man's wanderings, his cultural borrowings, his linguistic shifts, and his racial intermixture all are involved. The problem of classification is not made simpler in that definitive studies have yet to be made of many recessive languages and that even simple and accurate recordings are lacking for numerous refugee groups who are hidden away in regions that are hard to get at. It will be decades before all the oriental languages are well enough recorded and compared to permit even a simple classification.

Despite these linguistic conflicts it is possible to map the distribution of language groups in very general terms and to tabulate their proportionate usage among the peoples of the Orient. Early wanderers into southern Asia spoke tongues that sometimes have been grouped into an Austro-Asiatic family of languages. These at one time covered much more territory than they do today, and they left their marks on several other language families. Today the group is represented on the mainland by scattered languages ranging from northwest India to British Malaya and possibly by a few languages from the Indies. Austronesian is the name often used to cover another series of languages that variably includes several from Thailand and Indochina along with all those reaching as far out as Polynesia.

The Dravidian languages of southern India form another large family with four main groupings. Surely, race and speech have become disconnected in this case, with many borrowings and alterations. Certain subgroups have been increasing in frequency of use in recent centuries owing to population increase of their speakers, whereas others are quite recessive both in region and numbers. From Persia through the Pamirs and across northern India into Assam are spread nearly forty major languages and four hundred dialects that make up the three main branches of the Indo-European languages. In the northwestern mountain country there are many isolated groups that have lost their former close relations to languages now spoken out on the North Indian Plain. In general these three language groups have been steadily pushing back the Dravidian and other remnant tongues of central and southern India, but they have suffered modification in the process. Into the major languages of the Indo-Aryan branch have gone many contributions, increasing their differences. Hindi, with its dialects the most common north Indian tongue, has maintained its own grammar, but its alphabet and script are Persian, which belongs to quite another branch of the Indo-European languages. The modern vocabulary of Hindi is drawn from classical Sanskrit, several Dravidian languages, Persian, and Arabic. These effects largely were produced from within, by Hindu Indians rather than by outsiders or conquerors.

At the final count the Tibeto-Chinese language family may number over a hundred and fifty languages and some two hundred dialects distributed in the zone from southern Burma and Thailand through northern Manchuria, and from Japan and Formosa into western Tibet. Within this great area are many divergent linguistic elements, but there is less argument over the relation and affiliation of tongues than in the other main groups. Among the modern Tibeto-Chinese languages are a number of striking borrowings. Burmese and Thai are of this group, yet they use an alphabet and a script borrowed from India and quite recently fitted to the two tongues. Japanese is a marginal member of the family, an unwritten polysyllabic speech that borrowed the Chinese script developed for a monosyllabic speech. More recently the Japanese evolved their *kana* "alphabet" in an effort to bridge this gap, the result being an extraordinarily complex linguistic system in which relatively few Japanese really are at home. Korean has gone through a similar evolution. Mongol and Manchu, on the other hand, are written vertically like Chinese but with an Arabic script developed only after the thirteenth century. Even Chi-

nese itself has gone through many phonetic changes by virtue of borrowing and evolutionary change. The Mandarin dialect rapidly is dominating the spoken language picture; the continuity of the written language has given China a much closer bond of unity than that possessed by India or Europe.

THE GROWTH OF POPULATION

Enough has been said to indicate that many different regions have taken their turn at producing surplus human beings who irregularly wandered into far lands or who swarmed in mass migrations into neighboring regions. The process is an old one that in its early stages had more numerous checks and balances in it than are operative today. It is difficult to resurrect the population history by which the Orient has come to house over half the world's population, for the Orient seems always to have disguised its numbers or failed to handle statistics with finite accuracy, this being a modern occidental passion.

A good environment coupled with a certain degree of inventiveness and curiosity and backed by favorable social organization stimulated successful operation of certain early societies, and gave them an advantage over much of the rest of the world. It seems likely that some parts of the Orient have been among the most heavily populated parts of the world throughout much of human existence. All the common factors that make for increase of population in any part of the world operate with equal effectiveness in India, China, or Java, and, as the several cultural realms of Eurasia advanced in attainments and numbers, favored sections of the Orient probably kept ahead of the rest in population. India was in this favored list almost from the beginning, China entered it in the third or perhaps fourth millennium B.C., and Java and Japan worked their way into this position in the early centuries of the Christian era.

From India were made the first exploratory trade and colonial feelers by peoples possessing a certain sophistication in social and political matters. Thus it was Indian stimulus that sponsored the formation, growth, and development of the cultural centers that arose in each of several distinctive regional environments of southeastern Asia. Southeastern Asia had been a source of numerous groups that lacked a strong and cohesive culture and so spread themselves all over the western Pacific Ocean. The strength of Hindu culture gave rise to a series of states that slowly concentrated population on Java and near-by islands to give it a lead in numbers among the regions of south-

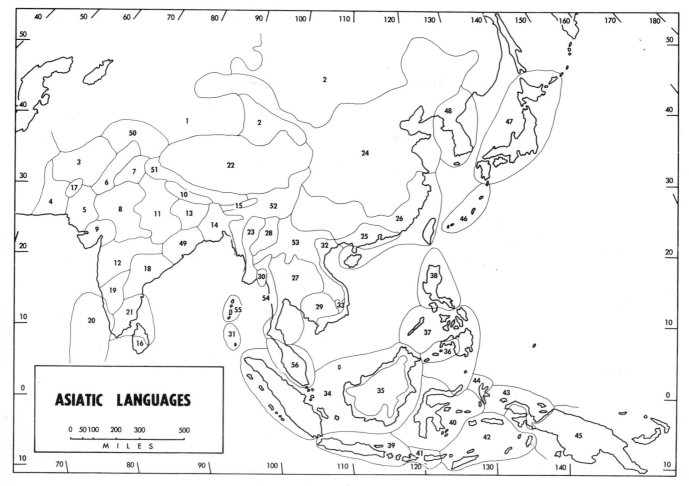

Fig. 32. Modern Asiatic languages. See accompanying table for identification.

A. Altaic family.
    I. Turkish branch.
       1. Turkish languages.
    II. Mongol branch.
       2. Mongol languages.
B. Indo-European family.
    I. Eranian branch.
       3. Pashto (Afghan).
       4. Balochi.
    II. Indo-Aryan branch.
       5. Sindhi.
       6. Lahnda.
       7. Punjabi.
       8. Rajasthani.
       9. Gujerati.
       10. Nepalese (Ghurka).
       11. Hindustani.
       12. Marathi.
       13. Bihari.
       14. Bengali.
       15. Assamese.
       16. Singhalese.
    III. Dardic branch, to which belong Persian and other languages spoken north and west of India.
C. Dravidian family.
    17. Brahui.
    18. Telegu.
    19. Kanarese.
    20. Malayalam.
    21. Tamil.
D. Sino-Tibetan family.
    I. Tibeto-Burman branch.
       22. Tibetan.
       23. Burmese.

    II. Sino-Siamese branch.
       24. "Peking" Chinese (Northern Mandarin).
       25. "Canton" Chinese (Cantonese).
       26. Mixed Chinese languages.
       27. Tai.
       28. Shan.
E. Austro-Asiatic family (relations very unclear).
    I. Mon-Khmer branch.
       29. Khmer (Cambodian, etc.).
       30. Mon.
       31. Nicobarese.
    II. 32. Annamese branch (relationship debatable).
    III. Remnant languages.
       Several languages belong here, but they no longer dominate regions, and are not shown on map. Many are not yet adequately studied and classified.
F. Austronesian family.
    I. Indonesian branch (Malay).
       33. Cham.
       34. Sumatran Malay.
       35. Borneo "Dyak."
       36. Mindanao "Moro."
       37. Visayan.
       38. Tagalog.
       39. Javanese.
       40. Celebes.
       41. Soemba.
       42. Timor-Ceram.
       43. West New Guinea.

G. Papuan family (poorly studied; relations unclear).
    44. Halmahera.
    45. New Guinea.

H. Composite languages (mixed linguistic patterns).
    46. Ryukyu (composed of B, D, and F?).
    47. Japanese (composed of B, D, and F?).
    48. Korean (composed of A, B, D, F, and ?).

I. Regions of multiple languages.
    49. Munda-Oriya-Kurukh (E, B, and C).
    50. Turkish-Tibetan-Dardic (A, B, and D).
    51. Indo-European and Sino-Tibetan mixtures.
    52. Chinese-Tibetan-Tai-Mon-Khmer-tribal (D).
    53. Chinese-Annamese-Tai-Shan-Karen-Group E, III.
    54. Burmese-Karen-Mon-Tai.
    55. Andamanese-Burmese-Groups B and C.
    56. Malay-Chinese-"Indian."

Metropolitan city areas and other local areas of the Orient possess highly mixed language patterns in such small areas that they cannot be shown on a map.

121

eastern Asia. To mainland regions the more gradual drift of Mongoloid peoples only much later gave the bases for real population increase, and the southeastern mainland entered the modern era with less than the normal oriental population density. Chinese stimulus in Korea and Japan operated somewhat similarly to

The rates of post-Columbian population increase are not so very different in the Orient from those elsewhere in the world, but, from large productive populations to start with, the sheer numbers that have piled up there are in excess of those anywhere else. Not only are the gross numbers greater but the net

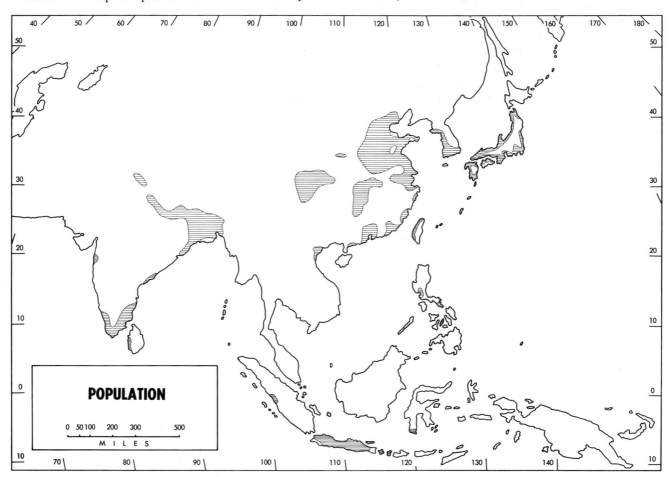

Fig. 33. Concentration of population. This map was designed to indicate only areas of heavier concentration of population in the Orient. Shown are those regions estimated at over 500 people per square mile. Individual metropolitan cities in scantily populated regions are omitted.

that of India in Java, with Manchuria and Inner Mongolia remaining relatively empty until the modern era.

The whole of the Orient shared in the increases that have affected the world during the post-Columbian era of environmental development and exploitation. Some regions, such as India, Java, and China, were the first to jump ahead under the new stimulation. Next came Japan and Korea, a little late owing to their self-imposed hermitage. More gradual have been the increases of such regions as Thailand, Borneo, and New Guinea. A few spots like Manchuria and the Philippines have attained large totals only during the present century.

totals per square mile are higher, and the densities per square mile of food-producing land are far above those of the Occident. The accompanying simple map of population concentration suggests only a limited distribution of this state of crowding.

The disturbing feature is that the West has helped remove many of the traditional checks and balances from population growth in the Orient without supplying the productive means to feed the increases. Preventive and curative medicine, and public health facilities, if incomplete, have been effective in lowering infant mortality rates, preventing huge killing epidemics, and keeping child-producing age groups alive.

Flood and famine relief, the discouragement of infanticide, the relative peace, and the prevention of tribal and interregional wars all have been factors making for modern increase in population. The standard of living has been declining for well over a century. Unless new keys to agricultural production can be put into the hands of all oriental peoples rather quickly, distress and unrest may unleash a series of militant, bloody, and disease-filled checks and balances throughout the Orient. On the other hand, if such provisions are devised and successfully inserted into the oriental economy, the resultant net increases may well overwhelm the world in a migratory exodus out of one great incubator realm, such as the world has never known.

The population prospect is startling from any approach. Oriental economy, fed on the products of an intensive hoe culture, long led the world in achievement. It has been placed at a temporary disadvantage by the flowering and spreading of the mechanical civilization of the West. What will follow when the East masters western tools can either be alarming or inspiring. Detailed regional consideration will be given to population growth and problems in the second section of this volume.

Religion, Law, and the Social Orders

RELIGION AS A FORCE IN CULTURE

The occidental often feels that the Orient is motivated by deeply mystical religions that not only shape the cultures of the several countries but emanate eerie vibrations that color the landscape and affect the very atmosphere. This is, of course, the exact aim of the authors of fiction thrillers, oriental movie intrigues, and the so-called "oriental music." At the same time, however, the Occident does not often openly admit the strength of religion as an operating force in shaping its own cultures. Many of the great religions show an earlier common body of culture, out of which each sprang. Each religion has in it ideas, rituals, and symbols that are drawn from or motivated by the landscape of its home environment. In so far as these tangible attributes vary and seem strange, the whole religion appears alien and a cultural world apart. Each, in its own realm, is a force making for the perpetuation of a particular culture. There can be no question that certain religions exert greater influence upon a culture than others, and that in a particular region one creed will make headway at the expense of another with consequent changes in culture.

Throughout the whole of southeastern Asia one must reckon with primitive tribal animism as a reservoir of ritual, symbol, and practice which, over the centuries, has fed a great deal of material into the organized religions of every eastern country. In some cases this material today is reflected only in limited ways, having been thoroughly digested and transformed during its absorption, but in other cases the symbolism and ritual are little modified from the animistic prototype. Similarly, there are peoples that variably can be labeled tribal animists, pagans, or heathen, who have not taken up any of the organized religions. The animistic regions, and their peoples, have been de-creasing steadily over the centuries, but they are not yet fully absorbed.

One must reckon also with the unaccountable missionary urge, for the application of this tendency is one of the very significant causes of cultural change. A missionary drive is not a part of every religion, nor is it a permanent characteristic. Important geographic aspects of religion are tied up with architecture, art, and sculpture. Significant to agriculture is the presence and variety of tabus against the use of particular foods.

The accompanying map presents a simple story of the distribution of religions in the Orient.

THE RELIGIONS OF THE EAST

Hinduism

Of the major religions of the East Hinduism is the oldest and, in many respects, the strongest of all. Its origins go back to a cultural memory housed outside India, and its earliest documentary texts related the invasions of northwest India and the settling down among a primitive people. Much of its added symbolism and ritual lies deep in the pool of primitive animism that belongs to the Dravidian peoples and their cultures. Hinduism always has been an amorphous religion, without finite creed or theology, tremendously absorptive in character, with unlimited numbers of deities and with infinite variety of permissible worship. Its absorptiveness has allowed the conversion of many alien peoples who have thereby been taken completely into the Indian cultural realm. Having no finite body it is a hard religion against which to organize revolt, because it has time and again absorbed and enveloped its dissenters. In this way its textual body has increased through the centuries, until it has become more and more restrictive of the freedom of society.

The increasing bonds of the caste system of India are an emphatic example of the one-way road down which India has traveled for over 4,000 years, until the accumulated cultural weight of Hinduism in mod-

Buddhism

Buddhism appeared in India in the sixth century B.C. as a protest against the accumulated evils of Hinduism, and it was the most successful of a series of early protests that were made over the centuries. Theologically it protested the growing materialism of Hindu creeds,

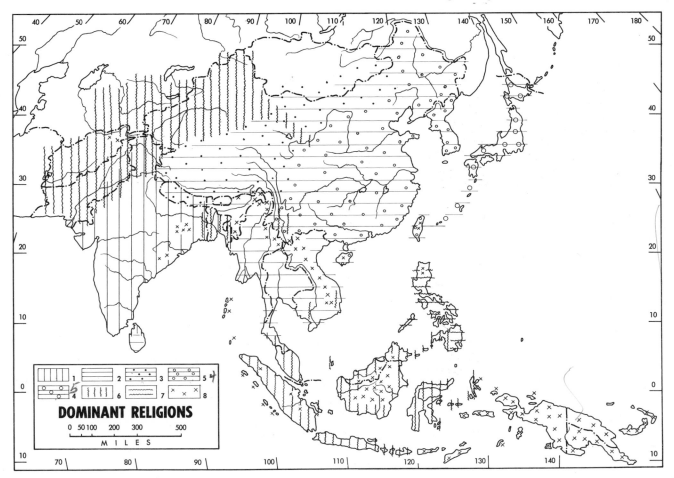

Fig. 34. Dominant religions: (1) Hinduism; (2) Hinayana Buddhism; (3) Mahayana Buddhism and Tibetan Lamaism; (4) Mahayana Buddhism and Japanese Shintoism; (5) Mahayana Buddhism and Taoism; (6) Islam; (7) Christianity; (8) Animism.

ern Indian life is almost more than society can bear. Similarly the evolution of the sacred status of the cow is a costly item to modern India. Earliest Hinduism had no such tabu on the use of meat, whereas the preservation of the 200,000,000 animals of modern India condemns millions of Indians to permanent malnutrition. The architecture of Hinduism is bewilderingly complex and varied, and a significant factor in almost any south Indian landscape. Both regional and historical changes have taken place in the form and decoration of Indian temples, shrines, and symbolic monuments to give them multiple variety in a crowded landscape.

and socially and economically it protested the shackles of caste and the dominance of the Brahmans. But rather than take a course of positive action as a modern American might suggest, Buddhism chose the nonviolent route of ascetic withdrawal from the world into a realm of contemplation, prayer, and passiveness. Its calm theologic superiority over Hinduism spread it wide over India and gave it favor which lifted it to the status of a state religion. A missionary drive then spread it over all southern and eastern Asia, though not without sectarian factionalisms. If its protest within India achieved no truly permanent good, Tibet, Mongolia, China, Korea, Japan, Burma, and Thailand owe a good share of their religious beliefs to Indian Buddhism. On most of the areas converted to Buddhism many of the original tabus, such as that against taking animal life, have rested rather lightly, while gradual growth in each country has produced special variations in its Buddhist faith. In the various countries architecture has taken as varied paths as theology, and in some the architectural heritage is today more noticeable than the social or philosophic one.

Taoism

It is often said that the Chinese are not a religious people. Clearly they are a more pragmatic people than the Indians, but they have taken their religion no more lightly than the Americans, to whom they are quite similar in many ways. While Confucius and his followers were formulating a moral and ethical code, Laotzu and his adherents were developing a spiritual philosophy known as Taoism, which promised immortality to those who accepted its complicated formula of "doing everything by doing nothing" and followed the mystic Tao or "Way." As Taoism evolved it borrowed heavily from Chinese Buddhism, and the two similar creeds satisfied those Chinese who had leanings toward spiritual and mystical things. A loose organization and a non-militant spirit kept Taoism within the bounds of China except as Korean and Japanese student visitors observed and reacted to it.

Certain features of Chinese life, such as ancestor worship and the moral bonds of the family system, are older and stronger than any one religious faith and are a common part of each Chinese religious pattern. A slow decline of both Buddhism and Taoism in the modern era left the Chinese without a strong native religion to help them face the modern world. But Chinese culture has not been weighted down with the accumulated burden of outworn religious institutions. In part this is due to the practical realism of the Chinese and in part to the vigilant and never-ending opposition of the Confucian bureaucracy to the too-great expansion of any religious movement which thereby might constitute a danger to the state. To the occidental tourist the visible architectural and sculptured expression of Taoism is easily confused with that of Chinese Buddhism, from which it borrowed physically as well as theologically.

Mohammedanism

The most militant of eastern religions has been the Moslem faith which came into India demanding the alternative acceptance of conversion and conquest or death by the sword and taxation. Without waiting for full assimilation of India its missionary drive carried it on through Malaya and deep into the Indies, where it played out in Mindanao, Borneo, and Java. From Persia and Trans-Caspia it spread through central Asia into northwest China and has deeply infiltrated western China clear down to the Burma border. Such forced conversion often was superficial and resulted in the perpetuation of older cultural traits. This arid-land faith with its desert symbolism is as much out of place in the tropical Indies as is Christianity and its Mediterranean complex. The only significant tabus of the Moslem faith are bans on the use of pork and alcohol, both of which rest lightly upon much of Malaya and the Indies. With Islam came the mosque and all of Moslem architecture to strongly alter the urban landscape of northern India and to give a lesser though noticeable change to the monumental building of many parts of southeastern Asia.

Where the Buddhist faith sought its ends in quiet contemplation away from the world, the Moslem faith has worked with political tools, with the strident emotional appeal in the marketplace, and with the sword. In time, therefore, the superficial acceptance of the Moslem faith often has become a full and ardent thing, with the result that wherever the Moslem faith is practiced today, latent political turbulence is found in which Moslems never have refrained from militant action when it seemed to promise results.

Christianity

Christianity and imperialism go hand in hand throughout the East. It probably was good fortune that tempered imperialism by Christian contact, for certainly it was not consciously arranged. Modern Christianity is a somewhat practical faith that never can let spiritual considerations blind all its advocates to the values of material improvement. Hence the evangelist preaching salvation has been accompanied by the medical missionary, the agricultural experimenter, the trade school man, and the teacher dealing in democracy, athletics, and the alphabet. If at times these things have boomeranged, the evolution of a new political system and an independent economy was implicit in the whole process of contact of the Occident with the Orient. The oriental sometimes feels that the missionary was the only check upon an exploitation by occidental imperialism that would have had no cessation short of complete prostration of oriental society.

There are almost as many kinds of Christians as Hindus, but normally the Christian native is an individual more literate and better prepared to face the modern world than the average non-Christian member of any oriental culture. In any event the Christian missionary has ranged more widely than the missionary of any other faith, and has touched every culture in every country of the Orient. There is some competition between Catholic and Protestant, and between Protestants themselves, but finally a regional division of territory has evolved by which the main force of Christian mission effort can be brought to bear upon the whole of the Orient as a part of a world-wide mission program. Christian architecture is more difficult to isolate from occidental architecture at large, and religious building by the missionaries often has adopted older regional motifs. In India one can hardly hold up the stuffy Victorian style as the result of Christianity, though in China perhaps one can point to "modern Chinese" as at least partly owing its inspiration to the builders of schools and colleges who sought to fit their structures into the Chinese scene. One country in the Orient can claim to be predominantly a Christian land, the Philippines, a result of the long and diligent, if strangling, efforts of the Spanish Catholic priesthood.

Sikhism

The Sikh religion arose on the turbulent fringes of an earlier era of Moslem-Hindu conflict. In the last century and a half it has prospered greatly under conditions of peace and friendly tolerance guaranteed by British rule in India. With Buddhism, Sikhism stands as the second successful revolt against the Hindu religion. Socially a protest against the multiple corruptions of Hinduism, the theology of Sikhism has been at pains to distinguish itself from its older sources. Many orthodox Hindus refuse to separate it from their own multiple faith, and there is mutual tolerance between Hindu and Sikh that is entirely missing between Sikh and Moslem.

More noticeable than its theology or its architecture has been the personal costume of those Sikhs who became members of a militant order developed to protect the faith against persecution in the open and mixed settlements of India's Punjab. The new order gave every adherent the new, common surname Singh, a turban, long hair, a full beard, and other minor distinguishing features. The rest of the Sikh community cannot be distinguished from the lower ranks of the Hindu rural farming population from which most of the converts to Sikhism have come. From the knightly order of the Rajputs, however, has come a virile leadership that has kept Sikhism an active faith. It had its center in the Punjab, a region now split by the boundary between Pakistan and India, but the Sikhs today are well spread over northern India. Since 1900 Sikhism has been the most rapidly expanding religious faith in India, surmounting even Christianity and losing very few adherents to the latter religion. Persecution during the continuing struggles over Indian separatism may well go hard with the Sikh community.

The Minor Creeds

Significant among the smaller religious orders of the East is the Zoroastrian faith of the Indian Parsees. Originally a Persian development, most of the adherents migrated to India in the early eighth century A.D. to escape Moslem persecution. They settled along the west coast of India between Bombay and Surat, and became quiet farmers and herdsmen. With a hereditary priesthood and a number of distinctive beliefs such as the "Towers of Silence" upon which the dead are exposed to the elements, the faith has been a clannish and closed group, seeking no converts from other faiths. Its total community today numbers about 100,000 people, scattered among the cities of India as a wealthy merchant class whose economic power in modern India far exceeds its religious impact upon the life of India. This position was achieved only with the rise of modern trade and the growth of Bombay and Surat as trade centers.

Jainism was a contemporary of Buddhism in protest against Hinduism, but its extreme asceticism long limited its growth. Without developing a missionary push, it did develop a simplified theology which had vitality and durability against the absorptiveness of Hinduism. It remained an Indian religion only, widely distributed over the country, but did not die out as did Buddhism. Today its 1,500,000 adherents are mainly located in northern Bombay Presidency and Rajputana. Many orthodox Hindus consider the Jains only a separate caste of the Hindu community today.

The Lingayats arose out of a twelfth-century protest against Hinduism in southern India, and, though they have maintained themselves as a separate group today numbering about 1,500,000 people, they are slowly becoming submerged again in the sea of Hinduism. In this they are but representative of other less successful protests which have already been fully reabsorbed into the parent faith, except for a current caste distinction.

Tibetan Lamaism is perhaps the most spectacular offshoot of the missionary drive of Buddhism. In the seventh century A.D. Buddhism was grafted onto a complex Tibetan shamanism having many highly developed cults whose operations bordered upon near magic. Several factional struggles have involved temporal as well as religious domination. The sects dominating for some centuries have been committed to priestly celibacy, unlike earlier sects, resulting in an almost universal Tibetan custom by which a family seeks to place at least one son in a monastery. This has operated to maintain a large parasitic class and undoubtedly to prevent population increases of spectacular proportions. In many parts of Tibet the only permanent settlements are lamaseries. By holding temporal power the leaders of Tibetan Lamaism have been able to restrain occidental missionary inroads into their fold more effectively than has any other oriental religion. Few alien visitors of any kind have been permitted in Tibet, but many followers of the faith succeed in making a pilgrimage to the religious capital, Lhasa, in southern Tibet.

The Shinto religion of Japan is the modern representative of early tribal animism heavily interwoven with ancestor and emperor worship from China and given theologic body by adoption of Chinese Buddhist doctrines. Shinto often is said not to be a religion at all, but a code of ethics and points of view as is Confucianism, but it contains more religious content than does Confucianism. During more recent centuries many of the native myths and items of nature worship have been eliminated, but Shintoism is still primarily a simple nature worship, with innumerable *kami* or "gods," surrounded by many fanatical concepts. Most of the latter have promoted nationalism, in opposition to the long influence of external Chinese culture, and have championed the divine status of the emperor. As such Shintoism played into the hands of modern expanionist industrial and military clans seeking justification for their programs of aggressive nationalism.

Confucianism often is termed a religion whereas it more properly is a political-ethical state philosophy. It could better be compared with Democracy and Communism than with Christianity and Buddhism. Of course, all developed religions contain points of view regarding the state, and economic and social affairs, and such political cults as Confucianism, Democracy, and Communism contain patterns of ethics and an emotional aspect which borders on the theologic. The pragmatic Chinese often have been somewhat agnostic as regards strict theology, just as many Americans are sometimes termed non-religious. Confucianism, therefore, took the place of religion in China among a share of the population. As it has lost its hold in modern China an agnostic society first resulted, which currently has switched to Communism as a state cult.

CURRENT CHANGES IN RELIGIOUS AFFAIRS

In several countries today many religions are represented, some exhibiting closed-order tendencies and some openly aggressive and zealous in their appeal for new adherents. In a sense there is a competitive re-

ligious struggle going on in parts of the Orient as, for example, the Christian and Moslem vie for converts among the tribal animists of interior Sumatra. Among many of the cultures of the Orient, however, there is an awakening among many of the older religions that is carrying out reforms and enlivening the cultural scene generally. Often this aspect seems buried under the political and economic turmoil of the East, but it is a process definitely at work. In the same sense, in some countries the greatest growth of Christianity is not achieved by occidental missionaries but by the spontaneous growth of the native Christian churches. In China at least Christianity was slowly throwing off its missionary controls and launching forth on a program of its own, when Communism took over. Though China was not yet a Christian nation, Christian leaders ranked high in political and economic circles. Despite the strong hold of Christianity in almost every country, it is doubtful if any one culture, except possibly that of the Philippines, will become as fully Christian as that of the United States within a long period to come.

After its ascendancy, Communism first declared for religious freedom, misleading both Chinese and occidentals. Gradually, however, the Chinese Communist Government restricted that freedom and then bent all religious bodies into machines to further Communism. These may be first and second steps in the abolishing of religious organizations which, in any respect whatsoever, could challenge the Communist Party in terms of group emotional mobilization. It will be interesting to watch Chinese communists essay to control Tibet, in which the Lamaist Church has performed so many of the functions of government. In Outer Mongolia the power of the Church has largely been broken, though its earlier power in no part of Mongolia had been equivalent to that in Tibet.

SOCIAL STRATIFICATION

Everywhere in the Orient the value of a human life is far lower than in the Occident, and it is so much below the current American evaluation that it is hard for our average citizen to think realistically about the question. Interestingly enough, however, there are oriental cultures in which there is a tremendous separation between the top and the bottom of the social order. Among some cultures the upper ranks have become surrounded by privileges and rights that have given them vested positions of tremendous power in their society. To these relatively few the oriental cheapness of life does not apply. And at the other extreme are those hereditary classes who have no rights and privileges at all, but only the duty of performing the onerous and distasteful jobs which must be carried out in any society. To these numerous folk the phrase "value of a human life" is but an empty mockery. No oriental society is completely free of these distinctions, though in some the degree of development is relatively slight. Perhaps in India and in Japan hereditary social stratification has become more fully developed than anywhere else in the oriental realm.

Back of all human social stratification is the simple classification of human beings by their occupations. In all societies the men who were the agents and exponents of religious cults and doctrines have held privileged positions. The warrior and soldier group inevitably occupied another niche in early and primitive social orders. The artisan and the cultivator frequently fell together in that often the same people concerned themselves with both lines. All societies have maintained tabus the breaking of which lowered one's social position toward the bottom. These simple patterns hold in American society today just as they hold among the simple Papuan society formerly labeled "headhunter." Each oriental society has embroidered this simple classification with its own particular design in social matters, and if some of the patterns seem fanciful to Americans, the reverse also is true. Oriental society has recognized from the start that differences among men are fundamental, in stark contrast to the views of the framers of the American Declaration of Independence. Both religion and the force of law tend to support the maintenance of the native social order.

THE INDIAN CASTE SYSTEM

Outstanding in oriental social patterns is the terribly complex system of social castes that prevails in modern India. The earliest Hindu annals record a simple system of three established castes and a fourth bottom layer: the Brahman priesthood, the Kshatriya military group, the Vaisya artisan cultivator, and the Sudra menial group made up of varied low-ranking elements. Slowly this simple grouping has become a host of over three thousand social strata today, eighteen hundred of them being Brahman subdivisions as the upper crust surrounded itself with more and more restrictions. The Lingayat religious faith mentioned above has, since the twelfth century, become subdivided into seventy-one separate castes.

The chief factors in caste distinctions are the rules of marriage, rules covering domestic food consumption, rules covering conduct of the individual, and rules concerning economic work habits. Individuals are born into their caste and cannot raise themselves. Every transgression that is not atoned for through elaborate ritual results in an individual sinking lower in the social order. Every revolt against Hindu society has ended in the enlargement of the caste pattern and in the formulation of yet more rules for human conduct. Migration, change of occupation, invention of new techniques in artisanry, all lead to lower caste levels. Particularly the last feature has tended to restrict and hamper the economic strength of Indian society.

And as time has gone on multiple transgression of caste rules was inevitable, resulting in the accumulation at the sheer bottom of the Indian social order of some 60,000,000 "untouchables," outcastes to whom, and to whose descendants, there is no prospect other than the lowest of menial labor, the fewest prospects for betterment, and the barest of marginal existence. Such religions as Christianity, Sikhism, and the Moslem faith offer only a partial escape from the binding laws of caste. Modern occidental influence has been thrown against caste but sometimes it has worked to heighten the effects of caste rather than to lessen them. Though this one-way road, all down hill, is not a material piece of the physical landscape of India, it is of utmost significance in the cultural geography of the country. India now is moving legally toward abolition of many of the restrictions upon the untouchable, but many decades will pass before caste and its problems are banished.

THE DEMOCRACY OF CHINESE LIFE

Often it is said that China is almost totally lacking in social stratification, and that it is nearest of all oriental societies to the concepts of American Jeffersonian Democracy. Perhaps the latter is true, but hardly the former. The literate Chinese ruling classes have been at some pains to maintain the notion that any individual could rise from the bottom to the top in one generation, and are fond of quoting the stories of famous men and women who did it, just as do Americans.

Detailed inquiry into Chinese history reveals that the minority who actually did rise to the top illustrate what is but an ideal principle in Chinese society. Confucius came not from the bottom but from a middling upper level, and the whole code of Confucianism was erected with a view to the maintenance of the established position of the cultured classes who were the proper managing agents of Chinese society. Confucian bureaucracy operated with this thesis in mind and bitterly opposed the rise of too great strength in the religious orders, too great wealth among a trading class, and too great a growth of industry in the hands of a social class. In other words, the scholar bureaucrat was set up as the highest level in Chinese society. The military class was steadily played down, as a widely quoted Chinese proverb will attest: "Good iron is not made into nails, good men do not become soldiers." Into the Chinese bureaucracy of landed families were admitted always sufficient numbers of new and poor scholars to maintain the ranks in effective numbers and proficient ability.

At the bottom of the social order in China have always been certain occupations and those who flaunted and disregarded Confucian standards of personal conduct and morality. Always there have been the marginal cultural groups who failed to practice the accepted social patterns. They have been termed "barbarians" in a variety of linguistic terminology and forced to put up with lesser social positions, economic privileges, and political freedoms.

The foregoing is written not to criticize the standards of Chinese society but to clarify commonly misunderstood ideas. With some drawbacks the most populous society in the world did maintain more widespread personal dignity and individual freedom than have most other societies in oriental or occidental worlds, and this, in itself, was no mean achievement.

In the modern period the position of the scholar bureaucrat has weakened noticeably. The rise of new professional classes is based on many new culture traits. The modern bureaucracy is a more varied group than formerly, but tendencies toward perpetuation still are visible. Through the growth of modern trade and industry the trader, the engineer, and the banker have risen to levels never before attained in China. The military group has varied in favor according to whether they have been war-lord plunderers or defenders against external aggression.

JAPANESE MODIFICATIONS OF CONFUCIAN DEMOCRACY

In Japanese society much of the Chinese Confucian pattern is visible, but at the same time important omissions, alterations, or additions have been made. The continued importance of clan organization in Japanese life has maintained vertical patterns which have tended to prevent a strong horizontal alignment of social life. Certain hereditary groups occupy underprivileged positions at the bottom of the social order. The scholar bureaucrat never became a dominant figure in Japanese internal administration, but only an assistant, a tool for the imparting of lessons learned from China. Out of a long history of military expansion the *samurai* or professional soldier came to hold a more strategic position in Japan than in China, one which was duly exploited in the last century. The early *za* classes of

artisans and merchants eventually grew into the *zaibatsu,* wealthy clans who held most of the land and the available wealth of Japan at the opening up of Japan in the 1860's, a position which allowed them to further rise to positions of industrial barons in modern Japan, socially and economically set apart from the balance of society.

Thus the evolution of a social pattern in Japan has produced a less complex order than in India, but one with a number of sharply set-off groups, some of which have been able to achieve positions of privilege and strength not equaled elsewhere in the Orient. While this has been achieved, a code of conduct has at the same time evolved by which the mass of the population were urged to be obedient to the expressed will of the emperor, regardless of what special group had been successful in pushing through a particular decision. This has resulted in a quite different social pattern which, in its own way, is strikingly significant in the cultural geography of Japan.

THE OCCIDENTAL AND THE PROBLEM OF FACE

Within any oriental culture, and between oriental cultures, there is operative a somewhat elaborate social ritual which has come to be known, from the Chinese, as "saving face." "Face" is best defined as a combination of self-respect and personal pride. In the elaborate social custom of every culture of the Orient the maintenance of self-respect and personal pride while participating in the operation of a complex society is, in itself, a somewhat complicated business. The criticizing of personal actions without destroying face requires tact, patience, and a kindred feeling for the niceties and mores of a culture. When not at war with each other oriental peoples have been at some pains to meet others half way in their social and trade contacts. In no oriental culture was there ever much feeling of inferiority, and in China at least was very positive the feeling that Chinese culture was superior to that of every other people.

When occidentals first arrive in the Orient, themselves suffering no inferiority complex but knowing little of oriental ways, they invariably run afoul of the problem of face. The attitude of occidental superiority throughout the centuries of contact, implemented by military, political, and economic exploitation, usually has been rudely expressed, with no concessions of any kind to the face of the individual or group concerned. Some occidentals naturally handle their contacts well, just as there are blunt and abrupt orientals who can meet an American at least half way.

This problem of culture contact is alive today and will continue to mark oriental-occidental contacts in the future. The time has passed when an American can casually kick a Chinese ricksha puller out of the way or physically mistreat his servants. The same is true of every other occidental nationality also, for the colonial empires have crumbled and the future well being of international relations depends upon tactful cooperation.

THE GEOGRAPHY OF THE LAW

Space does not permit an adequate discussion of the role of law and the development of legal institutions in the cultural geography of the Orient. The following general discussion is intended only to introduce the topic and to suggest a few of its ramifications and implications. The basic developments of law in human society lie very far back, and it is difficult to determine clearly whether there are many really different systems of law. But there clearly are many different sets of legal institutions that have been developed among the many societies of our world. Within the Orient itself there are different kinds of legal institutions, so that law has been differently applied in the several regions. In many respects these institutions differ from the corresponding ones in the Occident, and their cultural results sometimes are strikingly different.

Many legal institutions seem to have grown up around the subject of religion and its organization, and around the issues of ownership and control over property and water. In that property in different environments varies tremendously, legal institutions reflect something of the environment. In that legal institutions are the means of enforcement of tribal tabus and the more formal religious sanctions, a system of legal institutions inevitably embodies these tabus and sanctions. A simple culture in an environment made up of similar regions may formulate a relatively simple group of institutions, whereas a highly complex culture occupying different kinds of landscapes and involving both rural agricultural and urban industrial occupations develops a complex and voluminous variety of institutions. A complex social order may include within its formal legal patterns many social controls which modify basic legal principles according to social level, or it may allow many social decisions to be made on an extralegal basis, often labeled "social custom."

Since a pattern of legal institutions goes with a culture complex, human migrations have moved institutional systems from given environments into totally dissimilar ones. The basic Moslem law of the Koran, with its desert concern over water rights, is a little out of place in the rainy Indies. Such contrasts eventually produce regional modifications in basic legal institutions. In the migration of cultures, groups of legal institutions come into opposition and conflict. Sometimes they exist side by side with continual strife, whereas at other times one system supplants another, as its native culture becomes regionally dominant. Out of the workings of each group comes political control and the operation of a political area by the leaders of the culture group. This may be only the tribal food-gathering range, or it may be the complex national state of modern times. Political regions seldom remain static, either expanding or contracting according to the relative level of culture strength in the regions round about.

The East shows a wide variety of legal institutions, from the primitive group of institutions governing the Sakai of Malaya to the complex patterns of Brahman Hindu India. Some of these institutions have been stable for centuries, whereas others have been expanding and increasing their territorial scope since 1880. In the case of small but distinct tribal groups variations in the institutions are few. The Indies, however, scattered over thousands of islands, has a great many local variations in its *adat* or customary law, and in the institutions developed to administer it. Most of the native cultural groups of the Orient possess their own customary law. Thus, under the modern political statutory law of Burma, Thailand, or Annam lies a distinct body of customary law stemming from growth patterns of earlier centuries.

In the history of the Orient three species of institutional pattern developed and spread out over south and eastern Asia in the course of centuries to overlie most of the tribal institutions of primitive societies. In some cases the new and incoming institutions achieved only a thin and patchy veneer over the older codes, but in others the new systems supplanted the older native codes. The new systems were the Hindu, Chinese, and Moslem systems in that chronological order. Each of these species has developed regionally centered subspecies that slowly have grown more and more distinctive, having less and less in common with each other. From the Chinese parent species have come the Korean, Japanese, and Annamese subspecies. Mongol tribal-pastoral legal patterns always remained separate from the systems of the sedentary Chinese and did not spread far out of the dry lands. From the Hindu species have developed the Tibetan, Burmese, and Thai systems. From both Hindu and Moslem root stocks has grown the Indian Moslem system. The Indian Moslem legal institutions spread into Malaya and the western Indies to cover about the same territory as had been covered earlier by the spread of Hindu institutions. The eastern half of the Indies and the northern Philippines never received an oriental overlay over their local tribal systems.

Hindu and Chinese legal institutions were quite deeply entrenched on the Asiatic mainland when

European legal institutions came to the East in two related species, the Roman pattern of continental Europe and the common law of England. Gradually these have been applied to almost the whole of the Orient in another thin veneer. Where a colony was staked out the veneer has finally become quite deep, but where

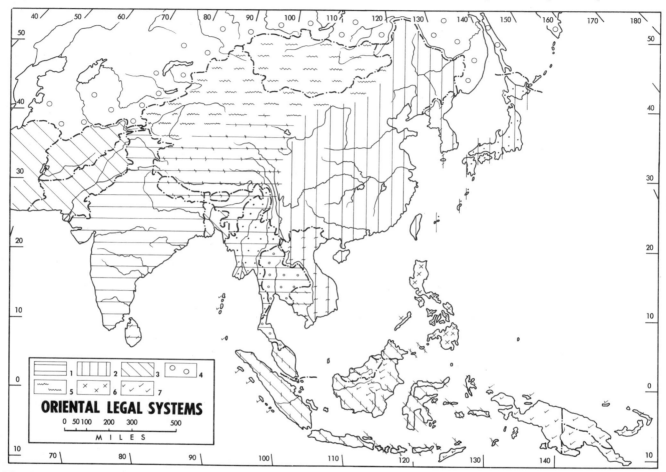

ORIENTAL LEGAL SYSTEMS

0 50 100 200 300 500

MILES

Fig. 35. Systems of oriental legal institutions: (1) Indianized codes: India, Hindu-Roman; Cambodia, Hindu-Khmer-Roman; Ceylon, Buddhist-Roman; Burma, Buddhist-Burman-Roman; Thailand, Buddhist-Thai; Tibet-Nepal, Buddhist-Lamaist; (2) Chinese codes: China-Formosa, Confucian; Korea, Confucian-Korean; Japan, Confucian-Japanese-Roman; Indochina, Confucian-Annamese-Roman; (3) Moslem codes: Pakistan, Moslem-Indian-Roman; Malaya-western Indies, Moslem-tribal-Roman; (4) Slavic codes: Soviet Russia, Slavic-Communist; (5) Central Asian mixed-pastoral codes; (6) Philippines, Roman-tribal codes; (7) Central Borneo and the eastern Indies, chiefly tribal, with Roman veneer of recent addition.

Moslem patterns were carried into southeastern Asia. Rather quickly the Moslem system replaced Hindu institutions in Malaya and the western Indies and spread to the southern Philippines. This replacement took place at the top of the institutional standard, being the operative patterns of political overlords. Under a thin veneer of Moslem practices lay parts of the older Hindu system, and under both lay Indonesian tribal institutions. This Moslem veneer had not penetrated much of the whole body of customary law when the European discoverers appeared on the scene.

no colonial overlordship was achieved the new European systems have not produced much change. An accompanying map attempts to present the distribution regionally.

One can visualize the prospects for real dissension in a situation like this: Suppose a Chinese shopkeeper and his Malay customer become seriously involved with a Sikh money lender in a small town in interior Malaya. The law of the land is Moslem, but Malaya is a British colonial holding and the court of last appeal is staffed by an Englishman. Each of the three litigants emotionally reacts in the sense of what is right in his own culture and would argue by his own native legal system. Unless the British judge were more conscientious than many colonial civil servants he might well decide the case by English common law and enrage all three principals.

Riding high on dominant political status the occidental seldom has been subject to oriental legal concepts of justice in the past. In several countries the occidental has possessed what were termed extraterritorial rights and privileges, and several oriental countries were subject to what they termed unequal treaties. The Chinese treaty ports were a case in point, about which more will be said in a chapter on China. There have been injustices on both sides. The failure of China to recognize and honor the institutions of patents and copyrights has been almost as annoying to Americans as the United States privilege of extraterritoriality to the Chinese. Out of such sources of conflict have come many of the "diplomatic incidents" of the past. During the Sino-Japanese War the United States took the lead in giving up her special rights and privileges in China, making Americans subject to Chinese civil and criminal justice and American firms subject to Chinese corporation and tax laws. The achievement of political independence in other parts of the Orient is repealing and replacing many other special privileges formerly used and abused by the Occident.

Control over Property

Legal institutions express themselves in many directions in the framework of a regional culture. To the geographer one of the more interesting directions in which law operates is in respect to property and in matters of land tenure. In the Orient added to this is the very intricate aspect of water control in relation to wet-field rice culture.

Throughout the Orient native culture groups have long existed with a wide degree of complexity, some of them living almost side by side for long periods. Different social and administrative systems exist, each with its own institutions for control over property, land, and water. The many simple tribal cultures as a rule have not highly developed their concepts of private property. Personal possessions may be privately owned, and tools, weapons, and houses are considered private, though in many such cultures there are age or group association houses that belong to all members of the tribe or village. Among such cultures the physical landscape usually is considered a common tribal resource range, though hunting, gathering, or cropping use privileges may be assigned to units ranging from clan societies to individuals. It is to such groups that one refers tribal or customary law.

Among higher cultures, rights of ownership of land and certain classes of property were claimed by the nobility or by regional rulers. Among these there was an extension of the concept of private property to more than personal possessions and homes, yet the concept fell short of the modern occidental concepts. Among such groups appeared a group of legal institutions pertaining to water rights, mineral rights, trade privileges, and customs collections. Early Hindu and Chinese institutions had approached this intermediate level well before the beginning of the Christian era, but few other culture groups at this time had progressed far in the growth of their institutional evolution. Out of the older Near Eastern kingly state cultures the full concepts of private land ownership spread to India and China before the beginning of the Christian era in company with the introduction of higher and more complex political systems. In India and China political-military nationalism appeared with the Mauryan and Han dynasties, and within the life span of both the institutional systems of both countries markedly matured.

After the appearance of the concept of private property in the Orient each of the more advanced cultures began to revise its institutions for control over land and property. No two systems developed along completely parallel lines or to equal extent. The appearance of Moslem elements in India and Central Asia-China, and gradually in southeastern Asia, brought an overlay of controls over land and property. The coming of the Europeans repeated the overlay in those regions in which Europeans developed control. Out of this long history has grown up the modern agrarian problem which besets almost every country in the Orient. Tenancy of farmers, landlessness of agricultural families, money taxes and land rental, heavy debt burdens upon tenants, whatever the local regional legal institutions, have become compounded into a tremendous problem for both the West and the East. It was largely because of this problem that Communism took over in China, and it is because of this same problem that Communism threatens in every country of the Orient today.

Settlements and Their Architecture

Roughly half of the world's people live in the Orient. They range from small, shy refugee groups to large collections of sophisticated city dwellers. How do they arrange their living patterns to accommodate themselves to roughly one seventh of the world's inhabited area, and what kinds of houses and settlements do they occupy? These basic features of human living supposedly are commonplace elements of cultural geography, but too little is known of them in the Orient, and the topic requires more space than can be allotted here. The present chapter is a suggestive approach to aspects of both subjects.

BASIC STYLES OF SETTLEMENT

Most orientals are village or town dwellers. Villages and small market towns accommodate perhaps four fifths of the total population. The inhabited area is today so densely populated that many compact, closely spaced settlements are necessary. Most oriental villages, towns, and cities impress the American as being jammed tightly together without the usual "living spaces" which he associates with multiple human residence. There are no accepted definitions for what, in the Orient, constitutes a village, a town, or a city, but on the basis of loose generalizations some totals may be estimated. There probably are close to 1,800,000 residential villages in the Orient, housing approximately 900,000,000 people. The many shapes, kinds, and sizes of residential villages range from two- or three-house clusters to villages of a thousand houses or more.

Towns are far less numerous but are of varied types and sizes. They range from small seaports and regional inland market towns to military garrison centers, resorts, mining towns, and political administrative centers. There are not more than about 10,000 such settlements, but they probably house in the vicinity of

150,000,000 people. Cities, thought of as complex settlements serving many utilitarian functions and having a population of above 50,000 people each, are still fewer in number. Urbanism is often held to be an occidental settlement trait, but sizeable cities in the Orient developed well before the historic period, are widespread, and are more numerous than is often supposed. Some of the large cities of the Orient have grown up only after the coming of the occidental. There are close to 500 such settlements, housing perhaps 90,000,000 people. Of this number of cities, perhaps 40 total more than half a million people each, and there are about twenty-five of these large cities, in turn, that total more than 1,000,000 people each.

Dispersed settlement in the Orient can be considered an abnormal form of residence distribution today. It is found among peoples of quite different culture levels and occurs, in variable degree, in every country in the Orient. These scattered rural homesteads probably account for almost 100,000,000 people throughout the Orient as a whole.

With hundreds of race and culture groups permanently living in situations that range from boats on rivers and on the sea to isolated mountain-top homesteads and villages, there inevitably is wide variety in the methods of arranging both compact and dispersed settlement. In some large regions, inhabited by millions of people, the settlement forms and the housing patterns are basically similar. But in contrast to this are the zones of fragmentation of race and culture, wherein many different patterns of living can be found in small areas. Within the Orient culture complexes range from the Stone Age to the Atomic Age, from simple hunting and gathering economies to technologically advanced, industrial export economies. No simple generalizations, country by country, or large region by region, may be made for settlement and housing systems.

DISPERSED SETTLEMENT

Though it is not the common manner of living, dispersed settlement is widespread, and it has been adopted by many kinds of people throughout the prehistoric and historic periods. It is found in many regions as a result of certain specific cultural stimuli though, at this date, not all the motivations can be diagnosed accurately. Some hunting-gathering or fishing peoples, remnants of earlier societies, still approximate dispersed settlement in parts of India, Burmo-Malaya, the Indies, and as far north as Formosa. In some cases this is by single family units, and in others it is by the hunting band, the smallest and simplest social group. Residence often is semipermanent in good local environments, but also it is often seasonal, temporary, or shifting. Though people of this simple type of economy are widely scattered, they do not bulk large in total numbers. Some of the fishing peoples, in single or two-family units, may live seasonally or completely on their boats, often tied up at night in the same locality.

Some of the earlier agricultural peoples, like the present-day remnant groups or small communities never growing into populous or powerful societies, lived in dispersed patterns that still are in use today. These peoples now are thinly scattered throughout the hill country of India, Burmo-Malaya, the Indies, and the Philippines. Some live in single family homes, some in small clusters, and a few are but seasonally dispersed throughout the farm landscape during the intervals of the chief agricultural production cycles, living in villages during the off-seasons. The earlier societies normally practiced shifting agriculture, moving their farmstead locations from time to time under different rules and systems. Shifting agriculture tends to foster dispersion of the population rather than compact permanent centering of a society in villages and towns. The modern continuation of shifting agriculture may be limited eventually by the regional pressure of men upon the landscape, but it still is widely practiced today. It has been maintained as an agricultural system by many peoples who have otherwise developed advanced cultures, thereby fostering rural dispersion of population in all parts of southeastern Asia. As far north as Korea and the highlands of eastern Manchuria a version of shifting agriculture, in Korea called "fire field" culture, still is used. This involves periodic shifting of location, the scattering of homes, and, essentially, dispersed settlement.

One large and significant region of dispersed settlement among a people of advanced culture is that of western China—the Szechwan Basin and near-by surrounding hill country. Here Chinese settlement took place in a landscape of irregular hill country, the Chinese settling down among, and displacing, an earlier population. Village and town settlement had been the earlier Chinese norm in the open landscape of North China. Towns as defensive rallying points were used in the advance stage of Chinese occupation of Szechwan. As regional pacification occurred and as the earlier occupants withdrew southward to get away from Chinese control, the Chinese found compact villages less practical than dispersed dwelling in the hilly environment. Gradually they spread out over the landscape the better to utilize the small and scattered bits of valley land. As population grew and terraces spread over the hills this pattern solidified, so that villages and towns now are service centers for the majority of the rural population rather than primary points of residence. The great majority of Chinese in this region live in single-family farmsteads distributed throughout the hilly landscape.

In northern Honshu and Hokkaido, where larger farms are both more necessary and possible than in the southern part of Japan, some farmers also have spread out upon the land in homes that occasionally resemble the Russian Siberian or northern American style. This is a recent development, and it accounts for only a minority of the population. In the Philippines, during the American period of control, as highways have improved, with consequent easier travel and transport, a rural scattering of homesteads along the roads has dispersed significant numbers of families to reverse the Spanish policy of concentrating the population in compact settlements.

Though India is chiefly a zone of village dwelling, there are several areas that today are marked by dispersed settlement. Whereas the Malabar Coast of southwestern India once was settled chiefly in villages and towns, dispersed settlement is widespread today. The whole southern end of the Indian Peninsula shows considerable dispersed settlement. The Northern Circars region, north of Madras, used to be a land of villages, but they are few and scattered today, with much of the population spread out upon the land. The eastern Bengal Delta region, perhaps because of the rise of jute as a commercial farm crop, is a region in which dispersed settlement is common today. The hill country of the lower Himalayas, in almost its whole length, and the whole of the Vindhya Hills show widespread dissemination of single farmsteads.

Among advanced societies who have developed complex living patterns, there always are a few families who prefer to live apart from their neighbors. Particular causal factors in local regions have promoted rural dispersion of residence. Commercial agriculture and the development of transport systems are important in this respect. In recent centuries, with heavier pressure upon farmland and living space, many local regions show rural dispersion of farm homesteads upon higher terraces, lands neglected until recently, along road and rail lines of easy access, in reclaimed areas, suburban fringes, and the like. Consequently, thin scatterings, or small patches, of dispersed settlement are to be found everywhere from Hokkaido and northern Manchuria to eastern New Guinea and to Baluchistan.

THE VILLAGE

Of the many kinds of villages a variety of classifications are possible. One Indian classic on village and town planning recognized some forty different kinds of villages. Essentially the oriental village is a collection of farm homes, but the homes of fishermen, of miners, of transporters, and of other functional groups are normally clustered in compact villages. The sheer compactness of many oriental villages is striking, particularly in north China and northern India, and the American often is impressed by the total absence of space between houses, of the lack of gardens, streets, and other types of "living space" which he associates with multiple human residence. When the pressure of men upon the land is great these features are often given scant consideration by the oriental, or they are provided for outside the village itself, on river banks, shore lines, waste spaces, or other "common" areas.

One is tempted to assert that the historic need for common protection and defense by the villager may be the chief causal factor for this tightness of dwelling habit, but this may well be an after-generalization too sweeping in scope. Close-order dwelling may have become habitual among Chinese, Japanese, Indian, and other peoples as an integral aspect of their evolving, closely knit social systems. It is hard to separate the social system of some of the southeastern Asian groups from their habit of communal living in a single physical structure housing dozens of families. In many parts of the Orient walled villages still are the common mode, reflecting a protective need of earlier peoples, but the good policing provided by the European colonial administrations and some modern native governments has caused protective walls to disappear

without markedly changing the basic compactness of settlements in many areas.

But not all orientals live in tightly compacted villages. The Bengal, Malay, or southern Japan village often is a loosely structured affair, with trees, clumps of shrubs, or patches of bamboo screening each house and providing shade for it. Garden patches may separate houses within a village. In many areas hamlets or clusters of houses constitute neither dispersed nor compact settlement, but administratively many of these groups or clusters constitute a village. This latter pattern is found in parts of Japan, the Philippines, in India, and in local areas in other countries.

Among many of the simpler social groups the village is built around a central feature, this varying from a shrine or a cleared threshing-ceremonial floor to a chief's house or a market place.

Ideally, the residential village does not contain stores, shops, fabricating plants, government service buildings, or other functional activities, but this cannot be taken as the sole characteristic of oriental villages. Probably a majority of villages show almost no secondary activities, but the Szechwan village today, in a region of dispersed settlement, has developed a particular tradition of social and economic service related to the market town, though it often is only a collection of thirty to fifty houses. The village through which a highway or rail line has been recently built may well have added a few secondary services without becoming a real town or city. Innumerable causal factors today make it impossible to define finitely what constitutes a village.

The pattern of livelihood, the social system, the presence of friction between local race and culture groups, the regional historic frequency of alien invasion, the habit of intergroup wars tied up with long preserved social patterns, the need for mass labor forces among peoples of simple power technology, all these are factors making for village dwelling of some sort as the normal thing in most parts of the Orient.

Villages in the Orient are arranged in many shapes and patterns. Some single patterns are common in large areas, or among particular race and culture groups. Conversely, many different shapes of villages exist in a given region wherein several causal factors have operated to determine the site and the space available for the building of a village.

Many factors have promoted the compact village of no definite shape or morphology, which is best labeled the cluster village. It is to be found in all parts of the Orient, in all types of local site and situation. In regional terms a great many of the villages of north and northwest India are of this type, very closely built, with a maze of alley and access lines into the house units. Many North China Plain villages are of this type, though here they are less tightly built. Many South China villages are cluster-shaped, concentrated at a river fork, a bridgehead, or on the only bit of flat surface available, showing a hodgepodge arrangement. Many of the villages built by the simpler social and culture groups of India and southeastern Asia are really clusters of houses arranged in disorderly array. Some of these are circular clusters, or clusters grouped around a focal point. Tibetan villages frequently are elongated clusters in cramped sites in those lower elevations in which sedentary settlements are found.

Elongated or string villages are to be found everywhere in the Orient. Often a site is chosen which promotes the string village. The seashore, a river bank, a natural levee or terrace, a highway, a dike line, or some other linear site form automatically arranges houses either in single file or double file over whatever distance is required to house the local population. Ten or twenty houses may be compactly grouped in a double row in less than 100 yards, or a thousand houses and their garden spaces may straggle out for several miles. The string village is an old form in the Orient, though it does not seem a natural one to the simpler societies. It is a culturally fixed form in many regions today in that a site for a new settlement may be chosen so that this form may be executed. The modern highway is a natural phenomenon upon which people may fix this type of village, and new dike lines are often chosen as practical sites for settlement.

The rectangular or grid-pattern village is a common form in many areas today. Though the grid-pattern settlement is a very old one, perhaps originating in northwestern India, its use in villages seems far less old than its use in town and city building. The form gradually spread over most of the Orient and was widely used among the more advanced culture groups well before the coming of the occidental. It is a traditional type in parts of southern Japan today, is old and widespread in China where plenty of space was available, and has been commonly used in many parts of India for a long period. Elsewhere it seems a more modern thing, perhaps promoted by the occidental in the recent period of developed transport.

Other forms of the village do not precisely fit into any of the three patterns mentioned above. The traditional Malay village is a straggly affair often built along the lower portion of a stream. But its scattered spacing of houses in garden patches, its lack of continuous road or trail connecting all the homes, and its orientation to water transport make it neither a string village nor a cluster village. The Javanese villages that cluster around the upper cultivable portions of a volcano's slopes fit none of these formal categories. The Borneo or Sulu Archipelago villages built on piles around accessible sea-water sites are more nearly cluster villages than anything else, but they are not type cases. The mountain-ridge or mountain-top villages built by many of the southeastern Asian peoples are often disorderly groupings of buildings that are hardly cluster villages. The villages of some of the peoples using the communal house, wherein a whole population lives in one large, subdivided structure, can hardly be called either cluster villages or string villages.

The oriental residential village serves one primary purpose, the housing of a local population. It normally is characterized by simple architecture and cheap utilitarian construction that serves the basic needs of shelter, storage, and privacy. The oriental village seldom has amenities as related to water supply, waste disposal, street cleaning, fly and insect controls, lighting, entertainment, and the like. In any of its common shapes and patterns the village reflects the culture level and variety of its inhabitants. House form and construction also reflect these regional culture patterns. Here and there, as among the Batak and Menangkabau of Sumatra, some of the Himalayan mountain peoples, or the Min Chia of Yunnan, architecture among village folk rises above strictly utilitarian patterns to create an artistic atmosphere not normally associated with village living.

Several kinds of differences can be noted in villages among the major culture realms of the Orient. Out of the strong Chinese demand for domestic privacy every village has an inn that provides shelter and meals, and travelers must patronize these services. In the Philippines, on the other hand, inns and hotels are never found in villages, and travelers always stay in private homes, for hospitableness is a highly cultivated national trait. Among some cultures a shrine is found in almost every village, but among others it is lacking. The Hindu Indian village always possesses zoning of residence, if inhabited by more than one social caste, with fairly strict segregation of residence quarters for the several groups. The villages of most of the simpler cultures of southeastern Asia and the Indies possess housing restricted to men, to women, or to other particular community social elements.

Considering the whole Orient, villages are located everywhere, on all kinds of sites, and no one generalization is possible as to where people choose to locate their villages. One can say that in floodplains where floods are frequent hazards villages most often are located on natural levees or dike lines. In the Indies some of the native peoples, being head hunters, always built on protected mountain sites, but the Dutch gradually suppressed head hunting and often required the building of villages near main roads and trails in more open lowland sites. Many of the earlier New Guinea villages were located in what once was forest but has now become grass country. Progressively village locations have shifted out of the grass country into the upland borders because of the lack of shade trees and construction materials. One can say that the Shan peoples of Yunnan and Burma prefer open, flatland sites for villages, but that the Palaung of northeast Burma and most of the other minority culture groups of upland southeastern Asia usually build on hill tops or ridge tops. In the hill country of southeastern Asia, from the flat lowland floodplain to the highest crest line one finds populations stratified at particular levels —a complex result of economy, military strength, cultural habit, and group aggressiveness. The Thai today are chiefly lowlanders, whereas the Lamet—a minority Kha people, descended from early Mon-Khmer stock —occupy ridge-top sites east of the Mekong River at about 3,000 to 3,200 feet elevation. These stratifications today are expressions of historic competition among many culture groups for living space and cannot be simple expressions of preferred choices, though they now often appear to be cultural patterns of some stability.

THE TOWN

The town is a more complex settlement than the residential village, in that it accommodates all kinds of secondary activities. It normally is larger than the residential village, but this is not always true. Its most common activity is its marketing operations and facilities, and most of the towns of the Orient are market towns. Most of them, of course, also serve a primary function as residential communities to such primary producers as farmers, fishermen, miners, or transporters, and to that population devoting itself to secondary activities. In connection with this marketing function are warehousing, processing, wholesaling, and retail merchandizing. At first glance these are ubiquitous human activities in which oriental towns differ only in specific terms from towns elsewhere in the world. The Chinese "cotton street" or "copper beaters' alley" each has a different appearance from those sections of American towns devoted to the same general operation, and the Indian "bazaar" carries a different atmosphere from the retail merchandizing section of a midwestern American market town. In these respects the oriental market town often is fascinating to the American tourist and offers both a cultural contrast and a

lure to explore that is lacking in his own chain store market area.

Beyond the ubiquitous facilities that provide for man all over the world, the oriental town does often seem to provide services in a way different from those provided by many occidental towns. "Coffin street" in many a Chinese market town permits the living to shop for a container that will eventually house his remains in a manner quite different from that available to Americans. Chinese restaurants, particularly in market towns, normally display their foods and do their cooking next to the street, so that passers-by may make a choice seldom available to an occidental in his homeland. The Indian silversmith, to take a random example, doing much of his work in an open-front shop where his customer may supervise, provides a kind of service seldom found in the United States outside of a "while-u-wait" shoe repair shop. There are many ways in which the oriental market town does seem to differ from its occidental counterpart in the kind of service it provides its customers. One could easily overemphasize these differences, perhaps, for many of them are intricately bound up with the whole of regional culture patterns and are not simply differences in the market town as a functioning settlement pattern.

Functions other than marketing are performed by the oriental town, of course. There are transport terminals or way stations, for both land and water transport, fishing centers, mining settlements, garrison centers, political administrative centers, educational centers, monastery towns, religious pilgrimage centers, mountain resorts, fortified emergency refuge centers to be used in time of unrest, and other types of towns. Except for the fortified center, which may be peculiar to China, their similarity to towns elsewhere in the world is perhaps greater than their intrinsic differences. Even residential suburban towns clustered around larger centers seem, in many ways, quite like those of the Occident. The small manufacturing town, often devoted to a particular commodity or category of manufacturing, is widely scattered over the Orient. In that it still uses simple sources of power and few complex machines, and often is organized on a pattern of community household industry, it has an appearance different from that of many occidental manufacturing towns.

Most oriental towns being centers of multiple operations and functions, often show a considerable amount of functional zoning. Traditionally this has come about without formal controls and ordinances in most countries of the Orient. Grain shops cluster together, dealers in construction materials often occupy a particular quarter, transport operators and their equipment most often congregate on the outskirts, whereas textile, jewelry, food, and other retailers most frequently are to be found near the centers of towns. Many Chinese and Japanese towns have a fairly intricate pattern of zoning of this sort, all accomplished in the earlier day without formal controls. The Indian market town, on the other hand, traditionally has been administratively controlled by some kind of town council, and often has rigidly set limits and patterns.

Most oriental towns are laid out on some kind of grid pattern, a feature adopted by town builders in all parts of the Orient a long time ago. Its actual execution depended upon how clearly a particular people understood the whole concept of a formally planned and arranged settlement pattern. Indian towns, near to the center of origin of the grid plan, have used it longer than have Japanese towns, situated far from that center, but the grid plan is centuries old everywhere. In those towns built on spacious sites a quite rectangular settlement normally resulted, whereas on irregular sites town builders normally accommodated themselves to the site and modified their plan as necessary. Normally many lanes and alleys gave access from the chief streets to block interiors, which usually were solidly built upon. A distinctive feature of many Chinese and Japanese towns lay in the failure to orient property lines to the grid plan, so that many Chinese cities today contain bewildering and irregular maze patterns within blocks. This is far less common in India, where the full implications of the grid plan were long ago appreciated. In parts of southeastern Asia in which culture levels and population long remained lower than in India or China, towns were necessarily fewer, simpler in layout, and normally less complete in the earlier period. In this region their growth in the period of occidental contact is a notable feature, but often the occidental had only slight control over the actual pattern of settlement as it appeared.

The protective wall was a common part of town building in most parts of the Orient, and most of the ancient towns possessed such a wall. Perhaps port towns possessed walls, whether on rivers or on the sea, least often. Gates, bastions, battlements, moats, and other features went with the wall as part of a complex. Wealthier communities first built in tamped earth or adobe brick, and later in kiln-burnt brick, or stone, though the use of burnt brick is far older in India than in China. The earliest towns in forested areas appear to have been surrounded by log palisades. In parts of southeastern Asia the wood or bamboo palisade was more common until the coming of the occidental. Many old towns still possess their walls, though often the walls have been breached in the modern period to permit modern transport to enter. Many old towns have long had suburbs lying outside the wall. The small town often had but four gates, one in each cardinal direction. This normally caused some of the interior streets to end against the wall, funneled traffic in and out along limited lines, and concentrated suburbs in particular locations outside the wall. Few towns founded after the coming of the occidental have had walls built around them, but many of the first settlements built by Europeans were surrounded with walls. Most of these European settlements have grown up into large cities since their founding and the walled towns now are small enclosures within the cities. Fort St. George at Madras and the Intramuros at Manila are examples of this development.

Many market towns appear to have remained relatively stable in population for rather long periods of time. Many Chinese and Indian market towns now appear little larger than they were centuries ago, but there are many more towns today, more closely spaced together, than were to be found in earlier periods. With limited facilities and sites, this suggests that the market town has an approximate maximum size and level of efficiency. No specific total population can be designated at this maximum level for the whole Orient, because different culture groups have developed different technologies and different cultural reactions to the functioning of the town.

Other kinds of towns, particularly administrative and religious, also have increased in number and closeness of spacing, as the total population of individual countries and particular regions has grown over the centuries. Many of the ancient port towns have disappeared, with silting up of river mouths and harbors, with changing political fortunes, and changing sea-trade patterns. Many of these port towns have remained small in size and restricted in regional functioning, particularly in the modern period in which the type and size of shipping has changed and grown, so that many ports formerly significant in international or interregional trade have become only local trade centers. Many of the modern, occidental-built towns grew up around the fishing villages or small trading shops of the native pattern, particularly the coastal port towns of India, the peninsular coast of southeastern Asia, and the Indies. Many of the towns of an earlier period have, of course, grown and matured into modern cities of large size and complex function.

THE OLDER ORIENTAL CITY

Some students of urbanism consider that the ancient oriental city was a product of the kingly state, in which developed agricultural systems dependent upon domesticated plant and animal exploitation, metals technology, intraregional trade and transport, and political systems, and in which social systems had matured sufficiently to permit the highly organized political-military state. This state depended chiefly upon an agricultural base for its support, but it had sufficient manufacturing and commerce to provide a broad variety of consumer goods and a multiple income pattern for much of its citizenry. The city specifically was both the point of organization and control and the center of manufacturing and commercial exchange. Manufacturing is here thought of as handicraft-community workshop, dependent chiefly upon human and animal power and the high personal skill of the artisan, and commerce is akin to what today is internal or domestic commerce. The city was the chief consumer of agricultural surpluses, the point of accumulation of wealth and tradition, and the chief developer of culture patterns—the center of civilization. It was the nerve center of the state, and the chief object of attack by an invader.

The earliest kingly states were not large, and perhaps were dominated by one such city, supported by towns and villages, but as states grew into real empires the cities of conquered states were turned into subordinate cities as regional points of control of the enlarged areas. If no such cities were in existence as the empires matured, regional city control points were built. I believe that this concept also fairly well fits the ancient city in most parts of the world, and that this is not uniquely oriental. But certainly the ancient Indian cities and the somewhat later cities of Central Asia, China, Korea, and Japan developed within this kind of framework. And certainly the early oriental city was a different kind of cultural mechanism from the modern large city of today, whether it be in the Orient or the Occident.

The ancient oriental city, in terms of physical structure, was dominated by walls and defensive construction, by temples, palaces, and governmental buildings. Such construction showed tremendous application of labor and skill, and often these were the only types of construction to rise above the second story. There always was great contrast between these types of buildings and the homes and workshops of the artisan citizenry. In the matter of size of the settlement and in the presence of this type of building lay the classical distinction between the city and the town or village. In Chinese the most common early words for city relate to walls and gates in contrast to the many terms for market town and village which relate to gathering, display, and trade of commodities. The very connotations of the Chinese terms for city carry with them most of the above implications. In modern urban political administration the Chinese have taken an old term for market and redefined it to cover the modern urban metropolitan settlement. There is still an aura about Peiping, as the long-time center of the Chinese world, which was lacking in modern Nanking or Shanghai, and it may well be that Communist removal of the political capital to Peiping contained an element of effort to recapture this in order to surround the Communist regime with a little more sanctity. There also is an aura around Delhi as a long-term Indian capital which the British sought to capture by moving their capital from Calcutta to Delhi in 1912, an aura that is lacking around the old port town of Karachi, now become the capital of Pakistan.

All the early cities of the Orient were built on some interpretation of the grid plan. Perhaps their builders did not understand it completely or possessed too little political and cultural control over the populace to carry it out with high efficiency. The early core of many of the old cities today is hard to recognize and map, but the grid plan is at the bottom of every one of them. With varying political or cultural impact, different kinds of modifying influences were brought to bear on the old cities with the passage of time, and many of them today show but imperfect remainders of their origin and pattern.

On the mainland the chief early cities were cities of the land and overland traffic. But throughout the Island Arcs and along some mainland shores the early city was often oriented to water routes, located on shore-line or river-bank sites, and thus often of necessity cramped into less than the proper space. Such cities often required both special types of water-front building and modified zonal arrangement, and often a share of their populations lived on boats on the water. The early shore-line or river-bank cities, therefore, frequently were at physical variance with the inland city. In that these sites often were subject to silting up, and the cities were organized by seafarers, the city oriented to the water was almost a transient thing, depending upon the fortunes of nature and sea power. These shore-line cities were often strange mixtures of peoples from many cultures, this in itself contributing to the transient nature of the cities when a harbor silted up or political power waned.

The city in southeastern Asia was a feature brought in by Indian or Chinese influences, depending upon the area. In ancient times no development of the complex political state took place here, and it was only with Indian contact that the higher levels of culture and the more complex patterns of economy and political administration developed. Indian influence largely was felt around the coastal fringes, whereas early Chinese influence penetrated southeastern Asia overland, with the migration of peoples away from the expanding Chinese empire. In such an area as the Philippines no city had grown up prior to the coming of the Spanish, and in New Guinea even the occidental has not yet produced a true city. In such countries as Burma, Thailand, Indochina, Malaya, and the Philippines cities are few today, and there is only one really populous cultural center in each of the five countries. Indochina, being a modern political unit composed of several separate early culture regions, has a number of smaller cities. Java and Sumatra were exceptions in the Indies, each having several early cities, but the whole of the rest of the Indies has produced few real cities. In Central Asia Indian and Chinese influences, plus the natural motivation of settlement around sources of water, produced a small number of cities at an early date.

It must be pointed out that in several parts of southern and southeastern Asia early cities existed but that they have disappeared with the demise of the political states they controlled. Thus, Angkor in Cambodia, the capital of Sri-Vijaya in the Indies, several cities in Java, Sumatra, and Burma have all disappeared except for certain architectural remains. In Central Asia the drying up of sources of water, plus the passing of political states, has caused the disappearance of a number of cities. In both China and India changing political patterns connected with the rise of empires out of kingly states and the changing fortunes of empires or attempted empires have caused the abandonment and gradual disappearance of a great many cities. In India and Ceylon historian-archaeologists are engaged in the identification and uncovering of many ancient cities, and the list is a long one which ranges from Mohenjo-daro and Harappa of the third millennium B.C. through Taxila and Anuradhapura to such cities as Kamatapura, the fifteenth-century capital of the Khyen kings of eastern India. The latter's size is demonstrated chiefly by a massive earth rampart over a 100 feet wide, 30 feet high, and some 15 miles in circumference. Kamatapura was laid waste by a Moslem conqueror in 1498 and has never been rebuilt or occupied since except by village dwellers.

In contrast to this decay and abandonment of some of the early cities, is the long life of others. Modern New Delhi is at least the ninth city that may be enumerated, in terms of buildings and streets, which has occupied a site in this locality, and Peiping became a city in the ninth century A.D. Canton now covers a larger area than ever before, but the general site has been occupied by a city for over 2,000 years. Many other oriental cities now stand on sites long serving as a regional cultural center, even though they have been torn down and rebuilt many times. Some of them have progressively changed both in morphology and architecture and in cultural pattern during their long histories.

NEWER ORIENTAL CITIES

No sharp demarcation between the ancient and modern cities of the Orient can be made. But in part one can suggest that those cities founded since the coming of the occidental, and since the development of modern economic and political systems, differ considerably from the classical city of the ancient Orient. Not only is there a difference in architecture to be found in the newer cities, but many of them are located on different kinds of sites, their organization is different, and their very reasons for existence are different. Singapore is one of the newer cities, less than two centuries old, possessing more skyscrapers than many European cities, a gathering of people from many cultures and countries, held together only by the concern with world trade relations, and not the expression of a regional mold of culture. So too was Shanghai, to a degree, before the Communists closed it off from the world of trade. Hongkong, Colombo, Manila, and Calcutta are examples of this new kind of city. Though these cities do resemble the ancient shore-line cities, they differ from them. The modern commercial port city often has grown out of an early local trade center, as did Shanghai and Jakarta, but as often it may be on a new site, as are Hongkong and Calcutta. And very different is Jamshedpur, the new industrial city growing up in the long neglected Chota Nagpur hill country of eastern India. But here the reason for being is not trade with the world, but the modern industrial fabrication of metals on a huge scale. Yawata, in Japan, Fushun, in Manchuria, and Wusih, west of Shanghai in China, are such cities. In every country of the Orient cities of this type are now growing up, some of them into large industrial centers.

Another modern factor in city development is the garrison or cantonment center built by occidental rulers in the cementing of their political colonial systems. Many of these have become sizable urban settlements. The appearance of modern transport, with its reorientation of regional traffic, has produced a good many new cities that differ from the older ones by virtue of the changes in transportation. There are several other sources of motivation for some of the newer cities of the Orient.

In the building of these newer cities there are notable departures from older urban patterns. Most striking is the trend to tall buildings, with the skyscraper now a common feature of most of the newer cities also invading the older ones. The bund, or improved harbor shore line, and docks and port equipment for large ships also are in contrast to the facilities of the older city. The wide streets and mechanical, wheeled transport of the new city contrasts with the narrow lanes and irregular surfacing of many of the old cities, and this too is invading many of the older centers. The physical morphology of the newer cities usually is on a more spacious pattern than in the older city, but one can seldom say that occidental control of city building has produced either beauty or efficiency. The land-transport terminal, with its rail yards and truck depots contrasts with the arrangement of transport handling in the old city. The large factory sites, and the large workers' residential quarters contrast with the arrangement, size, and distribution of these items in the cities of the handicraft era. The garrison quarters for military and police units and the occidental residential quarter also form a strong contrast with earlier cities. The very styles, patterns, and kinds of architecture in themselves form a contrast.

Often the newer city of the Orient seems to retain many of the poor features of cities native to both the East and the West. Too many attributes of the old remain, and the builders of the new have failed to build as well as they should have done. Of all the cities motivated by the occidental only New Delhi, the most recent of the nine cities of Delhi, seems effectively to have profited from occidental city planning. Some of the new, currently building suburbs and cities, under native political control, may fare better than those of the last four centuries.

The very term city is harder to define today than it was in the past. I once resided in a settlement of over 100,000 people in eastern China which contained all these attributes of the occidental city except piped water and piped sewage disposal. To the Chinese of the region it was not a city, in classical terms, for it was new, without a wall, not a political administrative center, and not a settlement of very much culture. I, also, found it hard to think of it as a city. Impressive totals of trade and manufacture, contributed to by large numbers of people packed into a small area and tabulated by a chamber of commerce do not clearly define a city. The very concept "city," in the Orient at least, has become as heterogeneous as the architecture and the things that go on there.

Admittedly, populations have grown larger in the oriental city. Tokyo, Shanghai, and Calcutta today are larger than were any of the cities of the pre-Columbian Orient, though the pre-occidental Tokyo of 1800 was one of the largest cities in the world, and it is possible that Peking in 1700 was the largest city in the world at that time. Today there are many more huge metropolitan settlements than ever before, and these are less a product of the Orient itself than of world-wide developments. The larger settlements of today are functionally diverse, multiple creations of both the East and West, the old and the new. All of them are changing rapidly. The Batavia of 1941, with its half million people, hardly resembles the Jakarta of 1954, with over two million inhabitants, but in this case so far there has been only a change in size. The Manila of 2,000 will be far different from the Spanish Manila of 1650, or the American Manila of 1940. Probably the large cities of the Orient, in another half century, will trend more and more to a common pattern and tradition than they do today. The newer city, motivated by the occidental, differed greatly from the classical city of the agricultural empires of the past. Perhaps, in the next half century, all cities of the Orient, both old and new, will come to resemble each other more closely, though, of course, the Japanese city will still possess an individuality different from that of a West Pakistan city.

DOMESTIC ARCHITECTURE

There may well be a half dozen living traditions of house building in the Orient, and more than that number of methods of working out each tradition, so that there are many basic kinds of domestic housing. When one adds the impact of local cultural custom upon domestic architecture, one is confronted with a bewildering variety of product.

Perhaps the most common building tradition is that of building in pounded earth or adobe blocks. This method relates to the very ancient Near and Middle East where it seems to have evolved when primitive cultures first began to abandon the pit house and build above ground. From the Middle East it spread both into India and through Central Asia into China and Korea, replacing the pit house en route. Replacement of the pit house was very early in India where adobe blocks are preferred to pounded earth. China began using both pounded earth and adobe blocks perhaps shortly after 1500 B.C., whereas in Korea above-ground building did not become common until the early centuries of the Christian era. The tradition first employed small-dimensioned floor plans, solid walls, few windows and doors, and the compound building of several house units together so that a given wall often could serve more than one family. It used the flat mud roof supported on beams, and it lent itself to either one- or two-story construction. Stone as a building material was utilized when available in such shapes that it could be used without much working. Since its introduction into the dry margins of the Orient this tradition has spread throughout most of China, very widely in India, into parts of the Tibetan highland and into parts of southeast Asia, well beyond what might seem the climatically dry and safe areas. In some of the more humid areas, such as central and southern China and Korea gabled sloping roofs were adapted for use on adobe housing and have gradually become common to most Chinese builders, and to all parts of Korea. In contrast the flat roof is often found along the central east coast of India in what is not really a dry climate.

A second basic tradition is that of the use of bamboo, reeds, and some of the grasses. The use of leaf and brushy materials may well be related to the bamboo tradition, but it seems older and more primitive, just as the pit house also was a tradition older than the pounded earth-adobe system of construction. Bamboo reed-grass housing had its regional development in some part of moist southeastern Asia. It produced a lightly constructed, airy house with numerous openings, that seldom is elaborately finished on the inside and often gives what an occidental terms a "barn-like" appearance. Widely overhanging roofs and single-story construction appear normal, with room sizes ranging from small to large, as needed.

A third basic tradition employed wood in almost all construction, except possibly a stone foundation and sometimes lower parts of walls. Poles and crudely formed planks were the first construction materials, but the tradition gradually matured into an architecture which employed well-formed planks and boards, flooring, plank- or shingle-type roofing, and very elaborate carving of projecting timber ends. Multiple-story building on variable floor plan dimensions, many doors, windows, balconies, and numerous decorative features go with this tradition, though today not all wooden housing is equally elaborate. Well-developed domestic architecture in wood may possibly be younger than either of the foregoing systems, but its roots reach well back into the past. Regionally the developed tradition seems associated with the forested hill country of the Himalayas and the Chinese-Tibetan border zone, but some use of wood construction is found almost everywhere in the Orient as a development preceding the coming of the occidental.

A later, but prehistoric, tradition is that of the kiln-burnt brick, which is an improvement upon pounded earth or adobe blocks, in that it permitted of more variety and greater adaptability. This may also have come out of the Middle East into both India and China, but the two regions interpreted it quite differently. India has long made excellent fully fired durable brick, red in color, in a wide variety of sizes. China shows a technique of only partial firing of the brick to produce a soft and short-lived gray brick in a range of sizes that was quite limited until rather recently. The Indian system of red brick firing spread clear out into the central Indies and is far more widespread than the Chinese interpretation of brick firing. In the Middle East, in northwest India, in Central Asia, and in northwest China brick construction required no new roofing techniques beyond the old flat-roof system, but in the moist areas of southern China, eastern India, and southeastern Asia new roofing techniques were required. Straw thatching and sloping roofs were old features in southeastern Asia, spread from moist India around to southern Japan, but such roofs did not fit burnt-brick wall construction. Here seem to lie the origins, for the Orient at least, of fired roofing tile and also the curved roof now often thought of as typically Chinese. The curved tile roof with its elaborate ridge-line decorations belongs to mainland southeastern Asia rather than to China proper.

Plaster construction, as a well-developed building technique, is a relatively late feature which may be related to Indian architecture, so far as the Orient is concerned. A simple mud plaster to cover pounded earth or adobe block architecture appears to be a very old feature, but this long preceded white burnt-lime plaster used as a primary construction material. If well-developed plastered construction matured in India, it eventually spread rather widely throughout southeastern Asia and into South China and involved different materials and systems of preparing the basic wall to which the plaster was applied. Plastering also is well developed in Japan and Korea. Plastered construction probably always was somewhat more costly than that using some of the simpler materials in many parts of southeastern Asia, so that it seldom became a dominant regional type. In the south, only in South India did it ever mature into a regional pattern of architecture.

The use of cut stone in building construction, in the Orient, is younger than the preceding systems. With minor local exceptions, it was slow to develop. Architectural working of stone in the Orient seems to have come out of the Near and Middle East several centuries before the beginning of the Christian Era and seems to be related to the upheavals of the Iranian and Greek culture worlds and to owe its technical skills and its motifs to that Iranian-Greek world. India received better teaching in the art of stoneworking than did China, not only in the first periods, but also later. In India, and in those parts of southeastern Asia to which Indians traveled, there gradually appeared a high tradition of building in stone, whereas the Chinese stonework, except in bridges, often gives the impression of being thought out in wood and executed in stone. However, cut-stone building always was too costly to be common in domestic architecture, but it gradually became the medium of construction in religious and public building, in palaces, fortresses, and in monumental construction. It is these historical remnants of stone architecture, of course, that dot the Orient with interesting tourist vistas, be they the great temples of Cambodia, Java, and India, or the many bridges and memorial arches along the old-style roadways of China. In those parts of the Tibetan highland where sedentary settlement is found above the tree line crude stone replaces wood in housing construction.

With the coming of the occidental new trends in domestic architecture appeared. At first these were mainly in the details of design and construction, but gradually some new basic elements are finally entering into the traditions of housing construction throughout the Orient, to modify the long-standing habits of all parts of the Orient.

From another viewpoint housing construction traditions may be worked out in several ways. The Chinese most commonly use a skeleton of wooden posts to hold up the roof, the walls being panel walls that fill in the space rather than support the roof. This is often done even when the building is in adobe or pounded earth, and sometimes even when the flat roof is employed. This principle may have descended from the tradition of late pit-house building, in which the roof frequently was raised above ground level on posts. But it could well derive from the bamboo building tradition in which a separate skeleton often is constructed and the walls covered with some kind of thatching. Normally the earlier Chinese preferred to build on a raised but solid platform, using earthen floors.

The skeleton of posts and panel walls are seldom found in India when wall construction is of materials strong enough to serve as bearing walls. But everywhere that well-developed plastered construction has become common, there is the use of the wooden skeleton to hold up the roof, the plastering normally covering some type of panel unit. The Japanese house followed the Chinese technique of using a wooden skeleton which supports the roof, the walls being commonly plastered panel walls, except for the south-facing walls—the front of the house when possible—which often are movable panels that can be removed to admit sun and air in

warm weather. The Japanese house uses much more wood than is common in China, and floors of the main rooms normally are of wood. The Japanese housing patterns follow little of the pounded-earth or adobe-block techniques of Chinese architecture, but rather follow the tradition of the warmer parts of southern Asia in being light, airy, and open houses. Korean housing has gradually become a blend of Chinese pounded-earth and adobe-block construction, plastered over, and Japanese housing with its wooden floors, mats, and floor living habits.

Quite another thing is the pile-built house, standing off the ground 3 to 10 feet. The pile house may be built of wood, bamboo, or thatching materials, it may be a single or multiple dwelling, and it sometimes is two story. The pile dwelling is today associated chiefly with the moist lowlands and aquatic fringes of southeastern Asia, but as a type it does not seem to be of great age in this region. Some students of oriental culture history incline to the view that the pile dwelling originated on the mainland of southeastern Asia among peoples parent to those groups now termed Malay. The pile dwelling is used from Upper Burma and South China into the Philippines and the middle Indies. It used to be very common in South China but is less so today. It now is the most common traditional housetype in that vaguely defined region termed Malaysia, but it is not used by every people. The early pile house most commonly was floored with spaced split bamboo, dust, dirt, and unwanted scraps dropping through to the ground or water below. The split bamboo floor gradually is being discarded today. Japanese housing in general seems to use a modification of the pile dwelling, after the southern tradition, most houses being set on short posts from 1 to 3 feet off the ground. The split bamboo floor is not employed in Japan.

The communal dwelling is one of the peculiar house-types found in southeastern Asia. It is a type used by simpler cultural groups possessing active clan organization, though there seems no universal simple criterion for determination of its use by any particular people. Today communal housing patterns are spread from Assam to Tonking, Palawan, and through Burmo-Malaya, and the Indies to New Guinea, but gradually the communal house is being discarded in areas having contact with more advanced cultures. There are two types of communal housing, but their respective distribution is not well known. One of these is the multiple-family dwelling of no specialized shape in which several families live together without separate quarters for individual family units. This is a housing pattern intermediate between the single-family dwelling and the true communal house, and is widespread in the Orient. The true communal house, limited in distribution as suggested above, is a "long house" which on occasion may reach the extreme length of 400 yards. In such houses there normally is one long common hallway running the whole length of the structure, and dwelling compartments are located on either side of the hallway. In shorter structures entrances normally are located only at the ends, but in the longer houses many entrances are provided. In most cases there is but one single physical structure to a village. Most commonly such houses are constructed of bamboo, matting, and thatch.

The courtyard is a distinctive feature often associated with architecture in the Mediterranean and the Near and Middle East. But as a feature of housing it runs through Central Asia, is widespread in China, occurs in Tibet, and is occasionally used in India. It may well have descended from the threshing floor, which gradually became walled in for simple protection of stored crops or for more adequate protection from robbers. Nowhere in the Orient is it a dominant feature, but the Chinese, with their desire for family privacy, have often aspired to the closed courtyard both in rural and village or city building. The threshing floor, as such, is a feature associated with housing in every agricultural section of the Orient, but only where the courtyard has developed in rural housing does the threshing floor almost become a part of the floor plan of the house. Commonly the threshing floor may be the front or back yard for a home if settlement is dispersed in nature. Village settlements sometimes incorporate threshing floors within the physical plan of the village but more normally place them on the outskirts.

The summer home in the fields is a common housing feature which is very widespread throughout the Orient, but it is nowhere a regionally dominant type. The structure serving such needs may be a fully built house used for several months every year, it may be a very simple structure requiring almost a kind of camping-out living pattern, or it may be the very simple and small structure termed a crop-watching shelter, just large enough to protect one person from sun and rain, by day and by night, during the period between ripening and harvesting of crops.

The Loess Highlands of northwestern China possess one of the most peculiar developments of housing in the modern world. Here one might say that the ancient pit house went below ground rather than came out above it. The loess is soft, stands well in vertical columns, and can be left in arched but unreinforced overhead vaults. A great many Chinese families live in homes excavated horizontally into the face of a loess bank or bluff. Large cave rooms can be easily dug out, a door fitted into the opening with a frame of windows around and above it to admit light, and there is a reasonably weatherproof house. Where vertical cuts are not numerous enough or properly distributed, Chinese have dug large square pits to house depth, retained a ramp along one wall, and excavated caves horizontally behind all four walls. This provides a courtyard and several rooms, again weatherproof. Many thousands of families in the Loess Highlands live in such homes. Though they are relatively weatherproof, they are not earthquakeproof, and in recent centuries the occasional earthquakes that have been centered in the Tibetan foothill zone have killed thousands of people in the western portion of the loess country.

The flat mud roof supported by beams and covered with reeds, poles, and brush is common in dry northwestern India, throughout Central Asia, in much of Tibet, and in northwestern China, an importation from the Middle East. Throughout the rest of the Orient the earlier patterns of roofing have all employed the gabled roof and steeply slanted surfaces to shed water. Straw thatching long has been the great common material employed in surfacing roofs. In special local areas, such as the Tibetan border country or upland Japan and Korea, wood materials in the form of planks, shingles, or bark have been used. In parts of southeastern Asia bamboo has been split and used, and perhaps bamboo "tile" gave inspiration for the common oriental curved clay tile so widely used in Japan, China, Indochina, Thailand, and Burma. Rural housing seldom has employed tile roofing, unless it be the occasional rich householder. Tile gradually supplanted thatch as the common roofing material of well-to-do city builders, owing to the inflammability of thatch, but the poorer sections of cities everywhere seldom were able to follow suit. In a few local areas slate roofing is found, but this depends clearly upon local availability. In parts of southeastern Asia, particularly in the Philippines and the Indies, nipa palm thatching commonly replaced straw, and in local areas other types of leafy thatching has long been common. The outline and appearance of the roof has many variations. Peaked, curved, and variable gable roofs are widespread. Double roof units, one underset and projecting, are common, and in many areas very wide overhangs are normally used.

Examining floor plans and house sizes, one is impressed with the fact that most of the Orient has lived in homes with small square footage per person. Though there are few data on the subject, one- and two-room houses per family unit probably outnumber all others. Middle-class families tend to have three- to four-room houses, and only the wealthier families can afford what amounts to a room or more per person. This has led to certain kinds of use patterns not common in contemporary America, except among the crowded city tenements or among the inhabitants of single apartments. The simpler social groups seldom build houses with compartmenting of space by rooms; they normally place the cooking hearth in the center of the floor, either in a pit or on a surface of stones. Advanced culture groups have tended to place the kitchen in an annex to the main house or even in a separate building to get rid of the smoke that normally goes with the oriental cooking stoves and fires. Many oriental groups do not compartmentalize such living functions as dining, living, and sleeping. Furniture is often at a minimum and tables and stools or benches are all-purpose items. Sleeping areas often are used for other purposes during the day, so that sleeping on mats on the floor is common, the bedding being rolled up and placed to one side during the day. In both Japan and southeastern Asia this is the common rule, but wherever the one- or two-room home is found the sleeping area must serve other uses by day.

Bathrooms and indoor toilets were rare in older oriental housing, as they were in the Occident. Public baths are an old institution in the towns and cities of the Orient, and toilets are commonly public also. The modern occidental, carefully coached in a convention of privacy, all too frequently finds himself embarrassed and nonplussed in those parts of the Orient where his own modern conventions have not taken hold. In the crowded Orient such matters are taken very casually and only in the larger cities is there a noticeable trend to change, except in a few local regions where modern public health programs have been vigorously carried out. In the Philippines programs of public health sanitation make the American feel less unhappy than in any other country in the whole Orient.

In much of the Orient the chief need is to cool or ventilate houses, but in the Tibetan Highland, North China, Manchuria, Korea, and northern Japan the winter heating problem is the more serious. Where the winter is cold the American finds the oriental home both cold and drafty; it is endured but not enjoyed by the local populace. Aside from the helpful but inadequate underfloor or underplatform heating device, sometimes used in North China, Manchuria, and Korea, no oriental heating techniques are effective or satisfactory.

Many of the oriental culture groups have developed particular twists to their housing patterns. In the Philippines and in parts of the Indies a bathing verandah is common, also often used for washing and drying clothing. In much of South India a wide-roofed verandah is a common feature of house construction, and in Japan a narrow south-facing verandah is often found. In Ceylon and South India, also, compartmentalization of the floor plan into functional rooms is common where the space can be at all afforded, and some such compartmentalization often occurs in China. When at all possible the Chinese reserve one room to be used as a dining room and a room where friends may visit.

Related to the floor plan and house size is the matter of crop and tool storage, the maintenance of animals, and the presence or lack of auxiliary building. Where the pile-built house is found on land, the space beneath the house normally is used to pen chickens, goats, dogs, even cattle and horses, and it also often serves as a crop-storage area. Along the Tibetan border, where multiple-story building is common, the ground floor often serves in the same way, the family living in upper levels. In China and Korea it is common to use one room of the house as a crop-storage area. Everywhere roof overhangs, ceiling space, verandahs, and other free spaces are used for crop storage by farming peoples. Many peoples throughout the Orient build special individual structures for rice and crop storage, special pig pens, animal pens, tool houses, and the like. There is almost infinite variety in this matter, but one finds that culture groups tend to act alike, so that there is regional variation in the patterns by cultural regions. Nothing like the American elaboration of farm buildings is to be found anywhere in the Orient, even today.

In common with modern trends all over the world certain changes are appearing in housing patterns in the Orient. Where the use of paint, varnish, or lacquer on wood surfaces used to be a peculiarly local matter, a few houses in every country are beginning to be painted and decorated, inside and out. Galvanized-iron or sheet-aluminum roofing commonly is replacing the inflammable and short-lived thatch roof. Wooden floors are spreading. Functional division of the floor space is increasing, and occidental floor plans are appearing here and there. As piped water becomes available kitchen sinks, shower baths, bath tubs, and flush toilets are being installed. Cement for pilings and foundation blocks, for porches and kitchen floors is becoming increasingly used. Glass is replacing paper, skin, or shell in windows, and windows are becoming hinged rather than fixed or sliding. And though the shine on a new galvanized-iron roof in Bengal is like that on one in the Philippines, housing throughout the Orient is not yet trending into one common tradition. Regionality, individuality, and peculiarity remain in the homes of the Orient.

It is difficult to suggest how many regions of housing there are in the Orient, and it is almost impossible, as yet, to present a clear map of them. In the broad sense one can distinguish a few regional patterns, but there remain discrepancies within each such region. Northwestern India, the Himalaya hill country, eastern India, the Deccan, and South India-Ceylon form recognizable divisions of India in which materials, form, and arrangement of housing vary one from the other. Throughout Burmo-Malaya the hill country everywhere is a region of many localized types, whereas in the several great lowland zones each lowland possesses its own regional pattern. The Indies show a mixture of house types, by islands and by culture groups, with Sumatra perhaps possessing the most striking individuality to be found anywhere in the Orient. The Philippines has zonal patterns within it but forms one regional major pattern. South China, the southwestern uplands, the Szechwan Basin, the Yangtze Valley, the North China Plain-Manchuria, the Loess Highlands, and northwestern China are perhaps possible regional divisions within such a large zone. Korea has a pattern of housing related to but distinct from that of China. Within Japan there is basic similarity again, but northern Honshu and Hokkaido can be distinguished from southern Japan in the way in which the house has been closed and made more weatherproof or in the way in which occidental housing patterns have been adapted.

COMMERCIAL BUILDING

In the older market towns and cities of the Orient one did not find much specialized building for stores, shops, manufacturing plants, warehouses, and the other buildings of commerce and trade. Characteristics of retail shops common to all parts of the Orient were the small street frontage, the open shop front, and shallowness in depth away from the street. And to a surprising degree these features remain common at present in the "native quarters" of cities today, and in the market towns, forming a contrast to similar buildings in the Occident and to the modernized sections of the larger and newer metropolitan settlements. In many areas the open air markets or "bazaars," and the roofed, temporary stalls on fixed sites took the place of formal stores and shops. Within the common older tradition of the Orient most commercial building seldom rose to more than two stories, though offices and shops seldom were located on second levels, these being reserved as dwelling quarters. Dwelling areas of single-story commercial building normally lay behind the store units. Warehousing in the earlier Orient seldom required special construction. Any kind of building, otherwise unused, could serve as a warehouse for the small packages and cases handled by crews of manual laborers. In the handicraft manufacturing of the Orient any home, building, or open space could be adapted to the simple processes and machines normally used.

Apart from these common features the architecture of commercial buildings normally has reflected the general regional patterns of private building. An adobe-brick market town of North India has shops varying only in detail from the pattern of housing, and in the Philippines the shop has long been housed in the same nipa-palm-leaf or wood patterns that house the residents. One of the easily noticed features is the fronts of shops and stores that may be closed at night, on holidays, or in times of civil strife. Store fronts that are fully open by day require more than simple doors as closing devices for the off-hours. The common older tradition involved some kind of movable panels, be they the solid wooden boards of China or the lighter thatch panels of the Philippines and the Indies. Wherever Chinese influence in architecture has made itself strongly felt—Korea, Japan, Indochina, Thailand—the practice is to use slotted ground and ceiling plates into which narrow vertical boards are fitted to fill most of the open space, with one or more door units, so as to present a solid front. Some variation of the movable panel is employed almost everywhere in commercial building.

The earliest occidentals in the Orient rented, bought, or built native structures. Only gradually did they replace native construction with their own styles in the older cities and towns. In the newly founded settlements construction normally was that of the country from which the occidental came. British-built cities in India are full of ill-assorted old British buildings, Saigon came to resemble a French provincial town, and the Spanish in the Philippines built much as they did in southern Spain.

As more and more occidental business concerns came to operate in oriental markets, and as orientals returned from abroad, steady changes came about in commercial building of all sorts. Stores gradually became modeled on occidental designs, with changes in architecture resulting. Closed fronts and fixed doors appeared on retail stores along with newly styled false fronts and rearranged interiors. Warehouses gradually became specialized buildings, newly designed and built, and often located in particular sections of cities and towns. Factory buildings became specialized as power and machines came into general use, with formal layouts and occidental building materials and styles.

This pattern of change in commercial building began in those port cities to which the earliest occidental traders came. These cities, along with the new cities founded by the occidental, became the centers of architectural influence from which some of the styles, methods, and materials gradually infiltrated the broad hinterlands of the Orient. As native artisans and designers gradually gained familiarity with the new features they have adapted and adopted them more and more widely, and it is a rare city that does not now display something of at least pseudo-occidental commercial building. Some cities have become so transformed that, in their business, warehouse, or factory districts they are almost indistinguishable in architecture from occidental cities. This will be a continuing development, and gradually a blending in motifs and styling will increasingly spread a "modern oriental" architecture that revitalizes some of the old native elements in architecture to combine them with useful elements in occidental architectural design.

PUBLIC ARCHITECTURE

In the fields of religious, monumental, and administrative architecture there have been many separate traditions of building in the Orient, perhaps dominated by six main sets of influences: Babylonian, Greek, Chinese, Indian, Persian, and occidental. Babylonian here is used with reference to the ancient tradition of the Middle East, the town and city building of the Tigris-Euphrates region. It is evident that this tradition strongly affected the architecture of fortifications, castles, and administrative buildings in North China from the first appearance of adobe-brick and pounded-earth walls around towns, cities, and states. It is difficult to distinguish clearly the continuing results of this tradition, amidst later developments and, as yet, to be sure of its relationships to religious and monumental building as such. Greek ideas in public architecture spread widely into Asia in the late centuries of the pre-Christian era, with other Greek ideas variably entering into regional complexes, and the resulting Hellenistic influences later and slowly spread almost completely throughout the Orient to some degree.

Chinese public architecture, as it finally matured, was a blend of local, Babylonian, and Hellenistic ideas, techniques, plans, and materials. Local is used here to include both the northern Chinese culture hearth and the southern regions sometimes called "barbarian."

Developed Chinese influences affected Central Asia, Tibet, and the whole of the Far East, Korea, Japan, Indochina, and Thailand, though the influences in Malaya, the Indies, and the Philippines have been more recent and lesser in strength.

Earlier Indian architecture was also a blend of local, Babylonian, and Hellenistic components, but it developed profuse ornamentation in which native Hindu religious motivations came to dominate Babylonian and Hellenistic features and which led it to far different ends from those achieved in the plainer and more realistic Chinese architecture. Indian architecture spread its influences throughout parts of southeastern Asia, touching southern Burma, Thailand, and Indochina, all of the Malay Peninsula, reaching deeply into the Indies, and lightly touching the Philippines.

Persian influences were introduced late into the Orient, chiefly into India and beyond under the control of the Moslem immigrants. Gradually the older Indian construction in the northwest and north became replaced by a new kind of Moslem construction which eventually became dominant. This new pattern spread, to some degree, wherever the Moslems gained a foothold, but its effect beyond North India is light and incomplete. A Persian would scarcely recognize a Moslem mosque, palace, or government building in the Moro country of the southern Philippines.

Occidental influences in public architecture have been the last in the long series to enter the field of public construction in the Orient. In the early centuries of occidental contact this set of influences, diverse in itself, produced some real monstrosities, designed by occidentals but executed by orientals who never quite grasped the full artistic implications of occidental design. Gradually some synthesis of East and West has here been achieved, with basic design, materials, and techniques from the occidental side, artistic motifs and execution from the native side, the whole revitalized into such creations as "modern Chinese" or "modern Japanese." Many of the newer Chinese university and administrative buildings are masterful combinations of occidental and oriental materials, design, and execution, and the best in modern Indian construction is an artful blend of Hellenistic, Indian, Persian, and occidental influences, erected in stone, steel, concrete, and brick. In the Philippines, Thailand, or Sumatra this artful synthesis has perhaps not yet come to full fruition in a regionally independent architecture. Every culture region of the Orient today is moving toward some such cultural blending of public architecture, interweaving the various traditional elements of design and materials with the modern elements.

The Patterns of Historical Contact

THE PRE-COLUMBIAN OLD WORLD

In pre-Columbian times the two ends of the Old World lay a long way apart, with never a clear connection between the extremes. Though not at the same time, the Indians and the pre-Islamic Arabs operated early sea links in the south center, varied Mongols and Turks opened and closed Central Asian caravan routes, and Rome and the Italian city states operated the Mediterranean link in the southwest. Perhaps the most knowledgeable people of all were the Arabic and Indian traders who ranged the sea routes between the Red Sea or Persian Gulf and the South China coast. They were not men who told their trade secrets or wrote serious travel books, but they did relate many a good yarn, as can be found in any collection of "Sinbad the Sailor" stories. From these wanderers both ends of the Old World learned a little, but all too little. When a blight fell over the West during the Middle Ages the Chinese still were expanding their geographical knowledge, but they never did expand their horizon to include western Eurasia. A few curious Chinese always have wandered widely, but there never developed a widespread passion for geographical exploration, and the leaders of Chinese society never gave encouragement to travel and exploration beyond the margins of the Chinese known world. The Mongol "open door" administrative policy of the twelfth and thirteenth centuries allowed more travel in, and freer contact with, eastern Asia by its neighbors than had ever obtained before. A little of this knowledge reached the ears of such men as Marco Polo, to inspire exploratory travel. At the dawn of the modern era, however, no one had been everywhere in the Old World, and in no country could there be drawn a reasonably good map of Eurasia. The accompanying sketch map is merely suggestive of this regional ignorance.

As the European end of the Old World began to waken, it developed a curiosity about peoples and places, and a passion for new products, which never had existed anywhere in earlier historic time unless it was the curiosity of the early Japanese about Chinese culture. It was not, of course, merely pure curiosity that prompted wakening Europe to explore the edges of their known world. Their environment was not rich in useful products, nor was it favorably situated on the trade routes of the Old World. The blocking of those routes, or the levying of heavy taxes upon the products flowing along the routes, was of serious import to Europe. Out of this curiosity and self-interest flowered the government-supported great discoverers of early modern Europe, who finally did go everywhere in the Old World, and in the New World too.

In 1475 overland roads between West and East probably were in worse shape than they had been for centuries, and travel and transport were slow, costly, and full of risks. The Mongol empire had broken down, India was not a well-organized unit, and the Turkish peoples coming into ascendancy in western Asia had too little appreciation of interregional trade to facilitate it. Products like pepper, sugar, and sandalwood sold in Europe for fabulous prices, but the fact was that small volumes did get through. Per ton-mile costs were high, for goods making the whole trip from the Indies to England had to pass through the hands of many traders and transporters and to pay toll to many a regional overlord. The alternative sea routes were no cheaper, faster, or more capable of handling large volumes. Ships were small in size, poor in manageability, and inefficient in sailing power. Proper knowledge of the wind systems did not exist, there was no continuous sea route, and no charts existed that were reliable as to length of journey, possible alternative ports of call, or the sources of products.

In this situation both southern India and western Malaysia were in a peculiarly favored position. Whereas the Mediterranean basin was the focus of many of the land routes of the Old World, the coasts of southern India and western Malaysia were the meeting ground of the chief sea lanes of the Old World. Here Indonesians, Indians, Chinese, and Arabs met in scores of ports. South Indian historical records are rich in accounts of busy ports with crowded foreign quarters in which many races were common and the

of a voyage that a ship could not be properly worked. Though the West has made much of the leaders and commanders among the great discoverers, the lot of the common crewman was a hard one, and crews were hard to get. Though a few priests and men who were educated for their time went along, those of the crew remaining alive upon arrival in India or the Indies often

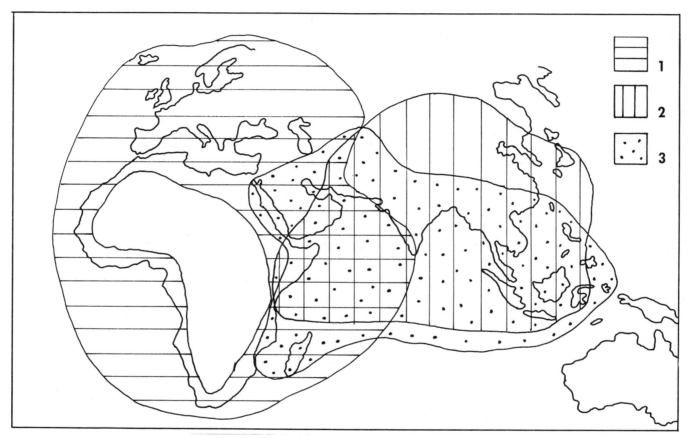

Fig. 36. West European, Chinese, and Indian known worlds before discovery of the Americas. (1) West European known world; (2) Chinese known world; (3) Indian known world.

economic products of the whole of the Old World were to be found. If the Malays inclined a little more to piracy, the Chinese had the biggest and fastest ships, and the Arabs may well have been the sharpest and most experienced traders.

THE COMING OF THE EUROPEAN

The sixteenth century sea route to India was a dangerous seaway strewn with death by wreck, starvation, thirst, and a host of malignant diseases. It was common for a fifth to a third of a crew and passengers to die on the way out, and for the story to be repeated on the homeward voyage. Not at all rare were cases in which so small a crew remained alive at the end

were tough characters. Seldom could they be called the best representatives of European cultures. But, curiously enough, the European brought two naive presumptions, that of the superiority of white skin over brown, yellow, and black, and that of the superiority of Christendom over the heathen and the infidel. And in their own way the Arabs, the Indians, and the Chinese had their own standards and judgments of the superiority of culture, religion, and trading ability.

The Europeans often were entranced with what they saw and found, but it was the attraction of greed under heavy odds. These first European traders came into markets, operated and frequented by races of men long skilled at sharp trading with each other. Prices of products were far lower than in Europe, and the potential profits were great, but the risks of an unsuccessful voyage home also were great. Then, too, the presence of interlopers in the Indian Ocean trade realm was widely resented, and the inexperience of the European in sharp trading often made him a loser.

The early European trader arriving in India found himself at a disadvantage, for European handicraft manufacture produced little that was of value to the high cultures of the East with whom first contacts were made. The industrial revolution had not yet begun to turn out its streams of products, and gold and silver soon were found to be about the only things the European had in which the East was interested. This also had been true in earlier days when much Roman Empire gold found its way to India in payment for eastern trade products. On the other hand, pepper, sugar, and sandalwood did not long remain the only items which interested the European. Cotton and silk textiles in many forms, the full range of spices, many kinds of scented and beautiful woods, ivory, jewels, porcelain, all manner of carved and enameled art goods, and a wide range of tonics and materia medica were to be had.

It is not to be expected that all the natives of the East got along perfectly before the European came. But it is true that the Europeans did not get along any better with each other in their eastern contacts than they did in Europe. Rivalry between Portuguese, Spanish, Dutch, English, and French, severally and in combination, was a standard part of the growth of eastern exploration and trade. This rivalry went so far as to justify piracy on each other's ships or to raid a native port with one ship out of an expedition, only to have a second ship turn up later as rescuers who blamed some other nationality for the outlandish actions. On the other hand, the sea-empire of Madjapahit, centered in western Malaysia, had finally collapsed only shortly before the Europeans came on the scene. Moslem politicians-of-fortune, local regional chieftains, and varied port rulers had not yet done squabbling over the division of the spoils. While the Islamic faith had spread rapidly in Malaysia, so had the renewed art of piracy. A vital corner of the Old World was in turbulent flux, but in a different way from that in Europe.

The above factors permitted a variety of situations in the early meeting of East and West. And if friendly contacts were not rare, unfriendly ones generated a greater height of feeling. For the first time the two extremes of Eurasia came face to face. They met as traders with products and profits as the goals on each side. But these first contacts involved more than the matching of skill and shrewdness at trade bargaining, with simple profit or loss their total result. They were the first meetings of the leading cultures of the Old World, such as they were. One group of cultures, that of Europe, was on the move, dynamic, eager, ambitious, and aggressive, but not completely unscrupulous by the standards of the day. The rate and the force with which Europe reached out into the several environments of the world to sample their products dictated the patterns of history and prompted the general trends in culture change the world over.

THE PROGRESS OF THE DISCOVERIES

The Portuguese went east, as the Spanish went west, toward the East. And to the Portuguese fell the job of first charting the new region. Their first visit to India, before 1500, disclosed the fact that this was but a wholesaling center and not the origin of the spices that were the first order of business. Portuguese contacts, therefore, quickly touched Ceylon, Malaya, Sumatra, Java, and Borneo, groping eastward toward the primary sources. By 1525 they had probed their way to the Moluccas and had skirted the coasts of most of the mainland of southern Asia as far around as southern China. By 1542 they had reached Japan. Somewhat rowdy and lawless conduct caused some setbacks in a number of places, but the middle of the century saw the preliminary reconnaissance of the East completed.

Many Dutch crewmen were on the early Portuguese voyages of exploration, and eastern goods reached the Low Countries via Portuguese ports. In the political patterns of the Europe of the day, the Low Countries had been under Spanish rule, but they rebelled in the late sixteenth century. With the Spanish ruler also holding title in Portugal, Portuguese ports were closed to Low Countries ships. This stimulated ambitious Dutch traders to begin making their own ventures into the East. The spread of geographical knowledge and the independence of Holland from Iberian rule changed things, and it was not long before both Dutch and English began competing with the Portuguese. The Spanish reached the Philippines early, but spread beyond only to a limited degree. The French were slow on the sea and were less active in the early period. On land the Russians were pushing out overland toward the Pacific, but their progress was slightly slower. Random explorers of several nationalities ventured to follow the old caravan routes eastward, returning to tell variations of Marco Polo's story.

By 1600 many islands were still unknown, and unexplored economic possibilities lay almost everywhere in the Orient. But by this date the Portuguese and

Spanish monopolies had been broken, and competition began to lower prices and to heighten the tension between the European principals. During the seventeenth century Portugal, Holland, and England led the trade war in the Orient. Such countries as France, Denmark, and Sweden made a few ventures by sea. Throughout the century there was considerable shifting about from port to port and coast to coast by the numerous expeditions, with traders of one nationality trying a port or coast given up by others. At first this was trial-and-error sampling, but eventually the contest became one of strength, the strongest squadron of ships or the strongest nationality laying more or less permanent claim to trading rights at certain ports or along certain coasts believed to be profitable sources of eastern products. By 1700 the primary discoveries within the Orient were completed, an economic sampling had been made, and things settled down to a political and military contest among the leading countries of western Europe.

FROM TRADER TO RULER

In 1600 "The Governor and Company of Merchants of London Trading into the East Indies" was chartered as a corporation holding a monopoly on British trade with the East, which for this purpose was defined as the region lying between the Cape of Good Hope and the Straits of Magellan. Two years later the Dutch set up a similar company, and in 1616 the Danes launched a third. These companies set up trading stations known as "factories" in port cities thought to be points of vantage. Each company attempted to monopolize the trade of the local region. Conflicts soon arose over prices, quantity measures, the monopoly aspect, the rights of Chinese, Arab, and other traders, and out of sundry religious and social causes. The Europeans often found themselves unable to enforce what they callously termed their trade rights, and they gradually began to assume police power over the local port, its settlement, and the immediate hinterland. India was in a state of political readjustment during the seventeenth and eighteenth centuries, and such events were not good for trade. Similarly, the numerous petty states and autonomous ports throughout the Indies made difficult the enlargement and extension of trade agreements. The Portuguese had first used this system, but the Dutch and the English soon followed suit.

Upon the heels of this self-assumed police power followed the trade treaty negotiated between the company "factor" or chief representative and a native governor or ruler. Treaty "violation" by the native brought reprisal by the European and the self-righteous extension of local police power. This slowly developed into regional political administration. The companies acquired armies, diplomatic staffs, and a kind of civil service corps having little to do with trade as such. Competition between Dutch, Portuguese, and English resulted in maneuvers on a constantly widening scale. The aims were economic spheres of influence in which each company's monopoly trade agreements would shut out traders of other companies and nationalities. Upon the sea naval squadrons and armed escorts were required to fend off resentful Arab shipping groups, unsympathetic rulers of native coastal states, and the ships of other European nations. In this struggle the Arab traders and many local Indian and Malay states stubbornly tried to maintain some independent privilege, but the Chinese rather rapidly disappeared from Indian Ocean waters and temporarily shifted out of the Malaysian sea trade. This increasing program ended with political conquest in each case. The program consumed the whole of the seventeenth century and most of the eighteenth. Such was the unforeseen conclusion to the competitive philosophy of a Europe that had not reconciled its economic and political ideas with the great world its discoverers had found.

THE COLONIAL EMPIRES

The aim of each European country in the East was to corner the best sources of eastern trade products in order to control the European market. In the hands of trading corporations operating at a distance and somewhat out of touch with political controls at home, the end product of a vigorous trade policy inevitably was political and military control over extensive regions. In the latter part of the period it became openly a scramble for colonies with no apology of any kind. A brief statement of the geographical distribution of these colonial acquisitions is necessary.

Portugal's early influence was spread so widely and so thinly that before her local trading posts had grown into extensive regions England and Holland had seized many of the choice spots. Portugal gradually came to hold only a few scattered ports more or less under sufferance by the British and Dutch. Today five holdings, scattered from South China to northwestern India, demonstrate the former range of the Portuguese. The Dutch East India Company sent out many more ships than did the English concern in the early years of the seventeenth century, so that the Dutch were able to forcibly exclude the British from the regions nearest the Moluccas, the chief home of the spices.

Gradually the Indies became a Dutch preserve, though many islands were left entirely alone in the earlier period. The weaker British company concentrated on peninsular India, and the Arabian trade bases in the northern Gulf of Arabia. As the British gathered strength they harried the Dutch, particularly, and

French port-territories remain as evidence. Anxious to have some part of a colonial empire the French moved on east to settle on Cochin-China and gradually to work up the coast and gain control of what today is Indochina. French efforts also secured a number of islands out in the Pacific beyond the Indies. Den-

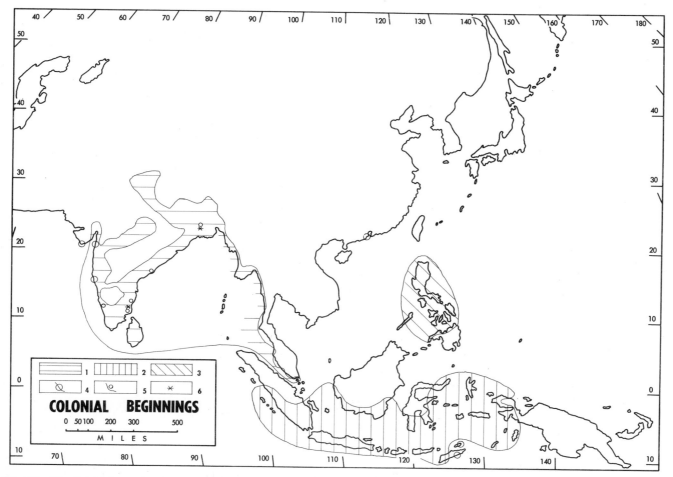

Fig. 37. The beginnings of colonial empires, 1823–1826: (1) British-controlled zone; (2) Dutch-controlled zone; (3) Spanish-controlled zone; (4) Portuguese port stations; (5) French port stations; (6) Danish trade stations.

gradually seized many ports and regions that the Dutch had taken from the Portuguese. In a last series of military adjustments between the two countries, Britain kept all Dutch holdings on the mainland of Asia, at the same time retiring from the island world entirely. This gave Britain full control of India, Burma, and Malaya. In the midnineteenth century a last British charter company picked a vacant space in the Dutch island world without being challenged and planted a commercial colony that has grown into the several British sections of Borneo.

France came late into the East, to be beaten off by the British in India, though a scattering of four small

mark, Sweden, and the other countries having trade interests in the East never were in a position to acquire regional control over territory, so that they do not appear in the list of colonial powers. The Danes lasted longest, finally selling out their last trading post to the British in the midnineteenth century.

Germany came very late upon the scene as a colony hunter. Little was left, but an unoccupied section of New Guinea, and some of the islands marginal to the Indies, plus others in the open Pacific, had to be the German share. These became Japanese and Australian during the First World War. Spain, having come early, concentrated upon the Philippines without serious challenge. Though her commercial effects were not great her cultural effects upon the Philippines were marked. Last of all came the United States, perhaps accidentally, to acquire the only Spanish colonial holdings in the East, the Philippine Islands and a few small islands in the western Pacific. The two accompanying maps present the colonial picture at its beginning and at its peak.

stricted by being located on a small peninsula at a distance from the great port of Canton, and here the Portuguese were satisfied to remain. The early Dutch, British, and Americans chafed at this sort of treatment but made little headway with the reluctant Chinese. The Dutch were similarly tolerated but restricted for a long period in southern Japan.

Only as the Chinese government weakened under a

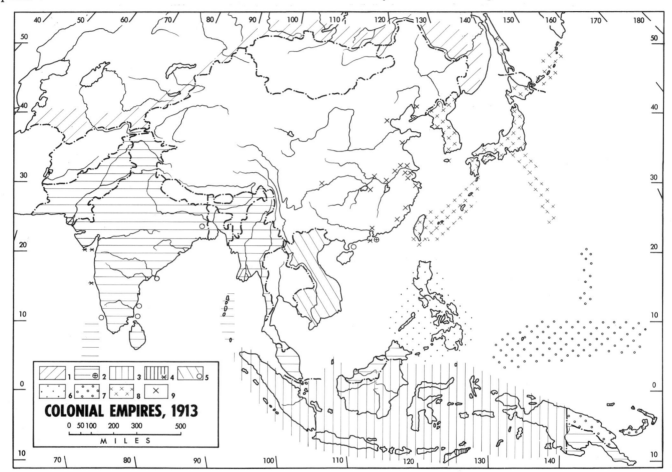

Fig. 38. Colonial empires in 1913: (1) Russian territory; (2) British holdings; (3) Dutch territory; (4) Portuguese holdings; (5) French holdings; (6) United States area, isolated Pacific islands omitted; (7) German zone; (8) Japan and Japanese holdings; (9) Settlement concessions in China granted to occidental powers.

By virtue of having few products of interest to Europe and by playing the Europeans off one against the other, Thailand was able to slip through the colonial net as the only part of southern Asia not a colonial holding. China, Korea, and Japan were far enough away from the center of trade attraction to be less molested in the early developments. Each country also was able, through a centralized government of some strength, to control European traders sufficiently to prevent the accretion of European colonies. In South China the Portuguese were tolerated but re-

decaying Manchu dynasty and the occidental powers gained strength did they finally succeed in securing concessions of territory and unequal trade privileges. These came in the shape of treaty ports and foreign concessions scattered along the China coast in the latter half of the nineteenth century. By then, however, every occidental country was wary of the other, though Japan was able to enter the picture and seize the Ryukyus, Formosa, and Korea. So-called spheres of influence were effective in limited degree, but the American Open Door Policy helped prevent further, final dismemberment of China. Germany, France, and Japan each were at one time or another prevented from carving a political holding out of China proper.

It thus seemed for a time that the colonial dismemberment of the Orient had ended, only to be renewed by the Japanese in 1931 with the grab of Manchuria, which expanded rapidly into the Japanese bid to take

TECHNIQUES OF EXPLOITATION

The formation of colonial empires and spheres of influence was accompanied by the shift of political power from the hands of native groups to those of occidental governments. In India, Burma, the Indies, Malaya, and the Philippines the process was carried

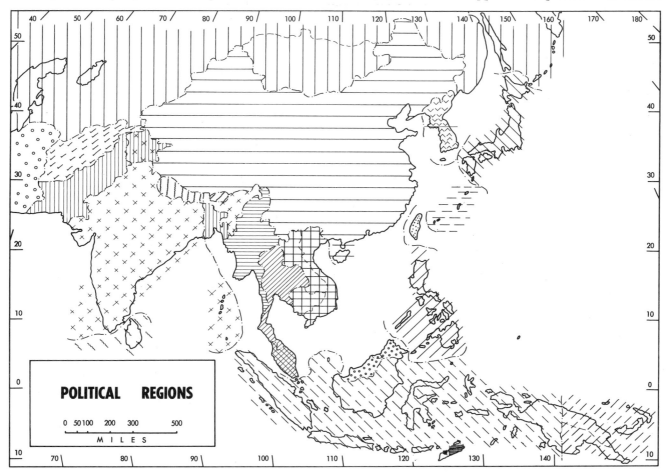

Fig. 39. Political regions of the Orient, 1953. Each political unit is shown in a different symbol. Two areas of conflict are in Korea and Kashmir. In New Guinea and Borneo formerly distinct units are now being brought together. Isolated port stations in India and China are not shown.

over the whole of the Orient between 1937–1945. In the heat of the struggle with Japan the "secession" of Outer Mongolia from China and the "annexation" to Soviet Russia was quietly achieved in such a way that it hardly resembled a colonial grab. Chinese Sinkiang is in danger of going the same way in time, and the alarmist fears for part or all of Manchuria and even for China itself. Colonial acquisition today is of a different pattern than formerly. Alignment of regions and political entities with Soviet Russia may have all the force of colonial acquisition, yet it must sometimes be described in other political terms.

out in such a way that only the end products were noticeable. Indochina was a marginal case more obviously gobbled up. Formosa and Korea also form a special case, since they were the result of a purely oriental contest. In China, and to some extent in Thailand and Japan, the techniques were applied in piecemeal fashion at a rather late date by various occidental governments, with rather different visible result. A brief summary of these varied methods will help to explain several features in political geography.

The least political of the techniques was the conscious and systematic breaking of the natural trade monopolies. The regional control over sugar, spices, cotton and its textiles, tea, and silk are the most obvious of these, though there were other lesser examples also. Sugar cane spread very widely just at the opening of the world discoveries, and no Indian export trade ever had a chance to develop. Spices were introduced into many other tropical lands, and their natural production was so scattered that the monopoly of the Indies had disappeared long before contemporary synthetic spices had become important. Cotton growing was introduced into several new regions to break the Indian production leadership. Tea was spread to India and the Indies from China. Silk was widely produced in small quantities but many local conditions prevented the easy transfer of production leadership from China to other regions. Its development in Japan came at a relatively late date.

The Opium War between England and China during 1839–1842 was a means of forcing trade upon China at a time when British economy still had not begun producing sufficient export products to pay for her own purchases in China. The development of the treaty-port system and extraterritoriality was the means of gaining legal entry into a resisting China without a deliberate military conquest. Consequent upon their limited victory in the Opium War, the British exacted the cession of the island of Hongkong and special economic and political privileges in five Chinese ports in 1842. The United States and France promptly asked for the same privileges, and the treaty-port system had begun. From time to time other nations secured privileges, and more ports were opened at foreign demand. These are shown on the accompanying map. In such ports many nations held special territorial concessions, each in effect a colonial holding inside China. The system lasted for a century, and the ports involved became the centers of social, political, and economic change in modern China. The special privileges accruing to occidental corporations and individuals came to be used by unscrupulous Chinese to help undermine their own economy.

In neither Thailand nor Japan did the Occident succeed in setting up the sequence of events that operated so well in China. Thailand lost territory to the French, but in 1909 bought off the special British privileges with the cession to Britain of the four northern states of the present Federation of Malaya. Japan was successful in throwing off the early efforts at similar penetration in her own home territory and at fending them off both in Formosa and in Korea.

In countries which became colonial lands the ability to control taxes, levy export and import tariffs, rearrange the land systems, and manipulate the growth of the transport systems all operated clearly in the favor of the occidental exploiters. The early practice of training in occidental schools only such skills as were of value to occidental corporations and the lower ranks of colonial civil service was perpetuated for too long. The similar pointing of other developments in modernization that were profitable mostly to the West is a part of the whole colonial program. The granting of foreign loans, with quite ample interest provisions, to native rulers or to political states too often had exploitive economic concessions tacked on as necessary evils. Even in China the existence of treaty-port bases gave outside traders extremely favored positions. The Japanese abused these privileges as heavily as did any occidental country. The Chinese for a time lost control over their own import and export tariffs but never did lose control over their land system outside the treaty ports.

A further feature of such special economic privilege lay in the growing occidental control over the carrying trade after the development of the steamship. Whereas all occidental lands have insisted upon the nationalization of their coastal trade by sea, occidental shipping interests exploited the trade of the Orient to the fullest. Only in Japan was there any real restraint upon this particular development. China's sudden ending of the freedom of coastal waters and the closing to foreign shipping of most of her former open ports, after World War II, made impossible the return of the former shipping patterns and aggravated her own economic recovery since she had no commercial fleet with which to carry her goods.

The Processes of Modernization

THE INITIAL IMPRESS OF THE WEST

Has China been improved by her relations with the West and have the Javanese a pleasanter prospect for having had contact with the Dutch for 350 years? Many orientals today would interpret the contacts of the whole period as resulting in distinct retrogression for the Orient. Others would point out that the terms modernization and westernization are not synonymous. Many would assert that the Occident came off much the best in the interchange of culture. A liberal and tolerant observer would recognize that, since the Orient contains at least half the population of the globe, there can be no simple statement of the results of culture contact. Political colonialism throws an unduly large shadow over consideration of the interaction of East and West.

The first impressions created by the West tended to be those of high-handed and lawless greed, occasionally touched by an irrational and cruel sort of kindness, governed by a new kind of religious intolerance, and backed by a militant power superior in effectiveness to anything known in the East. One must equate these judgments against the levels of regional and group culture of the period.

In the sixteenth century the lower and middle classes of north and western Europe still had not taken on a mellow cultural polish. Christendom was highly intolerant of other religions and, while curious about the mores of other peoples, was inclined to be suspicious of other cultures. In southern India at the time Vijayanagar was a wealthier, more highly developed, and more sophisticated state than any in Europe. The Ming emperors ruled a China whose cultural level surpassed anything in Europe for effete sophistication and maturity. But in the Philippines and the outer Indies were peoples still close to the Stone Age in their concepts of mechanics, tools and equipment, cult magic, and social organization. Throughout China, Burmo-Malaya, and India were refugee elements unable to cope with the higher levels of either East or West. And in Korea and Japan were people becoming obsessed with the odd notion that the world could be shut out at will.

Repeatedly it has been pointed out that race and culture contact at different levels produces varied results. Racial absorption may involve little culture change. Fusion of people and culture may occur. Race contact, without assimilation, may accompany side-by-side cultural evolution. Non-assimilative race contact may result in a large share of cultural synthesis by the simpler society. This cultural synthesis may include constructive and destructive elements alike. Generally speaking, in the Orient there occurred little of the racial extinction that followed the white man about the Americas. Trade and commerce of a high order were more important than colonization and settlement. Where the Dutch early tried a kind of limited assimilation in the Indies, the British set themselves up as a white super-Brahman caste in India. Side-by-side cultural evolution, with effective interchange, has taken place between the West and those eastern peoples of high native cultures. Cultural synthesis, partaking both of East and West, has occurred among simpler peoples. Some of the refugee tribesmen of the Indian Chota-Nagpur hill country today have living relatives who have become urban residents and semi-skilled workmen of Jamshedpur's great steel plant. If the West progressed more rapidly during the seventeenth through nineteenth centuries, the East now is rapidly gaining momentum and closing the gap.

THE OPENING WEDGES AND EASTERN REACTIONS

Several tools helped to start the process of change in varying parts of the Orient. Foremost was simple commercial trade, largely of an export nature, between the southern Orient and the Europe so anxious for spices, silks, cottons, and art goods. Those regions having the largest native trade and the most sought-after products received the greatest attention. Trading stations and permanent settlements became exhibitions of culture and "county fairs" in many a port throughout the Orient. Early in the process the zealous Christian missionary appeared, Catholic in the early period, often to intercede between the poor heathen and the avid trader. To put it bluntly, the economic advantages of becoming Christian soon became apparent to many orientals. The mission program, however, worked in ever-widening circles to originate an endless cultural chain reaction. The use of native personnel in police corps, clerical staffs, ships' crews, shops, and processing stations very early became a potent agent in teaching occidental techniques. The formation, by the European industrial revolution itself, of a whole new series of techniques, tools, equipment, and products produced reactions in many parts of the East.

Though no complete summary can be made, patterns of oriental reaction can be suggested. The widespread Arab trader class, with home ports around the Arabian Gulf from the south Indian coast to Zanzibar on the African coast, usually made war on the interloping European traders. A period of sea fighting eliminated them as a serious threat to European commercial trade. The more general Indian coastal and Malaysian attitude was one of willingness to trade upon reasonable terms, since flourishing trade was of long standing. Commerce was accompanied, however, by constant fighting over disagreements and unequal codes of conduct, accompanied by piracy and looting on both sides. In the Indies the lack of unified political and social control by any group over the thousands of islands permitted a great variety of conditions. In the more developed areas trade interests largely controlled reaction; in less advanced islands and regions simpler societies reacted negatively and submissively, as to a dominant force. Organized Indian states, themselves involved in a complicated game of power politics for the control of India, reacted variably. Sometimes they openly met the Occident on even terms, but the more frequent intrigue and counter-intrigue on all sides took the willing Europeans deeper and deeper into the Indian problem.

The Chinese met the Europeans with a tolerant disinterest, but with considerable control over events and the field of play. This resulted in a restriction of the exhibition and display of occidental culture to the Chinese, which made China slow to appreciate the dynamic power of the West. The very looseness of the bonds of Chinese culture covered the impact of early western penetration so that it seemed that China changed not at all in the early periods of contact. In Japan conditions were almost opposite to those both in China and in India. A very tight set of cultural bonds was strongly reinforced by tightening political control. The first contacts with the West forcefully impressed a few very influential Japanese. On the decision of a few leaders Japan closed her doors to East and West alike in an almost unprecedented manner. Somewhat similar was the reaction of Korea, almost as effective in delaying the process of modernization.

All this variety of reaction established very different patterns of contact between East and West, and set up interactions operating at very different rates. In a number of instances the original reaction patterns were radically altered by later events to completely redirect the whole sequence of culture growth.

THE EXPANSION OF NATIVE ECONOMY

Between 1500 and 1800 the Occident stimulated the growth of a large volume of export trade in the special products of the East. Trade had flourished for centuries, but its volume was slight compared to that which began when the Europeans brought in new wealth and increasing numbers of ships. Every country except Korea and Japan was affected to some degree. As an added factor for China, by 1750 emigrants to the South Seas had again started homeward the endless flow of cash remittances to South China.

Wealth from an increasing export trade reacted upon agriculture and the handicrafts, since many of the products were agricultural in origin. Increases in agricultural productivity began to stimulate population growth. Such increases were quite uneven in different regions. Areas suffering internal political strife failed to increase markedly until stability returned. Zones of lesser trade showed little early reaction. Perhaps the southeastern coast of India and the southeastern provinces of China were the first to show such increases.

A part of increasing agriculture involved new American crop plants, giving new range and depth to land use in almost every region. Some new plants became commercial products; others formed basic foods of local regions. The sweet potato, maize, the peanut, white potato, pineapple, tobacco, and the tomato are among the earlier crops. The export demand for farm products has never slackened, though the crop and regional focus has repeatedly shifted. More recently other new plants have come into the Orient, or into new regions. Tea from China into India and the Indies, coffee, cacao, cinchona, several oil seeds, rubber, sisal, and the oil palm have all been added. New trade has arisen in old oriental crops such as tung oil, soybeans, abaca, jute, and ramie, along with a host of minor products.

Occidental industrial maturity, the completion of the Suez Canal, and the evolution of the steamship introduced new elements. In the realm of handicrafts the oriental had been dominant, but the power machine gave the advantage to the Occident. Gradually the Occident began to ship goods instead of cash to pay for its purchases in the East. Machine-made goods were attractive, and most of the Orient could afford to buy. During the late nineteenth century oriental imports grew by leaps and bounds, to some seeming endless in limitation.

Acquaintance with new products of all kinds brought a changing consumer demand. This went hand in hand with learning to use new crops of all kinds. Such changes, along with sheer population increases, make up a significant aspect of the modernization of the Orient. The stimulation of greater trade, agricultural production, changing consumer habits, and population growth was also fundamental in the modernization of the Occident. In each major realm these changes were interrelated but subject to major regional cultural controls.

THE CHRISTIAN MISSIONARY

To the Christian missionary there is almost no unknown land anywhere in the Orient. Both men and women missionaries have been almost everywhere. Their primary business has been to preach the Christian gospel, but no aspect of culture has remained outside their concern. Many missionary schools and hospitals were started to secure students and patients to whom to preach, on the side resulting in generations of educated people and in thousands of doctors, nurses, clinics, and improvements in public health. The missionary architect, often working with strange materials and unfamiliar craftsmen, has devised and created styles of building that have been copied far and wide. Hundreds of newspapers, journals, and local publishers stand in debt to the missionary evangelists who, in order to get their literature printed in odd languages,

have done everything from devising new forms of writing to making type and teaching the craft of printing. Many a missionary has restored vanishing regional art motifs and handicraft skills through simple sewing guilds and workshops, and many a modern business family got its start on a loan from a missionary. The missionary often began by bringing from abroad seeds for his private garden and has gone on to motivate much of the work in improved plant breeding for the people of his region.

The Christian Church has made numerous assaults upon Asia, but none of the pre-Columbian programs lasted. With the early post-Columbian discoverers and traders went Catholic priests, restricted in program by the occidental culture of their period. The modern world-wide missionary movement began in the nineteenth century, and today it includes every form of Catholic and Protestant religion. In its modern program the Christian Church has confused many an oriental by its profusion of sects and contradiction of creeds, a condition made worse by the failure of occidental businessmen to follow a supposedly occidental code of life.

There can be no question that the modern mission program has succeeded in planting Christianity firmly in most of the Orient. Tibet-Nepal-Bhutan forms a blank void, the Mongolias and Japan are very weak links, and many parts of the Indies and Indochina remain yet untouched. Many individual mission stations seem only to hold their own in numbers of religious followers, while engaging in fruitful education and social welfare. Nevertheless, Christianity as such is growing. Since 1920 there has been rapid growth on the part of native churches, indicating that the Christian religion is now self-perpetuating, though not thoroughly independent of occidental sponsorship. In its further spread Christendom continues to be an agent of cultural change.

It is worth noting that the Christian missionary program, on the whole, has succeeded better among animist groups than among those with well-developed religions. Particularly is it notable that few Moslems have been converted to Christianity. It often is said that orientals adopted Christianity when economic profit was possible, but this is only a partial truth. Hindus of lower caste, socially underprivileged, have become Christians for more than economic profit motives. It may be questioned why the Christian program has not succeeded as completely as the earlier spread of the Moslem religion. This would require a rather complete analysis of comparative cultural positions of the Orient at the advent of both religious systems and is beyond present space limits.

THE GROWTH OF MODERN MECHANICS

Many an American has deplored the inability of an oriental peasant to use a wrench properly on a motor without pausing to reflect upon the situation. Many American youngsters grow up with tools and early become accustomed to the workability of metals and the fine tolerances demanded. Yet the American marvels at what the oriental can do with tools with which he, too, has grown up and fully understands. There are orientals who are fully at home in engineering mechanics, but the number forms only a fraction of the population. The automobile, for example, has been created wholly within the life span of men now living, and one cannot expect half the world's people to know just how to adjust a fuel pump when the total automobiles at their disposal at any one time number under 350,-000 vehicles. In the United States there now are over 25,000,000 vehicles, but many an American dares not tamper with his own car's engine.

Most of today's mechanical equipment is the creation of the Occident. Most of it is expensive, and only a minimum has reached the Orient, though the diversity of that equipment is great. Native skills in many lines are growing steadily. The changing equipment of transport reaches constantly into new regions. The world of print, and the technical manual, is opening steadily wider. The growth of power facilities is slow still, but it is widely distributed. Industrialization is spreading in varied forms, and that India had the largest steel plant in the British Empire was no accident. Since the Orient started late it well may skip many of the early stages which occidental countries went through.

The Orient long has lacked capital with which to launch many of the enterprises needed. Slowly capital resources are accumulating, and the ending of occidental exploitation will speed that accumulation. The slow growth of technical education remains one of the chief bars to the fuller modernization of the Orient. One cannot predict that overnight peoples quite unfamiliar with modern mechanics will industrialize fully. Nor can one predict that Chinese or Malays never will become mechanically adept.

THE WEAKENING OF TRADITIONAL CULTURE

When a student in school learns English or becomes a Christian there is an irreparable damage committed to a native body of culture. Perhaps the greater good will result from the switch in language or religion, but the fact is that such shifts in culture traits throughout the Orient have seriously undermined a great many native cultures. There once came to my room in the inn of a little village in western China an old man who alternately quoted Shakespeare and Li Po to me for a good share of an evening. He was a son of a landed family and by preference served as his native village schoolteacher despite a passably good education. He had turned his back upon the mechanical West but had retained some of its choicest flavor. Not numerous are such admirable combinations of culture. A language and its literature of oral folk tales or written classics is a significant share of a culture. The sloughing off of culture traits often follows rapidly upon loss of a religion, whether by an individual, a village, or a region.

Throughout the Orient the advent of machine-made goods wrought a terrible toll among native handicrafts. In textiles, iron and steel, paper, inks and dyes particularly, machine-made goods have driven out traditional materials, techniques, forms, and patterns. The introduction of celluloid and plastics has played havoc with brass, copper, leather, and lacquer work. The toll among the handicrafts is twofold. Not only have machine-made goods mutilated the materials and forms of native products but they have destroyed the livelihood of the millions who produced them. Handicraft production often was but a part-time occupation, but its decline left the scattered rural population without adequate means of support.

Close upon machine-made goods came the first factories into the port cities. They came for the cheap labor which could be easily taught the skills of machine tending. Without thought for labor conditions, human welfare, or culture conflict, factories were operated under conditions that were worse than in any occidental industrial city. Only since 1920 has this begun to change for the better.

Almost everywhere in the Orient the village was the basic operating unit of society. Stimulated agriculture, new machine-made consumer's goods, the decline of handicrafts, the visiting missionary, governmental orders concerning schools, taxes, and labor contributions tended to undermine the control of the village over its culture. With the weakening of village authority went a decline of general civil authority, perhaps to be replaced by an alien police corps.

The growth of the factory, foreign trade, and new means of communication undermined many of the older upper classes and set up new ones. The rise of the Chinese compradore class, equivalent to the American commission broker, was an essential part of trade between Chinese and non-Chinese-speaking occidentals. Much of the wealth of this new class came from joining in the exploitation of China. The shifting basis of education replaced the time-honored scholars with people slightly learned in an alien culture and often quite ignorant of their own native culture. The established operators of government frequently were quite at sea when faced with new technical requirements for administration. Over the course of a couple of centuries a considerable economic and social upheaval has occurred in almost every country.

This is but a partial survey of some of the disturbing factors that have gone with modernization. The weakening of traditional culture is as much a part of modernization as the acceptance of brand new culture traits. It is consideration of some of these unfortunate results that has caused many orientals to question the ultimate values of the mechanical West.

ACCEPTANCE OF THE MODERN WORLD

The Indian Hindu often has been characterized as a negative, submissive mystic who clings persistently to his own creed and culture. How then do new traits spread among such people? Cautious and careful experimentation with new traits, while zealously guarding the old, is a universal attribute of human societies. But no human society has permanently refused acceptance of new culture traits when their advantage clearly has been demonstrated. Too frequently the occidental has characterized the oriental as "unchanging." One cannot seriously hold the idea that the Orient has fundamentally rejected such a device as the railroad, for the individual objections have been little greater than those among our own parents. The occidental must understand that the Orient did object to accepting the railroad as a device for speeding his own transport at the unreasonable financial profit of the occidental stockholder, builder, and supplier of materiel. One must be sympathetic to the wish of the holders of an ancient culture to retain such of that culture as they choose. No occidental country is lacking in those that protest the passing of "the good old days." In effect, then, the Orient has objected less to new culture traits as such than to the terms of acceptance which they found forced upon them. No group has differed greatly in this regard, from the Andaman Island Negrito to the Chinese.

If anything, many in the Orient have wished for, and worked for, too full and too rapid an acceptance of the modern world. The machinery of occidental international trade and industry are more difficult of operation than that of a confederation of self-sufficient village economies. The Occident has expected a greater fee for its cultural tutelage than the Orient has

wanted to pay, resulting in the complex struggles toward independence. Too many orientals have taken up the notion that when a small fraction of a population has learned to use an occidental language, give a political harangue, use a cigarette holder or a telephone, and wear occidental clothing styles their society readily can take its full position in the modern world.

Within each oriental country there have been slow-changing, conservative, and insurgent radical elements. Often their differences have concerned the degree of acceptance of some part of modern occidental culture. There are Chinese and Indians more pronounced in their exhibition of British culture than most Englishmen, Filipinos who out-do the American, and those who will have none of the foreign world. The great mass of the population in every society seeks for the retention of the most useful and precious elements in its own culture, to be combined with similar elements of occidental culture. No one who has been in any part of the Orient has failed to see both amusing and harmless, or sad and tragic, anomalies. There is a common search for that combination which will permit retention of the oriental spirit. Not every country has made equal progress in blending unlike cultures, but no two have reached a similar point in the process. Some of those who have moved most rapidly in the past now have much to do over.

HISTORICAL AND REGIONAL VARIATIONS

No two countries of the Orient have reacted alike in the face of occidental expansion. Above were mentioned some of the earlier reactions to the coming of the European. The British introduced many features of modernization into India well ahead of Indian request and made efforts to prune back some of the pernicious growths that had appeared in Indian culture. English has become the one really common language of India's mixed races, and many forms of the modern culture complex are fashioned upon British models. A significant feature in the whole development has been the physical shape of India, permitting relatively easy access from both flanks.

Burma was a relatively quiet colonial holding, showing slow growth of modernisms, until the explosive developments of World War II. Burma thus achieved colonial independence far sooner than might have been expected. In Thailand the process of change never was conditioned by colonial status. This had its assets but also its drawbacks for, if political freedom remained, there did not result the same amount of technical training and long-range economic investment.

Indochina has suffered at the hands of chronic French maladministration, and in some respects is the least able of the lands of the southern Orient to manage its own affairs with satisfaction to all its varied peoples. Here most of the drawbacks of colonial status are to be found, with few of the long-range progressive advancements. The military contest between the French and the Communists was the result of this backward state of affairs. Malaya, with a large transient population and a protective policy toward the Malay, is perhaps least advanced toward political independence of any oriental colony, though it is otherwise quite modernized.

The Indies present one of the most complex problems. The steady development of Java stands in sharp relief against the retention of tribal culture and economy in New Guinea. Here processes of modernization can be found in every stage of the island landscape. The Philippines possesses an equal degree of contrast. The United States program to educate the islands to political freedom in the shortest possible time differed from the Dutch program. There are many indications that Philippine political maturity was declared achieved overly soon for some elements in the population, and quite far ahead of economic and social maturity in general.

China long was the prime example of the "unchanging East." Having barely escaped political colonialism in the full sense, she experienced the imposition of a system of unequal treaties that facilitated major economic exploitation by the outside world, including Japan. Restricted in form and scope in the earlier period, the process of change has been in full swing in the last half century. The very size of China and the single coastal approach has required time for the deep penetration of many cultural elements. The Chinese are a pragmatic people, given to full discussions of new proposals, and they will not be rushed. There is great occidental impatience at continued social and political instability. On the other hand, the Chinese will to acceptance of most of the material equipment of the Occident is well beyond their own speed in learning to use the new machines and gadgets. The process of modernization of China will take a long period still, but once completed it will be among the most successful of any oriental country.

Korea has not had a fair chance at the modern world. Awakened out of a long hermitage, she was made the economic slave of Japan with every possible restriction upon the progress of her people. Material development of Korea, in Japanese hands, has been remarkable, but it has been entirely for exploitive purposes. Against this is the education and training of a significant number of Koreans outside her own country in the last generation, which could partially offset the handicap. The mechanical division of Korea into two parts at the end of World War II may be a short or a long tragedy.

Japan offers a quite different case history. Japan has been opened and closed at the will of a few since the very first contacts were established with China. She is unique in the tightness of the bonds held around her by her rulers. At the time a few Japanese decided to end the period of hermitage in the 1860's she had been affected less by the Occident than any other country except possibly Korea. The concentration of energy applied to copying the material equipment of the Occident could never have been achieved in any other oriental country. The speed of change and development in mechanical, industrial, economic terms was greater than that of any other country. But also the controlled preservation of Japanese social and spiritual culture was greater. At the end of World War II, therefore, the sum total of Japanese cultural change had been less than it appeared on the surface. Under American military control it remains an open question how much true social and spiritual change can be induced. Our success in the Philippines was not complete, but it was coupled with an atmosphere of hope and impatient expectancy which was not clouded by the ghost of crushing military defeat.

It is impossible to generalize accurately, but what has been called the "equation of development" is rather interesting. In 1300, in respect to technical, economic, and social standing, the East and the West were roughly equal. In 1850, the East, in most respects, stood about where the West had stood in 1750, by then a full century behind. In 1935, the East, very roughly in many respects, had reached a point the West had reached about 1890, having recovered a half of the earlier separation. It remains an open question what period will elapse before the East and the West again are equal.

Regions: Physical, Cultural, or Geographic

It is customary among scholars dealing with large portions of human affairs to seek units of division of their material, so that specific discussion may bring out details, contrasts, likenesses, uniqueness, or ubiquity. Many scholars use regional or territorial patterns of divisions and apply to them the word "geographic." Geographers naturally use these territorial patterns of distribution of the phenomena with which they deal. Among some geographers a cult of regionalism has developed which attempts so to refine the divisional units that by the use of a map and a key there can be expressed the essential core of the message to be told. In those parts of the world where data are precisely gathered upon all manner of subjects, the geographer, by the use of statistics and cartography, can produce all manner of mapped distributional phenomena and translate combinations of these into regionalisms. But in those parts of the world where data are scant upon many subjects the undue pursuit of this tendency can produce only imaginative, artificial, or partial results. The Orient is such a region.

In a crude way it would be possible to delimit a bewildering number of different kinds of regions for the Orient. On the many maps of this volume there are sketched many distributional matters, but it does not seem possible to combine all these things into a composite, and have it produce a meaningful result. The incomplete map of languages has little relation to the map of crop regions, and neither of these concurs with the maps of religion or of climatic areas, incompletely as these areas are understood. On a more restricted scale, the map of zoogeographic regions of Thailand would have little resemblance to any maps of climate that could be drawn from the scant data available. For the whole Orient the map of customary beverages has never been drawn, but one cannot expect that it would be closely related to the crop map, the language map, or the map of religions. The map of native costume has not been drawn either, and to what other map it would closely correspond there is no way of knowing at present. Yet these two latter subjects would seem to be important items in the fuller delimitation of meaningful human regionalisms.

Too often the geographer has presented a concept of geographic regions that bears close relation to the maps of landforms, climates, and dominant crops. This is an obvious kind of related regionalism, and its application in the Orient produces a map of some real utility. Such a map, however, has no overwhelming relation to many of the details of the daily life of many of the peoples of the Orient. If this volume fails to present a summation pattern of geographic regions for the Orient, it is because this seems impossible to accomplish in view of the limited knowledge of those things that are significant to the issues of geographic regionalism in the Orient. In the Chinese proverb "The North is salt, the South is sweet, the East is sour, and the West is hot," there is expressed a significant factor of regionalism. That this corresponds to the use of salt, sugar, vinegar, and pepper in the daily diet of millions of people makes it important, but it is extremely difficult both to draw lines between the separate dietary regions and to fit this into a larger framework of Chinese regionalism.

The geographic region, if there be such a thing, should be a regional territory in which the whole complex assemblage of factors, affecting nature, area, man, and his culture, expresses itself in collective terms, since geography is concerned with all of these. Since culture is a changing thing, since man himself changes location constantly, since man alters his landscape, and since both plants and animals also possess mobility, it is likely that the geographic region never can be identified as a fixed territory for a long period of time. The interrelations of man, culture, and environment not only are complex but also are subject to constant change. It requires maintained censuses of data of very great variety to identify the status of separate elements of this complex at any one time, and to map its alterations. In the Orient too much of the pertinent census data is lacking to make possible the identification of the complex geographic region.

As man increasingly has adopted more complex political systems, the political region has emerged into the position of steadily greater importance. That man has not correlated this region with other kinds of regions often is extremely evident. The recent division of India into the two political states India and Pakistan is perhaps the most obvious illustration in all the Orient. The administrative utility of the political region has grown with the passage of time, regardless of its obvious clash with the simple environmental regionalisms based upon landform and climate. But the political region in an old and stable culture often tends to become, in itself, a synthesis of the factors of regionalism. In China proper the political province often seems as effective a regional division as any other that the geographer can conjure up based upon a few selected criteria only. Both the tangible and the intangible seem well expressed in the Chinese proverb "In Kweichow there are no three steps on the same level, no three days without rain, and no man has three coppers in his pocket to jingle." Obviously the new and still unstable political subregions of Thailand or Burma are susceptible neither to the formation of regional proverbs nor to the use of political areas as significant regional entities.

This volume falls in the fields of cultural and regional geography, and in it there have been utilized many kinds of regional criteria. In the early chapters of this first section there have been presented some matters of regionalism, though many of them are incomplete or inconclusive. In each regional chapter in the latter section of the volume there is concern for the matter of regionalisms, but again they are incomplete and sometimes intangible. At no time are these precisely delimited matters prescribed by sharp lines. There is an obvious political regionalism to the regional chapters upon separate countries. I have conceded to this but lightly in the case of India and Pakistan, perhaps all too lightly. I have declined to follow political regionalism in the Indies, in Central Asia, and in Manchuria. But in the Philippines political regionalism has been growing rapidly on a national scale, and it would seem to be working to the end of separating from the Indies a new kind of region despite the landform regionalism that places the Indies and the Philippines together. Ceylon is going in a different direction from India in many matters, because of political regionalism, entirely contrary to environmental regionalism and many of the elements of cultural regionalism.

Many regionalisms are the slow workings of cultural change and are unconscious matters of peaceful operation. The development of regional patterns of legal institutions in the native *adat* of the Indies shows this, as does the Philippine abandonment of bark cloth for woven textiles. The changes in cropping patterns of the Indus Valley or of Szechwan, in which rice and the sweet potato, respectively, have altered agriculture and food supply, amount to these kinds of changing regionalisms. Other changes are militant matters accompanied by the force of arms and the willful action of a population. The northern expansion of the Japanese into the territory of the Ainu for several centuries altered the regionalism of Japan. The leaders of modern Japan attempted to construct a regionalism, called the "Greater East Asia Co-Prosperity Sphere," based upon militant political and economic criteria. The separation of India and Pakistan was less a matter of militant procedure as such than of the political inflaming of religious and cultural prejudices that had been long ago implanted upon the soil of Mother India. The spread of the Annamese throughout the lowlands of Indochina, or of the Thai throughout Thailand has been a militant matter at some times and a peaceful one at others, but both operations have altered the regionalisms of this part of southeastern Asia.

In some manner or other I have tried to take these and other developments into account in this volume. But the easy diagraming of the issues of regionalism remains largely undone. The Orient as a whole is a cultural realm rather than a physical one, though it has as a supporting base a broad regional matter of physical climate throughout much of its area. Its primary divisions now are political ones, with an increasingly important role to play in the lives of all orientals. Two large bodies of culture traditionally have given to the Orient much of its peculiar cultural climate, those of India and those of China. Southeastern Asia and the southern Island Arcs find these two bodies of culture overlapping and competing with each other in some respects. The cultural climate of the Occident has so broadly entered into the life of the Orient, however, that it threatens to obscure much that is environmental and much that is native. And more recently a Communist cultural climate is invading and infiltrating the whole, to threaten new patterns of culture and new patterns of regionalism. The entrance of state trading agreements into the economic operations of the Orient is threatening to establish a totally new kind of economic regionalism, equaled only by the regionalism that proceeds out of Yen-bloc, Dollar-bloc, and Sterling-bloc developments. The latent nature of a superpolitical regionalism based upon the affiliation of all the countries of southeastern Asia into a regional unit of the United Nations, similar to the North Atlantic Treaty Organization of the European world is still another of the new items of regionalism that may well have a long-run effect.

There are, then, many bases for regionalism in the Orient. Some of them geographers have dealt with, but many remain untouched and unmapped. In this volume a considerable amount of this material is presented, but much of the highly pertinent material is lacking. Failing the data on which to outline adequately based geographic regions, there still remains the problem of how to break down large areas into units sufficiently distinct to permit comparison and detailed study. For such purposes, therefore, I have presented in the maps that follow a variety of regionalisms based upon selected criteria. They are presented for convenience and, collectively, are best described as maps of regions of convenience.

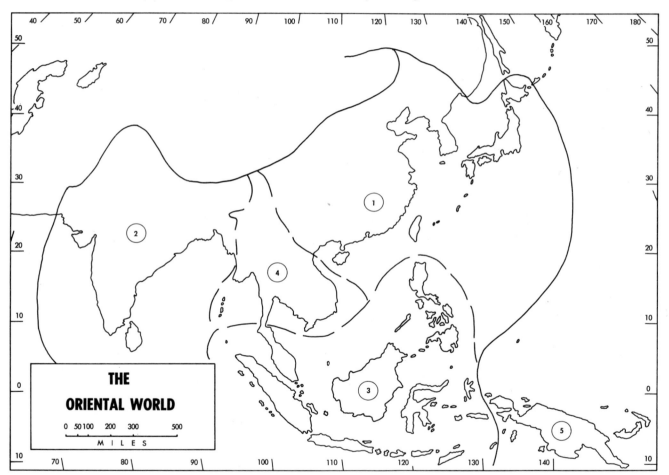

Fig. 40. The major divisions of the oriental culture world, as zoned by Russell and Kniffen, based upon a composite set of criteria: (1) Chinese realm; (2) Indian realm; (3) Malayan realm; (4) Indochinese shatter belt; (5) Pacific world.

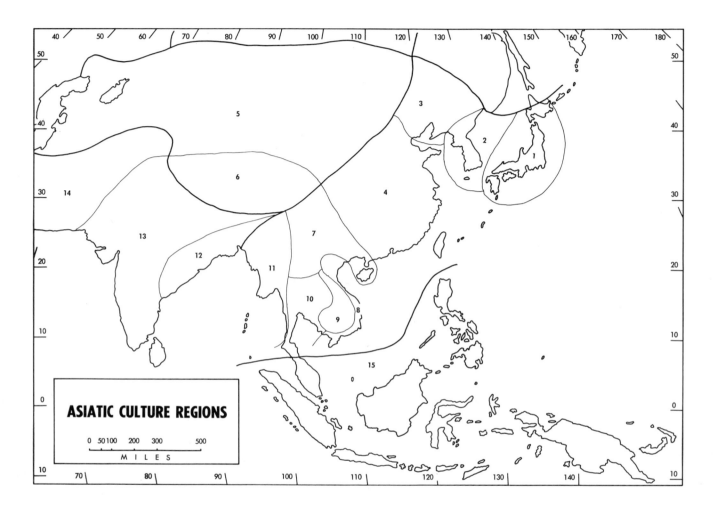

Fig. 41. Asiatic culture regions, after Bacon. These divisions are based upon arbitrary anthropologic criteria considered some-what debatable in some items. Numbers have reference: (1) Japan; (2) Korea; (3) Manchurian transition; (4) China; (5) Central Asian steppe; (6) Central Asian Tibetan zone; (7) Southwest China; (8) Annam; (9) Cambodia; (10) Thailand; (11) Burma; (12) East India transition; (13) India; (14) Southwest Asia; (15) island zone, undifferentiated.

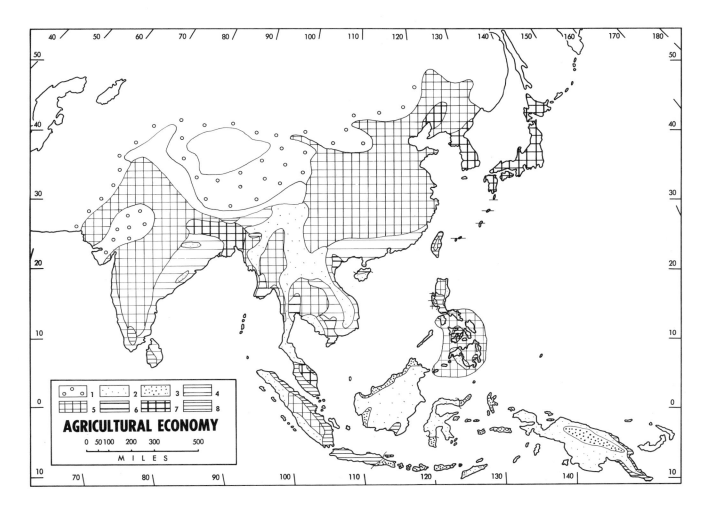

Fig. 42. Regions of agricultural economy. Blank areas are non-agricultural. Numbers have reference: (1) pastoral economy; (2) shifting cultivation dominant; (3) rudimentary sedentary cultivation; (4) intensive subsistence culture, rice being dominant; (5) intensive subsistence culture with mixed crops; (6) intensive commercial culture, rice being dominant; (7) intensive commercial culture with mixed crops; (8) mixed native and plantation cultivation. Modified from Whittlesey in *Goode's Atlas*.

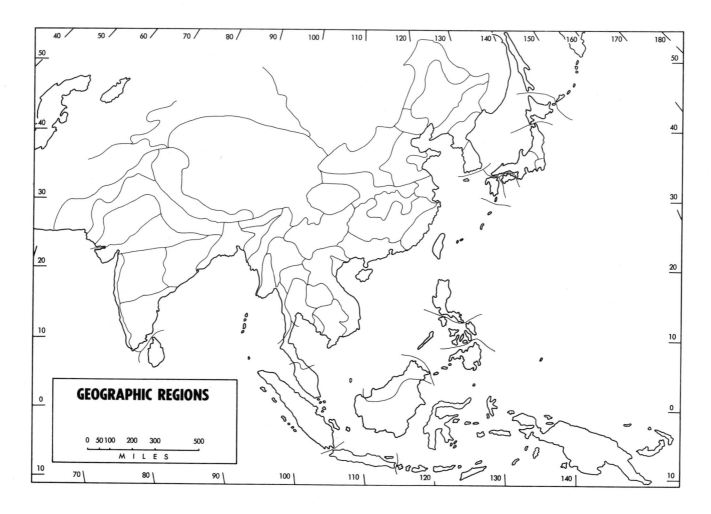

Fig. 43. Boundaries of geographic regions, after Cressey. Approximately 65 regions are outlined here, based upon an assemblage of criteria, chiefly those of the physical environment.

The Regional Growth of Culture

Mother India: in the Beginning

THE EARLY ENVIRONMENTS

As the last pulsation of the Ice Age relaxed and the contemporary Indian environment began to take shape the greatest significant change lay in climate. The yearly temperature cycle lifted a few degrees, and now no part of lowland India suffers cold winter weather. The moisture cycle receded somewhat and probably increased its variability. Cloudiness and humidities probably decreased a little. Subjective comfort of the body has been increased, but so has mental anguish over whether the rains will come on time and in adequate amounts. Most of these changes were complete well before the historic period began, but not before man began trying out the utility of various parts of the Indian landscape.

Much of southern India is a warm, moist, and muggy environment in which plant growth is rapid, and one in which early man probably found it difficult to cope with the plant world about him. As long as he was content to gather its products, however, the plant world was a productive one. There were some good spots in the south of India, but none of them were very large, and their complex of conditions was less useful than that of some other regions. The highlands of northern India, on the other hand, were a difficult landscape to use for two reasons. The handicap of strong relief was great, and a wet, heavy forest cover contained fewer items of value than did the plant cover of the lowlands. Parts of the North Indian Plain and certain portions of the central peninsula seem to contain a combination of elements that facilitated the gathering culture of earliest man and also permitted the exercise of the curiosity and initiative that resulted in agriculture. In early postglacial times these lowland zones were better than they are today in that slow desiccation had not then caused rainfall variability to become as serious as it is today. The zones of greater than average utility were widely scattered and covered a considerable total area. They are not contiguous regions, nor are they all alike in their local conditions. The upper Ganges Valley, the Narbada, and other similar valleys of Rajputana, a few of the peninsular river valleys, and some of the deltas of the east coast are among the more useful spots of early India. These regions constituted a number of similar ample environments that facilitated the parallel growth of several culture patterns. The cultures had certain things in common but also possessed numerous unlike features.

It is in the nature of the plant and animal resources that these local environments notably differed. Northwest India lay not far from the southwest Asian plant and animal nursery and shared most of its products from a very early date. Apparently the horse was one of the few animals not used in India before the Caucasian invasions. The Ganges Valley and peninsular Indian sites, on the other hand, shared a great many of the plants and animals that were at home in some part of southeastern Asia. It still is a moot question where rice originated. If India is not within its original home region the origin is close by, and rice became one of the earliest plants cultivated in eastern and southern India. Sugar cane is a plant that seems to have been at home in eastern India, being extremely valuable at all times. Both zones had available a wide range of plants and animals, usable at different stages of economic organization. It is difficult to suggest which environment had the greatest potential value, but it does seem probable that no local area in either environment stood out very far above the others.

THE EARLIEST SOCIETIES

The beginnings of Indian cultures cannot be even approximately dated or adequately described. From

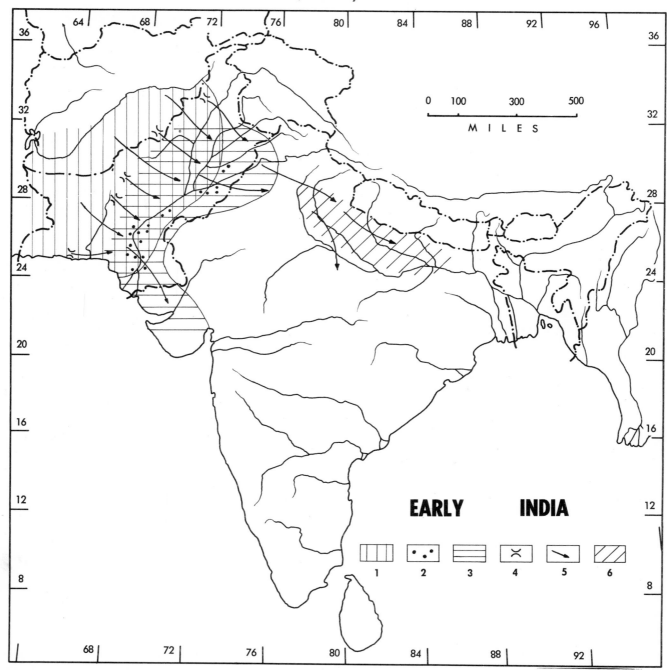

EARLY   INDIA

1   2   3   4   5   6

Fig. 44. Early India: (1) zone of pre-Indus peasant cultures, possibly 3500 B.C.; (2) known important sites of Indus culture, flourishing 3200–2000 B.C.; (3) probable extent of Indus culture in India; (4) chief passes from north to south: Khyber, Gomal, Bolan, Mula, Makran; (5) invasion routes of Caucasoid peoples; (6) historic-era Indian culture hearth.

archaeologic sampling it is clear that India was populated during the Paleolithic both by peoples who used the Stone Age culture of Europe-Africa and by Far Eastern peoples of a rather different Stone Age culture. The western realm reached into northwest India and throughout the peninsula, whereas the eastern zone reached northwest India at least. The samplings make clear that almost all parts of India were inhabited sometime during the Paleolithic. There is a marked gap between the Paleolithic and Neolithic in India. Knowledge of the Neolithic still is very spotty and inconclusive, and it is likely that many peoples moved into or through southern India then. The peasant cultures of the Iranian highland certainly included parts of the Indus Valley. Data for what now is termed Indus Valley culture indicate a tremendous advance in many ways, but the regional extent and affiliations are not yet clear. The accompanying map suggests the extent of pre-Indus and Indus culture. Southern India, contemporary with Indus Valley culture, is even more vague. Another gap exists between the Indus Valley culture and the Caucasian invasions. From this point on the story reads fairly continuously, though confusedly, since the Indian peoples never have possessed the historical passion that documented Chinese or Roman culture history.

The tentative picture of the Indus Valley is one of a rather sophisticated urban culture, well-planned cities of flat-roofed, multistoried buildings occupying the alluvial lowlands along the Indus River. Fired brick were expertly handled in building homes, baths, drainage systems, and wells. Many a modern Indian town compares unfavorably, item for item. Fortifications were massive and well developed around key cities at least. Craftsmen's skill in gold and silver work, in seal and bead making, and in pottery manufacture was first class. Irrigation agriculture grew most of the crops common to southwestern Asia, plus cotton at least and very likely a number of others domesticated in India. The Indus Valley of that day possessed more easily available fuel than it does today, much of which was cut off to fire the bricks used in building construction. More big game animals also were available then than are present today. The lack of remains of formal religious architecture suggest a religious and social pattern still simple and undeveloped as compared to that of India today. In pottery, art motifs, trinkets, brick types, and other relevant features the Indus Valley clearly shows an active relationship to other lowland cultures of the Near East. The duplication is not complete and there are a number of items that show real individuality. Undoubtedly there was a flourishing trade with the Near East.

It is thought that Indus Valley culture belonged west of a line drawn from the southern neck of Kathiawar peninsula to the modern Himalayan hill station of Simla. It seems possible to suggest that Indus culture was properly a northwest Indian culture using items from each major realm appropriate to its local environment. In a somewhat drier environment than possessed by much of the rest of India this would suggest that the main trade relations, racial contacts, historical ties, and social motivations lay with southwestern Asia. The beginnings of this culture unfortunately lie below the present valley water table, buried by recent alluvial deposition of the Indus. The ravages of severe floods and changing river channels may be read

in the local landscape today, suggestive of causes of abandonment of Mohenjo-daro, at least, the best-known city. In the time sequence Indus Valley culture appears contemporary with that of the Mesopotamian lowland.

No such clear presentation of typical south Indian culture can be made. Later less formal and less well-executed building in smaller settlements indicate a lower level than that achieved in the Indus Valley. They also suggest competition among peoples for possession of a landscape. More religious architectural remains of a varied sort indicate more concern with the mystical side of nature and life. Suggestions are toward greater contact with southeastern Asia than northern India, though whether by purposeful trade movement or by accidental folk migration is not yet clear. A subtropical agriculture which shared many things with southeastern Asia possessed a few unique items and shared a few with the Indus Valley.

Nothing positive can be said at this point on racial affiliation and linguistic relations between the Indus Valley and the rest of India. It would seem that the south possessed more diverse peoples than the north. At the close of the Neolithic as the modern period began, it seems almost as though Indus culture and southern culture held less in common than each held with its outer marginal realm. That is, in southwestern Asia and northwest India were the several parts of an early common culture realm, whereas southern India and southeastern Asia were the variant parts of another and separate realm. If this is true it may indicate a reversal of the regional relations that appear to have held true during the Paleolithic when southern India's connections lay mostly with Europe and Africa and North India was connected to the Far East. The argument in such matters often becomes partisan and in the face of insufficient evidence, it is too early to make more than a suggestion to this end.

THE CAUCASIAN INVASIONS

The dating of the earliest expansion of peoples from the Caucasian racial incubator is impossible to predict. Around 2000 B.C., however, the peoples of southwestern Asia again were in flux, competitively pushing about their home territory. For a little more than a thousand years this process went on, constituting an important chapter in the race history of Eurasia. Early during this period groups of people began moving eastward through Persia and Trans-Caspia, as they also moved westward toward southern Europe. Finding the numerous gaps in the western Mountain Wall, they began to filter through Afghanistan and Baluchistan and to scatter out on the lowlands of the Indus Valley. The Mountain Wall proved no more an isolating barrier then than it had during the stone ages. In fact the physical situation may have stimulated some movement into India. Passes through the high country were low and short enough so that crossing was practical at all seasons of the year. Wood, water, and pasturage undoubtedly were better than today, after centuries of overuse. The Mountain Wall was often a sufficient physical barrier to divert elsewhere. the attentions of predatory tribes seeking territory in Persia and Trans-Caspia. The old culture connections were sufficient to make known the existence of a land beyond the mountains. Across them lay relative safety in the turbulent period of Caucasian expansion. Figure 44 depicts the invasion routes.

The peoples who came into India at this time were not all of one physical mold, nor did they possess the same culture. They are variously named Aryan, Indo-Aryan, Caucasian, and Indo-European. They were crude farmers who also grazed animals. They brought some of their own breeds, including the horse for the first time. They were not pastoral nomads in the full sense, nor were they builders of a high order of cities. They were a belligerent folk who had fought for their living space previously and who fought for a place on the North Indian Plain. They were less sophisticated than had been the city folk of Mohenjo-daro and Harappa. It is not clear whether the newcomers drove out, or wiped out, the remaining city culture, or whether flood, famine, and pestilence earlier had achieved much the same result unaided. From the earliest folk sagas of the newcomers it is evident that the North Indian Plain was inhabited by people who impressed the "Aryans" as dark skinned and of an inferior culture. Successive waves of immigrants pushed the line of settlement out across the Indus. Semipermanent villages became scattered over the dry country of northwest India, and the newcomers employed an economy that still combined their own crude agriculture with open-range animal breeding. This economy was like that of their previous home, but it involved some new Indian crops and irrigation of a higher order than they had employed previously. There still must have been ample wood for human use and range fodder for more animals than were present.

In the course of the thousand or more years during which the Caucasian invasions took place the line of infiltration and settlement spread steadily outward from the Mountain Wall. The spread always was a militant one, and it always involved the kind of race mixture that results from conquest, with men often slain and women and children taken as slaves. The color line caused some trouble socially, and feeling about it undoubtedly aided the other basic causes in the slow evolution of the caste system. There always remained the change in skin color from northwest to south and east, and with it went a difference in culture, in language, in social organization, and in political sense. Gradually these Caucasian invaders grew less Caucasian and became definitely a part of the North Indian landscape as the Indian bonds tightened at the expense of the Near Eastern ones. Little was clearly defined about their culture as yet. It was a village culture, concerned with a generalized arid-margin agriculture, but possessing considerable mobility in animal care. There were many groups in varying stages of this cultural shift.

THE FORMATIVE ERA

At the close of the Caucasian invasions India was an amorphous collection of many peoples and many simple cultures, all scattered over a physical landscape whose natural and human divisions were seldom finite in character, boundaries, or qualities. Everywhere social stratification still was simple, though slowly growing. Religion was slowly combining Aryan priestly philosophy with Dravidian cult magic. Livestock, wild fowl, and wild animals still were items of commonplace consideration, eaten, worked, hunted, and used in many ways. Little was being done in the way of roads or irrigation works, but a progressive deforestation was stripping the growth from the lightly covered arid and dry margins as population and settlement increased. The good spots in the Indian realm were productive enough for population to grow, villages to increase in number, and a few towns to evolve at favored points. Much of humid India still was jungle, rainforest or scrub parkland, occupied by an abundant wild life, among which the scattered cultural landscapes were a very minor share of the total area of India. Even in the heavily forested regions, however, migratory agriculture and selective usage had its effects upon both the plant and animal resources, and probably by this period no truly virgin landscape existed. In this situation there were few human controls over progressive cultural change. No one region was held by a people whose cultural mores were a standard, or whose strength dominated a wide area.

The several centuries between 1000 and 500 B.C. were a formative era in which an unmistakably Indian stamp became clearly visible in all parts of the realm. It was a turbulent period in which tribal priests matured into religious philosophers, tribal chiefs became regional sultans, soldiers acquired formal social posi-

Sabha

tion, and strong groups pushed weak ones toward refuge zones. Artisan craftsmanship multiplied its skills and its products, and trade began to grow again, connecting all of India's subregions and reaching out to the Near East and to southeastern Asia. The domination of the Brahmans clearly set the tone for all higher societies as the priests spread throughout all parts of India with the steady growth of Hinduism. The simple social framework of Caucasian society hardened into the patterns of caste stratification. Many protests over Brahman usurpation and corruption of the old simple cultures set in motion waves of culture change which spread throughout India.

Despite primitive transport facilities India became surprisingly mobile. Pilgrims, missionaries, traders, artisans, soldiers of fortune, migratory clans, emigrating tribes, political opportunists, and many others surged north, south, east, and west throughout India. Some true blood mixture occurred in all this movement, working toward a composite Indian type, but far less resulted than should have been the case. Such things as Hinduism, Buddhism, and Jainism became known everywhere, caste, and customs of dress spread very widely, and local crops and practices spread to the simple limits of climatic tolerance. These common features were not enough to unite India. The written languages of Brahman and Buddhist priests never replaced local languages. Though innumerable common customs spread over the country they did not tie India into one unit. There is a curious contrast in the period, of trends toward unity of culture but the failure of regional cohesion. This same conflict appears again and again in Indian culture history. Many efforts to ascribe it to specific causes have been made, but perhaps there is no one answer to the query of why human cultures achieve the results they do.

Out of clan and tribal politics and village settlement came the institution of the *sabha* or village council government. Essentially a democratic political institution, it operated by elected representatives who formed a permanent managing body that handled every aspect of village economy and local culture. Gradually the democratic process became selective, representation in some villages being restricted to Brahmans; but a large percentage of the villages were non-Brahman, so that the village council became one of the most significant of Indian institutions. Out of this primary control came important features of land ownership and systems of taxation. Joint village tenancy, all-private ownership, and varied mixed land systems gradually developed, often depending upon caste composition of a village or geographic factors of local economy. In the hands of the *sabha* lay the

power of taxation and the use of funds in the maintenance of such public features as temples, market places, the assembly hall, streets, and monuments. This village development, throughout the breadth of India, most often skipped the mobile, simpler tribes of peoples practicing a hunting-gathering economy. To them the open jungle and forest ranges were ample, and they chose retreat into the back country rather than accept a lower position in a society involving irksome changes in their mode of life. Such a village development also, unaccountably, skipped other peoples and limited areas within the Indian realm. This evolution of an autonomous village system preceded the appearance of more formal and large-order political systems. The village system persisted into the modern era as one unifying feature which resisted the encroachment of all superimposed political authority. The durability of the system is responsible for the settlement patterns of modern India and for the relative scarcity of sizeable cities.

And out of tribal politics and priestly domination of social and religious rules came the domination of the Brahmans and the formulation of the essential laws of Hinduism which, ever since, have motivated the largest segment of Indian life. The Sacred Law became what the priestly class made it over the centuries. Political states headed by despotic rulers, administered by Brahman priestly ministers who surmounted a graded bureaucracy, composed the central theme around which political theory, Hinduism, caste, and the ordinary rules of society were grouped. Rulers were as subject to the laws as were other human beings. Militant competition among the kingdoms that appeared in the Indian realms was conceived as the normal circumstance. Out of this competition came the earliest regional dominance of the Indian realm by a part of the North Indian Plain.

THE FLOWERING OF EARLY INDIA

Sometime in the sixth century B.C. the growing turbulence of Indian culture began to produce results. Evolutionary achievements surpassed anything in the past but changed the direction of Indian culture growth not at all. The Caucasian peoples from beyond the Mountain Wall had grafted themselves tightly onto basic Indian culture. Landscape, plant and animal resources, and man were about to achieve a synthesis in the first Indian empire. This was the century into which Gautama Buddha and Mahabir were born, the founders of Buddhism and Jainism, respectively. Both were born into good places in society, in the central Ganges Valley, but both became dissatisfied with the increasing Brahman domination of Indian society. They and their movements were expressive of one side of the yeasty stirrings in Indian life of this period. On another side were the growing concept of the political state and the gradual enlargement of the petty kingdoms that had been growing out of tribal domains during the past centuries. Indian history does not record the long struggle that must have gone on among the new ruling class, their military aides, the soldier caste, and the priestly lawyers that both operated Hinduism and formed the new and growing bureaucracy.

If one examines the regional focus of the center of this cultural emergence, it appears to center in the middle Ganges Valley, as shown on Fig. 44. There are sound reasons why this should be so. Though the primary Caucasian invasions had tapered off some centuries previously, northwest India still was subject to invasion from Persia. This was the era of the great Persian rulers from Cyrus to Xerxes, and the Indus Valley section of the North Indian Plain was either an outlying sector of the Persian empire or a marginal zone constantly subject to predatory raids. So unprotected was northwest India by the Mountain Wall that the Indus sector was not the wealthy and prosperous part of northern India. Far to the east the very wet lower Ganges valley and delta were yet too hard to use, were but lightly populated, and also were marginal parts of northern India. The best conditions were found in the central and upper Ganges basin. Here was a landscape that was easy to use, was well equipped with those natural resources most useful to the age, and was at a distance from troublesome invasion and raid. This was the region into which the early Caucasian invaders had pushed, out of the way of later invaders. Here there combined native peoples and cultures with Caucasian peoples and cultures. The higher political sense of the Caucasians perhaps made the difference in promoting the effective political state before it was conceived by any native group or earlier mixture in any south Indian region. The critical element seems less the environment than the superior mixture of race and culture achieved in this particular region. Earlier in Indian history the dominant culture had lain in the Indus Valley, until militant invasion had made the zone untenable. Later Indian history was to see the center of gravity shift to other regions, under a variety of causes.

A declining Persian empire was terminated by Alexander and his Greeks, who also pushed across the Mountain Wall into the Indian lowland, only to be lured eastward by stories of wealth and prosperity of the Ganges Valley kingdoms. The inability of Alexander to permanently bridge the distance between Greece and India gave India its chance for expression of its cultural maturity. This came in the Mauryan Empire set up by Chandragupta somewhat before 300 B.C. Its capital was Pataliputra, on the site of what today is Patna, in the central lower Ganges Valley. This had been the base of the small kingdom seized by Chandragupta, from which his conquest of North India began. Under several able successors this minor kingdom grew to include the territory from Bengal to the Hindu Kush and from the Himalayas perhaps into modern Mysore. The extent of the Mauryan Empire is shown on Fig. 45. The greatest Mauryan ruler, Asoka, became a Buddhist convert and turned his energies from political and military conquest to running his realm peacefully, morally, and happily. The Mauryan Empire lasted, as an entity, until about 185 B.C., when it split into a number of pieces.

The Mauryan era was a mature expression of Indian culture of the time. Buddhism and Jainism were then most successful in their attempted reform of Hinduism. The Buddhist missionary push outside India was sent off by Asoka himself. Within the North Indian Plain, at least, man had learned to operate his environment to the maximum extent of his cultural concept. A productive agriculture based on rice and tropical tree products had been developed for the moist lands of the east, and a wheat-millet-sorghum agriculture had spread with increasing efficiency over additional territory on the dry margins. Cotton, sugar cane, and many minor grains now were widely distributed, but the general expansion of acreage was the most significant item as the jungle and forest were steadily cut back. Range-animal culture had begun to decline in relative importance, and there began the evolution of the sacredness of the cow. This notion spread first to oxen and gradually to other animals and birds, under the urging of both Hindus and Buddhists.

Roads and a transport service linked the far parts of the empire. Pataliputra was connected with the Arabian Sea ports of Broach and Musiris, with Taxila in the upper Punjab, and with Tamralipti and Tosali on the Bay of Bengal. The practical application of new political theory of the empire evolved many of the basic concepts of government administration that were used later in history. Despite this mature political growth economic structure remained simple. A repetitive, self-sufficient village economy permitted little real growth in internal trade, as we understand it in the United States today. A fairly considerable export trade did grow in better-ruled and well-placed regions but this did not free India from the restrictions

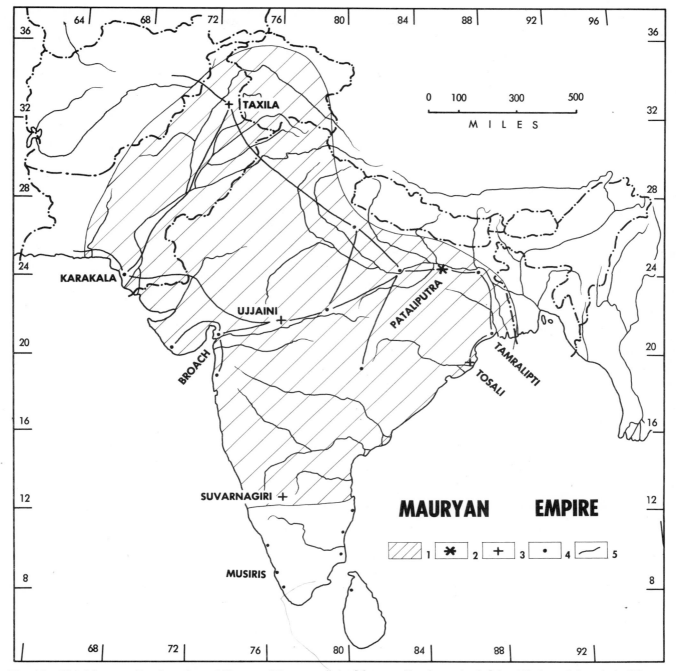

Fig. 45. The Mauryan Empire, about 250 B.C.: (1) area of the Mauryan Empire at its height; (2) imperial capital; (3) seats of Vice-Royalties; (4) trade centers; (5) trunk highways.

of its village economy. It is notable that early during the Mauryan era architects had begun again to build with the fired bricks that had characterized Indus Valley culture but which had not been commonly used in the interval of the Caucasian invasions. Mauryan architects used stone as though it were wood.

PATTERNS OF INDIAN HISTORY

There are three primary elements that compose the fabric of Indian history and that have been variably interwoven into its complex patterns. They are: invasion, the rise of a region to dominance, and the collapse of political power and the failure of regional unity. These elements must be described briefly.

Invasion

The early Caucasian invasions have been mentioned. In the period between perhaps 1000 B.C. and A.D. 900 there were no more major invasions of India by large groups of peoples looking for living space. Almost continuously, however, the northwest of India was subject to predatory raids and invasions of political conquest through the Mountain Wall, and much of the Indus Valley was in alien hands. Also to a minor extent in this period there were similar invasions in the northeast corner of India as various of the Yellow races crossed the great river trenches and touched the margins of India. In the northwest, seriously beginning in the tenth century, the spreading wave of Moslem religious and political conquest broke over the Mountain Wall and poured through the passes onto the North Indian Plain. Once this contact was established by land, the sea lanes between Arabia and the Malabar coast again became well traveled. For over 700 years in intermittent surges the invasions of Afghans and Turks continued, whereas in the last two centuries the pressure has lightened to become merely a border problem involving mobile and predatory tribes of hillmen. The Moslem invasions rather closely followed the pattern of the Caucasian invasions, surging across the Punjab and down the Ganges Valley to wear themselves out in Bengal and Assam. These invasions never penetrated deeply into the Himalayas, but they did infiltrate the peninsula in variable fashion, bypassing some of the strongest of the Hindu Rajput kingdoms in the Aravalli-Vindhya hill country to establish a foothold in the Deccan, and to carry raids to the very south of India. The use of mercenary Moslem soldiery by southern rulers and the gradual enlargement of the Mogul Empire in the sixteenth and seventeenth centuries carried varied mixtures of Moslems rather deeply into the peninsula. Many of these latter folk, however, were north Indian converts to Islam rather than fresh newcomers to India. The progress of the Moslem invasions is shown on Fig. 46.

By sea since the dawn of the historic period had come innumerable traders to India, but never had a lasting invasion struck until the Europeans appeared upon Indian shores. Out of the Indonesian island realm came one short and troublesome attack, but it produced no lasting racial or cultural effects. From the Arakan coast of Burma pirates for centuries harried the east coast of India, and from the Persian Gulf coast they intermittently had disturbed the west coast. The Europeans, however, were a new element with a new power and new techniques. Gradually their invasion of India spread almost all over the country, but the British, like the Moslem Turks and Afghans before them, and like the still earlier Caucasians, never succeeded in penetrating all the physical pieces that make up the mosaic of India. No people, clear back into the Paleolithic so far as one yet can tell, ever has swept completely over India, planting their stock and their culture in every region of that great land.

Regional Dominance

It has been suggested that during the protohistoric period the Indus Valley probably was the home of the dominant culture, and that during the formative era the Ganges Valley became the hearth of modern Indian culture and the seat of the earliest political empire. Certainly environment had something to do with this, in that the landscape of each area was amenable to development of extensive social institutions. But certainly too, it was people that made of each environment a definite cultural landscape. Each used selected resources to specific ends, and each altered that landscape by cutting back its plant cover, changing its water distribution through irrigation, running trails and roads across it, and building settlements upon it. With the variety of landscapes in India possessing inherently useful characters, it is hard to suggest one outstanding region. Throughout Indian culture history, however, one area has stood out above the others in cultural attainment during each period.

This regional superiority or dominance may be a partial illusion, the historiography of India being sufficiently intangible so that a flat statement cannot be documented satisfactorily. After the Mauryan era there stands out the Punjab under the Kushan, in the first century A.D., with the Gandharan schools of art a significant development in Indian culture. The Guptas again brought the Ganges Valley to the fore in the fourth century. The Pallavas made the country between the Godavari and the Kistna outstanding from the fifth to the seventh centuries, and the western Deccan under the Chalyuka rivaled the later Pallavas. The Colas developed the lower east coast as the outstanding region of India between the eighth and twelfth centuries. Several groups holding the Delhi Gap in the thirteenth and fourteenth centuries fought most of the rest of India, and came to exercise control over most of India, as shown on Fig. 46. The central Deccan under the Bahmani was an important region during the fourteenth and fifteenth centuries, only to lose out to the southern peninsular combine of Vijayanagar for the next century. The sixteenth century was shared by Vijayanagar and the Moguls before the latter domi-

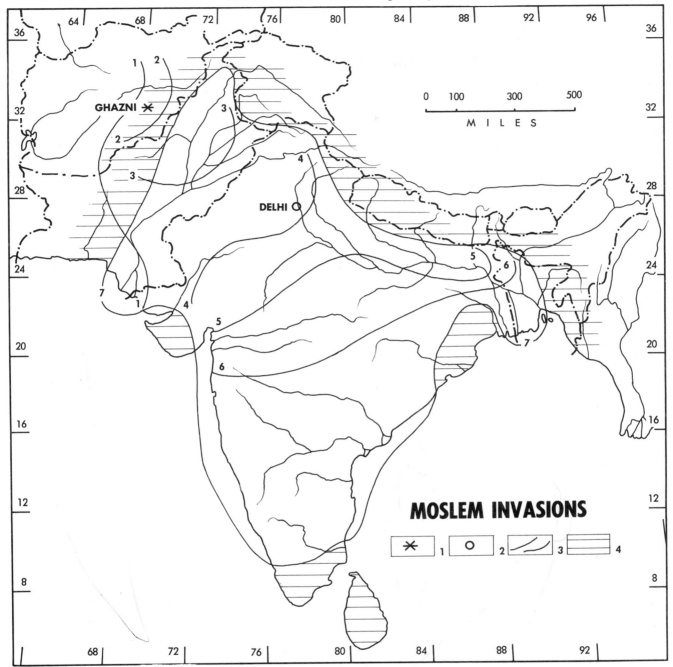

Fig. 46. The Moslem invasions of India: (1) base of operations through the twelfth century; (2) base of operations, thirteenth through fifteenth centuries; (3) numbered lines indicate: 1, advances of eighth century; 2, line of advance to A.D. 993; 3, advances to 1026; 4, advances by 1193; 5, advances by 1202; 6, advances by 1300; 7, maximum control by Delhi Sultanate about 1320; (4) regions independent of Delhi Sultanate.

nated the scene from their home base in the upper Ganges Valley and the Delhi Gap. This regional dominance is more than political or military strength alone, for it involves the integration of agriculture, handicraft industry, interregional and international trade, manpower, social organization, and Hindu or Moslem religious unity. These were mobilized behind an aggressive leadership of a family, a clan, or a racial minority either newly come to India or long kept from race mixture and diffusion by the restrictive caste system. These eras of regional dominance seemed to come about when a group could unite and mobilize the resources of landscape and of society for a period of creative effort.

Failure of Regional Unity

If the history of India reads with a bewildering change of pace and locality, it in part is owing to the lack of regional definition in the landscape of India and in part to the fact that new competitors were constantly surging through the Mountain Wall to engage in the struggle for control of some part of India. Often the Punjab, the Ganges Valley, or the Deccan was the scene of a mad scramble during a whole century, producing a regional anarchy and a wild struggle for paramountcy which failed to produce a positive result. Sometimes in widely separated parts of India two regions stood out above the remainder at the same time. If this happened side by side there ensued a bitter struggle, often resulting in the final dominance of one contestant. On the other hand, the contest sometimes ran for centuries, as that between the Colas and the Pallavas, with one side and then the other having the upper hand. Significantly, too, there are negative spots of rough hill country, desert or overwet mountain fringe that never have been the seat of a leading culture or group.

The struggle for regional dominance, as a natural part of things, is a segment of Hindu political philosophy. As an undercurrent in Indian life it has been present as far back as any record can be read. In the competitive struggle of the parts of the subcontinent of India there seems to be something akin to the struggles of another Eurasian subcontinent: Europe. Always before one group could bring the whole of India together and cement the unity into a fixed pattern, its energy or its resources ran out or some new invasion came to overwhelm the waning leaders. The Mauryan rulers failed to achieve complete hegemony over the Indian realm, though they codified the administrative and political principles that were to be used in every later empire. Innumerable Turkish tribes possessing only the common bond of Islam never could dominate Hindu India. The British, coming with new tools and new political concepts, have given up the task. Currently Moslem leaders have raised the cry of Pakistan around the myth of Islam. The prompt division of the realm into Pakistan and India when the British removed their restraining hand is completely in keeping with the long-range failure of regional unity of the Indian subcontinent. It is beyond my present ability to determine whether this is an inherent characteristic of the Indian landscape or whether it is primarily a product of a migratory and argumentative human race that cannot rise above the personality and psychology of some of India's first inhabitants.

THE ERA OF THE COMPANY

The coming of the Portuguese heralded a new era in Indian life, but it took a century for the preliminary skirmishes of Portuguese, British, Dutch, Arabs, and Indians to establish the pattern of development. The end of the skirmishing came with the formation of the British and Dutch East India companies and the reduction of Portuguese strength. Since the Dutch effort focused mainly on Malaysia, the British settled upon the Indian coast, slowly working inland. A concerted French attempt to gain control of India was thwarted. This British geographical spread was accompanied by economic and political penetration along the lines suggested in an earlier chapter. The European came at a time when the Mogul rulers were building their own empire and making one more attempt to unite India. The Mogul rulers brought little that was really new to Indian culture to bear on their problem. Occidental culture, on the other hand, was virile, expanding and ingenious in its maneuvers, if crude in its techniques and social approach. In the face of the traditional stumbling block of Indian regional disunity, and badgered by increasing swarms of disruptive Europeans, Mogul power faltered and faded slowly away. A mosaic of political regions scrambling for autonomy, hegemony, or loot fell prey both to British offers of friendship and to accumulated animosity. The growth and decline of Mogul power is shown in Fig. 47.

Not only was India the chief entrepôt of pre-Columbian trade in the southern Orient, but she was the chief source of manufactured goods. Iron and steel products and many types of cotton textiles led the list of Indian handicraft products that found their way to the markets of all southeast Asia. Indian ports were the meeting ground of Chinese, Arab, Indonesian, and Indian traders. Slowly the British came to comprehend the nature of this going economic operation, and gradually they excluded the other participants. Relegated to the role of petty traders, native shipping interests often took to piracy to make a living, in itself no new occupation in the East. The growth of British India is shown in Fig. 48.

The charter of the East India Company periodically was subject to review in the British House of Commons, and the more ruthless exploitation of India repeatedly was checked. Nevertheless India was made to carry the whole of the expenditures of Company operations, while tremendous profits flowed away to England to stockholders and private employees, and

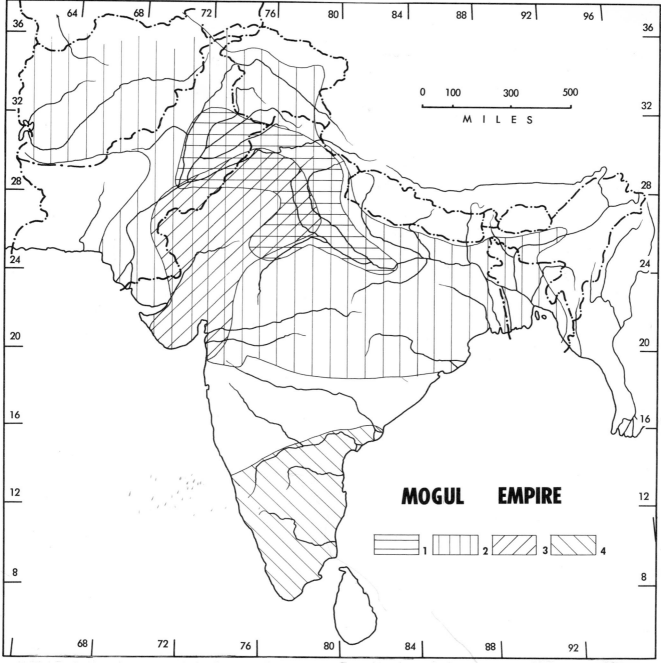

Fig. 47.   Rise and decline of the Moguls: (1) extent of the Mogul state in A.D. 1561; (2) Mogul state in 1705; (3) Mogul state in 1751; (4) the state of Vijayanagar in 1561.

almost no permanent investments in the future of India were made.   Though the Company kept the peace, developed certain port cities, and trained such clerks as they needed to carry on their trading operations, India benefited only secondarily.   However, the fact is that it did benefit during the eighteenth century.   The increasing assumption by the Company of effective police power and the functions of supervisory government left an Indian local community with a share of village autonomy not greatly different from that held throughout most periods of Moslem or Hindu imperial rule.   The well-organized trading efforts of the Company increased the market for Indian products abroad during the eighteenth century.

However, stresses began to develop within India, and within the Company, early in the nineteenth cen-

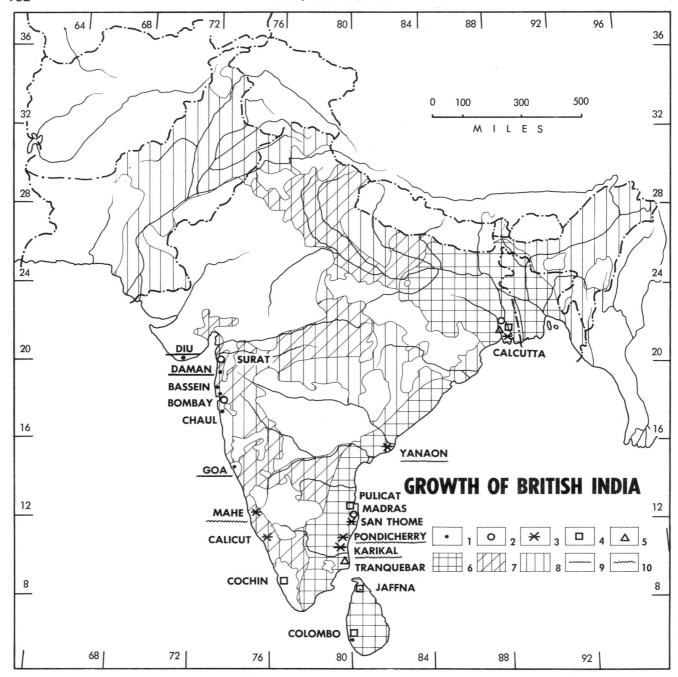

Fig. 48. The growth of the British Indian Empire: (1) Portuguese ports in 1561; (2) British trade stations in 1700; (3) French trade stations in 1700; (4) Dutch trade stations in 1700; (5) Danish trade stations in 1700; (6) British administered areas in 1796; (7) British administered areas added by 1823; (8) British India after 1857, including areas shown in 6 and 7; (9) Portuguese ports and areas in 1947, underlined; (10) French ports and areas in 1947, underlined.

tury. Commercial operations had become hopelessly entangled in governmental and peace-preservation machinery. The increasing cost of maintaining the Company's huge staff produced constantly heavier tax levies upon the regions under control. Attempts were made to enter the field of production and thus increase the earning span. Elements of trade were initiated that provoked great trouble, such as the insistence upon shipment of opium to China to pay for tea purchases. Within India unrest developed owing to the failure of the Company to develop transport, to attend to education, to supervise religion, to concern itself with Indian

Villages and towns

political and social institutions. Earlier Indian governments, however regional, had made efforts in all these directions. That none of these things were the recognized business of a trading corporation in the nineteenth century only increases the anomalous situation in which the British found their East India Company.

The British government began taking a hand in matters early in the nineteenth century, as the strains began to show more clearly. Concern over affairs in India, upon renewal of the Company charter in 1833, abolished most of its monopoly features. It checked any further tendency of the Company to increase its political control, leaving in the hands of Indian princes and rajas a large area of India, most peculiarly distributed over the country. Actually the Company had been making efforts in education for some years, aimed mainly at preservation of the traditional learning. In 1835 Lord Macaulay, newly arrived as a legal member of the Company's Council, keynoted a new policy, to educate as Englishmen a selected group of Indians who then were to become interpreters of occidental culture to the rest of India. This was a decision which was slow to bear fruit, but whose final results have had profound effects upon modern India. The increasing stresses finally led to rebellion in the 1850's, known in British circles as the Mutiny of 1857. In the next year the East India Company was abolished. The administration of India became the duty of a newly created British cabinet post, the Secretary of State for India. Thus India frankly became a British colony, most of which Britain ran directly, but in part of which she recognized the selective independence of native rulers. Unconsciously, therefore, the British perpetuated regional disunity, an old feature in Indian life.

THE MATURING INDIAN LANDSCAPE

India possesses a distinctive landscape in which cultural features today are fully as significant as the natural elements of landforms and vegetation. Many of these cultural elements are of great age, completely Indian in origin, whose distinctive stylistic lines belong to the whole span of Indian culture history. A few native Indian features belong to a particular period, and go with a religious or art movement. Others have been introduced from outside India at different times, eventually to become blended into or to remain isolated in the Indian landscape. Some rather distinctive cultural items are simply the result of the dense packing together of 400,000,000 Indians.

India is a land of villages and small towns. The 1941 census tabulated some 658,000 settlements in India, excluding Ceylon. Of these about 450,000 were villages of under 500 people; in each of 124,000 villages resided between 500 and 1,000 people. About 325,000,000 people live in settlements under 5,000 in size. Some 4,000 towns and cities house about 65,000,000 people. Of the latter group there are but 57 cities having over 100,000 people each. A simple average statement indicates that the average village has not far from a hundred houses, and that many small towns have from one to two thousand houses.

Smaller settlements normally are cluster villages in shape and form, with only occasionally an elongated shoe-string village or other shape definitely related to some local landscape stimulus. This is an old feature which goes far back into early Indian settlement history. Within the village narrow and irregular lanes, often ending in blind alleys, are the rule. In the often invaded northwest the cluster is tight and presents a protective solid outer wall, though newer villages established in the last two centuries often are more open. In moist parts of India villages often are less tightly clustered together than elsewhere. Normally villages are not walled, but they have around them strips or patches of uncropped common land on which animals are tethered, crop threshing is done, tools are stored, and manure heaps are piled for fuel storage. Around the village in fairly close order are grouped the fields and gardens. Field patterns are irregular and have been developed in accord with various local criteria. Often the Indian field system impresses the Chinese and the occidental as being somewhat inefficiently laid out, with considerable waste space and a certain amount of sheer disorder. This latter aspect is noticeably missing from those parts of Assam, south India, and Ceylon where plantation crops like tea, coffee, and rubber are grown today under occidental planning.

Above the small residential village is the small town, often fortified, that has matured out of the original market village and tribal political center. These today are merchandising and administrative centers as well as the homes of the landlords and upper classes. Such settlements almost always have been laid out on grid plans. The smaller towns may have but a single pair of streets, laid out to form a simple cross, and permitting a four-ward political organization. There usually are narrow lanes penetrating the blocks of houses which are densely packed together. Primary streets are of fair width, permitting two-way wheeled traffic, and along them are arranged the retail shops and professional offices that go with a service town. Near the gates or the edges of town are the grain shops, lumber yards, and those handicrafts requiring more space than can be afforded along the central main streets. Around the town margins are cleared spaces where crowds may gather, the wandering entertainment group may hold forth, animals and carts may be parked, the fair-day stalls may be erected, and barter may take place. Sometimes outside the town, but as often inside it, is the Hindu temple or the Moslem mosque. Often high-ranking castes reside exclusively in one section of town, while low castes and outcaste menials have huts in a suburb outside. Historic and religious monuments often are numerous and scattered about the town and its environs. Ruins of historic buildings and shrines sometimes occur, but durable building materials usually are gradually removed and incorporated into new buildings, so that the marks of ancient occupation are fewer than might be expected. Many a modern small town has a ragged fringe of suburbs strung out along the roads approaching the settlement.

Whatever may have been the history of house types in early India, there is a simple general zoning to these matters today. In the north and northwestern lowlands the adobe brick structure is most common, sometimes with a flat mud-over-matting roof and sometimes with a simple gable and a variety of roofing material. In much of the moist and warmer parts of India housing is flimsy as regards the walls, crude matting and even brush often being used by the rural peasantry today. In such housing the well-thatched roof with an overhang is more important than the walls. Such houses often have separate crop storehouses, built to a better standard. In the Deccan flimsy farmsteads often are surrounded by thorn fences. Everywhere in the villages the usual house consists of two rooms or less, mud floors are almost universal, windows are small or absent, and decorative features are few in number. In some sections whitewash is fairly common, whatever the building material. The small town possesses some better architecture. Two-story buildings are common, often with fired brick and plastered walls, whitewashed or color-surfaced. Balconies are frequent features of Indian town housing, as are good tile roofs and decorative tile floors in the better houses. Deep verandahs and terraces also are common features. The flat roof is a persistent feature of public and private building in towns and cities almost all over India and has led to characteristic use of rain spouts and drains, and the low, simple balustrade around the tops of the walls. Flat sandstone slabs on timber beams, with cement-caulked cracks, or cement over rubble stone in massive arched-roof building form the commonest roofs on better buildings. There has been considerable historical variation and repetition in building materials. In the Himalayan mountain zone wood is the primary building material, with considerable carving, gabled roofs, and interesting decorative features.

In northeastern India, the Himalayan foothills, along the Malabar coast, and in parts of Ceylon the gabled roof is normal, these being the rainiest parts of India.

Early in the historic period villages were few in number, set in small clearings scattered throughout the parkland, jungle, or forest. The small fortified town was slow to develop, despite the era of city building that had marked the Indus Valley. The Bactrian Greeks, Sakas, and Parthians brought into northwest India various Hellenistic features of architecture and decorative motifs that become woven into standard Indian concepts. The field areas and commonly used grazing lands were but a minor share of the total area in the early period. Gradually, with the native expansion of population and with steady immigration, the settlement clearings expanded against the native plant cover and, in populated areas, became fairly continuous. With this steady expansion of the cultural landscape its variety increased. The rice, palm, banana, and green tree-strewn landscape of Bengal, Assam, south India, Ceylon, and the Malabar coast has steadily grown more complex as more fields, new crops, and more settlements spread against the jungle and the forest. Whenever man has stopped for a time the jungle has reclaimed its own, and trace is soon lost of the earlier cultural works. In the drier parts of India the wheat, millet, small-grain, and parkland pattern also has grown more complex with more dense settlement. Irrigation canals and tanks have multiplied, and today there must be literally millions of shallow wells being operated by hand or by animals throughout the drier parts of the North Indian Plain. Steadily over the centuries this cultural landscape has been extended until today no more than 13 per cent of the total area remains in forest, largely in rough and permanently uncultivable parts of India. A considerable amount of cultivable waste and useless waste land is scattered throughout the cultural landscape.

Over the centuries there slowly matured several distinctive patterns of Hindu public architecture. Referring to a period in the fourth and fifth centuries A.D. one writer quotes the remark: "The architecture of the country is divided into three broad styles and ten types, corresponding to the geographical divisions and the political entities." * These three styles were a northern one involving mostly quadrangular shapes, a southern style using hexagonal and octagonal shapes, and an eastern style using rounded shapes. The introduction of Moslem architecture in Arabic, Persian, and Turkish styles since the ninth century has added sig-

* P. K. Acharya, *Indian Architecture according to Manasara Silpasastra*, Allahabad, 1927, p. 181.

nificantly to the cultural landscape of India, both in style and in building materials. Stone and cement became much more frequently used. In the Punjab Moslem building is mostly Persian in its stylistic relations; in the Deccan this Persian style has been Hinduized somewhat. East of the Punjab on the North Indian Plain Turkish or Mogul styling is most noticeable, but again it has been Hinduized to varying degree. South India possesses a great many historic temples and public buildings that are completely Hindu in their architecture, yet even here there are varieties that sometimes are regional and sometimes are sectarian in their relations.

The coming of the European introduced a new series of elements onto the cultural landscape of India. Often ugly interpretations of Elizabethan and Victorian styles of public buildings are to be found, somehow rendered unreal by Indian workmen and the Indian surroundings. In some of the earliest European settlements, Dutch, Portuguese, French, and British, are early buildings transplanted into the subtropical Indian landscape directly out of cool northwestern Europe. These styles have inocculated Indian builders sufficiently to produce some curious blends of products, found in and around some of the older urban centers, and in Ceylon. On the other hand the spacious layout, beautiful gardens, wide streets, and flat-roofed, tile-floored multiunit and detached houses of modern Indian urban suburbs derive part of their charm from the blend of Hindu, Moslem, and European styles.

In many new cities a combination of architectural styles has produced a variety not known before. Many of these new towns and cities are railroad towns or military cantonments built near the old and densely packed Indian centers. Most of the big port cities are new towns created within the span of occidental contact and are cosmopolitan settlements. In the very spread of the railroad, the road, the factory, commercial agriculture, and the plantation, both complexity and maturity have been added to the Indian landscape. The present scene is one of rapid change rather than stability and permanence. Many of the changes more recently introduced have entered only selected parts of the Indian landscape, or have not become Indianized as yet. In this next century both the spread and the Indianizing of these and other features will go on, to further intensify an already crowded cultural landscape.

RESULTS OF BRITISH RULE

Political conquest and economic domination are obvious results of British control of India. Many other effects of four hundred years of Indian contact with European culture are less obvious. If Britain did bring a kind of peace and stability to Indian life in the various regions as she took them over, one may almost question their worth. That very stability initiated economic programs which have saddled the Indian peasantry with a debt often estimated at thirty times their annual income. In the earlier eras, political change had been sufficiently frequent to permit periodically erasing the slate clean of accumulated debts, though, of course, this produced other handicaps. British efforts to simplify the land ownership and tax patterns of this complicated Indian landscape did indeed produce simplification in many regions. Often, however, the British raised the tax collector to a dominant position and slowly undermined the strength and vitality of the village *sabha,* thus destroying the small amount of freedom the rural peasantry retained. In the tax simplification procedures often the final result was to solidify the vested position of the *zemindar* class of tax farmer-collectors into a parasitic middle and upper class group.

Under foreign encouragement Indian foreign trade has continued to expand above the level it held in pre-Columbian times. Gradually, however, there has come about a change in the nature of this trade. India once a manufacturer and an entrepôt has become a producer and exporter of raw materials and an importer of manufactured goods. Once the trade monopoly of the East India Company was removed, British interests in India changed in nature and the flow of manufactured goods began. The decline of handicrafts and the growth of exploitative competition with other parts of the world in agricultural exports slowly has lowered the Indian peasant's standard of living. A decreasing standard of living is difficult to describe fully and document clearly, but, despite the science of the Occident and constructive British efforts, it does seem true that the Indian peasant is relatively worse off today than when the European first came to India.

Occidental contact with India has produced many significant benefits which clearly can be pointed out. Transportation and communication facilities compare favorably with those in many other parts of the world, and millions of acres now are cultivated through irrigation canals engineered by the British. The establishment of industrial plants, the development of Indian universities, and the spread of occidental medicine are concrete aspects of modern Indian life. British struggles against the burning alive of female widows, child marriage, and the caste system have been valiant efforts against strangling social customs, though only the first has been eliminated. The lowered death rate and the increase in total population are positive proofs of the benefits of British rule. And yet these things do not seem fully to compensate for the serious inroads upon Indian life, for the decreasing standard exists in spite of multiple benefits.

It perhaps is pertinent to ask whether the present state of Indian affairs can be laid on the doorstep of the British. It has been popular in some circles to do so. Certainly the British have been to blame for many evils in 400 years of contact of East and West. But Indian culture is not free from blame. In the post-Columbian changing world Indian culture has lacked the flexibility that characterized it during the formative period and the Mauryan era. The modern Indian people are the inheritors of one of the most restrictive and complex bodies of culture in the world today. This fact, itself, is partly responsible for the plight of the Indian peasant population. Recently change is increasing its tempo, but change still has far to go.

One of the distinctive results of British control over India has been the curious patchwork composing the Indian political pattern. When the East India Company was canceled the extension of police power and political administration had not yet taken over all of India. Still outstanding were about 700,000 square miles of area in very irregular distribution. Upon taking direct control over British India the Crown honored the existing treaties of the Company with the older independent Indian states. The difficulties that led to the decline of the Mogul line freed from supervision numerous minor kings, regional governors, petty princes, and ambitious feudal wardens. These then shared the same relationship to the Crown as other Indian states.

In the late nineteenth century over 600 separate regions claimed sovereign status. These ranged from little plots like Bilbari, 15 acres, to Hyderabad, 82,313 square miles. The Kathiawar Peninsula was the area of most numerous petty divisions. Slowly the number has been reduced slightly, at the outbreak of World War II totaling 562 states, with a total area of 715,964 square miles and a population of 93,189,000. To an American, with a passion for orderly arrangement of the obvious parts of government, the British arrangement in India has seemed most haphazard and inefficient. Obvious order has never been a primary component of British colonial administration, and so the British kept the system, making it work, and taking occasional advantage of a chance to increase administrative unity. Some of the native states had kept pace with developments in British India; others were striking examples of feudalism carried into the modern world.

Mother India in the Modern World

Today there are three political regimes operating in the region we have previously termed India. These regions now are separated politically and statistically, and increasingly in the future they will develop separate trends in many different ways. However, they have shared the same culture history, and in many respects they still are interdependent and complementary in their economies. There now is Pakistan, consisting of two separated but predominantly Mohammedan regions; there is the new state of India, the predominantly Hindu regions; there is Ceylon, the small southern island region; Kashmir is a territory in dispute between Pakistan and India. The separations are so recent, and so largely lines on the political map, that the discussion will pertain to all three areas—the historic India. In the latter portion of the chapter there is treatment of each of the three political units, and the statistical data presented in the last chapter of the book separates the three states. To distinguish the new and separate state of India from the older, larger India the two words "united" and "Mother" will be prefixed to the term for the larger region in this chapter.

THE AGRICULTURAL ECONOMY OF MOTHER INDIA

Problems in Agriculture

Mother India is a region in which two different systems of agriculture overlap and compete for space in the landscape. The two systems involve separate sets of plants and animals domesticated under particular combinations of climate, soil, and human sponsorship. These combinations were described in Chapters 5 and 6. The zone of meeting and the amount of competition have been steadily shifting, dependent upon the economy practiced by peoples newly immigrant or long settled in united India. Significant in this meeting are the plants native to united India which have been a variable part of each basic pattern. Important also is the variable use of irrigation during different historic periods. Vital to agriculture are the post-Columbian crop additions which have widened the range of Indian products. Of regional significance is the nineteenth-century introduction of the plantation and of commercial export agriculture.

A fundamental fact of modern united Indian agriculture is the low per-acre yield of crops. This variably has been ascribed to poor soils, the inroads of soil erosion during 5,000 years, small use of fertilizer, poor tools and poor cultivation techniques, a peasantry ignorant of beneficial practices, the increasing fragmentation of family holdings, voluminous pests, the irregular monsoon climate, and British imperialism. To this group must be added one more. Though for centuries he has employed practices only recently understood in the West, in most cases the Indian farmer is a somewhat careless operator. Here and there in united India there are illustrations of great agricultural skill among a people or regional group, producing impressive local landscapes, but these are unusual rather than normal situations.

Throughout much of the northern Deccan and the North Indian Plain west of Bihar the modern scarcity of wood for fuel has produced the standard practice of burning dung from such animals as cattle, water buffalo, horses, and camels as cooking and heating fuel. Nearly half the total animal manures are burned as fuel. Though this may be a very old custom its mass application is fairly recent. Its practice in any one village means that the lands of that village are permanently deprived of their major source of fertilizer. Where the fuel shortage is sufficiently severe to have promoted the practice, stubble and plant wastes also must be used as fuel, so that the land seldom receives any energy replacement. In many parts of united India, however, all animal manures and plant wastes are stored and used on the fields. Almost every village is ringed by a zone of better, more productive soils whose fertility is maintained by the disposal of human wastes, courtyard sweepings, and miscellaneous humus-creating wastes. The current fertilizer needs exceed the total supply of animal manures about four times, so that the replacement of fuel is but one aspect of the fertilizer problem. The fertilizer value of animal manures from the poorly fed Indian cattle is relatively low. The Indian peasant is too poor and debt ridden to buy commercial fertilizers.

In many parts of united India today soil quality and workability are low. Though the peculiar black soils of the Deccan retain their fertility without much human aid, the more widespread lateritic red earths are relatively infertile. And today soil quality is poor on much of the higher-lying, older alluvium of the North Indian Plain and the larger valleys of the peninsula. Over the centuries native practices maintained long-range productive capacity which now is being lost as extreme pressure upon the land forces agriculture towards short-range goals without provision for the future. Though the acreages under crop have been increasing it is discouragingly true that recent per-acre yields have declined in some crops, with smaller net yields than were formerly secured. Much of the rest of the world has adopted the use of commercial fertilizer to secure increased yields, united India having been left behind in the race for crop production. The problem perhaps can be handled, but now it calls for major improvement operations to be carried out by the governments of united India, since the problem has exceeded the stage at which haphazard individual initiative will suffice.

Indian agriculture already uses a larger share of the landscape than is common in many countries, and more reserve land is being brought under cultivation regularly. When this reserve volume is fully put to use approximately half the area of united India will be in cultivated fields. Somewhat less than one seventh of the fields are double-cropped, but about one sixth of the cultivated land is annually fallowed, some fields being left idle for several years in a row. Irrigation, in addition to the use of water on rice land, is employed on nearly one fifth of the fields, a proportion which has increased markedly within the last century as British engineering skill has developed massive irrigation systems copied the world around. In northwest India over half of the cultivated land is irrigated, in Sind the figure rising to about 90 per cent. In the upper and central Ganges Valley about one fourth of

the land is irrigated, and throughout Madras Province the figure is nearly one third. Figure 51 shows the regions possessing irrigation facilities. Coupled with the expansion of agriculture is the fact that, out of the detrimental impact of the Occident upon united India, the proportion of Indians in agriculture has been growing, rather than declining. In 1891 about 61 per cent of the population was dependent upon agriculture, whereas the percentage had grown to about 80 per cent in 1941.

India has the largest total of domesticated animals of any large country. There are about 200,000,000 cattle and water buffalo, about 90,000,000 goats and sheep, and perhaps 6,000,000 horses, donkeys, camels, and elephants. Even so; draft energy is insufficient, the dairy products volume is far short of the need and there is but a small surplus of low-grade wool and mohair. Many agricultural areas must share work oxen. Production of milk products annually totals about 26,000,000 tons, produced by some 74,000,000 dairy animals, approximately that of the United States, to be shared by almost three times the population. Mother India traditionally has paid scant attention to animal food crops, and today most livestock is downgraded, malnourished, and unproductive. Since 1930 fodder acreage has risen at a time when united India can ill afford to feed such unproductive animals. Overgrazing in many parts of united India, but particularly in the northwest, is causing increased soil and range destruction and a spread of the desert landscape. That meat is not used by Hindus or Buddhists is a matter of tradition. Religious prejudice also stands in the way of improving conditions by decreasing the animal population, and breed improvement can make little headway at present.

Food-producing agriculture is strikingly concentrated upon three grain crops, rice, wheat, and millet, which alone account for over two thirds of the food-growing lands. Since 1930 increases in sugar cane, vegetables, and the legumes have improved the balance slightly, but this has been partly at the expense of the cotton acreage, which cannot really be afforded. Tea, coffee, and rubber have been cultivated on lands taken from the cultivable waste volume rather than that devoted to crops. Increased production of a few other commercial crops has cut into food-growing acreage. Between 5 and 10 per cent of many crops now have been improved by the introduction of better plant varieties, but productive increase in this line barely manages to keep up with the increase in population. The introduction of more productive, but thereby more demanding, plants will boomerang in a short period unless some fundamental improvement is made in soil

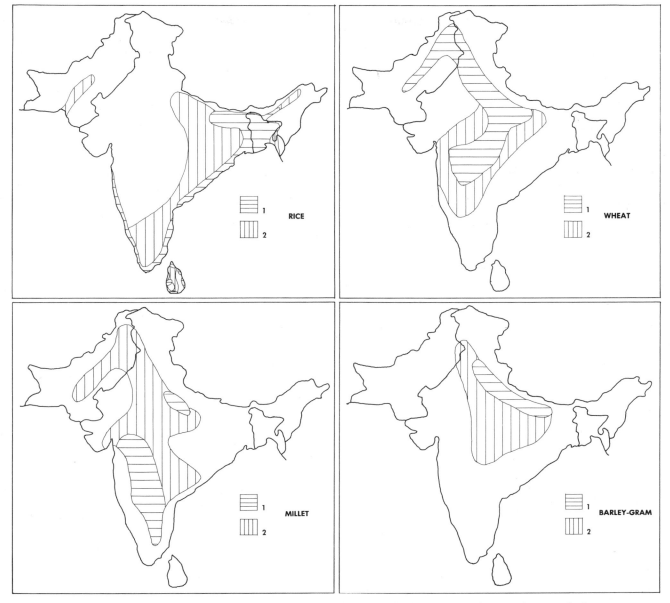

Fig. 49.   The major grain food crops of India: (1) primary producing areas: (2) secondary producing areas.

fertility.   In simple arithmetic, for each Indian there now is about three fourths of an acre of crop land from which to provide food and clothing, produce his exports, finance most of his imports, and attempt to raise his living standard in the modern world!

The Regional Crop Pattern

The accompanying maps present the regional patterns of the major Indian crops. The complementary position of the three primary grains, rice, wheat, and millet, is rather interesting. Conforming fairly closely to the regional pattern of rice are such subtropical crops as coconut, palmyra, and areca palms, of do-

mestic importance in the production of food and oil, sugar and toddy, and betel nut, respectively. Ceylon has turned coconut into an important commercial product within the present century. A number of spices, the mango, the banana, citrus, and other subtropical fruit once well matched this same pattern, but some have been taken outside it today. Wheat, grown in a different region of united India, competes with rice in a limited zone only. Durum wheats are grown in the peninsula and bread wheats in the north and northwest. Barley competes with rice a little more than wheat but has been a diminishing crop for some decades; it often is sown in mixed plantings with gram,

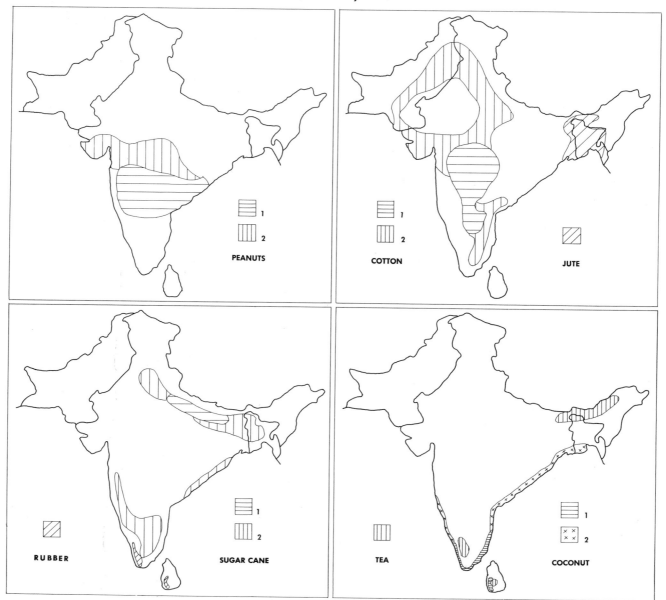

Fig. 50. Chief Indian commercial crops: (1) primary producing areas; (2) secondary producing areas. Unnumbered distributions refer to chief areas of production only.

a legume similar to the chickpea. The stone fruits, apricots, peaches, cherries, and plums, and such products as apples, pears, grapes, melons, and walnuts belong on the side of wheat and are found in the northwest and in the Mountain Wall uplands. There are vegetables that go with both zones too. Camels, horses, and donkeys fit the wheat zone fairly well, but cattle have spread all over united India as draft-energy and milk-products producers. The water buffalo, superior as a dairy producer to the average poor Indian cow, has spread outside the rice-growing zone as an urban dairy animal.

Millet, cotton, and several legumes, which go under the term "pulse," occupy a middle ground, being most at home in the Deccan and the edges of northwest India. Here often is mixed planting of two and even three grains in one field. Well-timed, plentiful summer rains stimulate the millet into producing the major grain yield, but light rains retard the millet and then sorghum forms the chief harvest. Long-range yields thus are better than from fields planted singly, particularly where a legume is interplanted. Various crops have been taken into both the rice and the wheat zones and fitted into agricultural patterns according to local

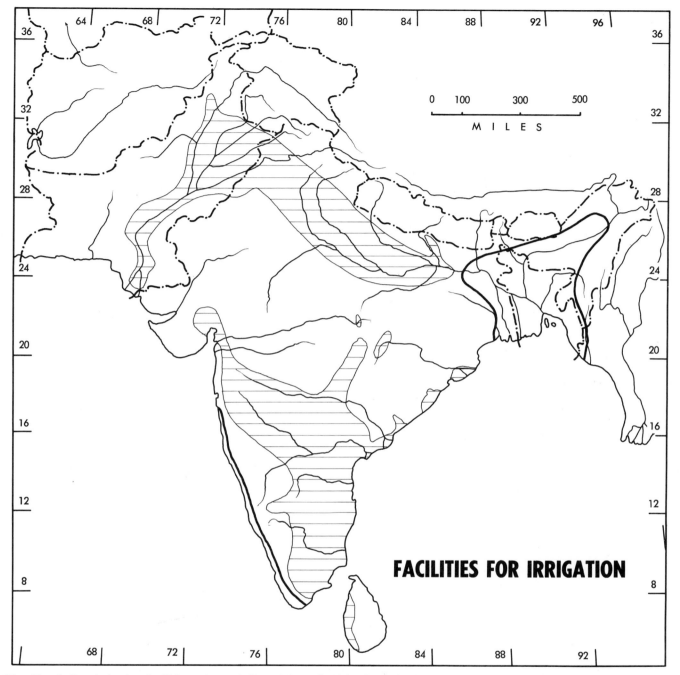

Fig. 51. Indian irrigation facilities. Areas indicated have facilities for irrigating much cultivated land. Used are stream-diversion canals, tank storage and canals, power-pumped deep wells, and shallow animal or manually operated wells. The heavy line along the west coast and in the Bengal Delta encloses the zone in which irrigation is not really required.

advantage. Sugar cane may be grown almost anywhere on the Indian lowland, but since 1910 has centered in the Ganges Valley. The oil seeds are spread all over united India, different crops preferring particular regions. Some are native field plants, others are tree crops, and a number are introduced plants. Some native crops such as jute or cinnamon are very clearly regional monopolies, belonging to Bengal and Ceylon, respectively. Such post-Columbian introductions as the peanut, tobacco, pineapple, maize, cacao, coffee, tea, and rubber were first tried in different parts of united India, then slowly have settled into particular regions or preferred types of environments. Tea and rubber are grown on plantations that

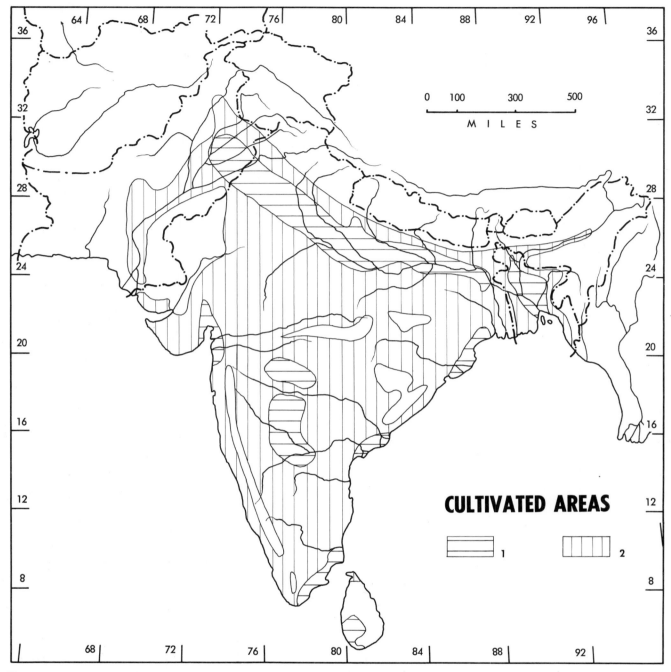

Fig. 52. Land in cultivation: (1) over 60 per cent of land in crops; (2) between 20 and 60 per cent of land in crops. Blank areas have under 20 per cent of land in crops.

mainly are British-owned. Coffee no longer is grown in Ceylon but is grown in South India on numerous small holdings. In Ceylon, British-owned plantations account for over half of the tea and rubber production and for the minor production of high-grade cacao. Indian labor is used on Ceylon plantations, whereas the Singhalese cultivate their own small holdings of both tea and rubber. Over 8,000 tea and rubber estates cover over 2,000,000 acres and employ a labor force of somewhat over 2,000,000.

Increasingly restricted in scope is migratory agriculture, once the typical economy of earlier, simpler societies of subtropical united India. Along the Mountain Wall from perhaps Simla eastward and down to the Bay of Bengal, in the Chota Nagpur upland, and in narrowing circles in southern Mother India variations of hunting, gathering, and simple digging-stick agriculture still are practiced today by some millions of people. In North Mother Indian this simple pattern is known as *jhum,* in Ceylon termed *chena.* Such irregular economy neither contributes much to the welfare of united India nor makes many demands, though it has played a widely significant part in altering the ecological balance of local environmental conditions in the past.

Forest Utilization

Forest trees are more typical of the remaining Indian vegetation than are grasses, a factor in itself important to animal culture. A large share of the united Indian landscape once was forested, under liberal use of the term. Today not more than 13 per cent of the total area is in forest and scrub cover of some sort, and for future self-sufficiency of wood products in general united India should maintain nearly 20 per cent of her total area in forest growth of some kind. Firewood is a major item in this consideration, not requiring timber forests. Of wood for lumber the united Indian forests today show little reserve, not more than 5 per cent of the total area. Over the centuries considerable cutting and reforestation has been practiced in varied parts of Mother India. Between 1850 and 1910 an increasing amount of timber was cut without any reforestation program. From 1910 onward forest management has improved steadily, and many good timber-producing trees now are growing in new forests. With continued good management, sufficient rough lands unavailable for cropping can be returned to forest production to provide for most domestic needs.

Forest woods of economic significance vary by vegetation zones. In the lower Punjab and driest parts of northwest united India today a thorny, shrubby tree *Prosopis spicigera* often is the only wood locally available for firewood and miscellaneous use. In better areas the long-ago introduced babul, *Acacia arabica,* provides lumber and tool and general-use wood. In and along the Himalayas a variety of woods are used. In the western zone deodar cedar, *Cedrus deodara,* chir pine, *Pinus longifolia,* blue pine, *Pinus excelsa,* silver fir, *Abies pindrow,* and Himalayan spruce, *Picea marinda,* are the most useful woods and today are marketed widely in the lowlands of the Punjab and the upper Ganges Valley. Further east in the Himalayan foothills, in the Chota Nagpur upland, and in preserved lowland tracts sal, *Shorea robusta* and related species, teak, *Tectona grandis,* sissoo or shisham, *Dalbergia sissoo,* and toon, *Cedrela toona,* are the most common forest timber woods, but bamboo and numerous minor woods are used for special purposes.

Sal is a better wood than teak for many uses, grows in pure stands, and ranges from the Punjab to Assam and from the Deccan into the Himalayan foothills. From Kathiawar to Chota Nagpur and from the Deccan to the North Indian Plain grows the mahua, *Bassis latifolia.* In early spring it yields very edible blossoms and in summer seeds rich in oil that are used as a butter substitute. It produces a good wood, but so prized are its other products that today it is cut for timber only when most necessary. In eastern Bengal, Assam and the Burma border hill country are found many woods that are also commonly used in Central and South Mother India. Teak, mesua or ironwood, *Mesua ferrea,* pyinkado in Burma or irul in South Mother India, *Xylia dolabriformis,* and padauk or rosewood, *Pterocarpus* spp., are the species common to both areas, along with bamboos, canes, and rattans. Kokko, *Albizzia* spp. is a much used wood common to the eastern Himalayan foothill. Sandalwood, *Santalum album,* is a South Indian wood much used for carving toys, figurines, other curios and utensils, and for its scented oil. Though cultivated for its nuts, the coconut tree is almost the most useful of all trees grown in South Mother India and Ceylon, since its wood, leaves, fiber, and shells have myriad uses. Over much of lowland central and eastern united India mango wood, *Mangifera indica,* is a commonly used, cheap wood in many villages and small towns. Usually it is only available in small quantities because the mango today is an important cultivated fruit tree rather than a forest tree.

MINERALS AND INDUSTRY

The people of the Indus Valley culture already were skilled in the use of most of the common metals of history. Indian bronze never equaled that of ancient China, and perhaps its gold work was excelled by that of some other region, but, after iron reached Mother India, Indian iron work compared favorably with that of any part of the world. Indian iron ores often contain small amounts of ferro-alloys in natural combination. In late pre-Columbian times Indian iron and steel circulated from the Near East to the Indies. Only slowly has modern industry replaced Indian handicraft skill in the metals. The village silversmith still thrives, and the modern urban united Indian silver and gold craftsman is one of the world's finest. Primitive iron furnaces and forges still are scattered throughout the peninsula, but the village and small town blacksmith today prefers to work with ready-made rods or strap rather than native pig iron.

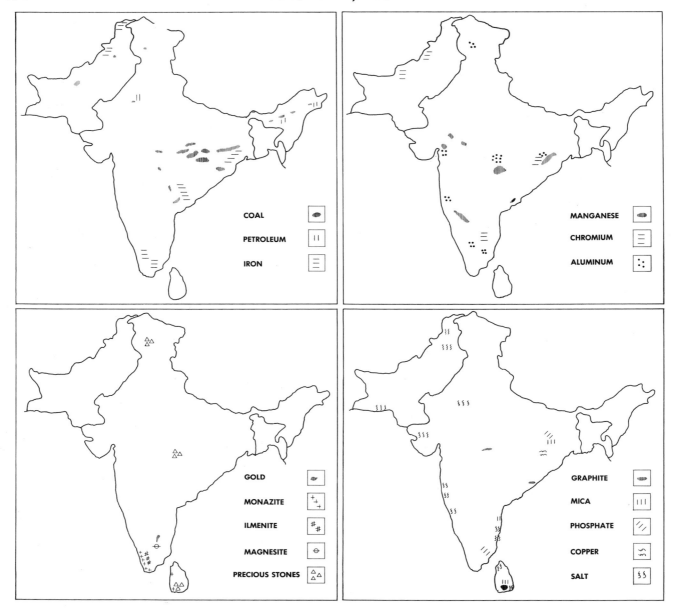

Fig. 53   Occurrence of mineral deposits in India and Pakistan.

British industrial investment in united India largely skipped metals production. The ores became significant as raw materials for expanding factories only in the West. The British early developed a bureau of geologic survey, and today the country has been rather well canvassed and its resources fairly well tabulated. The current assessment of mineral resources suggests that united India does not have either the volume or the variety adequate to the developed industrial needs of a populous subcontinent. Compared with an equally populous part of Europe, united India's resources are both smaller and poorly situated. The accompanying map shows the regional distribution of mineral resources.

Coal is the chief source of industrial power. United India ranks eighth among the countries of the world, with an estimated reserve of not over 60 billion tons. Neither quality nor variety is very high, and the volume is concentrated in the Chota Nagpur upland, with minor deposits in the Punjab, in Assam, and in southern India. An annual production of nearly 30,000,000 tons is used mostly in rail transport and in industry. Petroleum primarily is an import product. Small-producing fields lie in the Punjab and in Assam, and others perhaps may be found elsewhere around the folded fringes of the North Indian Plain. Hydroelectric power promises a rather high potential to united India, though the seasonal drainage of monsoon moisture is a severe handicap. Before this source can be utilized rather costly dam and conservation projects must be undertaken over almost all of united India, like that now being executed in the Damodar Valley west of Calcutta.

Widely distributed iron ores helped the traditional handicraft production, but they prove less helpful to modern industry, owing to the difficult nature of many of the ores and to the concentration of coal deposits. Good ores are found accessible to coal, limestone, manganese, and chromium in the Chota Nagpur upland, in huge volume, capable of meeting domestic needs for a long period. Mysore is the only other area possessing good iron ore in large volume. Manganese ore is widely scattered over the peninsula, and nickel and chromium occur in amounts sufficient for united Indian needs for some time. Mica and graphite from the peninsula and Ceylon, respectively, are two other significant mineral products of united India. Manganese, mica, and graphite have been export products, but their relatively low value lessens their cash contribution to Indian economy. Copper, bauxite, refractories, and mined rock salt are produced in small quantities. Most Indian salt is a product of evaporation of sea water, of domestic rather than industrial use. Gold still is the second most valuable mineral product, though its production is declining. Indian gold was one of the fabulous attractions of the East, but the chief producing region, the Kolar fields of Mysore, appear to be nearing exhaustion. Lead, zinc, tungsten, tin, and silver are not produced within united India, though the former inclusion of Burma within Indian statistical summaries suggested such production. Saltpeter once was an important export, but the volume has declined since the 1860's. Thorium-producing monazite sands from Travancore and Ceylon were a minor export used in making gas mantles until atomic energy projects advanced the importance of thorium, but the simple economic worth of the mineral product to united India will not be high within the near future.

Several precious and semiprecious stones have been Indian products, among them pearls, rubies, beryls, and topazes from the southernmost peninsula and Ceylon, diamonds from the peninsula, and sapphires from Kashmir. Chank shells from the Gulf of Mannar have been in steady production over the centuries, the whole shell used in religious ceremonies and shells being cut into bracelets and armlets as one of the old

Bengal handicrafts. It is likely that a steady export of these items reached wide limits within the pre-Columbian Old World, but modern production of none is particularly significant.

The new state of India is the proud possessor of the largest iron and steel plant in all the British lands. It is completely an Indian product, founded, developed, and managed by the Parsee Tata family, and owned entirely by Indian stockholders. It began production in 1911. The main installation is at Jamshedpur in the Chota Nagpur upland. Other lesser iron and steel operations are carried on near Calcutta and in Mysore. The latter region is far from coal and uses charcoal as a fuel in smelting iron ore. The Tata enterprises have included several other lines of industrial development, and will represent one of the major sources of industrial expansion in the next period. The Hindu Birla family enterprises somewhat resemble those of the Tata group, but have concentrated upon cement, sugar, and cotton textiles. United India is about self-sufficient in cement production, a rather critical item in the modern world of industrial expansion. Cotton textiles, the oldest industrial line, finally have become united Indian in capital and management. Domestic production does not supply the needs through a variety of factors. Politically sponsored revival of handicraft spinning and weaving has helped somewhat but has not put a stop to textile imports. Vigorous efforts in both Pakistan and India to supplement cotton textile manufacturing are beginning to achieve a better balance of sufficiency.

In the jute industry united Indian initiative and participation have been increasing slowly, though they do not yet control the industry. The division of India and Pakistan has worked hardships upon the jute industry. The factories lie in India whereas the crop is chiefly grown in East Pakistan. In a variety of modern consumers' goods a considerable stake has been built up in the face of competition. Glass, chemicals, paints, matches, paper, and pharmaceuticals all show such a beginning. Native industry will not yet properly supply the domestic market, nor can it compete in foreign markets. In producers' goods and transport-equipment lines hardly a beginning has been made.

United Indian industrial locations are somewhat scattered, though they are mainly found in the peninsula and the Bengal Delta. Jamshedpur, Calcutta, and Mysore are the iron and steel cities. Jamshedpur is beginning to add secondary manufactures, but it is located in a tribal refuge area and must import labor. At least two thirds of roughly 400 cotton mills lie within the triangle formed by Bombay, Nagpur, and Ahmedabad, though minor specialty centers are found all over the country. Cotton textiles employ about 500,000 workers. Just over 100 jute plants are in regular operation, of which all but three or four are clustered around Calcutta, employing about 200,000 people. Silk textile manufacture is not yet industrialized, and is scattered all over united India. The paper industry centers on Calcutta, as does match manufacturing. Agricultural processing plants are scattered over the country. Bangalore, Madras, and Calcutta lead in turning tobacco into cigarettes and cigars. Sugar refining is mainly centered in small towns on the Himalayan side of the Ganges Valley, from north of Patna to about Ambala. This is an industry now protected by import tariffs, so that cane acreage and refineries have recently increased. Cawnpore, Calcutta, and Madras lead in the modern tanning of leather for export. Rice and wheat flour milling are carried on at opposite ends of the country. Calcutta, Jamshedpur, Madras, Bombay, and Ahmedabad are the only cities properly termed industrial centers, though many towns have a beginning in some one industrial line. The total industrial labor supply of united India numbers under 2,000,000, to which should be added perhaps another 2,000,000 who are fully or partly concerned with cottage industry and handicrafts, about 1,000,000 concerned with transportation in all of its public forms, and about 600,000 engaged in mining.

TRANSPORTATION AND COMMUNICATION

As the British spread the modern network of roads and highways over Mother India they followed many an ancient route, sometimes utilizing the actual road embankment. Highways were developed with an eye to military movement and effective control of Mother India. More recently improvements have been made to provide transport for the population. The network today approximates 300,000 miles, of which about two thirds can be termed all-weather roads. The accompanying map shows the regional distribution of roads. A serious shortage of paving materials in the North Indian Plain puts the best roads in the southern peninsula. Some secondary roads are graded but still are narrow and poorly bridged. In addition to the above mileage are thousands of miles of cart tracks, bicycle and pack trails, not maintained, unbridged, and subject to flood and the Indian farmer. The automotive equipment totals some 250,000 vehicles. This would provide beautiful motoring conditions were it not for the thousands of darting bicycles in urban areas and what seem like millions of plodding oxcarts on the urban fringes and in the rural market towns. Bus transport is an important phase of motor transport, linking many towns not connected by rail. These services, overcrowded and badly equipped, are usually privately owned and often are irregular in performance.

The railway system started out to parallel the road system unprofitably. The railways use the European small-tonnage freight cars, compartment-type passenger cars, light engines, light rails, and a variety of gauges. Accumulated mileage for united India and Ceylon totals about 42,050 miles, shown on an accompanying map. Broad-gauge lines total 20,737 miles. This puts united India in third place among regions of the world. However, there are less than 27 miles of railway per thousand square miles of area, one of the lower figures among modernized countries. The railways now are government owned, with operation divided between government and private companies. Trains carry a large passenger traffic, mainly on short trips, at rather cheap fares, since most people travel third class in crowded, wooden-seated cars. Coal, for railway operation, and farm crops make up the bulk of the freight carried. Though the multigauge, patchwork pattern of lines fairly well covers the country, about half the mileage is in the Ganges Valley.

Both highways and rail lines focus on key points scattered over united India. Karachi, Lahore, Delhi, Bombay, Madras, Colombo, and Calcutta are major road and rail terminals. Secondary points are Attock, Ahmedabad, Jubbulpore, Nagpur, Dacca, Bezwada, Hyderabad-Deccan, Guntakal, Bangalore, and Trichinopoly. Both transport systems have more than their proportionate length in what was British India, whereas large districts that were in native states totally lack rail lines and almost lack highways.

The telegraph and telephone systems run with the road and rail systems, if less efficiently. "Telegrams" usually are despatched by mail, and the phone systems are hybrid combinations of old and new. Commercial radio had made little advance before World War II, but broadcast radio, linked to the home British system, had quite a following. Air transport, within united India, was uncommon before World War II, though united India was fairly well tied into world airways. Home-owned companies now operate several thousand miles of air lines, and in the coming era united India will take large steps forward in air transport. The major air terminals and air fields are shown on Fig. 54.

The chief ports during any past century are hard

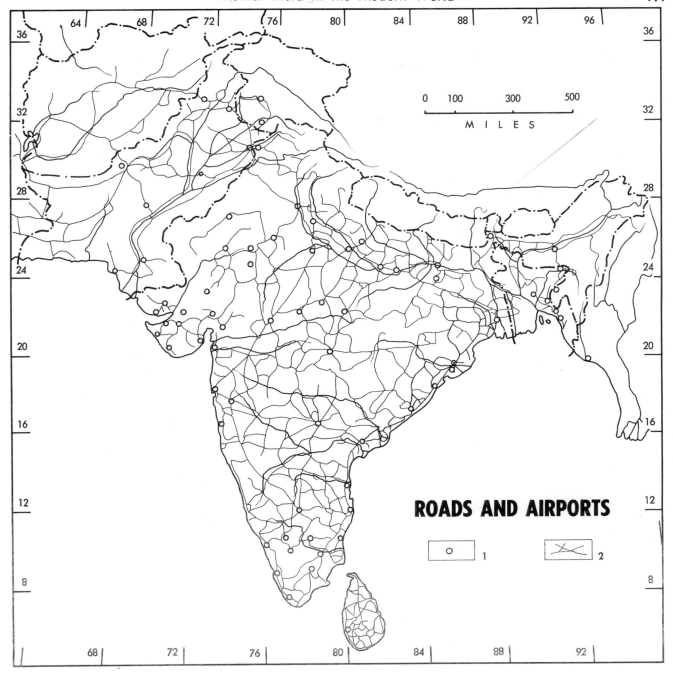

Fig. 54. All-weather roads and civil airports: (1) civil airports in regular use; (2) chief all-weather roads.

to locate now. Shifting sands, moving deltaic distributaries, naval conflict, and changing political fortunes have obliterated hundreds of them. The chief ports of the sixteenth-century European contact no longer are used by ships in foreign trade. The leading modern ports are those picked by the British East India Company. All are modern settlements. Karachi, Bombay, Colombo, Madras, and Calcutta form the primary group of big ports, given added facilities between 1920 and 1947 by the Government of united India. A second group of ports receiving planned development before 1947 were Bhavnagar, Calicut, Cochin, Tuticorin, Trincomalee, Visagapattam, and Chittagong. All these ports are shown on Fig. 55. Besides these are over 200 small ports used by coastal shipping. Significant in coastal traffic is the voluminous passenger movement. The Port of Bombay, during 1944–1945, handled about 2,000,000 people.

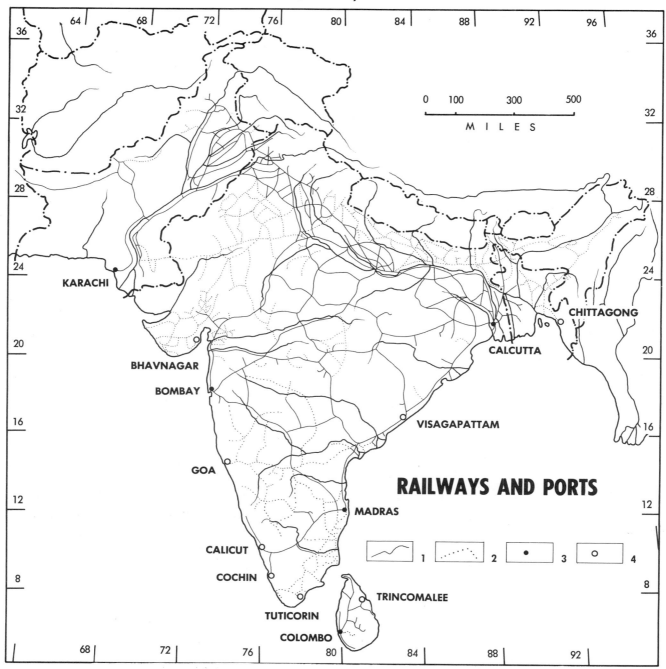

Fig. 55.   Railways and ports: (1) broad-gauge rail lines, 5 ft 6 in.; (2) narrow-gauge rail lines, 3 ft 3 in. or narrower; (3) major ports of long standing; (4) newly developed secondary ports.   About 200 minor ports with few facilities, mostly in peninsular India, are not shown.

THE TRADE OF MOTHER INDIA

It is unlikely that much produce has ever moved overland out of Mother India.   It has been suggested that Mother India was the chief entrepôt of oriental trade and that the main warehouses in this movement were the cities of the peninsular coast.   The impact of the Europeans was emphatic.   First they scattered

their trade among the many ports but drove all competitors away.   Next they concentrated on picked ports, leaving others to die off.   The British finally began to deal in Mother India's best export commodity on ever larger terms, selling cotton textiles everywhere. As the modern era approached and the Company faltered the export trade slackened, whereas the import trade grew steadily under new appetites for material goods. Within the last century the export trade has recovered, but on different grounds.

At present the export trade lists agricultural and mineral raw and processed products. Jute, raw cotton, tea, and oil seeds are the big items, followed by hides and skins, raw minerals, rubber, lac, and a series of minor, processed crop and forest products. Almost all are competitive products ranged against the same or related products of other lands. Even a monopoly like jute competes against sisal and hemp. No export is of high value, and in some cases the united Indian share has been mainly cheap labor, final profits going to British corporation investors.

The import trade lists fine cotton and its finished products far above other imports. Next come chemical products and machinery, both increasing since 1930. A third group is made up of petroleum, unfabricated iron and steel, tools and instruments, and motor transport equipment. These larger groups are followed by a long list of other manufactured products in smaller volumes. Notable for its present minor position is sugar, a declining import under a protective tariff and increasing home production. Statistically new since the separation of Burma from India in 1937 is rice, which for years has been imported at a rate of about 1,500,000 tons per year.

The big volume of foreign trade moves through the five ports of Karachi, Bombay, Colombo, Madras, and Calcutta, despite the development of some very new ports. Some export products focus upon particular ports. Bombay and Karachi handle raw cotton, Calcutta and Chittagong handle north Indian tea, and Colombo ships all Ceylon tea. Jute moves out of Calcutta; Cochin and Colombo ship the rubber. In contrast imports are spread among many ports.

The main volume of trade is with four countries. Of the chief products tea, oil seeds, hides, and skins go in largest volume to Britain, raw cotton to Japan, and jute to the United States. Germany long was the fourth ranking united Indian customer, taking smaller volumes of a variety of products. In supplying united Indian imports the order of rank was Britain, Japan, Germany, and the United States. Cotton textile imports were split between Britain and Japan before World War II, but Britain led in almost all other categories. Canada, Australia, Argentina, France, Italy, and Belgium were other countries with whom trade exchanges were significant. Rice and petroleum from Burma are the chief oriental imports, whereas distinctly united Indian products went to those lands containing an Indian population. In general Mother India has exported a larger value of goods than she

has imported. This flow has to some extent been equalized by the import of silver, gold, and services and by the drain of industrial and trade profits homeward to England. The total volume of united Indian foreign trade is rather small, and so long as India, Pakistan, and Ceylon can offer for sale only cheap agricultural products they can afford only a modest purchase abroad. Many Indians do not look forward to a tremendous expansion in foreign trade, preferring to plan for a continued modest trade exchange which will facilitate internal industrialization and gradual elevation of the standard of living.

With the growth of modern transport united India has developed a very important internal trade. What technically is foreign trade, between India and Ceylon, is only so by a quirk of history, similar to that which tabulated foreign trade between Burma and India as domestic trade. The separation of the three states now causes wholesale revision in the trade statistics, many former domestic trade items now becoming foreign trade commodities. The flow of actual trade has not been greatly affected by the statistical changes. In quantity terms coal and coke greatly exceed other items. Rice, oil seeds, jute, cotton, salt, wheat, sugar, and the fruits are the chief items. The fruit trade is growing, as shipping techniques improve. There is little trade in vegetables, but a fairly considerable one in wood and fiber products. The northwest frontier, the hinterlands around Calcutta, Bombay, Madras, and the island of Ceylon are the chief food deficit areas. Calcutta and Bombay both import wheat flour and rice, the wheat going to the upper classes. Ceylon consumes much united Indian rice, shipping to the mainland betel nut and spices. Fabricated metals, cotton textiles, and the whole range of manufactured goods shift from the port cities toward the several interior hinterlands.

MODERNIZATION AND POPULATION GROWTH

Lord Macaulay's cultural interpreters have been slow in producing positive results, but they have deployed themselves upon many cultural fronts. The impact of their programs upon united Indian life is rather irregular. The urban architecture of Bombay compares favorably with that of any city in the Occident. An Indian businessman may be as intelligent in international economics as his English opposite number. The Sikh congressman is as skillful as any United States representative engaged in a congressional filibuster. Change among some of the Indian refugee peoples is less than that among the refugees on reservations in southwestern United States. And Mother India still restricts its lower castes and keeps its "untouchables" out of some walks of life. Legislation since 1948 has abolished the status of the untouchable, but it will linger long. A flat statement suffices neither for the Occident nor for India.

In the long period of cross-contact many elements have entered into modernization. The establishment of British enterprise in varied forms was necessary, though exploitation went too far. A decline of handicrafts was perhaps inevitable. The Parsee factor in Indian industrialization finds no clear parallel elsewhere. The distinctive locations of industrial materials and agricultural surpluses produce in Mother India a peculiar scattering of modern enterprise. The operation of the Christian missionary movement has been far reaching, affecting secular and Christian education, medicine, agriculture, and modern artisanry. The leadership of modern united India has come mainly from students who have returned from England. A village-minded people still cling to traditional culture in spite of the debt that they have accumulated. An inclusive Hinduism that eventually has swallowed every effort at reform from within and a conservative Mohammedanism certainly are factors in this modernization.

Since 1940 much of the will to change has become galvanized into action. With British goading, India became an important productive element during World War II; with Indian prodding, Britain afterward let go the restrictive control that she had held over Mother India. If the prospect is bright on the one hand, and if change has been great, problems are arising on the other hand, and the need for further change is tremendous.

It is difficult to estimate the united Indian population at the time the European first came, but Mother India, along with China, perhaps constituted the most populous units on earth. Entering the modern world with a large population united India has grown rapidly. She possessed a fairly high standard of living when the European came, and modern population increase has come despite a gradually declining standard of living. Several occidental countries have increased greatly in population in the past century and a half, during an unequaled opportunity in world history, and occidental rates of increase actually exceed oriental rates. Oriental increase has been in spite of a disadvantage. In 1941 united India's people numbered 389,000,000, and by now probably total close to 430,-000,000. The accompanying map presents population distribution for Mother India in 1941 and for Ceylon in 1946. This increase in population is one of the most significant aspects of modernization. Much earlier British energy went into famine prevention made necessary by flood and drought. The growth of a transport network has alleviated the old form of the famine problem. Since 1920 more has been accomplished by preventive medicine. The single disease, malaria, annually has claimed well over 1,000,000 lives per year. Preventive measures have retarded the expansion of loss with population increase. Research identified cholera epidemics with religious pilgrimage, and preventive inoculations of endemic regions have reduced this danger. Prevention of childhood and infant ailments has been extending life expectancy for united India, which still rests in the vicinity of 31 years!

Medical study, however, has detected the fact that increasing numbers of Indians are permanently malnourished and close to the starvation margin, so that even small diet changes threaten disastrous results. Birth rates at such times are found to fall off. The wartime 1943–1944 Bengal famine, in which perhaps 1,000,000 people died from a variety of specific causes, was accompanied throughout Bengal by a crop only 6 per cent under normal. Admittedly local transport did not maintain normal food imports into a deficit region, nor could emergency food be brought in rapidly enough, with the Japanese occupying Burma, but the total food deficit was not of famine-provoking proportions to a people in sound condition. The excessive milling of wheat and polishing of rice are intangible but potent factors in this malnutrition, which does have some regional variation.

There are other medical indications that united India is not healthy, and that the increase in population coupled with a decreasing standard of living has brought the people of Mother India to the brink of a dangerous situation. In biological terms with an animal parallel, a ceiling has almost been reached in which a further increase might touch off some complicated biological reaction which would limit reproduction sufficiently to restore a balance. In human societies where preventive medicine and national and international relief programs operate, the natural biological processes are inhibited. So far the increasing productivity of modern united India apparently has not greatly exceeded the increase in population. An increasing standard of living and a deeper cushion of group resistance to minor economic fluctuations would be present if productivity really had exceeded consumption. Just how close to a balance and a ceiling united India now is cannot be stated. As industrialization proceeds, and as the reserve land of united India is put under crop, the slowly lifting level of balance may allow an ever larger total population. It is cer-

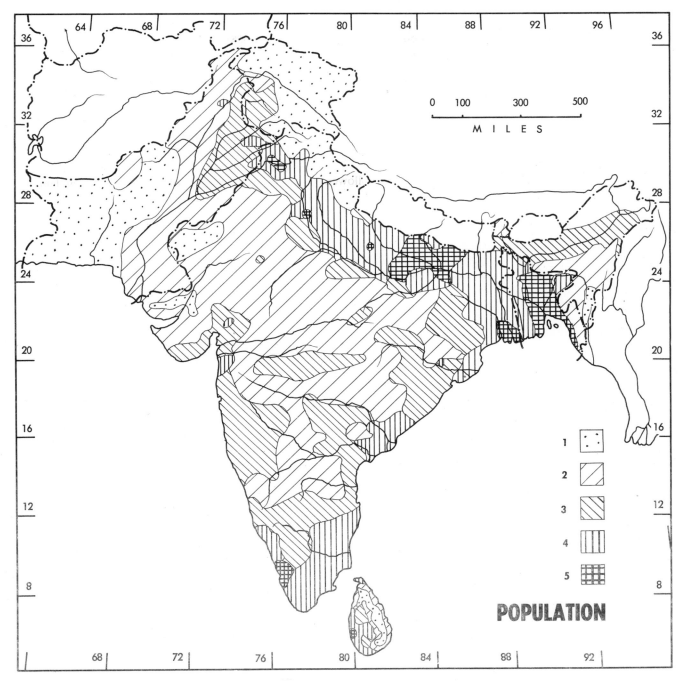

Fig. 56. Population density: (1) under 24 people per square mile; (2) 25–199 people per square mile; (3) 200–399 people per square mile; (4) 400–799 people per square mile; (5) over 800 people per square mile. India and Pakistan are generalized, after Davis, for the year 1941; Ceylon data adapted from *Ceylon Census for 1946.*

tain, however, that, unless some fundamental lifting of the ceiling can be accomplished, or some major voluntary reduction produced in the birth rate, the relative standard of living will not be lifted for the country as a whole. This is not a pleasant prospect to a people who have just secured their independence. As modernization continues it is likely that they will continue restive.

SEPARATISM IN MODERN MOTHER INDIA

Mother India has followed its historic precedent and broken apart again. Aided by modern transport in the last generation, Britain had come closer than any previous Indian overlord to operating India as one economic unit. Politically, Britain had to manage it in pieces, but all economic planning had envisaged one United India, so far as the mainland was concerned. Ceylon has been kept apart. The remaining political separatism, of the last generation, was gradually becoming less and less significant and has nothing to do with the current form of separatism. This chapter is written around a unified India, a sound major geographic realm despite the intermittent wish of a share of the inhabitants to operate it in three or more pieces. That wish was raised to a fever heat in the decade 1937–1947 by the propagandist efforts of the Moslem League, using the religious call of Islam. Nationalism and a will to independence had been growing in India over a period of some twenty years. No common, single formula for the political operation of an independent united India could be agreed upon by native leaders in the spring of 1947. Mother India was too united in a "hate Britain" and "quit India" campaign to hold back. Britain's postwar home plight forced her hand, and she reluctantly permitted Mother India to receive its independence divided into three political entities, Pakistan, India, and Ceylon.

In the divergent currents of internal opinion within united India there were many who would not have chosen independence from Britain upon divided terms in 1947. This group was composed of the rulers of Indian states, the Sikh community, many Moslems, industrialists, traders, the "untouchables," and many Hindu and Christian leaders. The reasons behind their agreement were many and varied. Rulers of most Indian states had considerable to lose. Sikhs feared a renewal of their old struggle with the Moslems. Many Moslems were Indian nationalists first and Moslems second, as were Christians. Since the tide of events could not be stayed many Hindus, Sikhs, and Christians went forward reluctantly, if hopefully, foreseeing

problems in the future. They rejected the name Hindustan on the ground that it did not fit a political state composed of Sikhs, Christians, and Hindus, and chose the name India. Moslems jubilantly but blindly surged into a future filled with problems that few had thought seriously about, hailing their Pakistan. Some Indian rulers promptly joined one side or the other, others slowly gave in, and some held out hopefully. Practically no long-range planning had preceded the division, since the major currents of thought and planning had been toward a united India.

The lines along which a division occurred are both old and new. The dry lands of northwest India are the core of Pakistan. Today a majority of the population is Moslem, whereas in the sixteenth century no more than 15 per cent of northwest India followed Islam. Various distributional criteria may be suggested to fortify the notion of Pakistan's validity. The distribution of the camel, the 20-inch rainfall line, the line dividing the wheat and rice crops, the zone of the historic invasions, the spread of the Islamic faith, these and more have been used many times by Pakistanis. No group of lines thus drawn proves very sound, however, for the actions of men in North India over the centuries have altered some natural distributions to suit their passing judgments. The inclusion of an isolated territory in the wet heart of the Bengal Delta violates every "dry land" criterion except that of religious faith. The division of the Indian realm into Pakistan, India, and Ceylon is a willful political separation of Mother India by articulate minorities who cry the unity of Islam, or the unity of Hinduism. Though considerable mass migration has occurred, and most Sikhs and Hindus have left West Pakistan, the Moslems had to leave behind a considerable minority, both in the west and in the east, and many Hindus remain in East Pakistan.

Pakistan took with it about one fifth of the area and the highways of the previous united India, about one sixth of the population and the rail lines, about one seventh of the cultivated land, a tenth of the army, a segment of reactionary large landholders, a minority of the educated middle class, very few of the shopkeepers, tradesmen, professional classes, and artisans, only a few thousand industrial workers, almost none of the minerals, a fraction of the industrial equipment, no mills for three fourths of the jute crop, a few small mills for one third of the cotton crop, one major port, Karachi, and one minor port, Chittagong. The agricultural surpluses, jute, cotton, wheat, and hides, were cut off from their normal internal and external markets. A Hindu middle class operated most of the economic machinery for united India, and, upon division, the

Hindus moved out of northwest India, along with the Sikhs, taking much of the liquid wealth and the technical skills. The Moslem element has been the most conservative group in Mother India, with the highest group illiteracy. Over 80 per cent of Pakistan is peasant farmer-herdsman stock, the total of industrial and business skill is rather slight, and experienced leaders are but few in number.

Aided by foreign loans and United Nations aid Pakistan is forging ahead. Karachi has been turned from a regional port into a national capital and has multiplied its population several times, the buildings and facilities being added after the increases of population. Concerted efforts have built new towns, new power plants, new schools, and new factories. Irrigation systems and leveling of desert lands in West Pakistan parallel drainage development and improved diking in East Pakistan. Productivity is increasing and slowly a little more balance will appear in the economy. This is still an artificial country, not yet smoothly operating and rounded in its activities, but certainly it is changing with great rapidity and shaking off the conservatism that has marked the Moslem regions in the past.

Pakistan may be made to live a long time by sheer human effort of the Moslems and tolerance of India. If it does succeed it will be a typical example of the separatism that, rather continuously, has plagued India in the past. But since the present separatism is not founded upon sound bases there are many people in the India that remains who hope for the day when economic and cultural good sense will prevail over religious fanaticism and political pride to bring Pakistan and India together again to build, in the modern world, a unified India stronger and more effective than any that has existed in the past.

Ceylon remains apart from India in a separatism that is aided by physical position. Ceylon was populated from Mother India and has shared her major cultural achievements. Today most of the Singhalese are Buddhist, following the missionary spread of Buddhism. During the last thousand years Indian Hindus have moved slowly into Ceylon, today composing almost one fifth of the population. Britain has operated Ceylon independently of India, since acquiring the island in 1796. A pattern of self-government has been worked out unlike that used in united India. With an individuality fostered by British control, it is unlikely that a political merger will occur in the very near future, though common economic interests will keep Ceylon and India tied closely together.

India suffered from the division of the country, but India, too, is shaking off some of the past. The centralization and ordering of the political structure of hundreds of states into fewer areas of administration is not yet perfect, land reform has made but a start, and the food supply still is inadequate. But the very amalgamation of hundreds of political regions, the start of land reform and agricultural improvement, country-wide planning, and new industrial projects will bring increasing change and growth. India's problems in some respects are more serious than those of Pakistan, for the area and population mass is much greater than that of Pakistan.

The separatism of Nepal and Bhutan is modern, even though the region is not completely Indian in blood and culture. A strong Mongolic element always has been present. Traditionally the area always was tributary to strong Indian states, becoming autonomous in periods of lowland weakness or strife. Modern separatism originated in Indian Rajput elements seeking refuge from Moslem domination during the fifteenth to eighteenth centuries. "Gurkha" consolidation of Nepal in the eighteenth century led to an isolationism against British encroachment which has remained a guiding principle ever since. Gurkha enlistment in the British Indian Army has been an economic opportunity compensating for the regional isolation. It will be interesting to observe whether this separatism will gradually change with Indian independence.

THE REGIONS OF MOTHER INDIA

Mother India is an interesting if puzzling study in regionalism. Among the varied kinds of distributions within the united Indian realm there are not many that show sharp, clean boundaries. The crest line of the Western Ghats and an upper line along part of the Mountain Wall are significant for many natural distributions. Man, however, has paid little attention to either line. Around the eastern two thirds of the Mountain Wall an important cultural line exists that is not matched in physical terms. Elsewhere in Mother India man has carried plants, animals, working techniques, and human institutions across, and himself has gone across, the transition zones and definitive lines of the united Indian landscape until today it is almost impossible to suggest rational division of the realm along sharp lines. Any such division is certain to disregard important criteria. Criteria then become selective, and the selection becomes variably subjective.

A certain number of divisions of the country have been recognized as valid from many points of view. These divisions mean something to Indians. They are useful in setting down a simple description of united Indian landscapes. To mention the major units only: the Northwest Frontier, Punjab, the Himalayas, Ganges Valley, Bengal, Assam, Rajputana, Deccan, Malabar Coast, Mysore, Madras, Madura, and Ceylon. To an educated Indian each of these carries connotations as to landscape, crops, people, and culture, but no one of them can be sharply defined except Ceylon, the island. Within certain limits they follow both natural and cultural criteria. For example, every North Indian distinguishes between the Punjab and the upper Ganges Valley, between "the Hills" and Assam. And he separates a Bengali from a Punjabi, a Tibetan from a Gurkha, a Sikh from a Baluch. But a Punjabi and a Sikh both come from the Punjab, the Tibetan and the Gurkha both come from "the Hills," the upper Ganges Valley has no one clear human type and Assam has nearly a dozen. Everywhere in Mother India simple divisions are compounded and regrouped to fit the occasion and the need.

At the one extreme Mother India may be divided into three pieces, the Northwest, the Northeast, and the South. This has its uses but tends to generalize too greatly. Detailed criteria may be assembled to show many kinds of regionalisms, some of which are shown on accompanying maps.

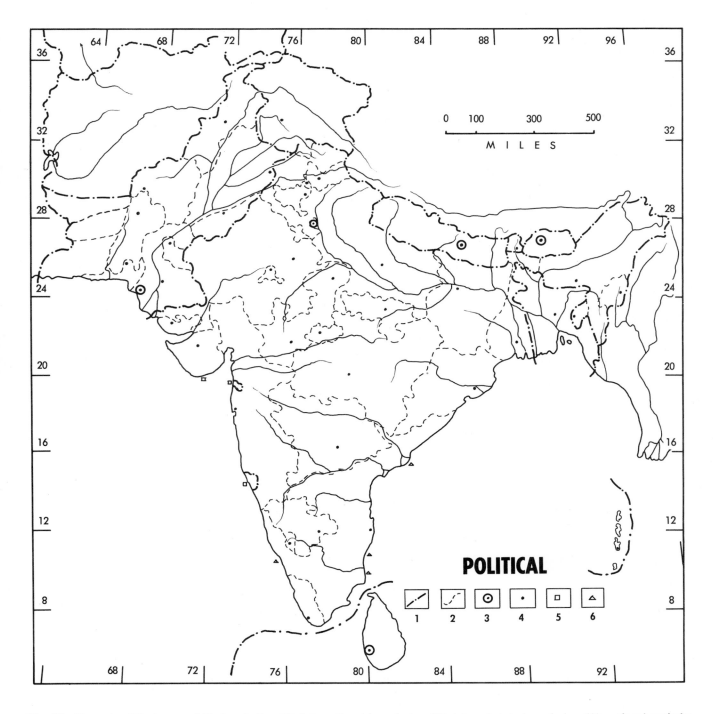

Fig. 57. Present political map of Mother India: (1) international boundaries; (2) internal state boundaries; (3) national capitals; (4) state capitals; (5) Portuguese territories; (6) French territories.

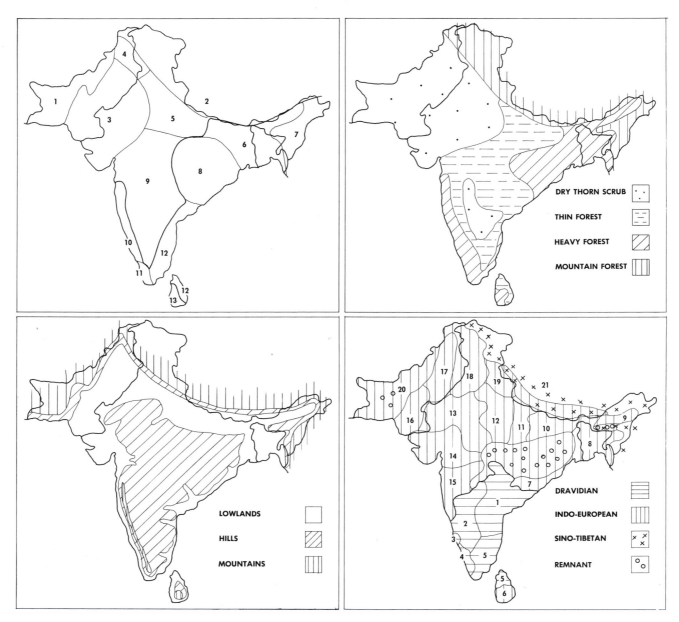

Fig. 58. Indian regionalisms. *Upper left,* climatic regions: (1) dry, hot summers and cold, barely moist winters; (2) cool summers and cold winters, moist all year; (3) cool, dry winters and hot, dry summers; (4) cool, dry winters and hot, barely moist summers; (5) cool, dry winter and hot, moist summer monsoon period; (6) mild, dry winters and hot, wet summer monsoon period; (7) cool, dry winters and hot, very wet summers; (8) mild winters and hot, very wet summers; (9) cool to mild dry winters and variably moist, hot summers; (10) mild, long, dry winters and hot, very wet, short summers; (11) warm all year, short winter dry season, and long wet summers; (12) dry, hot summers and mild, moist winters; (13) warm all year, dry winters, and wet summers. *Upper right,* vegetation. *Lower left,* physiographic. *Lower right,* linguistic: *A.* Dravidian: (1) Telegu; (2) Karnata; (3) Tulu; (4) Malayalam; (5) Tamil; *B.* Indo-European: (6) Singhalese, (7) Oriya; (8) Bengali; (9) Assamese; (10) Bihari; (11) Eastern Hindi; (12) Western Hindi; (13) Rajasthani; (14) Gujerati; (15) Marathi; (16) Sindi; (17) Lahdna; (18) Punjabi; (19) Pahari; (20) Iranian; *C* (21) Sino-Tibetan languages; *D.* remnant languages.

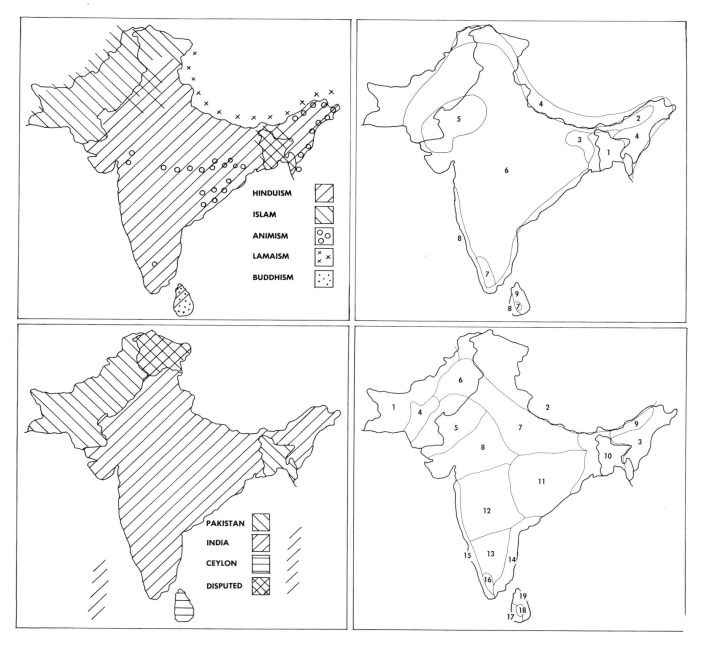

Fig. 59. Indian regionalisms. *Upper left,* religious. *Upper right,* agricultural crop regions: (1) rice-jute region; (2) rice-tea; (3) rice; (4) mountain mixed crops; (5) pastoral; (6) Central India mixed crops; (7) upland plantation; (8) rice-tropical fruit; (9) rice-subsistence crops. *Lower left,* political. *Lower right,* geographic: (1) northwest frontier upland; (2) Himalayan frontier upland; (3) Burma frontier upland; (4) Lower Indus Valley; (5) Thar Desert; (6) Punjab; (7) Upper Ganges Valley; (8) Aravalli uplands; (9) Assam Valley; (10) Bengal Delta; (11) Chota Nagpur Hills; (12) Deccan; (13) Southern Peninsula; (14) Coromandel coast; (15) Malabar coast; (16) Cardamom upland; (17) Colombo littoral; (18) Kandy upland; (19) Ceylon east coast.

The Irrawaddy Valley Becomes Burma

THE REGIONAL FRAMEWORK AND ITS EARLY PEOPLES

The cultural region known today as Burma lies within the most distinctive physical environment in the Orient, because it has but one core area placed within a bounding framework of mountains. This environment is a group of converging, lowland alluvial valleys ending in a broad delta fronting on the Bay of Bengal and surrounded by a series of mountainous uplands lacking good passes. In the north the framework is high and rugged and the valleys are narrow. To the south the mountain frame spreads out widely and the valleys become broader and flatter until they merge with the delta. The mountain frame encloses the delta, leaving it open to approach only from the Bay of Bengal. This regional environment is one part of the Burmo-Malayan Fan structure described in the first chapter. It is an elongated region in which all essential units have a distributional trend that is chiefly north-south. There are interruptions in landforms, stream patterns, climates, vegetation, soils, and other minor phenomena which prevent pure symmetry in these north-south trends, but none of these destroy the basic alignments.

To early man penetration of this region must have been difficult, but it also brought rewards in the good living to be had in the lowlands. How early man first entered lowland Burma cannot now be stated. In any case the river terraces of the Irrawaddy yield ample evidence of human occupancy at an extremely early date. And whether significant regional specialization developed here in the very early cultures is not yet clear. The whole environment has an extremely wide range of resources and potentialities. Early man in no way exhausted these resources, though he undoubtedly altered ecologic relationships and patterns of plant and animal life in both upland and lowland zones.

Who the inhabitants of Burma were, four to five thousand years ago, is not at all clear. Though there is little evidence of Negrito occupation, southern Burma may well have held such a population at one time. Pre-Mon-Khmer peoples are not well represented. The Mon peoples may have been the first of the alien stocks, drifting into the lowlands of Burma and the Menam Valley from India. Indonesian peoples are less represented here than in the lands further to the east. Four thousand years ago there were several different kinds of peoples scattered about the lowlands of Burma, doing a good deal of fishing, growing rice, fruits, and vegetables in jungle gardens, dwelling in villages, and sharing many other culture traits with the rest of southern Asia. They were already accustomed to using boats and aquatic resources, domestic garden crops, and the products of jungle and forest. Whether they were chiefly shifting cultivators or had learned sedentary crop practices is unproved. Since their numbers were not large their total productive ability would not today be impressive. It seems likely, however, that at this date life in the lowland was more bountiful than that in the upland jungles and forests that framed the outlines of the lowland.

As late as four thousand years ago the rich lowland region was a sort of human vacuum. Since that date this lowland zone has been drawing people into it, and supporting their natural increase, until it gradually has accumulated a total population of nearly 14,000,000 people. In a general way the lowlands have been the final goal of all the varied culture groups that have entered Burma, and the modern Burmese people and Burmese culture have been the final product. The Burmese of today are a lowland people, and their culture is a lowland culture, though the upland frame is home to a wide variety of culture groups with quite different patterns of culture.

Significantly, only two approaches have been commonly used within historical time to get to the heart of Burma, overland from the north along the mountains or the narrow river valleys, and by sea from the south. At few times in Burmese history has a lateral process of movement taken place either into or out of Burma. During World War II much of the drama attached to General Stilwell's famous retreat to India derived from the very fact that his little migration ran counter to the known patterns of historical movement in this part of the world. The one possible exception to this generalization pertains to the southern extension of the Burmo-Malayan Fan southward in the Malay Peninsula. On this southeastern corner lie the only easy land approaches to the heart of Burma, used occasionally in the past by Khmers, Burmese, and Thais and, during World War II, by the Japanese. A narrow strip of this peninsular zone was included by the British in their sphere of influence in Burma, and this strip has become a part of the modern political state.

The most significant cultural process at work has been the steady drift of peoples out of the north country, from the Tibetan corner of China, southward along the linear patterns of mountains and valleys into the confines of the region that we now call Burma. The final destination for all has been the alluvial lowland, and the pressures of group upon group have been southward and downward pressures. Some of the earliest groups were able to move into a part of the lowland zone and to develop a regional area. Others were able only to secure space on the margins of the lowland, from which individuals were able to infiltrate the lowland area and to become gradually a part of its culture group. Still others, both at early dates and more recently, were unable to secure a foothold in the lowlands, and have had to be content with living in the hill country or mountains of the upland frame.

The above patterns of movement have not been entirely chronologic, so that not all the earliest comers are lowlanders and the latest are mountain peoples, but it is true that some of the last culture groups to arrive have not been able to push into the lowlands. An early group, but not the first, to arrive who spoke a language akin to modern Burmese, were able to find a home in the lowlands. It is this group which has given the basic orientation of language and culture to modern Burma. As the lowland began to accumulate a significant population with patterns of culture distinct unto itself and with a stake in its own wealth and perquisites, it began to resist the raiding of groups from around the upland fringe and the taking over of parts of the lowland by these groups. This resistance slowly grew stronger as lowland political and military institutions developed, so that in later centuries the strength needed to gain a place in the lowland was greater than in earlier periods.

Though few of the southward-migrating peoples now to be identified in modern Burma can date their earliest movements as far back as 2000 B.C., some of these movements must have begun not far from that date. It was a slow drifting, and centuries went by before it began to produce a heavier population in the southern Burmese lowlands. The process surely had been going on before the recorded historic pressures of North China began to be exerted upon southern China and its peoples. I have presumed, therefore, to date the beginnings of this southward drift well back of the conventional historic dates for such migrational movements.

INDIAN TRADERS AND THE EARLY CENTERS IN BURMA

Conventional history suggests that Indian sea travelers began to make colonial and trade contacts at a wide variety of points in southeastern Asia just before the beginning of the Christian era. But Indian traders must have been probing the sea lanes and learning their way across the Bay of Bengal long before this date. Extensive sea travel in the Arabian Sea had begun much earlier, and it is inconceivable that seamen able to navigate the Arabian Sea refrained from similar voyaging in the Bay of Bengal. By at least 400 B.C. there must have been trading posts, with Indian trade agents permanently resident, all along the coasts of Burma and the Malay Peninsula. Earliest contact probably touched the whole coastal fringe, for the first voyagers did not know what lay behind the beach heads. Perhaps there were many local situations that rewarded these searching contacts with small yields of gold, precious stones, musk, rare woods, and the other items of interest to Indian traders. In the long run those contacts with the most favorable environments proved most profitable, and by 400 B.C. the choice territory must already have proved to be the delta coasts tapping the lowlands of Burma.

Trading stations set up by a people accustomed to specific social, political, and economic institutions among a people of different institutions leads to a contest of strength between both peoples and institutions. Indian contact with lowland Burma must have led to such a contest after 400 B.C. Indian culture was quite well developed by this date, whereas the peoples of lower Burma were yet simple in social structure, had only meager economic institutions, and were probably not more than tribal in political system.

It is quite probable that in the quickening political patterns of India of the time, refugees, soldiers of fortune, missionaries, and various other elements of Indian culture traveled with the traders to the ends of the Bay of Bengal seaways. In Burma the results of such contacts were small outposts of Indian culture populated by Indians who began to exercise economic, social, religious, and political control over the immediate hinterlands. Interplay between Indian and native peoples gradually led to some absorption of Indian culture traits by native peoples, ranging from religious to agricultural, and stimulated economic production of tradable raw materials and natural resources. Gradually these small trade stations grew into small port towns, the hinterlands expanded, and the culture of the little regions increased in complexity. Such additions to culture made life in the lowland more attractive to the southward-drifting hill peoples.

It is likely that this was not an entirely peaceful process between Indian and native peoples or between the several Indian centers. Nor was it a process that was rapid in its creation of cities, in its development of regional political institutions, or in the general effect upon the lowlands. In the early periods the native population never became large, its physical capacity in food production was not great, and the numbers of Indians cannot have been large. Therefore, only slow progress was made in the evolution of regional territories into kingdoms with a definite pattern of political, economic, or social structure.

By 100 B.C. it would seem that the delta land trade regions stood out as not only the most profitable, but the most populous, the most highly developed in social, economic, and political culture. These several little lowland centers became the nodal point around which the kingdoms of early Burmese history were organized. It is not until about the fifth century A.D. that the regional pattern of affairs comes tentatively into the accounts of the historian. By then there were a number of well-established place names that stood for towns, for petty kingdoms, for peoples, and for cultures. The names we can identify for such patterns are of Indian origin, for the native folk did not write and had little to tell of trade and conquest. Mon, Tailaing, Pyu, Pegu, Thet, Thaton, Prome, and Tenasserim, all are modernized versions of early Indian names applying to such regional units. The names Irrawaddy and Sittang also are of Indian origin. Chinese accounts carry both Chinese and Indian place name reference, further complicating the problem. Only in the ninth century A.D. do specific patterns become recognizable. The accompanying map presents an estimate of the early locational situation.

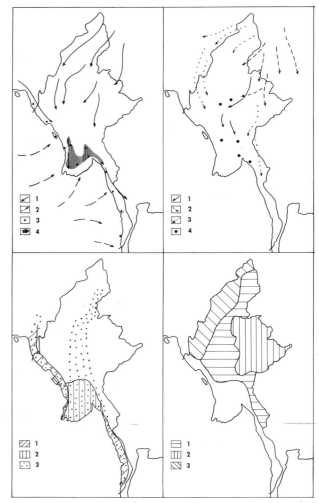

Fig. 60. Growth of Burma. *Upper left,* circa 400 B.C.: (1) tribal movements into Burma; (2) Indian sea contacts; (3) Indian trading posts; (4) zone of chief Indian tribal contacts. *Upper right,* A.D. 500–1400: (1) Burman movements; (2) Shan movements; (3) other tribal movements; (4) principal regional capitals: Prome, Pegu, Thaton, Pagan, Ava, Toungoo. *Lower left,* British beginnings: (1) acquisitions of 1824–1826; (2) acquired 1852–1854; (3) area of Burmese Empire, 1824. *Lower right,* British expansion: (1) Burmese-controlled areas taken over 1885–1886; (2) Shan-controlled areas taken over in 1890; (3) tribal areas taken over 1895–1896.

THE INTERNAL CONTEST

From about the fifth century onward the central theme of the regional geography of Burma has been the contest over who should control the lowlands. An auxiliary theme has been the contest over who should control what portions of the upland frame and the coastal fringe. To some peoples this latter was a chief objective, but to others it was preliminary to the main theme. Several different culture groups had filtered into the lowland from the north prior to the fifth century, and Indian groups had come by sea from the south. The northern sources had chiefly supplied population, whereas the Indian source had chiefly supplied elements of cultural organization.

Out of the mixing of these two product patterns came the early trading posts and the first regional kingdoms in the southern lowland. As these grew in size, strength, and capacity, the pressures of the hill peoples also grew, and the contest really began. The earliest regional kingdoms were represented by Prome, Pegu, and Thaton, in the areas of most effective Indian influence. These must date from about the late fifth century, and their influence remains dominant until the ninth century. Prome perhaps was the strongest in the earlier centuries, and Thaton in the later period. Their cultural influences probably extended well to the north along the Sittang and Irrawaddy rivers.

During the seventh and eighth centuries pressures greatly increased, and new peoples began to push into the northern and central lowland, to learn how to live in it. Burman peoples came into the central dry zone of Burma by the start of the eighth century. They improved their organizational abilities, took up Buddhism and other new traits, and by the middle of the ninth century founded the new regional kingdom of Pagan in central Burma. By midtenth century they had learned enough to expand their control to a zone some 300 miles north-south by 70–80 miles east-west —the dry heart of lowland Burma. In mideleventh century they added control over much of the southern lowland zone by conquest of Thaton. In this expansion process a Burman written language had appeared, regional organizational techniques had improved, irrigation systems had made rice agriculture prosper, and Pagan had become a large city. Pagan became the leading kingdom of the lowland, the "defender of the Buddhist faith" in the southern Orient, and its religious capital. An enormous volume of Buddhist religious building in brick probably required deforestation of a wide area for kiln fuel, perhaps contributing to the present arid-land impression of the dry heart of Burma. Burman culture traits spread, Indian and other old culture patterns were modified and adapted, and lowland culture began to shape into a Burman "Burmese" pattern. Education of a sort reached most Burmese youth, chiefly boys, and Burmese society developed a fairly unique pattern not attained either in India or China. A mixed religious and temporal pattern gave its members a general satisfaction seldom achieved elsewhere.

It is likely that control over the northern upland frame by the Thai peoples—then organized into the state of Nanchao in southwestern Yunnan—kept other northern tribal peoples in check and gave the Burmans their opportunity. The dry zone may well not have been usable by earlier peoples. Indian control over the southern zone had died out, and southern kingdoms were under pressures from hill peoples to the east and from piracy by sea, particularly from petty Indian kingdoms on the Arakan coast and from mobile groups along the Tenasserim coast. After the conquest of Thaton, thousands of captives were moved northward into Pagan's home area, to further the blending of lowland culture and racial stocks.

But the contest was by no means ended. Nanchao's control of the north failed, Chinese pressures increased, the Shan, a branch of the Thai, and other peoples began pushing southward more heavily, and Burman control of the lowlands had not become perfected. Regional rebellions fill the history of the time. In the late thirteenth century Mongol military operations pillaged Pagan and reduced its power, giving the Shan a chance both in the Shan Plateau and in the lowland itself. A Shan lowland kingdom appeared, based at Ava, northeast of Pagan, which pushed many Burmans southward and incorporated others into the kingdom of Ava. The Shan kingdom was perhaps the strongest single power until about the end of the fourteenth century, but it was a Burmanized society that composed it. The Burmans acted as a buffer, and a kingdom based on Pegu was able to assert itself as a trading state, its port handling a growing trade on the Bay of Bengal which probably serviced most of lowland Burma.

During the fifteenth century the lowland contained three major kingdoms, plus many smaller ones. In the upland frame many tribal peoples held regional control and occasionally were able to organize confederacies strong enough to trouble the lowland kingdoms seriously. Pegu, in the south, was the repository of old Indian culture and probably was made up of very early and later peoples in some kind of mixture. Toungoo was the center of the Burman kingdom, after the Burman shift southward, but its people were no longer a clear tribal strain. Ava was the northerly Shan kingdom, but one learning Burman and Burmanized Indian culture patterns, and itself suffering from infiltration of population from many northern tribal sources.

When occidentals first came to Burma in the sixteenth century, it was a complex of regional kingdoms and principalities, both in political and cultural terms. A lowland "Burmese" culture was becoming dominant regardless of the exact racial and cultural background of its peoples. The pressures from the upland frame were steady and strong. And from the sixteenth to early nineteenth centuries the whole pattern of regional control was in constant flux, as lowland kingdoms struggled for dominance. In the mideighteenth century Ava's conquest of Pegu thoroughly upset life in the lower delta zone, but the Burmans and Shans were not yet able to settle and develop the delta. Burma was not of prime importance to the occidental traders because of this cultural turbulence.

After the British gained control of trade in the Bay of Bengal they suffered nuisance raids from petty Arakanese and Tenasserim pirates and petty rulers. No lowland ruler of Burma could yet control these outer margins. British conquest of lower Burma and the Arakan and Tenasserim coasts resulted from this cultural turbulence and the raiding of British shipping. But once in Burma the British themselves had to cope with the old southward and downward pressures and the regional contest for control of the lowland. British colonial government during the nineteenth century was oriented in two directions. First the administration of the lowland, to permit the development of local and international trade. Second came the administrative patterns designed to control the peoples of the upland frame and to stabilize their regional zones of occupation. The British became the second major cultural force to affect lowland Burma from the southern sea approach.

In the hill and mountain country of the upland frame a sorting and mixing process had long been going on. There are perhaps today a dozen different basic culture groups, subdivided into dozens of local groups who have developed both horizontal and vertical stratifications of regional control. The Chin on the west, the Naga and Kachin on the northwest and north, the Shan on the north and northeast, the Karen in the east are the larger and dominant elements. The Palaung, Wa, Kaw, and Lahu are lesser groups of the northeast. Some are highland peoples living near mountain crests, whereas others are hill peoples. There is no fixed situation, however, and there are many intergradations as the struggle for position continues.

INDIAN, CHINESE, AND BRITISH OVERLORDS

Though Burma has often been under the influence or control of some outside power, this has been neither continuous nor competitive. At the time of the early Indian interest in, and colonization of, Burma's southern lowlands and coastal fringes China had not yet spread its control even into Yunnan. Indian influence in Burma never made for close attachment of the area

to India in political or economic matters, for neither area had progressed to the point of making this possible. Indian influence in Burma had become unimportant by the time the T'ang Chinese began to assert their overlordship over southeastern Asia in the seventh and eighth centuries. Most of the larger kingdoms of Burma sent tribute missions to the Chinese imperial court in Sung times at least, during the tenth and eleventh centuries, thus acknowledging the suzerainty of China. This may well have been a formality preventive of encroachment until in Mongol times the rebellious independence of the Shans and the Burmans of Pagan resulted in punishing military invasions. Consequent acknowledgment of subordinate status and occasional tribute missions prevented further too continuous and too active Chinese interest in Burmese affairs. Few Chinese have ever been among the migrants into Burma, and the country today has the smallest Chinese population of any part of southeastern Asia. Chinese culture, directly, has had but little real effect upon Burma or upon any of the Burmese peoples, for most of the peoples of Burma had come out of China to escape Chinese control.

British control over Burma, beginning in the 1820's, evoked no serious protest from China. Early British administration of Burma was independent of India, but in 1886 Burma was annexed to India and became a stepchild of the slowly maturing Indian Civil Service. British administrators and the British Colonial Office never seemed to appreciate the cultural separateness of Burma and India. The British in particular, and most occidentals in general, have greatly overstressed the early Indianization of Burmese culture. The British never administered Burma for the Burmese of the lowland or for the peoples of the upland frame, though there were many individual civil officers who saw beyond the general British program. Out of the annexation of Burma to India, during the late nineteenth and twentieth centuries, Indians gained a protected access to Burma that they had not had since perhaps A.D. 400. Indians became usurious moneylenders, urban shopkeepers, commercial agents, and soldiers in Burma, always protected by British law and civil administration. In 1941 there were nearly 1,000,000 Indians in Burma who were fast gaining an economic stranglehold on southern lowland Burmese economy through their ownership of farmland and their large financial creditor position in respect to the Burmese.

British political overlordship became more far-reaching than had either Indian or Chinese control in earlier centuries. The British brought with them cultural change, political control, and economic exploitation such as the peoples of Burma had never before experienced. As the pattern increased, the animosity and protest grew, though it scarcely was an organized nationalism. Separation of Burma from British India in 1937 was more formal than real, and too few of the mistakes were being corrected when World War II brought the Japanese into Burma. Lowland Burmese welcomed relief from the British, whereas the hill peoples of the upland frame, never much afflicted with the penalties of British rule and emotionally set against the lowland Burmese historically, remained loyal to the British. These two factors both were important items in the progress of the war in Burma. The accumulated animosities of lowland Burmese toward the British and their own regional dominance within Burma led Burma to declare for total independence after World War II.

ECONOMIC BACKGROUND

As the Burmese lowlands grew in population the regional capital towns and cities stand out for their political, historical, and cultural roles. But these urban control points housing only a minority of the population cannot describe lowland Burma. The area became a region of agricultural villages surrounded by garden plots and farmlands in which rice agriculture of a fair order of productivity formed the basis of a lowland economy that long has contrasted with the simpler and less productive economy of the upland frame.

The earliest lowland economy that first attracted Indian traders had been a simple one, combining jungle garden cropping with fishing and hunting, and to it the Indians undoubtedly contributed both plants and techniques. Rice, fruits, roots, and rhizome plants were intermixed in use, but the importance of fishing in this southern aquatic zone always was more significant than in the central dry zone or in the upland frame. The wettest parts of the southern delta section, subject to seasonal flood and high water situations, were then unusable for agriculture, since organizational and technological development did not make diking, drainage, and water control possible. This phase of lowland economy was not fully usable in the central dry zone of Burma, where a shortage of water limited garden cropping and where the aquatic aspects of the system could not apply. Occupants of the northern lowland areas and most of the upland frame, at the time of Indian contact with the coastal zone, most probably were shifting cultivators practicing a subsistence economy, based upon crude gardening, gathering, and hunting.

As simple culture groups came into Burma from the north they continued to practice shifting subsistence economies, gradually changing a few of their crops and some of their specific techniques as they became acquainted with a new economic botany-biology and with new climatic situations. Those peoples who got into the lowland were able gradually to learn a sedentary garden agriculture and many of the other things that went with lowland living. Such later groups as the Burmans and the Shans, upon coming into Burma, were already somewhat advanced in their patterns of economy, and were already familiar with sedentary cultivation and with wet-field rice culture. Their route of ingress lay through country with some open upland sites in which rice growing was possible, namely the Shan Plateau.

Once in the lowlands the Burmans were the first to be able to make real use of the central dry zone of Burma through their knowledge of wet-field rice culture, and perhaps were the first to develop rice culture into a dominant position in the lowland economy. In their dry-zone agriculture the Burmans made auxiliary use of a fairly wide range of crops that were adaptable to local climatic situations. Their development of irrigation facilities in the dry zone was the first big forward step in the intensive exploitation of the lowlands. As they were shoved southward under Mongol-Shan pressures, they carried their intensive system southward into the edges of the wet delta region, and the Shan took over the northern part of the dry zone, in turn to learn how to use this kind of landscape.

The southern wet delta lands presented problems that were slow in solution for a people without highly developed material technologies and without large-scale centralized organization. Earliest use of this area had made more of aquatic resources than of normal land resources. Agriculture remained jungle gardening or shifting cultivation in the heavily forested delta zone. Even in late Pegu times this was true, for Pegu was chiefly a trading-fishing economy. Only when the British came in to stabilize political and regional controls, bringing also an advanced technology, have the land-use problems of the delta been solved. Only within the last century, therefore, has the large-scale development of the southernmost lowlands occurred.

In the wide range of the upland frame many local situations gradually permitted some sedentary agriculture. Little of this showed up in the western portions, but in the northern hill country and northern humid lowland fringes simple sedentary culture gradually appeared. And in the Shan Plateau's open spots the Shans developed sedentary agricultural villages whereas the rougher uplands remained in the hands of shifting cultivators. The Arakan and Tenasserim coasts remained on a fairly simple level of economy, with jungle gardening, fishing, and mobile trading features characterizing the economy.

The central lowland dry zone of Burma, therefore, accumulated the largest population of any section of pre-British Burma. Pagan, Ava, and Toungoo show cultural remains, indicating a higher population and a generally greater development of the landscape than do those of Pegu, Tenasserim, Arakan, or the northern upland frame. The conquests of Thaton in the eleventh century and of Pegu in the eighteenth century probably were a combined expression of a greater population and a more mass-productive economy, as well as being an expression of the southward drive so evident in Burmese history. This central reservoir of population has supplied most of the new agricultural settlers that have turned the delta into a great ricefield in the last century. With the success of this recent colonial spread the population of southern Burma has grown greatly, and there has come about a shift of economic and political power into the delta region of Burma.

No single land tenure system can be described for pre-British Burma, owing to cultural heterogeneity, nor can there be just one simple description of a social system. The modern Burmese is apt to overgeneralize older Burman group patterns. There was both feudal and private ownership, but for all of Burma it is clear that cultivation rights were dominant over other concepts. And, though the different cultural groups had their own patterns of social stratification, no group in Burma ever developed the highly complex caste patterns of India. From the Burmese came a social democracy and a freedom for women unparalleled in an advanced oriental society. Burman and Shan concepts of law, rather closely related, came to dominate the conduct of lowland affairs. Personal authority within social and economic groups was superior to statutory authority. The village was a social unit, not a territorial one. Civil law developed out of Burman and Shan tribal law, criminal law being the particular code of an individual ruler, subject to alteration under his successor. Even in eighteenth-century times the economy was chiefly a subsistence economy marked by local barter trade, rather than by a money economy measured in currency values. Lowland Burma was in small degree only a part of any oriental interregional trade realm.

The coming of the British caused many changes. The villages became as much territorial administrative units as the British could make them, in civil, criminal, and peace-preservation aspects, introducing problems never previously faced. Education began to lapse as social and religious custom was interfered with. Land

was considered state owned, to be claimed by title, subject to foreclosure by individuals, and subject to taxation by government. Money trade patterns were introduced, and basic commodities not previously the chief items of trade began to be in demand in large volumes for export. The large-scale colonial settlement of the delta zone required governmental public works and sources of credit to colonists. Indians came in as laborers but shifted to the role of suppliers of credit. The rise of the rice-export trade developed in the delta a monocrop money economy in which consumers' goods became import commodities rather than the home handicraft products that they had been. The dry zone and the upland fringe shared in this development to lesser degree than did the delta region.

Though British administration early recognized the need for prevention of moneylender foreclosure of land and the rise of tenancy, it never perfected machinery to accomplish this end, and usurious lending practices took full advantage of the untrained Burmese agriculturist. In the newly settled delta, therefore, the Indian moneylender, after about 1870, began to achieve a significant position as financier of agricultural development. Slowly the control of credit and land accumulated in Indian hands, and tenancy on the rice farms of the delta increased. Indian investment in other parts of Burma remained small, owing to a variety of greater risks involved and to the little new development taking place. Between 1926 and 1940 there was almost a doubling in the land held by non-agriculturists, about half of which, some 3,000,000 acres, was owned by Indian moneylenders.

The development of interregional and international transport and trade patterns, under British ownership, altered the whole pattern of Burmese economy. Almost nowhere else in the world was a considerable area so easily exploited as Burma, a linear environment along which a system of water, road, and rail transport could effectively organize trade and control it through a single coastal port. British-built Rangoon quickly became that control port, an overgrown market village inhabited and run by the British trader, the Indian moneylender, and their Burmese laborers, but hardly a city, if cultural leadership be a requisite of a city.

AGRICULTURAL BURMA TODAY

Burma is often described as having an agricultural economy dominated by the single crop, rice. If all the agricultural lands of Burma were cropped as is the southern delta zone, this would be true, but the varied economies of the upland frame, and the generalized crop patterns of the central dry zone give more variety to Burmese agriculture as a whole than is true in either Thailand or Indochina. Rice is the one outstanding crop today, in terms of acreage and volume production, resulting from the settlement of the delta lands within the last century, and in recent decades Burma has contributed the largest single volume of rice to the international market. All other crops show small acreage and production volumes, as compared with rice, but the total of these auxiliary crops is large.

The total land in farms today approximates 22,-000,000 acres, and, with double cropping, the total annual crop acreage amounts to almost 16,000,000. Post-World War II unrest in the lowlands has prevented the full cultivation of much of the farmland, and it is likely that some years will elapse before the cropped acreage returns to the totals of 1940–1941. In that year about 12,500,000 acres were devoted to rice. In 1830 the total rice acreage for the delta region did not exceed 50,000. There are no data of this date for the dry zone and northern Burma, but the total must have been well above that of the delta. The Arakan coast and Tenasserim then had about 100,000 acres in rice. By 1890 the delta-region acreage was about 4,000,000 acres against some 1,750,000 acres for the rest of Burma. In 1930 the total rice acreage had increased to some 12,370,000, with the regional distribution somewhat as follows. The moist lower valley and delta zone of the Irrawaddy, Sittang, and Salween rivers contained some 8,700,000 acres, the dry zone held some 1,770,000 acres, moist northern Burma and the northern upland frame contained about 700,000 acres, the Arakan coastal and hill country possessed about 1,000,000 acres, and the Tenasserim coast had only some 210,000 acres. The general totals and the regional distribution of rice production has not changed markedly since 1930, though floods, droughts, and recent civil unrest have caused the year-to-year regional balance of harvested rice lands to vary considerably. The 1951–1952 crop year indicated only a little over 9,000,000 acres in rice.

Within the adequately moist portions of lowland Burma and the Shan Plateau rice is now a regular crop year after year, since the monsoon is reliable and there are few alternative crops available to the average holder of rice lands. The Burmese of today is a good farmer, within his physical and technological limitations, and the average yield of rice in Burma is higher than that of many other parts of the Orient. Small acreages of fruit, vegetables, sugar cane, sesamum, and cotton are supplementary crops on the humid lands toward the head of the delta region. It is in the dry zone and its margins, where irrigation is necessary for productive

agriculture, that most of the real variety shows up in Burmese agriculture. Sesamum and peanuts for edible oils, both grain and fodder millets, a variety of peas, beans, and related leguminous crops, chili peppers, onion, cotton, and tobacco are the chief crops that

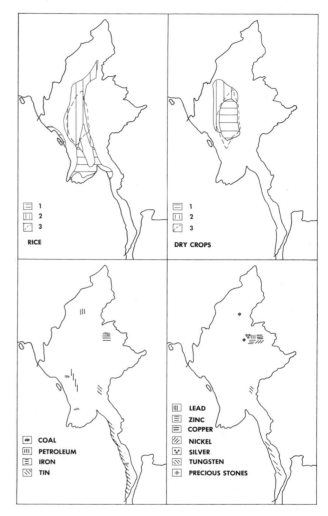

Fig. 61. Agriculture and minerals. *Upper left:* (1) primary rice-growing areas; (2) secondary rice-growing areas; (3) the dry zone. *Upper right:* (1) primary zone of production of dry-field crops; (2) secondary areas of growth of dry-field crops; (3) the dry zone. The lower pair of maps indicates zones of mineral occurrence.

compete with, and rotate around, rice in the dry zone. Irrigation facilities do not yet extend to all parts of the dry zone, so that some of the crops competing with rice are dry-land crops, whereas rice here is grown only on irrigated lands. Dry-zone agriculture involves both winter and summer planting, and much of the Burmese double cropping acreage is in this region.

A wide variety of vegetables are grown in small patches in the general farmland areas, in small areas around villages and towns, and in long strips along river banks. The rivers of Burma all fluctuate markedly in level from wet to dry seasons, and between late October and April the moist alluvial lands exposed by low water are utilized for vegetable culture, particularly in the dry zone. Among the food crops, maize, tomatoes, and varieties of beans occupy the largest areas, but more than forty different vegetable crops are cultivated on these river-bank lands. The largest share of Burma's tobacco is also grown on river-bank lands during the low-water season. Vegetable cultivation in all parts of Burma is chiefly a dry-season occupation, involves considerable regional variety, and almost supplies the total food needs.

Though a large amount of fruit is produced for home use, little of it is on the basis of formal orchards, and little cultivation is practiced. Many of the common fruits, such as the bananas, mangoes, oranges, limes, pomelos, lichis, palms, durians, and jackfruit, are either native here or have been common to this area for so long that they have become a part of the plant growth around villages and towns, along the roads and trails, and in the jungles of the yet uncleared lands. Into this same vegetation complex have gone such American fruits as the pineapple, papaya, sapote, and guava. Often it is difficult to determine whether production is from farmed lands or from wild jungle lands. The range and volume of fruits decreases in the dry zone, and in the upper parts of the upland frame.

In most of the rough upland frame shifting cultivation, on a subsistence basis, is still the rule for crop production. Normally a mixture of crops is planted together in the small patches and fields, but among some of the hill people certain crops have gained regional preference. In some areas one of the millets is dominant; in others maize, upland rice, buckwheat, or other millets are preferred. Elevation and microclimatic situation, as well as cultural preferences, have entered into this selection. Shan Plateau agriculture is more advanced than that elsewhere in the upland frame. Here wet rice is a staple in the open tracts among the Shans, with shifting cultivation used by other peoples living above them in the rougher areas. The Shans also have developed a specialty agriculture, dealing in commercial crops which are sold in the lowlands. Bread wheat, white potatoes for seed use, garlic, ginger, cigar-wrapper leaf, tung oil, varieties of oranges, tea, and European varieties of vegetables are all produced in various parts of the Shan Plateau.

The Shans also raise large numbers of animals for sale in the lowlands, particularly cattle. Animal diseases in the humid lowlands take a steady toll of most of the domesticated animals, and there is a regular flow of replacement stock from the Shan Plateau to all parts of lowland Burma. World War II took heavy toll of the animal population, but it is building slowly upward again and, in most cases, the totals are higher now than before the war. The further expansion of Burmese agriculture is related to this increase in animal population, since the majority of farms are large enough to require animal power for purposes of cultivation. The total number of work oxen and buffalo now stands close to 2,800,000, a total inadequate to the current need.

As previously indicated the delta region possesses a rather critical problem of tenancy and rural indebtedness. The Land Nationalization Act of 1948 was framed to restore the tenant to ownership status, to reduce the large holdings of non-farming absentee owners, and to stabilize a small farmer economy. It provides for reversion of land to the state in the earlier Burman tradition and, if properly administered, it may prevent accumulation of large holdings in the hands of a small group. The situation in the delta had developed within the last century, but by 1930 it had become so serious that large numbers of tenants had become almost migratory farmers, seldom staying with a given farm for more than 3 or 4 years, and a migratory landless laboring class was growing. It will take some years to straighten out the tenancy problems of southern Burma even under the best of peaceful conditions. The 1948 Act set 50 acres as the maximum holding of rice or sugar land, with small totals of other classes of land. Rubber lands and certain other small classes of land were omitted from the Act, but these omissions have slight effect upon the delta region. About 82 per cent of the delta agricultural population held farms under 10 acres in size. In the vicinity of 50 per cent of the farmers were full-rent tenants in 1948.

In the rest of Burma there are few serious problems of tenancy, since the expansion of agriculture has been in slow stages by relatively stable local populations. Within the upland frame the traditional pressures of movement have been stayed somewhat by British rule, and there is less of the push toward the lowlands. Here shifting agriculture on a subsistence basis among culture groups using traditional techniques of land control has not multiplied land problems in the degree found in the delta lowlands. Small farms, generally under 10 acres, are also the rule in the other parts of Burma.

Burma does not properly participate in the plantation agriculture found elsewhere in southern Asia. There is but a small acreage of coconut plantings, tea production is in the traditional Chinese manner rather than the newer occidental style, and there are no large plantings of sugar, coffee, cacao, or vegetable fibers. The Shan Plateau has a small acreage of tung oil trees, chiefly in large holdings. From near Rangoon southward through Tenasserim there are scattered plantings of rubber. Many of them are in small holdings, but the larger units are in occidental-style plantings. The future of rubber is not great in Burma, however, owing to the seasonal nature of rainfall, and thus it is unlikely that corporate plantation agriculture will encroach upon Burma.

The occupational censuses of Burma have never listed fishing as an occupational category, and there are few available data upon the yield of native fisheries. There is little doubt, however, that fish supply the second most important source of food, after rice, to the Burmese population of the coastal and lowland regions. It is likely that there are in the vicinity of 100,000 people whose basic occupation is fishing, and it is also likely that the part-time fishermen number in the hundreds of thousands. Burma's import of fish products is relatively small. Rivers, coastal waters, ponds, and other water bodies steadily provide a considerable volume of all sorts of aquatic products, and this traditional economy has not been lost in the elaboration of a dominant rice agriculture. There has been little development of fisheries, aside from the careful taxing of the yield, revenues which never have been utilized to improve this important facet of domestic economy.

AUXILIARY PATTERNS OF ECONOMY

The pre-British Burmese carried on a considerable variety of activities other than agriculture and fishing. Mining and lumbering are old occupations. Handicraft manufactures almost sufficed to fill the modest Burmese demand, though these declined under the impact of occidental imports in the nineteenth century. Today it is likely that some 75 per cent of the population is concerned with agriculture, and that about 20 per cent is concerned with industry, trade, transport, mining, and forestry. It is impossible clearly to separate such activities in a country like Burma, where part-time participation in varied activities is normal.

Mining is an old activity. North Burma jade has been mined and sent to China for centuries. The rubies and sapphires of the Shan Plateau were items of barter trade with the earliest Indian traders. Tin has been mined along the Tenasserim coast since the days of those same early Indian traders. Lead, zinc, and silver were mined at Bawdwin, and the petroleum of southern Burma was tapped and locally used long

before the European came east. The occidental has found few new minerals in Burma, though he has increased the annual outputs of several. Burma can be a regular contributor of significant amounts of petroleum, lead, zinc, copper, silver, tin, nickel, and tungsten to the markets of the world, though the 1953 production records are lower than those of prewar years. Coal and iron, however, exist in amounts too small to interest the industrial world. Mineral distribution is shown in Fig. 61. Hydroelectric resources are large, provided they are developed in such a way as to store the seasonal rainfall of Burma. As the Indians and Chinese controlled much of the mining in earlier centuries, the British control most of it today, and both the minerals themselves and much profit has gone outside of Burma in recent decades.

Lumbering is not a new-born activity in Burma, but it is not so old as mining. Since about 1800 Burma has become the chief source of teak in the international lumber trade, for teak is one of the strongest and most durable of the world's woods. With the rise of international shipping, in the late seventeenth century, Burmese teak found its chief use in ship building the world over, and its use therein has only recently declined somewhat. Expansion in other uses has maintained the commercial lumbering of teak. Not many other Burmese woods are well known and developed in usage abroad, but there will be such an increase in the future, for the forests of Burma possess many good woods exhausted elsewhere. Burmese forests also produce rattans, lac, tannins, a variety of resins, gums, and oils of value both in Burma and abroad. The domestic use of bamboos, construction lumber, tool wood, and firewood amounts to a large annual volume. Firewood and charcoal are the normal Burmese domestic fuels, and a large amount of both is constantly required. In addition to the volume destroyed by shifting cultivators, the total annual cut of timber for all uses, excluding bamboo, runs close to 1,200,000,000 board feet. Minor and auxiliary forest products can be expanded markedly, and Burma can long continue to produce a surplus of timber on a sustained yield system.

With the decline of handicraft manufacturing for home use in Burma, a chronic underemployment of the agricultural population has resulted. Modern manufacturing has begun on a small scale in a fairly wide range, but it absorbs the labor of but a small portion of the population. Burmese have not taken to modern mining, and much of the mine labor is Chinese or Indian. Much of the lumbering labor service is contributed by other than lowland Burmese. The Burmese are mechanically adaptable and make good skilled technicians, but their past opportunities have not been large. Most of the modern industrial enterprises still are British or Indian owned and staffed, as far as management and technicians are concerned. In the past most of the manufactured goods that replaced the handicraft manufactures have been imported products, distributed at the wholesale level by foreign firms, getting into local hands only at the retail level. There is a store in every Burmese village, however remote, which serves to spread these imported products.

In point of number the most common "factories" are rice mills, saw mills, cotton gins, and vegetable-oil mills. The roughly 875 such establishments employ about 60,000 persons, with the larger mills in each case being foreign owned. On the basis of a factory as any establishment using mechanical power in processing materials, there are in the neighborhood of 1,100 factories, employing about 100,000 workers. If the simpler home manufactures of modernized handicraft nature are included, several thousand more establishments must be added, employing another 300,000 participants, though these hardly can be termed factory employees. Cotton and silk textile weaving, along with lacquer-ware production, accounts for the majority of this rural handicraft manufacturing. In the past there has not been the demand for highly complex manufactured products that would have supported modern industrial developments in Burma, but the urge for such development is now growing and perhaps the need also. It is rather a normal pattern that has so far developed—agricultural processing, the textiles, the simpler fabrication processes, assembly, and machine-shop operations.

In the petroleum refineries, the railway shops, the dock and ship building yards, and the electrical-equipment plants, totaling some 15,000 employees in about 40 establishments, one finds more technical processes and higher skills developing. In the fields of general engineering, printing industries, and some of the chemical plants one also finds industrial skills and techniques beginning to advance industrial know-how. Burma has somewhat of a start in industrialization, and a small core of technical personnel, as well as a little management and financial control. They are sufficient to promote the general growth of industry and, taken with Burmese adaptability, will undoubtedly aid the growth of home industry in the future.

The first railroad, a short line of meter gauge built from Rangoon northward, came to Burma in the 1870's. By 1899 it had reached Myitkyina in North Burma, and gradually mileage has increased to just over 2,000 miles. In a linear country like Burma, a short mileage serves well to tap the important parts of the country, and the rail system was developed to tap areas not serviced by water transport. Continental meter gauge line and equipment, burning Indian coal, the lines serve a large passenger traffic and a moderate freight traffic whose chief items are agricultural produce going to markets and minerals en route to Ran-

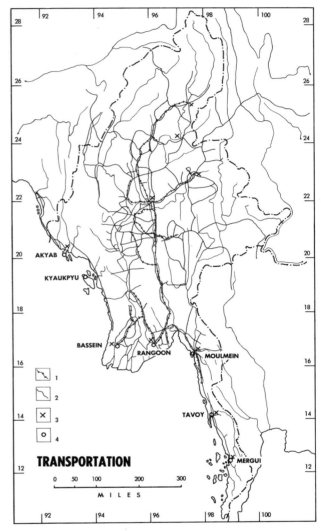

Fig. 62. Burmese transportation facilities: (1) rail lines; (2) primary roads; (3) civil airports; (4) major ports.

goon for export. World War II all but destroyed the railways, and physical reconstruction only now has been completed. Originally privately built, the rail system is now government-owned, but there remains a large financial debt unliquidated.

The linear build of the country, traversed by the Irrawaddy, has meant an easy development of water transport. Native traffic in considerable volume has flowed along the Irrawaddy, the Chindwin, and the Sittang for centuries, as well as along the whole coastal fringe. The British started developing steamboat service on the Irrawaddy before road and rail systems were started. A British-owned and -operated service has now been nationalized, and redevelopment after World War II provides cheap and effective water transport along almost the whole length of Burma, Bhamo being the head of steam navigation, 872 miles from Rangoon. The Chindwin is usefully navigated for about 400 miles. The volume of water transport throughout the Irrawaddy delta is large. The craft of the nationalized Inland Water Transport Board move well over half a million tons of cargo and nearly 3,000,000 passengers per year along the Irrawaddy and Chindwin. The Sittang is not of much real use for large craft, nor is the Salween, though many native small craft use both rivers.

Cart roads, packtrain trails and footpaths are old, long traveled, and widely spread in Burma and, in the upland frame, will continue so. The modern road-building program has achieved somewhat over 20,000 miles of vehicular roads, about a third of which are all-weather roads. It is not certain that all roads shown on the accompanying transport map are in regular adequate repair at present. In a linear country, again, this rather small mileage, supplementing the rail and water systems, can serve to a greater degree than might seem the case. In the vicinity of 750,000 animal carts haul an uncounted traffic. Burma has not yet really entered the automobile age, and only some 30,000 motor vehicles are registered. Of these only the trucks and buses really serve a public transport function, and most of the equipment is concentrated around Rangoon.

With its chief population and economic regions enclosed within the upland frame, it is only natural that Burma's chief trade contact to the outside world has been by sea through the delta zone. Rangoon, well located on that delta and linked to its eastern and western segments by interior canals, roads, and rail lines, has dominated the external trade and passenger traffic of Burma. The shipping has been predominantly British and Indian. Rangoon is the only important port, the center of import and export trade. Lesser coastal ports serve chiefly an interregional role, tying into Rangoon rather than serving as regional centers of external contact.

Rice has been the big export product in point of value within the last century. Second have been the petroleum products, followed by teak, lead, tungsten, tin, vegetables, rubber, cotton, and silver, in that order. Indian markets have been the chief goals of Burmese products, followed by British, Ceylon, and Malayan markets. The position of India as a buyer of rice, teak, petroleum, and vegetables has been a dominant one.

The export trade has been and continues to be chiefly in the hands of British and Indian firms, though Burmese participation is increasing.

Among imports, cotton and rayon clothing textiles and yarns have been for a long period the leading imports in point of value. Jute sacking for the grain trade has ranked second ever since the grain export reached large proportions. Machinery, iron and steel, vegetable oil products, chemicals, tobacco products, paper and its products, and assorted food products, in that order, have been the other significant imports. The total import trade has a wide range of products. India, followed by Great Britain, has long been a dominant supplier of the Burmese market. Within recent decades Japan and the United States have become significant suppliers of Burmese products, with Malaya, Hongkong, Netherlands, Germany, and Belgium following in approximately that order.

Burma's trade balance has been distinctly in her own favor for a long period, for her products have found a ready market elsewhere in the world. Indian deficits in rice, timber, and petroleum have given Burma a guaranteed market for those commodities. The rice market, at least, must always be a low-priced one, never producing huge profits to Burmese producers, but it is a steady market. On the basis of the rice and timber trade Burma cannot expect to be able to finance an extremely high level of living, nor can she afford out of such revenues alone to finance modernization and industrialization. Petroleum and other minerals will help, but their reserves are not endless and they are a rather ephemeral resource. Offsetting this favorable balance of trade has been the outward flow of profits and invisible items accruing to the British, Indian, and Chinese operators of, and investors in, Burmese economy. Most of Burma's public debt finds its creditors abroad. Nevertheless, Burmese economy today is sound, the per capita foreign trade value is higher than that of most of the Orient, and Burma finds her productive enterprise concerned with items that are not in competition with luxury markets or facing tremendous competition from other producing regions.

THE IRRAWADDY VALLEY AND THE OTHER BURMAS

The above heading is meant only in the sense that even today, after centuries of centripetal action, the peoples of Burma are not yet one. The process of fusion has worked towards a single cultural whole, but there have been counterinfluences, and one may well wonder whether it will ever completely succeed. Regionalism in modern Burma is strong. In part this is

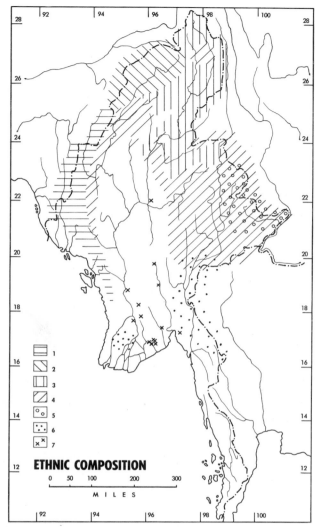

Fig. 63. Ethnic composition of Burma: (1) Chin peoples;
(2) Naga areas; (3) Kachin territory; (4) Shans and related
peoples; (5) Wa and Palaung peoples; (6) Karen areas; (7)
Indians. The Indians are chiefly urban. Burmese-Mon peoples
are to be found numerically dominant in all unlined areas except the eastern portion of the Karen regions.

environmental, owing to landforms, climate, and vegetation. In part it is cultural, the peoples of Burma
having developed variant cultures en route to their
present home areas. The British also have contributed
to the process.

British administration distinguished a Lower Burma
and an Upper Burma, and these terms remain in the
literature. The wet delta and the central dry zone do
differ, but the terms Upper and Lower Burma refer
rather to the historical growth of British rule. They
acquired Burma in two basic units, first the coast from
Mergui to Akyab, which became Lower Burma; the
interior came under control later, and since it was up

river, it became Upper Burma. Use of these terms only
confuses the regionalisms of Burma.

Currently, Burma is divided into 42 political districts, segregated into 8 divisions. These districts are
areas of convenience, based on tradition and on group-
culture criteria. Some are old in outline, but others
are still shaping up. The 8 divisions are somewhat
geographical, made on the basis of historical tradition
plus convenience. Divisional limits do not accord with
the regional patterns a geographer would draw, using
environmental and other criteria. It is common to find
that some of the upland frame areas regularly are
omitted from statistical summaries, but the omitted
areas are not always the same ones. This omission in-

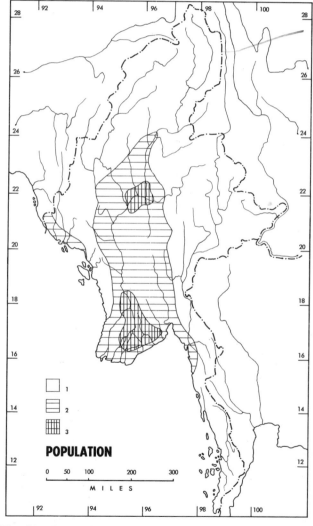

Fig. 64. Population of Burma: (1) blank areas have under
50 people per square mile; (2) 50–200 people per square mile;
(3) over 200 people per square mile. Densities here are estimated only, the 1953 census returns being unavailable at time
of drafting.

dicates inability of government to manage affairs in the upland frame where villages and farms constantly shift location, and where regionalisms are mobile matters of group culture rather than lines fixed on a map. Figure 65 presents various regionalisms.

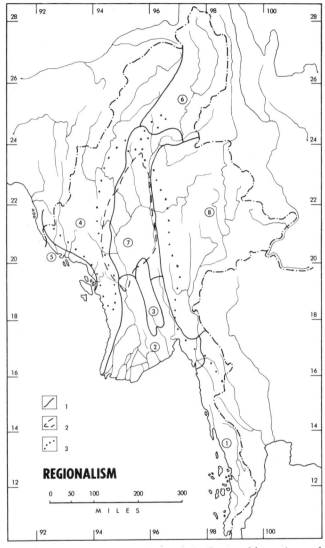

Fig. 65. Burmese regionalisms: (1) Geographic regions: 1, Tenasserim; 2, Irrawaddy-Sittang floodplains and deltas; 3, Pegu Yoma; 4, Arakan Yoma; 5, Akyab deltaic coast; 6, Upper Irrawaddy basin; 7, Central Irrawaddy basin; 8, Shan highland; (2) encloses the climatic dry zone; (3) encloses regions populated by culturally Burmese peoples.

In 1826 Burma's population was estimated at 4,000,-000. The earliest useful census is that of 1891, incomplete but tabulating a total of 7,722,000. That of 1941, still slightly incomplete, counted 16,824,000 people, indicating an increase of close to 1 per cent per year. The 1952 population is estimated at about 18,-500,000. The arithmetic density is the lowest for any country in the Orient, about 70 per square mile, whereas the physiologic density is about 740 per square mile. An accompanying map, prepared from incomplete 1941 census data, gives a representative distribution of population. The heart of the delta and the northern part of the dry zone exceed arithmetic densities of 200 per square mile. The Irrawaddy and Sittang valley areas carry a moderate population, and the upland frame is but lightly populated. The extremes are shown by Maubin political district, just west of Rangoon in the heart of the delta, with a 1941 arithmetic density of 261 per square mile, and by the Naga Hills district, in the far northwest, which had an arithmetic density of but 9 per square mile. Most of the upland frame areas, by 1941 data, had arithmetic densities of under 30 people per square mile.

There are few large cities in Burma. Rangoon, in 1947, contained about 600,000 people, and Mandalay's population in 1952 was about 175,000. There were another twelve towns and cities above 25,000 each in 1952. Burma is distinctly a village-dwelling region, and urbanism is not one of the natural tendencies of any of the peoples of Burma.

Though it is close to impossible to determine accurately the cultural regionalism of Burma today, some idea of its remaining strength can be gained from a linguistic or tribal map, and from data on mother tongues. In 1931 some 9,862,000 out of 14,647,000 people claimed Burmese as their mother tongue. A total of 1,341,000 claimed Karen, 1,021,000 listed Thai (meaning the Shans), 1,079,000 gave Indian languages, 343,000 listed Kuki-Chin languages, 305,-000 gave Mon, 176,000 claimed Palaung, 178,000 listed Chinese, and 153,000 returned Kachin. No later linguistic census data is yet available, but I estimate the tribal peoples at present about as follows: Karens, 1,500,000; Shans, 1,200,000; Kachins, 450,000; Chins, 400,000; Wa-Palaung, 275,000; Nagas, 80,000; and the smaller groups at a total of about 100,000. This would indicate just under 13,700,000 people culturally and linguistically considered Burmese, with about 600,-000 Indians and 200,000 Chinese, both of whom are chiefly urban. The regional distribution of these non-Burmese-Mon speaking peoples is shown on Map 63. It is noteworthy that no separate language is claimed by those residents of the Arakan or Tenasserim coasts. Many Shans formerly resident in the dry zone also now list Burmese as their mother tongue, as do the descendants of many another group which has gained space in the lowland. Burmese as a language has spread widely, and with it an indeterminant volume of cultural mores. On the other hand, the Karen are gaining political cohesion today and are no longer a shy group retiring before the pressures of others. Much of the political unrest of lowland Burma since World War II results from the fact that the Karen are demanding a share in the affairs of the State. Some of the strongest animosities and pressures within present-day Burma are those of the hill peoples against the lowlanders. Though this is traditional, it is now beginning to shape into regional political patterns, and, as the Burmese are achieving a political nationalism for Burma, these minority groups are beginning to develop political nationalisms for their own culture group. These regional developments are going to increase in the future, as cultural evolution and modernization affects the several culture groups that reside in Burma. This will be unlikely to grow into demands for total independence, but the domestic political map of Burma may well change continuously in the future, as these culture regionalisms further express themselves. The regional boundaries of such units will neither correspond to the so-called geographic regions drawn by the geographer nor to the political divisions drawn up in the past by governmental administrators.

The Irrawaddy Valley, from the delta to Bhamo, is the Burmanized cultural heart of Burma. This is the region with the greatest total population, the most productive agriculture, the greatest advancement in political and economic affairs, and culturally the most sophisticated. It will continue to dominate the affairs of all of Burma. But the Sittang Valley, and the eastern fringe of the delta, along with some of the eastern hill country, as the home of the Karen, now sometimes termed Karenni, constitutes another and slightly different Burma within the whole. The Shans of the Shan Plateau, heretofore politically fractionated by their strong individualism, may acquire political cohesion on some local regional pattern to change the regional balance of power and culture. Though the Irrawaddy lowland will continue to control the affairs of Burma, there are many smaller regional units that may alter the present life of the whole.

The Evolution of Thailand

ENVIRONMENTAL REGIONS AND EARLY CULTURE GROUPS

The political region today recognized as Thailand has a complex regional history. Though the Menam Valley is the heart of modern Thailand, and though the Thais are the dominant culture group, this is a rather recent development. Earlier cultures and political states were arranged on quite different regional lines. The 300,000 square miles of territory between the Annamite Cordillera and the Dawna Yoma contains three large physical units not well separated from each other. The Menam lowland, the Korat Platform, and the Cambodian lowland each are large enough to have housed a major cultural development of the past. The problems of organizing all three physical areas were too great for the earlier culture groups, and no one culture has ever controlled the whole region. The physical limits separating the three units do not constitute major barriers, and simple contact between units has been well-nigh continuous. But cultural and political beginnings took place on the margins, north or south, and, with simple transport technologies, distances and space proved too great for early competing cultures.

Many of the features suggested in the previous chapter hold for this major region. Around the three units the Menam Valley, the Korat Platform, and the Cambodian lowland, there is a mountain frame. From the north narrow river valleys and tapering hill ranges reach southward into the low country. The basic alignments of physical geography produce a north-south linear pattern, though this is less neat and compact than in Burma. Approaches by land have been via the north, and those by sea have come from the south. Two great extensive alluvial lowlands contrast with the surrounding uplands. The ranges of possibilities for primitive economies were somewhat the same

as in Burma. The aquatic habitats, the lowland jungle-forests, and the mountain zones here present much the same conditions for early man as in Burma, though the climatic aridity of the regional rain shadows is here less marked.

Who the first human groups were and where their centers were are even less well understood here than in Burma. There does appear more historic evidence of widespread Negrito occupance, and there are scattered reminders even today. Pre-Mon-Khmer peoples certainly were widely scattered, but their provenance and the duration of their earliest occupance remain speculative. Some Sino-Tibetan stocks must have come in at an early time, proto-Mongoloid to early Mongoloid elements that drifted southward through parts of the region. They are commonly identified as Indonesian peoples. The Chams are one of these stocks, at the dawn of history established in an east-west belt of the country, north of the delta, from the Mekong across the Annamite Cordillera to the sea-coast. There seems reason to distinguish somewhat between Mon and Khmer peoples, but they appear related, and both probably came from the west. The Khmer possibly did not arrive in the Cambodian lowland until after the first Indian contacts with the region. The Mon groups appear to have moved more into Burma and the Menam lowland, possibly earlier than the Khmer. As Burma was a kind of human vacuum, this region also early invited varied peoples into it, the lowlands being the chief goal sought by most groups. Some southward drift even now is continuing, for such newer elements as the Miao and the Yao are currently on the move southward in the northern mountain zones. Many of the more recent arrivals have had little opportunity to infiltrate the lowlands.

The chief cultural region of the past was based upon the Cambodian lowland, and composed the heart of the great Khmer Empire, of which modern Cambodia is the lineal descendant. The lower Menam Valley never acquired major status in the early period. The second cultural region became outlined in the northern-most Menam lowlands at a rather late date by the southward-moving Thais. It is this cultural unit which has expanded into modern Thailand. The Thais came so late as to have been unable to organize the full physical region before the European also came upon the scene. Internal struggles went on for several centuries to inhibit the Thais. And the French were able to incorporate the Cambodian lowland and the fringe east and north of the Mekong into their nineteenth-century colonial empire without effective Thai protest. The French thus set up a political boundary right through the major physical region that had never existed in the past. Had the Thai cultural and political pattern matured earlier, or had the European come later, the present outlines of political states in this area might well have been different from that found today.

THE EFFECTS OF INDIAN CONTACT

Indian sea traders not only touched the west coast of Burmo-Malaya but almost certainly traveled the Gulf of Siam and the fringes of the South China Sea. The Malay Peninsula never has been a barrier to an inquisitive people, though crossing it and setting out afresh in other ships doubtless preceded sailing around it. The sailing skills of the Bay of Bengal could sail the Gulf of Siam, for the seasonal winds are much the same, whereas sailing around the tip of the Peninsula involved other problems. Sampling of the coastal fringe by Indian traders went on clear around the coast of Indochina and as far north as Hainan. Before the Christian era China and India were connected by a known sea route, as well as by land routes across Yunnan-Assam and via Central Asia. And in this sampling, the two delta regions of the Menam and the Mekong must have been major attractions. Slowly, as in Burma, permanent trade stations grew into small cultural centers jointly inhabited by Indian and local populations. For some reason not easily determinable the centers of the Mekong Delta-Cambodian lowland grew more rapidly and achieved greater stature than did those of the Menam lowland. Perhaps it was that early aquatic resource economy of the Cambodian lowland was superior to that of the Menam area, as it still is today. Perhaps the total population of the Cambodian region already was greater, its products were more voluminous, and, therefore, the Indian trader concentration was greater.

The earliest historiography suggests that the political and cultural progress of the Cambodian zone was superior to that of any other section of the littoral facing the Gulf of Siam and the southern section of the South China Sea. Trade centers here also grew into little regional kingdoms controlled chiefly by Indian culture patterns but composed of local populations. As early as the start of the Christian era the first regional "state" appeared in Cambodia, centered west of the present Mekong distributaries and north of the delta itself. The first capital site that can be located lay close to the river somewhat south of the present city of Pnom Penh. An accompanying map depicts the early situation.

Slowly this "state" expanded northwestward into Cambodia proper, moving its capital and establishing new towns as population grew and more land was brought into productive use. Gradually the culture region included the lowlands lying east of the active Mekong distributary zone and south of the terminal uplands of the Annamite Cordillera, since this region appears to have contained the same native peoples and culture patterns as the section west of the active delta. The chief ports long remained on their original sites, west of the main delta. This "state" early in the Christian era came to be known to China as Funan, an Indianized culture group possessing a mixture of Hindu and native barbaric elements. Its people seem to have ranged from Negrito and early Indonesian folk, as the base of population structure, to Indian colonists forming the trader-ruler nobility at the top.

Funan spread its influence north toward Korat, west into the Menam Valley, and south over the South China Sea and the Gulf of Siam, even becoming involved in the affairs of the east coast of the upper Malay Peninsula. It was more of a maritime culture than a truly land culture, using aquatic resources and sea and river lines of communication rather than land resources and routes. It certainly was not the tightly integrated organism that we define as a political state today, but it did represent the best integration of region, people, products, and trade in Burmo-Malaya at the time. The early rise of local piracy in the southern Malay Peninsula, Sumatra, and perhaps Java interfered with regional organization there and kept Funan an important link in the China-India route, via a series of port way stations in the northern peninsula.

Khmer peoples, on the northern margins of Funan, infiltrating the lowland Chams and gradually becoming Indianized at second hand, grew in regional strength until by the sixth century A.D. their region, known to the Chinese as Chenla, became a rival to Funan.

Chenla, a landlocked lowland region of the middle Mekong Valley, shared the common lowland economies and culture patterns except for the sea-trading element. From the sixth to the ninth centuries Funan and Chenla are confused in the Chinese accounts. The historiography is perplexing, since it lacks a full writ-

region. Jungle garden culture, shifting agriculture, product gathering, and hunting also were standard parts of the economies. It is likely that small areas of sedentary rice culture accumulated around the towns and cities and in the most populous areas, but that shifting cultivation was the more common form throughout

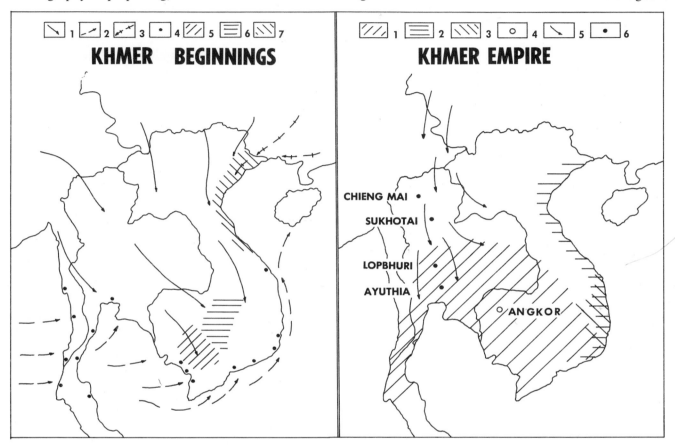

Fig. 66. The Khmer Empire and the advancing Thai peoples. *Left* (1) early tribal movements; (2) Indian sea contacts; (3) Chinese contacts; (4) Indian trade stations; (5) Funan core area; (6) Chenla core area; (7) Annam core area. *Right* (1) Khmer Empire at its height; (2) Annamese Empire at its height; (3) Champa at its height; (4) Angkor, the Khmer capital; (5) lines of Thai invasion; (6) Mon and Thai cities: Lopbhuri, the Mon capital; Sukhotai; Chieng Mai; Ayuthia. On both maps political boundaries are those of today.

ten record. Capitals frequently shifted, dynastic inheritances intertwined and alternated, domains were divided, grouped, and redivided, Indian influences varied, Hinduism and Buddhism competed and interwove their patterns, peoples migrated, and ancient site after site now is being uncovered which calls for reinterpretation of the patterns. By the eighth century Malaysian dynastic, political, and trade patterns became interwoven into the story as the "state" of Sri-Vijaya took form to dominate the South China Sea and to participate in affairs of the Cambodian lowland.

Fisheries were very important in the domestic economy of all the peoples of the lowland of this whole

the general countryside. Indian crop plants appear to have been introduced in some numbers. Little was done in road building, but small streams were canalized or canals were dug, and tanks and reservoirs were commonly dug where adequate water was not available in dry seasons. It is obvious that religious building early came to be a chief interest of the ruling elements of the population. Cambodia and the Mekong Valley are dotted with the ruins of innumerable religious buildings, the unearthing, reconstruction, and dating of which has become a passion with modern scholars of this region. Almost nothing remains of the earliest structures, which may have been built of wood. Domestic, commercial, and political building apparently always was in wood, bamboo, and thatch, whereas religious building came to be built in brick and stone. Laterite, easily quarried but durable in this tropical environment, was the chief stone used. A bewildering assemblage of Indian, Hindu, and Buddhist architectural patterns, with Cham, Khmer, and other local motivations, came to be the fashion, increasingly using the surplus wealth of all peoples.

THE CONTEST FOR REGIONAL CONTROL

The Cambodian culture region grew steadily in strength and population between A.D. 600 and 1225. Its political system matured, and the political state expanded. By the nineteenth century the capital had been shifted to the northwest side of the Tonle Sap. Lowland Cambodia was the core region, and around it lay local culture groups in many regional patterns with varying degrees of vassaldom tributary to the Khmer rulers. Khmer peoples themselves became settlers in southern Korat, in parts of the Menam Valley, and along the peninsular east coast. Something of a melting-pot process must have gone on, as Negritos, Chams, Mons, Shans, Malays, Khmers, and even a few Burmans, Indians, Chinese, Arabs, and other racial elements became intermixed in the population of the Khmer state.

Increasingly villages, towns, and cities grew in number, and the agricultural landscape expanded. Canals, tanks, and reservoirs multiplied in number. It has been thought that shifting cultivation always dominated the agriculture of these regions, but it is doubtful that this was so in the core area at least. Many of the larger tanks, reservoirs, and canals seem unrelated to temple and domestic water provision; they must have been designed for rice irrigation here just as they were in India and Ceylon. It is doubtful that the later Khmer population could have supported itself and its works on shifting cultivation alone, for the Cambodian population has been estimated at 4,000,000 in the thirteenth century. Certainly there were large reserve areas in which shifting cultivation did remain the normal system of agricultural land use, and not the whole of the lowland ever was put into permanent farm. Khmer culture at all times maintained an interest in foreign trade, and Khmer ports were cosmopolitan entrepôts. As economic strength grew, the expenditure of labor resources on religious building grew, as the size, complexity, and magnificence of temple architecture increased.

The Khmer political empire reached its height in the late twelfth and early thirteenth centuries. Its capital was at Angkor, northwest of the Tonle Sap. Though nothing remains of the domestic and commercial building of the city, the very number and size of its religious and politicoceremonial buildings, and its waterworks developments, indicate that it must have been a large city, even by present-day standards. The largest religious building in the world, Angkor Wat, was built here in the twelfth century, and its labor force alone must have been a large one. Indian and Khmer temples do not have large interior rooms, for they were not built to shelter congregations indoors, but the very bulk and detail of construction exceeds that of any other religious structure.

At its height the Khmer state came close to controlling all the great lowland region, but the outer parts to the northeast and northwest still lay without the state, and some of the inner areas were not integrated with the Cambodian core region. Korat, the central Mekong Valley, the central and southern Menam Valley, and the main portion of the peninsula were within the empire, and the Gulf of Siam was a Khmer lake. Through its lack of an effective land transport system, and through its dependence upon local subsistence economy, the Khmer Empire was never more than a loose political structure. And around these far-flung borders the Khmers finally were facing increasing pressures from other maturing culture groups, such as the Annamese, the Thais, the Burmese, and the Malaysians who, each in their own area, were integrating region and culture with the result that they possessed considerable combative strength and were themselves expanding regional entities.

Though the lower Menam Valley went through something of the same process as did Cambodia, the region formed no serious challenge to the Khmers. Indian trader stations developed into little principalities, and these matured into a kingdom, chiefly populated by Mons, long carrying the name Louvo. Lopbhuri in the central Menam lowland finally became the chief city and political capital. The area never developed the population, economic strength, or political maturity of Cambodia, and the Menam Valley became a tributary portion of the Khmer state, though its Mon peoples maintained some autonomy and a cultural contact with the Mons resident in the southeastern Burmese lowland. None of the other regional portions of the great lowland region ever early developed regional cohesion of culture or political strength of a sort to threaten Khmer power. It was from the northwest that strong and effective pressures finally accrued, at the hands of the Thais.

Tai — ⎡ Shans
      ⎢ Thais   Yunnan, somewhat Indianized
      ⎣ Laos
                    The Evolution of Thailand Mongol Pressure forced   **227**
                                                                    them
                                                                    South
                                                                    to
                                                                    Khmer

The specific environmental and regional derivation of the Thais is uncertain, for the basic Tai stock originally inhabited much of lowland central and south China just before the Christian era. Out of this Tai stock have come the Shans, Thais, Laos, and other of the present southeastern Asian peoples. When the Thais first come into the orbit of Burmo-Malayan affairs they were resident in southern and western Yunnan and composed the main populace and rulers of the ill-defined state of Nanchao. Culturally they represent an early and marginal phase of Chinese civilization, but in their Yunnan home they absorbed a degree of Indianization, and were then resident in a tropical upland region. They long constituted a major buffer to Chinese and Tibetan expansion, and they also had to deal with a variety of simpler culture groups moving into and through their area. Over several centuries they developed a skill at using and adapting varied culture traits to their own advantage. They learned city dwelling and wall building, military tactics of varied sorts, regional political administration, settlement infiltration, and the agricultural and economic use of a variety of physical regions. They were able to sustain themselves in Yunnan for a long period but, as southern Sung and Mongol pressures from China grew greater in the late eleventh to thirteenth centuries, they, like other peoples, yielded to those pressures and drifted southward.

Southward infiltration by Thai village farmers had begun pushing down the narrow valleys of northern Thailand as early as the ninth century. Fortified towns followed, with the taking over of the more favorable valley regions, the simpler non-Thai groups being forced into the uplands. The Thais thus came into loose contact with the Khmer realm before the latter had reached its fullest expression. Slowly this contact became closer and more competitive. Tributary vassaldom by Thai frontier regions to the Khmer state existed for a time, and Thais served as mercenaries in Khmer armies in the eleventh and twelfth centuries. Thai settlement infiltration of the lowland was, however, a more solid way of building regional control than was Khmer extension of political power without settlement. The Thai southward drift continued, their lowland population increased, and their lowland competitive strength matured. Local principalities consolidated and, by the thirteenth century, the Menam Valley Thais were a major threat to the Khmers.

The thirteenth and fourteenth centuries spelled the doom of Khmer control over the great lowland. First to occur was the evacuation of Champa, the southern cordillera, and that part of the lowland east of the Mekong, in the early thirteenth century. Almost con-

temporary was the loss of most of the peninsular coast and control over the Gulf of Siam. Consequent upon the strong pressures from China, the Thais and other peoples began moving in force down the valleys of the north country into the upper Mekong, Korat, and the Menam. First came greater autonomy, under nominal Khmer control, with Sukhotai made the southernmost Thai regional center about 1240. Then full Khmer control over the lower Menam region of Louvo was lost, as the Thais spread down the valley and into the peninsula. Chieng Mai became the chief Thai capital about 1296, still far north but out of Yunnan entirely. The development of a Thai written language, taken from the Khmer, acceptance of Hinayana Buddhism from the Mons of Louvo, the intermarriage of ranking Thais with members of high Khmer families, and the wholesale settlement advance by Thai colonists, all typify thirteenth-century aspects of growing Thai strength in the Menam Valley. An advance capital was set up at Ayuthia about 1350. The Thais became the overlords of the Menam region, over the old Mon population now intermixed with Khmers, and began organizing the valley into a political state. A century of Thai-Khmer sparring for control of the lowland began, with the Khmer state also having to combat the Chams of Champa, the Annamese, and the encroaching tribal peoples of the north. In the northern Mekong Valley, and in Korat, Thai and other peoples lacked the cohesion of those taking over the Menam Valley, and here many local tribal principalities and temporary confederations developed.

Khmer culture was at its height in the thirteenth century. The state was a loose political structure. Economy remained chiefly subsistence, but foreign trade dealt in a wide range of rare and exotic commodities. Society was considerably stratified, without the highly formal caste system of India, but with a definite hierarchy of nobility, priesthood, Khmer middle and lower classes, and slave-bonded servant laboring classes. The laborers were largely drawn from the non-Khmer populations of the outer regions of the empire. A tremendous labor force was required to build the public works such as palaces, monasteries, temples, waterworks, and raised, stone-surfaced roads which the Khmer had finally begun to build within Cambodia itself. The chief contribution of the Khmer civilization was its religious architecture, for it has left no great literature or other works of art. As the Egyptian kings were motivated to outbuild each other, the Khmer rulers seemed to focus upon religious monuments. This concentration required a huge permanent labor force, a constant source of raw materials, and a large volume of tool-food-housing supplies. The heavy demands upon the population, for ends that gained them little material result, certainly created an increasing separation between ruled and ruling, and certainly provoked unrest and increasing tensions within Khmer society.

The Thais were neither strong enough nor numerous enough to conquer the whole Khmer Empire in one great sustained campaign. They never became one politically united people. The Menam Valley Thais chose to try consolidation, studied Khmer culture, and by degrees expanded their own political system of regional control. They increasingly inhibited the operation of the Khmer Empire while strengthening themselves. Thai reduction of the areas from which tributary labor battalions and taxable wealth could be drawn must have played a role in the reduction of the Khmer Empire. Among the other factors that have been given partial credit for the undermining of Khmer power is the spread of Hinayana Buddhism. Hinayana Buddhism was a simple, ascetic, and rather democratic form of religion appealing to the lower classes, in contrast to the stratified and hierarchic codes of Sivaism, Brahmanism, and Mahayana Buddhism long in favor among the Khmer rulers. Another factor may have been a series of extensive floods in the early fourteenth century that rendered much of the Cambodian rice land unproductive, consequent upon changes in Mekong delta distributaries, thus undermining the economic support of the Cambodian core. Epidemics of disease, brought in by multitudes of refugees and religious pilgrims, have been given importance in the decline of Khmer power. Gradual soil depletion, under exploitive rice culture using no fertilizing and restorative techniques, has been suggested as of importance also. Lacking Khmer historical documentation of these matters, the several factors must remain unweighed in relative significance, but the cumulative result is quite clear.

By the end of the fourteenth century, suffering restriction upon all its borders and within its core, the Khmer Empire had been reduced to the core area, Cambodia. Its economic and political dominance over the great lowland was gone, and the Khmers built no more great religious monuments. But the Cambodian population was intact, if undergoing reduction, the Khmer state continued, and so did Khmer culture. Though many of its farmlands became overgrown with forest, and its innumerable temples and monasteries could no longer be manned or maintained, Khmer culture did not vanish as is so often inferred in popular writing about Angkor. In none of the many wars between Annamese, Chams, Thais, sea pirates, and the Khmers did there occur permanent conquest and

occupation of Cambodia. By 1400, however, the Thais were free to manage affairs in the lowland outside Cambodia and the Mekong Delta.

The Menam Valley Thais, with a capital at Ayuthia, gradually developed a political state that included the northern peninsula, the hill country west of the Menam Valley, the valley lowland itself, the northern mountain and valley area, and Korat. Apparently problems of political and cultural solidification of this region were sufficient so that the Thai rulers sought no permanent conquest of Cambodia. Nor did they successfully include the Thai-occupied upper Mekong region which remained a zone of small regional principalities. Cambodia never threatened resurgence to her former status. In 1432 the Cambodian capital was removed from Angkor to the vicinity of modern Pnom Penh, away from the dangers of Thai attack. The Northwest frontier districts of the Cambodian core gradually came under Thai control.

In the Thai dominance over the Khmers many Mon and Khmer culture traits passed to the Thais. In a sense this makes a third cultural orientation of the Thai—Sinicized, Indianized, and Khmerized. Thai rulers tried to become the absolute monarchs that the Khmer kings had been, and made efforts to pattern the social structure of the new Thai state upon that of the Khmers. Thai rulers developed temple and monastery building. The Khmer system of forced-labor battalions of slaves and bonded servants was taken into usage. Administrative structure and patterns of taxation, law and judicial procedure were copied in part. All these new forms were somewhat alien to the traditional individualities and social freedoms that marked earlier Thai societies and regional groups. The attempted impositions caused inefficiency and organized protest, and they may well account for the slowness of a stable Thai society and political structure to emerge in the modern world.

THE DELINEATION OF MODERN THAILAND

The fifteenth to the nineteenth centuries forms a long period of struggle for unification of the modern political state. Ayuthia remained the chief capital during the early part of the period. Thai ability at political organization of the large area came slowly and with difficulty, for the Thai peoples have been prone to division and individuality rather than to tight cultural cohesion. Both political rivalries for dominance and local regionalisms were frequent issues in contest. And the growing states of lowland Burma found many reasons for attempting control of the Menam Valley or the pennisula, so that there were recurrent military invasions. Though each of the several Burmese states could mount a military expedition for invasion, none could ever truly conquer or organize regional control of any part of the peninsula or the Menam Valley. Punitive expeditions by the Thais, in return, detracted from the main task. These invasions were sufficiently frequent to keep the Thais off balance for several centuries. One such sufficiently destroyed Ayuthia so that Bangkok was made the capital in 1768.

Such interregional feuding only ceased when the British took over political management of Burma during the nineteenth century. Under British manipulations a western boundary finally crystallized, running through the Dawna Yoma and into the peninsula. Similarly, a southern boundary, far down in the peninsula, finally became adjudicated in such a way that the predominantly Malay-populated areas remained in British Malaya, and the rest of the peninsula became part of Thailand.

When the French, in the latter part of the nineteenth century, began carving out their one mainland colonial holding, they commenced in the Mekong Delta. Cambodia came next, though not all the old Khmer core came under French control at one time, since the Thai had dominated its frontier units. French infiltration of the Mekong River region and the advance up the coastal front was roughly parallel. By 1907 they had maneuvered affairs to the end that all the Cambodian lowland and all the territory east of the Mekong was theirs. The northern ends of the British and French boundaries come together to preclude direct boundary contact with China.

Portuguese and Dutch traders first sampled the coasts of the Gulf of Siam and the South China Sea. They made contact both with the declining Khmer center and the new and yet unstable Thai region. Later came both the British and the French, the latter more concerned with the spread of Catholic Christianity than with trade. Neither region, one declining, one yet immature, produced large amounts of those products of chief interest to the European. The Thais adopted Khmer trade administrative controls and government offices, not previously having had much to do with foreign trade, and essayed to deal with European traders as though the Thais were the lords of creation, after the old Khmer system. Though they were slow to appreciate the realities of the modern world, they did become wary of all European contacts and entanglements. Often the Thai king chose among the smaller non-competitive countries, and began playing off the Dutch against the British, against the French during the seventeenth and eighteenth centuries, add-

ing the Americans to the circle in the nineteenth century. This was sufficiently well done so that Thailand came through the period of colonialism without falling prey to any country in the political sense, the only country in southern Asia to escape colonial status. But this very escape from colonial status has also left the Thais inexperienced in some of the ways of modern political philosophy and administration. Thai governmental administration of the affairs of society has less of the modern ways of the world about it than that of most other countries of the Orient today.

Though contact with China has been a traditional matter for the peoples of the whole lowland, in which the Chinese adopted the superior role, the Thais have never willingly accepted the role of a tributary vassal people. Ever since the Thai asserted their control over the Menam Valley they have maintained relations with China, in the form of trade embassies. In 1700 there were only a few thousand Chinese permanently resident in the country. Shortly after 1800 large numbers of Chinese men began to come in, marrying local women and engaging in trade, fisheries, and handicraft manufacture. A few always returned to China after some years in the country, but slowly the total Chinese population has increased. In recent decades Chinese women have come in with their husbands, causing intermarriages to decline in number. The children of Chinese men and Thai women have usually been brought up within the patterns of Thai culture, and they are considered native citizens before Thai law. The actual number of Chinese citizens resident in Thailand is slightly above 500,000, but the total mixed-blood Chinese population exceeds 2,500,000.

This Chinese infiltration may be considered a part of the traditional southward drift of peoples, but in terms of modern political nationalism it has inserted an alien minority into Thailand which is having repercussions in economic and legal matters. For some decades restrictive legislation has narrowed the freedoms of the Chinese and has provoked various forms of opposition. This is not a matter that affects political boundaries, but it may well affect the operation of the Thai state in both the political and economic sense.

The region early recognized as the domain of the Syam, as the Khmer termed the Thais, is thus not a well-defined physical region at all, but is a political region defined by the competing interests of two occidental powers, Great Britain and France. Thailand is far more a politicohistorical phenomenon than a cultural one, and not entirely one prescribed by physical geography. It is only a part of the great lowland region, and its present boundaries have little or no historical precedent. Thais live outside Thailand, and non-Thais are to be found within it. This political region is the chief zone in southeast Asia around which political boundaries form significant problems in political geography. Since these boundaries of today are recent creations of political manipulation, they are, and will continue to be, fluid items of continued contest. Modern Thailand is only that part of the great lowland, and a share of upland, chiefly settled by infiltrating Thais, which neither British nor French rivalry could further partition without invoking too great protest from the other. Political and cultural nationalism is new to the individualistic Thai peoples, and its rise among them may well provoke further boundary issues. This new nationalism shows up in the very name of the country, for the people of the "land of the Syam" changed their country's name from Siam to Thailand only in 1939. Its meaning, the "land of the free," is largely one of linguistic and political definition.

THE DEVELOPMENT OF AGRICULTURE

Much that was said of Burma in the section on Economic Background applies equally well to Thailand. Substitute Thais for Burmans and Shans, and Chinese for Indians, and the story reads similarly. Details vary slightly, for the dry zone of the Menam Valley is less pronounced than that of the Irrawaddy, the Korat Platform is not the equivalent of the Shan Plateau, and the culture history of the two areas is not totally alike. But the Menam Delta has come into full occupation as recently as has that of the Irrawaddy. Though the British here have no territorial political control they early secured a leading role in the foreign trade economy. The Thai have long been a people well acquainted with rice growing, and rice was the basic crop of the Khmer state throughout its long period.

And yet not all of Thailand is easily available to productive agriculture. The lower Menam Valley and its delta form an aquatic region in which the very volume of water make major diking and canal systems necessary. In most of the lowlands outside the lower Menam Valley the seasonality of precipitation and flood runoff has long meant that there has been a scarcity of water for crop irrigation. Even in the Menam Valley if the summer flood does not develop adequate volume much rice land today goes without water and the crop fails. The large areas of poor soils containing laterite horizons, and the wide expanses of heavy clays, have meant that soils in much of the country are poor and difficult to work. Many areas of Thailand have old and stable soils, now leached and impoverished; these areas actually would benefit from some erosion that would expose unleached soil materials.

Though rice has long been the basic food crop of the area that we now label Thailand, early agriculture was far more general than it is today, for it was a subsistence agriculture that grew a wide range of crops. Aquatic products such as fish and taro helped broaden the diet and the base of local support. Some of the fruits and vegetables have long been here, if they are not native, whereas others were brought in from the Indies or India by early trader-colonists.

With maturity of Thai government and the coming of the European diking, drainage, and canals began to be built in large numbers in the Menam Valley. With the development of trade in basic consumption products, and the decline in native handicrafts, the rice landscape began to expand. This expansion has continued so that Thailand today seems to possess a monocrop agriculture. Hundreds of rice varieties are grown, in situations closely adapted to local needs, though productivity is not always at the highest level. Actually the height of the dominance of rice in the agricultural scene probably has passed, owing to governmental stimulation of new crop and diversification programs, though much of the wet lowland is not easily put into other crops. The present dominance of rice is statistical, produced by its overwhelming acreage in the wet, lower Menam Valley. Outside the lower valley rice is the most common food crop, but its comparative position is less obvious. It would seem that over 90 per cent of the crop land is devoted to some kind of rice, but this may derive from inadequate data on dooryard and jungle gardens.

In peninsular Thailand rice lands are scattered in small patches only. Fruits and vegetables together bulk larger than rice in the income pattern. Rubber and coconut here are commercial crops, but they are minor in the subsistence culture of local communities. In the hill country along the western border shifting cultivation, subsistence culture, and a few local specialty crops dominate the economy. In northern Thailand wet ricefields string out along the valleys, and shifting cultivation ranges into the uplands in the hands of various tribal groups. A few specialty crops are also produced here, such as pickled tea for chewing rather than for use as a beverage, tung oil, and certain fruits. Much of the rice is glutinous rice, grown for home consumption, not acceptable in export commerce. Throughout Korat permanent rice lands lie along the rivers and around local sources of water. Glutinous rice for home use is more common than the non-glutinous varieties. Dry-land crops

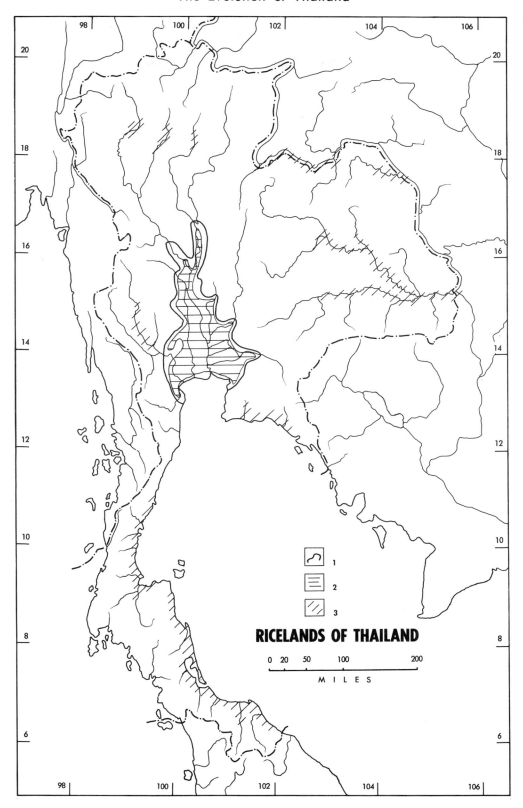

Fig. 67. The rice lands of Thailand: (1) encloses normal zone of flooding of Menam basin; (2) **primary rice-growing areas,** largely a monocrop region; (3) secondary rice-growing regions, in which rice normally is most important single crop.

and shifting cultivation are widely spread in small patches. Shifting cultivation is practiced on many hillside areas which actually have higher fertility than many of the highly leached lowland areas. Both Thai and tribal peoples practice shifting agriculture as a necessary supplement to their permanent farming. Mulberry trees are scattered on poor-soil areas for silk production.

Everywhere in Thailand fruits and vegetables are grown for local home and market village use. The commercial trends that have come to affect rice culture do not yet affect these garden and jungle crops, except around the larger cities, for the lack of transportation prevents a commercialization of this type of agriculture. There is not much specialization, the more common items being raised all over the country, though peninsular and southeastern Thailand find fruit culture relatively more important than elsewhere. Areas devoted to fruit culture resemble mixed jungle forest rather than orchards, because they are a traditional part of the economy and orchards are not segregated plantings on fully cleared lands. Vegetable culture on wet lowlands must use ridges for plantings, with numerous interspersed drainage ditches.

Besides fruits and vegetables some minor crops are of general and local importance. Tobacco, sugar cane, manioc, legumes, maize, pepper, betel nut, coconuts or sesame for edible oils, rubber, cotton, and such other crops as ramie, jute, sunn hemp, and kenaf are widely scattered in small plantings. Cotton has been a traditional crop in many parts of Thailand, but the poor success of the plantings has kept other minor fibers in small production. Coconut palms formerly were more widely distributed than at present, but diseases and pests have restricted their distribution and their local usages. Rubber plantings are now scattered in peninsular Thailand, but production is neither large in total nor per acre.

Animal husbandry forms a larger segment of Thailand's economy than it does in Burma. Both native cattle and water buffalo are numerous and distributed over the country. The whole of the Menam Valley does not produce adequate numbers of animals, and in Korat animal husbandry has both a domestic and a commercial aspect on small farms. Korat supplies the rest of the country with its draft animals. Chickens are kept in small numbers almost everywhere, and in aquatic situations Chinese breed large numbers of ducks. Among the Chinese pigs are common, as they also are in the north country where the Chinese tradition is stronger and the hold of traditional Buddhism is less restrictive. Korat exports live pigs to lower Thailand. In the north country horses are used chiefly as pack animals. Elephants are used in the teak forests, but elsewhere they are chiefly a religious and ceremonial animal. Though the Thais widely participate in raising animals, they eat but little meat, fish products taking the place of meats in the daily diet. The large number of Chinese form the chief domestic market for meat products, but Thailand in the modern era has developed a considerable livestock export trade.

The total land in farms appears to be about 19,-000,000 acres. Of this rice normally covers about 14,500,000 acres today. No other crop occupies a significant acreage, though the total of dooryard and jungle fruit gardens reaches almost 1,000,000 acres. Nearly 800,000 acres per year probably are cropped by shifting cultivation. In recent decades the rice acreage has been increasing steadily, from an estimated 2,500,000 acres in 1880 to the present total, some 5,000,000 acres of the increase taking place since 1910. Most of this large increase in rice acreage has been within the lower Menam Valley, since farmlands in other parts of the country have not increased markedly. And, just as the Irrawaddy Delta has a problem of tenancy, so does the newly settled area of the lower Menam Valley. Throughout most of Thailand farmers are neither deeply in debt nor tenants upon the lands that they occupy, but in the delta landlordism, tenancy, debt accumulation, shifting of tenants, rural instability, and rural dissatisfaction have accumulated in the wake of commercial rice farming.

SUBORDINATE ELEMENTS OF THE ECONOMY

Thailand appears to be one of the least mineralized countries in the world, but surveys are not yet complete. Peninsular Thailand shares in the tin resources of Burmo-Malaya, and tin for export is the most important mineral product. The country produces its own supply of salt for use in the fisheries industry, and for domestic consumption, from evaporated sea water or from springs and wells in Korat. There has been enough lateritic iron ore to permit handicraft manufacturing of such iron products as the traditional economy demanded in the past, but the prospective volume seems too small for industrial application today. Laterite as a building stone exists in quantity, and there are undeveloped deposits of several nonmetallic minerals. A few localities have produced precious stones, and there are geologic samples of many minerals. Modern survey may disclose enough of a few of them for commercial production. About 65 per cent of Thailand is still some kind of forest.

The northwest has shared the distribution of teak forests and long has been an exporter of this and a few other varieties of timber. The best of the teak is now gone, and cultural forestry has not adequately replaced it. Lac, rattans, some gums and resins, and a few other forest products are traditional exports which retain a place in foreign trade. Thailand today is one of the sources for wild animals for sale throughout the world. There is a considerable domestic trade in lumber, firewood, and charcoal from the margins of the country into the Menam Valley.

Aquatic resources have been a traditional part of lowland economy in all parts of Thailand. Everywhere in the lowlands some areas are flooded in the high-water season, and these form important fishing waters. Korat and the upper Mekong Valley have shared in this, and only the hill country of northern and western Thailand do not have local sources of fish and related aquatic foods. The Gulf of Siam and the coastal waters of the peninsula have long been important sources of fishery products, and, today, these waters play an important role in domestic economy of the country, since fishery products form the second most important article of diet. A few fish are raised in ponds, but this aspect of fisheries has never been exploited as it might be; it forms an important aspect of future development.

The waterways of the country have long been the most important routes of traffic flow. The main Menam Valley was thus oriented toward the Gulf of Siam. But much of Korat was oriented toward the Mekong, away from the Menam Valley. And the north country, not well served by the Menam river system, traditionally was connected to Yunnan and the Shan Plateau by overland pack trails. Modern Thailand is a country of numerous cart and pack train trails, but the modern development of canals in the Menam Valley has heightened the problems of road building. Surfaced highways are few even today, and the lack of good land transport is one of the most serious handicaps to the economy of the country. The short rail mileage was built with an eye to tightening the bonds of transport within the country. Though the mileage is only about 2,000, and though the traffic load is not great, the rail system has brought the peninsula, the north country, and Korat into better connection with the Menam Valley than they have ever experienced before. Though the rail lines cannot serve the whole hinterland of each of these outer regions, they do serve to establish a means of traffic routing which has now re-oriented each of these regions toward the Menam Valley. The Thai were among the first orientals to take up aviation, and, though the

number of fields is not large even now, air traffic also helps orient the Korat region toward the Menam Valley.

In the eighteenth century Thailand's handicraft production was a fairly considerable one, but it had not developed a mature pattern. Gradually imported consumer goods have undermined this volume and variety of manufacturing, and, as the expansion of rice agriculture in the lower Menam Valley developed after 1880, the Thais have lost more and more of their old technical skills and have become more fully agricultural. Chinese and occidental integration of control over the foreign trade of Thailand has brought the Chinese into rather complete control of internal trade and occidental firms into control of foreign trade, with the result that most of the manufactured commodities of foreign origin required in Thailand are imported and distributed by aliens. The Chinese are numerous in Bangkok, but they are scattered throughout the country in the towns and market villages, whereas occidentals have congregated chiefly in Bangkok. Very few branch manufacturing establishments have been set up since Thailand did not become a colonial holding in which governmental regulation could foster such development.

Since the late nineteenth century governmental awareness of the changing conditions of manufacturing and trade have caused numerous efforts to establish modern factory production in a variety of lines. In recent decades government policy has vacillated between taking over all alien-controlled industries and starting new ventures of a competitive sort. World War II interrupted this program, but it now is in process again. The chief problem is that Thais have acquired no modern skills in management or technology—there is neither an experienced governmental nor private industrial core of personnel available in Thailand such as has developed in India or the Philippines during the period of British or American colonial control. Though Thailand has escaped colonial domination Thais have acquired little of the training in modern management and commercial-industrial enterprise that a colonial population learns as it moves toward freedom and economic participation in the modern world.

Today there are not more than a few thousand trained managers and skilled workmen in the country, in modern commercial-industrial terms. Legislation toward nationalization of industry and trade cannot be effectively put into practice. Rice mills and saw mills are the most numerous "industrial" concerns, both largely controlled by aliens. Individual government factories do now produce paper, sugar, cotton and silk textiles, cement, refined petroleum, cigarettes,

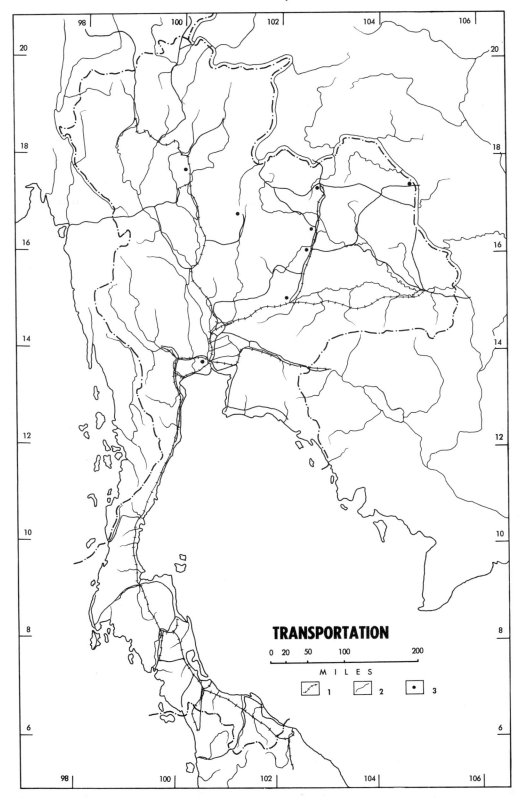

Fig. 68.   Transportation facilities of Thailand: (1) rail lines; (2) main motorable roads; (3) chief civil airfields.

boats and small ships, canned foods, and a few similar products. A start has been made, but it supplies only a small share of the needed consumer goods. Future progress will depend upon a realistic approach to the problems of technologic training and development of native capacity. The situation is complicated by the nationalistic trend of economic policy in advance of ability and by the controlling position of the Chinese in respect to internal trade.

Rice remains Thailand's chief export, making up almost half of the export trade by value. Tin, rubber, teak, and livestock form the other chief export products, followed by a variety of small-value commodity groups. In the import trade cotton textiles and yarns are by far the chief items. Prepared food products, petroleum, machinery, and sacking fibers are the other leading imports. Bangkok is Thailand's chief port, handling the trade of all except the peninsular region. As the chief port Bangkok is today a cosmopolitan city in which the full range of contrasts between the East and the West are visible.

THE REGIONALISM OF MODERN THAILAND

Conventionally the country is divided into four regions: the peninsula, the Menam Valley, the northeast or Korat, and the northern hill country. This division omits border areas and is a too simplified set of divisions based only on location. Culture history suggests that the present political unit is an artificial one, based more upon political strength than upon environmental elements. Thai governmental structure has steadily rearranged its administrative divisions. The late eighteenth-century pattern involved some sixty regional units. Since 1930 there have been ten major regional districts composed of seventy-one provinces or *changvads*. Thai operation of their geographical territory has not yet found stable regional bases upon which to establish administrative patterns.

The population map suggests that the central and lower Menam Valley is the key population region, correlating with the key agricultural region. Culturally the Thais have spread their patterns over almost all the lowland. The imposition of the Thai language upon the political state has today made almost all the lowland a Thai region, with the southern peninsula and the hill country people speaking variant tongues. South of the line indicated on the population map in peninsular Thailand Malays are numerous. In the west are Karen, and in the northwest both Shan and Wa-Palaung peoples overlap into Thailand. All through the north country are Yao, Miao, and other

peoples moving out of China. The Mekong Valley zone has many small remnant groups, some of whom also are found in the southeastern margin of the country. Near the Cambodian border are many Khmers. The Chinese are chiefly urban and market-town dwellers among the lowland Thai. Currently nationalistic education is attempting to nationalize all parts of the country culturally, aiming chiefly at the Chinese and the Moslem Malays of the southern peninsula, but its administration does not yet carry to all parts of the rural back country. Assessing the scene vertically, it appears that Thai culture dominates the lowlands and that, in the hill country, there are horizontal layerings of non-Thai peoples, each occupying an altitudinal plane, with the recent Miao immigrants out of China occupying the highest levels.

Among agricultural patterns five regional areas stand out: the commercial rice monocrop area of the Menam Valley is the area of chief importance; the peninsula is a highly mixed subsistence-commercial region; the Cardamom hill country of southeastern Thailand is similar to the peninsula; Korat is a region of subsistence food economy with increasing commercial trends in livestock and crop products; the western and northern hill country is a subsistence region with a few special cash crops. Putting the agricultural and population maps together brings out the fact that the area of maximum population and chief agricultural production also possesses the lowest physiologic density of population against cultivated land. The lower Menam Valley figure is slightly under 600 persons per square mile of cultivated land, whereas the Cardamom hill region has a density of over 3,000 people per cultivated square mile. Korat has a physiologic density about twice that of the lower Menam, and the northern hill country a density over three times as great. The western hill country and the peninsula are more lightly populated.

Except for the peninsula the outlying portions of Thailand are populated beyond capacity for an advancing standard of living based upon a simple agricultural economy. These are the regions infiltrated by the peoples out of China, and their continuing tendency is to push toward the Menam Valley where lies the greatest opportunity for an agricultural people. The total population of Thailand climbed slowly during the earlier centuries, but since the seventeenth century it has been rising rapidly. The earliest reliable figure is that of 1854, a total of about 6,000,000. The total had climbed to 14,500,000 in 1937, and was estimated at very close to 19,000,000 at the end of 1952. The chief volume of increase is settling in the lower

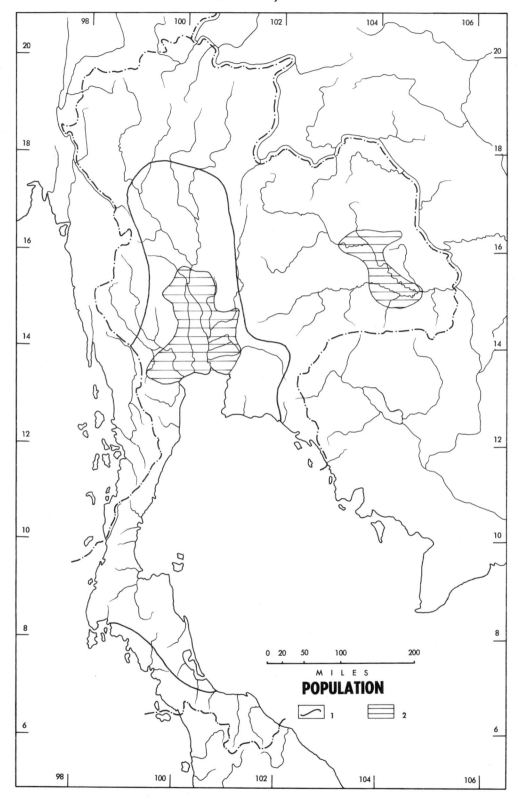

Fig. 69. Population, estimated, of Thailand: (1) except for southern Korat all areas outside heavy line are lightly populated, and this area encloses regions most fully occupied by culturally unified Thai peoples; (2) over 200 people per square mile.

Menam Valley. The Thai are a rural village-dwelling people chiefly, though there is a scattering of market towns all over the country. Bangkok is the only real city of large size, but there are perhaps a dozen sizable towns.

Environmental considerations suggest five major regional units: the peninsula, the western and northern hill country, Korat, the Cardamom hill region, and the Menam lowland. Detailed criteria of landforms, climate, vegetation, or soils indicate several subdivisions to each major region. Of these only the Menam lowland lies wholly within Thailand. If the physical, economic, political, and cultural regionalisms are weighed together, it would appear that this fivefold pattern expresses as well as any other the basic regionalisms of this new political entity.

Indochina, a State of Mixed Cultures

THE LACK OF A NATURAL CORE

The country known in the last century as Indochina is an illustration of the effectiveness of willful political force. It is an artificial combination of regions and cultures brought together by French military and political effort during the latter part of the nineteenth century, in a zone between the areas of Chinese and Indian cultural influence. Indochina of the early 1950's is also an illustration of the futility of political force artificially expended, for it is one country in political and military terms only. In geographic terms it is an assemblage of unlike geographic areas, dissimilar economic entities, and mixed but unequal cultural groups. The physical regions that make up the state are the easternmost parts of the Burmo-Malayan peninsula. The Annamite Cordillera occupies the center of the region, and its margins are a varied series of lowlands, coastal plains, deltas, and valley margins. The Cordillera itself is not all true mountain country, for it contains sections of subdued upland and small pieces of plateau. Several lowland areas are good enough to allow a people to develop economic strength and cultural force, but none is so placed as to facilitate the control or the cultural integration of the whole region now included in the state of Indochina.

If the limits set by modern political control are accepted, but if these areas are examined in their early situations, it is evident that there were several regions attractive to early man. The Tonking Delta in the north was an attractive lowland at a very early date, essentially similar to the tropical lowlands of most of southern Asia. Its moist to aquatic situation was also similar to that of the southern lowlands of China, from which it is not well separated by natural barriers. The Annam coastal plain is a relatively narrow and irregular strip of lowland leading southward from the Tonking Delta which, because of the possibilities of combining fishing and lowland plant economies, was an attractive zone. Its linear proportions presented no large resource in any one locality, but its very dimensions meant that many localities within it presented opportunity.

At the southern end of the coastal zone there broadens out the Mekong Delta zone, another useful aquatic lowland. Closely connected with it is the Cambodian lowland, previously discussed. The Mekong Valley is another large area of lowland, arranged in linear pattern, with numerous tributary valleys on the eastern side reaching back into the hill country. Though presenting different local environments from those of the delta or coastal areas there are many good localities, as far north as the sharp bend of the Mekong north of Korat.

The Annamite Cordillera is not one great mountain mass. Its upland areas, both plateau-like and mountainous, are variable and unequal in value. Though much of the more open uplands are today of value in tree-crop plantation agriculture, many areas always have been difficult for man to use. The uplands are generally moist and forested, except for areas of karst development in the north, and they are not so cold as to prohibit many of the more hardy tropical fruits and other useful plants. But the Annamite Cordillera appears long to have been one of the most malarial zones in the whole Orient. It is not the higher uplands that suffer, but the foothill country on both sides. This unhealthiness has kept the peoples of the lowlands apart historically.

The regions we know as Indochina today, therefore, present almost the reverse of the situation in Burma—an upland core surrounded by a loosely connected series of good lowland areas. On the one hand, these areas connect with the area of the Chinese world, and, on the other, they form parts of the great region that had early contact with the Indian culture world. This double exposure and the separation of the lowland regions have given to the peoples of Indochina their diversity. Though the evidence is not yet well assembled, it is clear that man has been here a long time and continuously. Negrito and many other early groups became resident in parts of the lowlands. This region shared in the early southern movements of proto-Mongoloid and Mongoloid peoples, and the continued southward shift of peoples has brought many different groups into the region. The evidence suggests that Indochina has always contained diverse human groups. Figure 66 presented the early occupance picture for both Thailand and Indochina.

THE LIMITS OF CHINESE AND INDIAN INFLUENCE

Though both Indian and Chinese cultural agents were active in Indochina in the centuries before and after the start of the Christian era, they never met in head-on competition, nor did they struggle for control of the area that we know as one country. Indian contact touched Cambodia, the Mekong Delta lowland, and the southern portion of the Annam coast at first hand. Secondarily, and through local inhabitants, Indian influence came to bear upon much of the Mekong Valley, and upon a larger portion of the Annam coast and as far north as Hainan Island. After the early centuries of the Christian era direct Indian contact with the Annam coast became negligible, and gradually ceased in the southern areas as well.

Chinese influence began to be felt in the Tonking Delta zone some centuries before the beginning of the Christian era, and, during the following centuries, Chinese influence grew steadily and gradually penetrated the northern portion of the Annam coast. Second-handedly Chinese influences spread slowly down the Annam coast and, through the steady drift southward of peoples exposed to Chinese culture, have continued to affect the culture of the country as a whole. Reference should be made to Fig. 66 in the previous chapter.

In the earlier centuries political and trade relations with India were strong in the southern sector, whereas in the northern sector they lay with China. At the height of Khmer power in Cambodia sovereignty was locally centered, and trade relations came to be with the whole of southern Asia. The Annamese, in the tenth century, threw off Chinese political domination but remained subject to cultural influence. After the twelfth century China exerted a nominal political overlordship over all of Burmo-Malaya, occasionally acting to prevent major turbulence, but it never came into actual local control of any area except for a brief period in the early fifteenth century when Chinese control over Tonking and Annam was asserted.

Thus one can generalize that the two chief peoples, the Annamese and the Cambodians, basically belong to different culture worlds. The Annamese are chiefly oriented to China, out of their cultural past, and similarly the Cambodians chiefly reflect Indian culture. Both have picked up elements that belong to the other culture world, and, therefore, the modern Cambodian pattern of culture contains something of China. Similarly the Annamese, through their conquest of Champa and their contact with the Khmers over the centuries, have absorbed many Indian features. The other peoples that make up the country today also have a mixed culture. The Thais of Indochina, resident in the Mekong Valley, have overlaid much of Khmer culture upon their earlier Chinese-oriented patterns. The tribal peoples of the Cordillera retain primitive elements and features both Indian and Chinese. Through the modern dispersal of Chinese, both in the north and in the Mekong Delta zone, Chinese influences now are being more strongly pressed upon Indochina than are those of India.

THE EARLY PATTERN OF CULTURE REGIONS

The earliest region to emerge above the primitive level was that of the Mekong Delta lowland, growing into the great Khmer Empire discussed in the previous chapter. Though this region now is part of Indochina its early relationships lay with the Mekong Valley, Korat, and the Menam Valley rather than with the Annamite Cordillera and the coastal zone.

On the southern and central Annam coast early Indian influences had established several points of contact among the several local regions that make up the coastal zone, but these trade contacts never were as productive as those of the Mekong Delta. This coast, and the hill country behind it, was inhabited by related groups of Indonesian peoples, commonly called Chams. Their origin is not yet clear, but they seem to have been a part of the early drift out of the north. Though related, there were cultural differences among them, and those with the greatest cultural attainments were lowlanders. The hill country Chams were thinly scattered clear across to the Mekong Valley. The coastal zone was narrow, small in total area, and divided into local regions by projecting spurs of the Cordillera that reached toward the coast. The hill country was irregular in surface and forested, and its economic productivity was low compared with that of the coastal zone. Reference should be made to Fig. 66 in the previous chapter.

Along this Annam coast events progressed much as in other areas of Indian contact, with trading port centers slowly growing into small regional principalities under Indian leadership. The competitive efforts of the several local areas, and the inability of any one region to achieve superior population, economic strength, and political power, prevented integration of the whole coastal zone into one unified state. The fragmentary history of the Indianized Chams suggests well-nigh continuous rivalry for leadership and constant regional turbulence. Though Champa achieved temporary unity under occasional dynasties, the essential limitations of the narrow coastal region prevented its growing steadily in strength, population, and cultural influence. A part of Cham turbulence regularly expressed itself in raids on the Annamese peoples to the north and on the Khmer regions to the south and west almost throughout the period of its separate existence.

In the Tonking Delta and the northern portions of the Annam coastal plain the Annamese had begun another regional development. It is not at all certain how early this began, but it took place several centuries before the Christian era. And it is not clear, either, how large a part was played by traders, settlers, or refugees from the area of China. The development may have been less a result of sea-derived traders-settlers than of the settling down of Annamese who had previously moved out of what now is China, after sharing something of very early Chinese culture. But in the late third century B.C. militant invasion of Tonking began to implant official Chinese control in administrative affairs and to formalize the organization of Annamese society along Chinese lines on a higher plane than would have been possible among the Annamese alone. This direct Chinese control continued for about four centuries, during which time the evolution of Annamese culture along Chinese lines was made relatively complete. This cultural development of the Annamese core produced marked material progress, the growth of population, and the beginning of expansion southward along the coastal plain.

The Chams for centuries had raided the Annamese lands to the north, primarily venting their spleen on the Chinese rulers of Tonking, but necessarily including the Annamese in their actions. As the Annamese began pushing southward they were less inclined to conquer and rule than to exterminate and themselves settle the coastal zone. Slowly this pattern extended itself until by the late fifteenth century the Annamese had overwhelmed the lowland coast and restricted the Chams to upland principalities of little real strength and simpler culture level. This destruction of the Cham power opened the whole coastal zone to Annamese settlement, and the Annamese spread steadily down the coast, absorbing the remnant Cham population and taking over some of their culture traits.

Into the northern hill country various peoples had been filtering out of China for centuries before the rise of Khmer, Cham, or Annamese power. Most of them were simple tribal peoples out of the uplands of South China. They scattered out down the Cordillera, sometimes mixing with earlier resident groups, sometimes pushing them into more restricted localities. Some of them made some contact with the lowland peoples, but here there seems to have been less infiltration of the lowlands by hill peoples than was true in Burma. As the Thai peoples began their southward moves some of them moved into the upper Mekong Valley and into the better parts of the northern hill country, known as Laos today. Tribal units, small principalities, confederations, and changing political patterns were the rule, this upland and north country never becoming the seat of a strong and politically integrated group. There developed a stratification of peoples by altitude and culture level, with a very great amount of regional intermixture. Localities with considerable resources developed nuclei of population, but generally the up country remained thinly inhabited with few regional centers of cultural significance. The more recent arrivals among these hill people were basically Chinese in their cultural orientation, but almost all of them gradually learned Indian cultural elements.

THE DOMINANCE OF ANNAM

Within the large area that we recognize as Indochina there matured three competing groups—the Khmers, the Chams, and the Annamese. The Khmers and the Chams were motivated and led by Indians, but there never was either formal cultural control or direct political organization by Indian political states. The Annamese, in contrast, benefited from formal control and organization by the Han dynasty government of China, one of the most effective societal organizing groups of the oriental world. Chinese influence gave them a superior working system and a tight cultural cohesion never achieved by either the Khmers or the Chams. Spreading itself far north and west from its good lowland base the Khmer state became a loosely structured affair encompassing many different peoples and culture elements, and subject to many disruptive factors and destructive forces. Restricted to a narrow coastal plain and unproductive hill country, and composed of loosely related peoples of variant levels of culture, the Cham state failed to achieve a close cultural cohesion and never gained access to a large productive lowland. The Annamese, starting from a productive base in the Tonking Delta, achieved a cultural unity before they began to expand. Choosing to restrict themselves to the healthier coastal lowland, and facing fewer disruptive factors, the Annamese retained their cultural cohesion during their low southward expansion. Refer again to Fig. 66 in the previous chapter.

Relatively independent after the tenth century the Annamese were able to overwhelm the Chams and appropriate their territory just at the time the Khmers were suffering their destruction as a powerful people. Thus the Annamese were free to expand into the southern margins of the coastal zone and begin infiltration of the Mekong Delta lowland as the Europeans came upon the scene. By this time the Annamese held the whole eastern coast of the upper portion of Burmo-Malaya, though they by no means populated the area equally from north to south. Concerned less than either the Khmers or the Chams with the building of great religious monuments, they retained considerable of the Chinese pragmatic outlook upon life, while at the same time absorbing many of the personal cultural traits of the Chams and the other southern peoples with whom they traded along their long seacoast.

Though continuing to disregard the hill country, even around the crowded Tonking Delta, the Annamese have steadily pushed southward. Since the coming of the Europeans they have been filtering into the Mekong Delta and its lower valley lands, even seeking entry into Cambodia. Their numbers have long far surpassed those of the hill peoples, and for centuries they have outnumbered the Khmer peoples as such. Today the Annamese dominate Indochina. The very extension of Annamese down the long narrow coast has made for regional differences and north-south rivalries which have lessened the early cohesion, but the Annamese still bulk as one people in the complex ethnic patterns of Indochina.

THE ASSEMBLING OF FRENCH INDOCHINA

Portuguese and Spanish missionaries visited Annam and Cambodia in the sixteenth century, and Portuguese and Dutch traders often touched the coastal ports of both regions in the seventeenth century. The Annamese rulers were hard to deal with, the desired products were not in good supply, and in general the Europeans found trade more profitable elsewhere. The French East India Company made late efforts but never achieved much success in attempts to gain a foothold in Annam. French missionaries appeared in the seventeenth century in considerable numbers, and their communications with the homeland slightly acquainted France with Annam. French missionary participation in Annam's internal political struggles in the late eighteenth century restored a southern dynasty to the throne, but it left suspicion of the missionaries and their trader friends.

About the middle of the nineteenth century the French began looking for a route into interior China. The Mekong Valley was first tried, followed by the realization that the valley of the Songhoi offered the only practical access from the south. As the Annamese attempted to prevent missionary-trader-political encroachment by expulsion of the missionaries, the French began using punitive military expeditions to avenge their ill treatment. One event led to another in a somewhat haphazard chain marked by personal decisions of both French and Annamese officials. First came French control over the Mekong Delta, then a protectorate over part of Cambodia, followed by another over the southern portion of Annam. Tonking and Laos, in the north, were the last areas to come under French domination in a late nineteenth-century effort to get into western China before the British took over the region. Late maneuvers with Thailand settled western borders and rounded out a half century of imperialistic conquest. See Fig. 74 for the political pattern of states.

A political state finally had been delimited. At the outset the French had had no realization of the physical and cultural complexity of the regions that they were taking over. Finding themselves in control of regions having different culture histories they followed expediency and ended with five different units, in each of which policy and practice differed. These five units on paper formed the Indo-Chinese Union, and made up the standard political map of Indochina before World War II. The Mekong Delta, in the 1860's actively undergoing Annamese settlement, became Cochin-China, in which the French themselves largely ran things. Cambodia, with its Khmer traditions and a descendant line of royalty, was operated indirectly as a protectorate under guidance. This same pattern was applied to the southern portion of the Annamese regions, now designated Annam. Tonking became a partial protectorate, and, centering on the delta of the Songhoi, this has become an important holding. The northern hill country and the Mekong Valley margins on the west, a maze of tribal territories, confederacies, and old principalities, was lumped into the so-called protectorate of Laos, to be administered as casually but as practically as possible.

Though a political state had been delimited and divided into administrative segments, the nineteenth-century French knew too little of their colonial people and their ways to govern for the governed. Vacillation at home, governors appointed for short terms, too great use of the military, a tremendous ignorance of oriental ways, and the exploitive urge have long joined to prevent either a happy or an efficient pattern of colonial rule. The French efforts have done much to undermine the traditional close bonds of Annamese and Cambodian village culture without replacing them with constructive modern elements. The pattern of divide and rule has prevented the formulation of any modern cohesion around the new state that the French created. Indochina remains a somewhat artificial assemblage of regions, peoples, cultures, animosities, and political forms. Belatedly, in opposition to the Communist problem of Indochina since the close of World War II, a start was made in 1948 to repair the damage, but now it is an unfair race against time and the growing seeds of destruction. The cultural unity of the Annamese is now recognized in the new state of Vietnam, which has replaced Cochin-China, Annam, and Tonking in the administrative structure of the country. Cambodia remains the unit that it long has been. Laos continues as the arbitrary grouping of the rest of French territory, a not entirely happy pattern. The very name now given to the whole is both recognition of the facts and a warning for the future—the Associated States of Indochina. As this volume goes to press the future is uncertain. French popular unwillingness to support a wholesale change in colonial policy and an all-out military effort, Annamese dislike for the French on any terms, and Communist ability to capitalize on political disunity prejudice the future status of Indochina. Either the United States or Soviet Russia may win the political-military maneuvering going on in 1954 that may determine the future outlines of Indochinese political regions.

THE TRADITIONAL ECONOMY

Subsistence economy by hamlet and village groups based upon rice and fish, supplemented by the small use of a wide range of auxiliary crops, is the tradition of almost all the culture groups of Indochina. Though there have been water shortages in some regions, there are no rain shadows of such magnitude as to motivate the culture of a wide range of dry-field crops as in Burma. The contrast in land use between the lowlands and the uplands is at least as striking here as in

any other part of the Orient, for most of the population clings to the lowlands, and the agricultural landscape is a decidedly lowland one. Rice dominates rainy season cropping, and most secondary annual crops are grown in the dry season. Receiving its moisture from both monsoon systems, Indochina exhibits considerable variety in planting and harvesting in different parts of the country. Rice, for example, is being harvested in some region during almost every month of the year. Most of the lowlands have practiced a permanent cropping system, whereas throughout the uplands shifting cultivation is the normal system. Well over half the country has been reduced from its natural forested condition to grasslands or parklands, largely at the hands of the shifting cultivator. Many abandoned tracts in the lower Mekong Valley and Cambodia reverted to forest after the decline of the Khmer Empire, and now are gradually being cleared as the agricultural landscape again expands.

In the Tonking Delta and the northern Annam coast the physiologic density of population has long been very high, decreasing southward to the newly settled wet portions of the Mekong Delta. The areal density of the upland territories always has been low, though the physiologic density of many local regions has perhaps been rather high. Cambodia and parts of the lower Mekong Valley declined in population after the decline of the Khmer Empire, and, though now they are increasing in population, they today carry only a moderate density. In Tonking and northern Annam continuous occupation and the full development of the agricultural landscape have produced extreme fragmentation of farmlands. In parts of the Tonking Delta, land now is divided into as many as 10 to 14 parcels per acre. In these areas of traditional occupation there is only a small amount of tenancy, land is high in price and always in strong demand. The fragmentation of farmland decreases southward along the Annam coast. Much of the lower Mekong region and Cambodia is divided into parcels of roughly an acre each, whereas in the more recently settled wet portion of the Mekong Delta there are many large holdings. On these new lands tenancy is reaching serious proportions, and it is common for tenants to remain on a given farm for short periods only. In the Tonking Delta Chinese diking practices have long been followed, and most of the delta now is in farmland, but in the Mekong lowlands that have suffered from too much water during a long flood season only modern diking and drainage-canal building has made possible the agricultural occupation of large areas.

In some respects the peoples of Indochina may be called simple growers of crop plants rather than technically efficient farmers. The rice yield for the country as a whole is among the lowest in the Orient, and the relative yields of other crops also are low. Regional differences are apparent in this matter. In Tonking the Chinese practices of using all available fertilizers, including night soil, have long been followed, whereas in the far south practices of soil fertility maintenance are poorly developed. Too few draft animals have been used, and, particularly on the very small holdings, manual labor is the chief source of farm power. Until very recently all farmers have used only the simplest of wooden tools. In many areas, and with many crop plants, planting is in garden patches and dooryard plantings. Few of the peoples of Indochina are highly skilled in the handling of shrub and tree crops.

Though fishermen have worked hard in all productive waters, they have achieved but low relative yields for the second-ranking dietary commodity. And though silk and cotton are traditional home textiles, their quality is low both in raw material and finished product, and their yields have long been inadequate to the need. Basketry, mattings, and bamboo and wood-tool and utensil making are widespread traditional occupations. In some lines the Annamese have shown high skills, and the most highly developed handicrafts are to be found in Tonking where Chinese influence has motivated the activity. Elsewhere in the country handicraft manufacturing is less well developed. In 1950 perhaps 1,500,000 people were principally engaged in handicraft manufacture of all sorts. In religious architecture the Khmers, of course, reached levels seldom attained elsewhere, but this was Indian motivated and came at tremendous cost. Road building was an almost unknown art, even compared with other portions of the Orient, and the regional interchange of commodities has been slight. The water channels of the Mekong drainage system and the coastal waterways of the Annam coast have been more important than the avenues of land transport.

Rice has been the dominant crop of all parts of Indochina, and the country rivals Thailand in having a monocrop economy. Nearly 13,000,000 out of about 16,000,000 acres of crop land are devoted to rice, when peaceful conditions permit normal agricultural planting. The agricultural activities surrounding rice culture set the seasonal rhythm of life in Indochina. In the wet lowlands it has been a wet-field crop, though many of the fields have lacked enough water in mid-season. There is some double cropping of rice. On some lands of deepest flooding a tall floating rice is grown, to be followed by minor crops during the dry season. Throughout the uplands rice has been the chief crop of the sedentary and shifting cultivator, but

the per acre yield is low. In the last century the acreage of rice has increased markedly, as some of the Mekong Delta lands have been diked and drained. The increase in settlement and land use is as marked here as it is in the deltas of the Irrawaddy and the Menam, with most of the consequent problems of tenancy and shifting of farmers from farm to farm. On these new lands agriculture is distinctly monocrop, and in much of the Mekong Delta rice is the only crop for which there are statistical returns.

All the traditional auxiliary crops of oriental agriculture find their place in some local environment of Indochina, but government statistical services have been unable properly to plot their occurrence and distribution. The native fruits of the Orient have been traditionally planted in dooryard clumps and small patches throughout the lowlands, but they only selectively reach into the uplands. Some of them are regionally centered, following local climatic criteria. The lichi is more frequently grown in the northern lowlands than in the south, whereas the coconut bears fruit only southward of Tourane on the central Annam coast. The durian is restricted to the southern portions of the country. Bananas, citrus fruits, and the jackfruit are among the most tolerant of altitude and location, are the most commonly grown, and, taken together, probably cover several hundred thousands of acres, though no specific data are available.

Sugar cane, taro, yams, beans, pepper, betel, some of the lesser spices, sesame, cotton, mulberries, sugar palms, and a variety of green vegetables, all find a place in the crop patterns of the lowlands, and some of them in the uplands as well. None of the crops is to be found everywhere, but in the older and more stable areas most of them are represented. Mulberries normally are grown on the edges of the lowlands, or on hillocks of well-drained soils. Some of these crops are grown on the river-bank strips of light soils at low-water season. In only a few cases is there adequate production today, for their cultivation has not increased in recent centuries at the same rate as the increase in population. The only items in this group to exceed 100,000 acres per year are the beans and sugar cane, with perhaps 200,000 and 110,000 acres, respectively.

Such American plants as maize, the peanut, tobacco, manioc, white and sweet potatoes, and some of the beans have fitted well into the traditional subsistence economy. Several have regional specialization, and some are river-bank low-water seasonal crops. Maize has been increasing steadily in acreage until today it ranks as the second crop in area, covering about 1,300,000 acres per year. As a dry-season crop it is widely grown, following wet rice. The potatoes cover

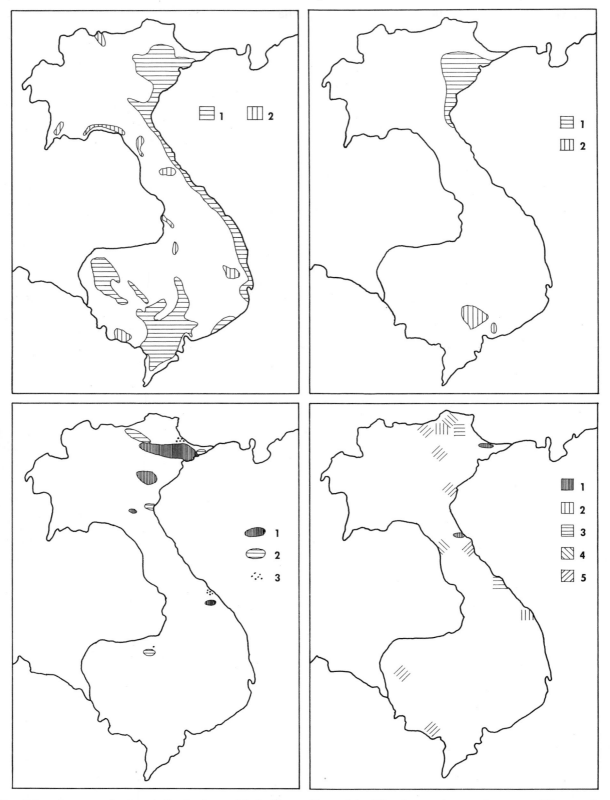

Fig. 70. Selected crop and mineral distributions of Indochina. *Upper left:* (1) primary rice-growing areas; (2) secondary rice-growing areas. *Upper right:* (1) regions of important maize production; (2) chief areas of rubber production. *Lower left:* (1) coal; (2) iron; (3) bauxite. *Lower right:* (1) manganese; (2) lead; (3) zinc; (4) tin; (5) phosphate.

perhaps about 300,000 acres per year, to rank third in area among the food crops.

Animal husbandry is not highly developed. Small native pigs are the most numerous animal, totaling close to 4,000,000. Though they are to be found everywhere, they are important only in those lowland regions of Chinese influence. Cattle of a mixed zebu-taurus breed are used sparingly as draft animals where they can be afforded. In the Tonking Delta and the more crowded portions of Annam there is little room for cattle, and they supply only a small volume of draft power or meat supply. Water buffalo also are sparingly used for the same reasons. Cambodia has a larger number of both animals than do other parts of the country. The cattle population approaches 2,000,-000, with water buffalo perhaps numbering 1,400,000. Horses are few in total number. In Cambodia and the south they are used chiefly as carriage animals around the towns and cities, and in the northern uplands they are pack animals. The elephant is more an honorific animal than one of husbandry. Fewer than 1,500 elephants are used in economic activities. Such other animals as goats or sheep are few in number, neither understood nor well cared for, and are not of economic significance. Chickens, ducks, pheasants, and geese are widespread in use, are kept in small numbers for meat and egg purposes, but do not make a large contribution to the food economy of the country.

Fishery products probably supply the second most important source of food for all but the upland population. Both coastal water fishing and that of the estuarine and inland lowlands is a traditional part of the economy. The Tonle Sap and the Mekong waterways, in flood season, along with smaller streams everywhere, provide a very rich resource tapped by simple methods. Only in restricted inland areas, or along the Annam coast, where year-round fishing is possible, are professional fishermen numerous, and most fishing is a seasonal or part-time occupation. The total annual catch probably amounts to some 260,000 tons, but reliable data are scarce. Pond culture is sporadically practiced but is not highly developed. Along with fishery products of the normal sort goes the harvesting of many aquatic plant foods. In season a share of the catch is used fresh, but the more normal methods are to salt, dry, smoke, or process the product into fish pastes.

Outside the areas of intensive lowland agriculture forest gathering supplies an appreciable annual return. Bamboo for matting, construction, tools, and utensils, lumber, firewood and charcoal for domestic or handicraft use, gums, resins, turpentine, lac, fruits, and roots, plus a variety of other vegetable products, are among the resources tapped. There is some hunting of game by the upland population. The forests have been stripped of most of their good timber resources and no longer supply the lowland with adequate good lumber. There has been little redevelopment of any of these resources in any part of the country, for the forested areas have not been thought of as areas of potential cultural development of resources, but chiefly as a natural reserve to be stripped or as a source of arable land when clearing.

FRENCH ELEMENTS IN THE ECONOMY

It is difficult to distinguish fully between French-introduced and native elements in the changing economy of modern Indochina. In a land once lacking effective land transport systems the French have built almost 20,000 miles of all-weather highways that traverse most of the major regions of the country, in addition to the many miles of dry-weather highways and the local service roads and trails also laid out. An accompanying map presents the transportation facilities. A railway system of about 1,800 miles now extends from one end of the country to the other along the Annam coast, though it does not serve the Mekong Valley at all, and its evolution was marred by financial scandal and mismanagement. The highway system connects both to China and to Thailand, but the rail system connects with neither Thai nor Chinese systems. Both roads and railways were built more with political considerations in mind than purely economic utility, but regional interchange of commodities has markedly increased. Harbor and port development and improvements of Mekong River and Tonking Delta water navigations have allowed the French to develop a variety of international trade, and also to tap the trade of southwestern China. With the diking and draining of heavily flooded lands in the lower Mekong Basin, achieved under the French, the expansion of rice agriculture has taken place, and Indochina has joined Burma and Thailand as the chief sources of export rice. The disruptive situation in Indochnia since 1949 temporarily prevents normal planting, harvesting, and export, so that Indochina may not contribute properly to the export market for some years. The demands of the French home market have drawn a number of commodities out of Indochina, so that a share of production has developed a cash-crop production pattern. Recently most of the surplus of pepper and corn has moved to the French market.

Considerable French effort has been expended in the attempt to develop commercial plantation agriculture. Cotton, mulberries, castor beans, jute, coffee, tea, coco-

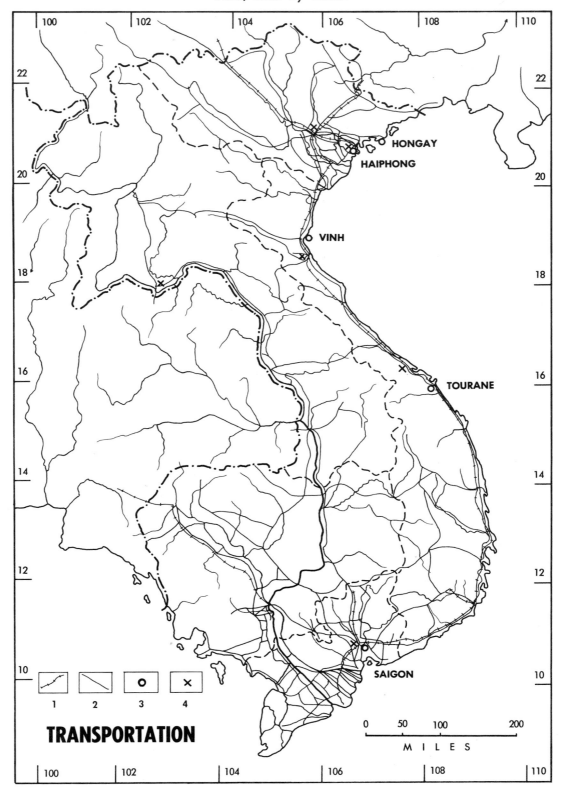

Fig. 71. Transportation facilities in Indochina: (1) rail lines; (2) motorable roads, Mekong Valley and some upland roads being impassable in rainy seasons; (3) chief ports; (4) chief civil airports.

nut, sugar cane, lac, ramie, kapok, tung, rice, and rubber, all have been tried within the last 75 years in an effort to match the plantation agriculture of Malaya, Ceylon, and the Indies. Only rubber has been at all successful, it today ranking third in crop acreages with a total of about 325,000 acres. Rubber production has slowly increased until today it more than supplies the French home market, and an increasing volume is going elsewhere abroad. French-owned rice "plantations" were established in the new lands of the Mekong Delta, but in the main these have become absentee holdings farmed by native tenants and no longer are true plantations. The first four crops mentioned are no longer grown on plantations at all, having totally failed in the hands of French plantation operators, who frequently came out from France inexperienced in the ways of tropical agriculture but hoping to become wealthy. Coffee, tea, coconut, and sugar cane are today grown on a few plantations to the amount of a few thousand acres each, but none has become a real success. Lac, ramie, kapok, and tung, all have been tried on small plantations in recent years, and the final success or failure cannot yet be determined, but the acreage of none amounts to more than a few hundreds or thousands of acres.

The development of French-owned agricultural enterprise has been assisted by land laws very favorable to French citizens, whereas other non-citizens of Indochina are prevented from acquiring land. Some of these plantation efforts were located in the southern uplands, though most efforts have chosen the better soils of the Mekong Delta margins. The rubber plantations are located in the edges of the uplands, about at the climatic margins for rubber trees. Though inexperience has been a cause for the small success of French-operated commercial agriculture, other factors have been the failure to adjust homeland import tariffs, the attempts to turn Indochina into a supplier of raw materials for the homeland, and the excessive effort to exploit native labor and land resources.

Late in the nineteenth century industrialization efforts began. Many starts have been made in mining, but only that in anthracite coal has been really successful. See Fig. 70. The coal is well located near the sea just north of the Tonking delta, and an increasing annual production reached 2,600,000 tons in 1939. Soft coal is found at several points in Tonking, and it is mined in small amounts. Tin, lead, zinc, tungsten, manganese, chromium, antimony, iron, gold, bauxite, graphite, phosphates, and precious stones complete the list of known mineral resources. Petroleum has not yet been found. The mineral deposits are widely scattered, but the Tonking uplands form the chief mineral-ized region. Native and Chinese miners have produced small amounts of most products over many centuries, but the modern French record is very irregular, production, except for coal, varying greatly from year to year. Though admittedly costly, most mining efforts have failed through bogus stock, flotation schemes. In good years perhaps 50,000 native and Chinese miners are employed in the mines, which are almost entirely French owned.

Other forms of industrialization have developed slowly, handicapped by the lack of native labor skills and by the French policy of not favoring colonial development of manufactures in competition with home industry. Cement manufacturing is probably the most successful, producing close to 300,000 tons per year, with ample markets in Indochina and the whole of the Orient. Brick and ceramic products are a related type of product which has increased in production in recent years. Small ships and boats, chemicals, glass, paints, soap, matches, paper, textiles, rubber goods, firecrackers, alcoholic and other beverages, and a few other products are being produced in factories located in Hanoi, Haiphong, Hue, Tourane, Saigon, and a few other cities and towns. The largest share of industrial output occurs in Tonking. Steam electric power plants are becoming widely scattered, and the larger towns and cities are electrified. The larger factories are French owned, but native participation in ownership and management is increasing.

In agricultural processing the milling of rice, of course, is the leading activity, largely in the hands of Chinese. Milling is widely scattered, but Cholon does more than any other center, since it is the chief port for export rice. Sugar, tobacco, vegetable oils, rubber, lac, and leather are the chief products processed in native and French-owned plants. The wood industries are scattered and not very significant as industrial performance, since Indochina no longer possesses woods sufficiently valuable for large-scale production or export. Teak, if it ever was voluminous, is almost entirely lacking in the remaining forests. Bamboo, building lumber, firewood, and charcoal are chiefly products of native handicraft operations, locally produced and distributed. Beyond the labor employed in mining not more than 100,000 laborers are engaged in activities that can properly be labeled industrial.

Though portions of present-day Indochina actively engaged in international trade at various times in the past, these regions were not very active in trade in the early nineteenth century. Chinese, Indonesians, and others carried on some coasting trade, particularly with Tonking and northern Annam ports, but not many of the natives of these regions were themselves active

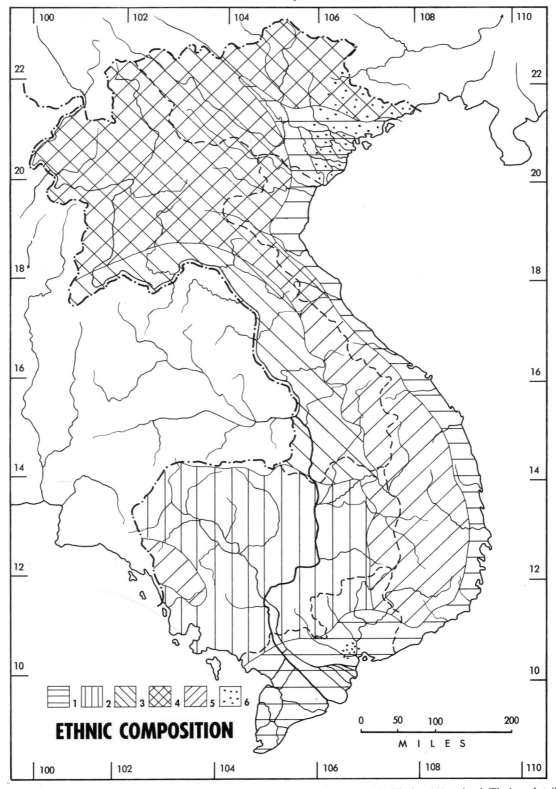

ETHNIC COMPOSITION

Fig. 72. Ethnic patterns of Indochina: (1) Annamese peoples; (2) Khmers; (3) Thais; (4) mixed Thai and tribal peoples; (5) mixed remnant tribal peoples; (6) the Chinese are concentrated in cities, towns, or coal mines.

traders. The Europeans who had begun to participate in the regional and international trade of the Orient in the sixteenth and seventeenth centuries did not have much success in Indochina. During much of the eighteenth century Tonking and Annam ports were frequently visited by oriental traders, but the Europeans still had little success along this coast.

After the French took over the region they began to develop trade between Indochina and France, drawing raw materials and agricultural products out and shipping manufactured consumers' goods inward. Slowly this volume of trade has increased between Indochina and France, but the trade with other occidental countries has not grown large. Some of the native products developed production patterns too large for the French homeland market, but restrictive control of trade has caused production to decline. The pepper trade is an illustration of this, and production now is about balanced at the figure needed to supply the native and French market. Other products such as coal, cement, and rice find their export market primarily within the Orient. Recent liberalization of policy is permitting such commodities as rubber to achieve its own level of production by competing in foreign markets after supplying the French home need.

The current economy of Indochina is dominated by French financial control, for most of the productive capital operating the economy is French. The Chinese elements and interests correspond to what often is termed the middle-class portion of a society, though native elements increasingly participate. Through the development of modern trade patterns native farmers are increasingly producing commodities for a commercial market on a money basis. At the present time rice is the leading export commodity, followed by rubber, maize, coal, fish, tin, pepper, and cement. The import trade finds cotton and rayon textile products in the first position, followed by machinery and metal manufacturing, petroleum, processed foods, iron and steel, and sacking fibers. Practically all foreign trade is carried on through the ports of Saigon and Haiphong. Tourane and Ben Thuy are but minor ports and Hongay is a coal export port only.

THE PROBLEMS OF INDOCHINA TODAY

Indochina was the last major occidental colonial holding carved out of the Orient, and perhaps the least skillfully. It now forms one of the last problems for solution in the long history of occidental imperialism and, because of its complications, is one of the most difficult to solve. This is not merely a case of integrating French interests with those of a maturing nationalism of one large culture group. Several culture groups are involved, and the issue is the solution of the problems within the framework of the democratic world or within the expanding framework of a Soviet world. France and Indochina could, themselves, finally arrange the details of cultural and political independence upon some basis satisfactory to the several culture groups involved, but France alone cannot direct or effectively influence the choice of culture worlds to which Indochina will adhere when there is active participation by strong forces interested in achieving a choice of the Soviet world pattern. France already has spent far more in manpower and resources on Indochina since World War II than she ever received in profit from her colony, but she has not the economic or political strength to deal both with internal problems of the country and with the forces of Soviet imperialism now so active in Indochina. The solution of the whole group of problems is bound up together, and, as this section is written, the member nations of the free world have not yet taken on their just share of the task.

To gain perspective on the whole complex problem it is necessary to mention the internal problems first. It seems that the area that we label Indochina has always been the home of diverse human groups and cultures. Here is the most critical meeting ground in the Orient of diverse peoples and of the influences of the Indian and Chinese culture worlds. France willfully but unwittingly chose to make of this shatter zone one political unit in the modern world. If she had not done so others would have tried to cope with the integration of region and culture. France did not easily come to frame a satisfactory administrative grouping of peoples and regions, and beyond doubt her early pattern did little to integrate the whole, but the diversity was not of French making.

The delimitation of five political states had simple bases in physical geography and culture history, as well as in the chronology of conquest. Of these Cambodia combined both physical and cultural elements. That the Annamese were spread from the Tonking Delta to the Mekong Delta did not integrate the area, for both the physical and cultural history of the area pointed to a threefold division, however poor these limits may be. Tonking, Annam, and Cochin-China, as French political units, only furthered the old separatisms. The rest of the country contains no natural unity, physically or culturally, and placing it in one unit was a negative action. To set up fully effective administrative regions in Indochina is a difficult matter. The Annamese and Khmers are lowlanders, the Thai prefer lowlands but live also in hill country, the Miao and others are mountain peoples in present culture

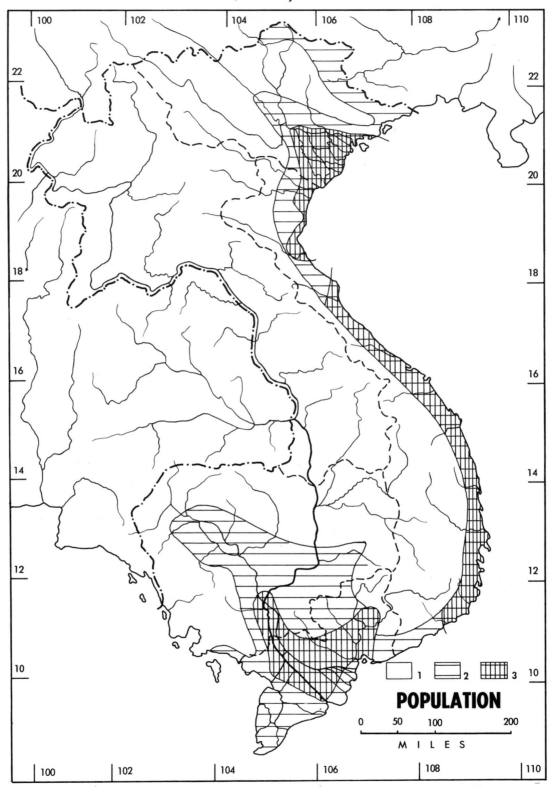

Fig. 73. Relative distribution of population: (1) under 25 people per square mile; (2) 25–200 people per square mile; (3) over 200 people per square mile, with some small regionally dense clusters omitted. Map, not based upon real census data, shows relative distribution only.

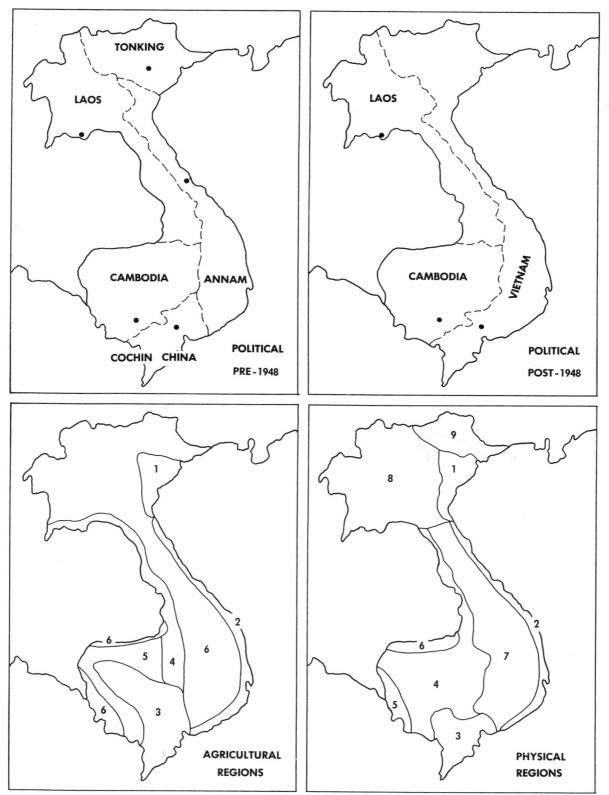

Fig. 74. Regionalism of Indochina. *Upper left:* the five political regions created by French colonialism. Capitals were: Cambodia, Pnom Penh; Cochin China, Saigon; Annam, Hue; Tonking, Hanoi, functioning also as national capital; Laos, Ventiane. *Upper right:* present Associated States of Indochina. Capitals are: Cambodia, Pnom Penh; Vietnam, Saigon; Laos, Ventiane. *Lower left:* indigenous agricultural regions: (1) Tonking delta subsistence regions; (2) Annam coastal region; (3) Mekong-Tonle Sap commercial crop region; (4) Mekong Valley lowland region; (5) Cambodian lowland subsistence region; (6) upland shifting agricultural region. *Lower right:* possible physical regions: (1) Tonking Delta; (2) Annam coastal plain; (3) Mekong Delta; (4) Mekong Valley-Cambodian lowland; (5) Cardamom Hills; (6) Phanom Dongrak; (7) Annamite Cordillera; (8) Laos plateaus and mountains; (9) Northeast Tonking Hills.

habit, but administrative regions cannot be simple ethnic regions. There are grounds for laying out nine major physical regions, six rather different regions of indigenous agricultural economy, perhaps six ethnic regions of still different extent, plus several other kinds of significant regions. None of these agree with the five past political regions or with the three new political regions, Vietnam, Cambodia, and Laos.

One of the chief problems is the severe pressures of men upon the land in the Tonking Delta and northern Annam. An accompanying map of population distribution too greatly generalizes the facts. Here fragmentation of farmland and the very high physiologic density of population make a rising standard of living almost impossible. In recent decades many of the rice farmers of the delta have not been able to afford to eat rice. Population growth here is outstripping productive returns from the environment. If public health programs could free the hill country of its malarial infestation, there are land resources surrounding the lowland, but there would remain the cultural habit of the Annamese as a lowlander. Resettlement of the many open lands of the hill country, the south, the Mekong Valley, and of Cambodia raises issues not only of economic development but of cultural integration.

There are now some 27,000,000 people in Indochina. Of these over 20,000,000 are Annamese, perhaps some 3,000,000 are Khmers, 1,500,000 are Thais, 350,000 are ethnically and culturally Chinese, 100,000 are Chams, and the rest are hill and mountain peoples of many ethnic-linguistic-culture mixtures. All of them except the Chinese are rural peoples in culture habit. Increase in population adds some 400,000 people per year, chiefly Annamese. Urbanism encompasses about 5 per cent of the total population, whereas the rest are hamlet, village, and market-town dwellers. A small share of the lowlands carries a heavy majority of the population and the uplands do not produce an adequate share of economic support for the whole population. To date not all of the lowlands are occupied, and, though they have not easily been open to the Annamese, the pressures of population in Annamese lands will cause steady Annamese colonization throughout the lowlands.

The need is great for an agricultural revolution in Indochina in both lowlands and uplands similar to that which has taken place in the United States in the last century. There is also a need for a modest growth of industrialism, but the economic problems of the country cannot be solved by industrialization alone as an American often uses the term. What really is needed is means to lift the level of economic produc-

tivity for a rural people so that an increasing standard of living may be achieved. Foremost is the need to lift agricultural productivity from almost the lowest average in the Orient, coupled with such development of urban centralized and rural decentralized industry as will restore the auxiliary occupations and incomes of all segments of the population.

The political-cultural patterns of regionalism now being attempted by the French in their new Associated States of Indochina make sense in many ways. They are long overdue, but their development does not abolish all problems with the drawing of new political lines. The realistic setting up of three spheres of political-cultural operation, with the recognition of Annamese, Cambodian, and Thai-Lao unities is an advance, though it will face the problem of the spread of Annamese throughout all lowland areas. With these new patterns must go effective land reform, economic reform, extended education, progressive public health programs aimed at preventing rather than curing, and the furthering of native direction of their own affairs. Were the French free to develop these matters, perhaps their own readiness to do so could result in modernization within the next generation which would materially lift the standards of living and the levels of culture.

The external aspect of the situation indicates that the French alone are not in a position to carry out the above changes. Born out of cultural unrest well before World War II was an Annamese nationalism not much shared by the other culture groups. Out of Japanese occupation and the fumbling of immediate postwar developments crystallized a large anti-French feeling among all groups, but particularly among the Annamese and Chinese. With Soviet sponsorship this unrest grew into a communist movement which threatens to destroy all postwar French development and to orient Indochina toward the Soviet world. Soviet sponsorship continues in the form of military and political aid expressed chiefly through communist China. This the French have been struggling against without either sufficient statesman-like leadership or military support from the democratic world. It is a French problem only in detail; it is a world problem in sum total. As this is written the issues are joined, but the solution is not yet in sight. In 1950–1951 it appeared to be a losing battle, but by 1952–1953 there came signs that perhaps the struggle was not yet lost. The political negotiations of leading United Nations Foreign Ministers, in 1954, find both France and Indochina almost bystanders as Democracy and Communism grapple for the upper hand in a world-wide struggle that involves such other distant and unlike regions as

Germany, Korea, and China. If the democratic world acts energetically and in good faith upon opportunity, it can both maintain a region and assist in modernization. So much headway has been gained by communist forces that it will take time to eliminate both the cultural scars and the material destruction even if the democratic world does at last discharge its obligation to keep Indochina within its own cultural world.

ADDENDUM. Between proofreading and printing these pages, there came a kind of respite in Indochina. The French too anxiously sought cessation of a long war they could not win by themselves. The rest of the Free World views the settlement with misgiving, whereas Communism views it with anticipation. In a British analogy, a long inning of cricket has been called and the sides have adjourned for tea. During the lull the French will lick their wounds and ponder how to hold the rest of Indochina. The Communists will organize their new territory and plan to win the rest of the country. Another round at bat in the inning will come sooner or later. The game certainly is not over, for the present lines of demarcation correspond to nothing in either the physical or cultural landscapes— they are but temporary lines created to facilitate the adjournment. The major problem remains just what it was prior to adjournment, a contest between the Free World and Communism.

One may wonder how the Annamese and Laotian small farmers felt on August 12, 1954, if they yet knew, though no one asked them. Their own spokesmen had received short shrift at the conference making the settlement. It had previously been evident that many Annamese were unhappy enough under the French to make them uncooperative. Such action in effect lent passive support to Communism; ignorance of life under Communism has betrayed those whose homes were north and east of the demarcation lines. The will of the peoples of Indochina can only be expressed slowly and cumbersomely, for the institutions that express public opinion are but poorly developed. The full independence granted the Associated States just prior to the settlement may galvanize energy among a share of the population in each state; the creation of a Communist state in northern Indochina certainly will produce action in that region. There remains much uncertainty and no unity of working plan. The cause of the Free World has been damaged by the action of the French in handing over a large region and perhaps 12,000,000 people to Communism. To whom can the peoples of Indochina now turn for help, and on whom can they rely? Unless Democracy translates itself down to the local level of a better life for the village farmer, further passive support will accrue to the Communists who promise improvement in things that farmers can understand. The settlement turns the tide again in favor of Communism.

The current lines of demarcation set up a fourth state of Viet Minh and alter the political regionalism indicated in Fig. 74. Its southern line is the seventeenth parallel of latitude across Vietnam. Its western line follows the Laos-Vietnam boundary north to the eastern bulge of Laos, cuts across the bulge, and then swings northwest to the China boundary. Two portions of Laos are therefore lopped off and joined to the northern part of Vietnam to create the new state. In the terms of the unhappy settlement are provisions for a supervisory commission, for the regrouping of troops, for resettlement of civilians, for military alliances for Laos and for Cambodia, but not for Vietnam, and for elections in July, 1956, to choose for the future. These terms give Communism a fertile field in which to mature a program to win all of Indochina, but they also provide some small bits of ground on which the Free World may grow Democracy, if it can still arrange a realistic planting program.

Dien-bien-Phu

FIN.

CHAPTER
19

Malaya: Malay, British, and Chinese

THE PENINSULAR ENVIRONMENT AND ITS EARLIEST OCCUPANCE

As a land appendage of Asia the lower portion of the Malay Peninsula forms an environment different from any of the other regional units and political states of the Orient. It is not a large region, being little larger than Pennsylvania and less than a third the size of California. It is ill arranged as to uplands and lowlands to serve as a core area for the regional development of a culture group, for its uplands are scattered and partly discontinuous, and its lowlands are strung out as coastal plains or as irregular strips of lowland around and between the upland masses. Many of the interior lowlands are poorly drained and were earlier rather unhealthy. It is a wet landscape, with many stream channels that carry more water than their length and breadth would suggest, but there is no one great river valley, and no large delta of dominant area and utility. Its chief historic function has been to serve as a landfall for navigators on the Bay of Bengal and the South China Sea.

Malaya is a region naturally covered with heavy forest which repelled early human occupance and which inhibits modern use of the land. At the end of the long peninsula Malaya has not been highly modified by waves of shifting cultivators or by immigrant groups of vigorous sedentary farming peoples until the coming of the British plantation farmer of the late nineteenth century. The plant cover repeatedly was able to spread back over the small scars intermittently produced by occupation of small coastal pockets. Even after a century of modern exploitation of soil and minerals only about a third of the total surface has been laid open to use. The forest only in small degree has been exploited for its own resources, both in the past and today.

Though today interior Malaya is still inhabited by perhaps 50,000 refugee jungle peoples of all sorts, comprising several groups of varied ethnic composition, few peoples chose the interior over the coastal fringes and estuarine reaches of the rivers. Though the earliest immigrants certainly were land travelers, they most probably preferred the coastal fringes even then. Among the simpler culture groups, there still were Negrito remnants in the late nineteenth century. There are small groups of mixed peoples, linguistically related to the Mon-Khmer peoples, and a few proto-Malays, but the chief population of Malaya has been composed of Chinese and Malays. The Malays for many centuries have been a people preferring boats, fishing, shore-fringe crop lands, and the riverine and coastal fringes to the interior areas and ways of life. Only in recent centuries have the Malays spread inland, penetrating those river lowlands where they could follow a living pattern related to that of the coastal zone. Sometime before the coming of the European, Sumatran Menangkabaus settled in Negri Sembilan on the west coast, intermarrying with the local Malay population. During the eighteenth century Celebes Bugis, a navigating, piratical people, came into Malaya, scattering out along the coastal settlements.

The Mon and Khmer peoples who spread across Burma, Thailand, and Indochina apparently never came down into Malaya. When the first Indians came across the Bay of Bengal their chief zone of contact lay north of Malaya, in the Kra Isthmus. The shallow sea currents around Malaya, affected both by the seasonal monsoon winds and by tidal irregularities, plus the vagaries of the monsoon winds themselves, made trader navigation around the peninsula difficult in the centuries before the Christian era. When Indian contact did slowly touch the lower part of the peninsula it remained chiefly interested in ports as landfalls, or was concerned with tin mining. There was some colonial settlement by Indians, but Malaya then was lightly populated by mobile peoples and must have presented fewer opportunities than other lands touched by Indian contact. Though small port trading stations developed, with some claim to area control, it is doubtful if significant regional development of Indian-controlled principalities ever evolved in Malaya.

The daily living pattern of the early Malays or other inhabitants of Malaya shared in the common tradition of the southern Orient. It revolved around the use of aquatic resources, lowland fruits, and such root crops as the yams and the taros. Rice appears to have been a late introduction, perhaps coming out of Indian contact. Mobile living patterns related to boats and the coastal waterways, and riverine and coastal habitation in scattered clusters became the tradition among the Malays. Though Malaya presented no large rich lowland as did Burma, a small and mobile population possessed an ample set of resources for a simple type of culture. In time Malay culture became somewhat Indianized, for Indian culture elements underlie the Moslem culture patterns of modern Malays.

SEA TRADING, PORTS, AND PIRACY

As Indian contact expanded in Burmo-Malaya and the Indies in the early centuries of the Christian era, there gradually appeared two centers of regional focus. That of Burma, Thailand, and Indochina already has been dealt with, and that of the western Indies will be discussed in the next chapter. Malaya, lying between these two centers, became a site for way stations and landfall ports in the early patterns of sea travel and interregional trade. The local Malays probably participated but little in this trade to begin with, whereas Indians and Arabs were numerous, along with some Mons, Khmers, Sumatrans, and Javanese. There were many river mouths and island-protected harbors on the west coast of Malaya that served as way stations as knowledge of navigation developed and sea trade grew more common.

As the evolving political and military strength of the several focal centers developed in Burma, in the Mekong Delta, in Sumatra, and in Java, Malaya constituted a no-man's land between these two spheres of influence. Malayan ports began to be used by the free trader from outside realms and by those in political disfavor in any one region. There gradually evolved the art of piracy, with Malaya providing home ports for many of those preying upon trade in these waters. In this some of the Malays may well have joined. None of these ports ever grew large, for the patterns of power were personal and subject to constant alteration, based upon through trade rather than upon local population and resources.

As Sumatran and Javanese principalities grew into political states, built partly upon the basis of sea power themselves, each tried to control Malaya, but the Burmese and Cambodian states rarely could exercise control so far south. Locations of some of the early Indonesian sea-states are debatable, and one school of thought holds the idea that no separate, long-lived political state was ever organized on Malaya, whereas the evidence may also point to the existence of several small states successively located on Malaya. The Indonesian state Sri Vijaya exerted some control over Malaya for several centuries, and Madjapahit for a shorter period exerted some control also. It is obvious that there were many shifting patterns of regional control as ephemeral sea-states rose and fell. Piracy based upon Malayan ports was a strong element in this shifting pattern. Few of the regional combinations on Malaya ever developed hinterland areas, settled agricultural landscapes, or sedentary populations as land-using peoples.

This ephemeral pattern of occupation of Malayan coastal ports was concentrated chiefly on the west coast, largely because of the better weather and navigational conditions. The east coast suffers from high surf, adverse winds, and difficult navigational conditions during the months of the winter monsoon, whereas the west coast is somewhat protected by the reach of Sumatra. Though the little ports were busy trade centers, the ships were small, the cargoes never were large, and the sheer volume of trade was slight as compared with that of today. No extensive port facilities were ever required, such as are found in modern ports, and, therefore, none of the ports ever acquired extensive docks, warehouses, or buildings, and none of the ports ever grew into a large city.

A few Malayan products probably entered the interregional trade of the time. Tin was mined by many different peoples, a little alluvial gold was produced, a few forest products were extracted, but the total demand for these products was not great, and they led to no permanent development of settlements, dependent populations, or cultural landscapes. Today the small scars of tin mining are widely scattered; evidences of buildings are repeatedly unearthed, but the marks in the landscape were slight and easily overgrown by forest.

MOSLEMS, PORTUGUESE, DUTCH, AND BRITISH

The control over the western Indies and Malaya by the east Javanese sea-state of Madjapahit collapsed under the invasions of the Moslem Arabs and Indians in the fourteenth century. There followed a resurgence of autonomy among the ports and small regional entities of western Malaysia for, by this time, a considerable cultural individuality had developed among the peoples of this region. The Moslems were able to take over political and trade control of these port states in piecemeal fashion without an organized military conquest. This Moslem entry was not a politically unified movement but a series of independent ventures by relatively small groups of Indians and Arabs whose chief common possession was their Moslem religion. Militant effort organized small sultanates around the numerous ports and converted the Malays into Moslems. Many of these little port states were extended into the hinterlands sufficiently to incorporate the Malays into the political and cultural structure of the sultanates.

Though the levying of tribute upon passing ships and a form of piracy again became frequent in these waters, the Malayan ports became active way stations in an increasing trade pattern, with ships of almost every oriental country touching Malay ports. The decline of the Khmer state and the immaturity of Thai economy helped to cause the decline of the transpeninsular trade route, so that Malayan ports were now on the chief route. The tribute levies and piracy by Malayan port sultans did cause many ships to use the route around Sumatra, through the Strait of Sunda, avoiding the Strait of Malacca, but this was a variable detail in the main route.

Moslem initiative expanded trade and travel contact all through the southern Orient and, with the open-door Mongol policy in China, Chinese traders appeared in considerable numbers. Malaya reached a new peak in its trade activity, now being on one of the chief trade routes of the world, so that its ports were busy and knowledge of it spread far and wide. Not many of the products passing through its ports were either domestic exports or imports, for this was a transit trade and Malaya but a landfall en route. Nor were the Malays themselves the chief traders, but the quiet local population that supplied food, water, tools, labor, and services to the passing traders.

When the Portuguese arrived in Indian ports they soon learned of the importance of Malacca, which then perhaps was the foremost port of Malaya. Malacca appeared to dominate the trade route, and perhaps the stories led the Portuguese to think of it as a producing area also. If they were to monopolize the trade with Europe, control of Malayan ports was necessary. So, with a few ships and men they were able to take over port after port, and to turn each into a base in much the same way as Moslem traders before them. They did not expand areal control over Malaya, once they found it a non-productive region. They failed to convert the Moslem Malays to Christianity, and changed little of Malay life. The transit function of Malay ports continued much as before, but with a new set of traders participating from certain ports.

Somewhat later the Dutch attempted to break the Portuguese monopoly, seize what appeared to be the chief ports, control the trade routes, and use the transit ports, but they concerned themselves only casually with Malaya as a region. There also appeared British, French, Danish, and Swedish traders, all concerned with the same objective. The arrival of these competitive European traders added diverse elements to the traffic, increased the variety of shipping, added to the competitive struggle for control of ports, and complicated the life of the Malays, but did little to develop Malaya as a region. Chinese, Indonesians, Indians, Arabs, and varieties of Europeans all engaged in a competitive trade contest, with piracy, looting, trickery, naval warfare, and varying group alliances-of-the moment all techniques in the struggle. The Portuguese lost out fairly early, the French, Danes, Swedes, Chinese, and a few others gradually dropped out and avoided Malayan ports. The Indians, Indonesians, Arabs, Dutch, and British became the chief contestants. Some Moslem port sultans, as native regional rulers of the hinterlands, were able to profit from the contest, but the Malays as a whole, and Malaya as a region, were changed but little. The contest was long drawn out and, only in the 1820's, did the British finally oust the Dutch from control of the Malayan ports. The final agreement between the Dutch and the British recognized territoriality in the sense that Britain withdrew any claims to the ports in the Indies, and the Netherlands gave up claims to ports in Malaya. But this did not, as yet, mean that Britain began to exercise regional control over all of Malaya—the interest still lay in the ports and their value in trade with the East.

THE GROWTH OF A BRITISH COLONY

The island that we now label Singapore has sheltered waters behind it which served as base point for traders and pirates for centuries. Sir Stamford Raffles, in the 1820's, dreamed of a great port here, at the very apex of the Malay Peninsula, which could become the primary hub of all eastern trade. Modern Singapore, as city, port, guardian of the British sea routes, and present Crown Colony, has grown out of that dream, but in the 1820's it was still only a decadent village port. The British concentrated on a few spots,

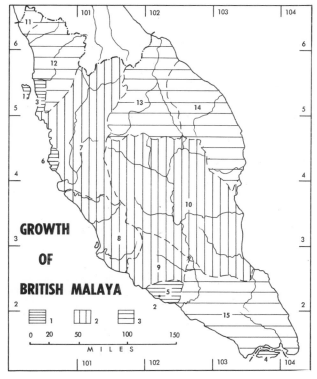

Fig. 75. Growth of British Malaya: (1) *Straits Settlements,* which date from: 1, Penang, 1786; 2, Malacca Port, 1795; 3, Province Wellesley, 1798; 4, Singapore, 1819; 5, Malacca territory, 1824; 6, Dindings, 1874; (2) *Federated States:* 7, Perak; 8, Selangor; 9, Negri Sembilan, all dating from 1874; 10, Pahang, dates from 1881; (3) *Non-Federated States:* 11, Perlis; 12, Kedah; 13, Kelantan; 14, Trengganu, all having been transferred by Thailand to Britain in 1909; 15, Johore, accepting status in 1910.

such as Singapore, Malacca, Port Dickson, Port Swettenham, Port Weld, and Penang, to use current British names. Singapore soon outdistanced the others, though Penang for some decades remained the base point of the British East India Company's administrative operations. Slowly, as settlements grew, and as food and raw-material needs increased, administrative problems led to the extension of police power, treaties with local sultans, and a growing concept of territorial domain. In the latter half of the nineteenth century British investment in tin mining and plantation agriculture began, and the need for territorial administration increased.

Since the frequented ports were on the west coast, economic development began here also and the growth in territorial administration focused upon the west coast. The chief ports and their immediate hinterlands were grouped into one pattern run by the British Colonial Office as the Straits Settlements, to which for convenience were joined such other stray British holdings as the Cocos-Keeling and Christmas Islands south of Sumatra. Nine Malay sultanate states were recognized, and with four of them Britain had treaties which led to a group termed Federated Malay States. Over these the British exercised considerable control, through devious administrative patterns, for these were chiefly the west coast states in which British tin mining and plantation agriculture were carried on. The remainder were grouped as the Unfederated Malay States, in which there were less British control and smaller economic investments. This triple administrative pattern kept Malaya disunited, kept regional development unequal, and kept it a kind of no-man's land still, for there was no such thing as Malayan citizenship.

The Moslem Malays, for the most part, during the period of increasing British territorial control and economic development remained a rural, unobtrusive people of agricultural-fishing economy, village dwellers along the coastal fringes, the estuarine lowlands, and at certain inland localities in which they could live their traditional life. Though many came to reside in the ports and cities and to provide domestic services and some labor, they were disinclined to become tin miners, plantation laborers, stevedores, and manual laborers. Throughout the centuries of European comment the Malays have been termed "lazy, indolent drones," the meaning being that they were not willing to do the menial work desired of them by the European. Consequently, as tin mining and plantation agriculture began, other labor had to be found, for the British, of course, would only manage and direct. Many Chinese traders had taken early advantage of the peaceful British ports and were willingly enlisted in tin mining, so that there began a steady influx of Chinese laborers. They were less efficient as plantation workers, being disinclined to remain on the job once they had accumulated sufficient resources to set up shopkeeping and trading enterprises. Indian laborers were brought in on term contracts, and proved more satisfactory than the Chinese.

As Indians and Chinese came into Malaya in increasing numbers, and as greater economic development took place, protection of the Malays became necessary. A land policy evolved that prohibited other than Malay ownership of rice land, but permitted the expansion of tin mining and plantation agriculture. Only slowly were Chinese and Indians allowed to own any kind of agricultural land, and there grew up considerable restriction upon both the Chinese and Indians. Both came to Malaya as temporary residents, the Chinese to go home when they felt rich enough, the Indians normally at the termination of their contracts. Neither Chinese nor Indians participated in government but remained separate cultural groups, and both thought of Malaya only in terms of economic opportunity. Gradually a few Indians and many Chinese became second- and third-generation residents of Malaya but retained their cultural ties to their homelands.

The British developed such roads, railroads, ports, and telecommunications as were requisite for economic development. Government effort in geological survey, agriculture, port development, the postal service, and public health was carried out as necessary. Some education of the Malays was slowly provided for, but seldom for the Chinese and Indians, who came to support their own schools, furthering their own cultural traditions. Malaya became one of the most productive British holdings, but never was administered as one country for its own sake. Gradual changes in government patterns came about, but before World War II no real integration of the threefold administration of Malay was made. By World War II the 2,500,-000 Chinese exceeded the Malay population of 2,100,-000, the Indian total stood close to 600,000, the Indonesian population at about 40,000, and the occidental population at about 30,000. Yet there was no integration of peoples, region, and culture, and the British held administrative control with only incomplete participation by the Malays.

THE MALAYAN FEDERATION

During and just after World War II it became obvious to the British that they had failed to integrate the Chinese, Indians, and Malays into the culture and social structure of Malaya. The Chinese and Indians had been given neither responsibility nor opportunity to consider themselves citizens of Malaya. The Chinese controlled most of the non-British wealth of the country, and dominated retail domestic trade and much of the foreign trade. They had supported Nationalist China, but after 1949 their allegiance began to waver. And in 1950 many Chinese held the attitude that they would inherit Malaya when the British lost control of the region in a few short years. The Indians presented no political or economic threat. The Malays had become aware of the Chinese problem and finally were

developing a spirit of social and political nationalism. The present Federation of Malaya plan was put into effect in 1948, but by 1951 there was serious question whether it would succeed, since there still were severe restrictions upon both Chinese and Indians.

During 1952–1953 far-reaching changes in procedures concerning citizenship, education, resettlement, and land tenure promised well for social integration and the cultural development of one Malaya. Several hundred village and town communities totaling over a half million people have been moved from shacky, ill-provided sites to newly built and planned settlements, each provided with schools, dispensaries, shopping areas, truck-garden zones, and other local facilities. New land laws permit the long-term lease of land by all nationalities. This has been a step taken to control communist guerrilla activity, but it will have long-term constructive results. Primarily affected have been Chinese residents who, in the absence of most civic privileges, have shown no civic-mindedness toward Malaya and have devoted little of their capital resources to the public good. It has been the Chinese community that has tacitly supported communist activity.

The schools of Malaya have been chiefly built, financed, and staffed for the Malays, Chinese, and Indians as separate communities, without attempting either to provide for all children or to integrate the educational aims of the separate nationalities. Increased facilities provided education for about 850,000 children in the Federation and Singapore in 1952. Action is being taken to create a single public school system for the country as a whole. Radio programs in the public schools, community radio receiving sets, vigorous adult education programs, and other steps are being taken toward the creation of a common social community.

The population of Malaya is increasing at almost 200,000 per year, with the highest rates of increase among the Malays. The population is a young population and its rate of future increase will be high. The cessation of Chinese immigration is tending to stabilize the Chinese community as long-term residents, though within itself it shows a high rate of natural increase. The population of the Federation of Malaya in mid-1952 was estimated at 5,500,000, composed of about 2,750,000 Malays, 2,150,000 Chinese, 590,000 Indians, and a few thousand other peoples. Singapore's population totaled close to 1,100,000 at the same date, composed of just over 800,000 Chinese, 150,000 Malays, 80,000 Indians, and a few thousand others. Included under Malays are an indeterminate number of people born in the Indies but not easily separated from Malayan Malays. This yields a total population for all of Malaya of close to 6,600,000, whose distribution is graphically represented in Fig. 80. With not more than 1,100,000 acres of food-producing agricultural land, which provides less than half the total food requirements, Malaya presents the outstanding oriental example of a region which has departed from the traditional oriental self-subsistence economy.

Under the Federation of Malaya plan Kuala Lumpur became the federal capital in 1948. In 1951 this city had a population of about 180,000 people. The Federation consists of the nine Malay states, each under its own ruler, and the two former Straits Settlements of Penang and Malacca. The Straits Settlement of Dindings reverted to Perak in 1935. Singapore Island is a Crown Colony and is not included in the Federation. Names and boundaries of the states are shown on the map of ethnic composition. A variety of legislative and administrative patterns now are being set up to develop self-government at all levels. Those people born in Malaya now are citizens, and residents born elsewhere may become citizens. At the end of 1952 about 4,000,000 people had been designated citizens. Malaya has been a land simultaneously occupied by several economic and social communities resident in different portions of the country. Eventually effective mechanisms will appear to further the integration of people, government, and culture. At present Malaya remains the one populous and advanced portion of the oriental world still in colonial status, but if the present attempt at cultural integration is effective Malaya will graduate out of this colonial status in the not too distant future.

NATIVE LIFE AND ECONOMY

Three main sources of support are important in the traditional economy of the Malay: fishing, rice cultivation, and the mixed jungle garden. As the Malay population has markedly increased since the advent of British control, this traditional economy has both continued and expanded in its productivity. The Malay eats a large amount of fish products in many forms, and fishery products are secured from all available waters. Today the Malay provides fish for the Chinese and Indian populations, as well as for himself, so that fishing continues to be an important Malay occupation. The large increase in Malay and alien population has created a large and steady market, and many Malay families derive their chief cash income from fishing.

British land policy restricted ownership of developed rice lands to Malays, so that today the Malay is the rice farmer of the country. The total acreage amounts

to over 900,000 at present. The yield provides only about a third of the total rice consumed in Malaya, but despite this shortage the acreage is only slowly rising. The ricefields provide the one open landscape of the country, for trees are not grown along field margins, settlement avoids the field areas, and most of the other agriculture of the country involves trees and shrubs.

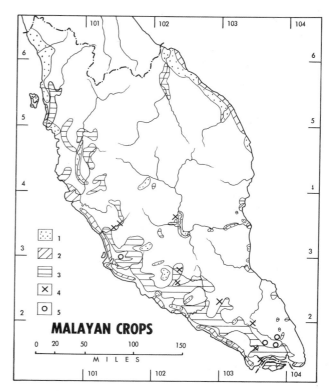

Fig. 76. Chief crops of Malaya: (1) main rice-growing regions; (2) chief solid plantings of coconut; (3) chief solid plantings of rubber; (4) areas of oil-palm plantings; (5) primary pineapple plantings.

Aside from rice planting the Malay is no real farmer in the modern technical sense—his jungle gardens are chaotic plantings of coconut and areca palms, coffee, bananas, durians, jackfruit, rambutans, mangosteens, and a few other fruits, plus tangled patches of taro, yams, manioc, pepper, gourds, sugar cane, onions, and a few other vegetables. This chaotic and tangled planting pattern is hard on the statistician, and it does not make for the ready supplying of town and city markets in large volume. For the Malay it was and is sufficient, and it is also true that jungle gardens of this sort are in far better ecologic balance in this moist and hot climate than are the orderly, weed-free, massed plantings of the occidental. Plantation agriculture in Malaya has abandoned its beautifully tailored appearance of the earlier years for a little more free growth of ground cover to maintain humus content and prevent soil erosion. Perhaps some 350,000 acres are devoted to these gardens, aside from the acreage of coconut, rubber, and other commercial crops which now also make up a part of Malay economy.

The Malay by preference lives in rural clusters of homes, each separated and screened by plantings. Originally these clusters of homes were just that, there being no shops of any kind, but the larger and more accessible clusters today are more village-like, and many of them have a shop or two. The pile-built house is almost standard, but there are regional patterns of design and decoration. To supplement his living pattern a variety of handicrafts were traditional until occidental machine goods and Chinese artisans came into Malaya in volume and numbers. Forest products such as rattans, gums, resins, and special woods have always been gathered and sold in small volumes. Gold and tin were mined in small amounts for sale in the past, and some Malay activity in both products remains in the economy today. Cattle, buffalo, fowls, and pigs were kept in small numbers by the Malay, the cattle and buffalo chiefly for ricefield cultivation and local land transport. After becoming a Moslem the Malay largely gave up pig raising. The annual dollar income of the Malay has never been large, but his self-sufficient pattern of living required no large income.

The Malay is not the indolent drone described by so many occidentals, but his pattern of living did not require endless labor. And in the centuries of piracy, despotic local rule by Indian and Moslem rajas and sultans, and competitive struggle by all manner of aliens, the Malay often found himself heavily taxed on any surplus commercial commodity. There constantly was a deterrent to labor and production beyond that needed for a subsistence economy. And in the modern period, when he has faced the competition of the money-zealous Chinese and occidental, he has been at the disadvantage common to every rural people practicing a subsistence economy.

Since 1918 the Malay has taken to planting rubber and coconut in small holdings for commercial production. He has gone into the cities and towns where British administration saved him some of the exacting taxation of his own native rulers, serving in domestic service, small trading, fishing, and similar occupations. His patterns of living have grown somewhat more complex as he has been surrounded by new peoples with new cultures. There are many gradations in living standards, from the rich sultan to the poorest

fishing villager, but the majority of the Malays live a simple life, on a relatively low annual money income. Under protective British policy the Malays have not been dispossessed of their lands or their traditional occupations, but education and changing opportunities are affecting the way of life of a large share of the Malay population.

COMMERCIAL ECONOMY

Tin mining is a key activity in Malaya's highly productive economy. Tin is a more valuable product

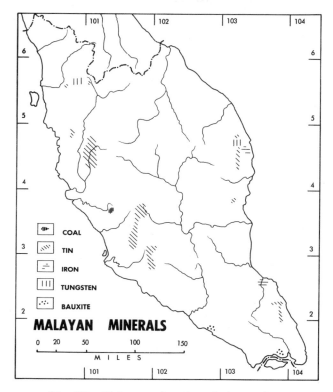

Fig. 77. Malayan mineral-producing regions.

per ton than most of the non-precious minerals, so that the 40,000–80,000 tons mined annually produce for Malaya a large financial return. Almost entirely an export product Malayan tin is an important item to British investment in Malaya. Alluvial tin ores are widely scattered around the western foothill margins where most of the mining has so far been done. Modern alluvial mining techniques severely scar the surface and produce a blighted landscape, so that modern mining is making permanent impressions upon western Malaya. Large-scale mining began during the nineteenth century, and steadily increased in importance until Malaya became one of the world's chief sources of tin. The ores first were exported to Britain for smelting, but local smelting has increased in importance, and now a share of the Burmese, Thai, and Indies' ores are also smelted in Malayan refineries. Earlier mining used simple machinery and much hand labor, which was contributed largely by the Chinese. Increasing mechanization has occurred, though the wartime destruction of equipment brought a temporary resurgence of simpler techniques. In 1950–1953 there were between 600 and 800 companies operating. Early ownership was entirely British, but Chinese control has been increasing steadily. In 1950–1951 British-owned mines still produced more than half the tin mined. Some of the alluvial ore mines in local areas are close to exhaustion, but there still are fairly large reserves of alluvial ore in Malaya as a whole. Lode mining in the ore zones around the edges of the granitic uplands already has begun and will increase in time.

Gradually other minerals have been produced in Malaya also. Soft coal good enough for steam power has been used for the railways, tin smelters, generation of electricity, and in various other industrial operations. Coal is mined in Selangor only. A traditional occupation in central and northern Malaya is gold mining, which continues as a small-operator pattern of alluvial mining, though there is now one corporate lode mine. Iron ore, bauxite, manganese, a little tungsten, some ilmenite, and a few other minor minerals are also produced. Iron ore, bauxite, and manganese mining was begun in the years before World War II along the east coast and in southern Malaya by Japanese companies operating concessions. Transport and shipping problems make iron and manganese mining difficult. Postwar renewal of mining in each of the three minerals is somewhat erratic, but each will probably appear in the mine output of Malaya in the future.

Plantation agriculture has grown to exceed tin mining in the commercial economy of Malaya. It began in a small way at Penang in the early nineteenth century when the British East India Company planted pepper, cloves, and nutmeg, hoping to become independent of the Dutch-controlled Moluccas. Depressed markets for pepper and plant diseases which destroyed the cloves and nutmeg trees disposed of the first efforts. But the plantation idea remained; during the nineteenth century there were plantings of sugar cane, coffee, gambier, cacao, tea, pineapple, and rubber. Sugar cane, tea, and coffee were minor successes for British plantation operators; pineapple succeeded but its cultivation passed into the hands of the Chinese; and cacao and gambier failed as plantation crops. Rubber, of course, succeeded better than all the others and has come to dominate the agriculture of Malaya.

First planted commercially in 1895, the acreage reached 40,000 in 1905, and has continuously expanded until in 1951 the total exceeded 3,300,000.

The first plantings were British, but, once the international rubber boom began, Malays and Chinese began small plantings in patches and small-field totals, and by 1951 the total small holdings stood at about 1,400,000 acres. The 1,950,000 acres of plantation rubber are divided among some 2,200 estates, almost half of which are Chinese in ownership. The 760 European estates possess over 1,400,000 acres and contain the best varieties of trees. Chinese estates and many of the small holdings are in old trees of poorer varieties, so long tapped that their productivity is declining. Replanting of much of the total rubber acreage is needed, but the process is fairly costly and is only slowly being carried out. Since 1947 total production figures have run over 600,000 tons per year, and rubber is the number-one source of income for Malaya. Plantations require a large working force which totals just under 300,000 at present. Though the plantings are permanent features of the Malayan landscape, the houses and settlements of workers in the past have been rather shacky and makeshift, since there is a tremendous turnover in the working force. Guerrilla slashing of rubber trees during 1950–1953 seriously damaged a few of the rubber plantings.

Coconut is a traditional crop, but in the late nineteenth century a considerable plantation acreage was set out in coconut along the west coast. The total acreage of plantations and small holdings, slightly lower than before World War II, is about 500,000, making coconut rank second among the commercial crops. Only a small share of the production among the Malays is used at home, and coconut for them is a cash crop.

Sugar cane, coffee, and tea succeeded as plantation crops but could not compete with rubber, so that the total acreages never grew large. By 1910 sugar ceased to be grown on plantations, and coffee has almost disappeared as a plantation crop, but both are widely spread items in the Malay jungle gardens at present. Tea still is cultivated on a few plantations, but the acreage is under 10,000. The oil palm, introduced from West Africa, was set out on plantations after 1917, and now totals about 100,000 acres, with future expansion probable. Pineapple covers about 25,000 acres of Chinese plantations in southern Malaya. Experiments are again being made with cacao, and with abaca, sisal, derris, and a few other plants, with an eye to diversified plantation agriculture. No pronounced efforts have been made with any of the native fruits on plantations.

Cash-crop agriculture among the Chinese shows up in several forms other than pineapple. The Chinese do almost all of the market gardening in Malaya, with small but intensively worked holdings around the cities and towns. Many Chinese, in the past, have grown manioc on rented or squatted lands for a few years in a variant of shifting cultivation. Sugar cane, the spices, tobacco, peanuts, and various other minor crops are often grown by Chinese farmers as a part of a commercial agriculture on a small scale. The Chinese also raise pigs, ducks, and chickens, in commercial proportions for the supply of Chinese and occidental urban populations, since these items are not now common and in ample supply among the Malays.

The total of commercial crops, on plantations and small holdings, is about 4,000,000 acres at the present time, and the figure will undoubtedly increase. These commercial plantings represent the chief source of national income for the population of Malaya. The plantation-working force is slightly less than 350,000, but a much larger number of people are represented by the Chinese, Malay, Indian, and Indonesian small holders, who variably contribute commercial crop yields to the total production figures. The per-capita income of Malaya currently ranks the highest in the Orient.

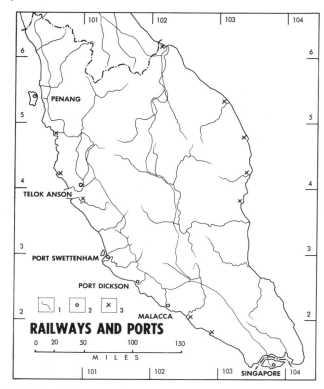

Fig. 79. Railways and ports: (1) rail lines; (2) major ports; (3) minor ports.

Forested Malaya traditionally supplied its own wood supplies and exported a small volume of exotic products. British nineteenth-century occupance considered the forests something to be cleared for agriculture, and most of the timber supply came to be imported. More recently forest utilization has begun to more than provide for domestic requirements, except for some of the special needs. Forest control and planned production of firewood, construction lumber, and export timber now is beginning to turn the forests of Malaya into an economic asset which undoubtedly can be expanded considerably in the future.

Ports naturally were the first features in which transportation development occurred. The rail system was laid out to connect the tin mines and growing plantations with the ports. Roads first were service lines for the railways, which also was true of telecommunications. All these features became located along the west coast of the peninsula. Slowly all forms of transportation have been expanded into other portions of the country, though there still is regional imbalance in the distribution of facilities. Singapore soon outdistanced the other ports of the country, to become the hub of all land and sea transport. Penang and Port Swettenham are the other important ports. Present government planning is taking large steps in these

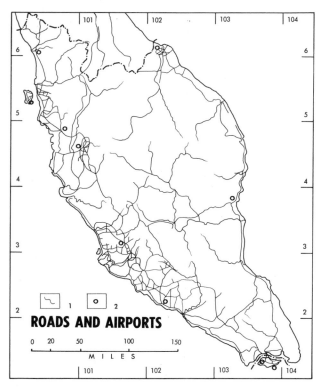

Fig. 78. Roads and civil airports: (1) main all-weather roads; (2) chief civil airports.

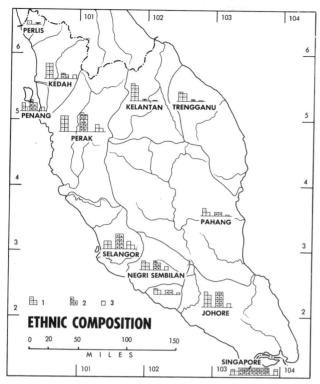

Fig. 80. Ethnic distributions in Malaya by states: (1) Malays; (2) Chinese; (3) Indians. Each square represents 50,000 people. As of June, 1951, about 85,000 occidentals and Indonesians are not represented.

matters, including radio communication. The installation of village community receiving sets on a wide scale is not only a feature of commercial economy but also one with far-reaching social and political implications.

Malaya was not developed with an eye to industrialization, but changing economic patterns have brought about a considerable amount of industrial processing. Tin smelting, vegetable-oil and rubber processing, and lumber milling, now important elements of Malayan economy, are scattered among the port towns of the west coast. Trade figures reveal that Malaya imports more copra, tin ore, and raw rubber than is exported. Malayan processing centers absorb a share of the raw-material production of Burma, Thailand, Indochina, and the Indies. Processed rubber, smelted tin, vegetable oil, and lumber products rank high in the export trade. Rubber and tin, by value, contribute about three fourths of the total income from trade. The political and statistical separation of the Federation of Malaya and the Crown Colony of Singapore make summary tabulation difficult, though in practice the two units are closely integrated. The concentration upon commercial agriculture and tin mining causes an unbalanced economy that requires a large import trade. Rice and other grain foods, meat products, clothing textiles, machinery and electrical supplies, and a variety of consumer goods swell the import trade. Singapore and Penang, as far eastern entrepôts, produce total returns that make the per-capita trade of Malaya rank among the highest in the Orient.

The Several Indies

A VARIETY OF ISLANDS AND THEIR FIRST SETTLERS

The ancestors of some of the culture groups now resident in the Indies doubtless walked overland to the regions they first occupied. When modern man first came to the Indies the present patterns of land and sea had not yet become established, for glacial ice bound up much of the sea water, and many of the present islands then were the uplands of old Sundaland and its eastern counterpart on the Sahul shelf. Land connection between Asia and Australia was not complete, but the deep water gaps were narrow and somehow a few culture groups made their way across them. As the last glacial period slackened rising sea water spread across Sundaland and the Sahul shelf, gradually creating hundreds and then thousands of islands. Sea currents developed in the shallow seas, coral growth spread, the present climatic regions developed, vegetation patterns regionally altered, and faunas developed their modern local regions. The major divisions between the floras and faunas of the Asiatic mainland and Australia remained effective, along Wallace's and Weber's lines, with man the chief transgressor across the primary environmental boundaries. The changes in local environments have been considerable, all within the time of occupance of modern man.

As this contemporary environment came into being change in the detailed outlines of islands and interiors continued to take place. Volcanism built up the uplands, created new islands, and blew landscapes apart. Estuarine lowlands became sedimented and shore lines changed, while coral reefs grew and created new islands. Mangrove and other wet-lowland plant associations appeared in new ecologic situations. Early man found some islands easily productive of food and other resources, whereas others were difficult to exploit above the simplest levels. Thus the contrasts between

Java and Borneo, Tidore and Billiton have been present throughout the occupance by modern man. Java always has been a productive island; Timor always one with severe limitations.

The very wet and heavily forested islands presented difficulties to early man as they do to contemporary man. The rather dry Lesser Sundas also presented handicaps to early culture groups lacking techniques of water control. Java and some of the islands just east of it probably presented a fairly optimum situation to early cultures. Moist enough to provide abundant plant cover and animal life, but too dry to permit dense rainforest, possessing rich volcanic soils and lowlands that were not fringed by deep marsh, Java must have been inviting to early man and provided him a good living. Such regions as the east coast of Sumatra and the south coast of Borneo possessed adequate aquatic resources in their marsh fringes but their forested interiors were handicaps.

This island world offered great variety, but it was a world separated into fragments, and it lacked a core region around which one great pattern of culture could mature into a land-based society. Its separation into pieces early led to great cultural diversity among its parts, but this very separation also stimulated sea traffic which in time bound many of the shores together as opposed to the regional isolation of the interiors of the larger islands.

It is generally held that the Negrito peoples were the earliest groups of modern man to arrive in the Indies, and their survival in such islands as Timor and New Guinea is a matter of simple survival in regions not heavily subject to the immigration and mixing of later peoples. Early Caucasoid wanderers perhaps were next on the scene, moving through the Indies and leaving their chief imprint in such groups as the Papuans, who now are generally held to be a mixture of Negrito and Caucasoid. Mixed peoples from mainland southeastern Asia came into the Indies in gradually moving pulsations, contributing such stocks as the Polynesians who largely moved through and out into the islands of the South Pacific. Early mixed Mongoloids appeared and spread rather widely, themselves mixing into previous groups. Increasingly the later peoples became more and more Mongoloid. As the present pattern of many islands took shape with the final adjustments of sea level, routes of travel shifted to the sea lanes, many islands became by-passed, and quite mixed populations developed along coastal fringes. It is popular to describe crudely concentric arrangement of the racial stocks, the earliest arrivals being in island interiors, and the last comers being the coastal peoples, but there is nothing simple in the regional disposition of the racial stocks, hundreds of languages, and innumerable local culture patterns that have evolved in the Indies.

No two islands are alike in race, language, or detailed culture patterns. Some small islands became homogeneous in population and culture, whereas other islands, both large and small, came to possess several racial mixtures, many languages, and a variety of local cultures. Later arrivals often penetrated the Indies less deeply than did earlier peoples. The Malays were among the last comers, themselves mixed but predominantly Mongoloid peoples, who spread as far into the Indies as the Lesser Sundas in their initial movement. The western Indies became the home region of the Malays for a considerable period of time. At some early date, however, Javanese, Sumatran, and south Borneo Malays took to the sea lanes in earnest, spreading west to Madagascar, into the Philippines, out into the Melanesian islands of the Pacific, along the China coast, and as far north as southern Japan. Sumatran Malays were late in occupying a part of the west coast of Malaya before the arrival of the European. Whereas New Guinea remained predominantly Negrito and Papuan, except for a thin fringe of coastal peoples, Java, Sumatra, and near-by islands became predominantly Malay. The central group of islands became a zone of highly mixed peoples. Here and there individual islands, or island clusters, preserved old stocks in varying numbers.

INDIAN COLONIZATION

The formal historiography of the Indies suggests that Indian settlers, traders, missionaries, and political rulers were scattered along the coasts of eastern Sumatra, northern Java, and southern Borneo in sufficient numbers by the first century of the Christian era so that one can speak of Indianized principalities and states.

All three of the islands mentioned seem to have been roughly parallel in the early development of Indian contacts, but it is apparent that the south coast of Java, the west coast of Sumatra, and the islands off the Sumatra west coast did not share in this early story. The Indian contacts seem derived from the same efforts that led to the growth of trade centers in the Mekong Delta and along the Indochina coast, this contact spreading out over the South China Sea to the shores of Borneo, Java, and Sumatra during several centuries before the Christian era. A long process of probing and exploring was required to find those areas of sufficient interest. Greater knowledge of sea currents, weather, and sailing possibilities eventually led to the establishment of direct routes from Indian ports to the Indies, but such direct contact at the start is doubtful.

The evolution of Indianized states in the Indies proceeded much as in Burma and Cambodia. The peoples to whom the Indians were first attracted were chiefly peoples of the littoral, who lived both from the land and the sea, and who themselves were rather mobile. Trade stations grew into regional centers, local control evolved into political power, and loose communities matured into principalities. These were scattered along the long shore lines of Borneo, north Java, and eastern Sumatra without much competitive overlapping or delimitation of areas of influence. Dependent upon sea travel and sea trade, they became littoral principalities rather than land-based entities, yet they were chiefly concerned with spices, rare woods, forest products, gold, diamonds, and other products of the land surfaces.

Scattered along these coasts must have been many trade stations and local centers of contact. The areas inhabited by Negrito and other peoples of simple culture and low productivity were less attractive to the Indians than were the areas populated by the agricultural-fishing Malays of somewhat higher culture. Local environmental differences also had some influence. With slow growth on land the less productive spots became subordinate to the favored localities as sea travel and sea power matured. The mobility of all the peoples and the shifting fortunes of groups must have led to many local changes of port stations and settlements. The whole region was somewhat similar, geographic knowledge was not yet very complete, and neither Indian nor local historiography can be precise in specific location of the first sea-states. Nevertheless it is clear that Indian colonial effort was concentrated in the western Indies, and that the first regional sea-states were located in this section of the Indies.

In the Indies, as in Cambodia and Burma, the Indian brought to the area a pattern of culture superior to

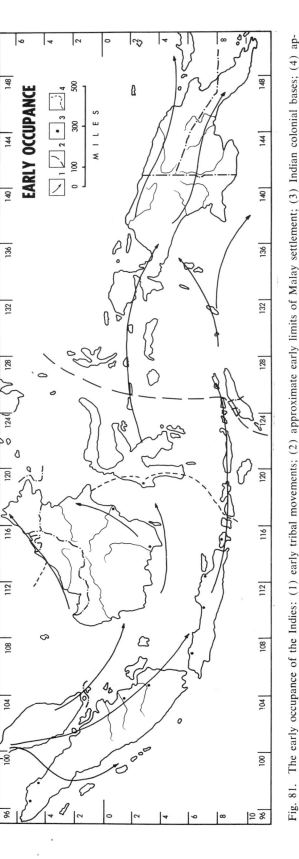

Fig. 81. The early occupance of the Indies: (1) early tribal movements; (2) approximate early limits of Malay settlement; (3) Indian colonial bases; (4) approximate limit of early Indian settlement.

that of any local population. Not only was some of this culture transmitted to the local population, but the Indians became the merchants, architects, religious leaders, and the political administrators of the little principalities and states that slowly began to appear in the western Indies. Underneath this new Indian veneer of people and culture each local region contained a variety of native populations and native culture patterns. The western Indies, for all its local variety, possessed a core of similar culture among the Malay peoples, much of which has remained to the present day.

SRI VIJAYA AND OTHER REGIONAL CENTERS

Once the canvass of the western Indies had been made, Indian effort focused upon regional centers. Probably over a dozen chief localities were scattered along the south, west, and lower east coasts of Borneo, the north coast of Java, and the lower east coast of Sumatra. In some of these centers Buddhist missionary influence seems dominant, whereas in others Hindu sects were primary. Trade contacts were extensive, for artifacts from both China and India of the second century A.D. have turned up in Borneo, Java, and Sumatra. Arabs, Chinese, and Indians were the chief traders, but seafarers from all southeastern Asia must have met in the chief ports. The collecting of various spice and perfume products gradually was supplanted by the cultivation of some of the major items. Plants originally domesticated upon the mainland were brought in and gradually became part of the product variety. Rare woods and a few other forest products were collected. Streams in many localities were mined for alluvial gold, and on Borneo diamonds and a few other precious stones also were produced in the same way. The western Indies thus came to be an important part of the oriental trade realm. As Buddhism died out in India Chinese students of Buddhism visited religious centers in southeastern Asia and came to include the Buddhist centers of the Indies in their travels. Diplomatic missions from several island states visited China, and it is clear that the western Indies had assumed a considerable status in the world of the East by the fourth century of the Christian era.

In the long run those areas inhabited by culturally advanced peoples, with good and productive local environments, came to be the most powerful and significant. In other less fortunate situations states advanced to a certain level and then retrogressed. Borneo is a region illustrative of this process. Among the first islands to be touched by Indian influences, in the early centuries Borneo possessed several Indianized states, but in the competitive struggle for regional dominance the Bornese states gradually lost out, and Borneo became one of the poorer and less populous regions only periodically exploited for particular resources. This situation has continued throughout the historic period and is true even today.

Java and Sumatra became the chief seats of competing states and regional interests, with a bewildering complexity of alternating rise to power and competitive defeat. The historian is yet unable fully to sort out the precise regional limits and the chronologic pattern of states based upon the Sumatran east coast and on the island of Java. Though the chief states always were those possessed of strong sea power, both commercial and military, the productive land resources of the hinterlands and the socio-political strength of the populations of the states were important factors in this competitive struggle. On Java and Sumatra the productive local environments were those of the rich volcanic uplands, which are located inland away from the coasts. The coastal sea-power pattern was always in conflict with that of the inland agricultural pattern. On Borneo the paucity of the inland resources kept regional development near the coasts, whereas on Java and Sumatra the productive land areas drew peoples inland. On the smaller islands east of Java the conflict between coastal and inland bases of development was less important, since the areas overlapped.

Though several Javanese states seem to have been important throughout the first millennium of the Christian era, the single strongest and largest state was that known as Sri Vijaya, based upon the southern east coast of Sumatra, with its capital near the modern city of Palembang. Sri Vijaya first grew to dominant position in the late seventh century, a combination of land resources, sea power, trade, and Indian political leadership. Its capital occasionally shifted to Java, out of the complex dynastic inheritance relationships, but it always was a west Malaysian state. At its height it controlled the seaways north to Cambodia, east to the Moluccas, and the whole of the Malay Peninsula, though in the ups and downs of sea power other island and peninsular states and pirate ports were able to compete for trade and political influence. Both close contact and friction with south Indian states were frequent. Sri Vijaya remained chiefly a sea power, never completely able to weld all land regions into one fully functioning political state. It reached its height in the twelfth century, and then faded away under the impact of piracy, regional competition, and the invasion of the Moslem from India.

Java contained several local regional centers in the early centuries. Island dominance at some times lay with one area, at others with another. Occasionally a dynastic family was able to combine most of Java into one state, whereas at other times as many as a half dozen regional entities were able to maintain independence. Religious differences, the overexpenditure of resources upon religious monuments, complex matters of interlocking inheritances by ruling families, and the ever-present issue of competitive sea power were factors in this regional problem. In the thirteenth century the decline of Sri Vijaya made possible the swift rise of the east Javanese sea-state of Madjapahit, whose zone of influence was almost as great as that of Sri Vijaya at its height, though located somewhat further eastward.

During these many centuries Java was the key economic region of the Indies, for its more satisfactory climate and its rich soils permitted its agricultural productivity to increase to greater extent than that of any other part of the Indies. Whatever state controlled the seaways, Java was the center of interregional trade, the chief island market for goods coming into the Indies, and the chief source of manpower and material resources. As piracy affected the outer islands at times when Sumatran or Javanese sea power was ineffective, outer-island productivity was inhibited, whereas Java was much less affected. Thus the ports of Java, particularly, became the chief centers of trade in this whole island world. Products and traders from all over the Orient came together in the several ports on the north coast, this in itself lending to Java an economic importance lacking in the other regions. The agricultural development, economic productivity, economic wealth, and the population of Java grew steadily greater than those of the other islands, to give a basic contrast to the regional development of the Indies long before the European came.

With the exception of a few localities and the steeper uplands Indianized settlements and culture patterns spread all over the relatively small island of Java, no part of which is many miles from the sea. Such small islands as Madura, Bali, and Lombok were fully brought into this Indianized culture zone, but the interiors of the larger islands were little affected. The uplands of Sumatra retained more completely Malay culture groups, and the inland regions of Borneo continued in their simpler ways of life. Such island groups as the Mentawi, off the west coast of Sumatra, largely escaped Indian influence. Though Javanese and other traders certainly traded as far east as Halmahera, the Indianizing of the islands east of Celebes was relatively slight. New Guinea and other islands remained almost

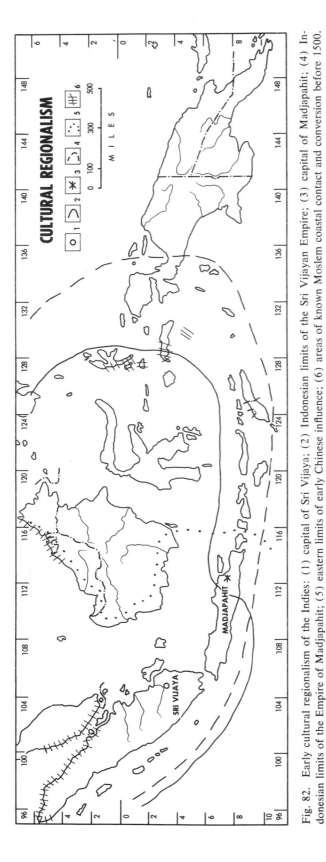

Fig. 82. Early cultural regionalism of the Indies: (1) capital of Sri Vijaya; (2) Indonesian limits of the Sri Vijayan Empire; (3) capital of Madjapahit; (4) Indonesian limits of the Empire of Madjapahit; (5) eastern limits of early Chinese influence; (6) areas of known Moslem coastal contact and conversion before 1500.

completely untouched by Indian influences. Certainly as late as the thirteenth century, when the Moslem invasions began, the peoples of New Guinea and many of the smaller islands off the main seaways continued their Paleolithic or Neolithic ways of life along with the peoples of interior Borneo and even some of the simpler groups on Sumatra. These patterns contrasted strongly with the cosmopolitan patterns of the coastal ports of Java and eastern Sumatra.

In the early centuries of Indian contact with the Indies, Indians were the political, social, religious, and economic leaders of port communities and principalities. In time Sumatran and Javanese Malays, by intermarriage and by absorption of Indian culture, came to have a large share in the leadership of society. In the late twelfth and thirteenth centuries Chinese began to become permanently resident in the ports of Sumatra, Java, and Borneo, and by the end of the fourteenth century there were large settlements of Chinese in many ports. Indian influences markedly altered the ways of life in the western Indies, increasing the contrasts between western and eastern islands already created by the coming of the Malays. Chinese influences, however, were primarily economic, increasingly concerned with the retail distribution of commodities and with the import-export trade of the islands.

Indian influences never penetrated the full depth and breadth of the Malay population and culture. Though the political state and its capital city might be run on Indian lines, with a close interweaving of religious and political leadership, the rural village communities remained democratic social entities, self-operative, mutually responsible, and Malay in cultural pattern. Acceptance of the shifting controls of political sea-states by local communities preserved local autonomy without risking destructive punitive action. Acceptance of state religious systems, of taxation, and of levies of labor and materials necessarily involved alterations and changes in village cultures, but preserved basic Malay cultural integrity.

THE INFLUX OF MOSLEM CULTURE

Arab traders had operated in Indonesian waters from the earliest centuries of the Christian era. After the rise of Mohammedanism the Arabs for some centuries did not mix religion and trade in their contacts with Indonesia. It was only in the late thirteenth century that Moslem missionaries came with the Arab traders. Though the record is not clear there appear to have been both Indians and Arabs from the Hadramaut coast of Arabia among the Moslem missionaries who appeared in Malaya and northern Sumatra. And quickly they learned to mix both politics and trade with their religious efforts. Finding opportunity in the ports of western Malaya they rapidly spread to the ports of western Indonesia. Their spread was not a solid line of advance but one that skipped about the seaways to such ports as presented opportunities. Moslem contacts touched some of the spice islands in the Halmahera group by 1440, and reached the southern Philippines by 1480, whereas parts of the Borneo coast were reached only shortly before 1600.

The entry of the Moslem missionary-adventurers came at a time when Sri Vijaya had declined in power, and much of the spread succeeded because of the rapid decline of the sea power of Madjapahit at the end of the fourteenth century. The disappearance of organized political sea power meant that the island world relapsed into an infinite number of small port and village communities, small islands and local regions, all independent, unprotected from the political adventurer, and connected only by the seaways and trade patterns. Here and there a local native regional ruler seized the opportunity to expand his own control, and was able to present some organized strength against the Moslem. But for the most part ports and local communities were wide open for the political opportunist able to capitalize upon the failure of political organization.

The newcomers proved adept at seizing the political leadership of port after port, declaring themselves rajas and sultans, converting the local populace to a nominal adherence to the Moslem faith, and organizing small regional principalities and states. The interregional trade continued to move, though the importance of individual ports altered under the new controls, and the Chinese role in trade expanded. The traditional antagonism between the Moslems and the Hindus and Buddhists caused the abandonment of the former state religions, the desertion of the great temples, and the superficial eradication of many Indian traits at all levels of society. The lack of unified political organization over the island world caused the rise of piracy which, in many cases, was less true piracy than the competitive attempts of local port sultans to control or profit from the sea trade.

Though not the whole of the population of western Malaysia had been converted to the Moslem faith when the Portuguese arrived, it is striking how rapidly the Moslem faith spread over the region. Perhaps it was but another expression of the willingness of the Malay to accept certain conditions thrust upon him in order to preserve his basic cultural integrity and the freedom of his village way of life. Under pressure from the Moslems many Indianized Sumatran and Javanese coastal peoples shifted inland on Sumatra, pushed up the rivers into interior Borneo, shifted eastward in the Indies, and even moved into the southern Philippines.

Certainly in the short space of two centuries the coming of the Moslems superficially altered the Indianized Malay culture of western Malaysia in a very marked way. The architecturally simple mosque replaced the ornate and costly Indian temple, social customs changed, the petty principality replaced the extensive political state, and economic decentralization followed political decentralization. Moslem influences never completely blanketed the western islands, leaving large island interiors untouched, and by-passing many small islands. The eastern islands were less attractive to the Moslems, who found simple subsistence economies and simple socio-political structures less easy to organize and take over, so that the regional spread of Moslem influences almost paralleled the spread of Indian influences. This new veneer of culture again added to the contrasts between Java and the outer islands, and between the western islands and those east of Halmahera.

THE COMING OF THE EUROPEAN

Rapid as was the spread of the Moslems over the western Indies, the process of applying a new cultural veneer had not been completed when the European appeared upon the scene to interrupt it and to inject new elements into the picture. In India the Portuguese quickly learned that the real world of spices lay further eastward. Upon taking the port of Malacca in Malaya, in 1511, the Portuguese felt they had secured an eastern base from which the exploration and exploitation of the Indies could be carried out. The Portuguese came as exploiters rather than as peaceful traders, and by early acts of piracy turned all nationalities against them from the start. They pursued with tactless force their ambition to destroy Arab trade in the Indian Ocean and native trade in the South China Sea and the local waters of the Indies.

Cannon, courage, and greedy ambition gave the Portuguese victory after victory in naval conflict, but the chief centers of the important products so long sought had but recently become converted to the Moslem faith. The new Moslem sultans of many of the Banda and Halmahera groups of islands saw profitable trade outlets in the Portuguese traders, but the Portuguese could not be content with normal trade, being bent upon monopolistic control of the world's spice trade. While they were unsuccessfully struggling with the issues of control of the trade routes and of the producing sources, the appearance of one of Magellan's ships in the Spice Islands forced them to even more ruthless action. There ensued a minor Holy War or Crusade, with control of trade the end objective.

Failing to make trade agreements with the Moslem sultans, the Portuguese turned to missionary activity but found that they could succeed only with the pagan peoples yet untouched by either Indian or Moslem religions, not many of whom were important spice producers. Animosity to the Portuguese stepped up the Moslem missionary efforts as a countermove, and the Moslem religion spread more rapidly than did Christianity in the Indies in this era. The ruthless greed and tactlessness of the Portuguese foretold the doom of peaceful European contact in the East and also ordained the shortness of Portuguese control of the whole region. In short order the Portuguese became thoroughly disliked throughout the whole of the East, thus arousing the suspicions of all peoples toward all occidentals.

The Spanish persistence in the Philippines and on the edges of the Indies, the voyage of the English Sir Francis Drake, Portuguese crewmen on the ships of other nations and, finally, the appearance of the Dutch at the end of the sixteenth century, all were factors in preventing the monopoly of the Portuguese in the Indies. But also important was the gradual growth of larger states, alliances, and confederacies among the Moslem ports and principalities. Atjeh in north Sumatra, the confederacies of the Sultans of Brunei and Ternate, and the state of Mataram in west Java, all grew large and strong enough to prevent the assumption of political and trade control over territory by the Portuguese. Though they were able to purchase and sell in Europe large volumes of spices, their monopolistic control of a great trade empire remained but a dream.

In spite of the failure of empire the coming of the European introduced new elements into the life of the Indies in the sixteenth century. The sea power of Java was broken, the spread of the Moslem religion and culture was furthered, a market-Malay language was spread about the ports, new trade patterns developed, important regional patterns of Christianity were implanted, and the political structure of the western Indies was altered. It is remarkable that many of the same small islands that earlier had been bypassed were again left untouched, that the interiors of large islands were but slightly affected, and that the regions and peoples east of Halmahera still continued the same simple patterns that they had followed for many centuries.

In the last years of the sixteenth century Dutch, English, and Spanish trading efforts in the Indies interfered with the activity of the Portuguese. Not every expedition produced large profits, but the Dutch were encouraged sufficiently to outfit more ships than did the Portuguese and to keep at the venture. The organization of the United East India Company aimed at a Dutch monopoly of the trade with the Indies. The weaker British traders followed the Dutch into port after port, letting them lead the way and do most of the squabbling. The Dutch learned to be somewhat tactful and careful in their contacts with Indonesians, but there still was trouble. Dutch field leaders planned a great trade empire, and worked toward it, though the home directors never sanctioned the plans. Batavia, on Java, was made the chief Dutch base, and Chinese merchants were invited to settle in the port. This early association of the Dutch and the Chinese really laid the foundations for the success of the Dutch East India Company.

THE DUTCH COLONIAL EMPIRE

The island of Java had declined in economic importance and population in the regional struggles of the various sultans and the Portuguese during the sixteenth century, but Batavia was a well placed base from which to carry on trade. The United East India Company was spread far and wide, from South Africa to Formosa and Halmahera, and the problems of running a monopoly trade empire became pressing. The Dutch in 1650 controlled the sea lanes of the Indies from Batavia, largely in the same way that Madjapahit had done at an earlier time from its capital in eastern Java. They governed only Batavia and its immediate environs, relying upon native sultans to govern the various islands, and relying upon treaties with the sultans to maintain trade relations. British, Portuguese, Danish, and a few other traders operated in various ports in the western Indies, conniving with local rulers against the Dutch.

During the latter part of the seventeenth century this uneasy state of affairs produced considerable unrest and military maneuvering. The Dutch East India Company was forced into military operations to control the territories of their trade realm, and by 1700 the Dutch not only controlled trade but had entered into political administration of the chief coastal regions. The Portuguese withdrew to Timor, the Danes were totally ousted, and the British retained only a fortified trading post on the west coast of Sumatra. The Dutch extended their monopoly trade system by which the agents of the Company, the Company itself, the Chinese, and regional rulers all handsomely profited from the production and trade of spices, but by which the rural villager and agricultural producer made but a pittance.

The policy of restriction cut down orchards of spice trees, depopulated some of the spice-producing islands, and reduced many regions to poverty. Piracy and interregional struggles were frequent and serious. Just after 1700 trial efforts at growing coffee on interior uplands of Java succeeded beyond all expectation, for by 1723 the yield amounted to some 12,000,000 pounds of coffee. This foretold a new era in Dutch trade in the Indies, the dealing with bulk export crops, and coffee became a regular export after this date. But the Company was not yet ready for volume trade, and economic theories of free trade had not yet matured in the Occident. The eighteenth century was one long struggle between the Dutch attempts to restrict trade, make profits, keep the peace, and extend political control over the Indies, against the Indonesian and non-Dutch efforts to circumvent monopoly, evade Dutch control, secure release from economic exploitation, and preserve the autonomy and freedom of the Malay way of life.

The United East India Company became almost bankrupt trying to manage both government and monopoly trade on a huge scale in the unsettled world of the late eighteenth century, and in 1796 surrendered its charter. The Indies suddenly became a political colony of the Netherlands, with the home government lacking both a knowledge of the problems of colonial government in the oriental tropics and personnel effectively trained to administer the new colony. Late eighteenth-century Dutch-British world-wide conflict reduced the widespread Dutch trade realm, forcing them out of South Africa, Ceylon, and Malaya. The latter phase of this struggle saw the British temporarily controlling Java and Sumatra, a peace treaty finally deciding that the Indies were Dutch and Malaya was British. Upset world conditions for a half century had made profitable trade difficult, and the restrictive patterns and vagaries of Company policy had left the economy of the Indies in an unproductive state, with the majority of the population living in poverty, but with many native sultans possessing tremendous wealth and power.

As the Indies became a political colony Java contained the base settlement used in trade and administration. Most of the Dutch populace was gathered in or near Batavia, with only small groups at outlying regional control points, particularly along the Sumatran east coast, on the south coast of Borneo, and at scattered points in the Halmahera and Banda Islands. Other non-natives were similarly scattered, with the most marked accumulations being those of the Chinese around the chief ports and trade centers. West of Halmahera most of the population had become Moslem in religion, except for scattered groups of non-Malay, animistic cultures on bypassed islands or large-island interiors. There was a small regional residue of Indianized peoples on Bali and Lombok, and Christianity had been planted in a number of small areas. Native sultans held direct political control in many portions of the western Indies, and several tribal confederacies were rather tightly organized culture groups highly resistant to Dutch administration. The Portuguese still controlled part of Timor, and there were significant areas of the western islands in which no regionally organized patterns of Company government or trade contact existed. East of Halmahera was a kind of no-man's land untouched by the cultural and economic currents that had been active in the western Indies for over 2,000 years. The by-passed islands and large-island interiors of the western zone also shared in this lacuna. Java contained the largest total population, but population densities were in strong contrast at many points throughout the whole of the Indies.

As Dutch colonial government began the Indies formed a region of immense contrast in language, law, religion, settlement, agricultural productivity, economic development, and other aspects of cultural development. Java and some near-by islands stood out as a region quite separate from the rest of the western Indies, and the area east of Halmahera was largely an unknown land. The multiplicity of regional divisions was complex, and no one system could be applied to the whole in any facet of the functioning of government as it operated in the early nineteenth century. The low economic productivity of the whole of the Indies, and the disorganized state of economic affairs, involved a large financial burden which the little Netherlands was in no position to assume. The Indies had to be organized in such a way as to become economically productive, and this primary requirement became the chief facet of early Dutch colonial policy. Various reforms and new procedures introduced by the first Dutch colonial government, and amplified by the British in the short period in which they controlled Java and Sumatra, were hindered by inadequacies, but they were serious efforts in the right directions. As the nineteenth century progressed the Dutch worked hard at the problems of colonial administration, and in the end achieved perhaps the best system of colonial government of any of the European colonial rulers.

THE INNER, OUTER, AND NON-DUTCH-INDIES

Possessing a small country with limited population and home resources the Dutch were unable to take the whole of the Indies into their early political and economic program. Late in the nineteenth century the British were able to stake out both political and economic spheres in both northwestern Borneo and southeastern New Guinea in areas yet untouched by the Dutch, and Germany was able to lay claim to northeastern New Guinea. Portugal clung to a part of Timor. Thus the Indies, as a group of over 3,000 islands, came into the twentieth century divided between four European political states. Germany lost her colonial region after the First World War, northeastern New Guinea passing into British hands, as a League of Nations mandate. Had other efforts been made by non-Dutch powers, in the nineteenth century, to attach others of the bypassed islands or regions they, too, might have succeeded and other areas would have passed from Dutch control. This sort of separation of the Indies into political regions has happened many times in the past.

The Dutch colonial empire, as it matured, included parts of all of the islands of the Indies, totaled the largest area, and contained the largest population. Though the Dutch were able to bring to all parts of their empire a certain degree of unity in administrative and cultural patterns, they were unable to develop all of it economically. They had come into a Malaysia with marked economic and cultural contrasts between islands. Their early efforts at trade led to a rehabilitation of Java and Madura, an increase in economic productivity, and marked increase in population. They were not attracted to those islands or areas of low economic productivity and simple culture which were lacking in commodities useful in the Dutch trade in Europe. The long-run efforts of the Dutch, therefore, furthered some of the long-standing differences between the islands. The contrast has long been strongest between Java and the rest of the islands, and in recent times this has been generalized in the term Outer Islands which includes everything beyond Java and Madura. The contrast shows most strongly in population, economic productivity, and in political nationalism. But it runs throughout all matters of culture.

The British portions of the islands have been under varied control. A portion of Borneo, Sarawak, was for some decades in the midnineteenth century a kind of personal preserve of the British Brooke family; North Borneo was originally a chartered company area, and some small territories were included in the Straits Settlements of Malaya. Southeastern New Guinea had been claimed very early by the British East India Company, but the lack of trade products prevented any development until the late nineteenth century. The German portion of the island had been the object of some economic experiment and missionary effort before being surrendered to the British World War I mandate under Australia. Today the several areas have been reorganized politically and administratively, and there is similarity in their British orientation but, lying at opposite ends of the Indies, inhabited by quite different peoples, and possessing a markedly different cultural history, the British Indies have no real unity. Sarawak and North Borneo today are Crown Colonies, and Brunei is a protected state. Papua is British territory and the Territory of Northeast New Guinea is a United Nations trusteeship under British administration. In 1949 Northwest New Guinea and Papua were combined into one administrative region under Australian control.

The small holding in Timor that remains the mark of Portuguese exploration of the Indies is not a rich territory, is inhabited by Negrito and early mixed peoples, and has a low economic productivity. Portugal has not actively attempted either economic or cultural advancement of the island in significant manner, and it remains today the bypassed island it has remained for many centuries.

Though biologically and botanically there is a major zone of demarcation through the Indies, both early and modern man have transgressed this boundary pattern. The cultural, political, and economic developments within the Indies in the last several millennia have not been primarily motivated by these environmental features. The interior of New Guinea, in matters of human development, more closely resembles the interior of Borneo than the Papuan coast of New Guinea, though Borneo and New Guinea lie on opposite sides of the Wallace-Weber set of lines. It is obvious that there is not just one, but that there are several Indies. Politically there are three Indies—Indonesian (formerly Dutch), British, and Portuguese—but in terms of population one might say that there are two Indies, Java and the rest of the islands. Linguistically there are many Indies.

THE BACKGROUND TO CONTEMPORARY AGRICULTURE

After the Napoleonic struggles in Europe the Dutch were in no position to embark upon a progressive program in the Indies, and some way had to be found to regain prosperity at home and to develop the Indies.

There resulted a system of government-controlled agriculture in the Indies conventionally termed the culture system. Local government, land control, taxation, crop production, agricultural processing, the export trade, and the import trade in consumer goods were integrated by government regulation in such a way that in Java there began a new era of commercialized agriculture and foreign trade. Monopoly thinking still prevailed but turned from restriction to increased production. Payment in money for crops beyond the tax assessment stimulated production, but the controls turned Java into one great farm estate. Dutch and Chinese managed the processing of exports and the external trade. The profits were great, and the Netherlands rapidly regained its prosperity. That the Javanese population increased, agricultural lands expanded, and a market for foreign goods developed did not lessen the stigma of exploitation and the native dislike for the system. The culture system increased the contrast between Java and the Outer Indies.

Coffee, sugar, and indigo were the chief exports of the Indies in this period. Subsistence production upon Java increased. The price of spices was declining, and with it the importance of the patterns of trade of the earlier era. During these decades government initiative introduced new crop plants to the Indies, and, though they did not immediately become productive sources of exports, their spread over Java and the east coast of Sumatra paved the way for later production. Tea, tobacco, manioc, and the oil palm were the most important of the new plants or improved varieties.

After 1850 liberalizing trends in Dutch policy began to make headway and, on private initiative, plantations were established. The term used in English translation in the Indies is estate rather than plantation, as in Malaya. The estates increased in number as government policy after 1865 abandoned controlled agriculture. The influx of Dutch settlers began, free trade for all nations was allowed, and participation by native small farmers in commercial production began on their own initiative. The incompleteness of Dutch control in the Outer Indies had prevented development equal to that on Java, but gradually the east coast of Sumatra and a few other regions began to participate in the new trends in agriculture. Tea, sugar, coffee, and tobacco were the first important private plantation products. Late in the century cinchona came into production, but this remained a government controlled forest product on Java. As the population of Java and Sumatra increased, with the accent on commercial agriculture, the production of basic food supplies began to lag. The wet ricefields of Java had been slowly expanding, but insufficiently. Interest in minerals led to some exploration and the development of tin, coal, and a few others, to add variety to the commercial patterns of the Indies. British activity in Borneo and British and German efforts in eastern New Guinea produced no marked expansion of agriculture or trade until the very end of the century when estate development began on a small scale.

During the present century the early trends were the increase of estate production upon Java and the east coast of Sumatra, with a limited growth of estates on the Dutch Outer Islands and in the British-controlled areas, the lagging expansion of subsistence culture and food-crop production, the increase in food imports, and the rise in native commercial agriculture in all parts of the Indies. Java constantly expanded its production and is the most important single producing region. The growth of small farmer and estate agriculture on the Sumatran east coast gives it second rank as a producing region. On the rest of the Outer Islands, both Dutch and non-Dutch, productive agricultural areas are small and scattered. The contrast between Java and the Outer Islands, other than the Sumatran east coast, is greater than it has ever been.

Native land systems involved both the concepts of hereditary land ownership and communal use ownership by shifting agriculturists, with many variations in local practice in different parts of the Indies. The Dutch East India Company sold large tracts of land on Java, regardless of native occupance and complicated traditional practices. After the abolition of the Company, government policy in the Dutch areas developed in the direction of prevention of alien land ownership, even for the Dutch themselves. But long-term leases for estates were permitted without real limitation, and short-term leases over small holdings accumulated as a means of debt settlement with creditors who often were Chinese. Non-Dutch regions first developed land practices along the British pattern, by which estates could be owned and land sold to creditors, but more recently the long leasehold system has been practiced. There has not developed in any part of the Indies a class of large landowners renting to numerous tenants that is characteristic of so much of the rest of the Orient. With the assumption of Indonesian independence land policy in the Republic of Indonesia is trending toward the restriction of large estates and the evolution of a nationalistic small-farmer policy. It is too early to determine whether this will involve elimination of all estates, and whether the traditional communal use-ownership policy will be stabilized or gradually supplanted by some system of hereditary ownership. In the British areas no marked change in current policy has appeared, though doubtless it will trend toward the protection of native ownership as an expression of enlightened colonial rule.

THE CONTEMPORARY AGRICULTURAL ECONOMY

The agriculture of the Indies today can be divided into four convenient categories, namely, shifting cultivation, sedentary subsistence culture, small-farmer cash-crop cultivation, and estate export agriculture. The first three types are small-farmer matters, out of which some export products come, whereas estate agriculture is large-holding plantation culture, producing little food supply but large volumes of export products.

The most widespread pattern of agriculture is the simple subsistence economy of the shifting cultivator, normally termed *ladang* in the Indies. This supports several millions of people in the Outer Indies, and it is a common generalization that nearly 90 per cent of the agriculture of the Outer Indies is shifting culture. It occupies large areas of land, for the total area required to permit cropping given plots for only one, two, or three years is enormous, even though the amount cropped in any one year is low. Few statistics are available, estimates suggesting that some 20,000,-000 acres are worked each year in the whole of the Indies. Most of Borneo and New Guinea are cropped by this system, most of the native agriculture on Sumatra operates by this technique, along with significant areas on Celebes, Flores, Timor, Ceram, Halmahera, and many of the smaller islands. In the western zone upland rice is a basic crop, and the taros, yams and sweet potatoes, maize, bananas, sago, and manioc are the chief crops. A number of fruit-tree crops are both planted and depended upon, though the use of some of these becomes a matter of gathering of semiwild and wild products. East of Celebes and Lombok rice drops out as a crop of the shifting cultivator, and the taros and yams-sweet potatoes are relatively more important in the food economy of the shifting cultivator. Rice growing has recently been started in three local areas in eastern New Guinea, shown on the accompanying map, but are not yet proportionately equivalent to rice growing in the western Indies. A small trickle of commercial products comes out of this agriculture, both for the domestic and export market, several of which are more the products of forest extraction than of formal agriculture. Shifting cultivation is, by and large, the agriculture of many of the simpler culture groups throughout the Indies, but it also is practiced by frontier and pioneer members of advanced groups in many parts of the Outer Indies.

The second category of land use is that of the sedentary small farmer engaged in subsistence agriculture. This is the system of the village dweller on Java, Madura, and the more developed parts of Sumatra, Celebes, the coast of Borneo, and coastal areas on other of the islands of the Outer Indies. It is an intensive hoe culture, a system on a higher level than shifting cultivation. The draft-animal population of all the Indies does not exceed 7,000,000, not all of which are work animals, and not all of which are available to the sedentary small farmer. Sedentary farmers are engaged chiefly in the production of basic food commodities, some volumes of which do enter the interregional and the export trade. In the western Indies wet-field rice is by far the dominant crop, occupying perhaps 11,500,000 acres in all. About 1,000,000 acres of the wet-field rice crop represent double cropping. Java is the outstanding rice producer, Sumatra, Borneo, and Celebes being significant also, along with a few of the smaller western islands. It is notable in the historic development of agriculture in the Indies that rice has not been important in food-crop agriculture east of the islands affected by Malay and Indian culture in the early periods. Upland rice is relatively unimportant among sedentary farmers. The accompanying map shows the important rice-growing areas.

Maize today occupies the second largest acreage and is chiefly an upland and dry-region crop, though sometimes a dry-season crop on rice lands. From central Java eastward through Flores maize is often the most important crop in local areas, many farmers growing three crops per year. The total acreage among sedentary farmers is nearly 7,000,000. The island of Madura is the chief region depending upon maize, about three fourths of its crop land regularly producing maize. Maize has been an export crop in part, but today it seldom goes abroad. Manioc occupies close to 3,000,-000 acres in all areas. Java and Madura are the chief producing areas, where poorer soils are devoted to manioc, but it is also a common crop in the southern part of Celebes and the Lesser Sundas. The accompanying map indicates the regional importance of the maize crop. Soybeans, peanuts, and yams-sweet potatoes are other important food crops of the sedentary farmer. Soybeans are rather new in the Indies and are steadily increasing in cultivation.

Dooryard fruit and vegetable gardens probably cover 4,500,000 acres in all parts of the Indies and produce a wide variety of fruits and vegetables. Coconut palms are probably the most important single fruit. Fish ponds on many small farms are almost integral parts of farm layouts, and they contribute significantly to

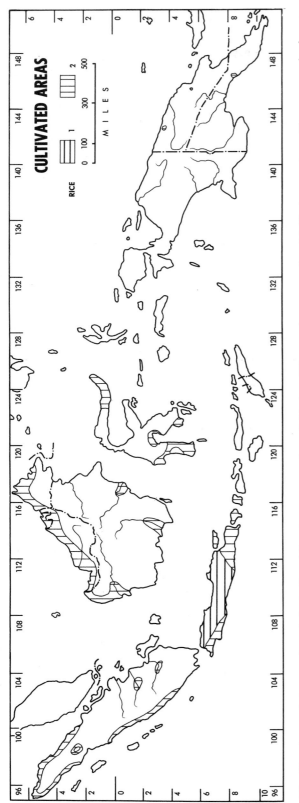

Fig. 83. Areas of rice growing of the Indies: (1) primary areas of wet-field rice; (2) secondary areas of wet-field rice growing. Rice as an upland crop among shifting cultivators occurs only in Celebes and the western Indies.

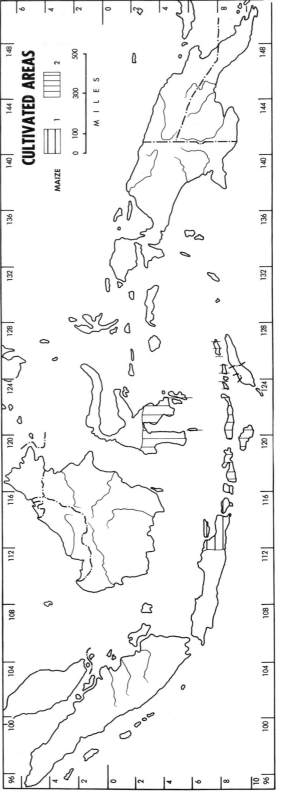

Fig. 84. Areas of maize growing of the Indies: primary producing regions; (2) secondary producing regions.

local economy. Some of the Outer Islands produce surpluses of coconut, rice, maize, and manioc, most of which flows into Java to balance the regional deficit in food supplies. On the swampy coasts of Borneo, particularly in Sarawak, and throughout the New Guinea coastal lands, the sago palm is an important item in domestic economy.

The third phase of agriculture involves the production of cash crops by the sedentary small farmer for sale on the export market. This has been a traditional minor part of agriculture in the Indies, varying in importance according to political regionalism and the vigor of international trade. For centuries it was specialized on Java and the Moluccas and has developed around pepper and the other spices, but seldom was it a dominant aspect of land use, for the trade never dealt in huge volumes. Often this cash-crop cultivation was carried on under duress, levied by native rulers and by the Dutch East India Company upon local regions. During the period of the culture system the small farmers of Java were required to produce large volumes of export crops. Since 1865 the small farmers have been increasing the variety of their cash crops, though even today the volume per farm is not large. The commercial crops have varied from time to time, but today coconut, rubber, tea, coffee, tobacco, fibers, spices, sago, kapok, and cacao are the chief commercial crops among small farmers. Since the small farmer does not depend chiefly upon these crops for his support his harvest and sale of them often depends upon favorable market prices. Seldom are such crop plants cared for as efficiently as on estates, and the per plant or per acre yield is much lower than on estates. The total production of some of the cash crops from small farms recently has begun to exceed the total produced on estates. As the population of Java has increased, with its food deficit in both rural and urban sections there is growing a trend to the commercial production of the traditional crops in the Outer Indies, a production which enters interregional but not the export trade.

Estate agriculture is essentially a product of the Dutch and British exploitation of the Indies. It began with the Dutch on Java and Sumatra in the late nineteenth century, after the abolition of the culture system. Tobacco, sugar, coffee, and tea were the early crops on Dutch estates, whereas tobacco and indigo were the first efforts in British Borneo, followed by coconut plantings. In eastern New Guinea a variety of experiments failed, and plantation agriculture primarily has grown coconuts, with rubber a second ranking crop. After 1900 rubber, tobacco, and sugar cane came to lead estate production in the Dutch areas, with rubber leading in British Borneo and coconut ranking first in eastern New Guinea. The chief region of estate agriculture has continued to be Sumatra and Java, though gradually a small acreage in estates developed on Borneo, Celebes, the Moluccas, and eastern New Guinea, as seen on the accompanying map. There are few estates on any of the small islands of the Indies. Estate agriculture reached its peak in 1930, dropped somewhat during the early 1930's, and recovered until just before World War II, when some 6,500,000 acres in all parts of the Indies produced over thirty different commercial crops.

Most of the estates are operated on lands leased for long terms. Estates occur in two different types of physical sites on Java. The tree and shrub crops such as coffee, tea, rubber, and cinchona are grown on the rougher uplands unsuited to wet-field rice or other small-farmer subsistence culture. The field crops such as sugar cane and tobacco have been grown on the smoother lowlands. As the pressure of small-farmer needs for crop land increased after 1940 there developed pressure against the estates located on the lowlands which are suitable for the small farmer's agriculture. At the end of World War II many small farmers moved onto estates and set up small farms, since operations on the estates were slow to reorganize. Trends are to short-term leases at higher rates, conditions which may make untenable the continuation of estate agriculture on the lowlands. On Sumatra, Borneo, and New Guinea most of the estates are on the lower coastal plains, but the issue of displacement by small farmers is not yet so acute as on Java, because there still is ample land available to all.

Of the more than thirty commercial crops grown on estates eight have long accounted for most of the commercial export volume. These are rubber, tea, coffee, sugar, tobacco, coconut, cinchona, and palm oil. In the former Dutch regions before World War II there were some 2,400 estates, and about 350 smaller ones in the British areas. Today about two thirds of the former Dutch estate-cultivated area is under cultivation, and about four fifths of the British area has returned to production. In 1900 estate production of commercial export crops amounted to some 90 per cent of the total commercial export volume. Just before World War II Dutch estates utilized less than 8 per cent of the cultivated land of the Dutch Indies, but still produced over 60 per cent of the commercial export total. In 1950, with many estates either no longer operating or working at reduced capacity, estate production amounted to barely one third of the total. The accompanying map indicates the regional spread of plantation agriculture. It is questionable whether estate production ever again will dominate commercial and export agriculture in the Indies.

In summary, some 47,000,000 acres are in farms throughout the Indies, ranging from annually shifting small patches to large corporate estates. About 44,-000,000 acres are cultivated in some manner each year, with a small share of double and triple cropping. Crop data can be crudely estimated for about 35,000,-000 acres, with the rest in mixed plantings of a variety not amenable to modern statistical measure. Rice is the chief crop of the Indies, grown on wet fields in the western Indies by small farmers as a home-consumption crop. Java is the chief producing region, but production no longer feeds the island, which now is dependent upon the Outer Indies. Maize is the second ranking crop, chiefly a home-food crop today with small-farmer production centered in the drier central zone of the Indies. Dooryard fruit and vegetable gardens, in combination, spread over the Indies wherever sedentary agriculture is to be found. Rubber, the leading commercial crop, ranks fourth in acreage, today scattered very widely over the whole Indies but centered on Java and Sumatra. The highest yields come from plantations, but the small-farmer volume today exceeds that of the estate operators. Manioc ranks fifth in acreage, a home-consumption crop which used to export a share of its refined product, tapioca. Concentrated in the central Indies, it is a widely grown crop.

Below these ranking crops are a wide assemblage of home-use food crops, both traditional and introduced, and an equally wide range of commercial crops, also traditional and introduced. Coerced production of selected crops by the small farmer has given way to a wide variety of both food and commercial crops which is coming to dominate the whole of agriculture. Estate agriculture, by pressure and policy, is declining in the former Dutch areas but not yet in the British areas. Java, Madura, Sumatra, South Borneo, and Celebes are the primary productive regions, both in respect to subsistence and commercial production. Shifting cultivation has almost entirely disappeared from Java.

The rest of the Outer Indies is the zone of traditional shifting cultivation but it is a zone of increasing sedentary and commercial cultivation. On Java particularly, agriculture today shows a quick response to market conditions, with farmers shifting from sugar cane to rice when the sugar market becomes unfavorable and shifting to other crops in response to changing market and demand patterns. On Java also there is an acute regional adjustment of crops to soils, local

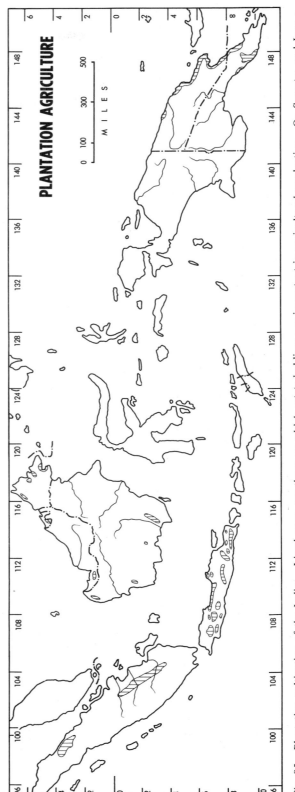

PLANTATION AGRICULTURE

MILES
0   100   300   500

Fig. 85. Plantation cultivation of the Indies. Lined areas are those on which estate holdings are important in agricultural production. On Sumatra and Java a wide variety of crops are grown. On Borneo rubber, coconut, and tobacco are the chief plantation crops, and in eastern New Guinea coconut is the chief crop.

climatic patterns, and other productive conditions that is not equaled on other islands.

Fishing has been an integral part of the food-producing economy of most parts of the Indies, only the upland peoples of the interior not doing some fishing themselves. For the coastal populations this, of course, has often meant a part-time concern with fishing, and for the inland peoples it has meant utilizing all sorts of fresh water sources, from rivers to ricefields and ponds. In the modern era not enough of the population has been able to participate in fishing, and there has developed a significant import trade in fish products for, among most parts of the Indies, fish ranks high in the daily food menu of the population. On Java whenever possible fish ponds are a part of the village-garden layout, and the cultural raising of fish is an old custom. Pond-raised fish form a significant part of the total production. Fishery products in the Indies have very wide range, from the turtle eggs and sea slugs of west Borneo through hundreds of species of salt-water fish to the small fish of inland rivers and ricefields and the varieties of carp that are raised in ponds in inland Java.

MINERALS, TRADE, AND INDUSTRY

The development of mineral resources in the western Indies is very old, going back to the early centuries of Indian and Arab traders. Tin, gold, diamonds, petroleum, and other products have long made up a significant part of the traditional trade of the Indies. During the eighteenth century traders bought tin, gold, petroleum, and other minerals from native sources. The Dutch were traders rather than miners or manufacturers and did little to develop primary production in minerals. After the Indies passed under government control only slowly did mineral production become part of the productive economy, in both Dutch and British areas. Mining, in the modern sense, developed only in the last half of the nineteenth century, and has continued to expand during the present century as geological surveys have been extended over the islands. Even today the knowledge of the mineral resources of the Indies is incomplete, and it is probable that both new minerals and new regional occurrences will appear in the future. Modern mining laws have matured slowly in the Indies, in the Dutch sector restricting rights to the government in the earlier period, but increasingly permitting private development since the 1850's until Indonesian independence began. It now is likely that restrictions upon aliens will begin to appear in Indonesian mineral legislation, trending toward nationalizing of mineral production.

Tin, coal, and petroleum were the first of the modern mineral developments, in the late nineteenth century, whereas manganese, asphalt, sulphur, phosphates, bauxite, and nickel came into production chiefly after the First World War. Huge deposits of iron ores are present, but the lack of coking coal prevents the growth of an iron and steel industry, and distance from markets restricts iron ore mining. Known mineral distributions suggest that the British parts of the Indies are less well endowed than is Indonesia, but this story is subject to change. The accompanying maps indicate mineral distributions. Mineral production today forms a significant aspect of the economy of the Indies, and the range and volume of minerals suggest that these resources will be of great value to the Indies in the future.

Petroleum is the most important resource, and the Indies form both one of the productive regions of the earth and the chief producing region of the Orient. Structural conditions for oil are scattered widely over the Indies, and new producing fields will appear in the future. Southeastern Sumatra and several coastal margins of Borneo have been the important producers to date, but it is likely that New Guinea will prove very productive. Tin is the second most important mineral, occurring in the islands nearest Malaya that are a continuation of the ore ranges of mainland southeastern Asia. Coal, sufficiently good for steam power, is mined in a number of localities, and domestic coal resources can provide an alternative fuel for a variety of industrial uses. Gold is mined in modern ways and in the traditional manner of river washing of gravels almost everywhere in the Indies. In the southeastern portion of the Territory of New Guinea about 1935 gold mining became a major element in economic development. Most of the other mineral resources go into the export trade, but they will become increasingly useful within the Indies in time.

Handicraft industry in the past has variably spread over the Indies in direct relation to the level of local cultures, but manufacturing has not been one of the important segments of the economy of the Indies. International trade between the various major sectors of the Orient has long taken particular resources out of the Indies and brought in manufactured goods. Textiles, tools, porcelains, and metal wares were brought in by Indian, Arab, Chinese, and Indonesian traders. The European traders took over the whole trade of the Indies and concentrated upon exporting the spices and chosen minerals, and eventually brought in the whole range of consumers' goods. Some handicraft manufacturing has persisted throughout this long

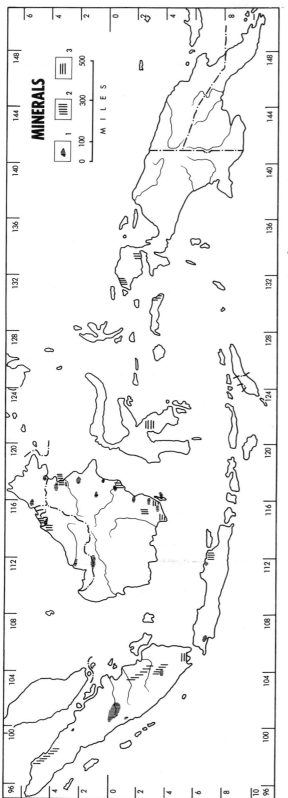

Fig. 86. Basic mineral product occurrences: (1) areas of voluminous occurrence of coal; (2) known producing petroleum fields; (3) areas of voluminous occurrence of iron ore.

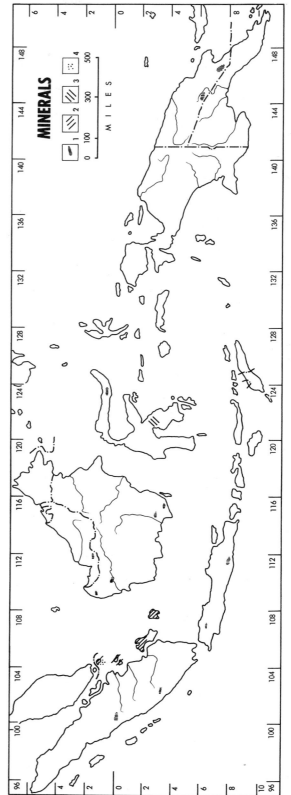

Fig. 87. Auxiliary mineral occurrences in the Indies: (1) chief areas of gold production: alluvial gold occurs in many stream beds; (2) tin-producing areas; (3) nickel ore region; (4) bauxite production chiefly on the island of Bintan to date.

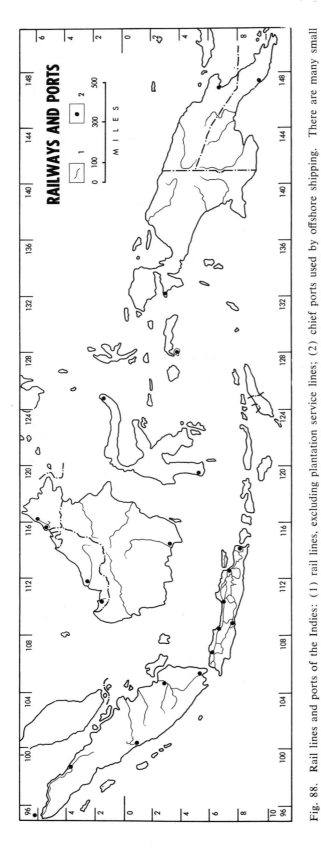

Fig. 88.   Rail lines and ports of the Indies: (1) rail lines, excluding plantation service lines; (2) chief ports used by offshore shipping.   There are many small ports used regularly by coastwise traffic and occasionally by offshore shipping.

period, in tool and implement making, clothing textiles, and in processing of export commodities.

In the modern period agricultural processing has steadily grown larger in volume and in regional location, and mineral processing has been increasingly developed. On Java particularly handicraft textile making has increased rather than declined, so that Java today has a significant village textile manufacturing. Modern Dutch influence furthered agricultural processing, using part-time village farm populations, began petroleum refining, rubber, chemicals, and cement manufacturing, aided the development of textile industries, and increasingly sponsored the development of decentralized manufacturing. About 3,500,000 persons may be classified as industrial workers. Few other than agricultural processing activities and traditional native handicrafts are to be found in the British areas. Indonesian government policy looks toward the establishment of a large volume and variety of industry. Nationalizing of ownership, the development of technical education, the protected development of home manufactures, and the local establishment of branch plants by international firms will be part of a long-range trend.

The trade patterns of the Indies are both old and varied, as previously suggested. In the modern era they have increasingly become oriented around the export of raw materials and the import of manufactured commodities. Before World War II the Indies supplied the largest share of the world's quinine, pepper, and kapok, nearly half the rubber, from a fourth to about a fifth of the coconut, palm oil, tea, and tin, and significant shares of the fibers, sugar, coffee, petroleum, and bauxite. In value terms rubber led the list, followed by petroleum, coconut products, tin, tea, tobacco, pepper, and palm oil. The Dutch Indies contributed the bulk of the total, but the British areas contributed significantly to rubber, petroleum, coconut, and tobacco. In the import trade, clothing textiles led in value terms, with foodstuffs, machinery, and metal manufactures being large items. Again the Dutch Indies took the great volume of total imports, with small shares only going to the more lightly populated and less developed British sectors. Since the destruction of World War II and the independence of the Indies, there has been a lessened volume of trade in particular lines, for the productive economy of the Indies has been only slowly restored to its former status.

In the historic development of the Indies water transport has played a far more significant role than has land transport. Java is the center of all such developments as roads, railways, telegraph and telephone lines and is followed by Sumatra. Elsewhere modern features of transport and communications are very spotty and restricted to local regions. The accompanying maps present the regional pattern of rail lines, roads, ports, and airfields. Of about 70,000 motor vehicles in all the Indies in 1952, some 65,000 were in Indonesia, and of these the great majority were on Java, with about 35,000 vehicles operating around Jakarta. Auto roads on Java and Sumatra often parallel rail lines, and current Indonesian government policy is to restrict public auto transport so as not to duplicate services provided by the rail lines. The growth of air transport has reduced the urgency of road building on Borneo and New Guinea particularly. In eastern New Guinea in 1949 there were over fifty landing fields being maintained for local air traffic, of which only the better-equipped airports are shown on the accompanying map. Many miles of truck and jeep roads have been allowed to deteriorate since the end of World War II in eastern New Guinea, since they are not required for local use. A large number of small ports are of value in local trade, but are not shown on the map of ports.

POPULATION AND REGIONALISM IN THE INDIES

The total population of the Indies today is approximately 81,000,000, but the following figures are not based upon accurate census returns. The total for the British regions is about 2,200,000; Portuguese Timor contains about 500,000; and the Indonesian Republic's total is approximately 78,000,000. Java-Madura contains slightly over 53,000,000 people on its 51,032 square miles, and this fact alone expresses one of the most significant regionalisms: Java is the center of the Indies. The arithmetical density for Java-Madura is close to 1,040 per square mile. Bali and Lombok are the only other large islands that possess a high arithmetical density, one close to 600 per square mile. Many small islands such as Ambon contain quite large populations, and many local regions have high densities, such as the Padang Highlands of Sumatra. Sumatra as a whole ranks second to Java in population, with a total close to 11,000,000, though its arithmetical density still is under 60 per square mile. The total population of Celebes is about 5,400,000, Borneo is close to 3,700,000, and all of New Guinea totals about 1,400,000. The population of the Lesser Sunda group of islands totals slightly under 5,000,000, and the Moluccas contain about 1,250,000.

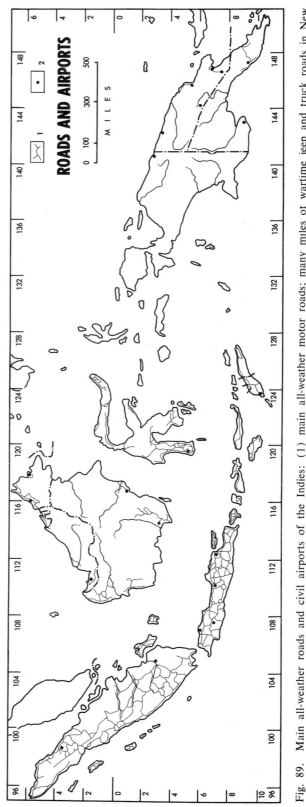

ROADS AND AIRPORTS

Fig. 89. Main all-weather roads and civil airports of the Indies: (1) main all-weather motor roads; many miles of wartime jeep and truck roads in New Guinea have not been maintained; (2) chief civil airports used by regular air services. On Java, Sumatra, and eastern New Guinea are many landing fields built for military use that now are maintained only at a minimum level of utility.

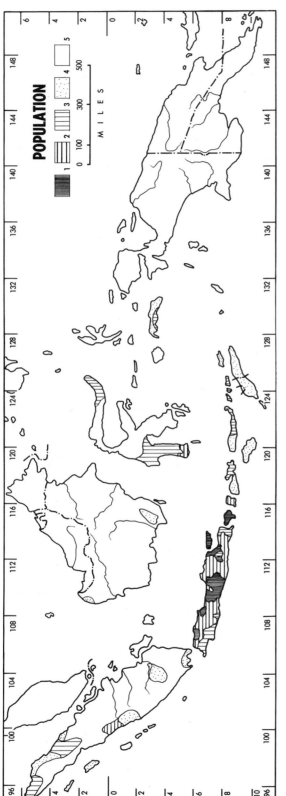

Fig. 90. Estimated population distribution of the Indies: (1) over 1,000 per square mile; (2) 500–1,000 per square mile; (3) 150–500 per square mile; (4) 50–150 per square mile; (5) under 50 people per square mile. No full census has ever been taken, 1953 Indonesian Republic data are not yet available, and for many small islands and large island interiors there are only estimates.

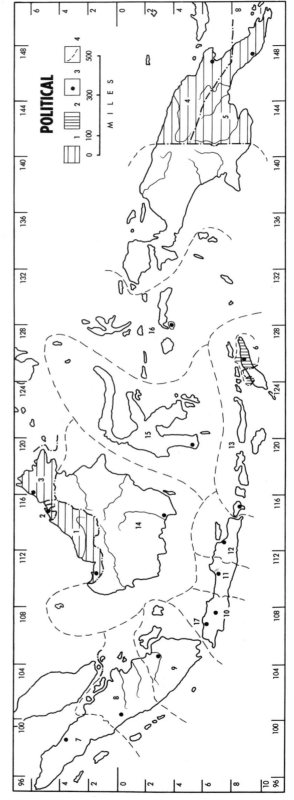

Fig. 91. Political map of the Indies: (1) British-administered units and capitals are: 1, Sarawak, Kuching; 2, Brunei, Brunei; 3, North Borneo, Jesselton; 4, Trust Territory of New Guinea, Lae; 5, Papua, Port Moresby; (2) Portuguese area: 6, Timor, Dili. Republic of Indonesia occupies unlined area; states and capitals are: 7, North Sumatra, Medan; 8, Central Sumatra, Bukit Tinggi; 9, South Sumatra, Palembang; 10, West Java, Bandoeng; 11, Central Java, Semarang; 12, East Java, Soerabaja; 13, Lesser Sundas, Den Pasar; 14, Kalimantan, Bandjarmassin; 15, Sulawesi, Makassar; 16, Moluccas, Ambon; the disputed region Irian (West New Guinea), no formal capital as yet; 17, Jakarta (Batavia), the national capital; (3) locations of capitals; (4) indicates boundaries of states in Republic of Indonesia.

Many of the islands of the Outer Indies can support far more people than now live upon them. To do so, however, will require the adoption of higher systems of land use than shifting cultivation, and the cultural improvement of many of the features of the environment. The building up of regions of poor soils, the development of water supply in the arid regions, the building of transport systems, and the regional scattering of social, educational, and technical education will be required throughout the whole of the Outer Indies, Indonesian, British and Portuguese alike. Few of the non-volcanic islands possess soils rich enough to permit the duplication of Javanese agricultural productivity, but in the past too little effort and investment has been expended upon the Outer Indies. Current British and Indonesian programs of cultural improvement and resource development can turn the Outer Indies into productive areas both complementing and supplementing the Javanese central core.

Most of the population of the Indies is Malay in racial background, though there are many subdivisions with different languages, group customs, and cultural affinities. The second largest single group of peoples is the Chinese, who total close to 2,000,000. They are scattered between Java, Sumatra, Borneo, Banka, and Billiton, though today a few Chinese are to be found in all ports of the Indies. The largest share is urban and commercial, but on Borneo and Sumatra they also engage in fishing, and on Banka and Billiton they engage in mining as laborers.

For decades the Dutch worried about the problem of overpopulation on the island of Java, and tried many methods of moving population to Sumatra and other islands. Some hundreds of thousands of Javanese have settled in southeastern Sumatra, but emigration from Java has not, and will not, alone solve the Javanese problem. Almost the last possible acre of Java's crop land has been utilized, and forested surfaces have been too greatly reduced for efficient flood control and water supply. The Indonesian government continues to share both the worry and the struggle to move Javanese elsewhere. There are few parts of the Indies in which Javanese can live in the manner that they know and prefer. The annual increase of the whole Indies continues to be marked; that of Java-Madura alone is striking, and Java may provide a living laboratory test regarding the possible maximum density of population that a portion of the earth can support. The break-up of commercial agricultural estates can, if carried out completely, provide some relief for a few years, and the growth of industrialization will permit further accommodation of some of the population, but within this century the Javanese way of life must materially change in any event.

Culturally and historically Java, Sumatra, Borneo, and related islands fall together into one group, as being the core area of the Indianized Malay peoples, the region in which the Chinese have been active, and the chief region of commercial agriculture in the modern period. The Lesser Sundas, Celebes, and the Moluccas form a second region of transitional character, both environmentally and in terms of culture history. New Guinea and related islands form a third region, often termed the Great East. This is the untouched and undeveloped part of the Indies that escaped the impact of Indian culture, that contains few Malay peoples, that was not reached by the Moslem culture wave, that contains almost no Chinese, and that has the smallest population and the simplest patterns of economy. This threefold division of the Indies neglects the facts that many of the smaller islands do not fit the broad generalizations just made, and that this large expanse of territory cannot easily be divided into such a small number of regions.

Another aspect of regionalism is political. The obvious divisional pattern is between the former Dutch, British, and Portuguese areas. Within the Indonesian Republic there have been many preliminary political groupings before the present division into political states, shown on the accompanying map. The international divisions are less a matter of native culture history than of the impact of modern political systems of imperialism. A curious twist of this pattern is the way in which the eastern British half of New Guinea is relegated to the Australian culture world, with which it shares almost nothing other than flora, fauna, and political administration. And the British sectors of Borneo, divided into several units in the past, have often been omitted from all discussions. There is little real justification for deleting the British areas from the Indies, despite the frequency with which this is done.

The Philippines: An Island Borderland

THE PEOPLING OF A MULTIPLE-ISLAND ENVIRONMENT

With all its 7,083 islands and rocks the Philippines forms one of the most numerous island groups on our globe. Its 20,000,000 people still do not fill it in a manner wholly typical of the Orient. Though many lowland areas seem alike in their surface patterns the archipelago presents a varied group of local environments within a certain range of physical conditions. A small world of many islands is set on the edge of the Orient, from which it has received most of its people and much of its culture.

All the lowlands are similar to other lowland regions of southeastern Asia in their environmental conditions. The islands belong more to the mainland regions of plants and animals than to the region of the eastern Indies. Here lowland gathering and fishing economies are as at home as in Malaya. Some plants do not reach to northern Luzon, but the basic ones abound everywhere. Many of the islands have hilly to mountainous interiors that call for altered living patterns, and it is only recently that the Malay peoples have gone deeply into these hilly interiors.

Once migration of modern man into the Philippines began, it has been fairly continuous, with overlapping effects. The first immigrants probably were land travelers who moved along the land connections with the Island Arcs in the periods in which these were open. They were simple hunters and gatherers. First came the Negrito and related small peoples. Each new group could find many localities suitable to its particular economy without undue conflict. Following the Negrito were the proto-Malay, who may have used the simplest ideas of agriculture to round out their hunting-gathering economy.

The first Neolithic people came by sea, sometime after the last major breaks in the land bridge routes. They brought crude agriculture and new criteria for the selection of settlements and landscapes. These people were mainlanders, originally from the Mongoloid racial hearth, and sometimes are classified as Indonesian A. They were followed by a succession of mainlanders, labeled Indonesian B, both groups coming during a period lasting perhaps from 6000 to 500 B.C. By 500 B.C. Malaysians began to appear in numbers. If in the earlier periods the several kinds of people occupied given districts with only moderate intermixture, conflicts gradually began to appear as people with varied cultures began a more active competition for picked landscapes. The Negrito have left to them few satisfactory landscapes today and, as the islands fill up with people, those few landscapes will be put to other use.

The Neolithic culture connection between the Philippines and the Asiatic mainland was a close one. Neolithic culture came to the islands already developed, though many questions on the subject still need answering. The first Neolithic men brought better tools, boats, houses, crude caingin agriculture and the first economic plant introductions. Indonesian B brought more and still better tools, the extensive use of jade, bark cloth making, the raised house type with a pyramidal roof, and an extensive agriculture with many more crop plants. As the late Neolithic connection with the mainland lessened, local specialization in weapons, tools, trinkets, and other culture traits became commoner. Some features like the use of jade were abandoned as the mainland contact was altered or broken. In date the Neolithic in the Philippines is tentatively set as covering a period from 6000 B.C. to about 200 B.C. The late Neolithic began about 1000 B.C. The Bronze Age falls across the Neolithic, roughly 800 B.C., and overlaps the Iron Age, which is thought to have begun about 250 B.C. in the islands.

Copper-bronze and gold working techniques came into the islands with the final Indonesian B groups from south China-Tonking, who terminated for a time the period of immigration from the mainland. With them also came irrigated and terraced rice culture, the domestic pig, and several minor items. Since the bringers of these new features were not very numerous their colonial zone was somewhat restricted. They contributed to about 3 per cent of the present population. Modern Igorot and Ifugao cultures are lineal descendants of the South China connection. The concept of very careful terracing of ricefields with integrated water supply did not spread beyond northern and central Luzon. In the rugged terrain of Mountain Province are to be found the only Philippine rice terraces executed in the full Chinese manner. Here cumulative effect of over 2,000 years of work in a durable landscape has been to outdo the Chinese at one of their own specialties.

From Malaysia after about 500 B.C. began the influx of peoples and cultures in a series of waves which finally spread all over the islands. Involved were cultures of late Neolithic through Iron Age, for this stream of people did not cease until the sixteenth century. These Malaysians have almost a 40 per cent share in the present population. With them came wooden and bamboo house types, mats and basketry, dress and tattoo patterns, boats and fishing techniques, and a great many domesticated plants and farming customs. After about 250 B.C. came pottery, cotton, and the textile loom, humped cattle and the water buffalo.* Then also came the knowledge of iron making and its use, trade goods from the Indian Ocean realm, and the sea trading habit. A great many of these traits were really Indian in origin. Many languages spoken in the islands today came with these peoples.

Feeding right into the Malaysian culture streams were the influences of the Indian traders, missionaries, and political organizers. By the third century B.C. their strength was felt over the southern and western islands, lasting some six or seven centuries. The actual number of Indian colonies located in the islands is not at all clear. The later Malaysians were excellent Indian cultural agents, who spread farther than the Indians themselves. Indian influence is shown in language, alphabets, crop plants, old architecture, old religious and art motifs, political and social organization. It is thought that nearly 5 per cent of the Filipinos are Indian mixtures.

* The modern Filipino term for water buffalo is carabao.

Cutting across the Malaysian-Indian line has been the later influence of the Chinese. After its quiet period in the early Christian era Chinese influence increased in Luzon by the eighth century A.D., and by the fifteenth century the Chinese were influential throughout the island and were growing steadily stronger as Indian influences died away. Today it is believed that almost 10 per cent of the population represent Chinese types assimilated over the last thousand years.

Racial mixing processes have been active for 4,000 years. A Filipino blend has been produced, ultimately and chiefly from Mongoloid racial types. Small additions are the Arab-Persian traces added through early sea traders and later Moslems, with some Japanese, Spanish and American blood added in the last four and a half centuries. In the multiple-island environment nature seldom repeated her proportions exactly. But the close proximity of islands and the liking for navigation prevented the regional isolation that might be thought possible. During the Neolithic the Philippines formed a major link in the island chain by which mainland culture traits spread throughout the south and western Pacific. Except for the remnant Negrito there are few contrasts in the Philippines of the order of those that mark the Indies. The Philippine environment is small enough for most incoming peoples and cultural influences to have been able to spread throughout the archipelago. Both the seeming variation and the considerable unity are a partial result of a multiple-island environment in which the same kind of local landscape is repeated over and over again.

MOSLEM AND MORO, SPANISH AND CHRISTIAN

The terminal wave of the stormy eastward flow of Mohammedanism reached the southern islands of the Philippine Archipelago about 1480. Its advocates were Indian and Arab Moslems, both scholars and administrators, successful in spreading their religion and expert at politically organizing small regions into Moslem principalities. In their wake came political chieftains of the little states in the western Indies, each with a band of followers, in the last Malaysian colonial spread into the Philippines. Within a short period the Moslem faith had encompassed the Sulu chain and had a foothold on both Mindanao and Palawan. This faith changed many aspects of native life, but the most significant changes were social and political. Social and religious organization developed a community of feeling, sympathy, and strength; political organization was

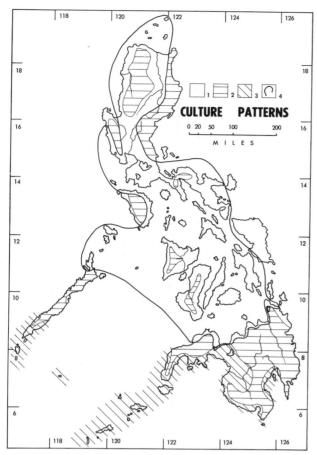

Fig. 92. Philippine culture patterns in late Spanish times·
(1) Christianized regions of mixed native-Spanish culture; (2)
Pagan areas of chiefly native culture; (3) Moslem regions of
somewhat mixed cultures; (4) enclosed region for which Spanish civil government was effective. Military government territories are not included in above.

expressed in small principalities of a more formal sort
than earlier ones.

Many Filipinos are amused at the phrase in occidental history books asserting that Magellan "discovered" the Philippines. In 1521 the islands had
long been well known to China, India, and all Malaysia, and in several ports the traders of many lands
met regularly. When the Spanish arrived in force in
1565, Moslem chieftains held power in scattered localities as far north as Manila, though the mass conversion
of the regional populace to the Moslem faith had
taken in only Sulu and parts of Mindanao and Palawan. The Spanish conquest went rapidly except in
the far south where the Moslem faith supported its
own political and military leadership; here the Spanish
never made their conquest truly complete during their
whole period of control. Constant Moro raiding and
looting, conducted from Sulu, Palawan, and Borneo,

caused annual losses along all Mindanao and many
Visayan coasts until the middle of the nineteenth
century.

Spanish rule markedly altered the culture of the
Filipinos and, of course, affected a much larger area
than had that of the Moslems. In the Spanish system
the Catholic priesthood worked hand in hand with
temporal power. By 1611 numerous churches had
been organized and a share of the population had accepted Christianity. Only in isolated island interiors
did there remain non-Christian tribes at the end of
Spanish rule. The fairly uniform acceptance of Christianity hastened other changes of a political and economic nature. The Spanish began with the barangay
and the datu (the native local political unit and the
chief), turning them into the barrio and the teniente,
in American terms the ward and the lieutenant.
Above the barrio they set the pueblo or town system
that they had used in the Americas, termed municipio,
now renamed the municipality. The barrio and the
municipality functioned to bring local affairs under
controllable heads, and served as the centers in which
fixed residence could be enforced. The centralization
of regional government in provinces grew out of the
granting of encomiendas, great tracts of land given
to greedy colonial officers, both political and religious.
The establishment of a central government superior
to the provinces placed the control of the Philippines
in Manila before the end of the sixteenth century.

The introduction of many American crop plants
enlarged the agriculture of the islands. In the nineteenth century the Spanish stimulated the development
of a limited commercial agriculture. The reorienting
of trade toward Mexico and the attempted operation
of the islands as an imperial monopoly altered older
trade patterns. The institution of new forms of house
building, food habits, forms of dress, social customs,
and the Spanish language made over the higher levels
of society and the masses to a variable degree. Spanish rule was monopolistic and exploitive. Spaniards
almost never engaged in primary production but lived
as gentlemen on the fruits of Filipino labor and Chinese trade. Forced labor and tax exactions were heavy
at the hands of both the priesthood and the political
administrators.

One cannot observe the impressive old churches
scattered over the Spanish-controlled parts of the islands without visualizing the heavy hand of the
Church. Only in the latter half of the nineteenth century were appreciable improvements made in colonial
administration, too slowly and in too little measure.
The weight of Spanish rule plus the effect of Moslem
raids retarded the growth of population until the nine-

teenth century. From a possible half million in the midsixteenth century population rose to about 1,500,-000 by 1800, leaped to about 3,500,000 by 1845, and stood close to 7,000,000 at the end of Spanish rule in 1899.

The Spanish furthered one pattern which now has grown into a major problem with no easy solution. In the sixteenth century the Chinese already were the leading merchants throughout the islands. Spanish encouragement of Chinese traders increased their numbers, even though periodic oppression temporarily reduced their operations. By the end of the Spanish period the Chinese controlled a good share of the interisland wholesale and retail trade. They were present in every large city and had infiltrated most of the profitable economic enterprises of the islands. They had intermarried among the Filipinos to such an extent that many of the present leaders of the islands are mixed Chinese-Filipinos. The Chinese population continues to increase and the problem grows greater with every year.

THE COMING OF THE AMERICAN

The Americans came into the islands with the avowed mission of improving conditions for the population. American control retained the whole of the Spanish regional administrative machinery, the barrio, the municipio, the province, and the capital at Manila. American procedure introduced the specially chartered city. These grew in number until in 1948 there were 18,859 barrios, 983 municipalities, 50 provinces, and 21 chartered cities. The last are supervised directly by the national government. Among the first acts of American rule were the separation of Church and state and the starting of a public school system. In consequence the Moros have become relatively peaceful members of Filipino society.* Their unity of religious feeling, and differences in food and dress, set them off against the Christians, but they are actively a part of the modern Philippines. Large blocks of friar-owned lands were bought back by the government and sold to private owners, in the first decade of American rule, but the Church still owns considerable property. Under American Protestant competition many recent improvements in the Catholic program have been instituted, particularly in the field of education.

By 1950 there were over 4,500,000 children in over 21,000 public and private schools of elementary and secondary level. Faced with some eighty languages and dialects American educators began teaching English, which now is the widely spoken lingua franca, even in Moro regions. Tagalog, one of the more widely used native tongues, now has been chosen as the national language. It is taught in public schools along with English but, though the radio and native movies help spread it, years will pass before it will become a truly national language.

Under American rule changes were made steadily to increase the role of the Filipino in his own affairs. Within the framework of government inherited from the Spanish many American democratic procedures were progressively installed. A limited pattern of free trade, within the tariff wall of the United States, came in 1909, and will continue through 1954. In 1934 Philippine independence was planned for the mid-1940's and given on July 4, 1946. During a 20-year period starting in 1954 the islands will retain a favored position within the United States tariff wall.† Unfortunately the Filipinos have also learned many of the political and social vices that inhibit good government. As American authority has relaxed these have increased disproportionately in number and volume. The short span of 50 years may have been too short a time in which to learn thoroughly the intricate workings of representative government. And unfortunately American rule did not completely finish many reorganization programs begun with good intention.

The recent influence of the American has increasingly altered the pattern of culture. As one travels over the islands today it is obvious that lipstick, chewing gum, and toothpaste are replacing the chewing of betel nut, that soft drinks and beer are replacing coconut and nipa palm tuba, that radios, newspapers, and comic books have become extremely popular. The Chinese merchant has been an almost ubiquitous agency by which a standard range of modern occidental consumer goods has been spread throughout the islands. The motor road and the bus, truck, and private car have recently been so widely adopted that motor fuel products now are one of the chief imports. In the homes of better-educated Filipinos one finds a surprising but purposeful reproduction of contemporary American life. Filipinos feel that they have

---

* A Moro is merely a Moslem Filipino. The old west European term for the Moslem was changed from Moor to Moro.

† The Bell Trade Act, negotiated in 1946, provided for annual fractional increases of United States tariffs upon Philippine goods until parity is reached in 1974, meaning that after 1974 Philippine products entering the United States will be subject to the same tariffs as those commodities coming from other countries. It also imposed various conditions upon the Philippines which impair political and economic independence. The United States retains several one-sided privileges in the islands which are not accorded Filipinos in the United States.

progressed farther than other Far Eastern countries on the road to modern civilization. Most of them look to the United States with affection, respect, and, it must be added, expectancy. There are some who feel that it was wrong to permit so rapid and full a reproduction of contemporary American culture in a small country which so far has not the economic maturity to support all its cultural aspirations. Through the American implanted educational system, today still somewhat lacking in vocational and mechanical training, the white-collar class has become the admired goal, rather than the mechanical craftsmen and artisans who have been the backbone of American material culture. In this the United States insufficiently countered the demoralizing impact of Spanish rule.

THE PATTERN OF RESIDENCE

In the pre-Spanish period there were several variations in living patterns, owing to racial and cultural differences. Some of the simpler groups were semimigratory in habit. The practice of shifting agriculture worked against permanently fixed settlements, and the linear coastlines made for random residence at any attractive landing. Fertile local landscapes brought heavier settlement and groups of villages. Perhaps the Moslems first fortified certain sites and turned them into strategic military and political centers. The Spanish carried the matter further, with formal and fixed sites. The poblacion, the central part of the municipio, with its church, convent, plaza, garrison barracks, administrative building and headmen's residences, gradually became a small town. The native barangay, upon becoming the barrio, often remained straggling and extended, more an administrative unit than a settlement site.

Today one finds homesteads scattered everywhere from the high-tide line to the high mountains. Houses seldom are screened for privacy by special plantings, though they often are partly concealed by a miniature jungle of fruit trees. A barrio often is a long and narrow shoestring alignment of houses along a road or a shore line. As new roads are built people sometimes prefer the convenience of roadside residence to scattered locations in the fields. One often finds the highway between towns almost continuously lined with houses. The poblacion of the municipality today retains its plaza around which are grouped the church, convent, schools, municipal offices, theaters, the municipal market shed, some of the shops, and a few of the houses. Spanish settlement plans, originally rectangular, have not always retained their alignment, as no force has been used in recent decades. New towns

in the colonial regions seldom have a formal plaza and do not show the massive stone churches and other buildings normally built under Spanish rule. Urbanism is a slowly growing part of the residence pattern of the islands, in 1948 slightly under 11 per cent of the people living in cities of over 10,000.

Field patterns are of every shape. Where physical conditions permit they often are roughly rectangular. Cane, corn, plantation coconut, plantation abaca, and many ricefields are fairly rectangular in shape and continuous in planting. Small holdings of most field crops, almost all of the fruit, and many of the vegetables are in very mixed plantings and are irregular in field pattern. The upland farm landscape always is an irregular one containing forest remnants or some of the rank grasses. In only a few places is the surveyor working ahead of the colonial settler, namely in the national land subdivisions. Most farms are delimited and identified by historic usage, customary acceptance, and the payment of municipality taxes. Specific land titles are rather new, and it is customary today in many areas to claim a given tract of land but to crop only a portion thereof, years ahead of the surveyors.

The house on piles, built of bamboo and thatched with various grasses, palm leaves, or mattings, was one of the early importations into the islands. Later crude timber and wooden planks became common for chiefs and wealthier families. There still are a few communal houses and special houses for men and women, but these forms have largely gone from the cultured parts of the islands. Almost basic today is the single-family house raised a few feet off the ground on posts of some sort. The height of these posts may vary from 3 to 10 feet. The house itself may consist of a single squarish room with a steep gabled roof, or it may be as large as a dozen rooms, multiple gabled and formed of a variety of separate rooms and lean-to units. The ground-floor section serves in the place of auxiliary buildings, as pens for animals and fowls, tool, and crop storage. This section often is not walled and seldom is floored. It is characteristic that roofs have a wide overhang and that the sliding windows of larger houses are provided with separate rain-shelter awnings.

Since perhaps 1930 urban cultural aspiration has been for the wooden house, set on concrete posts, with solid wood floors, a sheet iron roof, a formal entry stairway, electric lights, and a bathroom with running water. Most of the towns have piped water systems and electricity to support these hopes. In simpler economic situations, and in rural surroundings, bamboo may replace most of the wood, nipa palm thatch may cover the walls and the roof, and the floor may be of split bamboo. Running water and electric light are rare items in rural localities. Except in northern Luzon, whenever possible there are flowers around the house, in the ground, in pots, or in hanging coconut husks.

There are certain regional differences in house design and in materials, but for the main portion of the islands today the type is fairly standard. Where nipa palm is not available, cogon grass or split bamboo is used. In the higher mountain lands wooden slabs or rough planking are used. In the Batanes group of islands, north of Luzon in the main typhoon track, houses are strongly built of stone, and in the marsh country of parts of Mindanao houseboats form some homes. Some of the simpler tribal groups still use tree shelters and other special types of housing.

Modern urban influences have added to the changes in housing. Paint, glass windows, screens, plaster stucco, and garages are combined with the "modern" trend in architecture. This usually omits the posts and an elevated position. Since there is little zoning in practice, the elaborate homes of the wealthy in many communities are flanked by the one-room nipa houses of the poor. These newer features are spreading into the smaller towns and hinterlands, for commonly one may find a Filipino recently back from years in "the States" eager to retain accustomed living habits.

PHILIPPINE AGRICULTURE TODAY

The Philippines is primarily agricultural but does not feed itself. This became true in late Spanish times, and, despite efforts to correct it, it remains true today. American commercial stimulation of agriculture for export was not accompanied by enough teaching in scientific agriculture to replace the former simple crop growing. Agriculture today therefore is not as highly productive as it needs to be both to feed a rapidly growing population and to provide commercial exports with which to finance the higher standards of living made appealing by the cultural progress of the islands. Free entry into the United States, after 1909, gave export agriculture both a good market and a kind of guarantee. The share of land devoted to export crops is over 30 per cent. This would not be bad if the per-acre food crop yields were high, but they are among the lower yields for the world as a whole.

Farming Conditions

Farm equipment ranges from the simple digging stick to power machinery, and farming practices are a curious blend of science, easy-going tropical habits, and folk lore. Draft power of any kind is quite inadequate. Fertilization, crop rotation, and conservation practices are almost unknown to the general small farmer. But mechanization and improved farming have a greater potential in the islands than in many other parts of the Orient, provided that the right kind of government program carries it out, and provided that manufacturers can be persuaded to develop power equipment able to operate in wet and soggy lands.

Until about 1915 in no part of the islands was there a severe pressure of men upon the land. This has since developed in parts of Luzon and in the Visayas. There still is ample land for a larger population and, until the late nineteenth century, there was food enough for all the people. The very lack of intensive farming is responsible for a share of the low yields. Ricefields often are not level, so that the water must stand in pockets. Often what water there is is derived from immediate rainfall only. For years writers on the islands have commented on the need for irrigation. In north Luzon where the famous rice terraces of Mountain Province have been built over the centuries the chief engineering operation is the elaborate provisions of water for each field.*

As indicated previously the Filipinos developed their rice culture in the cheapest way possible, without always providing a water supply and without care for the soil. Animal power is used when available, but its inadequacy requires a large volume of human labor per volume of crop. As farmland has increased in amount, without concurrent provision of water, the cost of irrigation engineering needed has cumulatively grown until today the problem is a formidable obstacle in improving agriculture, both to private farmers and to the government.†

With rice the primary crop the future provision of water and the level terracing of small fields along the lines of the Chinese or Japanese system of intensive, man-powered farming is one avenue to greater crop yields. Enlargement of fields, mechanization of farm work, and the application of modern science in agriculture are another. The two routes to increased production are not fully compatible and cannot both be applied to the same fields. The islands still have a chance to use either or both on selected tracts of land. Several forces are at work, and it is difficult to predict the

---

* These fields total only some 70,000 acres, and include land planted to other crops than rice. In addition to the terraced lands there are many caingin and slope fields used by the same farmers, with practices as wasteful as those of the terraces are saving.

† It is estimated that the costs of projects to supply water to all fields needed for rice in another 20 years will exceed $250,000,000, for the islands a rather large sum.

direction of change. Though shifting cultivation is now prohibited by law, it continues on a rather large scale on the mountain hinterlands. Mechanization sometimes fails through improper training and equipment not suited to the task. Successful experimenters in mechanization are copied by their neighbors, but

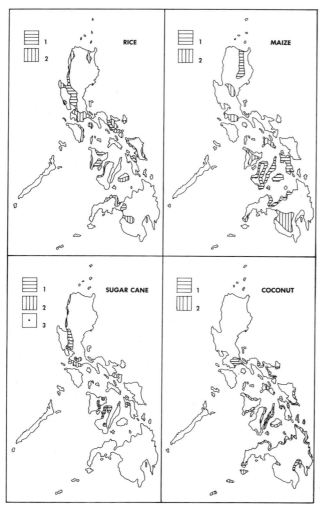

Fig. 93. Chief Philippine crops: (1) primary producing regions; (2) secondary producing areas; (3) sugar refineries.

the Filipino farmer is as hard to change as those elsewhere.

A little over one fifth the total area of the islands is taken up by about 1,700,000 farms. Of this area of some 15,000,000 acres about 10,000,000 are cultivated every year, the balance either lying idle or being utilized as pastures, wood lots, or non-crop areas. By double cropping the total land cropped each year is raised to about 12,000,000 acres. Expressed most simply, the average-sized farm is about 10 acres, but just about half the total farms are under 5 acres in size, and account for only one fifth the total farmland. Farms over 12 acres, totaling over half the land in farms, are run by fewer than 13 per cent of the farmers. Approximately 40 per cent of the farmers are tenants, the proportion ranging downward from a maximum of about two thirds in central Luzon. Recent land laws have improved the legal position of the tenant, but the actual position of the back-country tenant has changed but little, and tenancy reform is one of the most needed improvements in agriculture. About 9,000,000 people are concerned with agriculture out of a total of some 21,000,000. Accompanying maps show regional concentration of the five major crops.

The Crop Pattern

The outstanding crop is rice, of which there are hundreds of varieties. About 5,000,000 acres annually are planted with several kinds of rice, meaning just under 40 per cent of the cultivated land. About half the total agricultural labor is concerned with rice. Over 1,000,000 acres of upland rice, grown on plowed and hand-dug or cleared but un-worked slopes and dependent upon rain alone, consists mostly of quick-growing 3-to-5-month varieties with a light per-acre yield. Over 2,000,000 acres of rice are grown on plowed lowland fields that depend upon rain water impounded within their borders. These varieties require a growing season of 5 to 7 months, yield moderately but seldom are double cropped. About 1,500,-000 acres of irrigated long-season rice are grown every year, including a considerable second crop, with high yields. Some rice is grown in every province, but there is an uneven balance of sufficiency. Central Luzon is the chief surplus region, but metropolitan Manila more than absorbs this surplus. Rice lands are not adequately increasing in volume, and per-acre production has stood still for some years.

Maize totals about 2,600,000 acres, about 16 per cent of the cultivated area, and uses about 20 per cent of the agricultural labor volume. About 25 per cent of the population lives chiefly on maize the year around. Cropping practices vary markedly, from one to four crops per year on the same land. Most varieties are rather poor producers. Losses by corn borers often are heavy, and their seasonal life-cycle often controls the planting of maize. Some maize is grown all over the islands, but the coral limestone portions of the Visayan Islands unsuited to rice are the chief growing center. The lands of Mindanao to which Visayan colonists have gone are put into maize, rather than rice, out of cultural preference.

Sweet potatoes and bananas are of about equal importance as supporting food crops, the former occupying about 400,000 acres of land, and the latter about 300,000 acres. Rarely is either crop grown on wide acreage, but in garden patches around the farmsteads in many varieties. Each is grown almost everywhere in the islands, though the northern Luzon hill country has extensive areas of sweet potatoes and few of bananas. Manioc (for cassava) and mungo (mung bean) are other minor crops, usually occupying about 175,000 and 75,000 acres, respectively. Manioc is but little grown in northern Luzon. Sweet potatoes and manioc, with such other minor root crops as taro and several kinds of yams, vary considerably in cultivated area from year to year, depending upon food scarcity and the success of the major food crops. In bad years root crop plantings increase greatly, to slough off when better food can be had.

There are over a dozen minor food crops, roots, vegetables, and fruits that are scattered over the islands or concentrated in particular localities possessing attractive local environments. Such vegetables as tomatoes, green beans, eggplant and the bitter cucumbers, along with peanuts and such fruits as the mango, papaya, lanzone, jackfruit, breadfruit, oranges, coffee, and cacao are widely scattered and well liked, though almost nowhere are they grown in organized plantings of any size. Except for peanuts, tomatoes, and mangos, a few plants of each of the others share the jungle-like planting around many farm homes. Pineapple, a minor crop in acreage, is a significant export product grown in northern Mindanao on an American-operated plantation, but it is grown elsewhere in small home plantings only. The total acreage of these crops amounts to about 300,000 acres per year.

Sugar has been the chief commercial export crop in past years when free access to the United States markets was assured. Under the quota system adopted during the mid-1930's, the destruction of World War II, and the gradual increase of United States tariff barriers, sugar may decrease in importance. Something over a half million acres normally go into cane, grown both on big plantations and on small holdings. The island of Negros, central Luzon, eastern Panay, and northern Cebu are the sugar cane centers, where refiners operate "sugar centrals" to crush and produce raw and white sugar. Widely distributed over the islands are small plantings of cane used to produce the older style domestic brown sugar in small crushing and boiling plants. Domestic consumption takes about 12 to 15 per cent of the crop.

Coconut is coming to be the chief export product of the islands, despite the rather low quality of coconut products turned out, and is promoted by the steady planting of new lands both by the small planter and the plantation owner. There are now about 140,000,000 trees planted, almost 100,000,000 of which are of bearing age. Supposedly preferring low elevations and sandy to loamy soils near the seacoast, coconuts today are doing well under a variety of other conditions. Commercial plantings reach from central Luzon southward, southern Luzon being the most densely planted region. The northern part of Luzon and the interiors of the larger islands contain no commercial plantings, but a few trees around homesteads are common, up to elevations of about 2,000 feet. Most coconut products, fresh coconut, copra, desiccated coconut, coconut oil, and tuba (a fermented alcoholic drink made from juice extracted from the growing tip of the tree), are produced by the small landholder. He is individualistic in habits and slow to adopt progressive techniques. Less than 2 per cent of the yield is used domestically. Coconut lands often are planted to other crops when the trees are young. It is hard to tabulate the acreage devoted to coconut, but the figure is probably not far from 2,600,000 acres, about 21 per cent of the cropped area.

Abaca now is the third ranking agricultural export, covering about 700,000 acres, some 6 per cent of the land in crops. The southern end of Luzon, Samar, and Leyte, and eastern Mindanao are the chief producing districts, though the Visayan Islands generally produce some abaca. Southeastern Mindanao, before 1941, had developed as an area of Japanese-operated plantations, producing the majority of the export. Post-war land-holding readjustments have eliminated the Japanese and have greatly increased the role of the small planter who grows abaca as a cash crop along with corn, bananas, and vegetables as food crops. This has tended to production irregularities of some importance. As southern Luzon, Samar, and Leyte suffer occasional typhoons, very hard on the banana-like plant producing the fiber, the future of the export industry is not entirely an assured and happy one.

Tobacco, a major export crop during late Spanish times, was operated as a government monopoly on large land holdings. In the American period the crop first increased and then has gradually declined, being largely Spanish controlled. Since 1930 tobacco has occupied about 150,000 acres of land, used less than 2 per cent of the agricultural labor, and accounted for about 2 per cent of the exports. War-time destruction was hard on the organized tobacco industry, and imports of American tobaccos in the prosperous post-war era have made development difficult. Northern Luzon, particularly the Cagayan Valley, is the chief producing area, with Cebu also important, but small garden plantings are found almost all over the islands.

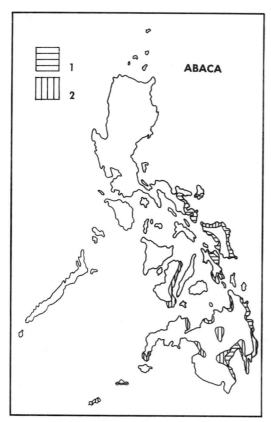

Fig. 94. Regional production of abaca: (1) primary production regions; (2) secondary areas of production.

There are a number of minor export crops, such as
maguey (producing a type of sisal fiber), derris root
for insect killers, and rubber. Rubber, so important
in Malaya and the Indies, ranks about twenty-fifth by
area and about twentieth by value of product in the
Philippines.

The ten major Philippine crops, ranked by area of
land, are: rice, coconut, corn, abaca, sugar cane, sweet
potatoes, bananas, tobacco, manioc, and the mung
bean. By value of product the first ten are: rice,
sugar cane, coconut, corn, abaca, bananas, sweet potatoes, manioc, tobacco, and the mango.

The animal population of the islands is considerably
less than needed, whether for draft power or for food
purposes, though totals had been climbing steadily until
excessive war-time slaughtering set the islands back a
good many years. In rank hogs, carabao, cattle, goats,
horses, and sheep, and chickens, ducks, and pigeons
are the most numerous among the animal and fowl
groups. Of pork, beef, and carabao the average urban
Filipino consumes a total of about 40 pounds per year,
which is far less than the American average, but well
above that of the Orient as a whole. Fish form a very
significant part of the island diet, and the annual con-

sumption per person runs above 50 pounds, though
unevenly divided between coastal and interior consumers. The average Filipino prefers a basic menu
of rice and fish in three daily meals, supplemented by
varying amounts of bread, meat, vegetables, and fruit.
The fish volume is made up of commercially caught
sea fish, locally caught fish from the sea, rivers, lakes,
and ricefields, fish culturally raised in ponds, and a
significant import volume. The fish-pond harvest is
substantially increasing as coastal mangrove swamps
are diked and turned into ponds for the raising of one
particular fish, the bangos.

About 22 per cent of the islands' area now is in
farmlands; other figures are somewhat tentative, since
the Philippines is engaged in detailed classification of
her land area. In 1948 nearly 60 per cent of the total
remained to be surveyed. Almost 20 per cent of the
total area now is in open grass and parklands, largely
the effect of shifting agriculture and annual burning.
Commercial forests are estimated to cover some 44 per

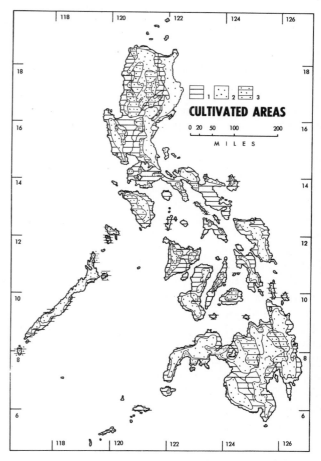

Fig. 95. Cultivated areas of the Philippines: (1) predominantly land in farms; (2) chiefly uncultivated land with scattered caingin clearings; (3) areas of partial cultivation, with
farm areas increasing under frontier settlement.

cent of the area, and non-commercial forests, being second growth and worked-over lands, about 15 per cent. Swamp and marshlands cover about 2 per cent. Estimates of the eventual permanent forest lands needed average about 38 per cent. The forest volume of timber is estimated at about 450,000,000,000 board feet, about half of which is inaccessible. The annual growth rate is thought to be over 3,000,000,000 board feet per year, whereas present commercial timber cutting has barely reached 1,000,000,000 board feet annually. About 97 per cent of the remaining forests are owned by the national government, though nearly two thirds of the municipalities have small communal forests. Besides commercial timber production, however, is an unknown but serious drain upon forest lands by the continued illegal practice of caingin clearing, and by the uncontrolled permanent removal of forests by colonial settlers.

Some 3,000 species of trees are said to reach commercial size, though most of the commercial timber is secured from some sixty species entering the market under about twenty different names. The chief commercial lumbering islands at present are Mindanao, Negros, and Mindoro, though lumber is widely produced by small operators. The Philippines already enjoys an export market in lumber, rattan, and minor forest products. This market, if properly developed, can increase, and, if the forests are properly handled, timber export can become a permanent and valuable aspect of Philippine economy.

TRANSPORTATION AND TRADE

In 1949 the Philippines still had not recovered its pre-war status as regards roads, railroads, the communications system, and domestic and foreign trade patterns. Recovery was largely being financed by American rehabilitation grants, which poured large sums of money into the islands. These funds upset the normal trend of domestic affairs and promoted a prosperity unlike that in any other country that suffered damage during World War II. The large demand in world markets for edible oils, sugar, and fibers has promoted high prices, and the Filipino national income has moved steadily upward. This income, plus the obvious need for reconstruction materials, has produced a great upsurge in the importing of manufactured goods. Despite huge war-time losses the Philippine situation, therefore, is somewhat different from that of other oriental countries suffering delay and failure of effective post-war reconstruction.

The Philippine highway system of about 18,000 miles of national and provincial paved and all-weather

roads, in 1952, fairly well opens up for contact the major regions of the country. Palawan and Mindoro are the islands most notably lacking in roads, but many sections of Luzon and Mindanao lack secondary roads. The total mileage is quite inadequate to the needs of

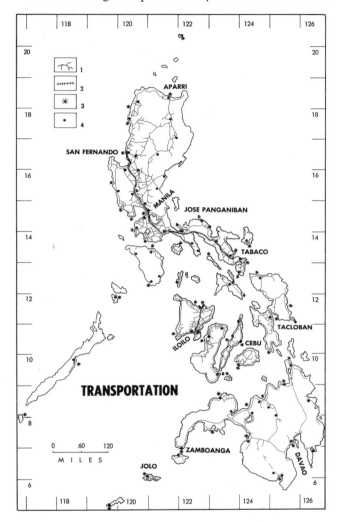

Fig. 96. Transportation in the Philippines: (1) primary road net; (2) rail lines; (3) national ports (ports open to foreign shipping are named); (4) civil airports.

the population, particularly in some of the frontier territories. About 95,000 motor vehicles in 1950 did not provide adequate services. A relatively large number of companies operate bus routes over all open roads, but there is need for many more vehicles of all types.

There were, in 1941, about 850 miles of permanent railway on the three islands of Luzon, Panay, and Cebu. The Luzon line was British built, a 42-inch-gauge system with a fair amount of antiquated rolling stock, a large part of which was ruined during the war years. The Cebu and Panay lines were American built light-rail systems which also suffered during the war. The Cebu line has not been rebuilt, the Panay line is in service, and the main line on Luzon is operative again. The railways have suffered from competition from coastal water transport, from parallel bus and trucking transport, and from unprogressive management. In a multiple-island environment railways are less serviceable than other forms of transport, and it is not likely that the railway mileage will ever become great. The sugar-growing and lumbering areas have small movable rail systems totaling nearly 500 miles in all, but these are not available for general transportation.

Many interisland shipping services, with a variety of ships, launches, and small boats, make regular runs throughout the islands and operate ferry services between islands. Most of the small ports are restricted to domestic shipping services. Today air services connect every large island and almost every large town to Manila, so that in a few hours one can get to every part of the archipelago.

In domestic trade there is an interesting dual pattern. Many American, some Filipino, a few British, and other European manufacturers, importers, and exporters have headquarters in Manila and selected towns appropriate to their lines. The American and Filipino firms handle the largest share of the major wholesale trading. The Chinese commercial investment is greater than the American investment, though on a quite different plane. Of approximately 72,000 commercial enterprises only about 14,000 are run by Chinese, but they are more highly capitalized than the majority of native concerns. The Chinese thus form a powerful group of wholesalers, retailers, and middlemen handling a large share of the domestic trade beyond the primary wholesaling ports. The number of Chinese is increasing steadily, and their share of trade likewise increases. The domestic trade involves moving manufactured goods from Manila throughout the islands, and the moving of rice, corn, and the export crops from the rural countryside to the major urban areas and major ports on the several larger islands.

In the field of foreign trade the islands have made steady growth. In 1855 the total foreign trade amounted to about $5,000,000, with exports slightly larger than imports. By 1899 this total had climbed to some $34,000,000, amounting to about $5.00 per capita, with imports slightly larger than exports. In 1941 the figure stood at almost $300,000,000, with exports a little larger than imports, and the per capita figure at about $17.00. During most years of American control the islands had a favorable balance of trade. The American share in the total trade in 1899 was very small; that of Spain was very small by 1941. In 1941 the United States supplied some 87 per cent of the imports and took about 60 per cent of the exports. The value of the 1947 trade, somewhat inflated by high prices, jumped to some $775,000,000, with imports about twice the exports, amounting to a per capita figure of $40.00. A considerable share of the imports naturally represented reconstruction materials, but too much was spent on expendable consumer goods. The bulk of the trade fell to the United States. By 1950 import controls had reduced the import of consumer goods and almost balanced the trade again.

In pre-war years the British and Japanese commercial fleets handled a large share of the total shipping, with Norway and the United States in lower positions. Under abnormal conditions United States ships now move the major volume of commerce, but the islands would welcome relief from the constant threat of United States shipping strikes. There now are eleven ports open to international trade.

By the 1947 trade returns some 41 countries did more than $1,000,000 total business with the islands. The leaders were: United States in a position by herself, followed by Canada, France, China, Great Britain, Denmark, Italy, Belgium, and the Indies, in that order. In the commodity pattern of exports sugar led in the pre-war years, but coconut products, taken altogether, now hold first place. Gold, from mines all over the islands, has ranked second or third, with abaca fourth to form a first group of really important exports. It is upon these four items that the economic structure of the Philippines must rest after the United States completes its rehabilitation financing. In a second category, in order, come tobacco products, embroideries, timber and rattans, iron ores and the ferro-alloy minerals, and canned pineapple. Certain items, like sugar, pineapple, and embroideries, go almost entirely to the United States. Mine products are rather new in the export pattern. Gold is the really valuable one, but iron, chromium, and manganese are certain to increase in volume in coming years. Mining is largely American engineered and at least partly American controlled.

Among the imports cotton goods have ranked first in more recent years. Iron and steel, petroleum products, tobaccos, paper and its products, grain and their preparations (mostly whole rice and wheat flour), rayons and other synthetic fabrics, automobiles and tires, meats and dairy products, and chemicals, cosmetics and drugs complete the list of major commodities. The import of tobaccos now exceeds the export, a post-war development. The importance of iron and steel and petroleum among the imports reflects the inability of the islands to produce its own metal products and the lack of adequate native petroleum supplies. Since the islands cannot grow wheat, but people demand breadstuffs and macaronis, the permanent import of wheat is likely. The full import lists are comprehensive in range, reflecting the industrial immaturity of the islands. Import controls, of some sort, will create an artificially stabilized pattern of imports for some years.

TOWARD THE GROWTH OF INDUSTRY

A wide variety of traditional skills still are practiced all over the islands. Basketry, several types of matting, hats, varied textiles, wooden clog-shoes, fish nets, ropes and twines, native boats and carts, metal tools and utensils, and varied ornamental and decorative items are among the commoner products. Certain regional specialties distinctly stand out, such as the brass products of Moro Cotabato and Lanao provinces, the abaca textiles of the non-Christian hill peoples of Mindanao, the cotton textiles of the Luzon Ilocanos, the wood carving of Luzon's Mountain Province. In the older household there was little formal furniture and fittings, and the Filipino was used to living and working with the simplest of materials. In general, however, there seems to be less regional specialization and rather a smaller volume of handicrafts surviving in the Philippines than in other parts of the Orient. Over a half million people are engaged full time in the making of handicraft products, with many more part-time performers. Many aspects of the traditional handicrafts have been decreasing during the American period under the impact of Chinese-merchandised, occidental-made machine goods.

Processing of the current chief crop exports has been carried on since Spanish times. The Chinese started exporting abaca and refining sugar, and they perhaps also processed some coconut products. Tobacco is a Spanish commercial product. Sugar processing still is done in two ways, the small and crude old "muscovado mill" making brown sugar and the modern corporation factory "sugar central" making raw and refined sugar for home use and export. Coconuts are processed by farmers, small concerns, and corporation factories. Most of the coconut oil and desiccated coconut are factory produced, but most of the copra and tuba are the work of small farmers using virtually handicraft techniques. Periodic shifts in the export of coconut products from oil to copra and back again are dependent upon world prices and tariffs. The tobacco industry, which has declined since the start of World War

II, is divided between the small home operator and the companies making cigarettes and cigars for domestic consumption and for export. Abaca gradually was becoming mechanized before the war, but the elimination of the Japanese plantations will increase the share of hand operations in fiber production.

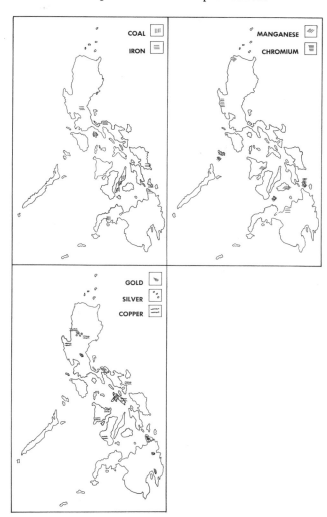

Fig. 97. Mineralized regions of the Philippines.

The processing of many other consumer products is under way. For export these are not yet numerous. Embroideries produced in small shops and homes, lumber and rattan manufactures from small concerns, and canned pineapple from a corporation cannery are the most valuable. Buttons, cordage, and vegetable fiber hats are others. For home use there are being manufactured a wide variety of food products, clothing, cement, glass, furniture, soaps, cosmetics, distilled and soft drinks, and metal products fabricated from imported metal shapes. The recent production of gold, iron, and the ferro-alloy minerals is promising, but the absence of adequate coking coal will require the special development of charcoal-fueled smelting plants not yet developed in the islands. The rise of the mining industry is the one spectacular industrial change in island economy, but the mineral base is not sufficiently wide to produce island industrialization.

Under private initiative industrialization would be a slow process in a country like the Philippines without large capital funds and accumulated technical skills. To hasten this aspect of the islands' economy government corporations with long-range plans had begun operation in widely separated lines before World War II. Fresh and canned fish, rice and corn milling, coconut and abaca products, cotton textiles, shoe manufacture, cement production, fertilizer minerals, metals production, and hydro-electric power are some of the lines under production and planned for development for government concerns. Government corporations now are engaged in rail, bus, and air transport. Well-planned and administered leadership of this sort can stimulate island industrialization, but the Philippine record has not been particularly good. It is expected that private industry will follow gradually and eventually replace the function of government in part of the industrial program. The industrialization of the islands has not yet gone far, but plans are laid to further elevate the Filipino's standard of living, to restore the normal balance of trade, and to increase the productive capacity of export products against the day when complete tariff separation from the United States makes world competition necessary.

ISLAND REGIONALISMS

The Philippines show unanimity in many essential characteristics but some regional differences in landscape, agriculture, psychology, language, and customs that divide the islands into the same intangible kinds of regions that exist in the United States. The Philippines culturally is one of the youngest portions of the Orient, and many of its regionalisms have not yet become clearly distinguishable. In broadest terms the three main portions of the islands are Luzon, the Visayas, and Mindanao, though this omits three minor areas, the Batanes Islands, Palawan, and the Sulu chain. Three rather well-defined parts of Luzon form distinct geographic regions, the balance of the island being divisible only by the selection of some arbitrary criterion. The three are the narrow Ilocos country of the northwest coast, the Mountain Province of north Luzon and the Bicol region of southeastern Luzon.

The narrow coastal lowland of northwest Luzon known as the Ilocano country is easily the most clearly defined geographic region of the islands. The four provinces on this coast do not form a rich region, but Spanish influence was very strong here. The area has a climatic regime with a distinct rainy season and a dry rainless one that limits second-crop agriculture and provides too little water for the coastal lowland. The Ilocano region is overpopulated and notable for the Ilocano people themselves. The coastal lands speak a distinct language. Frugal, industrious, and ambitious, the Ilocanos are the best handicraftsmen and the most seasoned wanderers of the islands. They use bamboo distinctively in house building but rarely enjoy the luxury of flower gardens. Their rice-producing techniques display a number of quite individual practices. A great many of the Filipinos in Hawaii and the United States are Ilocanos, and they are among the best and hardiest colonists of Mindanao. This population abroad constantly remits money home to support a share of the home population.

Mountain Province of North Luzon is a rugged and mountainous landscape widely covered by pine forest and, in spots, spectacularly terraced into rice and sweet-potato fields. It has an assemblage of racial groups with some old and distinctive cultures, a moist and comfortable upland climate, and rich gold mines. Southeastern Luzon is a peninsular territory heavily planted to coconut but growing considerable abaca and other mixed crops. The Bicolanos, distinctive among the peoples of Luzon, speak a dialect of their own. Mostly small landholders, good farmers, and not given to wandering, they are both provincial and proud.

The mass of central Luzon is a zone of conflicting subregions and is difficult to separate further. Here is some of the best farmland in the islands, producing large rice, coconut, and sugar surpluses. But here also are the worst tenant problem and the hub of social unrest in the islands. In one hill section live some of the simplest of the Negrito peoples, within a few miles of Manila. Manila is the chief port and by far the largest city of the islands. Its metropolitan area, with about 1,300,000 people in 1948, is a cosmopolitan world settlement. Here are the greatest amount of modernism and the home of the Tagalogs. The Tagalogs in their home area enter all forms of occupation, but they are proud people who seldom will go as farm colonists to other parts of the islands. However, as government officials and businessmen they are found everywhere. Within the central zone of Luzon is a citrus-growing region, a distinctive volcanic landscape, and some of the most rugged relief of the islands. Man has developed cultural boundaries here that cut across natural boundaries and make it impossible to separate or group the several sections of central Luzon.

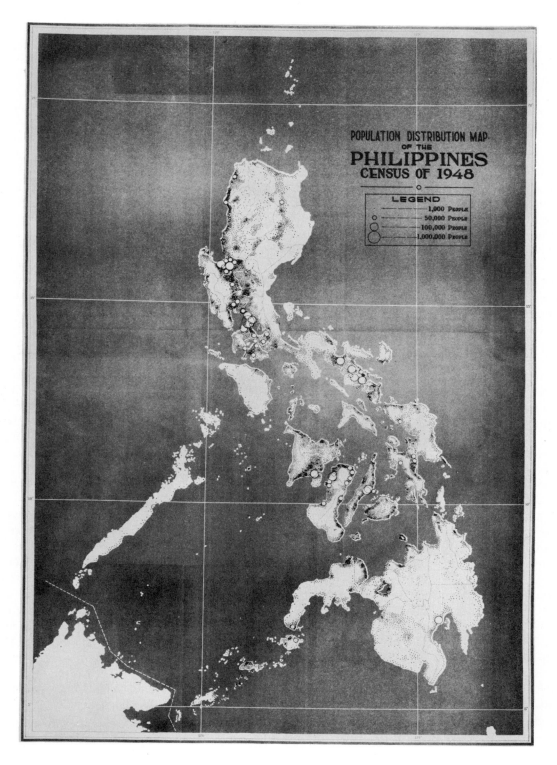

Fig. 98. Population distribution, 1948. From the *Census of the Philippines, 1948*.

There seldom is agreement on which islands make up the Visayas. Many somewhat related languages are spoken throughout the group. Whereas Panay and western Negros are culturally much alike and grow rice, sugar cane, and coconut, eastern Negros, Siquijor, Cebu, Bohol, Masbate, and Leyte are related and grow and eat corn and sell coconut and a few minor products. Samar stands somewhat alone, as do several of the northern islands of the group. There are numerous customs in which the Visayas differ from Luzon, and by which Panay in the west differs from Samar in the east. Most of the Visayan Islands are overpopulated, and people have been migrating for decades to the shores of northern Mindanao. Culturally and agriculturally, therefore, northern Mindanao today resembles the Visayan Islands.

Mindanao can be divided into several regions, but the lines must be drawn largely on physical criteria rather than cultural, since the frontier island is undergoing colonization and has yet to develop definite cultural regionalisms. The north coast and the Zamboanga peninsula have been colonized by Visayans and are becoming distinctive regions. Both the Lanao and Bukidnon highlands are attractive volcanic plateaus with mild climates and rather similar soils. But the Bukidnon country today is mostly open grassland, lightly populated and just becoming a colonial land. Lanao, on the other hand, is the chief Moslem stronghold, a land of small-scale agriculture and big bamboo, and the one region of the islands into which the Chinese merchant class has not yet gained full access. The Cotabato country is a broad basin with a great river system and a large area of lowland swamp that is as yet undrained. Its better lands are rapidly filling up with Visayan and Ilocano settlers and town-dwelling Chinese merchants, who are gradually submerging the Moros and the pagan peoples of the hilly margins. Some government initiative in soil conservation, hinterland and secondary road building, and pest control could turn this region into one of the most prosperous parts of the Philippines. The Davao Gulf Basin of southeastern Mindanao was the core of the commercial abaca business in pre-war days, a land of coconut and abaca plantations. The disappearance of the Japanese and the post-war entry of many Filipino small settlers have changed the direction of agricultural and cultural growth. The Agusan Valley of northern Mindanao is similar to the Cotabato Valley but still is largely forest or swamp country, thinly inhabited by pagan tribesmen, into which the colonist has barely begun to make his way. The mountainous east coast is a rugged land with a narrow and ragged coastal fringe that has but few usable patches of lowland. The Sulu island chain is a distinctive region. The most confirmed Moro peoples and a sea-going small-island way of life set them apart from other Filipinos.

This characterization obviously has omitted most of the 7,083 islands that make up the Philippines. The natural regional criteria of climate and landforms remain stable, but vegetation and soils are changing rather rapidly as the forests are removed and fresh soils are prematurely aged by repeated cropping without fertilizer, rotation, or cover crops. The rapid increase in population and the mobility of that population, along with the changing cultural patterns, make the firm characterization of regions particularly hard at this time.

THE PROSPECTS OF INDEPENDENCE

In the half century of American rule population has increased from about 7,000,000 to just over 19,000,000, a remarkable growth. The Chinese, the only large alien group, number somewhat over 300,000, though the total mixed Chinese-Filipino group numbers well over 1,000,000.* Will this same rate of increase occur in the next half century? It could be largely natural increase, from a high oriental birth rate coupled with the high birth rate of a Catholic country. "Within the memory of people still living, certain areas have been converted from grass and forest land, where few people lived, to intensive agricultural regions with heavy populations." † For how much longer can this go on and still be coupled with an increasing standard of living? Can the role of the Chinese be held within bounds, so that they do not dominate all Philippine society and economy? Can the Filipino acquire sufficient skill in management to operate successfully his own complex industrial and commercial concerns? Can industrialization, which so far has made little real headway, be promoted to assist an agricultural economy that cannot feed itself? Can social hygiene restrain the birth rate to compensate the decrease in the death rate being produced by preventive medicine in one of the healthiest parts of the Orient? Can Philippine society, now the least oriental segment of the East, rationalize practically its physical position in the Island Arcs on the border of the oriental realm, far from a friendly United States?

There still were, in 1949, more reserve lands than had been put into farms, though some of the reserve is not top quality. These may last another 30 years, after which time there may be only marginal lands remain-

---

* Official statistics are useless in this matter, since illegal entry of Chinese is known to be continuously occurring.

† *Report of the Philippine-United States Agricultural Mission,* page 9.

ing. Mechanization of farming can increase the yield, improve the quality of crops, lower the cost, and enable competition with other countries producing the same or similar crops, but can this be accomplished by the time American tariff protection ceases? A strong and well-integrated program of agricultural and soil-handling practices could advance the islands a long way toward permanent prosperity. The processing of export products is fairly well advanced, and the manufacture of finished goods for home consumption has begun. The modernization of the first and the proper extension of the second are necessary steps in domestic development. The absence of ample domestic supplies of coal, petroleum, and the fertilizer minerals, and the inability to grow adequate amounts of cotton are the chief handicaps that must be surmounted.

For many years Filipinos have stood against the large investment of American capital, fearing a delay in the granting of independence. Now that independence is a fact, even though American capital is legally assured equal opportunity with domestic funds, government pre-emption of many fields inviting to American operating concerns somewhat discourages large-volume financial investment. The possible threat of future ultranationalistic legislation also discourages the investment needed to accomplish the industrial growth desired. The new Filipino family-corporations with resources sufficient to undertake industrial operations may threaten to strangle the economic development of the islands. To offset this possibility, the pattern of government corporations will continue to be pushed and Filipino labor is becoming organized and articulate.

Coupled with the economic problem is the fact that independence has lowered the efficiency of operation of the Philippine government. The smooth operation of responsible representative government has not yet been proved practical in the Orient, with its intricate family systems and a historic pattern that operates somewhat on the Jacksonian premise that "to the victor belong the spoils." The tenancy situation is sufficiently bad in some parts of the country to cause dissident elements to focus social unrest upon the economic monopoly and government inefficiency and thus to promote real sectionalism and political turmoil. However, many Filipinos are awake to most of the above questions and problems, determined that their country shall make the most of its opportunities. Undoubtedly in the solution will be features unfamiliar to current Anglo-American, but the physical and cultural position of the islands on the borderland of the Orient, rather than deep within it, may permit effective integration with modern world cultural trends.

China during Fifty Centuries

THE AGE OF CHINESE CULTURE

Is there any truth in the popular idea that China has existed without change for the last four thousand years? Though the notion has been widely current it could hardly be more inaccurate. The Chinese probably are justified in claiming the oldest continuous living civilization, but this is owing to constant and steady change within certain limits rather than to no change at all. Scholarly opinion itself regarding the age of Chinese culture has gone through a full cycle of change in the last century, so that occidental literature today displays a wide variety of opinion on the question. Early in the nineteenth century the West accepted Chinese folk chronology which began seriously with the "Yellow Emperor" about 2700 B.C. Somewhat after 1900 historians became critical and would accept only dates proved by documentary evidence, reducing Chinese folk chronology by about 2000 years. Today about 1400 B.C. is commonly accepted as satisfactory. Studies by archaeologists have uncovered an impressive array of evidence pointing to a very old and long-continued occupation of China by the Mongoloid races, an occupation reaching clear back to Peking Man himself, perhaps 500,000 years ago. While the literal dates of the serious folk chronology have not yet been replaced, it now is evident that the nuclear body of Chinese culture must have been forming at a period at least as early as 2700 B.C. That formation certainly was conditioned, initially, by the environment in which it developed, but the Chinese eventually constructed a culture complex which became independent of a specific landscape and which has retained its traditional features in several different landscapes. It is the purpose of this chapter to inquire into this long process. First it is necessary to examine briefly the nature of the primary or hearth environment, along with other contrasting landscapes of early China.

THE QUALITIES OF THE ENVIRONMENT

The physical landscape of China today is rather different from that existing six or seven thousand years ago. The beautiful mosaic patterns of terraced fields did not exist, and the thousand of miles of dikes had not been built. Forests of several kinds covered much more of the country than is true today, and soil erosion had not dug its destructive fingers into many parts of China to lessen the value of the land to a farming people. It seems a fair statement that no other landscape in the world has had such a percentage of its surface made over by man, purposefully or because of him. As previously described the landscape of China is a checkerboard pattern of mountain strips and lowland plains and basins. The lowlands are scattered widely, and the dissected hill and mountain landscapes comprise by far the greater portion of the area of China. In soils, vegetation, and climate there is a tremendous variety from northern Manchuria to Hainan Island. After several thousand years of living in parts of the landscape the landscape today shows that the Chinese have made the most of its variety while at the same time planting certain common cultural traits everywhere. However, it certainly must have been possible, let us say, at 2700 B.C. to pick out several clear types of local environments, separated not by linear boundaries but merging through transition zones. Though this environmental complex is not able to support the present enormous population of China, it was more than adequate for any demands upon it in the earliest periods.

The area that was covered by loess and alluvial deposits, the Loess Highlands and the North China Plain, certainly must have comprised a unique region of North China. It probably was an open landscape without a heavy or difficult vegetation cover, with soils that were easily worked by simple means and that were rich enough to yield good returns under casual treatment. The hard-rock highlands projecting above the loess and alluvial cover probably never lost all their forest cover. The soft loess lands certainly were without widespread surface water supplies, but the scattered highlands, and their margins, must have had better water supplies all during the loessial period. The main streams throughout the area must have carried a seasonably variable volume of water. Climatically this whole region had a long, cold winter with much dust and wind, and a medium-length hot summer with low, variable precipitation. The precipitation total may have been a little greater than at present. If its winter dust and low temperatures and its precarious summer precipitation make it seem less attractive today than our modern conception of a Garden of Eden, it did have the very real advantages of rich soil, rock, wood, and water all relatively near at hand everywhere, with a wide variety of grains, fruits, and animals to choose from. Early man asked less of his environment than do we today. All these resources were present in an area of North China large enough to permit a scattering of several local centers or groups of tribes who did not, in the beginning, have to fight for possession of a single small prize area. The corridor along the northern footslope of the Tibetan Plateau afforded a passable connection to all of central Asia and constituted, from the very beginning, an important feature of the North China environment.

It is hard to suggest the regional limits of the open loess and alluvial landscape. To the northwest, however, it must have faded off into the more arid and monotonous landscapes of the Mongolian Plateau country. Here the shallow, open basins, with seasonal flood lakes or dry sandy and salty floors, alternated with the grass-covered aprons, basin margins, and rocky drainage divides. The better-situated spots were usable grasslands; the poorer localities were barren rock flats or desert strips from which the loess had been removed. No sharp line separated these two landscape types, but rather a broad and gradual transition. The structural elements of the Chinese checkerboard do not accord with the distribution of precipitation in this part of China. The lines of the Yin Shan and the Ala Shan lie well out in the grasslands and in no sense formed a significant environmental boundary. Farther and farther out in the grasslands the volume of easily exploited environmental resources became more and more limited, and this open grassland presented a poorer environment than that of the loess and alluvial landscape nearer the coast.

Southward from loessland there was a sharper change of another variety. Particularly in the west of China the high Tsinling Shan system sets a barrier across the land. The north and south sides of the Tsinling present one of the strongest and sharpest zones of contrast in all China. Eastward as the Tsinling Shan steadily lowers and becomes less formidable the contrast becomes less sharp and more of a transition, but the facts of contrast have been there at all times. This southern landscape was a subtropical environment, moist and rainy much of the year, with an all-year growing season, and with vegetation in the form of forests covering all except the floodplains. Bamboo, the citrus fruits, palms and a host of other trees, shrubs, and flowering plants were present. The water buffalo, rhinoceros, elephants, monkeys, and other tropical birds and animals replaced the fauna of North China. Here, less effort was needed to secure a fair existence in a mild environment, but the very lack of a natural nucleus probably prevented human concentration upon a particular region.

Other minor contrasts might be mentioned. The littoral of the coastal fringe, from southern Korea around to the southern coast of Chekiang, Shantung and Liaotung excepted, presented a marshy, muddy fringe of saline soils, high water table, and tall grass and reeds that was less usable than the higher, drier parts of the alluvial fill. A part of the Yangtze floodplain undoubtedly shared this same water-logged nature. Even today the Chinese only partially have mastered the appropriate uses for this kind of landscape, and in the earlier periods it was not a sought-after section of China. Similarly, northward into Manchuria where neither loess nor alluvial fill provided soft and easily tilled land, the shorter growing season, the colder snowy winter, and the heavier forest cover combined to frame an environment that has attracted the Chinese only within the present century.

THE PEOPLES AND CULTURES OF FOLK HISTORY

The discovery of Peking Man and his contemporaries seems to indicate that perhaps the same types of people have lived in China throughout much of human history, but it proves nothing with regard to the origin of the body of culture now labeled Chinese. And the continued presence in this part of eastern Asia of related physical types does not preclude repeated migration and countermigration across, into, and out of the separate local environments within the major region. It is quite impossible today to place the specific regional home of the Mongoloid races and, similarly, it is almost impossible to place the exact region in which the Chinese type of Mongoloid man first developed. From numerous bits of evidence much of Chinese folk history appears truly to point to migrations within eastern Asia and to long-continued residence in North China.

With respect to material culture, the earliest folk history indicated interest in problems of water control, in flood, drought, and irrigation. It relates the beginnings of agriculture, mainly concerned with the evolution of cultivation and crop handling. However, this folk history suggests that animals had a place in folk economy, and that there also was a place for fishing operations. It was concerned with several rather unique items, among them being silk and jade. It showed an awareness that in other geographical regions there were other ways of supporting existence. Metals and the fabrication of various implements are parts of the pattern but do not dominate it.

Beyond the material aspects of culture in this Chinese folk history the manner of dealing with human relationships was somewhat different from that of other folk histories. Calculations regarding the seasonal and calendar cycles became tied up with divination of floods, droughts, and other supernatural troubles, and rites propitiating the gods became intertwined with ceremonies honoring the ancestors. There accumulated a mass of folk culture rather unlike that accumulating in other parts of Eurasia, and with it came a peculiar awareness of the differences between this culture and those about it.

The specific statements of Chinese folk history are as impossible of application in a literal sense as the doings of the divine beings of Greek mythology or the accounts of the earlier eras among the American Sioux. But since 1930 a critical pursuit of archaeology and history has gradually pieced together a long and complicated story that promises to outdo the folk history not only in complication but in duration of time and sheer variety of performance. Only a start has been made in unraveling the Stone Age geography of China, and no critical judgment so far can be set upon the period. Chinese culture seems to be not as old as that of India and the Near East. Many of the fundamental inventions came in from the Indian-Near Eastern realm, but numerous features were acquired from southeastern Asia. It may well be that agriculture itself, as a technique, came from some other part of Asia, transmitted along the central Asian corridor. But under these additions is a basic body of Chinese culture, formulated in an early North China hearth, that even today is fundamental to an understanding of China.

THE PRIMARY CULTURE OF THE NORTH CHINA HEARTH

Good soils, water, wood, stone, and domesticable plants and animals in abundance all lay close at hand in the landscape of the Chinese culture hearth in the Huang River Basin. There certainly were variations in the region, and numerous local, superior sites were separated from each other in space and situation. The total central area of such landscapes is in the vicinity of 200,000 square miles. After the close of the glacial era, as loess deposition and alluvial sedimentation slowed down, this region would seem to have been the most attractive part of eastern Asia to groups of people just learning to handle the simplest problems of rudimentary agriculture and animal husbandry, settlement formation, and society organization. And if it was a superior environment it also was a malleable one which could reasonably be changed and shaped to fit the early group decisions and organizational politics of the peoples who permanently occupied it. This simple flexibility was, so to speak, an essential virtue of a hearth environment for any culture group just entering its formative stage and not yet crystallized into specific modes of operating a landscape or an economy.

Though this open landscape covered a large territory it graded off into other kinds of landscapes in all directions. Along these marginal transitions, in the earliest eras, there was no conclusive environmental stimulus in one direction only. It is only in more recent periods of culture history that we can begin, even, to draw sharp boundary zones between distinctive landscapes, after a long process of selective human use and development has accented certain features of the environment. Once development started, the pertinent natural resources gave the primitive economy an advantage over that of surrounding territories. Every forward step slowly increased that advantage to make this an outstanding region. Even under primitive conditions its population density must have exceeded that of neighboring regions, a fact which further favored the hearth area. In this central North China hearth there was organized an agriculture that drew upon many native plants, such fruits as the apricot, peach, plum, persimmon, and pear, such plants as several millets and buckwheat, and that early adapted plants and animals from other domestication centers. In addition there were forest-borne nuts and many wild animals available for the hunting. The irregular rainfall and the presence of streams in the alluvial lands fostered an awareness and a promotion of primitive irrigation once agriculture was understood. Already the initial step had been taken in setting up an inten-

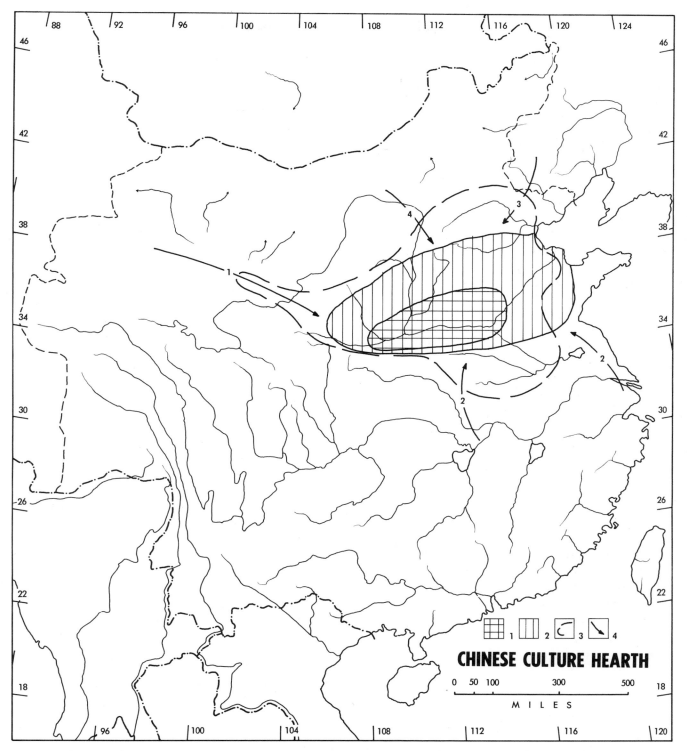

Fig. 99. The culture hearth of China: (1) the Shang region of the second millennium B.C.; (2) regions controlled by the Chou, early first millennium B.C.; (3) primary zone of loess and alluvium in north China; (4) regional sources of early contributions to basic Chinese culture, with numbers indicating: 1, ancient Near Eastern sources; 2, subtropical central and south China sources; 3, northern microthermal forest sources; 4, inner Asian grassland sources.

sive agriculture. The differences between portions of the hearth were slight and unimportant compared to the larger contrasts between the hearth and the grasslands or the subtropical southern forest.

Material culture was not only the product of the hearth. Inevitably certain culture traits were fostered in this homeland unlike those developed in outside, unlike environments. As the sedentary hearth developed there followed the universal tendency to look down upon those who did not practice the same customs. Gradually and somewhat unconsciously the hearth population came to think of themselves as "we, the cultured" and of all peoples of the transitions, margins, and lands beyond as uncultured barbarians. This is a common human tendency, but Chinese culture eventually developed this feeling into a very strong self-centeredness.

THE CULTURES OF THE BARBARIAN FRINGE

The self-centeredness of the North China hearth has a very real basis. On the Mongolian grasslands the mature pastoral economy that characterized Ghengis Khan's time had not yet evolved. The economic opportunities of the grasslands in the third millennium before Christ cannot have been great, even though repeated overgrazing had not yet worn them down. Then its contrast to the loesslands was less than it now is, but its resources permitted no great development without an integrated social organization. The simple pastoral economy of the grassland transition was in contrast to the sedentary agriculture of the North China hearth. The precarious environment constantly produced human surpluses which flowed toward the hearth in a steady movement that is one of the most marked features of the history of eastern Asia. The process, certainly was at work by the end of the Neolithic period, has operated throughout recorded Chinese history.

Northeastward short summers and cold winters combined with an irregular forest cover in pointing inhabitants toward some variety of hunting-fishing-gathering-pastoral economy. The Korean section and the southern, unforested, portion of the Manchurian lowland eventually became a Chinese colonial fringe, but in the earliest periods no regional economy here could compare with the pattern of the open lands farther south.

Southward in the Yangtze Valley a watery lowland landscape made reeds, boats, stilt houses, and aquatic food of greater human significance than in North China. Here human inventiveness was being exercised upon the innumerable potentialities of such plants as the bamboo. A marginal sprinkling of Negrito peoples in the coastal lowlands of South China, and a backwash of proto-Malay seafaring folk along the whole South China littoral, gave the coastal fringe a racial variety not found inland and pointed up the use of tropical items in the environment. South China was a big country, with much local variety, a hilly landscape with many local basins and a long and irregular coastline. There were many slight variations in its earliest sprinkling of population. A number of locally favored regions became minor culture centers. Most of them used the common materials of the subtropical environment, but there was no outstanding hearth, and none that rivaled the North China hearth.

THE FEUDAL ERA AND ITS FRUIT

The dawn of Chinese history found a pastoral people making the final move into the settled hearth area. The Chou were a simple people who had lived in the northwestern transition zone long enough to add the sedentary agriculture and the economic methods of the hearth to their own pastoral economy. Political and administrative organization had not then progressed far, but it was a military conquest by a semibarbarian group so closely related in racial origin that no clear distinctions can be made. The conquest was followed by the parceling out of fiefs and the setting up of an essentially feudal society. The conventional date for the Chou conquest usually is given as 1122 B.C., a date still subject to upward or downward revision.

The first few generations of Chou feudal lords rapidly picked up skill in handling the culture and the peoples of the hearth, becoming completely immersed therein. This was a period during which the techniques of intensive irrigation agriculture were being more fully elaborated in the hearth area. Village settlement and the walled city as a primary center of culture, wealth, and administrative power probably owe their final origin to this period. The local region, centered around a city, became the focal unit for group organization and operation in agriculture, flood control, irrigation, and public works, and from this time forward it formed the primary territorial unit in Chinese administrative operations. Iron first came into China during middle to late Chou times. The introduction of sufficient iron to allow use as tools came a little later, perhaps 500–300 B.C., but it marked a primary step forward in Chinese economy.

The several local centers of the hearth filled out, and a period of internal competition began. No longer were favored sites sheltered one from another, scattered throughout an extensive landscape. Centrally located feudatories, hemmed in on all sides by increasing pressures, sometimes were swallowed up in the conflicts. The marginal peoples, on the other hand, suffered attacks by the barbarian peoples knocking at the door of the hearth, seeking entry. The feudal period did much to heighten the contrast between the hearth and the outer barbarian lands. As a result there was a never-ending series of rival groups edging closer to the hearth to carry on the regional struggle for power within the hearth itself. Most pressures came from the north and northwest, but not exclusively. The late feudal era was marked by political arrangements which remind one of the League of Nations of the 1920's, and by an era in which protective wall building became a habit and the basis was laid for the final project of the Great Wall of China. Political historians consider the feudal era to end in the late third century B.C., but the last several centuries of the era developed an intensity of cultural activity that makes closer scrutiny necessary.

THE FORMATIVE ERA AND THE BIRTH OF "CHINA"   *600 B.C.*

The sixth century before Christ was a period of intense political and social activity in North China as it was in India and in the Near East. The struggles of the feudal era were becoming acute, and there was a great restlessness among mankind. This was a time when men were searching for a progressive, practical plan for the operation of feudal society when that society in the North China hearth was nearing the stormy end of an era. Confucius was born about the middle of the sixth century in what now is western Shantung, a member of an aristocratic family of one of the smaller feudal states. He was a scholarly leader in the search, formulating an ethical, moral code of human conduct based upon his editorial synthesis of the past history of Chinese hearth society. Undoubtedly he arranged a "lawyer's brief" to fit his beliefs and edited the chronicles of the past with a liberal hand to provide precedents for his case. Though that editing has confused historians no end, it did provide in shortened form a code of conduct and a concept of ideas that slowly became the central hallmark of Chinese culture.

Other scholars formulated bodies of philosophy, religion, and ethics during the period which took other directions than the political-social-economy of Confucius, though they all contributed to the culture complex. Many contemporary and later disciples and students of Confucius became government bureaucrats and practicing politicians, all eager to try out their ideas

of political economy in the complex political geography of the day. Many of them drifted from feudal state to feudal state, searching for the right combination of situations and opportunities. The more these practicing politicians applied themselves, the more acute grew the struggle, with marginal members constantly less honorable in their adherence to the civilized codes of conduct in war, politics, and economics. The advantage lay with these marginal peoples, semibarbarian still, constantly pushed by other peoples behind them. The fact that they were ignorant of many of the somewhat artificial ethical codes of the hearth made some of them welcome ambitious itinerant scholar-politicians who could be useful in the struggle for power. By the latter part of the third century B.C. the contest had ended in the conquest of the hearth by a semibarbarian people from the northwest who, in a generation, instituted political and economic changes of a kind and degree that permanently ended the feudal era and carried the formal culture of the hearth far outside its standard bounds. Much of the basic content of the hearth culture had spread much earlier.

The political-military process should not obscure other developments that were equally significant. The influx of new blood was sizable, and the population of the hearth was growing. The exchange of material goods increased between the barbarian south, the forested north, the pastoral northwest and the hearth. Contact along the central Asian corridor and the southern littoral brought new ideas, new crops, and new tools into China. Many of these things cannot be very closely dated as yet, but it must have been very early in the feudal era that wheat became the staple north China food grain, and wet rice spread northward and across into central Asia as a random, minor crop. During the later feudal era a new and formalized style of writing was developed; the system of private land ownership began to replace the serf, fief, and feudal lord, the growing skill in water control and the ox-drawn plow improved agricultural productivity. Then followed changes in the tax system, the growth of handicraft manufactures, the development of trade, and the appearance of a merchant class. The chopsticks so diagnostic of Chinese culture became common at this time. All these and many more new features attest to the fact that the hearth area had matured. The hearth was now the center of a political empire. It had become the key region, economically and politically, of a North China that stretched from the grasslands deep into the subtropical south. At this point one might venture, at last, to talk about a "China," and a "Chinese culture" in distinction to the less-developed, barbarian cultures round about, and opposed to the earlier feudal culture of the hearth area itself.

The accompanying map locates the approximate areas of the chief contending states of the feudal era. No precise list of states can be given, and boundaries often changed as the balance of power shifted. The State of Ch'in, which seized control of North China at the end of the feudal era, is underlined and capitalized. Various walls built in the late feudal era are sketched in approximate position, and the extent of the later Great Wall is also shown.

THE HAN EMPIRE AND IMPERIALISM

The date usually given for the political conquest of the hearth area by the semibarbarian State of Ch'in is 221 B.C. The new empire lasted but the remaining life of creator Ch'in Shih Huang Ti, until about 209 B.C. However, the forward steps that had been taken were permanent ones, and shortly a native of what today is northern Kiangsu had gathered the reins of power and established the Han dynasty, that was to administer China for some four centuries, 207 B.C. to A.D. 220. The early years of the new dynasty were a period in which changes initiated in the previous century were put into effect with greater thoroughness and were given wider regional application. This meant, in the broadest sense, a spread of "Chinese culture" outward over much of what today constitutes modern China. It was carried out by military conquest and political expansion of the simplest imperialistic type. Toward the north and west countermeasures were taken by the new Chinese state against the continuous encroachment of the pastoral nomads. These measures eventually led Chinese imperialism along the central Asian corridor into what today is Sinkiang. Contact with Rome along the overland trade route followed. Similarly imperialism touched southern Manchuria and northern Korea. Southward it bypassed the hilly negative blocks of central and southern China to encompass the basins scattered over the whole country, reaching into the lowlands of Tonking in modern Indochina. In the terms of political geography it was the dynamic drive produced by the unified force of the then most significant geographic region of eastern Asia. And it was expressed at a time when no other people had mastered the use of any landscape region short of India and Persia. See Fig. 101.

The key economic region of eastern Asia became the political center of the new empire, and the capital was located within it. As such it gathered the ambitious personalities from all over China. The hearth region began, in a simple way, to derive some economic profit

from the empire. It drew tribute missions and students of society from outside what today is China proper. And with them came strange goods to widen the material economy of the heart of China and strange ideas to expand Chinese culture itself. By the end of the Han many a barbarian trait had quietly slipped into Chinese culture to become so deeply embedded as to seem to later generations that it always had been there.

The process of cultural growth and expansion served to increase the strength of Chinese culture and to crystallize its structure. During Han times the scholar-bureaucrats cemented their gains tightly into the fabric of Chinese life. Though the scholar outside office often served as the cultural conscience of China to protest the action of the scholar-practical-politician in office, the combined results of their activity was to raise Confucianism to the status of an official state cult. The scholar-bureaucrats, as a group, became an integral part of the Chinese administrative system of government. That a system of political economy thus succeeded in becoming a state cult, while, in other societies, organized religions became state cults, is a fundamental distinguishing characteristic of early Chinese culture.

THE ECONOMIC PHILOSOPHY OF HAN SOCIETY

The Chinese culture hearth had developed as an intensive agrarian society operated by villages administered by regional city centers. Only a simple range of implements, tools, and mechanical agents were available. Self-sufficiency was not complete, but only a relatively small volume of trade was needed and commercialism was a minor aspect of hearth culture. The end of feudalism required time; practical methods of land ownership and the adjustment and shifting of taxation from crops to land and to the individual owners could not be devised overnight. Chinese hearth society had not developed a large slave labor force as did Greece and Rome, but corvee labor was exacted by the state to accomplish its public works projects. Convicts and "political criminals" also were used on public works. The last century of feudal time and the whole of Han times were a period in which the economic principles of operating an agrarian society were strongly debated. A few revolutionary reformers were rejected, and Chinese economy remained true to its older patterns. Confucian scholars divided into schools of thought over taxation principles, land tenure, the place of trade and handicrafts, and the admissible degree of state participation in agriculture and handicrafts. Some of the discussions read almost word for word like

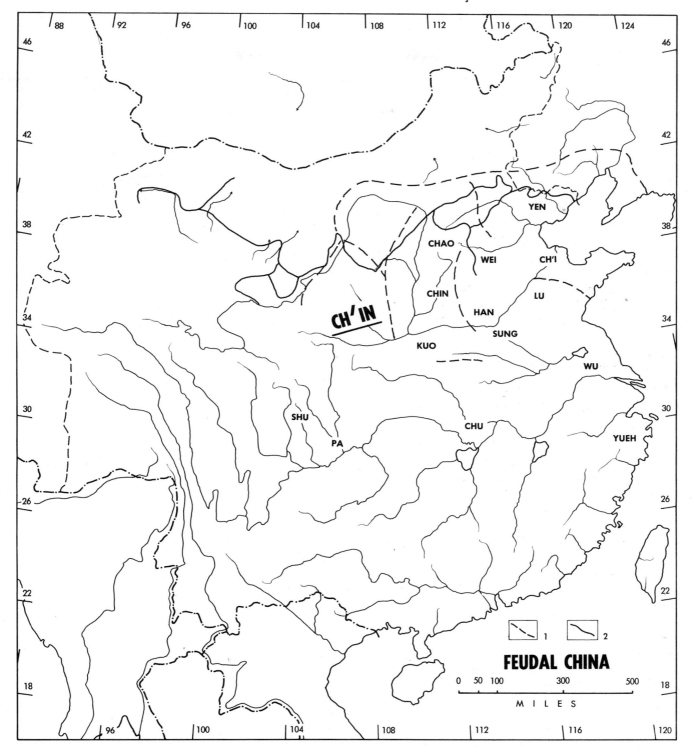

Fig. 100. Feudal China: (1) primary walls and alternative walls built in late feudal times; (2) Great Wall of China as it matured in later centuries. It used elements and short walls of the feudal era. Chief contending states of the feudal era are named. Ch'in, in larger print and underlined, emerged victorious.

current debates about the economic philosophy of American society.

In spite of the best intentions of government a landlord class arose, along with a segment of the population who became landless tenants. Similarly, a small though prosperous merchant class developed and maintained itself. The scholar-bureaucrats did very well by themselves economically. Han times were a period of settling into accepted molds and patterns of conduct, and of rejecting patterns that involved too great change from the past. Various ills of the state were adjusted, or corrected, or manipulated as they arose. There had been no real precedents to go on, though all adherents to a cause drew such justifications from the Confucian classics as could be found. Though there unquestionably were maladjustments in the patterns of society that crystallized by the end of the Han, the system worked reasonably well for all concerned. Successful molds had been poured for a regionally self-contained agrarian society that operated intensively with a minimum of equipment and a minimum of commerce and handicraft industry.

Modern comparative study of mechanized American agriculture proves that intensive oriental agriculture produces somewhat more actual food per acre than does the American system. However, the man-days of labor involved are far greater in oriental agriculture and the present volume of food production per capita in the Orient is far below that of contemporary United States. However, during Han times it is significant that the intensive system was an improvement over any other economy then operative in eastern Asia and led to a dominance by the Chinese hearth area. The spread of this intensive system was a part of the spread of Chinese culture. It was supervised by a centrally pyramided but very loosely articulated professional bureaucracy with a definite stake in the over-all success of the system. The system involved drawing enough food, manpower, and materials from the empire at large by imperial authority to properly maintain the hearth's political power, to maintain the military power to defend the empire from aggression, and to keep the system in operation.

SETTLEMENT MORPHOLOGY

From an incomplete study of the subject it would appear that at a very early time the inhabitants of the culture hearth came to prefer two definite settlement forms, the compact village and the centrally located city. Dwelling in fixed settlements was one of the fundamental features distinguishing Chinese culture.

The Chinese village is always a compact affair, though it may have various shapes. Houses are built tightly against one another, and there seldom are spacious yards and gardens as in the American small town or hamlet. The most common shape is the shoestring village, a double row of houses along a single street. The site often is a dike top or a stream terrace or bench. Sometimes among the larger trade villages is found the rough grid pattern with one or two streets dominating, and now and then irregular and odd-shaped villages occur. The village varies in size from perhaps a dozen buildings to a thousand houses, with about a hundred houses seeming to be a fair average. Common to all Chinese villages are tea shops, restaurants, inns, and a temple, plus the itinerant goods peddler. Only large villages have grain, cloth, metal, furniture, and other shops. Almost all shops double as private homes, and there seldom is zoning of functions in a village. In north China villages normally are walled, but elsewhere in China it is uncommon to find many walled villages.

The Chinese city is a settlement synonymous with the management of the affairs of society. Size or volume of commerce and trade are not at all the criteria for a city, though most cities are local trade centers. This means that a city is the center of political, economic, and cultural power in its regional landscape. The city is the location of the skilled handicrafts, the religious center of the district, the residence of landlord families, of scholars, and of political officials. Since early times the city has been walled, and today the common word for city is the word for wall, the wall being the personification of those features that distinguish the city from the village or the simple, overgrown mart of trade. Several types of cities are common to China, according to their rank and standing in the management of affairs. Lowest in rank is the frontier march site city, in the past a special rank of frontier outpost. Such a city often was but a walled village, crudely built and possessing little wealth or culture. The average county seat, scattered every 15 to 30 miles apart all over China, had something of a grid pattern to its layout. This might range from two simple cross streets with alleys and lanes to a regular multiple grid with rectangular blocks. The wall often was irregular in outline, conforming to the site, and of such size as the local economy could afford. Such cities generally show a zoning of economic functions, and frequently have one or more suburbs lying outside the walls. Today, in population they range from perhaps 5,000 to 200,000 people. District and provincial cities usually were laid out on larger, more formal lines involving true grid patterns, large walls, numerous gates, and considerable formal public architecture. After 1911 some cities tore down their walls, and turned the space into circular streets. Many also have gone through modernization programs of street widening and installation of water, telephones, and electricity.

In architectural features Chinese settlements show an amazing diversity while at the same time exhibiting a striking superficial similarity. Adobe brick is the commonest building material all over China, but many regional special forms are found. Roofs normally are of gray tile or of straw thatch. North China seldom spruces up its buildings, but west and south China frequently uses whitewash and decorative designs. Domestic architecture in China always has been plain and simple, but public architecture has had a flair for the ornate, elaborate, and highly decorated. The curved roof popularly associated with China is a feature chiefly of public building that has been developed in recent centuries, though some homes of the wealthy families also show it. Out of the culture hearth of North China came the basic features of Chinese building, which have spread wherever the Chinese have gone. These features are the rectangular room unit with few doors and windows. The roof is normally supported on a skeleton of wooden poles independent of the walls which normally are panels filling in the spaces. The room unit can be multiplied any number of times, arranged in L, U, or closed square shapes, the whole set upon a terrace foundation to get it above ground level. In compact settlements various modifications of the rectangular room are found. Most Chinese building is single storied in villages and single or double storied in cities. Only special public buildings and monuments normally reach more than two stories, so that the average Chinese settlement shows a flat skyline unlike that of the large occidental city. In their spread over China, however, the Chinese have taken on many extraneous building materials and housetypes, which actually provide, today, a widely varied architecture. The flat mud-roofed houses of the northwest of China contrast with the steel and concrete skyscraper of the port cities of the China coast, to suggest only two of the many.

THE EXPANDING COLONIAL FRONTIER

Following upon the Han military conquest of the neighboring regions was the process of implanting Chinese culture in the conquered areas. The devices that had accompanied the transformation of feudal China into imperial China worked with considerable satisfaction. The *hsien* or county, the *chun* or military corps area, and the *chou* or political district were the principal administrative regional units that were set up over the new territory. Each was subject to change according to conditions of the specific region. The *chun* was at first less a region of so many square miles than a route between the hearth and some outlying district. Eventually the *sheng* or province matured out of a variety of major political regions of control. Along with the regional devices went the walled city as the functional heart of each new region incorporated into the political administration. The walled city became an advance outpost in an alien landscape and culture. The walled city offered security in times of stress, but infiltration of the countryside was carried out in peaceful periods. The village became the normal rural unit in advance of the city, but not everywhere was it used. In Szechwan Chinese penetration had actually preceded the end of feudal times, and, here, with the walled city as a primary protective control, settlement spread out first over the Chengtu Plain and then the rest of the Szechwan Basin in the form of scattered homesteads.

Where there were barbarian peoples occupying the areas of colonization they were dealt with in various ways. In some areas forced transplantation was used, whereas in others continued residence eventually produced assimilation into the Chinese blood and culture complex. Some of the barbarian groups kept shifting southward ahead of Chinese colonization, themselves pushing still others in a slow drift southward into southeastern Asia. Regardless of what precise method of disposal was used, the Chinese were dominant in culture, administrative control, and numbers. Commencing with the best local centers and those most easily built into bases of operation, the slow process of Chinese colonization of the southland began to fill in the regions bypassed in the earlier military conquest. It was to be a long process, and one not yet complete at the present time. In Fukien the remainders of alien peoples and cultures today are but vestigial remnants. Hainan Island, Kweichow, and Yunnan, on the other hand, are regions in which the Chinese no more than equal the so-called "non-Chinese" at the present time. They have pushed these modern "barbarians" off the best lands, monopolized the political, economic, and social administration of the territory, and extended their lines of influence completely throughout the region. The "non-Chinese" have given the Chinese many things and have absorbed much of Chinese culture, but many of them persistently hang onto language, dress, ceremonial customs, and other marks of their own cultures. Along the Tibetan frontier the Chinese colonization stalled somewhat against the rough and rugged landscape not easily amenable to sedentary, agricultural settlement, and there are blocks of territory occupied by "barbarian" peoples over whom the Chinese even today possess only nominal control or influence.

On the north and west Chinese culture found landscapes not so amenable to the techniques of colonization used in the south. Out into Inner Mongolia, away from the old hearth and into the grasslands, the Chinese repeatedly have pushed. In wet cycles and periods of strong Chinese power they have advanced their lines, only to blow away in the "dust bowl" episodes of dry cycles, and to shrink back under nomad raids in periods of inadequate Chinese strength. Along the central Asian corridor the standard Chinese technique of making Chinese of all other peoples did not work well either, since the Chinese themselves were always a minimum element in the population totals. Repeated efforts in Sinkiang over the centuries have to date achieved only bitterness, unrest, and internal distress, as alien cultures have held strong against Chinese political and military pressure. Northward into Manchuria the Chinese, in this century, have swarmed in such numbers as to sweep all before them in the southern and central lowlands. The northern fringe and the hill strips on either border are not yet colonized. Though their political control has been, and still remains, shaky, Manchuria is Chinese in blood, culture, and economics. The process of Chinese colonization and frontier expansion is not complete on any modern frontier of China, and there is no indication that activity has ceased. In the remaining bypassed zones in southwest and west China it will go on to the inevitable end that eventually all people and all culture will be Chinese. Of course, there will be regional variations and specializations. The question of Chinese expansion on external frontiers will be considered later.

CHINESE ACCULTURATION THROUGH EXPANSION

The earliest expansion out of the hearth found the Chinese firmly convinced that they were superior to any and all barbarian folk of the marginal landscapes. This self-centeredness did not prevent Chinese assimilation of many barbarian customs, in a rather selective manner. Pastoral folk assimilated into Chinese culture brought relatively little; they never did cause the Chinese to take up the use of dairy products. South of the Tsinling the process was relatively more complete but still selective. Bamboo, rice, and the water buffalo were not parts of the original ancient hearth culture, but they are intrinsic parts of modern China wherever climatically practical. The elephant, however, was

apparently not liked by the Chinese as a domestic animal, though as an art form it is very common in many parts of China. These are but random examples of the process.

Chinese who went beyond their own borders, as the pilgrims to India, as the traders to the Indies, or as the diplomatic emissaries to tributary kingly courts, brought many things back to China not only of religion and the world of ideas but also of art, architecture, plants, tools, and methods of artisanry. Tribute missions to the Chinese court always brought the special products of their own home environments. The Chinese have taken these things into their culture and transformed them variably to their own ends. Not a century was without some new features; scarcely a generation did not witness the gradual increase in the ideas and the materials that made up Chinese culture. Naturally there were peak periods and low periods in this acquisitional process. The several centuries of the Han, the time of Sui and T'ang, the Mongol Yuan dynasty, the early Ch'ing dynasty, and the last century have been, possibly, the peak eras of cultural expansion.

But in all this contact the Chinese never have lost control over the process of acculturation. Though the process seems largely to have been an unconscious one, strong reaction has always set in against any feature that threatened the fundamental balance of Chinese culture. Never was the firm stable nucleus of the classical China of the North China culture hearth ever basically altered. Even the impact of the modern world has not succeeded in changing this balance, so far, though more will be said of this subject later.

THE CHANGING PULSE OF CHINESE HISTORY

Chinese scholars sometimes assert that there is a repeating cycle of rise and fall in Chinese history, though there is little agreement upon critical dates and cycle lengths. Regardless of the possibility of determining repetitive cycles as such, there certainly has been the repetition of a process and a comparable sequence of events. Once the Han dynasty had spread to its widest limits it began a slow decline under the endlessly increasing problems of empire, the decreasing efficiency of political administration, and the lessening prosperity of its populace. The rise and fall of the Han empire completed a sequence of Chinese cultural operations. The Han fell, in the last analysis, because the operating machinery of society became hopelessly cluttered and inefficient. Government slowly piled an overwhelming burden of taxes, vested interests, special privileges, and procedures which had outlived their need upon the populace whereas it grew less and less able to mobilize its strength to hold off the semibarbarian tribes pressing inward toward the hearth area.

accomplishments. The pattern of gradual decline under the weight of too much government and too great increase in the social and economic diseases of society, repeated itself in the later decades of T'ang. Next came the Sung, after a shorter interval of chaos, with

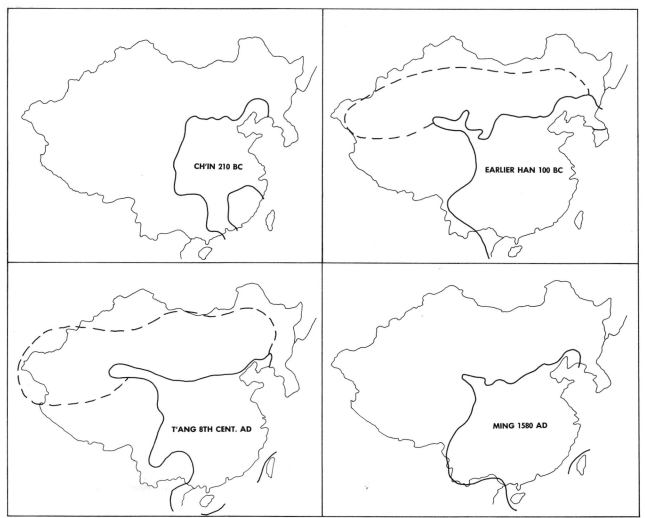

Fig. 101. The regional patterns of Chinese Empires. The outline is that of Greater China as of about 1890. The dashed lines enclose frontier zones of influence important to empire stability.

There followed a period in which these semibarbarian groups struggled with each other and with the peoples of north China for the mastery of the north, while at the same time the Chinese and non-Chinese in the southern parts of the empire struggled for autonomy or hegemony. Several centuries passed during which a variety of short-term alignments prevailed, but eventually the Sui achieved a near hegemony over all China, but then diverted their attention toward Korea. Out of this divergence the T'ang dynasty (A.D. 618–907) came to the top as a Chinese dynasty, aggressive, virile, dynamic, leading the energetic Chinese realm to new

its dynastic period (979–1278) repeating the story of a fresh start, a prosperous peak, and a declining segment of unrest, dissension and invasion. By the Sung dynasty, however, the Yangtze Valley had been developed significantly as an economic region, playing a vital part in empire affairs. When the pastoral invasions pressed too hard upon the north in the 1120's, the Sung were able to roll with the punch, withdrawing their capital to Nanking and continuing to operate a reduced Chinese state for another century and a half before finally falling to the Mongols. During that period a number of peoples fought for control of the northern marches and for the old Chinese hearth in the north of China.

Mongol control of China (A.D. 1279–1368) presented another, if slightly varied, cyclic act in the long historical pageant. Mongol rule was unique in that for the first time a people had cemented most of the power of the pastoral realm into a single political-military machine to batter down Chinese opposition and take over all China. A further distinctive feature was that the Mongols ruled, not with the self-centeredness of Chinese culture, but with an open-door policy that used Turks, Moslems, Italians like Marco Polo, and many others, in one great machine. More than any other Asiatic people until the modern era the Mongols had a concept of a kind of pan-Asia, controlled from their pastoral heartland, with interchangeable officials and ideas, a great political and military empire that enveloped many cultures but elevated no one creed of society to a position of dominance. This was a peak period of Chinese culture change, and it also was a period that spread knowledge of the East into the West.

Though the Mongol political concept was a vast one the machinery of operating it was unequal to the task. Accumulating unrest in China brought mobilized opposition in the Yangtze Valley which finally grew great enough to retake the hearth area in the north and give the Ming dynasty control of China proper (1368–1644). Though the capital was shifted northward again to Peking, the Yangtze Valley was a much more vital part of the Ming empire than it had been during the Han. Ming control never reached so far into central Asia as had Han power, but it was expressed much further southward, so that the Annamese, the Khmer, the growing Thai and Burmese cultures, and even the Indies, acknowledged the political hegemony of China. The decline of the Ming and the ascendance of the Manchus again repeats a very familiar theme, with its own special embroidery upon the patterns of history. Manchu China was a prosperous climax era of Chinese society, but the same accumulation of cultural rubbish finally weighed China down and gave voice and volume to a protesting people, to end Manchu imperial rule in 1911.

CHINA OF THE MANCHUS

The Manchus did not come into China the crude barbarians that history sometimes pictures them. They had spent a period upon the northeastern borders learning to use the tools of Chinese administration, and trying to devise some social techniques that would enable them to control a sedentary China while retaining their own pastoral mobility. These techniques worked well enough so that by 1900 Manchus still were a distinct nucleus in many a large Chinese city. However, racial independence and social separation were not sufficient to guarantee permanent dynamic leadership in a society that, at its height, was perhaps the most prosperous and complex society in the world, so that the Manchu rulers of China declined along with the society they headed.

The China of the seventeenth and eighteenth centuries was a mature and full-flowering plant in the oriental garden. Every rise and fall of a dynasty had enlarged the roots that fed the Manchu plant. Every era of peace, prosperity, and trade, every era of imperial expansion, every era of invasion and foreign control, every Chinese who ventured abroad, every stranger newly come to China, brought something that enlarged Chinese culture. A steady stream of new crops, new tools, new techniques, new ideas, and new blood added to the variety of material culture and to the depth of social culture. And with every passing century there had been an increase in the cultivated land, in the mileage of roads and canals, in the length and strength of the river dikes, and in the manpower available to intensively operate the Chinese economic system. China of the Manchus was a richer, stronger, more cultured, and more sophisticated society than any that had gone before.

There still was the perennial barbarian fringe upon the north and northwest, but the pastoral peoples now were knocking less strongly at the gates. Troubles in the southern imperial domains, beyond China proper, called for occasional expeditions, reprimands, and mediatory gestures. The trade and tribute that came from the South Seas, however, offset trouble from that quarter.

In organizational form Manchu China was genetically the same China that had flowered first in the Han Empire. The same Confucian bureaucracy administered the broad lands of the empire, using the Confucian codes and the classics, and the same machinery of government that had worked so well for the Han. This not only was a peak era for the mass of Chinese, but it was also a peak era for the Confucian Way. And in the pride and satisfaction of the Manchu rulers, the Chinese Confucian bureaucrats, and the Chinese peasantry there lay the old self-centered concept of China as the center of a cultural world, surrounded in all directions only by barbarians of lesser standing. These included the first Europeans who came to China by sea in the sixteenth century from a distant corner of the barbarian world scarcely mentioned in Chinese accounts.

Europe of the sixteenth and seventeenth centuries was just struggling out of the pinched and bare patterns of the Dark Ages. The geographical discoveries were on, but the economic fruits of empire had not yet fattened the lean societies of Europe. As much as Europeans were impressed by the spotty brilliance of India and the Indies, it was China that created the strongest impression. Undoubtedly China of the Manchus was the most prosperous society on the face of the earth at the time. It had greater and more universal prosperity, a greater volume of material goods, and a better standard of living than had India or Europe. Perhaps one must excuse the early, wealth-hungry European visitors for forgetting what little cultivated manners they possessed when face to face with the peaceful plenty of China.

THE OLD CHINA TRADE

The contact of European explorers-traders-pirates and sophisticated Chinese represented the greatest conflict of rival self-centeredness that occurred during the great discoveries. In the presence of the prosperity of Manchu China the Europeans were most eager for trade on any terms. The Chinese South Sea traders then were keen merchants, and the Chinese market was a large one for buyer and seller alike.

The first European purchases were made with cash payments of silver dollars from Spain, Mexico, and Portugal. Trade was administratively centered on Canton by the Chinese because this was the chief port to which foreign sea-going traders had come throughout Chinese history. The newcomers had little to offer so that there was not much interest in trade with Europeans. Arabs, Indians, Malays, and others had long carried on trade that took no special government machinery to administer; this new trade, therefore, evoked no new Chinese ministry or bureau to handle it.

The earliest period of trade was one in which the European sampled the wares of China and sought for something abroad that could evoke Chinese interest in order to lessen the cash outlay. Of interest to Europe were tea, silks, lacquers, porcelain, carved wood, and a wide variety of art goods.

The volume of trade gradually settled around tea and silk, which also spread out beyond the specified port of Canton to the whole of the south China coast. In return the Europeans found that a variety of items somehow attracted Chinese buyers. Furs for clothing in the north China winter, ginseng for medicine, opium as a luxury product for a prosperous society with a leaning toward some exotic outlet. The best products were the cotton textiles of India and a wide variety of luxury goods from the South Seas. It was not long before the British were ruthlessly pushing the opium trade because of its tremendous profits, Britain later going so far, in the 1840's, as to fight a war with China to force China to buy more of a vicious drug that the Chinese were already regretting that they had started using.

The European traders found that China had many a natural monopoly whereas Europe, by 1800, had no satisfactory line of goods to exchange with China. Gradually this led to efforts to break Chinese control over trade in such things as tea and silk. Later on other commodities came in for monopoly breaking also. Eventually a degree of success was attained, and India gradually became the tea-producing country wherein British capital not only profited from the trade but also from the initial production. Japan was encouraged as a silk producer and eventually took most of China's market. Other minor commodities have gone through somewhat the same cyclic patterns of trade, in that Europe pressed China to trade in a commodity but eventually moved the trade elsewhere. The normal European statement of this change concerns the fact that the Chinese refused to produce in sufficient volume in standardized units, sizes, or qualities. The facts were that the Chinese had never had a large trade in any of the products that Europe wanted in large volume, had an economic system which did not make for large production of such goods, were attracted by nothing the European brought in exchange, and saw no great reason for changing the long-accepted patterns of Chinese society. China could not see ahead to what was coming, but no more could Europe foretell the effects of clumsy dealings and avaricious pursuit of trade.

The Portuguese were the first to reach Canton. Not long behind them were the Dutch. The British were the first to intensively cultivate the China trade and to work it in conjunction with their trade in India. Gradually the British and Yankee colonists forged ahead in trade relations with China, France, Holland, and Portugal being minor participants. Colonial American trade was largely carried on by New England's seaport towns, carrying furs, ginseng, and a few odd products to China. The Indian textile trade largely was in the hands of the British East India Company, to whom also goes the black score of the opium trade.

EUROPEAN SPHERES OF INFLUENCE

The Portuguese came first to Canton in the decade between 1510 and 1520. They secured a permanent establishment at Macao in 1557, but no other permanent footing in China was secured by any European until well into the nineteenth century. Until perhaps 1700 the volume of trade remained small and its problems no more than minor vexations to Chinese bureaucracy. As the volume of trade began to grow in the early eighteenth century it coincided with the most vigorous period of Manchu rule, when an expanding

to be characterized as the "Sick Man of the Orient" during the twentieth century. These were: increasingly heavy economic and political pressure by Europe, the general economic and social decline of Chinese society toward the end of an era, and the steady weakening of what had been a dynamic Manchu leadership.

The Chinese failure to diagnose the increasing Euro-

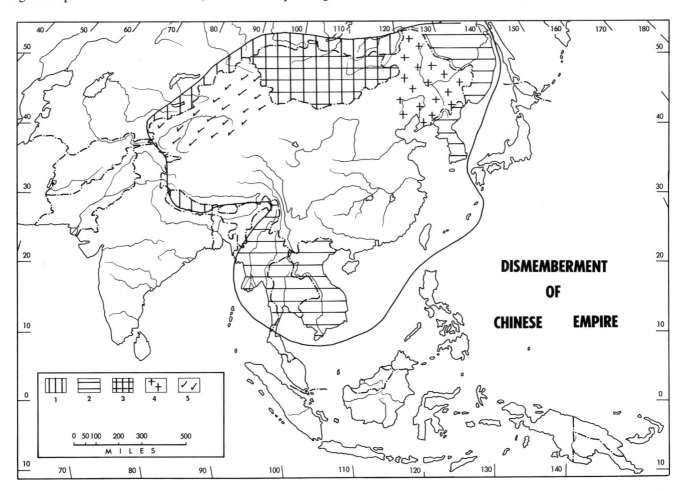

Fig. 102. Dismemberment of the Chinese Empire: (1) tributary areas lost in the eighteenth century; (2) tributary areas lost in the nineteenth century; (3) areas lost in the twentieth century; (4) temporary loss of Manchuria in the twentieth century; (5) zone of increasing Soviet influence. Treaty port concession areas are shown on Fig. 38.

economy in China could easily absorb the shock of a new orientation, or turn it to an advantage. European economic pressure upon China did not become significant until after 1800. The first civil unrest, expressive of an ailing society, had shown itself just before the death of the great Emperor Chien Lung in 1799. None of his successors more than fractionally measured up to the ability of Chien Lung, one of the most able men of his time. Three factors, therefore, coincided to contribute progressively to the social, economic, and political ailments that have caused China

pean pressure, exerted from the sea rather than from the pastoral northwest, as something totally unprecedented in Chinese history gave them no start in making those changes that were needed. At a time when the whole of the Occident was fast gathering energy through a creative period of invention, productive manufacturing, and exploitation of the world's economic resources, China had become frozen in the molds of Confucian bureaucracy, self-centeredness, and passive unresponsiveness. Chinese and Manchu officials made more bad moves than good, within a series of set patterns that led only to greater involvement rather than solution of the problem. And the aggressive West, with a taste of colonial imperialism, became steadily more rapacious. The Chinese realm was too big a series of geographic regions to be taken over by any one European power. The situation turned into a political-economic race for spheres of influence among Britain, France, Germany, Russia, and Japan. A series of political treaties were exacted from China, under various kinds of military pressure, giving European powers special concessions of an economic and political nature, usually accompanied by the lease of small areas of land in port cities along the coast of China and the Yangtze River. The first such "treaty port" arrangement occurred in 1842; the last such exaction was in 1898. Just before the close of the nineteenth century the drive of imperialism became more frantic. France held economic claim to most of southwest China, Britain to the Yangtze Valley, Germany wanted Shantung, Japan had Korea, and Russia was interested in Manchuria. The United States had no regional unit in mind, but held the newly acquired Philippine Islands. And in a spell of self-interested altruism the United States set forward the open-door doctrine, which proposed an end to regional, political imperialism in China. Its real effect, however, was to sanction economic imperialism for everyone, since the treaty ports and treaties giving the European special rights were not canceled. The Chinese of the last generation felt as seriously about these unequal treaties as American colonials ever felt about "taxation without representation" at the hands of Britain.

Not only did the Occident carry economic and political imperialism throughout China but also at least once inhibited the normal processes by which Chinese society, in the past, threw off a decadent dynasty. What is known to historians as the Taip'ing Rebellion (1851–1865) swept out of Kwangtung and forged a long black trail of destruction, possibly taking more than 20,000,000 lives, before it ebbed out in the Yangtze Valley. It is just possible that, had the Europeans not given financial and material aid, the rebellion might have succeeded. It is equally possible that the violent unrest that has marked the twentieth century would have begun at a time before the final acts of imperialism had been committed and that Chinese society would have shaped its reorganization into the modern world far differently from the pattern now being etched in blood, starvation, and unhappiness.

As the years of the twentieth century have passed the obvious occidental imperialism has slackened. More subtle and pernicious undercurrents in the form of financial loans, and large-scale commercial dealings protected by unequal treaties, have continued. And with the slackening of occidental imperialism there arose Japanese imperialism, a century late in the race, even more seriously to plague Chinese society. Commencing with the seizure of the southern Ryukyu Islands in the late 1870's and reaching its disastrous climax in the 8 years of the Sino-Japanese War, the Japanese effort exceeded any of the illustrative examples set by the Occident. There are those who hold that the economic imperialism of the outside world was rapidly beating China down to the role of an economic slave producing volumes of low-cost raw materials at the price of a steadily lowered Chinese standard of life. In the eighteenth century China possibly had the highest standard of living in the world, whereas in the early 1930's China was a rival for the questionable rank of "one of the lowest standards of living in the world." The self-centeredness and crystallized rigidity of Chinese bureaucracy both refused and were unable to change, but the Occident carried exploitation to completely unjustified extremes in fattening its own economy.

THE CHINESE WAY IN REVOLUTION

Throughout the long period in which Chinese culture has been subject to the impact of outside elements there has been a rather standard form of reaction. The Chinese are fully committed to the process of peaceful change by slow gradual election, with a Confucian maxim for justification. To the sudden major shift, the change imposed from without, the change that would create a break with the past, the change decided by a few key officials, the mass of Chinese have been unalterably opposed. In other words, steady change that is held to a rate and an amount that does not threaten the continuity and the major tenets of Chinese life is acceptable; change that threatens the continued existence of established Chinese society finds a weight of objection that usually is passive but that can break into sudden and violent storm upon occasion. During the major span of Chinese history the Confucian bureaucracy has been in charge, and anything that threatened to change the essential system of society enlisted the opposition of those in charge. It is worth noting here that the change of a dynasty did not involve the change of the system, but merely of the reigning family.

At times the scholar class unquestionably fattened upon the toil of the masses, but over the long period of Chinese history the scholar class has served as the cultural conscience of China, maintaining society on the path laid down in the Confucian classics, battling all divergent trends that threatened the Chinese state, serving as the repository of the permanent values of Chinese culture in a changing world. Made up of human beings drawn from all walks of life and all parts of China, there was a perennial air of democracy about the scholar class that was much more apparent than real, for only sufficient peasantry were admitted to the chosen calling to maintain the ranks of the scholar class. For 2,000 years this cultural conscience changed with the passing centuries yet remained constant to the goals of Confucianism to provide the thread of continuity in Chinese civilization. Within the last century has come the severest test of all, and it now often seems that the old scholar bureaucracy has totally collapsed under the impact of the West. In fact this is not so, and a new scholar bureaucracy is in the forming, though both groups are buffeted by the turbulence of changes taking place in Chinese culture today, and the new group has not yet developed a centralized body of culture to serve as the ideal and standard of society.

The Chinese have been stubbornly individualistic in their acceptance of change and their opposition to new culture traits. Always there have been reformers, experimenters, true revolutionaries, and men ahead of or behind their times. However, an unproved new cultural device has never been accepted. Objection to change sometimes has seemed the dominant motif of Chinese culture, but this, also, is much more apparent than real. Objection may be individual, by family, by village, by local region, or by major geographic region. Chinese culture never has been uniform throughout the whole country, a fact that never has bothered the Chinese, but one that often has caused foreign observers to reach simple generalizations falling far short of the truth.

The Chinese essentially are a practical people, even though the logic of their reasoning follows paths unfamiliar to the occidental. Sometimes their acceptance, rejection, or discard of culture traits seems odd to the occidental but is soundly based in their own psychological background. Selectivity in these respects ranges from matters of individual food and dress to regional adoption of a political creed, or general acceptance of electric light by the country at large. The process of nation-wide adoption of particular segments of culture, therefore, is an extremely complicated affair. It sometimes involves a long period of years before the protest dies down around a particular instance, like the railroad. Or it may involve civil uprisings that eventually lead to armed conflict, like the political manipulation that has grown into Chinese Communism. Variation of the procedure

is unlimited, but there is one certain feature in all cases, which is that the Chinese people eventually decide for themselves regardless of the dictates or the lobbying of special interests, groups, parties, or regions. It may take even as long as a century for the process of acceptance or rejection to work itself out. Chinese history is full of these periods of readjustment, periods that impress the reader of history as being full of chaos, anarchy, and disorganized political institutions. The last two generations constitute such a period, during which the cultural choices thrust upon the Chinese populace have been greater than at any time in the past.

One other certainty in the Chinese process of change, whether it be in religion, dress, or political machinery, is that no new culture trait, however simple, has come into the Chinese realm and long remained unchanged by Chinese group personality. In the spread of Buddhism from India to China, with its sculpture, its architecture and its metaphysics, the end product differed greatly from the original. In accepting the growing and smoking of tobacco the Chinese devised instruments and techniques quite unlike those of the bringers of the plant and the habit of smoking. In the progressive spread of Democracy and Communism in China from their respective homes, the future ultimate blend of both into a peculiar system of Sino-socialistic-democratism would no doubt equally astonish Washington and Jefferson, and Marx and Lenin. It took Buddhism several centuries to flower anew in China after its spread from India, though it never did produce the mysticism in China that marked its homeland India. So too, then, one should expect neither a full repetition of American Democracy nor Russian Communism in China in the long run. Though this progressive change is true of all cultural diffusion, it particularly needs to be emphasized for the China which suffers so much from conventional overgeneralization.

The Chinese definitely recognize that the Occident has some culture traits and some techniques of using a landscape that are superior to those of the Orient. There is a very positive appetite in China for much of the material equipment of the west, varying from preventive medicine and diet-balancing vitamins to radios, automobile passenger buses, and hydroelectric projects. These material advantages notwithstanding, the present-day Chinese, as a nation, retain their self-centeredness to the point that they reject occidental materialistic and scientific philosophy as epitomized in "pure science," the atom bomb as a military weapon, and "untouched by human hands" as a mark of engineering efficiency. In the apparent chaos that marks modern China there is at work the essentially Chinese spirit of individual rationalization and group compromise in regard to how much of the West can safely be accepted by the East without endangering the soul of Chinese culture. The Chinese way in these things is to tolerate enormous tribulation for this generation, and the next if need be, in order that future generations may live within a pattern of culture first crystallized into the Confucian code 2,500 years ago. The Chinese today are weary of the struggle to rationalize the East and the West, but until some kind of common denominator finds general acceptance the struggle will continue. As a well-educated Chinese said to me shortly after the termination of Sino-Japanese hostilities: "If we do not find peace in my lifetime, we will in that of my grandson."

China during Fifty Centuries

(CONTINUED)

THE AGRICULTURE OF CHINA

The agriculture of modern China still is essentially that of the ancient Chinese culture hearth of the loess-lands. This is in spite of all the new crops, the new tools, and the new climatic regions to which the Chinese have gone. Intensive hand labor with a minimum of mechanical power, closely integrated crop follow-up, and large yield per acre are as descriptive of Chinese vegetable gardening or rice culture in Yunnan today as of the agriculture of southern Shensi or Shantung in the sixth century B.C., when Confucius was alive. The taro and rice of the southern regions called for wet fields and terracing. American potatoes, maize, peanuts, and tobacco have greatly altered the map of cultivated lands since the Columbian discoveries by extension of the agricultural area in upland regions. The export of tea, silk, soybeans, and tung oil to foreign markets has seriously upset the balance of agriculture. But these are not changes in the system itself. The small size of the truck gardens and the intensity of cultivation apply to any of the fifty centuries during which the Chinese have farmed northern China. In point of fact, the intensification of Chinese agriculture has grown greater during the last two centuries than it ever had previously. This is a detailed sharpening of the system caused by the desperate struggle to keep ahead in the feeding of a hungry but growing population that has not been really well fed since the end of the eighteenth century.

The Land Problem

By the close of the feudal era communal and feudal land holdings slowly gave way to privately owned land. In the abolishment of the feudal system there can have been no even division of land among the population and many families must have managed to secure or retain title to various choice farmlands. Since agriculture already had been placed above trade and manufacture as occupational callings, land already was the chief depository of any surplus wealth, individuals and families adding to their holdings whenever opportunity presented itself. Out of the emphasis upon agriculture the Chinese had, by the beginning of the Christian era, much experience with the problems of land taxation, deeds and titles, sale and exchange, accumulation of land in the hands of the wealthy families, and the inevitable formation of a landless class of farmers who became hired hands and tenant farmers on the lands of the city-dwelling absentee landlords. At times monasteries and temples or guilds and speculative associations secured control over large land holdings, but these non-personalized owners never have seriously threatened the personal ownership of China's land. Individual family or clan holdings sometimes have reached huge proportions, but these are special forms of Chinese personal ownership not often found in the Occident. Most of the usable land of China became private, personal property as colonization spread out of the hearth, and the ownership of the farmlands of China has consistently remained in private hands throughout the whole of the Christian era.

Over the centuries land has changed hands continuously. Always families economically on the way up have been anxious to invest their savings, and families on the way down, for one reason or another, have been forced to sell off their lands. During waning periods in Chinese history, when the burden of inefficient government has been great, the peasantry has lost much of its land to the large landlord families. The return of peace, and steady colonial expansion over China, added to the total land volume. Resettling of unclaimed lands, building of dike systems, cultivation of new alluvial delta lands, lands cleared and newly terraced for cultivation, lands made cultivable by new crops, all have been means of increasing the volume. The peasantry thus has continuously acquired new lands. The pattern of Confucian society made it possible for certain peasants continuously to rise into the class of landlords and scholar-bureaucrats, while others again sank back into the tenant farmer group. The Chinese family and clan systems were important agents in this process.

At the beginning of the Manchu dynasty, in the seventeenth century, conditions were favorable to the acquisition of land by the peasantry. All the above-named factors were operative, plus the fact that the government generally gave anyone claiming new lands a tax-free period. However, by the middle of the nineteenth century the dynastic downward swing of Chinese history plus the force of occidental economic exploitation began causing a serious deterioration of land ownership. By the outbreak of the Sino-Japanese War in 1937 conditions, sunk to a level seldom reached previously, were almost impossible for an agricultural society trying to participate in an enlarged world of foreign trade, industry, and expanded material culture. It is a commonly accepted statement that for all China, in 1945, perhaps 60 per cent of all Chinese farmers were tenants of some kind, and that well over half of them were deeply in debt. This is more serious in agricultural China than is a similar figure of tenancy in industrial United States. The situation generally was held to be worse in the south of China than in the north, with Manchuria the best off of any section. In southwest China most good land was in the hands of Chinese landlords, with peasant Chinese as tenants and non-Chinese tribespeople often forced onto the barren hill lands or into the position of tenants.

Average land holdings vary considerably, but figures running from 1 to 10 acres per farm family could be found in many parts of the country, with an over-all average not far above 3 acres per farm family. There were many millions of landless families, many millions of owner-tenants, a section of the peasantry owning adequate land, and some hundreds of thousands of families that owned large amounts of land. Some estimates indicate that 5 per cent of the population owned 50 per cent of the cultivated land, whereas 70 per cent of the farming population owned but 20 per cent. This was one prominent factor in the internal trouble in China, usually designated the Kuomintang-Communist dispute of the period between 1925 and 1949. Inadequate and non-realistic government land reform policy by the Kuomintang was countered by over-emphasis on agrarian reform by the Communists, but this strong focus on land problems remains a vital part of any debate over which path should China follow.

One feature that is true today but that probably was absent in earlier China is the fragmentation of land in small patches. The Chinese inheritance system permits division of a father's land, between his sons, though many families and clans hold certain lands in undivided form. As the present dense population of China has built up, the constant division process has made for smaller and smaller holdings. Not only are the holdings small in total, but they may be made up of as many as ten or a dozen plots of ground, scattered over a distance of several miles. While all agrarian reform has urged the reshuffling of land to give farmers unified holdings, the peasantry objected, fearing another fleecing in the process. This fragmentation and division of an absolute maximum of 290,000,000 acres of farmland among possibly more than 375,000,000 farm people out of the total Chinese population indicates that, within this generation, there is one unsolvable problem in China— there is not enough land to go round. When the formative period in Chinese culture elevated land into the position of the primary economic good, there was more than enough for all. But the very fecundity of the Chinese soil has produced so huge a human crop that China now is facing a situation in which there will never again be land enough to satisfy the classic Confucian value. This must be taken into account in any study of Chinese agriculture, for it is one factor that accounts for much of the social and political unrest of the present generation.

Frequent reference was made by travelers of recent decades, economists, and critics to the fact that the Chinese waste land in several ways. Such items as the burial custom of placing coffins in the fields receives caustic comment, along with the neglect of river bottom or delta lands that could be cultivated, and quite arable land left in simple waste. It is only in the non-rice-growing parts of China that coffins are placed in the fields, and any close observer can perceive the speed with which local erosion, decomposition, and the seasonal plowing return this land to crop use. Locally grave mounds do reduce the crop lands, and the absence of country-wide flood control planning also prevents use of some river bottom land in a number of places. Civil unrest, punishing taxation, and economic dislocation cause the non-cropping of some land every year. Soil erosion, over the last 3,000 years, had made its inroads upon many parts of China, before terracing had put many areas into shape for permanent farming. These and other factors do reduce the net total of land cropped in any one decade, but the Chinese compare favorably with any other society in the best use of their land. The addition of every single foot of cultivable land in China would still leave the volume too slight to suffice both to feed China and to provide every family with a sound investment in the classical tradition.

Pre-Columbian Crop Patterns

The mainstays of Chinese agriculture are rice and wheat. Both were introduced before the colonial spread of the Chinese out of the culture hearth over China, and both became integral parts of food-crop patterns. Wheat came into China via the Kansu corridor from the west, and became the staple crop in southern Manchuria, northern Korea, and north China. Rice came into China from the south, becoming the staple crop of central and South China and of the Pacific littoral clear around to the east coast of Korea and southern Japan. The Yangtze River Basin became the meeting ground of the two crops, resulting in a seasonal division of the land, wheat being a winter crop and rice a summer crop. Both spread farther north or south as minor crops, eventually achieving a degree of balance in land use. This balance is of long standing and has not changed appreciably as the Chinese landscape gradually has filled with people. It resembles the balance struck in India.

In each of the two basic cropping patterns there are supplementary crops, some indigenous and some imported from neighboring regions in early periods. The second, fourth, seventh, and thirteenth centuries were notable periods in which numbers of crop-plant additions occurred, but this undoubtedly was a steady process. Such items as cotton, kaoliang (a sorghum), peas, and some of the beans, melons, and many of the garden vegetables, came from southwestern or central Asia, via the Kansu corridor. Taro, some of the spices, bananas, sugar cane, and some of the tropical fruits came from southeastern Asia or India. North China agriculture had as its native supplementary crop complex some of the soybeans, several millets, a variety of vegetables and fruits, hemp, and silk. South China's native supplementary patterns included the bamboos, citrus fruits, other soybeans, a variety of vegetables, tea, and tung oil. During the historic period there slowly developed many regional patterns of crop dependence based upon local soil and climatic conditions, smoothness of land surface, water and flood conditions and the ease of handling native plant cover. Native and imported crops shared in this re-

gional development. The evolution of the wet field for rice led to terracing for better water control and the extension of crop land.

Earliest China possessed only a moderate range of products, north and south. The steady accretion of new plants broadened the base considerably. However, it appears that China lacked supplementary crop plants that would make easy the exploitation of her rough hill lands. The main grain crops, rice, wheat, barley, millet, and kaoliang were all crops of smooth, plowed fields. The peas and beans, and a few oil seeds were not easily grown on the rough, hilly, poorer lands. The garden vegetables needed good soils and close handling. Though there were fruits available, fruit culture on a large scale never seemed to appeal to the Chinese. Pastureland and animal culture was not an important part of Chinese agriculture, north or south. A fairly considerable proportion of the arable land of China, therefore, was not well suited to any of the crops that had been brought into China prior to the Columbian discoveries. These marginal lands, then, never could be put into really developed food-producing agriculture. Perhaps this was one of the limiting factors that long held down the population to a figure which left considerable elbow space for all. In this early agriculture of China one final fact should be noted. The produce of China's farms was consumed at home, there being practically no international trade. There was, however, a significant drainage of surpluses from all over China into the key economic area of North China as a part of imperial tribute.

Modern Agricultural Factors

Few of the crops introduced since the Columbian discoveries has seriously or permanently displaced a previous crop. However, opium seriously upset the productive balance of agriculture over almost all of China during a 40-year period extending from perhaps 1880 to 1920. The opium poppy began to be grown before 1880 but reached its major proportions during the last two decades of the nineteenth century. It displaced food crops primarily, reducing the food volume at a time when the population was growing rapidly, and causing a hike in the land-tax structure consequent upon the very large returns from opium compared to food crops. Opium continued to be grown after 1920 but on a reduced scale, which gradually has tapered off over most of China proper. The cessation of poppy cultivation often caused a period of land abandonment until the land-tax structure again was lowered to fit the productive income pattern.

Maize, the sweet potato, the white potato, the peanut, tobacco, and such minor items as the tomato, pineapple, grape vine, and some vegetables, all fitted into segments of the agricultural complex in such a way as to round it out, broaden it, and increase the productive yield without the serious displacement of any previous crop. Thus the white potato became either a truck garden crop around the cities inhabited by the white man, and was consumed by him, or a crop of the back-country rough-hill or marginal lands suitable to no native crop. Maize filled in many local areas and was grown as a hill land crop. The sweet potato spread rapidly and in many areas became a staple crop on the hill crests above the terraced rice lands. Particularly in rolling, hilly Szechwan did the sweet potato find a natural home, becoming the basic crop of the poorer peasant farmer. The peanut supplied a more productive and plentiful cooking oil than any plant previously cultivated. The cumulative effect of these modern introductions, which are spread from the late sixteenth century to date, has been to tremendously increase the food supply available from lands that were not very productive previously, giving one more stimulus to population growth.

Commercial production of various crops for international trade has not altered the major regional balance of Chinese agriculture, though it has upset the productive economy within many individual regions. Thus the export of tea, silk, egg products, pig bristles, goat skins, soybeans, cotton, sesame, tung oil, grass cloth, and lac has affected the economy of one or more regions. The effects have been separately expressed during the period of modern foreign trade. At first the trade in each grew slowly, then boomed, and finally collapsed in a number of cases. Such economic reactions have not been permanent, but each has contributed to the economic problems of present-day China.

In spite of all the varied introductions Chinese agriculture has a very high dependence upon grains, particularly upon rice and wheat. Its per capita meat consumption is very low and the pressure of men upon land is such that modern China cannot afford food for many animals. Fruits, nuts, fish, and fowl likewise play a small part in the diet of most Chinese. Nutritional standards under a high-grain diet are today less high in China than in many other parts of the world. This is in part a question of sheer pressure of population and inadequate supply.

The occidental agricultural missionary, the university research station, and the provincial experiment station have done a great deal to stimulate the productiveness of modern Chinese agriculture. Much remains to be done both in plant breeding and in insect control. In spite of Chinese skill in maintaining soil fertility, many sections of China today seriously need fertilizer, particularly organic ones. Today, however, China cannot feed and clothe herself, and the deficiency appears to be growing, since population increase exceeds increasing productivity. The annual food deficit now stands at about 2 to 3 per cent of the total food consumption, and before 1950 it was met largely by imports of rice, wheat products, and sugar. There was a steady cotton import, much more than making up for the regular annual export to Japan, which was in the nature of a trade in quality differential. Whether this deficit situation is really here to stay or is partly caused by the constantly unsettled conditions of the last 75 years is open to question. There undoubtedly is a certain margin of increased productivity yet to be achieved, and a peaceful China could operate with greater efficiency than has resulted in the recent past, but the limit of reserve productivity cannot be far off. It would seem that the intensive system of agriculture, that first gave the Chinese culture hearth its regional advantage more than 3,000 years ago, has run near to the end of its line and now has brought the huge Chinese population up against a dilemma for which there may be no solution short of a revolution in the very nature of agriculture, the reduction of the Chinese population, or the development of an industrial export economy that will support the purchase of foodstuffs from abroad.

Regional Crop Patterns

The most significant regional line of demarcation in the agricultural picture of China is the Tsinling Line, which roughly corresponds to the northward limits of rice, water chestnut, taro, canals, flooded-field patterns, bamboo, citrus fruits, the palms, tea, and a number of minor crops or agricultural practices. The accompanying map suggests that it is possible to outline a number of agricultural regions by selection of varied cropping patterns and combinations. The individual distribution maps indicate some further details of agriculture. The table summarizes some simple data concerning these crop regions. The map of forested and cultivated lands suggests the regional concentration of good farmland and points up the fact that the usable volume is relatively small, even though China is no worse off in this respect than many other countries. Brief generalization about Chinese agriculture is difficult, for Chinese farmers, after centuries of trial and error have worked out rather complex cropping systems based upon many local factors. Changing conditions of transport, plant breeding, and marketing economics affect these patterns, but less rapidly than in our own country. Study of Table 5 will indicate that central China, particularly Szechwan, has the most

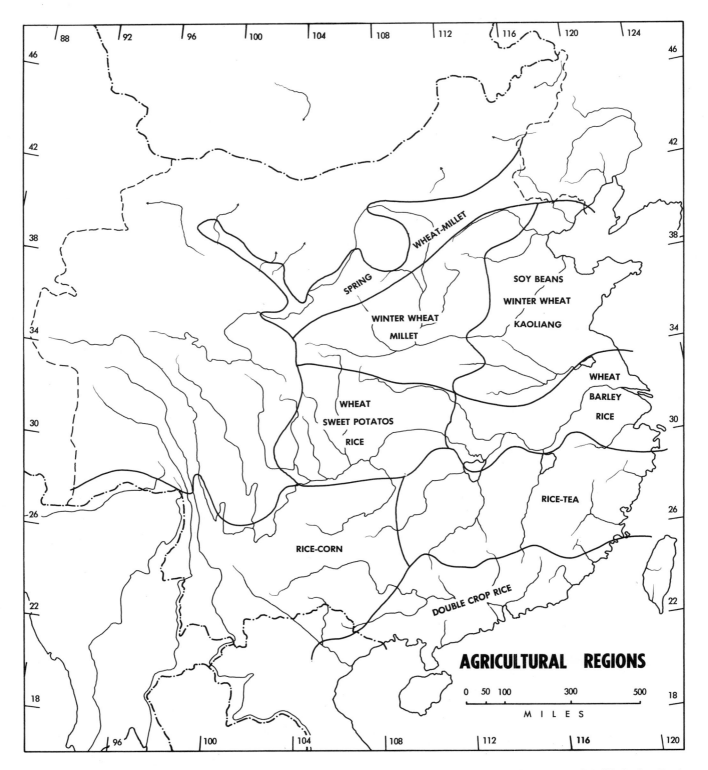

Fig. 103.   Agricultural regions of China, expressed by chief crops.   Crops are named in descending order.   Modified after Buck.

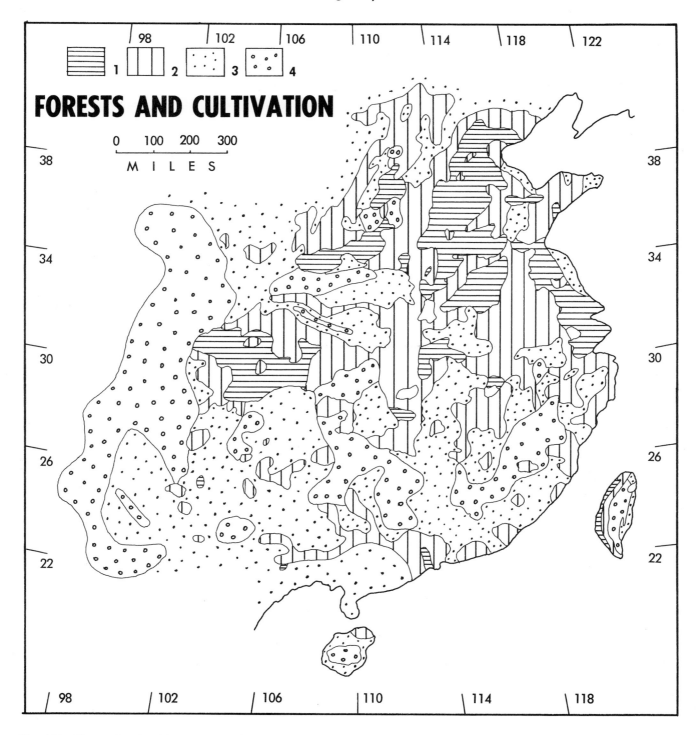

Fig. 104. Forested and cultivated areas of China: (1) over 60 per cent of the surface cultivated; (2) between 20 and 60 per cent cultivated; (3) under 20 per cent cultivated; (4) areas containing some real forest growth. Zones 1–3 contain usable wild timber trees tolerated in growth, but contain little standing forest. Modified from both Buck and Chen.

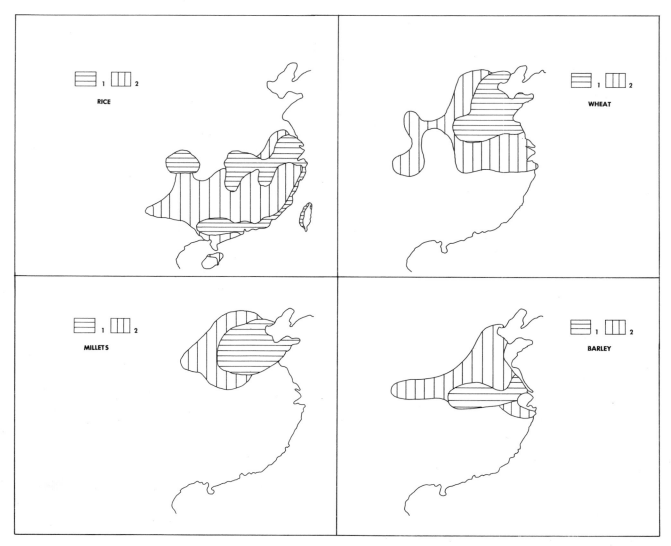

Fig. 105. The primary grain cereals: (1) primary zones of production; (2) secondary areas of production.

complex crop pattern of any part of China, growing a larger number of the common crops than any other agricultural region. Manchuria, the northwest and the southern rice double-crop regions have simpler crop patterns than the blended agriculture of central China.

Northward from the Tsinling Line double cropping becomes more and more unusual until in northwest China and Manchuria it is rarely met with. The Yangtze Valley has about half its land double cropped, combining southern summer and northern winter crops. Perhaps three fourths the land of southeastern China is double cropped, two crops of rice and minor subtropical products being grown in the extra-long growing season but with few northern-type winter crops. About half the crop land of China is irrigated, most

of this being rice, of course, with a minor amount of irrigation agriculture throughout the north until one reaches the dry Kansu corridor zone of oasis culture. Organized irrigation projects in the north could expand the irrigation agriculture of the north considerably. Over a third of the cultivated land of China is in small, terraced fields, and much of the total field surface has been so rearranged as to represent a man-made landscape. There is almost no square mile of China that does not show the cumulative hand of man. Almost all rice land is terraced, of course, but terraces of a sort are found throughout the Loess Highlands and in various other parts of the country.

The northwest and southwest of China are the only regions that have not significantly shared in the agricultural export trade. Northwest China has a very

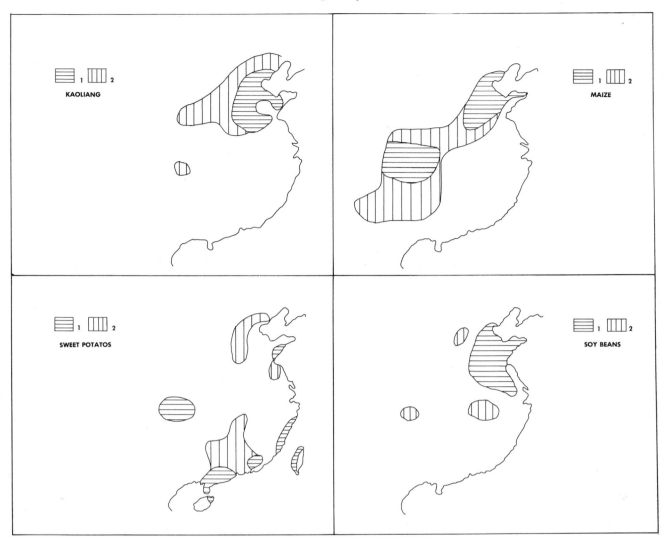

Fig. 106. Auxiliary food crops: (1) primary producing regions; (2) secondary areas of production.

strong dependence upon spring wheat, with a rather small crop range. Southwest China is isolated and also has the most dense packing of population per square mile of cultivated land of any part of China. These two areas today seem to have the poorest standards of living in the country. Despite the stake in international trade Chinese agriculture still is mainly a local consumption affair. Transport mechanisms are so inadequate and per ton-mile costs so high that very few common products will support a long haul, and it is only the unique products of Chinese agriculture that achieve an export volume. Agriculture is the chief source of income for perhaps three fourths of the Chinese today, and, since there are many factors limiting the over-all efficiency and success of agriculture, Chinese economy as a whole suffers thereby.

FORESTS AND THE TIMBER PROBLEM

Was all of China ever covered by forest? This remains an unsolved problem. It seems most probable that the zones of active loess deposit, and stream erosion, flooding and sedimentation in north China and the lower Yangtze Valley were never fully covered with forest in the ordinary sense. It would also seem that there was open grassland within a good share of southern Manchuria. Probably the mountain projections above the north China loess maintained their forest cover. Most of central and much of southern China are natural forest areas, though bamboo and subtropical grasses prevented the tree cover from reaching completeness. It is likely that bamboo, the grasses, shrubs, and some scrubby plants have in-

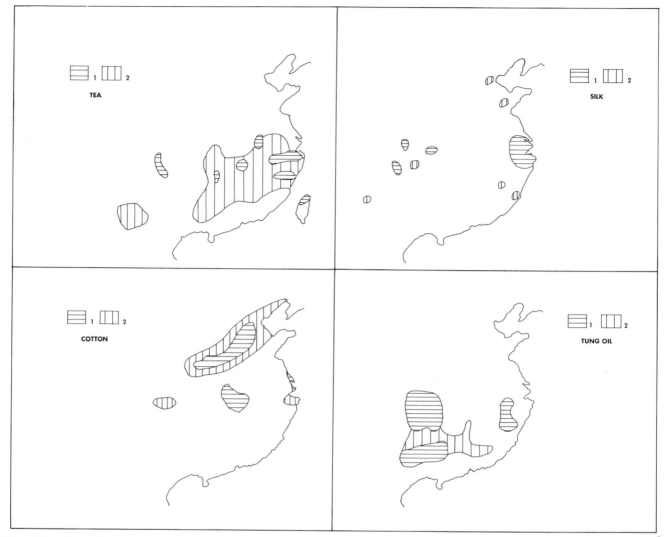

Fig. 107. The chief export crops: (1) primary producing regions; (2) secondary areas of production. Tea is widely grown in south China, but acid soils and microclimate center the main production. Silk is widely produced also, but accumulated labor skills historically have centered production. Mulberry trees do not grow in north China, and silk production there is from upland wild plants, chiefly scrub oak. Tung oil is grown on rough hill lands with trees seldom in orchard stands.

creased in area within historic time, since their rates of reproduction under tolerance are greater than that of forest.

Undoubtedly the Chinese have deforested large areas, not once but several times. In periods during which the economic pressures of men upon land for food, lumber, and fuel were less than those today the Chinese successfully practiced reforestation. Numerous replantings within recent decades have suffered at the hands of needy but irresponsible fuel gatherers. One has but to watch a wee north China lad spend his whole day trying to secure fuel enough for the evening fire by gathering grass, roots, and twigs broken from saplings to realize the pressure that exists.

Today most of China's good timber is gone, though there remain a few forested patches in isolated locations. Elsewhere timber is almost a farm crop that is regularly cut too young. China today is a timber importer on a steadily increasing scale without hope of reducing the import volume. Possibly one fourth of the area of China proper would be forest covered if man let nature take its course, but in modern China that is literally impossible.

FISHERIES

Every well-ordered Chinese menu includes fish in some form or other if possible. The list of aquatic

TABLE 5

CHINA'S CROP PATTERNS BY AGRICULTURAL REGIONS

Region	Primary Crop	Millet	Kaoliang	Wheat, spring	Wheat, winter	Barley, spring	Barley, winter	Broad beans, winter	Soybeans	Peas	Maize	White potatoes	Sweet potatoes	Peanuts	Rape	Sesame	Sugar cane	Bamboo	Citrus fruit	Persimmons	Pears	Stone fruit	Melons	Tea	Tobacco	Cotton	Mulberry	Silk	Pig bristles	Goatskins	Eggs *	Tung Oil	Common Animals (Listed in order of importance reading crosswise)	Growing, Season Days
1. Manchuria	Soy beans, Kaoliang	×	—	×	×				—		×																						Cattle	150–170
2. Northwest †	Millet	—	×	×	×							×			×																		Cattle, sheep, horses, camels	175–200
3. Loess Highlands	Winter wheat	×	×	—	×						×	×				×				×	×				×								Cattle, donkeys, sheep, horses	200–225
4. North China Plain	Winter wheat, Kaoliang	×	—	—			×	×	×	×	×		×	×	×					×	×	×			×	×					×		Cattle, donkeys, horses, mules, fowl	190–240
5. Yangtze Valley	Rice				×			×	×	×	×	×		×	×	×		×			×	×				×	×	×				×	Water buffalo, cattle, swine, fowl	260–300
6. Szechwan	Rice			×		×		×	×	×	×	×	×	×	×	×	×	×	×	×	×	×	×		×	×	×	×	×	×	×		×	Cattle, swine, water buffalo, goats	330–360
7. Southern Hills	Rice				×		×		×			×		×				×	×	×					×	×					×	×	×	Cattle, water buffalo, swine, fowl	300–330
8. Southern double-crop ‡	Rice							×				×	×	×				×	×	×					×	×		×	×				×	Water buffalo, cattle, swine	340–365
9. Southwest Plateaus	Rice				×			×	×		×				×			×		×	×			×		×	×	×	×				×	Water buffalo, cattle, horses, swine, goats	340–365

* Refers to important commercial production only.

† Oats, buckwheat, wool and pastureland are significant in this one area alone.

‡ A number of subtropical fruits are significant in this one area alone.

products consumed by the Chinese is smaller than the Japanese list, but considerably greater than that used by occidentals. The primary fishing waters are from Hangchow Bay southward to Hainan Island, but Chinese boats range the whole of the China coast, a distance well over 3,000 miles. Over 100,000 sailing junks are engaged in full-time fisheries work, and the total of professional fishermen, including fresh-water fishermen, is above a million. Few large, powered trawlers are used by the Chinese. The sea fisheries bring in the widest range of fish, shrimp, oysters, and edible seaweed. Canton, Ningpo, Shanghai, and Dairen are the leading fishing ports, from which fresh fish are sold to the immediate urban markets and salted fish shipped to wider, inland markets. Almost every port along the China coast has its fishing fleet of boats built and decorated by special local designs, though the fleets of the flat, alluvial north China coast are small and unimportant.

Fresh-water fisheries are significant in the Yangtze Valley and southeast China, but they are less important than the sea fisheries. Relatively few professional fishermen work the inland waters, but many members of farm families casually engage in fishing during slack seasons and free hours. In the rice lands of east and south China there are many reservoirs and ponds in which practically domesticated fish culture is carried on. Particularly in Kwangtung such fish culture makes an important contribution to farm incomes. It is difficult to assess the contribution of fish to the Chinese food supply, either quantitatively or dietetically. Certainly fish is a useful addition, even though the poorer segments of the population cannot eat fish at every meal.

TRANSPORT AND COMMUNICATIONS

The enormous contrasts in communications existent throughout the world today are occidental creations of the last century and a half. In the China and the Occident of 1800 transport and communications had not greatly changed for many centuries. Only the Roman Empire had had a system of courier routes and roads that were the equal of the Chinese system. Since the Chinese never made exceptional use of wheeled vehicles roadbuilders could use steps in constructing their routes through hilly and mountain landscapes. All main routes were paved with stone slabs to a width of several feet, and many secondary paths had single slab centers. Pack animals and the human carrier were the basic elements in transport, both of passengers and of cargo. In southwest China as late as 1930, it required some 60-days' travel to go from Chungking to Kunming, via Kweiyang, by native means over native roads. In 1939 I made that trip in 3 days by car over gravel-surfaced highways. On United States standard roads 2 easy days would suffice. Today in many parts of China the human carrier still handles almost everything that is moved, and over most of the country the human carrier, the sedan chair, the pack animal, the junk, the wheelbarrow, or the two-wheeled oxcart are the prevailing transport mechanisms. Per ton-mile costs are high, transport time is great, and the very roads and equipment limit the volume and type of materials that can be moved. Such introductions as the pony taxi and the rubber-tired two-wheeled cart pulled by two to eight men are costly and slight improvements in the face of tremendous need.

In central and south China natural waterways and the canal play a role of enormous importance. The barbarian Wu tribes, resident in the Yangtze Delta, developed the first sections of what came to be the Grand Canal. Various additions were made until a single waterway was developed from south of the Yangtze to the Yellow River in the sixth century. The Grand Canal has attracted much attention, though it was but one of a number of important waterways. The total of navigable waterways, river and canal, is estimated as high as 40,000 miles. The development of modern transport in China reflects both the conservatism of a people in accepting new devices and the severe exploitation by the Occident. At first contact with the

European the Chinese seagoing junk was a better vessel than any possessed by Europe, but the native sailing vessels of the Chinese today are little better than they were in the sixteenth century. Only slowly did the Chinese take to steam and steel, but at the outset of the Sino-Japanese War they had built a large fleet of steam launches, tugs, and small steamers. A fair coastwise shipping fleet had been purchased from abroad but it suffered severe foreign competition under unequal controls. British, Japanese, French, and American shipping concerns handled most of China's foreign trade, most of her coastwise trade, and much of her shipping on navigable rivers. Post-war nationalizing of China's shipping waters and the destruction of most of the former operating fleets have left China in a desperate fix. She has chosen, however, to suffer inadequate transportation at a time when it is most needed rather than to re-open the door to foreign ships and exploitation. This will take time to correct, and perhaps for a generation China will have inadequate water transport.

The first railways were built by occidental concerns on concession by the Chinese government. There followed a mad scramble which left China short of railroads, but with loans that still are to be repaid. Including Manchuria the railways operating in 1937 totaled just short of 10,000 miles. The war saw many lines ruined and new ones poorly built in the emergency. In 1952, using National Government surveys, the Communists had about 17,000 miles of railway operating. Eventually China will need perhaps 60,000 miles of railways covering the country in a well-planned network, so that the task has only begun. The accompanying map suggests the present operating coverage of rail lines.

There was less foreign exploitation in the building of modern highways, though the Occident controls the automobile business. The old stone steproads, the narrow winding paths of South China, and the rut-ridden earth roads of the northwest were unfit for modern wheeled vehicles. China is having rather suddenly, to revise a whole land transport system that has served for many centuries. It is both costly and slow going. The Sino-Japanese War greatly spurred the building of strategic roads to open up western China, but the campaign will be long, for China's highways at present are but a fraction of those needed. Before the war, the total road mileage was about 70,000 miles of all qualities of modern roads, and automobiles and trucks numbered only about 50,000. It will be a long time before many Chinese can ever hope to own cars. Provincial organizations to handle passenger and freight movement have developed everywhere, and it is likely that public management of most automotive

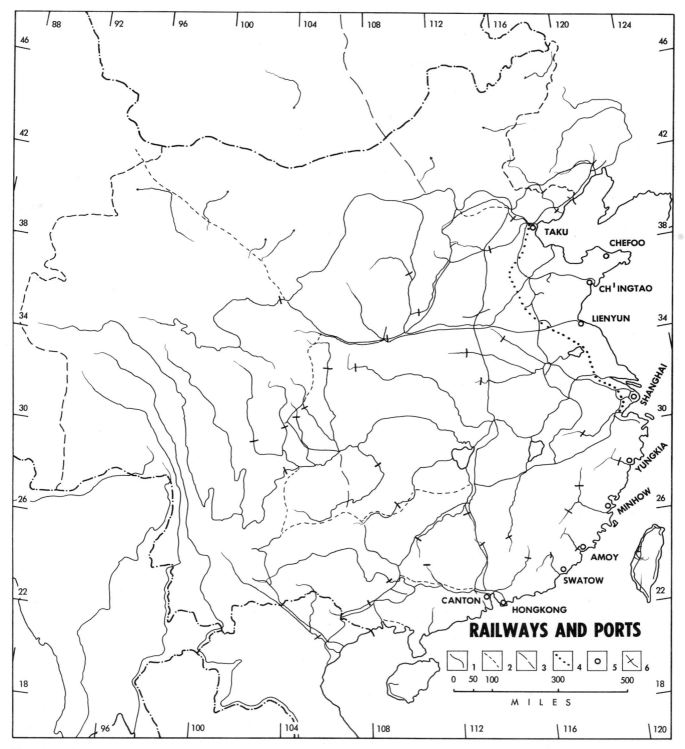

Fig. 108. Rail lines and water transport: (1) operating rail lines, 1953; (2) rail lines under construction; 1953, (3) projected rail lines; (4) Grand Canal, now navigable only in short sections; (5) chief ports; (6) upstream limit of water transport by raft and small boat. Ocean ships may reach Hankow on the Yangtze.

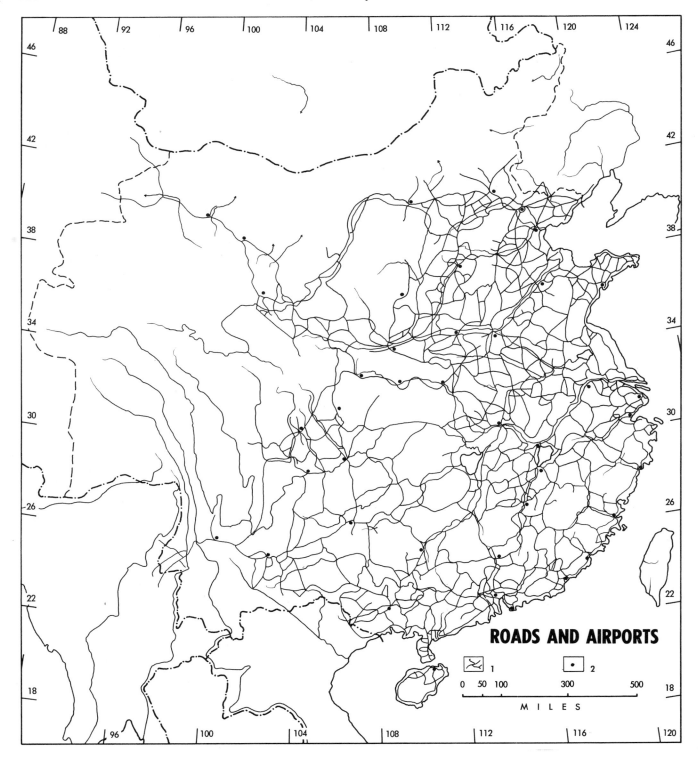

Fig. 109.   Roads and civil airports: (1) roads usable by wheeled traffic of some sort (not all roads shown can be traveled by
motor cars, and many roads are in poor repair by American standards); (2) airports regularly used by civil traffic.   Many air
fields are not shown, and amphibian planes may reach many areas without airports.

transport will characterize China's road system. The modern roads, though sometimes longer than the native routes, are on better gradients and afford easier travel, so that there is much profitable use of the new roads other than by auto.

In aviation the revolution has had to be even more sudden. Szechwan was familiar with the airplane before the railway and the automobile came. The Chinese like to fly but as yet have not mastered the fine maintenance techniques necessary to keep planes air-fit. It is likely that aviation will develop faster and to a greater extent than was true with rail and roadways, since the urgency of the times is greater and China must skip some stages in transport development.

In telecommunications the Chinese are more successful. Telephones, telegraph, and radio they have mastered and used increasingly well. The mileage of wire or the number of radio sets, after a long period of World War II, is no proper judgment of the use of these instruments.

Today one can pass quickly from one extreme to another, for China is only beginning to develop her modern transport equipment. In Shanghai, alongside a riverside street, one can see the modern ocean liner, the steam tug pulling a long line of barges, the stubby local passenger boat, the sea-going junk, the inland water junk, the one-man water taxi boat, and the raft of bamboo poles floating downstream to the lumber yard. And along the street will pass the private limousine, the scurrying taxicab with horn at full pitch, the trackless trolley, the motor truck, the coolie-pulled cart, the bicycle, the ricksha, and the human carrier. Close to Shanghai one can pass into the native scene where the small rowboat, the inland junk, the ricksha, the water-buffalo pack animal, and the human carrier still control the movement of goods and people.

MINERAL WEALTH

The Chinese appear to have learned the use of metals from their western neighbors, but they were among the first to burn rocks out of the earth, known as coal, for heating purposes. Once learned, this knowledge was used in the making of some of the world's finest bronze art goods and in the making of iron agricultural implements. Even gunpowder was developed and used in firecrackers and in the defensive forerunners of the rifle and trench mortar, but elaborate inventive effort in the use of metals was not continued, because the early decisions that agriculture was the preferred calling for civilized man and that minerals should only be used to assist man to the necessary minimum. The Occident did the first surveying of

China's mineral resources, and the early stories were phenomenal. The Chinese Geological Survey was founded only in 1916, and knowledge of the mineral wealth is even now only reasonably approximate. Certain minerals have been mined and exported for decades and represent one source of foreign exchange. In this list are tungsten and antimony, over which China held a monopoly until 1940. China is a small but significant contributor to the world supply of tin and has exported salt to Japan. Reserves of tungsten, antimony, and tin are ample for a reasonable future, whereas salt primarily is produced by the solar evaporation of sea water and is a limitless resource.

The chief mineral resource is coal, in which China ranks fourth in the world list, with about 240 billion tons. The best coal is concentrated chiefly in Shansi and Shensi, which is hardly the best location, but reserves sufficient for several decades at the very least are found in every province. The annual mine total has run about 30,000,000 tons per year, about half of which normally was used in industry. With this large coal supply goes only a scant iron-ore reserve of good quality of about a billion and a half tons, most of which is located in Manchuria. Most of the iron ore is rather poorly located at a distance from most of the coal, but Manchuria has the best combination of the two minerals. Much of the coal throughout the country is satisfactory for coking, but the good iron ore is limited in volume and most of it needs blending for the best results. In the third primary mineral resource of the modern world, petroleum, China appears rather lacking, though surveys are not yet complete. Northwest China has a small production and forms, with Sinkiang and Szechwan, the best potential area, so that China may yet be found to have sizable amounts of petroleum. In the alternative power source, China has a reasonably large water-power potential, but it is of such a nature as to be rather costly to develop, in which field China is only getting a start.

The balance of the mineral prospect is only fair. Such ferro-alloys as chromium, nickel, molybdenum, cobalt, and vanadium appear to be lacking, though a modest amount of manganese is present to go with the tungsten and antimony. Lead, zinc, sulphur, mercury, and gold exist in significant amounts, but silver, copper, and a number of minor minerals appear to be present in inadequate amounts only. Of the light metals the actual volume and value of magnesium and aluminum ores must await further geological field work, but they appear significant.

In summary, it would appear that China has the largest volume of mineral resources of any country of the East. This resource is quite ample for the present rate of use. However, if China is going to pursue successfully the path of industrialization, her huge population will certainly require more resources than are now known except for coal. It may be that in

try was permitted to develop to its fullest. Historically this meant that each local region had to be self-sufficient. With an approximately similar major culture pattern extending over the country there resulted a widespread duplication of handicraft industry

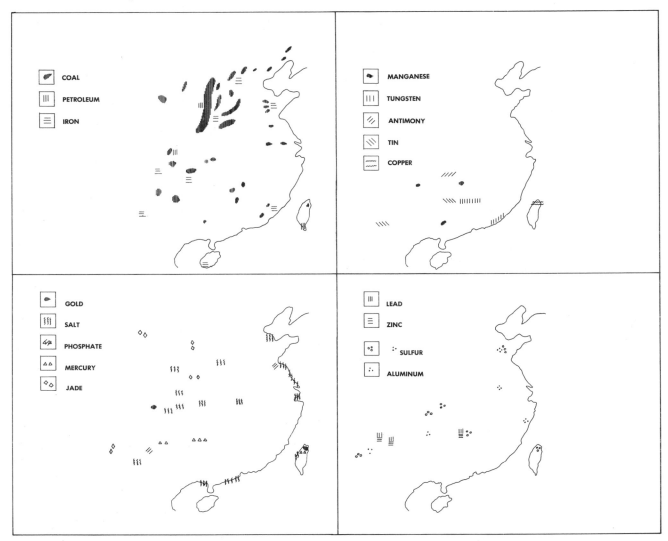

Fig. 110. Mineral occurrences in China Proper and Formosa.

the final geological canvass of the remaining back country sufficient resources will be found to permit an industrialization to reach large proportions.

CHINESE INDUSTRIALIZATION

In early Chinese society a preventive restriction to the growth of industry was repeatedly applied. Such restrictions were meant to insure that neither trade nor manufacturing dominated the agricultural society. Within its limited sphere, however, handicraft indus-

for the production of tools, utensils, weapons, clothing, and art goods. But with varied climate, agriculture, local resources, and local cultures, there resulted endless variety in the products of a handicraft society. Over the centuries there were ups and downs in the prosperity of this industry, as well as regional shifts in the centers of production. Government from time to time felt called upon to take over, regulate, stimulate, or restrict the production and distribution of goods. And certainly there was progress in the use of metals, woods, stone, textiles, and ivory, so that the handicraft industry of the early Manchu dynasty was a richer, fuller one than had been that of the Han. Thus it was that early modern Europe was so greatly impressed with the products of China at a time when Europe's industrial revolution was only beginning to produce results.

However, by the third quarter of the nineteenth century European products began increasingly to flow into China as industrial production grew. Occidental concessions extracted from China in mining, trade, industry, and settlement gave foreign-owned enterprise a foothold. Foreign control over Chinese import tariffs, special concessions to foreign-owned factories, and the manning of these factories by cheap Chinese labor produced a flow of goods within China that successfully competed with the products of any trial Chinese-owned factories. This foreign activity did considerable to train Chinese labor in modern industrial skills and, in fact, formed the only such training ground that existed. In the long run, the native handicrafts themselves have suffered tremendously, the Chinese found themselves outdistanced, and Chinese per-capita production of material goods during the 1930's was probably less than at any time since the establishment of the Manchu reign.

Between 1912 and 1937, however, in the cities along the coastal seaboard, a very considerable start was made in almost every type of industrial enterprise, and the pace was picking up. Chinese capital, organizational know-how, and labor skills were accumulating around every large city and slowly moving back into the hinterland. Had the Sino-Japanese War not intervened, Chinese industry would have made significant strides forward during the last two decades. This very fact undoubtedly was one of the causes for the decision of the Japanese to strike in 1937—it could not be put off much longer. Now Chinese industry has been set far back, through destruction and dislocation, and faces a slow recovery complicated by serious internal dissension.

Patterns of industrialization differ. In modern China the first efforts combined private industry and state ownership. Increasingly the state participated in all types of industry, and there is wide divergence of opinion as to correct future policy. Most Nationalist official government statements variably followed the plans of Dr. Sun Yat-sen, made during the early 1920's. The groups composing the National Government aimed at something part way between the free economy of the United States and the state-operated economy of the USSR, seeking to industrialize China to the fullest at the earliest opportunity. An opposition view held to the classical Chinese position that as an agrarian society China should have only such industry as is imperative and that this must be introduced only at such a rate that it will not dislocate that society. It is doubtful if China will reproduce fully the true pattern of either the United States or the USSR. The future role of the foreigner in Chinese industry will be significantly smaller than it was before 1937.

It is likely that industrial reconstruction, which must precede further progress, will relocate near former centers. These were a series of seaports and their hinterlands stretching from Dairen in Manchuria, to Canton-Hongkong in South China, including Tientsin-Chingwangtao, Tsingtao, Shanghai, and Foochow. Some inland locations will certainly be included. On these cities were focused the rail and road systems, the international trade routes, the capital resources, and such skilled labor as was available. In 1937, perhaps two million people were working in industry, exclusive of mining and transportation, and most of them were resident in the above-named urban concentrations. Communist patterns of industrial development may well follow many of the blueprints laid down in earlier decades, but the Communist control of China will probably result in a slower initial development of industrialization than would have been true in a Nationalist China which had committed itself to industrialization ahead of agrarian reform.

FOREIGN AND DOMESTIC TRADE

Trade, like industry in the classic concept, was an occupation to be held to the minimum consistent with the satisfactory operation of an agricultural society. Contact with the far ends of the earth naturally involved contributions of products from the outer areas to the Chinese capital, since all outer territories were considered tributary thereto. These shipments took the form of tribute sent by periodic political missions, with return gifts made by the Chinese court. On the side there usually was considerable barter and exchange of products by all such missions, to make life interesting. With the barbarian tribes immediately surrounding China there usually was some informal trade arranged for by the Chinese, not so much to make a profit as to secure a distribution of Chinese goods among the border peoples and perhaps limit the threats of invasion. The earlier organization of the Chinese government reveals no provision for trade administration, and there was no office corresponding to the United States cabinet position of the Secretary of Commerce. This provision never was made and, in the end, the occidental traders were forced to make their own arrangements, which eventually grew into the present Customs Bureau, and the Postal Administration. This is an oversimplified statement, but it indicates the directional orientation of historic Chinese thinking about foreign trade. But despite all restrictions domestic trade and the trader flourished, for the Chinese love of bargaining and the acquisitive instincts are strong.

Domestic Trade

Exchange ranged from local community barter to interregional trade. The self-sufficient local handicraft economy involved constant community barter and exchange on a small but active scale. Special commodities in food, jewelry, clothing, art goods, medicines, and charms circulated all over China to be purchased regularly by the upper classes and upon festival occasions by the lower classes. Besides the regular shops of the large village, town, or city, the agencies that handled internal trade were the guild, the periodic fair, the middleman, and the itinerant peddler. Trade guilds in effect took the place of the American Chamber of Commerce, Better Business Bureau, Growers' Association, and Interstate Commerce Commission. Guild houses served as clearing houses on financial settlements, warehouses, offices and hotels for traveling members, forwarding agents, and commission houses for merchants operating from a distance. The middleman performed much as does the American commission agent. These two agencies handled what might be termed the wholesale trade, as well as some of the retail business. The village fair was seasonal or periodic, depending upon the region, and most effectively functioned among communities too small for permanent shops or guild branches. The itinerant peddler is found all over China, in city and rural countryside, each with his distinctive sound identification, handling retail trade of the smallest caliber and including every kind of product. Though the modern bank, corporation, and department store have cut into the upper segment of urban domestic trade, the above pattern still operates everywhere in China today.

Foreign Trade

For many years China has been buying more abroad than she sells, and the statistician usually includes an item termed the "invisible trade balance" to square this deficiency. The optimist feels that the shortage is effectively made up by invisible items like the spending of missionary societies in China and the homeward remittances of Chinese residents abroad. The critic sometimes alludes to it as partial proof that Chinese economy today continues on the downhill trend that has characterized its whole contact with the Occident.

The truth rests somewhere between these two extremes. Since the 1920's world price fluctuations and China's variable foreign exchange rates have made difficult a true comparison of trends.

The first century of Chinese trade with Europe saw China gradually accustom herself to selling the European such natural monopoly products as tea, silk, and art goods. More recently exports have included minerals and non-monopoly agricultural products. That there have been a succession of new export items has been China's good fortune. As previously suggested, these monopolies have been broken, one by one, followed by declining trade in each. Though there has been an increase in total exports over the decades it has not been adequate for China's needs, since, for the most part, it has been made up of cheap agricultural produce and raw minerals. On the other hand, the imports into China steadily increased, once the Chinese acquired a taste for machine-made, occidental products. The import total has risen more rapidly than the export total, giving an increasing divergence in the trade balance. The war years naturally reduced all exports and imports of civilian goods and caused a huge increase in military imports, to further worsen the trade balance and require heavy borrowing abroad. And yet China has only begun to modernize.

Post-war Nationalist Government restriction of the import of expensive luxury goods by foreign firms to sell to the rich and to be used as speculative materials in an inflationary market is the kind of unpopular limitation on the import trade that will have to be practiced for some years, while China uses her limited sources of foreign exchange for her program of agrarian reform or industrial development to help achieve her own modernization. Now that Communist control has replaced Nationalist control in China, and international cold-war politics has replaced earlier patterns, China is temporarily restrained from trading with some sectors of the West and will develop more trade with Soviet Russia. If the restraint becomes long-time full embargo, China's foreign trade patterns will become peculiar ones, but, if relaxation of restraint occurs, a marked development of trade will be resumed, its nature dependent upon political factors and open markets.

The Chinese provided the West with a market for a period of time, and it is one that the West now misses. If it is restored in our lifetime, it is one that will have to be judiciously cultivated with careful long-range planning on all sides, and with a careful program by the West. The Chinese now have a consumer interest in almost all the material goods of the West, but, in order to buy them, China must export. Until Chinese modernization has developed some momentum, there will be only a limited range of products available for export.

Chinese trade has moved through many ports, but a few stand out in dominant position. Shanghai has handled nearly 50 per cent of all foreign trade, Dairen is the chief Manchurian port, Tientsin and Tsingtao serve North China, Hongkong and Canton handle the major share of South China trade.

The commodities of export within the recent past have been, in order, and subject to some yearly variation: soybeans and products, tung oil, silk, egg products, tea, raw cotton, coal, cotton textiles, pig bristles, hides and skins, tin, wool and camel's hair, tungsten, and antimony ores. Excepting Hongkong, which has been a special kind of center for Chinese trade, the direction of this trade in the past has been toward Japan, United States, southeast Asia, Britain, Germany, and France, roughly in that order. Many hoped that Nationalist Government post-war China would be able to take over the Japanese export trade to southern and eastern Asia, and undoubtedly Communist leaders would like trade with that part of the world to grow as China becomes able to provide the economic grades of products acceptable to that market.

Chinese imports since 1930 have been scattered over the whole range of world trade products, after a long period of importation of consumer goods. Despite Communist tactics and foreign embargoes China will continue to require petroleum, unfabricated metals, foods, raw cotton and cotton textiles, rubber and fibers, timber, and such manufactured articles as finished machinery, tools, and industrial equipment. There has been, and will continue to be, a steady increase in the import of capital equipment in the fields of transportation, mining, textile manufacture, electricity, smelting and refining, the chemical industries, and machine tools. In the direction of purchasing southeast Asia could stand high, supplying rice and other foods, petroleum, ores, rubber and fibers, and the balance of her imports will come from that part of the world which best cooperates with China's needs. It was to be expected that Japan would continue to play a large role in both the import and export trade of China, since both China and Japan would have to buy cheaply whenever possible, if they are to buy at all.

MODERNIZATION PROCESSES

The last century has thrown Chinese society into the greatest cultural turmoil since the formation of the empire over 2,000 years ago. Earlier it was suggested that the joint self-centeredness of the Chinese and the occidental provoked a considerable cultural clash. China had met and weathered clashes of culture before the European came. However, with a base beyond the seas and never-ending streams of people who never settled permanently in China as had previous invaders, a surplus of military power, and cultures that were both complex and dynamic, it was inevitable that Chinese Confucian culture should begin to give way. Involved was an about-face from the old frontier entrance in northwest China to a front door upon the Pacific Ocean, symbolic of the full shift in culture. The effects of the impact of the West are everywhere visible in the landscape of China today and in the social and political turmoil of her people. It is clear that the effects have not been equally distributed over China, and that some parts of the country have progressed further in the adjustment of cultures than others. In some group elements among the Chinese something of occidental culture has sunk deeply, though among others it is but a thin veneer which cracks occasionally to expose the Confucian core within. Still other groups apparently cling to the traditional patterns with no loosening, whereas there is a reservoir of population yet almost untouched by any visible part of the West. Regionally it appears that the coastal fringe of China has changed most and the Tibetan border least, but the situation is less simple than that. The urban seaports are perhaps the centers of radiation of non-Chinese culture, both material and social. The inland city felt the effects before the coastal village, the banker and merchant before the peasant farmer.

The modern Christian missionary has been a tremendous factor in the modernization of China. The movement commenced with straight evangelism; as it grew its effects multiplied. The agricultural, medical, and educational efforts of many mission groups were often begun in order to get clients to whom to preach, but these efforts spread far and wide beyond their original aims. Most agricultural research in China originated in mission work. Similarly modern Chinese medicine and education arose out of Christian mission programs. And out of the need for hospitals and schools came mission architecture and Chinese contractors, with distinctive effects upon Chinese architecture. The foreign slick paper and pen and ink spread far outside the schoolroom through graduated class members. The need to print evangelical literature produced modern print shops, which finally helped lead to the Chinese newspaper and periodical press. There are endless illustrations of the ramifications of the process.

Another potent agent of modernism was the occidental businessman who used a variety of innocent tricks to induce the purchase of his wares. Thus bobby pins, cigarettes, or tinned cherries could, in the 1930's, be purchased far beyond the limits of European residence and the advertising poster. The appetite for new material goods mushroomed in the last generation, but the process is really only in the beginning.

Not least among the agents of change have been the Chinese who went abroad. The letters home and the remittances of money came first, and then the family members returned with their new traits picked up abroad. Many South China villages and towns clearly show the imprint of money and ideas gained in the Netherlands Indies, Malaya, or the United States.

Change has not been in material terms alone. The mission school book often inculcated a strong brand of patriotism for China along with something that the teacher called democracy but the student failed to understand perfectly. In time there came a wholesale selling of this particular feature, but with it were unequal treaties, the treaty ports, and pinching economic exploitation. There came opium with its deadening effect upon morals, health, and family welfare. There came ideas about labor rights and eventually a labor movement. During the 1920's there was a potent vaccination of Communism into China from the USSR which has spread as far afield as did the democratic inocculations of the Christian missionary.

All this change began slowly and worked in small but widening circles. With each decade the volume of new material confronting the Chinese increased. Radio, the airplane, and the atomic bomb came in closer sequence than many of the earlier products. Vaccination upon inoculation, dose after dose until the patient has raised a fever. The individualism of the Chinese has seldom permitted sudden country-wide decisions by a few people as was the case in Japan. Not until masses of the Chinese have experienced much of the modern world can there be a satisfactory decision as to what course China will take. The fever still rages but must be allowed to slacken at its own pace. The tremendous amount of culture conflict within China today will require a further period of time to resolve. At first glance Communist control of China seems dictatorial action by a few people. The Chinese have often accepted programs put forward by a small group of leaders, but in the end either have rejected those leaders and their program, or have modified the program in the course of time.

IS THERE A POPULATION LIMIT?

China is the most populous country in the world though the exact figure can neither be stated nor agreed upon. For the purposes of this book the population of Greater China is taken as 500,000,000 and that of the 23 provinces of China proper as 440,000,000. Having served with the Chinese Nationalist Government for some years and knowing how tabulations of this sort were made up, I use these round numbers which probably are as accurate as any others now available. Expressed in simple average for all of China, the figure of about 114 per square mile is not impressive. Stated as population per square mile of cultivated land the total is 1,140. Another type of comparison, used by several writers on China, is illuminating. If a line were drawn from southernmost Yunnan to northernmost Manchuria, some 2,500,000 square miles of territory would lie to the west, along with 15 to 20 million people, while on the east would remain about 1,750,000 square miles and 450 to 465 million people. Expressed in averages, the eastern section would have about 260 people per square mile of territory and perhaps 1,200 people per square mile of cultivated land. This emphasizes the fact that both the cultivated land and the people of China are placed east of this imaginary line. With a landscape as described in an earlier chapter, that part of the Chinese checkerboard west of the line, and the central Asian lands, is made up of the higher blocks, the rugged parts of mountain massifs, the high filled basins. All the larger, useful lowland basins lie east of the line, including most of the Szechwan Basin.

The annual rate of increase in population and the total volume of increase for present-day China are among the highest in the world, with an annual excess of births over deaths of perhaps 5,000,000 a year. It raises the questions, how long has this been going on and for how much longer can it possibly continue. Useful data are scant throughout all of historic time and always have been made unreliable by the Chinese peasantry's fear that truth telling to inquirers into statistics can only end in heavier tax burdens. Interpretation of Chinese history would suggest that the hearth area became a population center, with several accompanying minor concentrations, and that China has not really been filled up until rather recently. Over the centuries ascribed totals are 30,000,000 for the first century A.D., 45,000,000 for the early eighth century, 60,000,000 for the late fourteenth century, 150,000,000 for the late eighteenth century, 380,000,000 for the late nineteenth century, and 500,000,000 for the present.

These figures indicate that China has long been among the world's more populous regions, but they indicate too that the modern totals show a tremendous increase over earlier ones, and that several stimulating

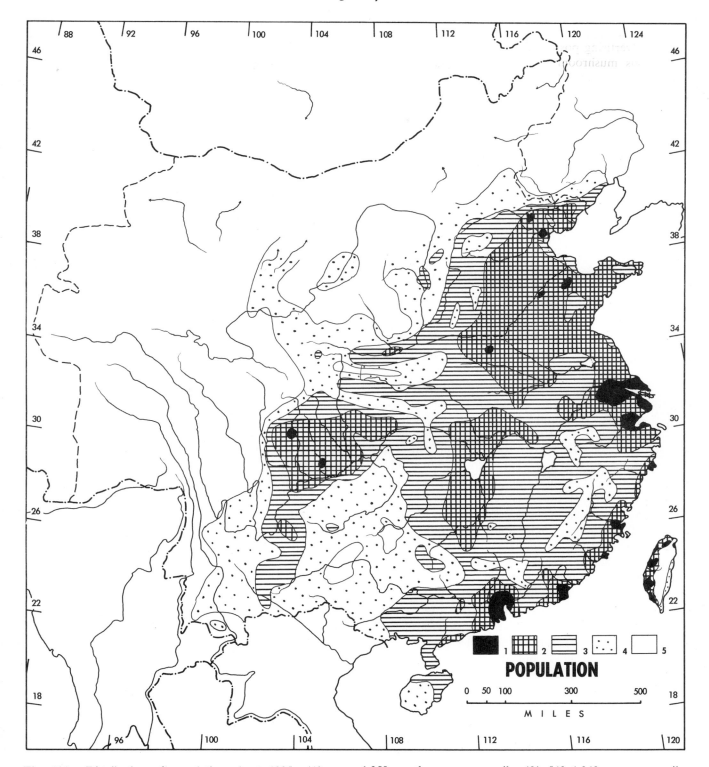

Fig. 111.   Distribution of population about 1935: (1) over 1,350 people per square mile; (2) 540–1,349 per square mile; (3) 180–539 per square mile; (4) 36–179 per square mile; (5) under 36 per square mile.   Generalized from Hu and Alexander.

factors have been at work within the last century or two. China shares this recent increase with the rest of the world. The effect of American crop plants and large-volume foreign trade has been mentioned. A potent factor has been modern curative and preventive medicine as brought to China by the Christian medical missionary and spread into wide Chinese acceptance. This has reduced the impact of endemic and epidemic diseases. Another factor of unanswerable but significant results is the discouragement of infanticide, a custom today relatively unpracticed. Modern transportation, and flood and famine relief projects have reduced perennial limitations. Civil wars probably are less effective checks today than formerly. Until China filled up and put to use most of her cultivated land, increases in population usually made for a higher standard of living, since they were accompanied by new bases of material culture. As suggested earlier, there are those that feel that China recently has been suffering a decreasing pattern of life, becoming a marginal-existence producer of low-cost agricultural export products only. The stimulating factors of the last two centuries may have run their courses without there coming into operation any effective new bases of support.

The growth process still sweeps forward, however, and it seems clear that China has outgrown her natural environment. Self-sufficient agriculture and widespread handicraft production were the historic sources of income. Today agricultural output is relatively less than formerly, handicraft production per capita is far below what it once was, industrial production still is small and unbalanced, there is an unfavorable balance of trade, and there is a national debt. Industrialization is the oft-proclaimed hope of the future, though a revolution in agriculture is desired. The present rate of population increase seems to more than keep pace with industrialization and agricultural improvement, though in a truly peaceful China the latter rates could be speeded up. Against this are the presently suspended natural checks and the historic process of breeding children in search of sons to farm the land and to maintain the family ancestral line. China is in a dilemma and is vociferously debating a program to follow in the future. Unless agreement upon the aims and plans of Chinese society can allow effective mobilization of energy, it is likely that the consequent unrest will unleash "the Four Horsemen" to start a real balancing operation. Alleged Communist programs to really reduce population may or may not be strongly put into practice.

THE REGIONALISM OF MODERN CHINA

It is customary for the rest of the world to speak of the Chinese and China as though everyone were alike and the country one homogeneous geographic region. An effort has been made to show how the several densely populated lowland basins are set apart by strips of negative mountain highland, how soil and climate divide China, and how culture history has added to the variations. There is something in Chinese culture that tended to negate the harmful impact of these natural regional divisions upon society. Perhaps part of it lies in the common written language that transcended all the bounds of spoken languages. Perhaps it is summed up in the Chinese proverb, "Within the four seas all men are brothers," applying to the Chinese realm only. It is worth noting that the large subcontinent of China historically has possessed far more unity than the smaller subcontinent, called Europe. The temporary disunity of modern China often blinds the occidental to this regional unity that is a part of the cultural continuity of China.

The motives for regionalism in China are soundly based on the natural environment and have been historically developed over the centuries. The earliest distinctions between occupants of the culture hearth and the barbarians were matters both of material and social culture, growing slowly into regionalisms. The process of spreading over China, imposing Chinese culture, and absorbing the crops and customs of the conquered non-Chinese seriously mixed up the simple early distinctions that divided the cultured from the barbarian. Despite this intermixing, regional distinctions are quite clear to the Chinese themselves.

The proverb "In Szechwan the dogs bark when the sun shines" is matched by the name of Yunnan province, "South of the Clouds," both rather limited but effective characterizations. Shansi province for good reason is the recognized butt of the Chinese "Scotch" joke. Tientsin wheat noodles and Canton white rice are two major poles in a complicated pattern of regional dietary distinctions. Fukien faces the sea, and its separate river valleys are subregions of a physical and cultural province that turns its back on China and is the most sea-conscious of any section of the country. What seems significant here is that, although the Chinese even seem to foster certain of their regionalisms, in some way they never let them get out of hand to become separating factors, as happened in Europe. Modern Chinese regionalisms resemble the friendly, good-natured sectionalism of California, Texas, and Brooklyn.

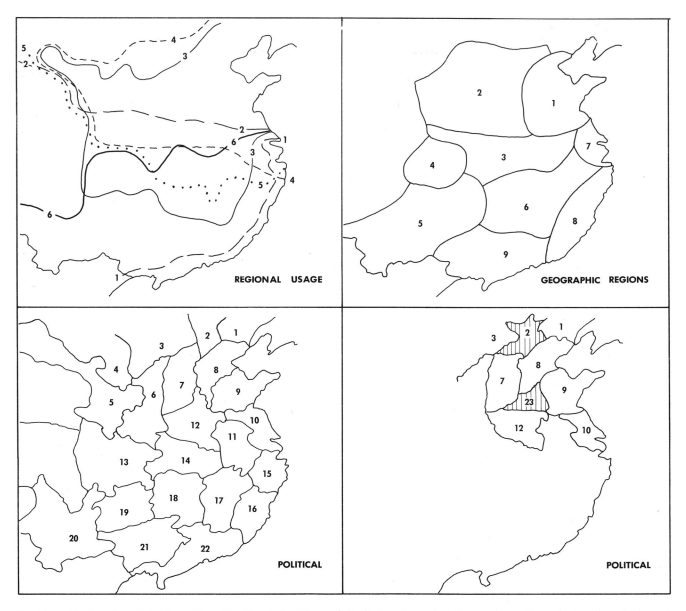

Fig. 112. Regionalism in China. See also Fig. 103. *Upper left,* factors in regionalism: (1) northern limit of marked southward emigration from China; (2) southern limit of marked northward emigration from China proper; (3) encloses zone of dominant Mandarin Chinese spoken language; (4) approximate limit of the brick sleeping *kang* in older usage; (5) approximate southern and western limit of use of padded cotton clothing; (6) primary division of dominant use of rice (south) and wheat (north) in daily diet. *Upper right,* geographic regions after Shu-tan Lee, based upon physical environmental criteria: (1) North China; (2) Upper Hwangho; (3) Central China; (4) Szechwan; (5) Yunnan and Kweichow; (6) Yangtze River and Lake Region; (7) Shanghai-Nanking region; (8) southeast coast; (9) West River region. *Lower left,* political provinces in recent decades for the traditional China proper. *Lower right,* Communist provincial boundary changes in northern China Proper. A new province, Pingyuan, has been created out of parts of north China provinces Honan, Hopei, and Shantung. Kiangsu has been reduced in size on the north. Chahar in Inner Mongolia has been reduced in size but given some of northern Shansi. Several other changes have been made in Inner Mongolia and in Manchuria.

The political divisions of early China repeatedly shifted about but gradually settled into a system of fairly fixed regions that has been stable for centuries in some parts of China and is still being formulated in others. Under early Manchu rule China was divided into fewer provinces than at present. In part the provincial boundaries were arbitrary lines drawn for administrative convenience across a section of landscape that possessed few good natural boundaries. Others are the crystallized acceptance of environmental lines that appealed to the common people who made up and administered China. As such they usually are drawn through the negative zones surrounding the several positive nuclei. As Manchu China grew more populous, boundaries in the marginal parts of the empire were formally delimited. In the central portion of the empire, often termed China Proper, the lines are significant of many things, but in Outer China they are still ephemeral and subject to change. The compounding of human events has been too fluctuating in a landscape in many places lacking sharp natural divisions to allow closely drawn lines that stay put. The Communist organization of a new province in the North China Plain reflects a population pressure and local administrative problems of modern development.

Modern China is a complex group of cultures, regions, physical zones, and psychological concepts. Within the old China proper one could do worse than to accept the old administrative boundaries employed by the Chinese Imperial Government. Accenting the subjective reaction of human events to the physical landscape, the provincial boundaries serve reasonably well and accord with statistical summaries. Most of these lines mean more than do the boundaries of Nebraska, Wyoming, Colorado, and Kansas. The so-called geographic region, setting more emphasis upon crops, climate, vegetation, and landforms, produces a map with some agreement with, and some divergence from, the political region. Other selective criteria can be used to draw still different maps. Not yet is enough known about China and the Chinese to permit drawing a map that satisfactorily delimits the distinctive and significant portions of the Chinese realm.

A FEW ALTERNATIVES FACING CHINA

China is overpopulated. She cannot feed herself. She is an agricultural country in a world rapidly industrializing. There is too little land. There is but little technological skill in China. There is a reasonable but not abundant volume of mineral resources. China has little available capital and a considerable national debt. The mass of the peasantry is poor.

The Chinese standard of living is far from the top in the list of countries of the world. Many Chinese are opposed to departing from the intuitive, humanistic pattern of life summed up in Confucianism. Many are eager for a full and complete change to the material, scientific culture of the Occident. Many seek to blend the two, keeping the best of each. Some seem to practice the worst in both. Most Chinese wish to prevent any recurrence of nineteenth-century economic and political exploitation. The services to China of the Occident cannot immediately be replaced. Many Chinese like what they have learned of Democracy. Others strongly advocated the creed labeled Communism. There is a strain that lends itself to Fascism. China has been boiling with unrest and change for a century. Which way to go, which path to choose, how best to employ the landscape of China, what form of society to shape for the future?

Listed thus, modern China has a profound dilemma. To some occidentals it seems discouraging that China cannot in a decade solve all her problems. Americans forget that they have not always been strong, and that they have had much help from Europe. By admitting oversimplification, some of the incongruities above can be stated quickly as a series of alternatives.

First and rather fundamental in interest to the masses of China, with their agrarian background, has been the problem of agrarian reform. Of the many ideas as to how the reform should be accomplished, most encounter the difficulty of insufficient land. This has been untrue in the past, but is very real today. The improvement of tenancy conditions can only be achieved through real effort and the curbing of special interests. Involved in the problem today, however, is the new and additional question of a section of Chinese society possibly abandoning the classic Confucian pattern of the past, even as the United States abandoned the concepts of Jeffersonian democracy. If a portion of the population becomes permanently town and city dwelling, with a consequent change of economic habits and no vital tie to the land, then the problem of agrarian reform for a rural farming element may be tackled with possibly greater success. The approach through agrarian reform became the program of the Communist Party in China, subordinating other issues in their campaign for support by the masses of rural Chinese. The program was motivated, and participated in, by Chinese and Russians trained in the patterns of Soviet Russia, and its success aligns China with Soviet Russia, rather than with those other parts of the Occident with which China has dealt chiefly in the past.

Second is the problem of the degree and kind of industrialization. China now possesses a little of the several kinds of industry in her remaining village handicrafts, decentralized cooperative industries, and her small segment of modern, city machine-and-power industry. Big industry of the corporate urban variety seems to some Chinese, and to the West, the more attractive and productive prospect. But big industry in a few urban centers filled with residential slums has also seemed unattractive to many Chinese and to be no answer for the immediate needs of the millions of Chinese who would have to leave the land to permit an effective agrarian reform and agricultural revolution. Small-scale industry, moderately powered, locally controlled, and widely decentralized all over the country, coupled with centralized key industrial enterprise, would seem the best answer to many liberal Chinese. This pattern would, in a sense, constitute an effective replacement for the traditional handicrafts that complemented Chinese economy before the invasion of the Occident. The Kuomintang and the National Government of China in the end came to support and advance the cause of big industry, foreign trade, and a close linkage with the industrial West, subordinating other issues thereto.

Next is the basic question of the nature, form, and administrative organization of the governmental system of Chinese society. Government has been ineffective for over a century now, including the last decades of the imperial system of the Manchus. After 1911, departing from the imperial pattern of the past, varying forms, machinery, and ideas have been in use for over a generation. Warlordism, fascism, communism, one-party-tutelage, representative government in varied forms, foreign concessions, and international council forms, all have been operating in some part of China during the last half century. The Chinese, more than any other developed society, have wanted as little government as possible. Traditionally China was governed by men of good will, and not by laws, a government effectively fitting an assemblage of agrarian families, but one ill fitted to the management of a complex society based upon a wide assemblage of different economies having the world as a whole for their scope.

Next, there is the question of the size and area of China as a political state. If the traditional loose articulation of government were to remain, it would be doubtful if the huge Chinese realm could stand against the powerful economic and political pressures of the modern world. The alternatives in the handling of the parts of Outer China present themselves. Two thousand years of trying to make Chinese of the occupants of Sinkiang have not succeeded in an environment not fully congenial to the Chinese form of life.

The USSR detached Outer Mongolia from China in a short span of years by developing local political and cultural autonomy within a major controlled framework. In the last century China has lost Tonking, Formosa, the Ryukyu Islands, Korea, Manchuria, and Outer Mongolia, but now has temporarily regained Manchuria. Manchuria, Sinkiang, and Tibet are the units most in question, though there is even question concerning the adherence of Formosa, Inner Mongolia, and the northern part of China proper. Formosa, at this writing, is in a peculiar situation, belonging to Chinese, but not ruled by the *de facto* rulers of China. Sinkiang and Manchuria are serious in their implications. Some of the best mineral reserves and mineral potentials lie in these two outer regions, and their permanent loss would be a heavy blow. The adherence of so large a territory to one functioning state is not a matter of any geographic law, but a problem in managerial ability.

Finally there is the alternative of preservation, retention with synthesis, or abandonment of much of Chinese culture in favor of the material, mechanical culture of the Occident that, for the first time since the formation of the empire, has proved the stronger. The city and the farm village are farther apart today than they ever were before. This is one of the deepest problems of all, the answer to which will automatically color many of the answers to other alternatives. Today China is a curious blend of the materialistic and humanistic, with proponents for many courses and exhibits of the virtues and evils of each.

ELEMENTS IN THE SOLUTION

For a adequate final solution of China's problems, there must be taken into account issues of the kind and variety of economy, the population and its increase or decrease, the pattern of the government of society, and the very orientation and content of Chinese culture itself. In a satisfactory solution of all the problems, all these issues must be interwoven simultaneously.

For the moment, at least, one solution has been reached, for China now has a Communist government. During the years between 1924 and 1949 various kinds of struggles took place between the several interests, programs, groups, and factions, concerned with the future modernization and development of China. Both Soviet Russia and the rest of the West took part in the maneuverings, and Japan played her own role, complicating the issue for all parties. That portion of the West, now calling itself the Free World, concerned with world-wide industry, trade, and various kinds of representative government, lost out in the maneuvering. The choice was not made by the failure of any one occidental negotiator or Department of Foreign Affairs, but rather it was made by the masses of China, finally electing the traditional choice of reform of an agrarian society. The rural agricultural people of China chose agrarian reform, not Communism, for most of them had no comprehension of the implications of Communism. They responded to the appeal of the group that seemed to promise most in relation to better arrangements with regard to daily living, the burden of taxes, the rates of interest, tenancy charges, and the exactions of the upper classes of society. This does not mean that the people of China have chosen Communism for all future time. Much depends upon how the other issues at stake can be handled.

The Communist government of China now faces the problems of developing the agricultural revolution, initiating such industrialization as they deem needed and possible, and deciding upon at least some of the issues concerning the content of Chinese culture. Agrarian reform can be only a palliative for the moment, even to the former tenant-farmer class, for the present system of agriculture will not feed a population still growing larger. Communist government has taken, and will continue to take, steps toward altering the structure of Chinese society and the content of its culture. Some kind of industrialization is inevitable in China, regardless of the system of government followed. An industrial revolution may occur in Communist China as it occurred in Communist Russia. If the Communists can somehow arrange all three of these things out of the material resources of China, while holding their power, and coping with the problems of population, they could become the permanent government of China.

The inability of Communist government to increase the productive capacity of China within a relatively short span of time could lead to the more vigorous attack upon the population problem as a means of achieving balance of human needs and resources. There is a capacity for impersonal realism in the functioning of Chinese society in the past that makes this a possibility. Failing satisfactorily to achieve this balance by activity on any one of the possible fronts, Communist government would become open to replacement in the management of Chinese society. The population of China, in the past, has been tolerant of much mismanagement by government, but has never failed to turn out a set of managers when it could stand no more. Much recent occidental judgment of what the population of China has wanted has erred by judging from the desires of the middle and upper classes rather than from those of the lower segments of society. It always has been the lower segments of society that have made the real choices between programs put forward by its upper classes.

Though there seems no immediate hope for a Communist collapse or for a real split between Communism in China and in Russia, there is ground for belief that Communism will fail again in China, as it has failed in the past, and that eventually Chinese society will return to a system of operation more nearly in harmony with many of the chief values of the Chinese as a people. In view of the fact that the present issues are more critical than those facing any Chinese society in the past, there is little hope that this can be accomplished in a few short years. The long-term solution of the problems of arranging the patterns of Chinese society gives no solace to those in the West who hope for change in terms of a few short years. It may well be that the West will need to acquire some of the patience of the Chinese themselves.

The Inner Asian Fringe

THE BALANCE OF HUMAN PRESSURES

On the chief central Asian stages the peoples of the oriental realm have performed only intermittently. The Tarim Basin is Chinese in neither people nor culture despite the common use of the term Chinese Central Asia. Though the lines of piedmont oases and the wide grazing ranges are of primary importance in the very early spread of peoples and their cultures, the several great blocks of central Eurasia really are marginal to the primary story of the Orient. Therefore it is the intention of this volume to deal but briefly with the great inland regions.

Throughout the evolution of the complex cultures of the humid Orient and the mobile pastoral cultures of arid central Asia, there has existed a delicate balance. One or the other normally has been aggressive, shoving into the territory of the opposing realm. In this long process of cultural thrust and counter-thrust the Tibetan Plateau has been less important than the open grasslands and the strings of piedmont oases. The process, therefore, has been focused upon two zones, the northwest Indian frontier and the dry margin of northwest China, with the difficult Tibetan Plateau between them. On other sides of the central Asian stages pressures from the humid lands never equaled those of the arid lands until the appearance of modern Russian expansion. This pressure differential caused much racial movement to pass toward Europe, after the rise of China, and prevented any clash by elements on opposite sides of the dry lands. Within the last century, however, Russia has approached the dry heart of central Asia with steadily growing energy, while Chinese power has been declining.

In the future the principals of any struggle in central Asia will be not nomad and farmer but the governments of two great countries. Involved will be differences in colonial policy. Always the Chinese have tried to turn the pastoral and oasis peoples into Chinese, both in economy and in customs. Never has the effort succeeded, and never has it changed materially. The result has been that in periods of stress China never has been able to count on the continued adherence of any racial or culture group. Chinese influence in central Asia has waxed and waned directly with the military power of the Chinese state, and according to whether a recessive or forward policy was being followed. Russian colonial policy, under Soviet management, has been exhibiting a flexibility which has developed and furthered native cultures while fitting groups and regions into the larger framework of the Soviet state. If this is not completely true, at least it is subjectively so to some of the central Asian peoples when compared to the policy of China. By this means Russia detached Outer Mongolia from China after a period of infiltration. If further expansion in central Asia is part of Soviet policy, there is a long boundary along which Sino-Russian conflict may develop. What happened in Outer Mongolia may also happen in Sinkiang within the near future, and perhaps elsewhere.

India has been far less positive in her thrusts into the central Asian heartlands than has China. Since early in the Christian era no northern all-Indian state has had the power to carry its rule beyond the frontier hill country. Most of the expansive activity of Indian culture has taken other directions. Consequently central Asian peoples have pushed into India along what has been principally a one-way road ever since the Caucasian invasions first began.

THE TIBETAN ROOFLANDS

Only the Andean highlands of South America compare to the difficult environment presented to man by the Tibetan Plateau. The best part of Tibet is the

343

southern fringe and the southeast corner in which most of the 4,000,000 people reside. Over most of the country agriculture is impossible and grazing quite limited, since most of the plateau is both too arid and too cold. The southeastern corner, however, drops below 6,000 feet in a small area, and the lower lands permit a rather wide range of agriculture which even includes rice in a few spots. Barley, peas, wheat, mustard, buckwheat, radishes, and turnips form the primary crops in order of importance. Irrigation is a necessary part of a good share of the agriculture. Yaks, sheep, donkeys, ponies, and goats are employed in the very vital animal economy which seasonally ranges widely over Tibet. Except for the large amount of tea used by every Tibetan, the food economy is a self-supporting one, the surpluses of the southeast corner moving over much of the rest of the inhabited country. Tibetans much prefer Chinese tea to the Indian product. From China also come silks, horses, and silver; from the Indian lowland cotton textiles form the most important import. There is a steady export surplus of wool, animals, hides and skins, musk, and medicinal herbs, each of which is exported both to the Chinese and Indian lowlands. Highland economy is one involving a large amount of internal transport and trade to adjust the strong regional inequalities. In the long run Mongol pilgrims have added to the mobile traffic and to the economy.

Pack-train roads and trails cover the country fairly well, being fewest and least used in the Chang Tang. The main trunk road of Tibet runs east-west along the upper courses of the Indus and Brahmaputra rivers, joined by many small routes that cross the passes of the Himalayas. Today the route that proceeds through Sikkim is the most important of the routes into Tibet. Within the country most of the routes converge on Lhasa. Northward and eastward several routes extend to central and north China but, since these cross the grain of the country, they are difficult to travel. Large monasteries are scattered through eastern and southern Tibet, many being towns in themselves. The only other sizable settlements are the towns of southern Tibet, scattered along the upper valley of the Brahmaputra River, locally known as the Tsang Po, at the medium elevation of about 12,000 feet. Of these Lhasa, at least, has become somewhat modernized, with electric light and telephone systems, a radio station, and various other occidental cultural features.

Though some new features steadily have been added over the centuries, Tibetan economy is a relatively static one, without the great population growth that has marked the lowland zone. The growth and continued presence of a strong monastic system renders partly parasitic a segment of the population, though many monks engage in part-time agriculture, animal care, or handicrafts. The social custom by which every family tries to secure monastic membership for one male member is a form of social insurance, but it does seriously inhibit population growth. Though the ordinary diseases of the hot lowlands are lacking, Tibetans seem peculiarly susceptible to smallpox, and changeable, mixed polyandry and polygamy have caused serious development of venereal diseases, so that there are other inhibitions to population increase.

The age of human occupation of the Tibetan Plateau cannot clearly be estimated, but both white and yellow peoples have pushed into its ragged fringes during a long period. Some have been retreating refugees, others adventuresome explorers. Most of the culture traits that have spread over Eurasia have been evident here too, but their acceptance has been limited both by the environment and by human conservatism. Tibetan pastoral nomadism is a complex matter slowly developed over a long period. Tibetan society was essentially simple, tribal, and Shamanistic when Buddhist missionary currents from both India and China began infiltrating southern and eastern Tibet in the late fifth century A.D. Increasing invasions of Indian and Chinese culture continued through the seventh century, bringing religious, social, and material features which have dominated Tibetan culture since that time.

There being no strong control over local society the monastic aspect of Buddhism rapidly extended itself, and the oldest monasteries date from the seventh century. By the late eighth century a combination of earlier Shamanism and Indian Buddhism grew into a special form of Buddhism, known as Lamaism, which discarded celibacy and poverty and developed cults of semimagical powers. The leading group, known as the Red sect, dominated the plateau, taking over political, religious, and economic controls. Its great monasteries, under hereditary leadership, ran Tibetan society despite continued attempts at reform. Early in this growing process Tibet went through its one expansionist period, spreading its influence outward in all directions. Though only the fringe of the North Indian Plain came under their rule, they dominated all the Himalayan mountain country. On the north they controlled the Chinese corridor into the Tarim Basin through forts located along the northern slopes of the Nan Shan. Raids into the Chinese lowlands occurred during the interval also, which ran for perhaps a century. Permanent occupation of the populous lowland by a relatively few militant highlanders was not possible, however, and by the end of the ninth century the Tibetans had retired from low-country affairs.

Religious reforms in the fourteenth and fifteenth centuries produced the Yellow sect of Lamaism, which slowly has become dominant in Tibetan affairs. The Red sect continues but is split into several groups of lesser strength and power. Adoption of the pledge of priestly celibacy by the Yellow sect involved change in the mode of selection of the chief Lama. This now involves reincarnation of a *buddha* into successive bodies and the search for the new ruler when the previous high priest has died. Restoration of the early Buddhist pledge of personal poverty has served to increase the economic role of the monasteries as corporate institutions. Since the fifteenth century the Yellow sect has had its seat at Lhasa and the sect leader, the Dalai-Lama, has been the chief priest of the religion. Yellow sect monasteries are among the largest and most influential in the country today. In theory the reformed Yellow sect was not concerned with political affairs, but in practice the Dalai-Lama and his group are by far the strongest element in Tibet. This makes Lhasa in effect the political capital, though many local regions are practically autonomous. The traditional spiritual head, the Panchen Lama, has his seat at Tashi-lumpo, outside Shigatse, but in recent years he has spent much of his time in China.

Chinese concern with Tibet has been quite intermittent since the seventh century. The several Mongol rulers of central Asia and China became so interested in Lamaism that it became the religion of the Mongol peoples during the thirteenth century. Religious pilgrimage to various monasteries and to Lhasa resembles the centering of the Moslem faith upon Mecca. The Mongol rulers of China favored the Yellow sect and helped it to supremacy, at the same time securing the peaceful adherence of Tibet to China. Both Ming and Manchu dynasties intermittently continued this favor and assistance. The modern relations between Tibet and the Chinese Republic have been intermittent and not completely friendly, though Tibet nominally is under China. With considerable British interest in the Himalayan zone, the British have developed their routes into south and eastern Tibet, so that after 1900 the Chinese often used the Indian approaches to Lhasa.

The physical region of Tibet amounts to nearly 1,000,000 square miles, roughly separated into the five sections enumerated in an earlier chapter. Politically Tibet is a much smaller area, since the Chinese have included in neighboring provinces a large amount of the plateau. Culturally there is a variable line of demarcation. Tibetans dislike the low country. The lowland cultures that surround Tibet have pushed into the high country, each to its own limit of operation. Indian cultural invasion has taken place on the south

from Kashmir to Bhutan, Moslem and other minor invasions have occurred on the west, and various Chinese elements have intruded all along the east and in the northeast. Only along the very arid northwestern boundary ranges is there a true no-man's land with few claimants for space.

THE MONGOLIAN AND DZUNGARIAN GRASSLANDS

From the Great Hsingan westward across the north of China extends the grassland strip of Inner Mongolia. Northward these open ranges thin out into a dry belt that is the heart of the Gobi. Fluctuations in precipitation cycles over north China extend and contract the width of the grassland strip, or make agriculture possible in the open ranges. Within the Gobi sand wastes are very small in area, but bare rock or gravelly pavement is widespread, and the Gobi is a transitional belt of minimum utility and some truly barren country. Here lies the main source of the loess that has covered much of north China. Westward the Gobi shades into the sandy Takla-makan desert of the Tarim Basin. Much of the open country lies at elevations between 3,000 and 6,000 feet, and several mountain ranges rise above 10,000 feet. North of the central dry belt of the Gobi and the Takla-makan lie the cooler, moister grasslands of Outer Mongolia and Dzungaria. These grass ranges vary in character from wide, open basins to summer mountain pastures capped with good forests. Water is no great problem to a mobile economy in ordinary years north of the Gobi. It is these northern ranges that formed the main home of the many pastoral races that swarmed out of central Asia during nearly 2,000 years. Expansionist waves spread into China, the Tarim Basin, and toward Persia and India, into Russian Turkestan and Europe. These cool northern lands had a high carrying capacity most of the time and were in every way better than the grasslands of Inner Mongolia, which in good periods were subject to infiltration by Chinese farmers. Not often have non-sinicized peoples permanently made Inner Mongolia their home. Here usually have ranged those peoples who were knocking at the gates of China.

Throughout this great area today a wide range of economies is practiced. The Soviet section is changing rather rapidly from the older, simple pastoral economy to a diverse and complex Soviet economy. Mineral wealth, long untouched and still not really surveyed, has become one of the primary modern interests. The Chinese section has become predominantly Chinese in population, using an extensive version of Chinese agriculture. Many Russians today are scattered over Outer Mongolia, and Chinese are to be found almost everywhere in the towns as traders. Over 1,-500,000 square miles of territory are involved, about one third of which today has been annexed to Soviet political holdings, and a share of which has been incorporated into the Chinese realm. Perhaps 3,000,000 people and 30,000,000 animals are to be found in the area. Sheep are the most numerous of the animals and always have been of primary importance. Horses lend greater mobility but sheep supply many more of the nomad material needs. Trade patterns that once were focused entirely upon the towns of north China have been broken apart rather badly. Much of the area now is economically directed toward Russian border towns, and the Japanese have temporarily oriented part of eastern Mongolia toward Manchuria. The coming of the automobile, the radio, the airplane, and the miner have permanently upset the old, if shifting, pattern of economies.

Mongol life, where not too affected by Russian or Chinese influence, still retains its mobile form of sociopolitical organization, with the banner and the khan the local and regional group units. Tibetan Lamaism still is the primary religion of Mongolia, but Dzungaria and other western ranges have become Moslem. In areas of Lamaism the monastery functions as in Tibet and often forms the basis for permanent settlements. Soviet and Chinese influence both tend to lessen these religious influences.

The Chinese have no real liking for open grasslands where their traditional economy is restricted and their tight socio-political organization is weakened by enforced mobility. Neither the limited garden culture of small oases nor the precarious and shifting life of the pastoralist ever has attracted many Chinese. Individual Chinese concern with the lands beyond the settled margins usually has involved trade relations. The concern of the Chinese state primarily has been with regard to frontier policy and control of the mobile peoples who periodically have invaded agricultural China. Occasionally the rulers of China have been interested in the great overland trade routes. Over the historic period these rulers have used either a recessive policy involving retirement within the Great Wall, or a forward policy reaching out into the grassland ranges to control the pastoral peoples. When the passive policy has been followed Chinese settlements and outposts often have been abandoned in the outer lands, to be renewed in the periods of the forward policy. Seldom has the Great Wall been the dividing line between nomad and farmer.

The pastoral folk learned the riding of horses, to become more fully mobile, only during the sixth to the fourth centuries B.C. A serious period of invasions then began as greater mobility stimulated both pastoral economy and aggressive ambition. Following upon this the first Chinese positive, forward policy was put into operation by the early Han dynasty during the second century B.C. Its reach took in only the inner fringes of the great pastoral zones, those that lay on the China side of the Gobi. Such control was sufficient to permit westward extension of Chinese influence through the Kansu Corridor and into the Tarim Basin, from which contact with Rome was made. Though this long line of trade contact was maintained during the Han, it was not until the seventh century under the T'ang that the Chinese successfully crossed the transition belt and carried their influence into Dzungaria and Outer Mongolia. Chinese control never was more than lightly applied in this outer zone and frequently was thrown off completely. Several strong Chinese empires levied tribute or exerted a restraining hand over territories as widely spread as the upper Indus Valley of western Tibet, the Oxus River country, the Ili River valley, the trans-Altai lands, and the trans-Amur region.

On the inner side there always has existed a very uneasy balance of affairs. When the Chinese have not been pushing outward, pastoral folk have been pushing inward. In more recent centuries these have been supplemented by peoples who were originally forest dwelling but who took on a mobile pastoral economy until they could edge their way into China. Chief among the latter were the Manchus. At the end of the seventeenth century almost no Chinese were settled outside the Great Wall. Groups of Mongols had become rather permanent users of Inner Mongolian ranges upon losing out to the Manchus for control of China. In the latter half of the eighteenth century Chinese agricultural settlement of Jehol began, with seasonal trader-craftsman penetration of the whole inner range country, already well developed. Settlement moved rather slowly until the 1870's when it began to quicken markedly. On the better eastern end settlement has fairly well ruined the ranges over a depth of about 250 miles outside the Great Wall. Such settlement has resulted in the demoralization of Mongol pastoral society, with a low grade sinicization of the population.

On the outer fringe Chinese control has been marked more by its chronological absence than its exercise. Tradition, however, hangs heavily and persistently around the Chinese realm, and a control once asserted has been reclaimed at a later date. China, at the height of its power under the Manchus, pressed its controls to the maximum historical limits during the eighteenth century. The nineteenth century, on the other hand, was an era of steadily weakening controls and constant shrinkage of power. This shrinkage has been shown on all fringes of the realm, but its largest area is in central Asia. Until the appearance of modern Russian activity in central Asia the Chinese were opposed only by pastoral elements from within the grassland ranges themselves. Positive Russian pressures from beyond those ranges steadily have increased, speeding the retreat of Chinese regional influence.

THE DRY TARIM HEARTLANDS

The Takla-makan, occupying the central lowland of the Tarim Basin, is today one of the world's great and true deserts. Alternating zones of waterless sand dunes, loess deposits, and bare rock expanse blown clean by the wind cover an area over 800 miles east-west by nearly 300 miles north-south. The basin is open only on the east where it is continuous with the central Gobi. The desert slowly is expanding outward toward the mountain rim surrounding the basin. This is not a matter of simple desiccation within the basin itself during the last thousand years, but one involving a much longer time span and complex regional relationships. The basin, away from the Turfan depression, has a general elevation ranging from about 2,800 feet on the east to about 4,200 feet on the west, and it is surrounded by mountain systems that range between 12,000 and 24,000 feet. Glacial era precipitation upon ranges bordering the Tarim must have been heavier than that today. Then innumerable streams poured water and sediments into the basin. Along the footslopes of these bounding ranges now runs an almost continuous alluvial piedmont, much of the upper fringe picked clean of fine materials by the wind. Since the end of the last glacial period precipitation upon the mountain ranges has decreased, mountain glaciers have wasted away and become fewer in number, the volume of water crossing the piedmont has lessened, and many streams have dried up entirely.

Early in the human occupation of central Asia the piedmont zone of moisture availability was rather wide, since many streams penetrated deeply into the central desert. Many streams joined to enlarge the volume of the Tarim River. That volume has decreased and its terminal lake, Lop Nor, has changed location repeatedly as alluvial sediments have blocked the terminal channels of the Tarim River. Today a narrow line of widely separated oases surrounds the piedmont fringe, but in the earlier period this must have been one great, well-watered piedmont, with close connections between its stream zones and piedmont springs. Since the time of earliest man the routes through the basin have been used. Many of the primary cultural inventions were

spread east or west by these routes long before the historic era began.

At the dawn of history increasing aridity already had narrowed the strip and reduced the number of streams, thus increasing the distances between water sources. Lowland precipitation is very slight in amount and spasmodic in occurrence, certainly too small to support plant life of significant economic value. All during the historic period the wasting of glacial ice has continued, with the diminution of stream flow and the total failure of some sources. Decreasing surface water finally led to the use of the Persian *karez* or artificial underground tunnel so placed as to lead water down piedmont slopes to cultivable lands. Many former oases have been abandoned over the centuries, the line of settlement retreating toward the outer rim of the basin. Not all oasis decline is caused by declining climate and water conditions. Collapse of *karez* channels, overwhelming by drifting sand and loess, civil war, nomad raids, shifting terminal river channels, and a variety of other causes have contributed. Some water supplies still are sufficient to support a large area of cultivated land; others maintain but little patches. The oasis of Kashgar contains about 1,000 square miles of irrigated land. Almost all sizable streams are snow fed, increasing in seasonal flow with the summer snow and ice melt. No indications point to further rapid, contemporary reduction of water supply, so that no early abandonment of remaining oases seems necessary. Occupation now could benefit from really good management.

Specialized oasis culture developed techniques of water transport and conservation, the varietal selection of plant strains, and a limited range of animal culture using the mountain pastures surrounding the basin. The basin floor itself possesses almost no grazing lands. Each major oasis developed a basic economic autonomy that made it self-sufficient. During active trade periods every sizable oasis town supported a considerable foreign colony of traders and caravan operators, as well as military garrisons. In periods of unrest, when trade dwindled, the roads became inactive and the towns became isolated settlements dependent upon their own local resources.

The earliest occupation of the Tarim Basin by Chinese and Indian peoples found a complicated mixture of Caucasian and Yellow races then in possession. Already, over 2,000 years ago, the Tarim was a forbidding area with but a small share irrigable. Regular use of the piedmont routes required organized maintenance of peaceful conditions in the oases. This meant protection from the pastoral peoples of the northern grassland ranges. The mobile tribes of Dzungaria and the Tien Shan habitually raided the oases but never permanently occupied the basin, owing to its limited grazing resources. The first forward policy of the Chinese Han dynasty turned from its primary foreign policy goal of securing the frontiers of China to clearing and maintaining the piedmont routes through the Tarim Basin. On the southern route the Chinese met Hellenized Indian traders and administrative posts in the western oases. In some of these western towns Indian influence preceded that of the Chinese. The northern route was more useful but took more protection and administration, since the passes through the eastern Tien Shan from Dzungaria were open all year.

Organized Indian administrative control of the southwestern Tarim ceased by the end of the fourth century A.D. Chinese control over the Kansu Corridor was maintained a majority of the time, but its permanence decreased toward the west. An extension of the Great Wall, built in early Han times, ran north of the piedmont corridor, past the Suloho Basin and almost to Lop Nor. The Chinese ruled the westernmost oases only during a few periods in the long history of the Great Silk Road. Chinese control everywhere had wide gaps in time, which left the basin open to other influences. The eastward spread of Islam during the eighth to tenth centuries and the constant shuffling of the northern pastoral peoples turned Dzungaria and the Tarim Basin into zones of Turkish and Moslem cultures. Though this involved new languages and customs on the one hand, any new immigrants settling in the Tarim Oases necessarily accepted the sedentary oasis economy.

With slight regional variation, and periodic new additions, oasis economy has been standard in pattern. Slightly terraced fields are arranged snugly around the water sources, bordered by irrigation ditches and by mulberry, poplar, and willow trees. Wheat, barley, maize, melons, sorghums, millets, and cotton are the primary field crops. Alfalfa, rice, and a variety of vegetables are minor or garden crops. A large volume and a wide range of hardy fruits and grapes are grown in orchards and arbors. Dried and candied fruits and melons are important food export commodities. Animal economy, if limited, is vital. Cold winters cause agriculture to be seasonal everywhere except in the Turfan depression. Village and town settlement is the rule, most of the arbor-strewn, flat-roofed mud settlements resembling each other closely. The population of the basin is in the neighborhood of 2,500,000 people. Fifteen per cent, perhaps, are Chinese traders, shopkeepers, and artisans; perhaps 10 to 15 per cent of the total are pastoral nomads ranging the upland country.

Minerals have not played any large role in past political policy, though from the mountain country has long come jade, gold, and a variety of precious stones. Though not well surveyed the mineral resources of the basin margins appear sufficiently promising to make the area important in future central Asian policy. Even more important in this respect are the Ili Valley and Dzungaria which, in Chinese practice, have been included in the "New Dominion" of Sinkiang. Contemporary Soviet development has tended to upset the traditional balance of trade, communications, and transport between China, southwestern Asia, and Russian Turkestan. Russian rail and highway terminals lie far closer to Dzungaria, Ili, and the Tarim Basin than do any Chinese terminals. The Great Silk Road was a trans-Asian route in which central Asia afforded little but the route. That traditional trade route died out with the development of modern ocean shipping, but China has done little to change the situation in central Asia. Most of her attempts at control in the last century have been of the traditional order and, coupled with mismanagement, have produced periodic unrest or actual civil war. Russia has been developing her own vast central Asian territory and now finds herself in a position to tap the resources of all central Asia in a way that the Chinese cannot now match. Economic penetration may well be followed by political penetration.

The Northeastern Frontier: Manchuria

THE CONCEPT OF MANCHURIA

Northeastern China is a curious part of the inner Asian frontier zone. The Occident speaks of Manchuria as though it were a definitive region. The name supposedly means the "land of the Manchus," but there never was one Manchuria until the Japanese created the puppet state of Manchukuo during the 1930's after seizing territory that the Chinese had administered under the group name "Tung-san-sheng" or Three Eastern Provinces. Thus Chinese administrators seem to have recognized three "Manchurias," variably occupied by different peoples and cultures. There can be no easy and sharp division between these three parts of the frontier zone, for the physical and cultural factors have constantly shifted for thousands of years.

In simplest terms this so-called "Manchuria" consists of a great central lowland of rolling plains and shallow river valleys surrounded by ranges of hills and mountains. The uplands are parts of the massif and mountain elements of the Chinese checkerboard, and the central lowland is a subsident basin further hollowed out by denudational forces. It opens southward on the northern gulfs of the Yellow Sea; one broad gap at the northeast corner allows more than half the lowland to drain northward into the Amur River. Looking outward from the lowland, except toward the two gaps mentioned, the surrounding uplands are rather formidable, without obvious passes. The Central Great Hsingan do not present a very great obstacle, it is true. From the outside, however, entry into the lowland is relatively easy, since the way is mostly downhill through country that is rough but not impassable either on foot or with animals.

On the basis of all the physical factors the territory displays three kinds of environments. These were recognized very early and have predominantly motivated occupation throughout most of the historic period.

Modern man has made possible a new usage pattern and new criteria for regional grouping, so that there have been both disputes over the region and important changes in the manner of its use. Formal geographic terminology must follow usage and common need though the formalizing of terms often lags in time. The Chinese dislike and do not use any translation or full equivalent of the term Manchuria, preferring their own term Three Eastern Provinces. It is unlikely that a major three-part division of the region will occur in the near future, whatever the internal administrative pattern. Use of the term Manchuria permits easy reference to the large lowland and its surrounding hill and mountain borders.

The southern littoral is a physical environment quite similar to that of the north China hearth lands, though the Jehol uplands extend right into the sea to separate it from north China. There is a narrow coastal pass at Shanhaikuan, where the Great Wall met the sea. Historically, control of this pass either gave the Chinese control of the Manchurian littoral or gave a Manchurian group ready access to the northern part of the North China Plain. The littoral extends clear around the Gulf of Liaotung to include the lower parts of the Liaotung Peninsula. It has extended some distance northward up the valley of the Liao River, depending upon a number of variables. To the far north and to the east there is a forest environment which originally housed people who did everything but cultivate the soil vigorously and steadily. The region normally utilized by such peoples included the highlands of eastern Manchuria, the Little Hsingan ranges in the far north, and a considerable portion of the north and eastern lowlands. This still is a cold country with much forested upland and with marsh and bog lowland tracts. Active deforestation rapidly is changing much of the area under modern commercial exploitation.

The central, western lowlands, and a large share of the Great Hsingan mountain country is almost fully continuous with the pastoral ranges of eastern Inner and Outer Mongolia. Much of the area is too dry to support continuous forest cover. Grassland ranges shade upward into parklands on the eastern fringes and the uplands, whereas some good forests cap the mountain ranges. The pastoral peoples of central Asia always have been at home in either the lower open grasslands, the parkland fringes, or the mountain pastures with forests capping the crests and providing shelter in deep and well-watered marginal valleys. Traditionally, western Manchuria has lain within the domain of the central Asian pastoral peoples. There has been no single, long-lasting tri-point boundary stake in the lowland between these three zones, but the mythical dividing point often has lain in the stretch between the modern towns of Hsinking and Szepingkai, not far from the Sungari-Liao drainage divide. This corresponds to the common distinctions of south and north Manchuria.

HISTORIC CONTROL OF THE LOWLAND

At the dawn of history three sets of people had formulated three different patterns of living in what today is Manchuria. To the north and east the forest peoples used wild game, reindeer, sleds, sled dogs, canoes, forest products, and furs in a variety of localized combinations. From the peoples of the open country to the west and south they learned about other animals, but, in the early period, they made the most use of the Chinese pig, though they also copied a little casual agriculture. Their environment was a difficult one, requiring a moderate mobility and considerable ingenuity, and not offering extremely rich returns. For the expansion of their economy, and the improvement of their way of life, it was necessary for them to come out of the highlands onto the more open and more productive southern lowlands. To do that meant changing their economy, material culture, and customary social organization. It meant using some of the same tools, techniques, and ideas that were used by the peoples already in the lowland. One after the other, during the historic period, some group has come out of the forest realm into the Manchurian Lowland to attempt its control. The more successful of these groups expanded further and sought to include some part of North China and the Mongolias.

Along the southern littoral the Chinese very early had spread their sedentary-village and town-dwelling agricultural economy based upon a tightly knit social

system. The land connection, past Shanhaikuan, between the main north China hearth and the littoral, often was tenuous, particularly the connection with the eastern, peninsular portion. This led to the development of water connections across the several gulfs, particularly with Shantung. The littoral often served as the route of contact with Korea and Japan in the earlier periods. Expansion of the Chinese northward was conditional upon complete mastery of agriculture and land use. In the earlier centuries the shortening of the growing season by severe late and early frosts, too cold winters, or droughts reduced this mastery and decidedly limited northward penetration. In addition there was the opposition of alien populations who could not be controlled by the early Chinese social and political system.

On the west the open grassland ranges and the hill country parkland called for a different economy. Here was a sector open to and used by the pastoral peoples of central Asia. In the early period their economy, too, was limited by their incomplete mobility, and their territorial control was not yet implemented by a sociomilitary organization capable of banding together large populations. Cycles of cold years or short seasons were allies of the forest peoples in restraining northward Chinese penetration; dry cycles were allies of the pastoral peoples.

With the expanding Chinese Han empire, a formal attempt was made to increase Chinese influence in Korea and Manchuria beyond the colonial littoral. A certain success resulted until the empire weakened and became recessive. Then began an alternating period of expansion and contraction like that in central Asia. The T'ang restored Chinese influence in Manchuria, only to see it fade in time. The Liao were the first ex-forest people to really make good their shift into the new orbit, which included much of north China and eastern Mongolia. Their tenth-century empire was known across all central Asia. The Jurchen, also an ex-forest people, were next, establishing the Chin empire in the twelfth century, the first to make Peking a renowned capital city. Then came the pastoral Mongols, utilizing many of the techniques of the Liao, their empire including much of Manchuria. The Chinese Ming dynasty rulers dominated the play during the fifteenth and sixteenth centuries, for the first time fully setting up effective tools of frontier military government. The Manchus came next upon the scene, originally being a forest-dwelling Tungus people. They mastered the Ming frontier system in Manchuria, made many changes in their own administrative machinery, and understood much of Chinese culture before moving into China.

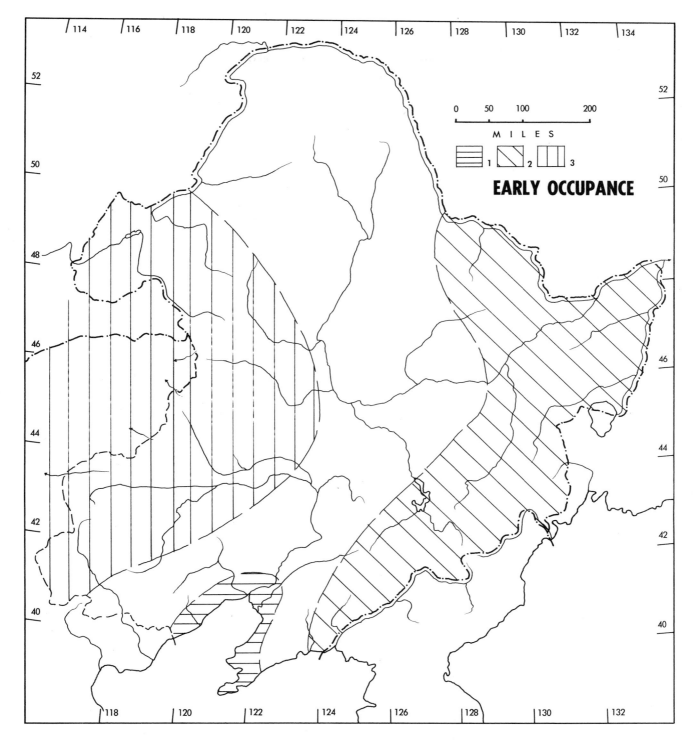

Fig. 113. Early occupance of Manchuria: (1) Chinese littoral; (2) East Manchurian forest zone; (3) West Manchurian pastoral region.

At no early point did the Chinese succeed in planting their own economy and settlers far within Manchuria. Under early Manchu rule the whole of the northeastern frontier beyond the littoral still was preserved as pastoral and hunting range. Population pressures in north China had not yet become greatly intensified. As these pressures did increase in a prosperous China they met a gradual weakening of Manchu administration and Chinese settlers began to inch forward in Jehol and Chahar, as previously indicated.

About 1820 there began a slow colonial infiltration that finally became a steady movement as Chinese from Hopei and Shantung provinces of north China spread over southern and central Manchuria. Forests began to disappear, and pastoral ranges went under the plow as a southward stream of agricultural exports began. In this way modern Manchuria became separated from the stream of events in the wider frontier zone of inner Asia. About 1880 the colonial spread widened its range toward the margins of the lowland. After 1900 the volume began to increase by leaps and bounds. Since 1920 immigration has headed for the open lands of north Manchuria and the hilly lands of eastern Manchuria. Only the dry western hill country and the cold northwestern corner now lie outside serious colonial range.

Credit for opening and developing Manchuria goes to different groups. Both Britain and Japan had a hand in opening south Manchuria, though Japan eventually froze Britain out. Russia played the major early role in north Manchuria. Britain's participation, of course, was limited to economic matters. China supplied the main volume of colonists. Japan tried colonization repeatedly, using different techniques, achieving almost no real success in getting Japanese onto the land. Russians did settle in parts of north Manchuria prior to 1919, to be joined by many refugees during and after the Soviet Revolution. Rarely, however, could they compete in agriculture with the spreading Chinese, so that the Russian element tended to gather in urban centers. Japan froze Russia out of Manchuria during the early 1930's. Koreans began crossing the border into the hill country of eastern Manchuria shortly after 1900. Though this has remained their primary area of concentration, they have scattered widely over the whole of Manchuria. Chinese, therefore, have been the primary colonial element, though the modern control of China over Manchuria has been tenuous and uncertain. Estimates suggest a total of 3,000,000 people for all Manchuria in the midseventeenth century, two thirds of whom were Chinese in the southern littoral. Of about 45,000,000 people in Manchuria, including Jehol, before post-war changes

began, at least 40,000,000 were Chinese. The Mongols numbered no more than a few hundred thousand, Japanese perhaps slightly over 1,000,000, largely urbanized, and the Koreans not quite a million. This predominance of Chinese has resulted in the translation of the whole Chinese social and economic milieu into Manchuria in a way that must affect the future of the region.

Chinese colonization had begun when both Russia and Japan began to exhibit their interest in the eastern holdings of a weakening China. Decades of maneuvers, both political and economic, ended in 1931 when Japan swept Manchuria into her expanding empire. Chinese colonization then slowed down a little, but Japanese controls increasingly restricted the pastoral peoples in favor of Chinese agricultural settlement, since the latter produced food and trade products for Japan. Japanese concern with the pastoral zone inevitably progressed into infiltration into Inner Mongolia. Jehol was added to "Manchukuo" by force in 1933. The Japanese like the earlier Liao and the Manchus, found no natural boundary upon which to rest a frontier policy, once they moved into the pastoral realm of western Manchuria. The defeat of Japan in 1945 supposedly returned Manchuria to China but found the Russians in occupation. Thus the other active interest in the inner Asian frontier again was able to come into the Chinese realm. What followed was at least the planting of a political-economic yeast in an active loaf of dough, with the expansion of Communism taking over the whole of China from a Manchuria-North China base between 1945 and 1949. Perhaps Russia stands ready to annex another block of territory at the next opportunity as she did in the case of Outer Mongolia.

A CHANGING AGRICULTURE

In the long Chinese littoral of southernmost Manchuria agricultural life is like that of the North China Plain. It is characterized by village settlement, small land holdings that often are fragmented, intensive cultivation, a somewhat self-sufficient economy that has suffered modern inroads from the world of commerce and international trade. Here kaoliang, soybeans, millet, and wheat long have been the staple crops which, supplemented by a little cotton and silk, a few vegetables, and some hardy fruits, make up a cropping pattern quite like that of north China. A pig and a chicken or two go with almost every home, and a draft animal of some kind to almost every family is normal.

The earliest modern colonial expansion attempted to reproduce this standard economy. Farms could be

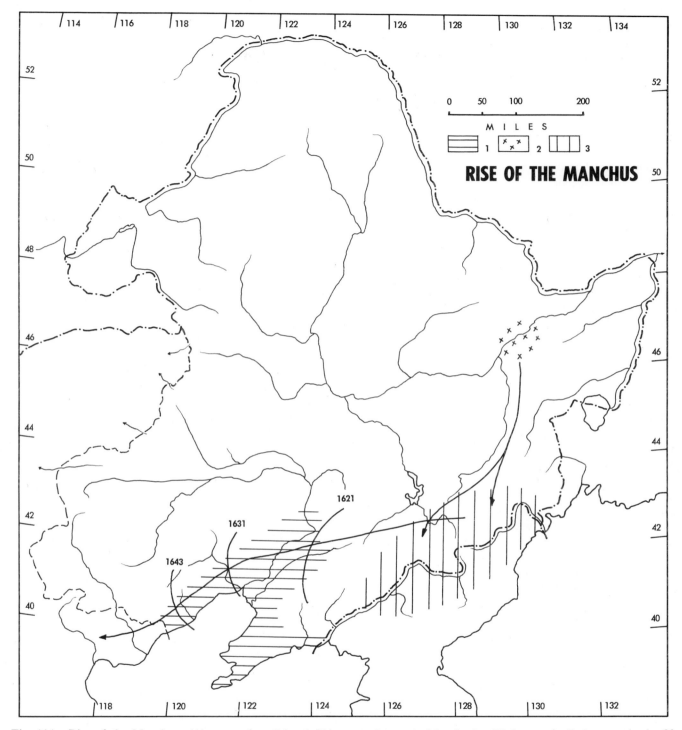

Fig. 114. Rise of the Manchus: (1) zone of traditional Chinese settlement in Manchuria; (2) home of tribal groups in the fif-teenth century who later became the Manchus; (3) area of political control, after migration, of tribal groups on edge of Chinese world, in late sixteenth–early seventeenth centuries. Dates on lines indicate expansion of Manchus into China in seventeenth century. Modified from Michael.

larger, however, and fragmentation of holdings occurred less often, since this is a result of repeated division of land among family descendants. More liberal use of animal or forest products also was characteristic. Under peaceful conditions the compact village was less common, and scattered farmsteads spread out ahead of the main flow of settlement. Chinese trader contact with the pastoral Mongols brought some changes found only on the frontier.

The introduction of occidental systems of transport produced profound and rapid change. Movement of colonists was speeded up, long-range shipment of agricultural produce was made possible, and new regions were opened for colonization. Modern transport greatly changed the economy that developed. Farm holdings increased in size, scattered settlement became quite common though not exclusive, the farmer narrowed his range of crops to increase the volume of each. The shorter growing seasons of the northern sections and the poorer soils of the hilly margins required selected seed varieties and special cropping practices. Combinations with animal culture were profitable. On the open lowlands an extensive agriculture appeared which resembled American midwestern commercial farming far more than the traditional intensive oriental hoe culture. Around the eastern margins Korean and Chinese farmers alike took to the hills with a modified transient slope culture, burning off the forests and cultivating their crops in a short-range, destructive exploitation. Timber-cutting concessionaires planted agricultural colonies in forested districts in the east and north without providing community services of any sort in a rush to skim the value off the land, leaving the colonists to struggle with agriculture afterward. In some years 1,000,000 acres per year were added to the cultivated landscape in all of Manchuria. With ready markets abroad and a lighter pressure on the land the Manchurian farmer usually attained a higher standard of living than was possible in his crowded homeland, though it often had much of rude frontier improvisation about it. The seasonal nature of agriculture, plus fairly good transport systems, made for a large seasonal flow of labor back and forth between Manchuria and north China.

Kaoliang, soybeans, the millets, and wheat were the staple crops in the spread of agriculture. With the rise of foreign trade in soybean products this crop surpassed kaoliang in the acreage total. Soybeans and wheat largely have been cash products for sale abroad. Kaoliang and the millets have been domestic foods both for human and animal consumption, though under Japanese control a considerable amount of millet went into Korea to free Korean rice for shipment to Japan.

Maize has been a somewhat lesser crop in the north, but in the littoral and the hill country of Jehol it assumes major proportions. It has been used both for human and animal food, the latter mainly being domestic swine. Rice is grown both as a wet-field and upland crop clear into northern Manchuria, mostly by Koreans, using north Japanese short-season varieties of low per-acre yield. The northern Chinese use but little rice, so that most of the small crop was consumed by Japanese and Koreans. Mongol range cattle are fattened on Chinese farms during the summer before moving to urban markets, but the Chinese are not skillful at this aspect of agriculture. The white potato is an important crop in the most northern part of settled Manchuria. In the southern littoral cotton is a very old crop, but its production never has been large, even under Japanese stimulation. Wild-silk production in the littoral and the Jehol hill country also is of old standing but of minor proportions at all times. Tobacco, buckwheat, sugar beets, and hemp are other crops with local production centers, stimulated by the Japanese. Fruit culture has been but little developed. Japanese experiments suggest a real future for the hardy fruits such as the native pears and peaches, and for apples, plums, and grapes. There are perhaps 10,000,000 sheep, goats, cattle, and horses in Manchuria, with almost that many swine. A significant volume of hides and skins, bristles, wool, and mohair is available though the trade is not well organized. Trade still is augmented by wild animal furs secured from the upland regions. With development there could be a considerable export of meat products.

Accompanying maps indicate generalized distributions for the major crops. More detailed maps would reveal that cultivation is concentrated along the major lines of communication—river, road, and rail. There is considerable reserve land in the several regional hinterlands. Subject to disturbance by war and political juggling Manchuria should be a zone of continuing colonization and increasing agricultural production for some decades. Estimates suggest that the population can increase at least 50 per cent on existing standards and patterns of land utilization before the agricultural landscape becomes maturely filled. Development of irrigation projects in western Manchuria, managed forest economy in selected regions, the full substitution of sedentary animal culture for range culture, and similar techniques could extend that population limit considerably. It seems doubtful, however, that Manchuria could be filled to anywhere near the level of north China today and maintain a standard of living reasonable for even the Chinese farmer class.

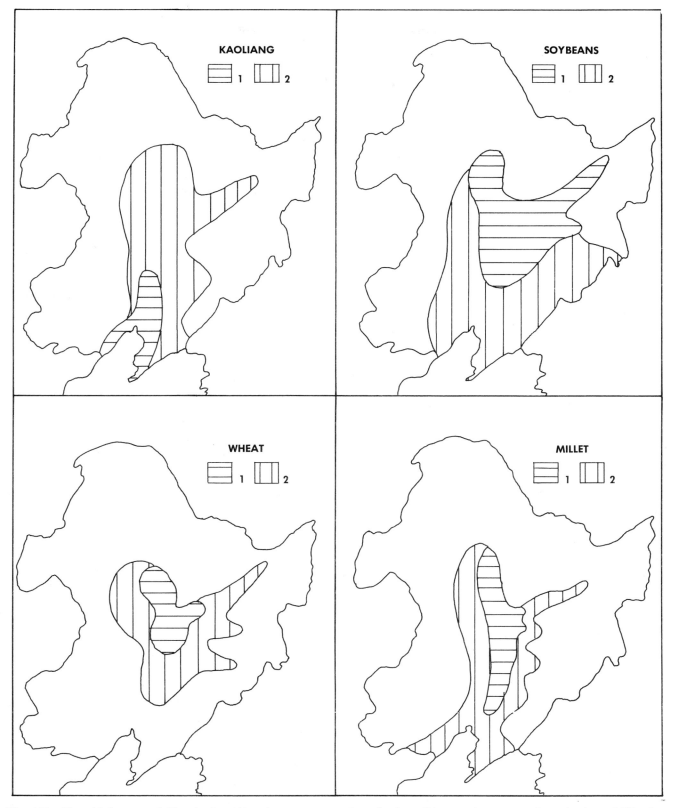

Fig. 115. The chief crops of Manchuria: (1) **primary** centers of production; (2) secondary areas of production.   Millet here means Italian millet.

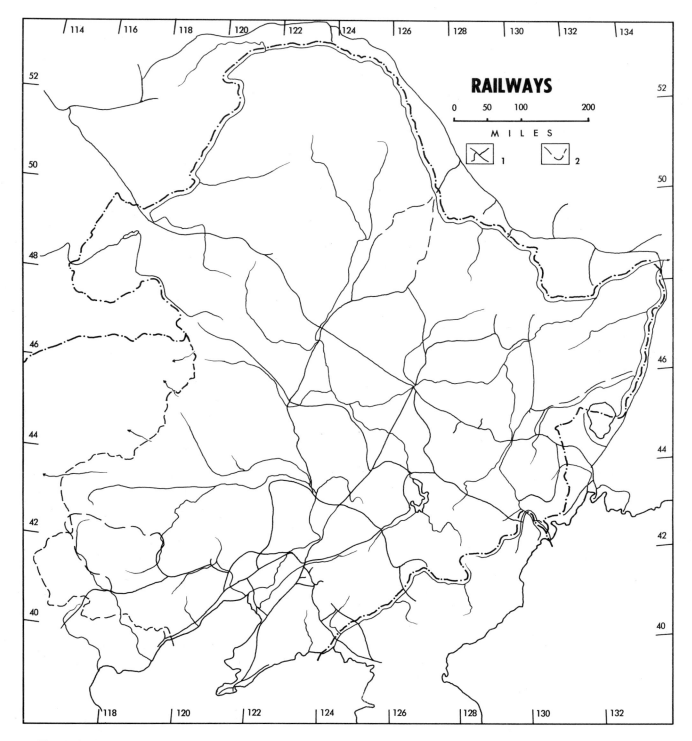

Fig. 116. Manchurian rail lines: (1) operating rail lines; (2) lines uncertain as to present existence or operativeness.

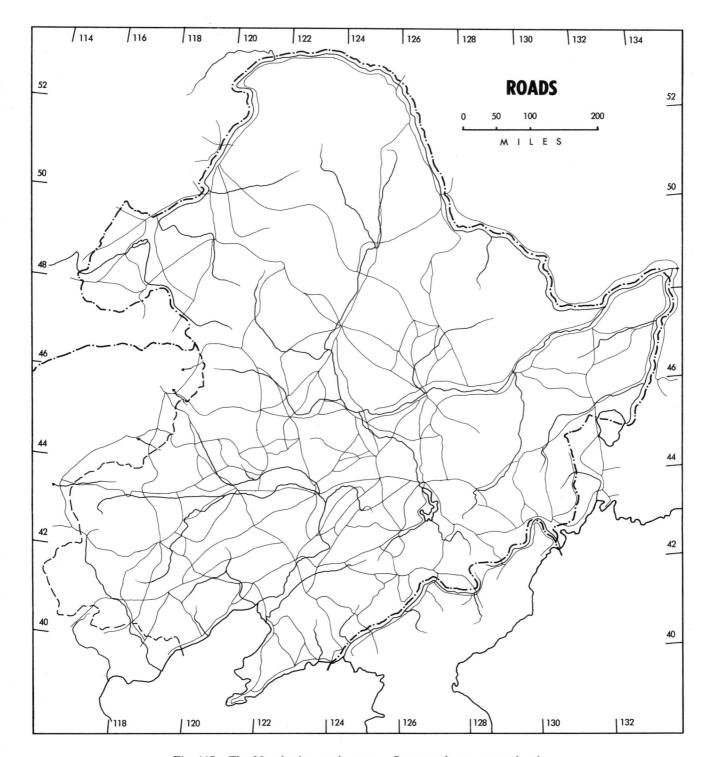

Fig. 117. The Manchurian road system. Some roads are seasonal only.

COMMUNICATIONS, TRADE, AND INDUSTRY

On the basis of transport, minerals, industry, and trade in the period prior to post-war disruption, Manchuria was the best-developed region of Greater China. This was the result of a period of progressive development unhampered by regional disorganization. Several countries had a hand in the growth, though Japan squeezed all others out and inherited a largely undamaged economic region. The immediate post-hostility months saw Russia loot industrial installations as she withdrew her occupation troops, during 1946, and saw increasing Chinese civil conflict between Communist and Nationalist factions take in Manchuria to disrupt transport and weaken the productive economic strength of the region. Manchuria had been developing at a faster rate than any other part of Asia, but cumulative difficulties now have set back the level of achievement many years.

Russian, British, Chinese, and Japanese engineers and money had built a rail system in Manchuria the equivalent of that of all China proper. A good share of the system was heavy-duty railroad, with a large carrying capacity. Though not ideally arranged, as it could have been under unified control from the start, it tapped the Manchurian lowland rather effectively. Japanese control maintained the connections with north China and with Russian outlets, but developed those with Korea in order to improve Japanese contact with Manchuria. The rivers of Manchuria had long carried a considerable traffic but were not suitable to rapid, large-volume cargo movements in the right direction. Manchuria never had any significant canals. The highway system developed more slowly than did the rail system in the earlier years. Under exclusive Japanese control it expanded considerably but never carried the load that moved by rail, owing to the shortage of automotive rolling stock. Under Japanese control, too, an extensive system of airfields was built, and the telegraph and telephone systems developed in proportion.

Mineral surveys in Manchuria began concurrently with those in China proper, but they had not been completed by the period of Japanese control. Exploitation of coal and iron resources had begun, and a number of other minerals were in production when Japan took over. Japan considered Manchuria an exploitable workshop in her program of empire building, and she invested great sums of money and a very considerable amount of research and survey work. During the war years Japan, therefore, was able to draw out of Manchuria a large volume of strategic minerals, metal products, and fabricated equipment. It is doubt-

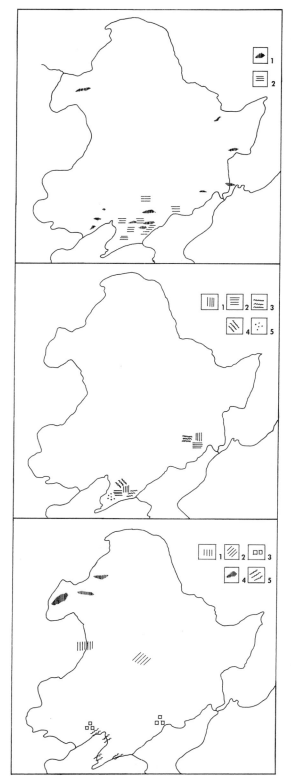

Fig. 118. Manchurian mineral occurrences. *Upper map:* (1) coal; (2) iron. *Center:* (1) lead; (2) zinc; (3) copper; (4) fluorspar; (5) aluminum. *Lower:* (1) tungsten; (2) antimony; (3) asbestos; (4) gold; (5) salt.

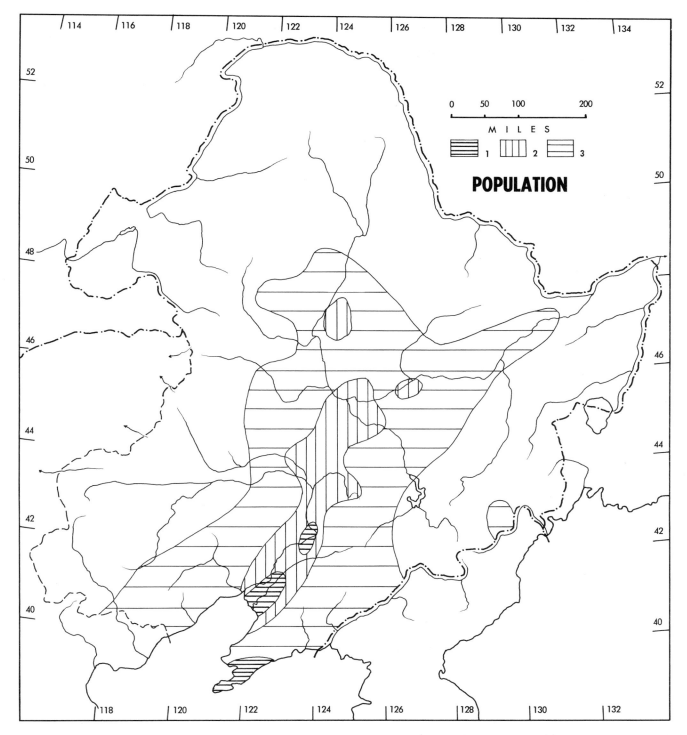

Fig. 119. Population distribution: (1) over 300 people per square mile; (2) 180–299 per square mile; (3) 36–179 per square mile. Blank areas have but slight population. Generalized after Hu and Alexander.

ful, however, if, by the end of a losing war, the returns had paid a profit on the investments of money and energy. On the basis of present knowledge, Manchurian mineral resources are rather extensive, fairly well distributed, and sufficient to support a very considerable regional pattern of industry. Though production volumes have decreased greatly in the immediate postwar years, the restoration of production can be a more rapid matter than the original development.

The Japanese put tremendous energy into programs of industrialization on a planned basis. Established mining, industrial, and transport centers were rapidly expanded during the 1930's and early 1940's. As the cities grew corporate industrial expansion definitely shaped and controlled the patterns of growth. At their peak there were a number of large cities, concentrating a wide variety of growing technical skills. Those industries essentially of value in preparing for military operations proved somewhat temporary in their effects upon Manchuria, but others will be of lasting nature. With only a short period of industrial training and development, followed by some years of disorganized internal affairs, it is impossible to assess the productive capacity of the region within the near future.

THE PAWN OF MODERN EMPIRE

Manchurian developments, almost from the beginning of modern expansion, have been affected by corporate investment, foreign trade stimulation, and the lesser and smaller aspects of a commercial-trade economy. The north Manchurian farmer fed his animals and his family largely upon homegrown foods, but the balance of his living economy came out of a significant foreign trade in soybeans, wheat, and animal products. Since this was modern colonial settlement, the region had no long history of local self-sufficiency in respect to village handicrafts, even though many of the Chinese were individually skilled in a variety of lines. In many ways Manchuria continues part and parcel of the Chinese culture realm, but in other important respects it forms a different, separate region. These divergent trends represent a source of potential trouble both to China and to Manchuria itself. The region forms, in this century, one of the great colonial and economic frontiers of the world. China has not yet filled it, but it cannot possibly be the full solution to the Chinese population problem. Although the population is so largely Chinese, organized Chinese interests have played a lesser part in the modern development of Manchuria. Chinese political control has not provided efficient administrative management. Despite the strong Chinese ties, it is very probable that from within regional separatisms will grow stronger, particularly if such are prodded and fostered from without while China proper continues to mismanage Manchurian affairs. Japan proved unable to colonize Manchuria and held it solely as an economic workshop, though giving it a somewhat more orderly administration than had been supplied by China. If Russia can sponsor an administration more orderly than that provided by China, accompanied by a lesser exploitation than that of Japan, it is entirely likely that Manchuria will be attracted permanently into the Russian orbit. It is doubtful that much Russian colonization as such could take place, but this would be of less interest to Russia than having the transport-communications outlet on the North China Sea.

Korea, the Land Between

A PENINSULA OF HILLS

Korea presents one of the hilliest landscapes in the world. Few elevations are outstanding, since but one volcanic mountain, Paektu-san, with its white rock crest resembling perennial snow, reaches 9,000 feet elevation, far to the north on the Manchurian border. Only some thirty-six peaks exceed 7,000 feet, most of which are in northern Korea. The highland spinal chord runs southward from Paektu-san along the east coast, with ridges tapering off to the west and south to fill the whole peninsula. The uplands reach into southern Korea, which has some crests higher than 6,000 feet. Almost every lowland plain is so small that hills are a part of the landscape. Small patches of lowland are scattered around the coastal fringe, the largest occurring on the west coast.

The higher north country is a cold, rocky, and rather grim region, surfaced with volcanic lavas, covered with coniferous forests, and deeply notched by river gorges and canyons. The narrow east coast is but a slim shelf set between the mountains and the sea. Most Korean rivers are short, drain south and westward, and empty into deep estuaries that would form many good harbors were it not for the high tidal ranges. Locally west-coast tides exceed 30 feet, whereas those of the east coast seldom exceed 3 feet. All along the west and south coast are hundreds of islands, which nearly double the long coastline. The south-facing valleys and coastal plains of southernmost Korea are the mildest and most hospitable part of the country.

The hilly and divided Korean landscape contains some very beautiful and picturesque scenery, but it presents a rather formidable environment to the 30,000,-000 Koreans. The East Manchurian Highlands set a barrier between the peninsula and the Asiatic mainland which is increased by the canyon of the Yalu River. One might look to this peninsular environment for a story of continued isolation, such as Korea tried to maintain during the seventeenth and nineteenth centuries. However, the peninsula stands between the northern mainland of China and the Japanese Island Arcs. As the land between two regions of active cultural development, Korea has been subject to the expanding energies of both.

On the one hand, Korea was the land link in the long-continued contacts of China and Japan, but, on the other, the Koreans have been mauled in the struggles for control of the peninsula. Throughout this hilly country inviting spots have always attracted man. None is very large, nor has Korea possessed extremely high value in soils, useful plants, or climatic assets. Not an outstanding assemblage of local regions, Korea nevertheless has been made into a productive territory by the diligent efforts of its peoples.

THE PEOPLE OF KOREA

It is hard to distinguish the diverse human elements that have combined to produce the modern Koreans. Far from being a single racial type, the Koreans are a heterogeneous people. Into their racial history has gone a little of almost every known east Asiatic group, plus a number of unknown components. Within the historic period the additions have been Chinese, Mongol, and Tungus-speaking peoples as well as Japanese blends. The Japanese blends are a complex factor, however, for a rather important element in Japanese racial development itself has been the Korean one. Korea always has been a connecting link between the mainland and the island world. Refugee colonists, invading conquerors, temporary residents, and passers-through have left their mark upon the present inhabitants.

This process began when man first started to migrate about eastern Asia and has continued to the present time. Despite the constant mixture, one can distinguish between northern and southern Koreans. In general, northwestern Koreans possess more Chinese and Tungus elements than do other sections, and southern Koreans possess more Japanese elements. Several different language groupings were present but were never mutually unintelligible. These simple differences were lessened in the past, however, by a rather closely unified group psychology, surrounded by a culture that has borrowed much on all sides but somehow managed to develop an extremely distinctive individuality of its own.

THE ROAD TO JAPAN

The Koreans take real pride in the age of their own culture, but there is little that is purely Korean about the earliest culture history of this region. It shared the ideas and traits of all early eastern Asia and gave many of them a local twist. At the end of the Manchurian littoral extension of North China, northwestern Korea became a marginal part of that pattern at an early date. But northern Korea adjoined the forested and mountainous East Manchurian Highlands, and so shared in a second pattern of culture. The southern coast, however, had affiliations with the Island Arcs and the separate growth of a third culture. There was no great distance between the margins of these zones of influence. Though it is difficult to place a date upon their linking this must have occurred in informal and unplanned ways long before the beginning of the Christian era. The first known and conscious contact of China with Japan occurred through Korea just before the start of the Christian era.

Chinese movement in this direction was an intermittent process. As feudal strife in classical China sharpened toward the final struggle and organization of the empire, in the third century B.C., dissident elements sought refuge in the surrounding regions. The Korean Peninsula was one of these, and numerous Chinese refugees scattered into vacant localities or were given sanctuary by resident tribal peoples. Within a century this leavening effect began to show in a quickening and development within the peninsula itself. Formal Chinese contact came first in northwest Korea in the late second century B.C. as the Chinese Han empire reached eastward along the Manchurian littoral. Several frontier districts were set up taking in the northwestern half of Korea. As Chinese home strength waxed and waned, so did her influence in and upon Korea. Before the Mongol conquest of Korea, Chinese control never was exerted over the whole peninsula. Only the Mongols tried to go beyond Korea into the Island Arcs. The attention of the Ming Chinese was little drawn to

Korea, and Manchu China was satisfied with a tributary Korea. Throughout the historic period Chinese showed a tolerant and scholarly interest in both Korea and Japan, China playing the role of tutor and donor. Chinese culture actually was enriched by a number of items both from Korea and from Japan.

Conscious Japanese contact with Korea began in the first century B.C., but a link with Chinese culture beyond soon became the chief interest. In the early period contact was by land, along the southern and western Korean lowland and through the Manchurian littoral. Later contact was by coastal waters when the Korean principalities became too unruly. Military action became a standard part of the Japanese program to maintain and enlarge the link with China. Japanese attempts to control south Korean principalities seemed less a matter of imperialist expansion than a matter of keeping open the route to China. Japanese headquarters in Korea served as route stations and forwarding offices in this process of culture contact, in which the Japanese definitely were the active agents. Koreans often were intermediary tutors, themselves going in large number to Japan. In historical retrospect Koreans usually considered China the benefactor and Japan the interloper, while strongly resisting the efforts of either to control their peninsular regions.

EARLY KOREAN REGIONALISM

The Korea that before 1945 appeared one national unit, divided into thirteen administrative provinces, is a result of a long process of accretion. Earliest Korea seemed to be a land of innumerable tribal groups, each occupying a small, separated lowland or upland tract in the hilly landscape. Chinese and Japanese influence now hindered one group, now favored another. To skip the earlier outlaw regions, the first regional entity to appear in the Korean Peninsula was the Early Han dynasty border region of Lo-lang, which took in the country south of the Yalu River to a line drawn approximately from Kaesong to Wonsan. South of this lay a march zone serving as a refuge to outlaw Chinese, into which the native tribes began to push from the south.

North of the Yalu lay mountain country in which a northern forest people who had taken up Chinese agriculture and absorbed some Chinese culture organized a petty kingdom that began expanding southward at about the end of the first century B.C. Northern Lo-lang fell to this new principality of Kaokuli at about the start of the Christian era. As the third century opened, Chinese power from the Manchurian littoral was strong enough to organize the southern remnant

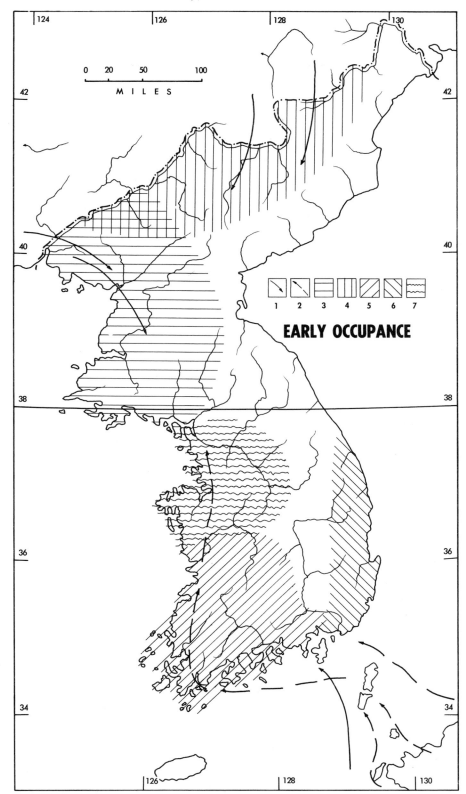

EARLY OCCUPANCE

Fig. 120. Early occupance of Korea: (1) lines of earliest approach; (2) Japanese route of contact with China; (3) approximate region of Lo-lang, Chinese colonial province; (4) approximate main area in Korea dominated by Kaokuli; (5) Chen Han territory, later the core of Silla; (6) Pien Han territory, the southern portion of which became Imna; (7) Ma Han territory, later the core of Paikche, which expanded southward.

of Lo-lang and the marches into the Chinese province of Tai-fang. This did not last long and was the last Chinese effort to colonize, or themselves organize, a region of Korea. The marches later became a zone of contest between the sinicized forest-mountain peoples of Kaokuli and the south Korean agricultural peoples of Silla and Paikche.

At an early date southern Korea was occupied by three groups of mixed tribes, the San Han. The Ch'en Han tribes occupied the lower east coast, the eastern hill country, and its marginal valleys. The Pien Han tribes held the low country and hill margins of southernmost Korea. The Ma Han tribes held the western lowlands and the adjoining hill country.

Of these many tribes the Ch'en Han had developed the most complex culture, were town dwelling, produced and traded in iron products, and were good farmers. The Ma Han were simpler, village-dwelling agricultural tribes. The southern Pien Han, least affected by Chinese culture, were village-dwelling farmer tribes who had considerable in common with the earlier Japanese tribal groups. A part of the Ch'en Han territory first reached formal organization under the small state of Silla as early as 57 B.C. The first petty state in the Ma Han regions was organized as Paikche about 18 B.C. The Pien Han tribes were slower in reaching political unity, perhaps owing to Japanese interference. Here a petty state, named Imna, finally united the remaining Pien Han tribesmen during the fourth century. At an early point in this whole process of growing unity there had been nearly eighty tribal "states" in the southern half of Korea alone. Silla, Paikche, and Imna were the political results of tribal and regional amalgamation.

Imna often came under Japanese domination in the efforts to keep the route to China open. Paikche received intermittent assistance from Japan in her struggles against Silla and Kaokuli, since this also furthered Japanese interests in the route to China. Silla never was more than nominally under Japanese control at any time, though she suffered from continued Japanese piracy along her coast. Chinese influence increased in the sixth century, and rather rapidly Silla grew stronger and larger at the expense of Imna, Paikche, and the northern marches. Kaokuli was too often engaged in fighting China.

Aided by Chinese culture and Chinese military assistance, Silla, by the start of the eighth century, had amalgamated all Korea except a northern, central mountain tract. The latter zone was taken over by P'o Hai, the successor to Kaokuli. During the eighth and ninth centuries Silla was a brilliant facsimile of Chinese culture flowering on the periphery of the Chinese T'ang Empire. The Mongols were the first to unite the whole of Korea in the thirteenth century. They split the region into 64 administrative pieces, presumably along somewhat natural lines. Under unified control since then, different administrative units have been employed, varying from eight to the present thirteen.

It thus appears that Korea evolved out of a wide combination of hill-and-valley peoples sparked largely by Chinese culture. The better western and southern central lands were too open to Japanese interference and control. The rugged mountain lands and forest regions of the north could not permanently support a strong population. Both these regions were drawn into the maturing Korean state, once a vital and growing core had developed. Occupation of the hill-and-valley country by an agricultural people using many Chinese farming practices and united by the common cement of Chinese culture made effective unification possible in a landscape that possesses many small divisions but few clear natural regions.

UNITY, HERMITAGE, AND CONQUEST

Ninth-century Silla was an honorable, tributary member of the Chinese cultural realm. It suffered no interference from the Japanese, who now were using direct sea routes to North China. Silla retained an active Buddhist monasticism that made the Diamond Mountains an object of pilgrimage from all over China and Japan. But social and economic defects were growing in number and volume in the Korean state. Revolution and reform produced reorganization during the early tenth century, and a new ruling group appeared, calling their state Korai, from which is derived our English term Korea. This change brought the Buddhist religious orders to power, and promoted a number of unhappy and unprogressive economic features.

China now had less contact with Korai, since various barbarian empires ruled parts of Manchuria and North China. The Liao included northwestern Korai within their empire before shifting their emphasis south and westward toward China. The Mongols never quite understood the relationships between Korai and China and, being "barbarians" themselves, soon were at outs with Korai. This ended in full conquest, economic loot, and thorough disruption of Korean economy, which increased as Mongol power declined. The fourteenth century ended with another reorganization of Korea, a new dynasty, and a new government, plus a re-alignment of Korea with the new Ming Empire of China. Even a new name for the country resulted,

Chao-hsien, familiar recently as the official Japanese name Chosen.

The fifteenth and sixteenth centuries became the golden age in Korean history, a period in which liberal government rested lightly but efficiently upon the unified people of the peninsula. Korean inventiveness came to the fore, agriculture expanded, the standard of living increased, and relations with both Japan and China were peaceful. Toward the end of the sixteenth century, however, Japanese piracy was renewed and culminated in military invasion of southeastern Korea and some years of difficulty, in which the city of Seoul changed hands several times, reminiscent of its recent trials of war. Korean loyalty to the Ming Empire brought the Manchu invasion of Korea and loss of freedom in the 1630's. A restoration, as a Manchu vassal, produced no illustrious developments like those of the two earlier centuries.

A protective Manchu influence and a dislike for the European derived from the earliest contacts produced in Korea the cultural isolation that gave rise to the phrase "The Hermit Kingdom." This lasted from the middle of the seventeenth century to about the 1860's. The breakdown of this self-isolation resulted from the inability of China to hold off the Occident, and from the sudden expansionism created in Japan by the West. Japan actually was the first country to breach Korean refusal to deal with the world. A series of commercial and diplomatic maneuvers between Korea, China, and various foreign powers soon stripped Korea of her position as a tributary to China. But before any occidental country could take advantage of this independence, Japan suddenly, in 1895, turned Korea into a part of the new and growing Japanese Empire. This time a united Korea became wholly Japanese, in contrast to the earlier puny Japanese efforts to control the overland route to China.

JAPANESE-DOMINATED KOREAN AGRICULTURE

This section is written as a general commentary on Korean agriculture for the whole country. Data for North Korea are not available and, where South Korea is not explicitly mentioned, application is to a united Korea of the early 1940's. The general use of the terms northern and southern is merely geographical, but North Korea and South Korea are employed as political area terms.

In 1945 just over 3,000,000 farm families cultivated about 11,300,000 acres of farmland, divided into millions of tiny plots. The Koreans are predominantly village dwellers, and systems of land inheritance and

control have become rather complex during a long history. The fragmentation of fields has reached considerable proportions. In the central and southern lowlands agriculture is a stable matter, involving wet fields and water control. In the northern hill country this gives way to a dry-field culture and to a great deal of transient culture, locally designated "fire-field" culture owing to its consistent practice of burning off fallowed grass, brush, and tree-grown lands. This is squatter agriculture carried out by poor families on lands that can be cropped only for one, two, or three seasons before a shift must be made to other fallow lands. Nearly a half million acres were annually cropped in this way, the total having actually increased under Japanese control. In Korean agriculture a variable amount of double cropping is employed; it is frequent in the warmer south but less common in the cooler north country. The 463-mile length of Korea is increased, in climatic contrast, by the elevation of the northern hill and mountain country, and there are many agricultural differences between north and south. These involve crops, farming techniques, tools, animals, and food consumption. The accompanying maps present this contrast graphically.

Expressed most simply the farms of Korea average between 3 and 4 acres. In fact, however, the most common size of farm is between 0.8 and 2.5 acres broken into disconnected plots. A small landlord class of Koreans owns a goodly share of the total farmland. Tenancy is most common in southern Korea and, before 1950, was least common in the north. In southern Korea, where Japanese inroads upon land ownership were most pronounced, the proportion of landless farmers had reached about 75 per cent by the end of World War II. Well over half of the total farm families then were landless. When owners who also rented a little land were included, the proportion of tenancy for all Korea reached a figure of about 80 per cent, one of the highest in the world. Agrarian reform measures introduced after 1945 by American occupational forces expropriated nearly 700,000 acres of Japanese-owned lands in South Korea and sold them to almost 600,000 tenant families on a long-term payment basis. Subsequent land reform measures have moved more slowly. In North Korea all large farms were expropriated and cultivation rights turned over to tenant farmers on a purchase plus "contribution" basis. As the population has grown the size of farms and the per capita acreage steadily has decreased.

In southern Korea there is but little reserve land available, particularly little that is suitable to rice culture. In the hilly and more northerly areas there still is some reserve land amenable to dry-field culture.

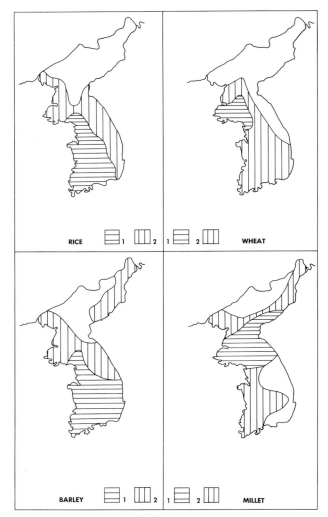

Fig. 121. The chief food grain crops: (1) primary producing centers; (2) secondary areas of production. Millet here includes several varieties.

That 30,000,000 people must try to live on the produce of no more than 12,500,000 acres of land, lacking an organized industrial output and a favorable foreign trade, is but the bare statement of a hard fact. With the steadily deepening exploitation of Korea by the Japanese the situation grew worse throughout the period of modern Japanese control. The wiping out of Japanese investment in land and control over agriculture after 1945 can prove only a partial amelioration. The crowding of North Koreans into the southern half of the country has greatly aggravated this condition.

The crop patterns of southern Korea long have been dominated by rice. This single crop, grown on summer-flooded fields, totaled somewhat over 4,000,000 acres per year. Barley, the next ranking crop, totaled more than 3,000,000 acres per year. Barley chiefly is a winter crop, grown on rice, bean, and cotton lands.

Cotton is an important summer crop, expanded greatly by Japanese stimulation in this century to a total of about 625,000 acres. Ramie and other industrial fibers, some of the less hardy fruits, such as persimmons, grapes, peaches, and plums, and a wide variety of vegetable and root crops supplement the crop patterns of southern Korea. Tobacco is also a southern crop, closely controlled by the Japanese to promote a taxable monopoly.

Toward the northern border wet-field agriculture becomes increasingly less important. Rice gives way to several kinds of millet, the dominant crop, covering over 2,000,000 acres. Here double cropping is less often found, agriculture operating primarily on a single summer cycle. A variety of beans, maize, buckwheat, sorghums, oats, and white potatoes are the auxiliary crops. Only the hardiest of fruits can be grown and the range of vegetables decreases.

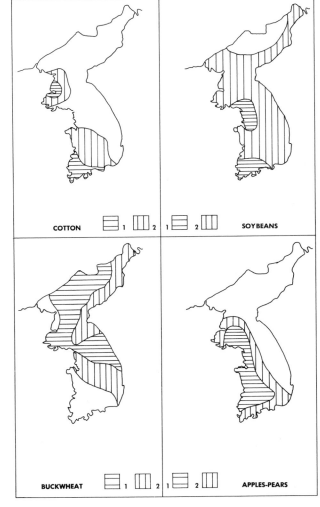

Fig. 122. Important auxiliary crops: (1) primary centers of production; (2) secondary areas of production.

A certain range of crops is sufficiently tolerant, or is bred into local varieties, to be grown almost all over Korea. The soybean is the chief of these, forming one of the ranking crops in all parts of Korea, and formerly totaling about 2,000,000 acres. The mulberry tree, for silkworm feeding, is another which is evenly distributed, to total perhaps 150,000 acres. Hemp, peas, radishes for home use, sesame for cooking oil, and pirilla for lighting oil are widely distributed crops having rather small total acreages. Pirilla is much less important since the introduction of kerosene. Wheat, a major crop, totaling some 800,000 acres centers in central Korea, is unimportant either in the far north or far south. Apples and pears, the chief commercial fruits, are centered along the lowlands and hill country of the western half of Korea.

Animals play a relatively small role in Korea agriculture. About 1,725,000 light-weight cattle of all types in the early 1940's provided but a small amount of draft labor, little meat, and almost no dairy products, the latter being in disfavor. The 1952 draft-animal population was considerably less than this figure. A few thousand sheep, goats, and horses are insignificant, despite Japanese stimulation. Pasture lands and forage crops do not figure in Korean agriculture. About 1,500,000 pigs are kept in the villages, and, like the cattle, add to the food supply only in a minor way. This total now has been appreciably reduced. An estimated 6,000,000 fowls of all types provided a few eggs and little meat in relation to the total food supply, but the present total is not more than half this figure. A small export of animal products to Japan drew off most of the annual surplus.

The strong hand of the Japanese can be seen in the changing crop patterns and food habits. Since 1900 the rice acreage has increased but, despite the large increase in population, Korean rice consumption had decreased to a low figure in 1945. Marked increases had taken place in the production of millet, barley, maize, buckwheat, and potatoes. A large import of Manchurian millet had developed. The answer to the low local consumption lies in the increasing export of rice to bolster a growing Japanese deficit. Millet, barley, maize, buckwheat, and potatoes formed an ever larger share of the Korean food supply, all cheaper products eaten from necessity. The increases in cotton, tobacco, wheat, and commercial fruits were at Japanese urging and were turned to Japanese profit. Japanese development of irrigation facilities and the reclamation of tidal lands in southern Korea were motivated by the desire for an increased rice export. Little effort was expended by the Japanese to increase the total of dry fields on a permanent basis. There can be

no question but that in a single generation the Japanese forced the people of Korea to accept a markedly lower standard of living.

Attempts, in South Korea, to increase food production to meet the needs of a swelling population have met with some success, and in 1952 South Korea is self-sufficient in basic agricultural needs. The fishery catch has not yet returned to normal, fisheries ranking second to agriculture in Korean domestic economy.

MINERALS AND THEIR USE

For a small region Korea has a very considerable mineral resource, which is distributed rather widely over the country. Koreans themselves have made some use of their resources in the past, having a respectable development of handicraft manufacturing. The development of modern mining began under American engineers during the late nineteenth century, but the ex-

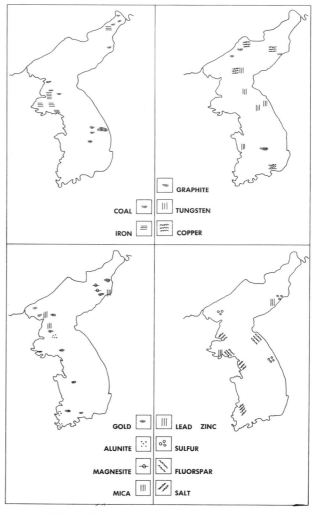

Fig. 123. Mineral occurrences in Korea.

ploitation of minerals chiefly has been at the hands of the Japanese, who utilized them in Japanese industry rather than for the domestic development of Korea. The distribution of minerals is shown on an accompanying map.

Of the primary industrial minerals coal and iron are widely scattered and voluminous in total reserve, but petroleum is lacking. The coal is chiefly anthracite, and some of the iron ores are relatively low grade. The hydroelectric potential of Korea is very large, and the Japanese developed a widely distributed system of hydroelectric power plants.

Of the ferro-alloys tungsten is present in important amounts, and there are small resources of manganese, molybdenum, and nickel. Korea is an important producer of low-grade graphite for the world market. Lead and zinc are rather widely distributed over the country. Gold has been one of the most valuable of the auxiliary Korean minerals, scattered all over the country. There are deposits of alunite, an aluminum ore that cannot economically be utilized to date, though the Japanese did make aluminum from it during World War II. Copper is scattered as a mineral secondary to zinc, lead, and gold in a number of areas. There are small resources of a few lesser minerals.

For a unified territory able to utilize its own mineral resource this list is fairly large for the modern world. However, most production, heretofore, went to Japanese industrial development and did Korea but little good. More recently a political line across Korea and disruptive conditions both inhibit mineral production and make problems of local occurrence far more significant than these would be in a peaceful and united country. In general one can say that most of the minerals are widely scattered, both north and south of the 38th parallel; the most important of these are shown on the accompanying map. Unfortunately, some of the best coal and iron resources lie in northern Korea, along with more than half of the hydroelectric resources. Some of the other mineral resources also have been chiefly produced in northern Korea. This has meant that the current economy of South Korea is restricted in its power volume, and in its other mineral volume, making difficult the normal production of goods both for the civilian population and for the protective effort against Communist aggression.

When Korea again is able to settle down to a period of reconstruction and peaceful living, the mineral resources of Korea will have been mapped and their productive exploitation begun. Many of them will be adequate for a modest program of industrial use, and others will be available in such quantities as to form useful export products. Until that time comes, however, mineral production in Korea will continue on an emergency basis, disrupted by military operations and uneconomical patterns of use.

COMMUNICATIONS, INDUSTRY, AND ECONOMIC RAPE

In the Korea of the old order, roads and the system of communications strongly resembled those of China. Stone-paved step roads traced their routes across the landscape, regardless of landforms, and were traveled chiefly by human carriers, pack animals, and riding horses. An elaborate country-wide system of signal fires implemented government couriers. Considerable coastwise water traffic probably handled most of the long-distance movement of commodities. The Japanese proceeded to install all the modern forms of transport and communications during their period of control. They developed a railway network and at least one urban street car system. They turned many of the step roads into vehicular highways. A telegraph system was developed, telephones became common around urban centers, and radio communications systems were developed. A government postal system was organized, ports were built, and coastwise shipping improved. A considerable network of air fields was developed after 1930. Transport facilities are presented on accompanying maps. Though these facilities do not compare with those of the Occident and were relatively smaller developments than those of Japan, they gave Korea a better set of modern services than were available in China.

Statistical tabulations of industrial production and of foreign trade during the period of Japanese control indicate that a considerable volume of manufacturing had been developed before 1945, and that Korean trade had risen to large proportions. The range of manufacturing was considerable, and some of the activities were in advanced and highly technical lines. Heavy industry and the chemicals accounted for a very significant share of the total production. The number of concerns increased markedly, and the value of the total output was progressively enlarged. Household handicraft industry was encouraged and somewhat expanded. Trade patterns showed a large volume of export products in both raw materials and manufactured goods, and a large import trade in semiprocessed and manufactured goods, in fuel supplies, and in consumers goods. Korea, as a Japanese colony, seemed to be developing along the lines of industrial capitalism.

Close examination of the situation, however, as indicated in several recent studies of Korea, indicates that the transport map and the statistical records give

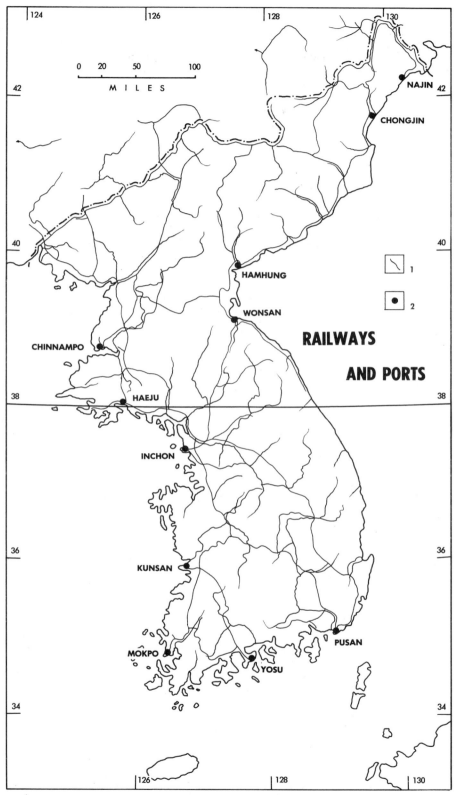

Fig. 124. Rail lines and ports in Korea as they existed in 1950.

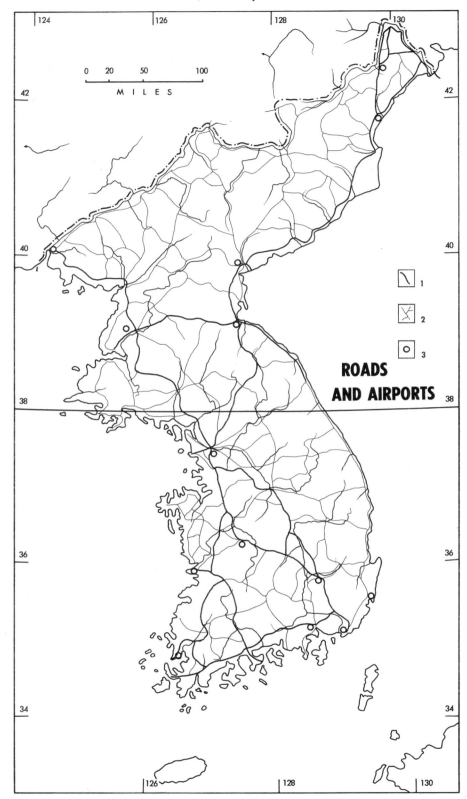

Fig. 125. Roads and civil airports in Korea: (1) first-class highways; (2) secondary roads, which are narrower than first-class roads. In addition there are many miles of narrow and unimproved village and local roads suitable for animal-cart traffic; (3) civil airports as of 1941.

a quite false impression regarding the economic development of Korea under the Japanese. By far the greater proportion of all these developments were carried out, not for the essential good of the Koreans, but for the strengthening of Japanese economy. In many lines industrial production in Korea was not independent and self-contained, but interlinked with operations in Japan. It is perfectly true that on Korean soil the Japanese were effecting an industrial revolution, but it was not of, or for, Korea, and it had little constructive impact on Korean domestic economy.

Korean industry was manufacturing close to raw materials, but it was an integral part of Japanese economy. This was unlike British-developed manufacturing in India, which in part was designed to produce goods for the Indian market. Banking, the financial system, economic regulations of government, controlled patterns of trade with Japan, all were arranged to the one end. Increasingly after 1930 Korean industry was military industry aimed at increasing the military striking power of Japan. Transportation and communications were aids in this process. Their further utility lay in the better draining of Korean minerals, fishery products, rice, wheat, soybeans, and other agricultural supplies out of Korea for the benefit of Japan. Korean trade during the late 1930's was almost exclusively with Japan. Korean participation in this whole development was limited to agricultural production, mineral production, and to unskilled and semiskilled labor in Japanese manufacturing plants. Only occasionally were Koreans permitted to acquire modern technical skills and to participate in the ownership of manufacturing enterprise. Korean participation in government was either at the clerical level or at the median level of collaborationist activity of a few Korean landlords and merchants. This all amounted to a more efficient economic exploitation of a colonial holding than that carried out by any occidental colonial ruler. Koreans became a kind of "lesser Japanese" working for the advancement of Japan.

Though the record would suggest that Korean economy developed broadly under the Japanese, that manufacturing and secondary economic activities rose in productive value, and that agriculture and other primary activity production declined in relative importance, this was largely a statistical illusion so far as the Koreans were concerned. Domestic economy remained unchanged in its patterns; a force of over 800,000 Japanese operated a secondary economy on Korean soil drawing its strength from, but also keeping it divorced from, domestic economy. The great majority of Koreans remained agricultural, and after 1930 the Japanese restrained the use of raw materials in domestic handicraft manufacturing, forcing a further dependence upon agriculture. But as larger and larger supplies of agricultural products were squeezed out of Korea by the Japanese, the Korean dietary position declined along with the economic position of Korean farmers, who increasingly had to sell their products at prices fixed by their overlords.

After 1945 much of Korean industry was dismantled and stripped of its productive capacity by Russian and American military teams. Much of Korean industry was of no purpose in a peacetime, post-war Korea. The sharp drawing of a line across Korea resulted in the separation of many elements in Korean economy. The northern and southern portions of the country were complementary parts of a whole, and the effect of drawing a line at the 38th parallel was to make the economic operation of either half extremely difficult. Soviet refusal to permit the regional interchange of raw materials, power, food supplies, and other items were continuing elements of a process rendering Korean life difficult. The steady stream of emigrants out of northern Korea increasingly compounded the problems of southern Korea from all points of view.

The events after June, 1950, have only furthered the long process of disturbing Korean life and economy. Though many efforts and much money have been put into increasing productivity of southern Korea, much of it has a wartime pattern, and the draining of economic resources continues. Regardless of what detailed pattern of settling the issues of control in Korea finally results, the balance sheet of over a half century of exploitation, war, and regional disruption can show only a net loss for the Koreans.

POPULATION AND REGIONALISM

Though the Koreans have a diverse racial background, by the present century they had become one people, with one language, one culture, and with few basic regionalisms or cultural origins such as those compounded in the Indies or Indochina. As a village-dwelling people they have had few really large cities, but there have long been many port and market towns of some size, and the capital city has been a large city for some centuries. An early eighteenth-century population figure of slightly less than 7,000,000 seems fairly accurate. The first real census of population was that of 1925, after Japanese exploitation had begun, but also after some Japanese public health measures had been introduced. The 1925 total was 19,-522,000. The 1944 census totaled some 25,900,000.

Both of these censuses failed to include those Koreans who had left the country, a figure which steadily

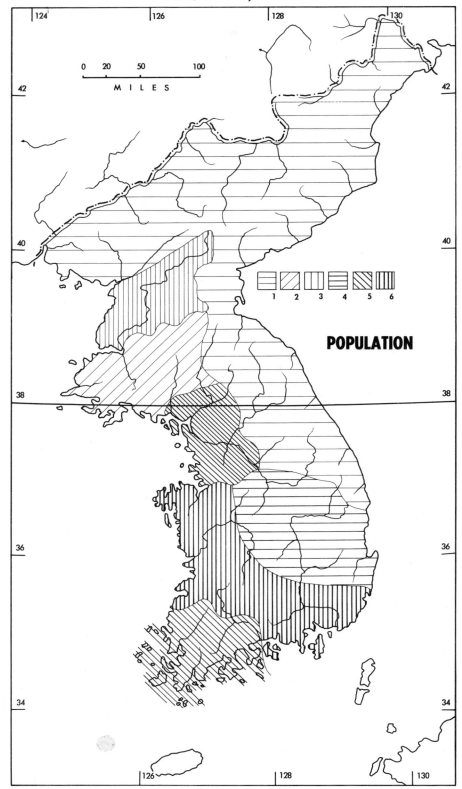

Fig. 126. Population distribution, 1946. Distribution is arithmetic by provinces, interpolated in general terms by regions, and estimated for all parts of Korea. Numbers have reference: (1) under 200 people per square mile; (2) 201–300 per square mile; (3) 301–400 per square mile; (4) 401–500 per square mile; (5) 501–600 per square mile; (6) over 600 per square mile. Generalized after Taylor.

had increased since just before 1900. As economic and political exploitation had increased, large numbers of Koreans had moved into Manchuria, some of whom moved on into Siberia after the Japanese took over Manchuria in 1931. Large numbers of Koreans went also to Japan as industrial labor, a few to China, and a very few scattered elsewhere in the world. This emigration was chiefly of rural Koreans, and it replaced the more normal modern growth of urbanism. After 1945, Japanese were sent back to Japan, and most of the Korean population abroad returned to Korea. The 1952 estimate of the total Korean population suggests a total very close to 30,000,000.

The marked increase in population is recent, and most of the population is a young rural population. This means that the future increases will be rapid, and that the population will continue its present rate of increase for some years, unless the current disruptive conditions continue both severe enough and long enough to materially affect population structure and its rates of growth.

In 1944 the present area of South Korea, somewhat less than half the total territory, contained slightly under 16,000,000 people of the total of just under 26,-000,000. The 1952 estimate of the total population for South Korea suggests a total very close to 22,000,-000, though no precise data are available. This estimate is rendered difficult by continued emigration out of North Korea, much of which cannot be tabulated. If the estimate for all of Korea is at all accurate, it would appear that North Korea is declining slightly in population but that South Korea is rapidly increasing. The latter increase is compounded of three elements: the natural increase, the post-war repatriation of Koreans abroad, and the steady influx of emigrants from the north.

In South Korea, at least, there has been a marked increase in urbanization since 1920, promoted by the lack of space in the rural countryside, and by the congregation of refugees in urban areas. Seoul and Pusan have grown markedly in their total populations, the former in 1952 exceeding 1,250,000, and the latter nearing the total of 450,000. There were, in 1945, at least a dozen other cities of over 50,000. The termination of hostilities in 1953 could produce a reverse drift of population from the cities to rural areas, and from the southern part of the country back toward the north, provided some effective settlement of military-political difficulties between North and South Korea results in 1954.

Before 1945 the chief regionalisms of the country were those arising out of the natural environment. In

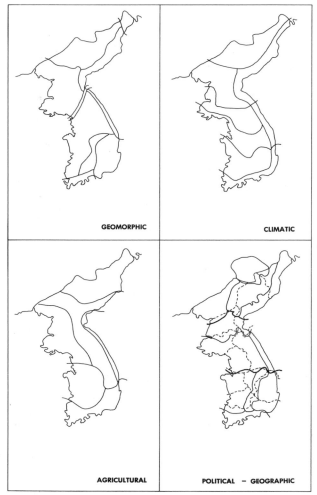

Fig. 127. Regional patterns of Korea. Geomorphic and climatic boundaries after McCune; geographic region boundaries after Lautensach.

an agricultural society, uniform in its major cultural patterns and living in an environment of marked physiographic and climatic variety, these regionalisms become chiefly matters either of environment or of population distribution, agriculture, diet, and detailed patterns of living. Southern Korea has a heavier population pattern, more cultivable lowlands, a more widespread rice landscape, and auxiliary agriculture containing a wide variety of crops applicable to a milder climatic regime. Northern Korea is a rougher, upland landscape, chiefly of dry fields, fewer and more hardy crops, shifting "fire-field" agriculture, and lesser and scattered population patterns. The accompanying maps depict various elements in this picture.

The insertion of such items as the 38th parallel and markedly different kinds of political systems into the issue of regionalisms may have a long-run future effect.

Though the 38th parallel is but a line on a map, corresponding to nothing in the physical environment, its cumulative effects over the years can be significant. Not only political systems but also education, psychological reactions, and social change are involved. The northern part of Korea has been subject to greater disruption than has southern Korea since 1950. If some kind of settlement is reached that could permit a united Korea before too long an interval passes, these new factors of regionalism may not become too deeply established. Since they run counter to the cultural currents of the Korean people, the temporary effects could be erased through a unified program of cultural action. However, if the separation of north and south goes on long enough for one or more generations of people to reach maturity with different political and social orientations, a pattern of cultural regionalism could be developed that might long stand against the trends toward unity. There is the danger, therefore, that the opposing cultural programs of Communism and Democracy may produce a lasting impression upon the Korean people and their culture.

Japan: A Small Island World

A SERIES OF ISLAND ENVIRONMENTS

The Japanese islands lie toward the northern end of the long line of Island Arcs that rim the eastern margins of the Asiatic continent. They form a relatively small environment situated between the largest land mass and the largest ocean. The lands of Japan are mostly uplands, the tops of steep and rugged mountains projecting above, with most of the mountainous mass lying below, the present sea level. In earlier human time the level of the ocean was slightly lower, and Japan then was a larger region of land grouped into a small number of islands fringed by considerable areas of relatively broad and open lowlands, particularly in what today is the Inland Sea and the coastal shelf toward Korea and China. The rise of the ocean level in post-glacial times has subdivided Japan into many islands, and has taken away from modern man a significant area of lowland. Today one tends to think of Japan as a very small country made up of steep surfaces, but it really is small only in terms of the amount of its arable land in relation to its large population. The earliest Japan known to man was neither so small in actual area, nor was it small relative to need and population. The smallness is clearly relative even today, for Japan stretches some 1,200 miles from northeast to southwest.

The Japanese islands form a mosaic of small individual units, blocks, peninsulas, and islands, broken by fault and fracture lines, grouped into a number of major units, and littered with the products of volcanism. There are a number of structural depressions between these major units, and one of the largest of them is occupied by the Inland Sea, in itself a very real part of the Japanese environment. Maximum elevations reach 12,000 feet, and the steep uplands dominate this environment. In many places steep rocky coasts drop directly into the sea. Scattered around the fringes of islands and between some of the less deep structural depressions are small lowland patches, alluvial areas filled with coarse to fine sediments, which provide agricultural surfaces. Many coastal sections show uplifted marine terraces and benches, for some of the areas of Japan have been above sea level only in Recent geologic time. These areas provide additional relatively smooth and open areas which have been put to agricultural use, though many of them are of comparatively low value. Much of the volcanism has produced acid materials which weather into poor soils, though volcanism has provided many beautiful and scenic landforms.

The south-facing portions of southwestern Japan possess mild climatic regimes and some subtropical plants, whereas the north coast, the southern uplands, and all northern Japan is cold and snowy in the winter and possesses mixed and coniferous forests. These conditions are amenable to occupance and use by modern man, but for early man they presented a somewhat difficult set of conditions. Natural food supplies are not abundant for a population of limited technology, and living conditions were on the rigorous side. The best regions were the coastal fringes in which early man could combine the use of land and aquatic resources, but the range of possibilities was far less in the Japanese environment than in the more varied regions of southeastern Asia.

The Japanese environment is one not bountifully provided with those natural complements of soils, plant resources, animal life, and other features which made for easy productivity of material goods for early man. The aquatic resources around these island shores are rich, but they were less available to early man than to modern man. By dint of hard work through a long span of time the Japanese have made their environment a productive one, but many of these advances had to await the introduction of techniques developed in other parts of the world, and then carefully fitted to the local scene. The historic pattern of the introduction of developed techniques into Japan has led to the false conclusion that the Japanese have been only an imitative people, whereas in the perfection and fitting of techniques to their environment the Japanese have displayed almost as much originality as did the Chinese, who also copied and adapted many alien features of culture.

Earliest man may well have been able to walk overland from the mainland to the lowland fringes of southwestern Japan, and it is notable that the Japanese archaeologists have turned up almost no record of the Old Stone Age in Japan. The inference is that occupance areas then lay on the lower coastal plains and lowlands now covered by the Inland Sea, the China Sea, and the immediate shore waters around the Japanese islands. The Ainu aboriginal population, proto-Caucasoid in origin, established themselves in such numbers that they have steadily contributed to the racial composition of the modern Japanese. Man moved upward onto the present alluvial lands and the lower upland fringes as the post-glacial patterns of islands and coastal outlines developed. Neolithic man came into the islands by sea both from the north and the west, bringing different elements of culture and probably representing different and mixed racial strains. The northerners brought useful elements of fishing economies, but they did not add greatly to the population as such. The main line of immigration lay through Korea, and the chief elements were proto-Mongoloid and Mongoloid in origin, to set the racial basis for modern Japan.

Out of the south, probably South China, moving along the coastal fringes came some southern peoples after the present lines of land and sea had developed. In popular thinking this stream of peoples bulks high in contributing to the Japanese population, but it is doubtful that this is so. These southern peoples undoubtedly did bring many culture traits into Japan related to the use of the sea and the subtropical elements of the environment.

Since most of these migrants came into southwestern Japan, bringing higher culture traits, it is natural that this was the early center of Japan. In a rigorous environment not bountifully providing for early man, the coastal lowlands of the southwestern portion were both the most livable and the most productive. Here the mixing of the early racial stocks and patterns of culture took place, and here also began that conversion of alien traits into traits distinctively Japanese.

THE SOUTHERN CULTURE HEARTH

The southern part of Japan was not only a more productive environment but also in closer contact with that part of mainland Asia in which Chinese culture was expanding and maturing during the late feudal era. Refugees from China, during the final bitter struggles of feudalism and the appearance of the Han state, carried Chinese culture into Korea and brought it into range of southern Japan, whose peoples were themselves in contact with Korea. These contacts can be traced to at least the third century B.C., and they gradually raised the culture level of southern Japan out of the Stone Age, though central and northern Japan lagged behind. The peoples of southern Japan were grouped in matriarchal tribal and clan patterns, each occupying small coastal sections. A competitive situation developed among these local groups, with the Yamato of Kyushu gaining the ascendancy and moving their headquarters to the eastern end of the Inland Sea by about A.D. 300. There was a general eastward movement of tribes and clans, including immigration from Korea and perhaps from the China coast.

Though the precise racial and cultural origins are not clear, rice culture, horses, cattle, the pig, and the dog appeared in southern Japan during these centuries. The horse came with the cavalry-warrior complex and was taken up by clan leaders and tribal chiefs as a means of solidifying their regional and group controls. Rice culture brought with it other crops, agricultural practices, and domestic use techniques. Metallurgy, domestic architecture, village settlement, and social patterns, all filtered in slowly. Many of these items came from China but not all from the North China culture hearth, some coming undoubtedly from the Yangtze Delta and coastal country, and others from Manchuria and the Mongolias. A few features may have come from South China, from the same centers that had spread many culture traits southward into southeastern Asia, but it is doubtful if much of Japanese direct cultural origins lie as far afield as southeastern Asia.

Kyushu, Shikoku, and the portion of Honshu fronting on the Inland Sea were the regions in which both human and culture migrations occurred. Water movement and fishing economies remained strong, mixing peoples and the details of culture. Replacement of primitive practices occurred, and new ideas were blended into old ones. Population grew, and most of the lowland alluvial tracts were settled. This whole process of development was restricted to southern Japan, and gradually there came to be marked differences between this southern region and the areas

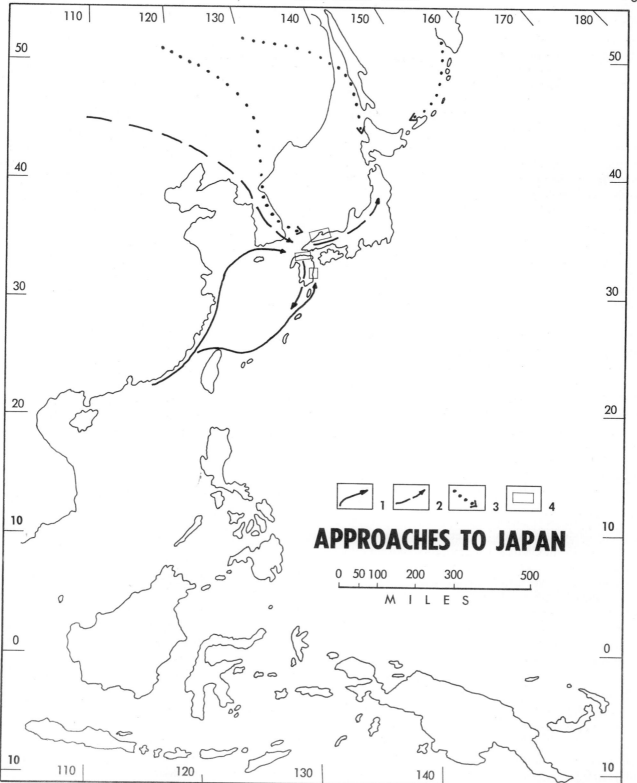

Fig. 128. Approaches to Japan: (1) possible migration routes from southern China coastal areas to southern Japan, source of the so-called "Malay" elements; (2) possible migration routes of the proto-Caucasoid Ainu and Neolithic Mongoloid groups; (3) possible northern routes of Paleolithic and proto-Neolithic elements; (4) location of earliest "centers" of Japanese culture.

north of the Inland Sea. In the north country the
Ainu and possibly other Stone Age peoples were thinly
scattered and culturally undeveloped. As time passed
the contrast became greater, and, as the southern peoples more and more fully occupied their lowlands, local
pressures for space began to develop. Slowly the
southern peoples began moving into the edges of their
own upland regions and also pushing northward along
the lowland fringes of Honshu. This southern section,
therefore, as the culturally advanced region, became
the source for the colonizing of the rest of the Japanese
islands and the local source of the cultural patterns
that gradually have grown into modern Japanese civilization.

THE CHINESE CULTURAL IMPRINT

Japanese culture possesses many similarities to the
culture of China, some of which trace back to introductions before the Christian era. And during the
early centuries of the Christian era, when the southern
peoples were making their first real advances in civilization, many Chinese traits were taken up in an unconscious pattern of acceptance. This hit-and-miss
learning process went on until the late sixth century.
By then Japanese leaders appreciated the value of Chinese culture, appeared to realize that their knowledge
was incomplete, and set out to broaden their contacts
and patterns of learning. Early in the seventh century
Japanese leaders despatched commissions to the Chinese court that compare with the modern system of
organized despatch of students abroad to centers of
learning. The best educated young Japanese were selected to study all possible aspects of Chinese culture.
Some remained in China for many years and upon their
return to Japan became leaders in a program of "modernization," as it were, that spread elements of Chinese
culture throughout southern Japan. All manner of
subjects were studied, from Buddhist theology to city
planning, from painting to manufacturing. This constituted an enormous program of cultural borrowing,
but the learning can hardly be called mere copying,
for it had to be integrated into a whole and blended
with the elements of native existing culture. And the
very organized manner of approaching the problem
was far in advance of any process of cultural development in vogue elsewhere.

The whole program perhaps evolved because China
had just begun to blossom again into one of its high
periods of development. The Sui had begun to organize North China into one state, and the T'ang were
just completing the task of making China the greatest
empire in the world at that time, politically and cul-

turally. The Japanese thus were able to study China
during one of its best periods, when Chinese culture
perhaps stood foremost among the world's cultures.
But another significant element in the picture was the
fact that administrative power in Japan was already
sufficiently centralized in the hands of a small group
of leaders for a major program of action to be decided
upon and carried into effect without a long period of
debate or struggle. It is important to note this early
illustration of the far-reaching results of the decisions
of a small number of people, Japanese leaders at a
particular point of time, because it is a phenomenon
that has occurred repeatedly throughout Japanese culture history.

The first cultural missions to China were so successful that they were repeated rather continuously for over
two centuries. By the middle of the ninth century official sponsorship for study of China came to an end,
though privately the process continued for almost two
centuries longer in lesser degree. By the latter part
of the ninth century the T'ang were declining in China,
and perhaps there was less to learn that could be of
use to the leaders of Japan. This long period of study
made the leaders of Japan familiar with the workings
of Chinese civilization and spread Chinese culture traits
throughout those parts of Japan inhabited by the peoples spreading out of the southern hearth region.

The impact of Chinese culture showed up in many
ways. In the early eighth century the Japanese set
out to build an imperial capital city of Nara, off the
Inland Sea, which they modeled upon the great T'ang
capital of Ch'ang-an. Grid-plan streets were laid out,
buildings were built in the Chinese style, functional
zoning was applied, and the city had come to stay.
The matriarchal society of early Japan finally disappeared in favor of the patriarchal system of China, and
the social status of women became permanently altered.
The tribal and clan leaders saw utility in the nationalized political system of China, topped by an emperor,
and so they installed it and in so doing rewrote Japanese history to give the system an ancient status. But
the leaders of Japan could not bring themselves to
install the full pattern of Chinese education, the examination, and the civil service, which would have
meant throwing open to all Japanese the opportunities
for political power. Thus they kept alive the clan
system which facilitated the preservation of real power
in the hands of hereditary leaders. Similarly they reorganized the land system and systems of taxation, but
in the end let the land system of China degenerate,
while keeping the tax system, so as more effectively
to consolidate power in the hands of the few.

Japanese religion grew into a mixture of Buddhism and native animism, but the study of Chinese Buddhism was serious and it became an important element drawn from China. Chinese art, handicraft manufacturing, and agriculture were studied and adapted so far as practical and possible. Here there was less danger to real power in the hands of leaders if a full application of Chinese practices took place. A far-reaching item that was taken from China was the written language, but the results have been less than satisfactory. At the time of earliest contact with Chinese culture no system of writing was known in Japan, but the spoken languages were polysyllabic. Chinese is a monosyllabic language easily written by single ideographs or characters. The first writing employed in Japan was Chinese, written by people brought from Korea. These immigrant scholars became the first recorders of Japanese historiography, the first scribes, and bookkeepers. Slowly the Japanese learned this complex system of writing, and it gradually became the written language of Japan. The grafting of a monosyllabic writing onto a polysyllabic speech resulted in a cumbersome system that never has been outgrown.

Though the adapting of only a few features of Chinese culture have been discussed, it must be obvious that the process involved selective adaptation rather than indiscriminate imitation. A close study of Japanese culture in this period suggests that a clear imprint of Chinese culture was spread throughout much of Japan with the result that Japanese culture is modeled upon that of China. But it is equally discernible that slavish copying was never permitted in many lines and that the leaders of Japan were extremely skillful in checking those trends which would have truly converted Japan into a little China in all respects. Chiefly the checks were applied at those points which preserved in the hands of the old line of Japanese leaders the power, wealth, and control of Japan.

SYNTHESIS AND OUTGROWING THE HEARTH

As the knowledge of Chinese culture began to pile upon in Japan there arose the increasing problem of how to integrate the new elements into Japanese life. The earlier solutions were to adapt it wholesale, but slowly Japanese became sufficiently skillful in the manipulation of Chinese culture traits to be able to discriminate between the merely new and the really useful aspects of Chinese traits. Not only was this process operative among the political leaders of Japan who dropped out features they did not like, but it gradually became applied throughout the whole range of Japanese life. In the mild climate of southern Japan the domestic architecture of North China was hardly necessary, and its strictly utilitarian features were too subdued to appeal to the Japanese. Slowly there evolved several distinctive Japanese housetypes, variably using movable panel walls, designed to let in light and sun, clean floors and mats, and a minimum of furniture reminiscent of southeastern Asia. Taken from Chinese patterns, Japanese housing still resembles its origins in many respects, but it is distinctively different.

Japanese agriculture basically resembles that of China in many respects, but it has developed its own distinctive methods, tools, and customs. The early arts of Japan closely resemble those of China, but gradually there have evolved subtle distinctions that often are hard for the occidental to recognize but that the educated Chinese and Japanese know well. This holds true in painting, sculpture, literature, drama, and the whole range of decorative and utilitarian arts. It holds true for many of the social customs, such as the ceremonial greeting, for dietary habits, such as the use of tea as a national drink, for the patterns of clothing, and many other elements of culture. In all these things the Japanese have slowly modified the basic elements into something peculiarly Japanese.

The process of converting Chinese cultural examples into Japanese customs and material developments was not done rapidly. The earliest elements in this adaptation of Chinese culture came early during the period when the Japanese were still consciously studying Chinese affairs. The most distinctive transformations, of course, came in the centuries after the Japanese had stopped observing China, and were independently living their own lives. The culture historian is apt to classify the centuries between about A.D. 900 and A.D. 1400 as the most important era of activity in the field of cultural transformation. The political historian is apt to divide the time span between about A.D. 800 and A.D. 1550 into two eras in which he first distinguishes the attempt to install a system of political nationalism and, second, the development of feudalism in Japan after about A.D. 1000.

In the sixth century A.D. the Japanese already were pushing northward beyond the Inland Sea and into the edges of the hill country of central Japan. As their culture developed more and more, and their population increased, the contrasts between the southern peoples and the aboriginal population of the north and the hill country heightened. There began a process of expansion northward out of the hearth that can be likened to the expansion of the seaboard American colonies westward across the United States. It was a slower process, and it involved different kinds of issues, but there are similarities. The Japanese had to fight their way northward against a stubborn resistance on the part of the hunting and gathering aboriginals who did not want to see their hunting ranges turned into farmlands. There developed a professional soldiery on the frontier who resembled the American "Indian fighter," settlers often found their advance locations raided, and forts and a frontier force of farmer-soldiery were employed. Some Japanese left the settled areas for various reasons and took up residence among the Ainu, often inciting them to resistance. By the end of the eighth century the lowlands well north of modern Tokyo had been cleared of Ainu, and considerable settlement by southerners had taken place. During the eighth and ninth centuries the Japanese pushed steadily northward, slowly learning the military techniques required to conquer the Ainu. By the end of the ninth century the strength of the Ainu had been broken, though groups remained in the uplands to bother the Japanese for another century or more. Some intermarriage steadily introduced Ainu blood and physical types into the Japanese people.

The Ainu had been a hunting and gathering people who lived along the shores of the islands and used the lowland interior regions that provided fish, game, and some plant resources. In the north country they found little in the mountain country of value, and increasingly found their range of support reduced as the southerners conquered the coasts and lowlands. Ainu had also inhabited the shores of Hokkaido for a long period, and some of them retreated to Hokkaido when dispossessed on Honshu. In Hokkaido, however, the upland country was largely barren of resources useful to hunters and gatherers, and the Ainu stuck to the coastal fringes and some of the more open lowland areas. In taking over Ainu territory the southerners found little developed land upon which to base their own occupation. They faced a forested environment with a cooler climate having few directly useful land resources to begin with. Their occupation of the north country, therefore, was a slow matter of clearing forests, developing fields on rough surfaces, changing their crops, and finding short-season varieties of crop plants that would mature in the cooler, shorter growing seasons.

Throughout northern Honshu, therefore, settlement and resource development was slow. Many Japanese settlements came to depend more upon fishing than upon agriculture. In many respects the southern people moving northward did not basically alter their southern patterns of culture. Housetypes, clothing, food patterns, customs, and habits remained much the same. The northern, colder parts of Honshu were slow to fill up with settlers, many of whom found this northern country unattractive in comparison to the milder portions of southern Japan. It was almost A.D. 1400 before most of the easily settled land of northern Honshu was occupied.

FEUDAL PATTERNS AND THE ECONOMY

It was noted previously that the leaders of Japan carefully rejected those elements of Chinese culture that would have endangered their positions of control over Japan. They were even anxious that the utilitarian arts be learned well, that agriculture develop, that settlement of all of Japan through northern Honshu be possible, but they were also anxious that the early patterns of social stratification remain strong, and that there remain a sharp line of demarcation between the mass of the population and the small group of leaders, rulers, holders of wealth, and large owners of land. There slowly developed, therefore, a complex set of multiple rules and standards which reminds one of the patterns of feudal Europe in which the commoner lived by one pattern and knighthood and the nobility lived by another. Out of this feudal development Japan has emerged with a set of social patterns second only to India in stereotyped inequality between the bottom and the top of the scale.

Since the leaders of Japan never really installed the Chinese centralized system of political administration and let clan leaders gain control of large areas of land all over Japan which became tax-free estates, these leaders retained the real control of Japan. When it suited the most powerful clan, the emperor and national authority was invoked, but provincial administration never grew in strength and the emperor remained a figurehead for centuries. This situation inevitably led to competitive struggle between the leading clans, with the most powerful actually holding the balance of power throughout Japan. In the early periods this placed the center of power in southern Japan, but since the Japanese were expanding northward, the center of power gradually shifted eastward and northward also. These struggles for power also developed a professional soldiery, some of whom were concerned with the northern frontier problem, with others concerned only in the interclan struggles. The power of the Buddhist church alternately grew and receded, often becoming an important element in the feudal struggle as monasteries and church leaders sought themselves to gain commanding position.

After the Ainu frontier was pushed into northern Honshu the slow shift of the center of population, of agricultural productivity, and of general economic

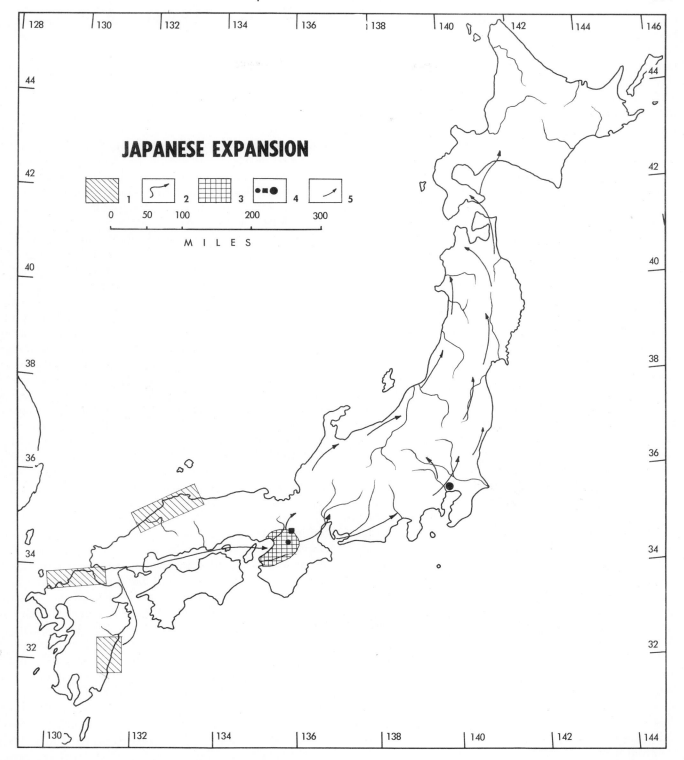

Fig. 129. Japanese internal expansion: (1) earliest culture "centers"; (2) shift of Yamato peoples from Kyushu to Nara Plain; (3) Yamato culture hearth core area; (4) successive northward shifts of imperial capital, from Nara to Kyoto to Tokyo; (5) successive stages in northward expansion from culture hearth.

wealth finally made it possible for the regional rulers based upon the Kwanto Plain, around modern Tokyo, to assume the lead in the regional struggle. Tokyo was developed into a city, connected by roads with the rest of Japan, and made the *de facto* capital of Japan. This occurred in the early seventeenth century, and by ingenious devices the Tokugawa clan became the real rulers of Japan. Tokyo soon became a large city, reaching a total of over 1,000,000 by 1800.

After the frontier problem ceased to be important the professional soldier turned his full attention to the regional and clan struggles. Considerable destruction of property and loss of life occasionally followed the more bitter struggles for power. The professional soldiery gradually became a parasitic class, entrenched in social and legal position, and entrenched economically with a considerable annual income derived from taxation of the peasantry. Out of this pattern comes the modern Japanese tradition of the soldier, the semi-religious cults, and the other military elements that were so successfully exploited by the leaders of Japan within the last century. In the late sixteenth century this military tradition took the form of the first Japanese attempt to conquer the known world, which then meant Korea and China, and a decade of fighting in Korea followed. The effort failed because of the inability of the home base to maintain and supply a large army at a distance, and because the leaders involved could not command the resources of all of Japan. The effort was a factor in the last major shift of regional power to central Japan.

Throughout the feudal era Japan remained primarily an agricultural country, dependent upon an intensive small-farmer economy which paid taxes in kind to support the upper classes. Handicraft manufacturing developed a fairly broad base, regionally concentrated in southern Japan and following slowly upon the eastward and northward shift of population. Northern Honshu, until the late nineteenth century, remained an underdeveloped region dependent chiefly upon agriculture, fishing, and forestry. Road systems were laid out sufficiently to connect all parts of Japan together, but these were chiefly of use in administration and local movement. Fishing grew steadily in importance in Japanese economy, developing skills and familiarity, but it still was chiefly a subsistence matter in which only coastal and shore waters were exploited.

From prehistoric times the southern peoples had maintained sea contact with Korea. And during the period of studying Chinese culture the Japanese traveled around the coast of Korea at first, and later directly across the North China Sea to the China coast. Water transport along the coast in Japan, within the Inland

Sea, and to the north country is of long standing. From about 1200 to 1620 Japanese traders engaged in a considerable sea traffic, consisting both of legitimate trade and of piracy. In this period Japanese merchants and traders established connections with, and had trader colonies in, the Philippines, Malaya, Thailand, Indochina, the China coast, Formosa, and Korea. Some of their ships steadily ranged into the South China Sea, and a Japanese pirate looted an English ship off Singapore in 1604. It was in the latter part of this era of sea trade that the Japanese made their first contact with the Occident, that the occidental traders found their way to Japan, and that a few products and ideas of the West got into Japan.

The luxurious living patterns and fighting of clan leaders that went on over the centuries consumed a goodly share of the surplus of the country, but did not really destroy the productive economic base. The population grew rather steadily until, by about 1600, it probably stood close to 25,000,000. The agricultural area had steadily developed and, except for some of the marginal and upland areas recently brought into use, had developed close to its maximum. Manufacturing, fishing, and trade were productive phases of the Japanese economy. Japan had reached a mature plane of economic development of the pre-industrial variety.

Throughout the whole feudal era the peasantry of Japan had protested their treatment, sometimes with local effect but never with the success that attended Chinese rebellion during the decline of a dynasty, so that by 1600 there were many stresses that had developed in Japanese society. The leaders of Japan saw in the arrival of the occidental a possible threat to their continued control of the country. Particularly was Christianity a threat, for its acceptance carried with it allegiance to a God who lay beyond the sea outside Japan. Though tobacco and firearms were willingly accepted from the European, the Tokugawa clan, just coming to power at the start of the seventeenth century, decided that continued contact with foreign elements might overbalance an already touchy and unstable set of affairs in Japan. For the third time, therefore, the leaders of Japan rather abruptly made a decision for all Japan that changed the whole pattern of events. They decided to close Japan to the outside world, both in respect to outsiders coming into, and Japanese venturing out of, Japan. Within a few years, in a series of edicts, all backed up by severe penalties and successful in result, they closed the ports of Japan to occidental and Asiatic traders, expelled the troublesome Spanish and Portuguese, stopped the conversion of Japanese to Christianity, stopped Japanese going abroad, limited the size of ships that could be built in Japanese yards, and sealed Japan up in an unprecedented kind of existence which evokes the word "hermitage." They also took many internal measures to weaken the strength of other clan leaders, such as forcing the permanent residence of hostages in Tokyo, allowing internal land transport routes to deteriorate, rearranging fiefs and land grants, and reducing the power of regional subordinate rulers.

These measures were all carefully planned and rather well executed. They succeeded in stabilizing the economy of Japan, and in stabilizing the patterns of regional control in such a way that Tokyo became the real seat of power in Japan, and the Tokugawa clan became the real rulers of the country. This procedure also had other results, of course. It kept occidentals out of Japan, except for the one small Dutch trading post which served as a listening post. Thus Japan escaped the fate of colonial status, so distasteful to the Orient. But in so doing Japan also lost touch with the rest of the world and with the progress of world events, for the knowledge gained through the slight contact with the one Dutch post was, on the whole, inconsequential and of little value to the Japanese leaders and the Japanese population alike.

The long period of hermitage did accomplish one other thing, culturally speaking. The control of the Tokugawa clan was sufficiently tight so that no large-scale internal changes or developments took place in Japanese culture. But the period of self-containment did serve to make the Japanese self-dependent in economic matters, and it tended to stabilize the population of Japan at a figure between 25,000,000 and 30,000,-000. When population was growing rapidly in most other parts of the world, this is a rather remarkable demographic event in world history. And it served also to put the finishing touches upon Japanese culture, developing many kinds of things into even more distinctive patterns. By the middle of the nineteenth century, when Japan opened up to the rest of the world again, Japanese culture had become a rather specific pattern of its own. One could easily see the Chinese influences in things Japanese, but the detail of the pattern was clearly different from that of Korea and China, more clearly so than at any previous time in Japanese history.

EMERGENCE AND MODERNIZATION

The Tokugawa clan still ruled Japan in the 1850's when Admiral Peary sailed into Tokyo Bay and called upon the Japanese to end their two and a half centuries of hermitage. Repeated overtures to this end had been declined earlier, and Japanese administration had been extended to Hokkaido early in the nineteenth century to prevent Russian encroachment. The American overture was more than a casual invitation, however, for it was made through a show of military force which was not lost upon the Tokugawa. Though they still held firm control internally they were quick to realize that Japan could not stand up to outside forces that could muster many large guns in the big steam naval vessels such as those in the American fleet. Within a few years they had signed trade treaties with several occidental countries, and had taken the first steps to modernize their own military establishment. This was the fourth time that a small group had changed the whole course of Japanese history.

The changes could not be undone, but they were the undoing of the Tokugawa and of the old order of feudalism in Japan. The emperor and the other clans that ruled Japan under Tokugawa control had not had the foreign fleet in their own home ports and were inclined to expel the foreigners. A few "incidents" soon convinced other leading clans of the futility of resistance to the outside world. The Satsuma clan of western Japan turned to developing a modern navy, and the Choshu clan began the building of a modern army. General opposition to the long rule of the Tokugawa took the form of restoring the emperor to a kind of power than the imperial family had not exercised for centuries, swept the Tokugawa from internal control, and started Japan on a course of modernization that both startled and impressed the whole world in the 75 years between 1866 and 1941. The Tokugawa had committed Japan to this program without the original support of the country, but other clans took over the lead, carried on the program, and managed to retain control of Japan until the end of World War II. Japan entered upon this new era in sound economic, social, and political circumstances, for there had been no time for a long series of disastrous internal wars to dissipate either population or resources.

A first step in modernization was the abolition of landed feudalism and the outmoded administration of government. Direct rule by the emperor and a bureaucracy, the abolition of feudal fiefs (for a reasonable price in government bonds), the establishment of new political administrative regions, and the pensioning off of the old regional rulers and the parasitic soldier group were the first steps in internal organization. This process, of course, gave to the ruling classes privileged opportunities for those members discerning enough to take them. Some old clans rose to new political power, and others acquired new economic strength, but it is notable that in general the control of Japan continued in the hands of the same general groups that had run Japan for many centuries.

Though the Tokugawa had actually sent a few observers abroad before the opening of the country, Japanese culture was sadly out of date compared to the industrial, military culture of the West. Realizing this the new leaders of Japan fell back upon a useful precedent, that of sending students abroad to study the superior cultures. Since many of these new leaders were derived from the old military clans and the professional soldiery, their first concern was the building of a strong military force which could deter the colonial imperialism of the Occident. Appreciating also that such a force could now be built only upon the basis of an industrial technology, they undertook a thorough-going industrialization. So for nearly 50 years the Japanese government sent commissions, study groups, observers, and students all over the world to study the material economy of the West in a determined effort to bring Japan up to date as quickly as possible. German military and medical science, French and German law, British ship building, and the railroad and manufacturing techniques, and the business methods of the United States were all carefully studied. Observers all over the world studied the patterns of trade, colonial imperialism, the developments of agriculture, mining, transportation, and architecture. Educational systems and political institutions were examined.

The Japanese government took the lead in these matters, paying for the studies and then subsidizing the developments in Japan. The first railway was built between Tokyo and Yokohama in 1872, and by the end of the century hundreds of power plants and factories were operating. The operation of concerns was turned over to private companies formed by the leading clans, so that not only did Japan industrialize rapidly, but also the control of the modern aspects of the economy remained in the hands of the old leading elements. It is a commonplace to say that in a non-industrial country the evolution of manufacturing begins slowly and somewhat on a hit-and-miss basis. Not so in Japan, for by 1900 most of the kinds of things being done abroad were also being done in Japan. As new industrial developments occurred abroad Japanese continued to study them and to adapt them at home.

In the first few decades of modernization industrial skills were not sufficient to keep pace with developments of the economy, operating efficiency was rather low, and the occidental rather easily came to the conclusion that the Japanese were not creative but only imitative. It should be sufficient to remind an American, however, that as late as the end of World War II the United States was still following the lead of Germany in many matters of industrial evolution to put the question of copying in proper balance. The amazing thing is that Japan went at modernization in a wholesale manner, in the way in which she had studied Chinese culture centuries earlier, and in a way seldom attempted by any other society. This was long-range planning well before five-year plans became the vogue. The process of synthesis always follows slowly after the process of learning about new culture traits, and Japan even today has hardly had the time to synthesize the mechanical economy of the industrial West.

It is notable that, whereas everything industrial was accepted, the leaders of Japan chose carefully in the fields of social, political, and cultural institutions. They did not disseminate many of the cultural ideas of the more democratic countries of the Occident but showed a preference for many of the elements of such an authoritarian society as Germany, wherein there were fewer dangers to the vested interests that had controlled Japan for so long. This repeated the sequence of events in adapting Chinese culture. A great many aspects of Japanese society went untouched by the hand of modernization, and there continued to exist a rural, agricultural Japan which neither participated in, nor received benefit from, the process of modernization. At the same time the rural farm youth became easy subjects to indoctrinate with the military tradition, the divinity of the emperor, the acceptance of the new order, the need for colonial expansion, and the continued leadership of the upper classes.

The Japan of Yesterday, Today, and Tomorrow

THE PATTERNS OF MODERN ECONOMY

The Japanese economy of today is compounded out of agriculture, fishing, transportation, manufacturing, international trade, and colonial imperialism. Of all the countries of the Orient Japanese economy most closely resembles the variety of economies thought to be characteristic of the Occident. This is what the leaders of the late nineteenth century wanted, and they reproduced much of the bad along with the good. But, since this modernization was grafted upon an oriental base already mature in most of its features, the resulting blend is neither typically occidental nor oriental.

The settlement patterns of Japan were well fixed, and the agriculture of Japan was thoroughly matured, when modernization came, so that few striking changes were introduced into the agricultural economy. Some new crops, a few tools and practices, some processing methods, commercial fertilizers, and an increased productivity resulted, but agriculture and its population have remained essentially that of the older Japan. In the several parts of the colonial empire changes in agriculture were introduced in contrast to the static situation in Japan proper. Some mechanization occurred in parts of Manchuria, and the plantation system appeared in Formosa.

The Japanese have been fishing around their coasts for centuries. After the restrictions of the Tokugawa were lifted, the fisheries of modern Japan benefited tremendously from the freeing of the population, and from the introduction of the larger, powered boat, the new types of nets used with trawlers, the canning of fishery products, the advanced ship-cannery techniques, and the expenditure of financial resources upon the fishing industry. Japan has advanced to the rank of the world's chief fishing country, with techniques and practices in advance of those anywhere else. These developments have resulted both in an increased home use of fishery products as food and in the production of a significant item in international trade.

The rapid development of industrial power of both thermal and hydroelectric variety, the wholesale establishment of industrial plants in a wide range of production, and the acquiring of advanced technical skills have produced a large amount of corporate urban manufacturing in Japan. This was designed to give Japan both military strength and a productive export economy. In the process both mining and forestry have been modernized. Corporate urban manufacturing has not replaced the older community workshop manufacturing entirely, but rather has blended with it to supplement and extend its range. An early concentration upon producer goods for Japan and consumer goods for the export trade meant that Japanese retail consumers were not greatly benefited.

Railroads, urban and lowland highways, ports, ocean shipping, airfields and the airplane, telegraph, telephone, and radio communications have all been significant elements of the modernization of Japanese transportation and communications. These elements have been part of a complex system, so that Japan ranks among the leaders of the modern world in most of these matters, while at the same time keeping many of the features and means typical of the older Orient in the rural and upland areas.

As the modernization of Japan took place the scarcity of many raw materials became evident. To aid the acquisition of these needs the Japanese became active in international trade. The foreign trade of Japan more closely resembles that of Great Britain than that of any other oriental country.

As Japan became increasingly modernized, and as its population grew, the limitations and shortages of the home environment became more and more obvious. A colonial imperialism was developed from the first, designed to supply such shortages as they appeared. The first step was the taking over of the Ryukyu Islands in the 1870's, followed by the militant acquisition of Korea and Formosa in the 1890's. Then followed the stemming of Russian strength in the Far East in the first decade of this century. Japan acquired the Kurile Islands, the southern half of Sakhalin, and control over valuable fishing waters. Japan also gained the opportunity for economic exploitation of Manchuria, though political title remained in the hands of China. Attempts in China during and after World War I were not very successful, but a mandate was secured over the Marianas, and the Marshall and Caroline Islands. Political control over Manchuria in 1931 was the next step implementing economic control. The attack upon China in 1937 was one of a series that followed upon control of Manchuria and the spread of influence into Inner Mongolia, but other than simple issues of markets and raw materials had now begun to enter. The Japanese phase of World War II came as a logical development of colonial imperialism, but it, too, involved factors other than those of raw materials.

Modern Japan is a unique blending of oriental and occidental cultures in all their forms. The American dime stores full of handicraft goods marked "made in Japan," the Japanese freighter in almost every port of the world, the cultured pearl, Tokyo University, the Japanese Army, Mitsui as a supercorporation, the earthquake-proof Imperial Hotel of Tokyo, the American-type farmstead of Hokkaido, and the religious shrine-summer resort-tourist center, all are expressions of modern Japan. Japan, in 1945, was given an ultimatum to further reorganize this blend into something more suitable to the rest of the world. Now hedged about with international limitations, and forced to live upon her home political area, Japan is attempting the balance of a process that involves many serious questions. Having grown so in population during the first phase of the process can she now continue to feed herself? Can she arrange peaceful patterns of industry and trade so as to fill the shortages and lift her standard of living sufficiently to remain at internal peace? Can she find that blend of East and West needed for peaceful existence on the international plane? Can she modernize her social and economic institutions in compliance with demand without losing her own soul? It is obvious now that the past modernization of Japan was of a special sort only, advanced yet incomplete. The finishing of this program will require a considerable span of time.

CONTEMPORARY AGRICULTURE

As of 1950 the per capita area of cultivated land in Japan was the smallest of any oriental country, and one of the smallest in the world. Japan provides no more than three fourths of her own food requirements at present. Agricultural productivity, measured in output, is up to the pre-war level but, since population has increased, the per capita return is not more than 80 per cent of the pre-war total. In 1950 there were some 6,200,000 farm families, totaling about 38,000,000 people, of whom some 21,000,000 are considered gainfully employed in agriculture. The total land cultivated in 1950 was somewhat in excess of 12,500,000 acres, the exact figure being difficult to ascertain owing to underreporting by farmers. The total cropped acreage was probably slightly in excess of 16,500,000 acres. Changes in crops and increasing productivity mark the agricultural record since 1945. Agriculture has gone through several readjustments during and since the end of the war. During the war many non-food lands were converted to food crop use, resulting in a decrease of mulberry and tea acreages. There was also a marked decrease in the animal population during the war. The most significant post-war change has been the tenancy reform program demanded by the American occupation forces, but it appears likely that there will be a slow drift toward increasing tenancy in the future years, since the real position of the farmer in Japanese society has not altered. For the present total tenancy has been reduced from over 60 per cent to about 35 per cent, with pure tenants dropping from about 30 to 5 per cent. Tenancy was more marked on rice lands than on other crop lands, and this remains true today.

Rice has long been the dominant crop of Japan, in 1950 amounting to almost half the total cropped land. Other grain cereals total about a third of the cropped land, with wheat being the most important single crop, totaling about 1,900,000 acres, and the others being several kinds of millets and barleys, along with oats and maize. Sweet and white potatoes, and a variety of peas and beans fill out the range of major food crops, with sweet potatoes yielding the largest caloric volume of food after rice. The accompanying maps indicate the regional distribution of the chief crops.

About 1,000,000 acres of green vegetables are grown every year, in wide variety, these being a repetitive short-term crop occupying a small share of the total land. The fruit acreage of Japan is not more than 250,000 acres, notably less significant than in other parts of the Orient. Fiber crops occupy less than

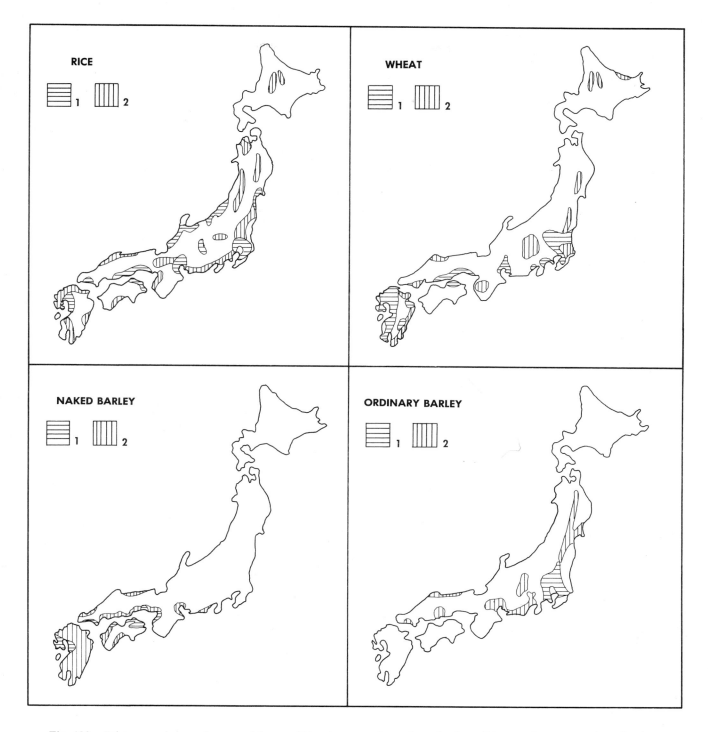

Fig. 130. Primary grain cereal crops of Japan: (1) primary regions of production; (2) secondary areas of production.

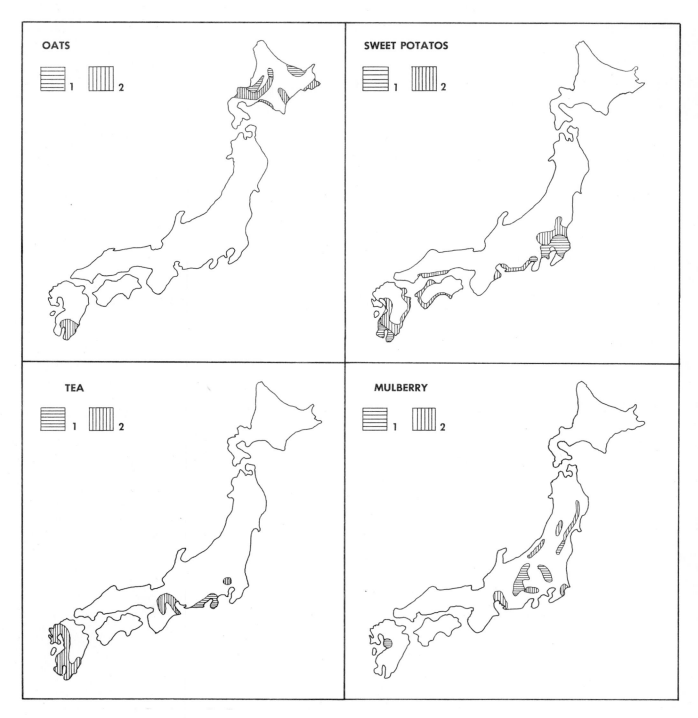

Fig. 131. Auxiliary crop patterns of Japan: (1) primary centers of production; (2) secondary centers of production. Mulberry distribution is that of 1948, much reduced from the areas utilized before 1945.

100,000 acres, with other miscellaneous industrial crops about doubling this figure. Green-manure crops cover some 600,000 acres and form an integral part of cropping practice. Tea now covers only some 75,000 acres, grown on perhaps 30,000 farms only. Silk mulberry trees occupy no more than 450,000 acres, against the total of about 1,250,000 acres in 1940. Silk production has decreased notably since the start of World War II; it may never recover its former importance. The total number of cattle in 1950 stood at its maximum figure, 2,461,000. Pigs are again increasing, the 1950 total being about 625,000, some two thirds of the total of the 1930's. There are close to 400,000 sheep and a slightly larger total of goats. Chickens total some 22,000,000, and rabbits number about 3,500,000, both figures being markedly lower than the pre-war totals.

As the above rather tabular paragraphs suggest, Japanese modernization included setting up of statistical services, and there are better data for Japan than for most parts of the Orient. In agriculture and rural economy in general the data are somewhat under-reported, owing to a traditional fear of the tax collector.

In the modernization of Japan in the last century the percentage of the population concerned with agriculture has steadily declined. The total of farm families today is only slightly higher than it was in the 1860's, and the total agricultural land is also only slightly greater. But the percentage of farmers dropped from about 80 per cent to close to 41 per cent in 1940, there being a small increase in farmers after the end of World War II. This latter increase may or may not be a temporary thing, dependent upon the success of industrial rehabilitation in the near future. Though the total land and farmers have increased but little, the volume productivity of agriculture has increased significantly in the last century. The introduction of new crops and cropping practices, the marked increase in the use of commercial fertilizers, and a general intensification and efficiency of crop growing, all have been contributing factors. Japan for centuries has followed Chinese practices of using night soil, green manures, stream and pond mud, and other forms of fertilization. Per-acre yields for many crops put Japan among the leaders of the world today.

The dominance of rice in the agricultural scene suggests that as the southern peoples spread northward over Japan they carried southern land-use patterns with them. Slowly short-season rice varieties, terracing, careful water control, and other cropping practices spread with them. Rice is the single most important crop on the northern island of Hokkaido, just as it is in Kyushu, but few of the other subtropical crops reach this far north. Rice is cultivated on over half of the farms of Japan. Almost all rice grown is of the wet-field variety, upland rice everywhere being a minor item. Rice is chiefly a crop of the alluvial lowlands, but in many areas of lesser slope the terracing has reached well into the uplands.

Many of the upland fields of Japan today are only crudely terraced or leveled, and they lack water control facilities. Dry-field crops thus are significant items in the total agriculture. Though the crop list is a large one, and though rice does not dominate the agriculture of Japan as fully as that of modern Burma or Thailand, Japanese agriculture remains essentially that of the Orient, intensive but not extremely efficient, varied in crops but limited in the range of its application. Agriculture is what the Japanese farmer could make it, with hand tools and a limited range of examples from which to choose his land-use patterns. There has been no agricultural revolution in Japan, corresponding to the industrial revolution that has taken place in the last century.

It is normal to suggest that much of Japan is too steep in slope to permit a significant increase in the amount of agricultural land beyond that cultivated in recent centuries. It is also a common generalization that in all Japan today there are only a few hundred thousand acres of reserve land that can be turned into productive farms, and that most of this is marginal land for which the costs rival the potential return. This is a traditional view, and it is the traditional attitude of Japanese leaders, both in and out of government. It fails to take into account the most efficient developments in mountain agriculture elsewhere in the world. There is ample ground to suggest that, if a realistic program were conceived beyond the traditional oriental pattern, looking to tree and bush crops, upland animal economy, industrial crop production, the extension of mountain and arctic-margin varieties of land use, there are many upland areas of relatively gentle slope that could be brought into effective land use.

What is needed is a fresh outlook upon land use, a program of the world study of agriculture, which could promote something of the same kind of revolution that the Japanese leaders brought to the manufacturing economy of Japan. One is duly impressed by the facts that in Japan today there is very little wastage of lowland arable lands, and that on the existing farms there is no small patch of ground wasted. It is also impressive that in the industrial expansion of Japan a minimum of farmland was diverted from agricultural productivity, in contrast to the situation in parts of the United States where urban land developments of the last century have often driven the farmer off the very best crop lands. Nevertheless, a large area of uplands is still unused, and it does not seem true that there is no opportunity for the expansion of Japanese agriculture.

· The physiologic and agricultural population densities of Japan are among the highest in the world. The regional crowding of farmers and farmland is strongest, of course, in Kyushu, Shikoku, and parts of southern Honshu, and naturally least in Hokkaido, which is the least productive portion of Japan as to agriculture. Most of the farms are very small, the country-wide average being a little over 2 acres. The Japanese farm often is fragmented in location and is divided into wet and dry plots, so that an individual farm often consists of from two to ten individual field plots in several locations. The farms of the south are smaller on the average than those of the north.

The size of a farmstead itself has an influence upon the frequency of draft animals kept on Japanese farms, many farms being too small to maintain an animal. Cattle are the chief draft animals; horses originally came into Japan as part of the military cult but now are often used as draft animals. Fewer than 3,000,000 animals of draft age are available, and a larger number would unduly tax the present food supply. Since some farms keep more than one animal, it appears that less than half of the farmers have their own power supply for ploughing and certain other selected chores. Cattle predominate in the south, with horses more popular in the northern regions of larger farms. The small Japanese cow eats less and poorer food than the horse, and its lower work capacity is adequate on the small southern farms. Even so draft animals are not fully utilized, and too much agricultural labor remains hand labor in all parts of Japan. Water buffalo are not used anywhere in Japan. Farming in Japan is essentially a family matter, there are few permanent agricultural laborers, and the seasonal or part-time labor supply on farms is a small volume only.

Multiple cropping of farmlands is a normal part of agriculture in southern Japan, but it lessens northward and is seldom followed in northern Honshu and Hokkaido. This is true both on rice lands and on dry and upland fields. Related to this multiple cropping is the variety of regional cropping patterns. Southern Japan shows the greatest variety of crop production, with most of the crops cultivated in Japan showing up in some degree. Northward of Tokyo many crops progressively drop out of the productive pattern. Crop variety is still slight in Hokkaido. In part this reflects climatic limitations, but the recency of the occupation of northern Honshu and Hokkaido is also important.

Hokkaido, in particular, shows many of the features of the frontier fringe, in which the full variety of land use has not yet had time to develop. In southern Japan the most favorable areas produce two rice crops per year. More common is one summer rice crop followed by a winter crop of another sort. The difficulty of properly draining them of excess water has limited winter cropping of many ricefields. There is increasing use of furrow irrigation for crops grown on what are termed dry fields. Multiple cropping also involves intercropping, with several crops planted in alternate rows, with harvests variably timed, and with replanting on rows vacated by previous crops.

Though Japan has moved steadily toward an intensification of agriculture, there remains even today in the upland regions a considerable amount of shifting cultivation. This practice is declining slowly as upland farms are roughly terraced, but terracing is expensive, and little of it is being done today. Shifting cultivation is seldom found in the uplands south of central Honshu. The very continuance of this rather primitive system of land use suggests that there are areas in which a more efficient permanent land-use system could be installed, to the productive advantage of the agricultural economy of Japan.

FISHERIES

The Japanese have long shared the common oriental liking for fish and other aquatic food products. Japanese fishing techniques include most of those common throughout the Orient. Fishing of the shore waters of the Inland Sea was one of the basic elements of economy by the beginning of the Christian era. As the Japanese spread northward along the coasts of Honshu fishing villages were among the early settlements. During the centuries prior to the closing of Japan by the Tokugawa, fishermen ranged over much of the Yellow Sea, the Sea of Japan, and the offshore waters around Japan itself. During the Tokugawa period only the immediate shore waters were fished, but by this time the Japanese had learned to use many aquatic foods, in a range of variety well beyond that common in the Occident. The rise of population in the last century, and the modern techniques learned abroad, have led to a remarkable development of the fishery industry in modern Japan, with the result that the Japanese eat more fish per capita, harvest a larger volume of fishery products, and export more fish than does any other country.

Fresh-water inland sources of fish are not very important in Japan. The pond raising of fish dates only from the nineteenth century, and the culture pearl industry from 1915. The Japanese fishery industry, therefore, is essentially a marine fishery. Japan lies close to the zone of mixture of northern and southern ocean currents, and is surrounded by waters rich in aquatic life. Though the number of fish species is less than that found in southern waters, the Japanese have developed their modern fisheries to a greater extent than those of any other oriental country. The use of simple power boats has been an integral part of this modern development, along with the application of line and trawl techniques. After 1920 the Japanese in the fishing industry developed to a greater degree than found elsewhere, the floating fish cannery, the mother ship serviced by many small power boats. Japanese concerns have engaged in fishing along the whole coast of Asia, as far south as Singapore and the Indies, and as far north as the Bering Sea and the Gulf of Alaska. Though this extensive distribution of fishing sometimes was handmaiden to military intelligence, it was a profitable economic venture in its own right.

Many of the fishermen of Japan are farmers who engage in seasonal or part-time fishing, using small sail boats and working the shore waters within a radius of a few miles only. This variety of fishing has produced the largest share of the total catch, and has in good part supplied the domestic supply of fish, seaweeds, shell fish, and miscellaneous aquatic foods. This is the traditional fishery pattern, which ranges from following the ebb tide as a beachcomber to the small boats that dot the shore waters and fill the harbors. The offshore fisheries are chiefly those developed by organized groups and corporate concerns, fishing with modern equipment. Most of this catch is canned and is a contribution to the export trade. Since early in the present century the Japanese export of fishery products has been a major item in foreign trade. This trade was carefully built up, with such consequences as herring being shipped to Great Britain and tuna to the United States.

The productivity of the offshore Japanese fisheries in part depended upon the spread of political power with the growth of empire. Japan now finds herself restricted somewhat as to fishing waters. She is prohibited from ranging widely in the Pacific, and no longer can she fish Soviet arctic waters. This will restrict the volume of the catch and will reduce the export trade quota, but fisheries will continue to be important in the over-all Japanese economy. It is likely that the immediate shore waters and the offshore regions open to Japan will be fished intensively in the future, as population rises and the pressure upon food supply increases. In 1949 almost 500,000 fishing boats of all types were again operating, with a larger tonnage than during pre-war years. The total number of fishermen of all types well exceeds 1,000,000 persons at the present time. In 1951 fisheries production was over 8,500,000,000 pounds, reasonably close to the pre-war total. Government restriction of fishing in shore waters, to prevent depletion, may well prevent the further increase of fish production.

COMMUNICATIONS AND TRANSPORT

The earliest Japan of which we know was essentially a region using the waterways of the many bays and the Inland Sea of the southern parts of the country. The northern folk used a network of mountain paths and trails. The Japanese learned to build the stone-paved step roads used by the Chinese in hilly landscapes, and adopted the shoulder pole and the sedan chair for primary use on these roads. They also took over the ox sled, the wheel barrow, and the two-wheeled ox cart for use on locally smooth surfaces. They also learned the better building of boats from the Koreans and possibly the Chinese. From the continent the horse was adopted by the Japanese leaders as an element in military tactical transport for their own better control of the peasantry.

Slowly the Japanese adapted these mechanisms of transport to their own home environment. Small boats and ships, and also the detailed patterns and uses of land transport, were altered to fit the local situation. The coasts of Japan were dotted with harbor and port facilities, and the network of roads gradually spread thickly over southern Japan, increasing in the north also to a fairly close network. The trunk roads of this old system were important elements in the system of political control of Japan. Before the coming of the occidental, however, the Chinese and Korean origins of the Japanese transport system remained very clear. In the program of modernization of the last century the Japanese effectively revolutionized most of their system of transport and communications.

They soon began building both naval and merchant shipping and, within recent decades, the Japanese sea transport equipment, naval, mercantile offshore, and coastal, has ranked high among the world's fleets. Port and harbor development has accompanied the growth of boats and ships. The opportunities offered by World War I were capitalized upon effectively, when other shipping was scarce, and the Japanese mercantile fleet has been among the world's large fleets since that time. Scarcely a port in the world of any significance is unfamiliar with the Japanese freighter, and this commercial fleet has not only facilitated the growth of

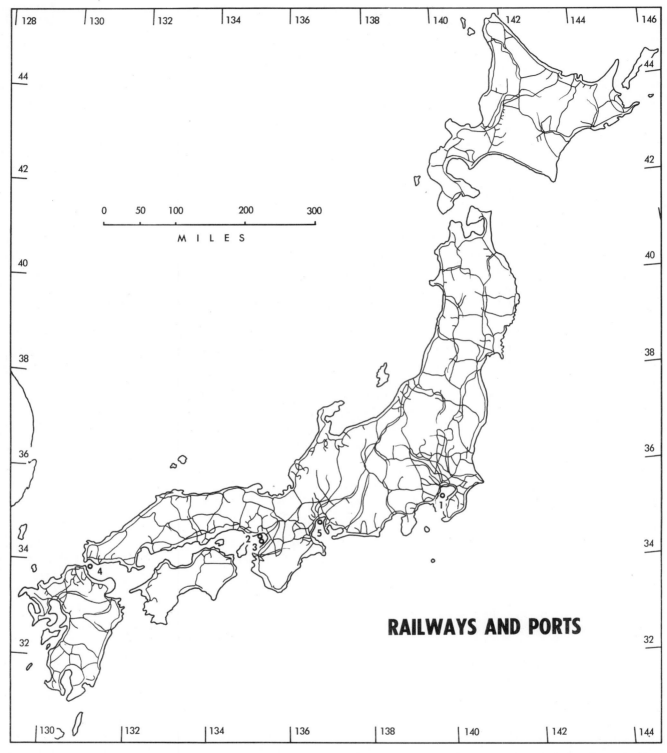

RAILWAYS AND PORTS

Fig. 132. Railways and chief foreign trade ports of Japan. All rail lines are shown, regardless of ownership and gauge. There are over 700 ports used by domestic coastal trade. About forty ports are open to foreign shipping, but over 90 per cent of the foreign trade by value is handled through: (1) Yokohama-Tokyo, (2) Kobe, (3) Osaka, (4) Moji-Shimonoseki, and (5) Nagoya.

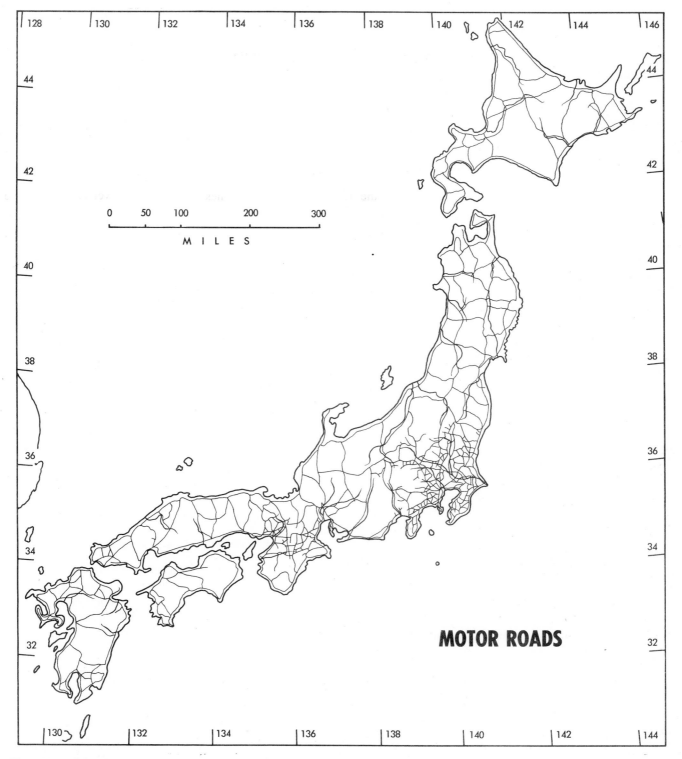

Fig. 133. Motorable roads of Japan. Included here are national and prefectural roads, usually improved and surfaced. There are many more narrow local, village, and town roads suitable to wheeled but non-automotive equipment.

Japanese world trade but also earned its way in the world's general ocean trade.

On land the Japanese launched into a program of railroad building that has given it the most effective rail system of any part of the Orient. Since Japan is a small country, elongated and divided into many islands, it has no region that is far from the sea, and so the actual mileage of rail lines and roads required was far less than that needed by China or India. Sheer mileage is here of less significance than the utility and efficiency. Rail lines are of several sorts, ranging from the long-distance railway carrying freight and passenger trains, through the rapid interurban transit lines around large cities, to the urban street-car systems found in several cities. The Japanese railways are of meter gauge, for economy of building in a mountainous country, and their rolling stock is light weight. The main rail system is government owned and operated, but there are numerous private short feeder lines. Compared to Great Britain the rail system is neither as dense a network nor as efficient a system, but it carries a tremendous passenger traffic and a respectable freight volume. Many of the key rail lines follow the old trunk roads of earlier periods, serving political ends as well as economic ones.

Roads in Japan have never been fully modernized, since they are less necessary in the political control of the country. Only a small mileage of modern motor roads has been built, and these are less effective in modern transport than are the rail lines. A network of narrow roads of relatively steep gradient in the mountainous terrain has resulted, many of them but little wider than the old step roads. Roads are chiefly of local utility in the rural regions of Japan and were not key items in the industrial modernization of the country. Around the large cities fairly adequate road systems were laid out to facilitate industrial development. Many of the roads on the alluvial lowlands are narrow and elevated above the ricefields. Most road traffic is local in character, and involves carts, wagons, bicycles, and foot traffic. Interlocking with these roads is the old network of local paths, trails, and step roads that long has serviced the villages and hamlets of rural Japan. Even though the road system is less well developed than the rail system, the road map indicates that Japan is fairly well connected by roads open to modern vehicular traffic, though few of these roads could carry the types and volumes of traffic that roll over many American highways. The number of motor vehicles puts Japan second in rank to India among the oriental countries, with some 165,000 in 1952. These vehicles chiefly provide transport services in and around the cities of Japan. Cross-country bus lines and long-distance motor transport services in Japan are relatively unimportant, trains here chiefly providing for passenger traffic.

Air transport was relatively slow to develop in modern Japan which, itself, does not greatly need air services. It was only with the political and economic development of the colonial empire that air services began to be developed. The decade of the 1930's showed a striking expansion of civil air services. Aviation became chiefly a military function with the growing imperialism of Japan in recent decades. There is a good network of airfields throughout Japan which can serve whatever ends the Japanese wish in the matter of air transport.

Telecommunications were of interest to the leaders of Japan in the furtherance of modernization, and Japan today has a widely distributed set of telegraph, telephone, and radio facilities. The rural population has not made much personal use of modern communications systems, but they are a significant element in the governmental, industrial, and urban development of modern Japan. Japanese developments in this field were greater than those of other parts of the Orient to the end of World War II.

The Japanese port and the city impress the occidental visitor, as he is impressed elsewhere, with the variety and multiplicity of transport and communications facilities. Some of the oldest forms still are in use, along with many features still quite new in the Occident. Human porters using the shoulder pole, carts, wagons, bicycles, rickshas, street cars, trucks, passenger cars, and scurrying taxis are jumbled together in a kind of traffic pattern never seen in the occidental city.

THE GROWTH OF MODERN INDUSTRY

Prior to World War II Japan was the best example of an industrial country outside the Occident. Other portions of the world today are rapidly undergoing industrialization, and Japan now is going through a period of rehabilitation and reform in her industrial patterns. The present is a period of transition, but Japanese industrial production still is a noteworthy volume, and it is reasonable to expect that it will increase in the future.

In the 1860's there was a considerable volume and variety of manufacturing in Japan, modeled upon the handicraft patterns of Korea and China. Household industry of a primary sort was very widely spread, and less widespread, simple powered and community workshop patterns were highly developed. Japanese artisans were skilled in the textile manufactures, in bamboo and wood, porcelains, lacquer, and in many of the metals. There were few large urban centers of man-ufacturing, and there was but a small volume of power available, other than human energy, the auxiliary power being chiefly derived from water wheels. Charcoal was the primary source of fuel and energy. Japanese leaders quickly realized that these facilities, skills, and products were inadequate in the modern world.

As previously suggested an interlocking pattern of government and private initiative sponsored the modernizing of manufacturing in Japan. A determination that Japan not become a colonial holding of some occidental power predisposed part of the program. The refusal to utilize foreign capital concentrated control and ownership in the hands of a few leading combines, but also meant that only as capital resources accumulated could the program increase its own rate of development. The periods between 1890 and 1900, 1913 and 1920, and 1930 and 1941 were important periods for the growth of industry.

An early concentration upon light manufacturing and the textile industries was rather natural, since it could call upon many old skills at least partially usable in the new patterns. Most of the rural population of Japan was too poor to buy the industrial output, and the need for additional income led to a development of the export trade, which could help pay for the needed imports of raw materials. Gradually developments in the chemical industries, the iron and steel industries, and in general metals manufacturing began to rise. There was an early concentration upon hydroelectric development to provide an adequate power supply, but there has been a steady increase in power development throughout the whole period since the 1890's.

Cheap labor and the fairly close integration of community workshop manufacturing of many individual parts in small shops associated with the larger factories permitted Japan to undersell many occidental firms in supplying consumer goods to the world. Lower operating efficiency often was compensated by multiple shift operation of factories at a time when the "swing" and "graveyard" shifts had not yet become common in the Occident. Though the Japanese home market consumed but a small share of the industrial output, rural Japan contributed to the growth of industrialization through bearing a much heavier share of the national tax burden than did the commercial and manufacturing sectors of Japanese society.

About 1930 it was commonly stated that Japanese industry was concentrated upon the textile and light manufacturing fields but had not yet made great headway in heavy industry. Of this the Japanese were well aware, and after 1930 a noticeable shift in the industrial program took place. Consumer goods, textiles, and light manufacturing were steadily reduced in emphasis as a concentration began upon the heavier variety of manufacturing. Increasing efficiency and greatly increased labor skills made possible this sort of shift, but the increasing capital resources of Japan were also significant.

In the early stages of the growth of manufacturing the regional development was most marked in and around the large cities from Tokyo southward along the Inland Sea. Here were concentrated the larger share of the artisan skills and the older patterns of manufacturing. As hydroelectric and thermal power development made power available in many parts of Japan there was a gradual regional diffusion of manufacturing. As the development of mining, and the growth of the iron and steel industries took place, some activity began to show up all over Japan. With the maturing of secondary manufacturing, using by-products, related skills and new materials, there developed an industrial region stretching from Tokyo to the northern part of Kyushu, with nodal concentrations in and around the large cities. Smaller regional industrial locations developed in northern Honshu and southern Hokkaido. There began a drift of population from rural Japan to the industrial region and the large cities of Japan.

Early in the program it became obvious that Japan proper did not possess all the mineral resources necessary to a great industrial growth, either in volume or in variety. More and more the colonial empire was called upon to furnish raw materials, and gradually there developed a pattern of decentralization of manufacturing at various points throughout the empire. Korea, Manchuria, and Formosa, all shared in the growth of Japanese manufacturing, and both their raw materials and their manufactured goods were integrated into the industrial operations of Japan proper.

The most significant Japanese mineral resource is coal, but it lacks the range of quality needed in a strong industrial economy, being poor in coking coals. Kyushu and Hokkaido possess the largest reserves, but the mines of Honshu have been turning out the largest volumes. The volume is adequate to a small industrial use for a long period, but in the projected use pattern of the late 1930's the coal supply would be exhausted in a century. Korea and Manchuria supplied the necessary coals for blending with Japanese coal in industrial processes.

The petroleum resources of Japan are small, and the annual production has never been large. Northwestern Honshu and Hokkaido are the regions of Japan proper that possess petroleum, though Japan formerly drew an annual production from Sakhalin.

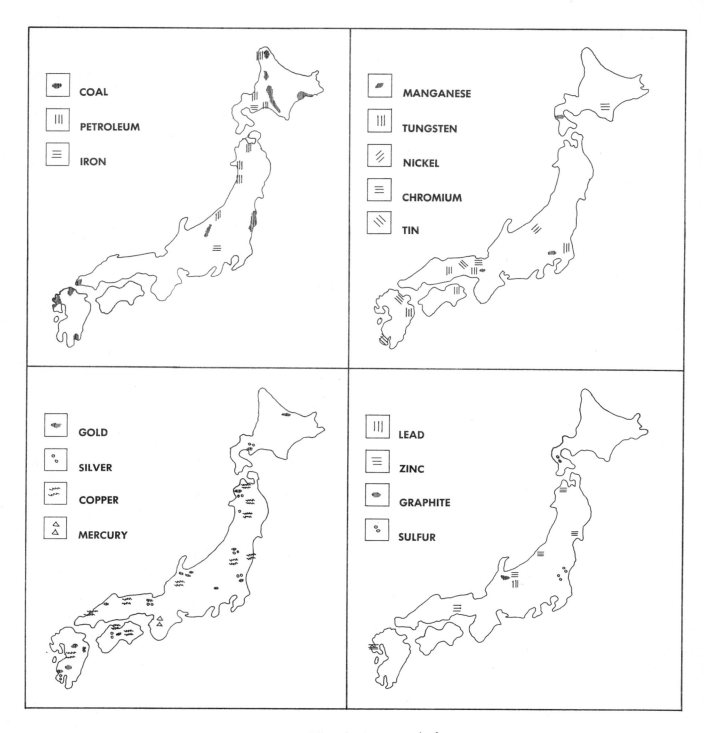

Fig. 134.   Mineral occurrences in Japan.

Compensating for this shortness of industrial fuel supply, Japan now has many hydroelectric plants, most of which are small in capacity but effective in providing a widely distributed power supply. Nearly 1,500 hydro plants have a maximum output close to 6,500,000 kilowatts, but not all plants can operate at the maximum rating, since there is a strong seasonality to water flow in many parts of Japan. There were, of course, numerous thermal power stations which raised the total power capacity to over 9,000,000 kilowatts.

Iron ores are widely scattered over Japan, but they normally are mixed ores of variable quality occurring in small volume, rather difficult and expensive to mine and to smelt. These were adequate to a handicraft economy, but not to an advanced industrial economy.

The emphasis upon electrification led to the development of copper mining and, for a peacetime economy, domestic sources are adequate. Ores are widely scattered over Japan. Military industry during the period 1933–1945 required more copper than provided by domestic sources, and a greatly increased manufacturing pattern probably would again make Japan dependent upon outside sources. Some of the copper ores contain sufficient amounts of gold and silver for normal Japanese use. Sulphur is a mineral present beyond normal Japanese needs, but for most of the rest of the auxiliary industrial minerals Japan has but partial supplies, and does not have tremendous reserves. Dependent upon the scale of industrial use Japan needs small to large volumes of many of the ferro-alloys, lead, tin, zinc, graphite, refractories, and phosphates. Bauxite is entirely lacking in Japan.

In summary Japan is not rich in minerals. Only sulphur is truly surplus to an industrial economy. Coal, gold, copper, and chromium are sufficient for a modest industrial program, but not for a large one. The shortages of iron ore, petroleum, the ferro-alloys, bauxite, and several auxiliary minerals are serious. The large agricultural need for phosphates makes the shortage in this mineral serious. So long as Japan possessed a colonial empire many of these home shortages could be bridged, but the post-war Japanese industrial economy is handicapped. How greatly it is handicapped depends upon what level of operation can be achieved and is permitted by the nations victorious in World War II. The shortages could be the very pretext for another effort at colonial empire when the situation is opportune.

As industrial development matured, government maintained a strong directive influence upon its course, but actual ownership increasingly trended into the hands of a small number of supercorporations owned by the big families. The chief of these, Mitsui, Mitsu-

bishi, Sumitomo, Yasuda, and Fuji controlled literally hundreds of industrial, mining, and trading concerns, interwoven in very complex patterns. With the development of the colonial empire a few lesser combines grew, and there were many small manufacturing concerns not directly owned by but tributary to the large concerns. Much of the remaining community workshop manufacturing was independent but also at the mercy of government control. During the 1930's there was considerable consolidation and streamlining of industrial ownership, and government again began to participate. With the end of the war there was attempted, at the behest of occupation forces, the complete dissolution of the great holding companies. By 1948 this process had been fairly well completed, at the cost of considerable industrial productivity. So long as any phase of the occupation continues a reconcentration of industrial power may be prevented, but it is doubtful if public ownership of industry through stock ownership will long continue once the occupation ceases.

As Japan began to consolidate her industrial machinery, after 1937, toward military production there was a steady decline in light industry, home handicraft manufacturing, and the production of consumer goods. These could no longer be sold abroad and were little needed in Japan. Industry became very markedly heavy manufacturing which increasingly was military industry. The end of the war brought Japanese manufacturing almost to a standstill, therefore, and rehabilitation has been slow both because of the necessary reorientation of production and because of the above-mentioned disruption of ownership and management.

Post-war manufacturing now begins to show a trend toward the production of high quality products for foreign trade rather than the cheapest consumer goods which had marked the trade of the early 1930's. The actual patterns of manufacturing in Japan in the near future will depend, to considerable extent, upon the admittance of Japanese products into foreign markets rather than upon the potentialities of Japanese industry itself. The simple index of production in 1951, compared to a base of 100 in the years 1935–1938, stood at 102.6, but, when readjusted for the increased population and labor supply, it stood at only 85.9. Metals, machinery, and chemicals stand highest in productive ratio, with textiles and non-durable consumer goods still markedly suffering from the wartime reduction. The home market still does not consume an appreciable share of the product of Japanese industry, since no strong appetite and cultural trend toward modernization of styles in consumer goods has yet developed, and since the Japanese population still suffers a lower purchasing power at the high inflationary post-war price levels.

In summary, it must be stated that Japanese industry is today capable of manufacturing many more goods than it now is producing. This productive capacity today is hedged about by many political restrictions both in the domestic and in the international fields. It is a frankly debatable situation as to future trends. On the one hand, there is the urge to prevent Japanese industry from again becoming too strong in those fields amenable to rapid conversion to a war potential—a very strong urge in the immediate post-war years—and, on the other hand, there now is appearing the urge to build Japanese industry into a bulwark to a free world against Communist aggression. These are both political issues influenced from abroad rather than issues of domestic potential and policy.

THE GROWTH OF TRADE

During the long period of Tokugawa control of Japan there had been very little foreign trade, and even domestic trade was restricted to little more than local trade. With the opening of Japan to the world, there began a tremendous change in patterns of productivity, with a consequent large-scale development of trade, both domestic and foreign. From the very start the leaders of Japan attempted to arrange a favorable pattern, by which she exported chiefly manufactured and processed commodities and imported raw materials. This was not always entirely possible, of course, but in the long run it is true that Japan never descended to the role of supplier of raw materials that is characteristic of so many of the other oriental countries.

During the early decades, after the 1860's, Japanese exports consisted of such items as raw silk and tea, both of which were really processed commodities, silk textiles, porcelains, lacquerware, and the other manufactured products of community workshop industry. Quite early there began the import of minerals, raw cotton and other fibers, food grains, and lumber. As industrial production began to rise there appeared in the export list cotton textiles, cement, glass, chemicals, varied consumer products, and simpler items of machinery. Accompanying this export trade, other raw products began to flow into Japan, such as rubber and sheet and shaped metal products to be further processed. Gradually a wide range of exports began to flow out of Japan, and the import volume continued to expand and to rise.

From the start oriental sources of raw materials were important, and oriental markets for manufactured goods ranked high on the list. The United States for a long period ranked high also, both as a source of imports and as a market for the products of industry and agriculture. The United States steadily consumed the largest share of Japanese silk and tea, Japan replacing China as a supplier on both counts. As Japanese shipping increased in volume raw materials were drawn from all over the world, and exports flowed to all parts of the world. The United States, China, India, and the Indies have been the biggest single sources of raw materials and markets for export goods. Japan successfully competed with Great Britain, the United States, Germany, and France in oriental markets for her export products, lower quality and cheaper prices being relied upon to appeal to the larger bulk of the population having a low purchasing power. In the American market Japan concentrated for several decades on low-priced products which could undersell the increasingly costly domestic manufactures of the United States. The dime-store trade was a significant share of this market for manufactured goods, and Japanese manufacturers were skillful in meeting the commodity pattern.

Within Japan, as mineral and forest products from many local regions began to be needed in the growing industrial centers an important coastwise shipping trade began which handled the bulk of internal commodity movements. Railway traffic in coal, wood products, rice, and a few other commodities has been significant, but is less important than water traffic. In respect to the wide range of domestic consumer goods, however, there has not developed a tremendous growth of internal trade in Japan, which still restricts its purchases to local products.

In recent decades Japan has added such new raw material imports as petroleum, bauxite, copper, lead, zinc, tin, and iron ore to its earlier list, as the shift in industrial emphasis took place. A serious decline in the export of raw silk was temporarily damaging, with long-range reactions in land use, as noted earlier. After 1937 the Japanese export trade began to decline in range and volume of commodities, and the import trade changed its character markedly in order to provide strategic war materials. The colonial empire supplied a considerable share of the imports of food products and raw materials, taking a share of the exports as well. And during the war years Japan drew a wide range of commodities from the occupied areas in an exchange which could hardly be called trade.

With the tightening of economic bonds after 1937, government restriction of production, local trade, and consumption patterns altered the range and variety of domestic trade. Adoption of controlled patterns of food collection after harvests from rural Japan distorted these domestic trade patterns.

The end of the war brought trade to a standstill, both in domestic and foreign markets. Political controls over manufacturing, fishing, exports, and imports have not yet ceased, and there still is government collection of several crops after harvest. In 1950–1951 between a third and a fourth of Japanese imports consisted of food products. The trade patterns of Japan still are abnormal in 1954, and are likely to be slow in reaching a stable level. Post-war Japan trade shows a marked contrast with that of pre-war years, a large adverse balance. This is partially made up of invisible items such as American Army expenditures, and government aid, but in turn this is offset by reparations payments to several oriental countries. Large food and machinery imports now complicate the attempt to achieve a balance. The loss of a large portion of Japanese shipping during World War II is a significant factor in trade difficulty at the present time. Slowly Japan's patterns of trade are reconstituting themselves, but it again must be noted that these patterns now are artificial and hedged about with political restrictions upon commodity movements and currency exchange in such a way as to make the whole subject of trade dependent upon political decision more than upon the relative need and opportunity for economic exchange.

THE COLONIAL EMPIRE

Rightly or wrongly the leaders of Japan decided that if they were to modernize and meet the world on its own terms they, too, must have a colonial empire. The opening section of this chapter itemized the steps taken to add to the territory of Japan. The Japanese leaders thought it was necessary and, with the changes that occurred in Japanese economy, the additions were necessary to provide additional resources required to follow the program that was adopted. But could a different program have been adopted? It is now a question of political and military history, but the question can be asked as to whether a colonial empire really was necessary to the modernization of Japan. Though the past phase of this question now is hypothetical, it has a bearing on the future of a Japan that was built up partly by means of a colonial empire.

Japan in the 1850's was living almost entirely on its own resources. The mass of the population lived frugally, but the upper classes lived very well by any standard in the world at the time. The total population was close to 30,000,000, and the cultivated land was not markedly less than it is today, though total food crop production was lower then than now. Many

mineral resources were not then being utilized, and the forest resources were more than adequate. It is probable that the stimulation of social and trade contact with the Orient, with its impact upon internal economy and patterns of living, would have resulted in some population increase. It was not required, however, that the leaders of Japan emphatically encourage a pronounced rise in the birth rate in order to reorient the economy of Japan. It was not actually necessary to build a large army and navy to prevent colonial encroachment by the occidental powers. Colonial encroachment had resulted in those countries in which governments were ineffective, and in which cultural institutions were not developed to meet changing conditions, but Japan in 1860 remained untouched by colonial infringement.

More careful and discerning planning, it seems to me, could have started Japan upon a course of modernization which would not have required a large army and navy, which would have remade the old patterns of economy on a comprehensive basis and which would have lifted the standards of living for all Japanese. If agricultural modernization had been carried out along with the introduction of an industrial revolution, the productive capacity of the country would have increased at a more balanced rate, and would have developed no tremendous shortages in any line. Certain it is that Japan could not have provided all the raw materials she needed to meet all requirements, but many of these were not provided in her colonial empire anyway. Capital investment in the colonial empire could have been used within Japan proper to accomplish ends never met in the other way.

There is room for much argument on this subject, but Japanese leaders did not have the perspective of the present and chose a particular path. Along that path they expended large resources upon military effort, invested huge sums in colonial development, increased the scope of their plans, and built up a pattern of political, psychological, and military thinking that in the end came to dominate over sound economic thinking with regard to the purposes of modernization and industrial expansion. If they had come out of World War II victorious, the whole program could have been rationalized as being justified. Japan having been the loser, it is obvious that there has been tremendous waste and that now certain problems have come home to roost very uncomfortably in the restricted physical and cultural environment of a post-war Japan that possesses no colonial empire into which to move population and out of which to draw cheap products.

The Ryukyu Islands were of no marked material profit to Japan, though their strategic value in a further colonial expansion was, and is, obvious. Korea was a profitable venture, in sheer economic terms, for every possible product was drained out of Korea for almost a half century, and the total value received must have been greater than that expended. Formosa, likewise, was a profitable acquisition. The economic balance in the case of Manchuria is not so obvious, and neither is that of Sakhalin. The ventures in China proper, from 1932 onward, were unprofitable in most respects. The Marianas-Caroline-Marshall Islands mandate possibly showed a net result on the economic balance sheet. The last venture, after 1941, undoubtedly did not end with economic profit. In a final kind of accounting, the cost of reparations, destruction inside Japan, and the economic repercussions of some years of post-war life must be set against the previous profits. And now Japan has too many people, too little economic reserve, a disrupted economy, an accumulated volume of hatred and distrust toward her from other peoples, and a tremendous sense of frustration. Perhaps she also has a lingering feeling that, if plans had been a little better, and the breaks of the game a bit more favorable, the whole long program would have succeeded; it would then be unnecessary to debate whether a colonial empire can be made to pay.

POPULATION AND REGIONALISM

The rate of population increase in Japan now appears to be declining, but is it declining rapidly enough? A hopelessly overpopulated Japan can only become another of the world's trouble spots. The physiologic density already is extremely high, and a large amount of the cost of imports now is taken up by food supplies. An excellent system of public health gives Japan the lowest death rate in the Orient. The population still has a large share of young people in the child-bearing age bracket. Unquestionably, therefore, the population total will continue to rise, and there no longer is a colonial empire to which to migrate or in which to earn a living by temporary residence. There is ground for the fear that it will be relatively easy to recruit an army intent on militant change. The 1952 population was close to 85,000,-000, and there is a net annual increase that can scarcely drop far below 1,500,000. Currently between 800,000 and 900,000 new family units are formed annually by marriage, requiring a steady increase in some form of remunerative opportunity. Only a small portion of this can be found in agricul-

ture, and Japan both must further increase her manufacturing economy and be given access to the world's markets. The alternative is that the Japanese standard of living will drop with all the dangers to world peace that result from national privation and political desperation. The prospect for Japan in the coming decades can easily be painted in gloomy colors, for the population of the country can hardly level off short of 100,000,000 unless some drastic factor of change enters the pattern of population increase. This is the specter that will continue to haunt the Japanese long after their leaders chose the path of militant modernization and the excessive encouragement of population increase.

The regional distribution of population in Japan shows considerable inequality. Regional densities are comparatively low for most of Hokkaido and northern Honshu, and for the central Japanese Alps, west of Tokyo. Many other local upland regions possess low densities also. Parts of the southwest coast of Honshu, and the east coasts of both Kyushu and Shikoku are well below the country-wide average. The regions of highest density naturally are those lowland territories surrounding the great cities. In regional terms the lowlands surrounding Tokyo and those fronting on the Inland Sea have the greatest areal densities.

Urbanization is an increasing trend in Japan. In 1920 there were but 16 cities having over 100,000 people each, with another 31 containing over 50,000 each. In 1950 there were 64 cities each over 100,000 in population, and another 84 containing over 50,000 people each. The 1950 totals of population resident in cities of over 100,000 approximated 21,000,000, and the total resident in cities between 50,000 and 100,000 was about 6,000,000. The full number of cities totaling over 30,000 in population in 1950 was 247, with a total population just over 31,000,000. The data for 1948 indicate a total of almost 10,500 compact settlements for the then total of just over 80,000,000 people. It is significant that under 1,100 such settlements contained less than 2,000 people each. The most common settlement category was that ranging from 2,000 to 5,000, with a resident population of almost 20,000,000 people. Almost a third of the total 1948 settlements contained more than 5,000 people each, housing almost two thirds of the total population of Japan. One must use population statistics with care in Japan, for the village and small town often include a considerable rural population, since the political unit often is a regional one which has been changed in area and meaning since 1900. Nevertheless, these data indicate that the Japanese no longer can be considered a rural people, and also that the population no

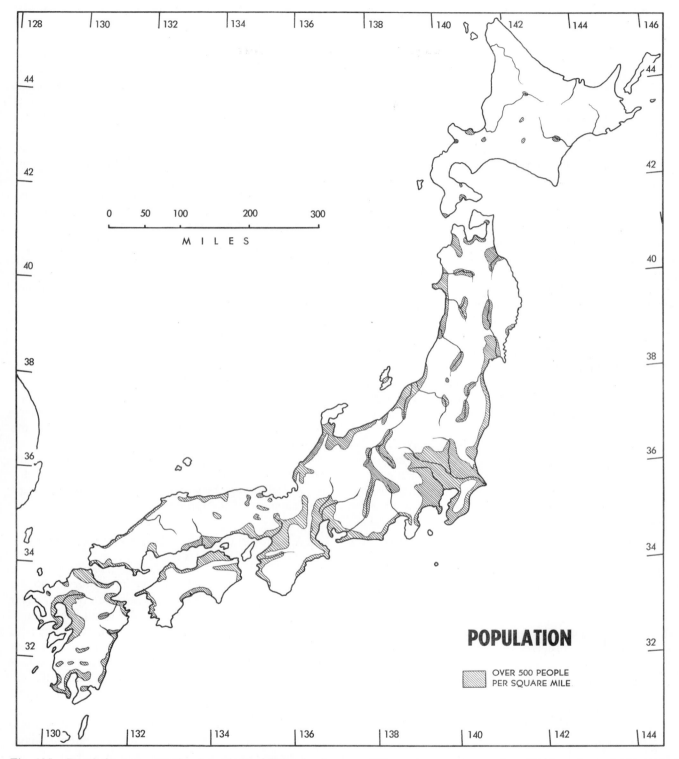

Fig. 135. Population concentration in regions of Japan having over 500 people per square mile. Northern Japan is increasing in density more rapidly than southern Japan at the present time. After Trewartha and *Japanese Statistical Yearbook, 1950.*

longer can be accommodated on farmsteads or in rural hamlets.

Particularly during the years after 1920 the trend to urbanism has been increasing, with many surplus rural persons drifting to the manufacturing centers to become industrial labor. In 1900 some two thirds of the Japanese population could be considered rural or village dwellers, whereas in 1950 the strictly rural population amounted to no more than a third of the total. In many of the smaller and medium-sized towns and cities the simple residence data are less useful, since there is part-time employment both in rural and urban occupations.

Of the really large cities of Japan in 1950 there were only four of over 1,000,000 people each. Tokyo contained 5,385,000, and the other three were Osaka, Kyoto, and Nagoya. Two other large cities were Yokohama and Kobe. If metropolitan limits are substituted for political ones all six cities just named rank among the world's great urban centers. All of them, except possibly Yokohama, are old urban centers developed as the control centers of an agrarian society. Tokyo was one of the earliest cities to exceed 1,000,000 in population in modern times. These key cities have, of course, grown into the chief manufacturing or port cities of modern Japan, and they lead in the urban trend recently developed. No really large city is located in northern Honshu or Hokkaido.

The post-war rise in rural agricultural population is a result of the post-war disruption of manufacturing and foreign trade. This conceivably may be only a temporary trend. The older pattern of inheritance, by which the first son inherited the whole farm, increasingly made for the growth of urbanism in the last century as the rate of population increase picked up. Inheritance laws have been temporarily altered, to increase the chance of an increasing number of younger sons staying on the farm, at the insistence of the occupation forces. However, this will rapidly produce the overfractionalizing of farms into such small units that they are economically unpractical and will shortly undo the whole program of land reform. As this paragraph is written there is occurring further manipulation with laws on land and inheritance, and it is likely both that the occupation forces and the Japanese government will continue to juggle legal procedures in these matters.

Tokyo and its surrounding lowlands today form the heart of Japan in politico-economic matters, and in point of sheer population concentration. The whole of the Inland Sea fringe, however, composes the cultural heart of Japan and also forms the key economic region, both in agricultural and industrial terms. This is chiefly a concentration in the lowlands, and the uplands of southern Japan represent a marginal zone. The central Japanese Alps form a relatively negative block in the center of the country. Northern Honshu still forms a marginal zone of economic and political influence, important in producing mineral and forest products, but one less densely settled and less steeped in the traditional culture. Hokkaido now is emerging from its frontier phase, but in important respects it still is a marginal unit, economically contributing toward, but culturally tributary to, the southern regions of Japan.

In simple terms each of the four big islands Honshu, Hokkaido, Kyushu, and Shikoku forms a regional unit of a sort. All four have important vertical zonations. Honshu consists of many different kinds of areas, lowland and upland, subtropical and microthermal, filled and empty, that break it into several kinds of local regions. By landform, climate, and human occupance Japan consists of hundreds of small units which, upon the application of specific criteria, can be turned into dozens of different kinds of local regional groupings. Such elements as language, race, religion, and cultural affinity are less significant in producing regionalisms within Japan than they are in most other parts of the Orient. In these matters settlement history and the spread of a composite southern culture have produced a marked degree of uniformity. Today one of the chief regionalisms lies between the rural agricultural folk and the permanently urban population, for differences in patterns of living here are as great today as are differences between ethnic and culture groups in other parts of the Orient.

CAN THE UNITED STATES REMODEL JAPAN?

Japan again is a small country in territory, with the population that should go with a large country. Her system of food production, in spite of all the changes and improvements introduced, still is that of intensive hoe culture, and is quite inadequate to her needs. Her modernization in matters of material economy still is incomplete. Her over-all demands of productive capacity require far more resources than are available within Japan itself. Her social, cultural, and psychological climate has been altered somewhat, by military defeat and the demands of the victors, but this modernization, too, is incomplete, and it is highly questionable whether it has yet become permanent and real. The material problems of living, compounded by the psychological problems of living on less than is sufficient, provide in Japan a veritable cultural powder

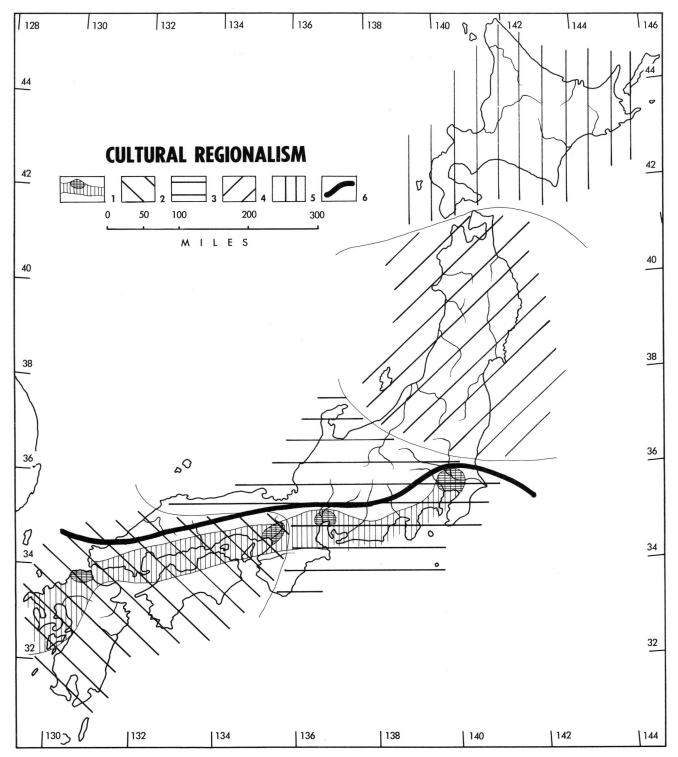

Fig. 136. Cultural regionalism: (1) modern industrial-urban zone and nodal centers; (2) Japanese culture hearth, historical core, subtropical region; (3) central Japan, the region of early historical growth; (4) Tohoku, the old northern frontier region; (5) Hokkaido, the newer modern frontier region; (6) limit of widest effective spread of the southern "subtropical" environment.

keg. No fuse has yet been lighted, but there are many fuses of different lengths leading to the fuel. A few sparks are flying about already, and more are certain to be struck as too many Japanese try to live on too little. If the sparks become too numerous, and too strong, it is only a question of time before one will light a fuse, long or short. If a long fuse became lighted there might be time to act and prevent the explosion, but the danger lies in the lighting of a short fuse that will set off an explosion before the world has time to act. The explosion might assume a Hitlerian form of militant expansion, or it could take the Communist form of advancing the Iron Curtain. It is not a complete certainty that a spark will set off an explosion, nor can its precise timing be suggested. But it is very clear that Japan will require far more cultural coaching and close examination, and will also need far more material assistance to complete her modernization than that given Germany after World War I if the explosion is to be prevented.

After World War II the United Nations established an occupational force in Japan that was directed to reorganize the economic and political patterns of the country. The first directives were clearly aimed at the war potential and at the monopolistic systems of political and economic control that had marked the decades of modernization. Somewhat less clear were the directives in other directions. The United States assumed the chief role in the pattern of occupation. A short period of explicit direction of Japanese affairs was to be terminated by a treaty, after which the Japanese themselves were to assume an increasing role in the further re-arrangement of their own affairs. At the outset American authorities knew too little about Japan, and learning has proceeded slowly. The world at large, and the United States in particular, has shown little appreciation of the real problems of Japan today, even though that appreciation is slowly growing. Economically today Japan is in much the same state as is Great Britain. She must have assistance in technical lines to a greater extent than Great Britain, but she must have real access to the markets of the world for her manufactures if she is to buy the raw materials needed. But culturally Japan is in a different position from that of Great Britain. She needs much skillful assistance in modernization in order that the peculiar and partial patterns of the present be rounded out into a successful blend of East and West.

The Japanese people have shown that they can reorient their cultural patterns. Few other people have so clearly proved their ability at cultural change. But Japanese history suggests that decisive leadership has been a critical element in the process of cultural change. Several times within the historic era a small group of Japanese leaders has turned the tide of cultural movement. When that leadership has limited the range of action to be taken the results have sometimes compounded problems.

The United States, through its directives to occupational forces in Japan, temporarily took over a partial leadership of Japan itself. There was attempted a many-faceted reorganization and further modernization of Japanese society. One facet of this was to attempt improvement in agricultural productivity. Another was to increase the productive efficiency of industry. Still a third facet was to introduce far more of the democratic processes of the operation of society into Japan than had been brought in, and to attempt to abolish the monopolistic control of the country by a small group of leading families. This, in particular, carries heavy implications. Formal occupational control, in 1954, is lessening, and will not continue endlessly. Will the changeable political climate of the United States reflect itself in a changeable set of directives or influences during the remainder of the occupation or the following period of diplomatic contact? Will effective democratic capacity be installed sufficiently to prevent the will of a few, be they the traditional clan families or the newer Communists, from directing the life of Japan?

China let the Japanese copy as they would, and Japanese leaders took what they chose. In the late nineteenth century the whole world let the Japanese copy as they would, and Japanese leaders carefully chose what they took. Can the United States now ensure that the Japanese people, or the leaders of Japan, choose wisely enough to ensure cultural, economic, and political stability, or will it carelessly let too few people do a restricted choosing, let too many sparks be struck, and let the Japanese powder keg explode in some pattern which can again involve the whole Pacific Ocean? The Japanese are a far more able people than has often been thought, and, if care is taken to develop their geographic environment in all its physical and cultural aspects in proper relation to the rest of the world, there is every chance that the destructive sparks can be so restricted that they will not soon ignite a cultural explosion. The United States first called upon Japan to join the modern world. The United States now has the opportunity, in Japan, to lead in the peaceful blending of the cultures of the East and the West.

For Use in Reference

Statistical Abstract

GENERAL AREA AND POPULATION DATA

Region	Area in Square Miles	Population	
The Orient (as treated in this volume)	7,604,879	1,253,000,000	
Pakistan	365,907	75,850,000	1951 est.
India	1,269,640	356,829,000	1951 census
Kashmir (disputed control)	82,258	4,410,000	1951 est.
Ceylon	25,332	7,943,000	1951 est.
Maldive Islands	115	95,000	1951 est.
Nepal	54,000	7,000,000	1951 est.
Bhutan	18,000	300,000	1951 est.
Portuguese India	1,537	680,000	1951 est.
French India	196	330,000	1951 est.
Burma	261,789	18,500,000	1952 est.
Thailand	200,148	18,800,000	1951 est.
Indochina	285,640	28,000,000	1952 est.
Malaya, Federation of	50,850	5,500,000	1952 est.
Singapore, Colony of (including Christmas Island)	286	1,100,000	1952 est.
Indonesia, Republic of (excluding West New Guinea)	575,895	78,000,000	1952 est.
West New Guinea	159,375	350,000	1952 est.
British New Guinea (main island only)	160,240	1,150,000	1951 est.
North Borneo	29,387	331,000	1951 census
Sarawak	47,071	565,000	1952 est.
Brunei	2,226	47,000	1952 est.
Portuguese Timor	7,383	460,000	1952 est.
Philippines	115,600	20,800,000	1952 est.
China	3,643,000	500,000,000	1952 est.
Hongkong	391	2,300,000	1952 est.
Macao	6	450,000	1950 est.
Formosa	13,886	8,700,000	1952 est.
Korea, the whole of	85,228	29,300,000	1952 est.
Japan	147,690	84,300,000	1951 est.
Ryukyu Islands	1,803	950,000	1952 est.

PAKISTAN

Physical Data:

Area in square miles:

West Pakistan	311,406
East Pakistan	54,501
Total	365,907

The two units are separated by a distance of about 900 miles.

Length of coastline: 900 miles.

Chief river: Indus, 1,900 miles long, drainage basin of 372,000 square miles.

Highest mountain: Tirich Mir (northern West Pak.), 25,263 ft.

Acreage Data:

Total area in acres:	234,000,000
Forest	5,500,000
Arable reserve	105,000,000
Annual fallow	10,000,000
Land in farms	56,000,000

Chief Crops: 1950–1952

	Estimates in acres
Rice	22,200,000
Wheat	9,550,000
Millet-gram	4,450,000
Cotton	3,350,000
Jute	1,900,000
Oil seeds	1,900,000
Sorghums	1,300,000
Maize	1,000,000
Sugar cane	850,000
Barley	500,000
Fruit	500,000
Tobacco	200,000

Animal Population: 1951

	Estimates
Cattle	15,000,000
Buffalo	6,000,000
Camels	4,000,000
Goats	1,000,000
Sheep	600,000

Fisheries:

	Estimates
Fishermen	80,000
Annual catch	250,000 tons

Mineral Production: 1951

Coal	513,000 tons
Petroleum	810,000 bbl
Chromite	25,000 tons

Communications: 1950

Railways	7,205 miles track
Roads	62,000 miles
Motor vehicles	26,600
Telegraph lines	27,500 miles
Telephones	18,800 sets
Post offices	6,700

Industrial Production: 1951

Steel	21,000 tons
Cement	507,000 tons
Cotton yarns	19,350,000 lb
Cotton cloth	127,660,000 yards
Electric power	217,000,000 kwhr

Foreign Trade: 1951

Total imports	U.S. $533,200,000
Total exports	U.S. $755,000,000

Banking: Currency: Rupee, value in U.S. $0.30
Banks: 108 with 201 offices

Population: Total in 1951 estimated at 75,850,000

West Pakistan	33,850,000
East Pakistan	42,000,000

Religion:

	Estimates
Moslems	65,000,000
Hindus	9,500,000
Christians	550,000

Cities: 1951

	Estimates
Karachi	1,126,000
Lahore	850,000
Dacca	273,000
Rawalpindi	240,000
Hyderabad	240,000

Schools: 1952

Primary schools	40,300	3,212,000 pupils
Secondary schools	6,500	1,164,000 pupils
Colleges and universities	132	?
Technical schools	221	?

Political:

Member of British Commonwealth, organized in 1954 as Islamic Republic of Pakistan.

National capital: Karachi.

Local divisions: 5 provinces, 9 states, 1 tribal border district, 1 federal capital area.

INDIA

Physical Data:

Area in square miles: 1,269,640 excluding Kashmir
Includes: Andaman Islands, 2,508 square miles
Laccadive Islands, 80 square miles
Dimensions: About 2,000 miles north-south by 1,830 miles east-west.
Length of coastline: 3,500 miles.
Rivers: Brahmaputra, 1,800 miles long, 361,000 square miles in drainage basin, part of which is in East Pakistan.
Ganges, 1,557 miles long, 350,000 square miles in drainage basin, part of which is in East Pakistan.
Godaviri, 900 miles long.
Kistna, 800 miles long.
Narbada, 800 miles long.
Highest mountain: Godwin-Austen (K2), 28,250 ft.

Acreage Data:

Total area in acres:	812,569,000
Forest	93,000,000
Cultivable waste	68,000,000
Annual fallow	60,000,000
Area in farms	340,000,000
Annual area sown	270,000,000
Irrigated area	50,000,000

Chief Crops: 1951

	Estimates in acres
Rice	72,000,000
Millet-gram	40,000,000
Sorghums	36,000,000
Wheat	25,000,000
Cotton	15,600,000
Peanuts	10,400,000
Fodder crops	11,200,000
Maize	7,800,000
Barley	7,000,000
Rape and mustard	5,000,000
Sesamum	4,000,000
Flax seed	4,000,000
Sugar cane	3,700,000
Jute	1,800,000
Castor seed	1,500,000
Tobacco	800,000
Tea	775,000
Coffee	200,000

Animal Population: 1951

	Estimates
Cattle	110,000,000
Buffalo	40,000,000
Goats	47,000,000
Sheep	41,000,000

Index of Agricultural Production (1935–1939 is 100) in 1951–1952 was 102.0.

Fisheries: 1951

Fishermen	400,000
Catch	514,000 tons

Mineral Production: 1950

Coal	32,300,000 tons
Petroleum	1,860,000 bbl
Iron ore	2,970,000 tons
Manganese	2,600,000 tons
Chromite	14,000 tons
Gold U.S.	$6,700,000
Copper ore	360,000 tons
Ilmenite	212,000 tons
Gypsum	206,000 tons
Bauxite	51,000 tons
Mica	16,300 tons

Communications: 1949–1951

Railways	33,860 miles
Roads	250,000 miles
Motor vehicles	151,000
Telegraph lines	110,000 miles
Telephones	171,000 sets
Post offices	37,000
Radio broadcast stations	22
Moving picture theaters	3,250

Industrial Production: 1951

Electric power	5,870,000,000 kwhr
Finished steel	1,094,000 tons
Cement	2,249,000 tons
Cotton yarns	588,000 tons
Cotton cloth	4,084,000,000 yards
Jute products	889,000 tons
Bicycles	114,000
Fertilizers	116,000 tons
Sulphuric acids	109,000 tons
Paper products	134,000 tons

Index of Industrial Production (1937 is 100) in 1951–1952 was 123.0.

Foreign Trade: 1951

Total imports	U.S. $1,804,800,000
Total exports	U.S. $1,594,200,000

Banking: Currency: Rupee, value in U.S. $0.21
Banks: 439, with 4,698 offices in 1950

Population: Total, census of 1951, excluding Kashmir and some of Assam hill country: 356,829,000.

Religions:

	Estimates
Hindus	275,000,000
Moslems	41,000,000
Animists	24,000,000

Christians	6,500,000
Sikhs	6,500,000
Jains	1,500,000
Buddhists	800,000

Cities: Census of 1951

Bombay	2,840,000
Calcutta	2,548,000
Madras	1,416,000
Delhi	1,190,000
Hyderabad	1,085,000
Ahmedabad	788,000
Bangalore	779,000
Kanpur	705,000
Lucknow	496,000
Poona	480,000
Nagpur	450,000
Howrah	433,000

Metropolitan area of Calcutta contains about 3,350,000 people, including Calcutta, Howrah, Tollyganj, Garden Reach, and Behala.

Schools: 1950

Primary schools	206,800	17,402,000 pupils
Secondary schools	19,920	4,700,000 pupils
Colleges and universities	780	335,000 students
Technical schools	25,800	780,000 students

Press: About 4,550 newspapers and magazines published in 1950.

Political: Autonomous member of the British Commonwealth.

National capital: New Delhi.
Local divisions: The hundreds of political units existing before 1947 now are in process of realignment, and in 1952 there were 27 states
Official name of India now is Bharat, with new names being installed for states and some cities.
English now is the official language, but plans call for making Hindi the national language.

CEYLON

Physical Data:

Area in square miles: 25,332; 270 miles north-south by 140 miles east-west.
Chief river: Mahaveli, 206 miles long.
Highest mountain: Pidurutalagala, 8,281 ft.

Acreage Data:

	Estimates in acres
Total area	16,250,000
Forest	3,500,000
Arable reserve	3,500,000
Land in farms	4,000,000

Chief Crops: 1950

	Acres
Rice	1,000,000
Coconut	1,070,000
Rubber	655,000

Tea	560,000
Cassava	185,000
Millets	110,000
Sweet potatoes	62,000
Citronella	34,000
Cinnamon	30,000

Animal Population: 1951

Cattle	1,072,000
Buffalo	658,000
Sheep	51,000
Goats	378,000
Pigs	104,000

Mineral Production: 1950

	Tons
Graphite	12,800
Salt	28,000

Fisheries:

	Estimates
Fishermen	30,000
Catch	60,000 tons

Communications: 1950

Railways	913 miles
Roads	10,500 miles
Motor vehicles	47,300
Telegraph lines	13,300 miles
Telephones (1951)	18,860 sets
Navigable waterways	160 miles
Post offices	1,360

Industrial Production: 1951

Electric power	105,000,000 kwhr
Cotton cloth	8,400,000 yards

Foreign Trade: 1951

Total imports	U.S. $327,300,000
Total exports	U.S. $382,800,000

Banking: Currency: Rupee, value in U.S. $0.21
Banks: 14 in 1951

Population: Total, estimated, 1951, 7,950,000

Ethnic groups: 1951

	Estimates
Singhalese	5,300,000
Ceylon Tamils	940,000
Indian Tamils	820,000
Moors	440,000
Malays	35,000
Burghers	45,000

Religions: 1951

	Estimates
Buddhist	5,000,000
Hindu	1,500,000
Christian	650,000
Moslem	455,000

Cities: 1952

	Estimates
Colombo	400,000
Jaffna	70,000
Galle	55,000
Kandy	54,000

Schools: 1949

Primary schools	6,242	1,247,000 pupils
Secondary schools	585	222,000 pupils
Colleges and universities	2	3,700 students
Technical schools	24	3,100 students

Political:

Dominion of British Commonwealth
Provinces: 9
Capital: Colombo

MALDIVE ISLANDS

Islands: 17 atolls containing several hundred islets, over 300 of which are inhabited.

Area: 115 square miles.

Population: About 95,000.

Autonomous republic administered as a protected state under Commonwealth Relations Office. Often grouped with Ceylon, under which it had been administered until 1948.

KASHMIR

Area: 82,258 square miles.

Population: 4,410,000 estimated in 1951. About 75% of the population is Moslem, and about 20% are Hindus, mainly resident in southeast.

Cultivated land: About 2,300,000 acres are in farms, with perhaps 1,900,000 acres in crop each year. Chief crops are rice, wheat, maize, and barley.

NEPAL

Area: 54,000 square miles.

Highest mountain: Everest, 29,002 ft.

Population: About 7,000,000 estimated 1951.

Capital: Katmandu.

BHUTAN

Area: 18,000 square miles.

Highest mountain: Kula Kangri, 28,870 ft.

Population: About 300,000.

Capital: Punakha.

BURMA

Physical Data:

Area in square miles: 261,789.
Dimensions: 1,260 miles north-south, 575 miles east-west.
Rivers: Salween, 1,750 miles long.
Irrawaddy, 1,250 miles long, drainage basin 160,500 square miles.
Highest mountain: Khakabo, 19,315 ft.

Acreage Data:

Total area in acres:	167,500,000
Forest	96,000,000
Arable reserve	19,000,000
Area in farms	21,600,000

Chief Crops: 1950–1952

	Acres
Rice	9,730,000
Sesamum	1,320,000
Peanuts	700,000
Coconuts	350,000
Millets	600,000
Beans	250,000
Chick peas	230,000
Cotton	220,000
Tobacco	135,000
Rubber	115,000
Maize	90,000
Sugar cane	45,000
Wheat	35,000

Animal Population: 1951

	Estimates
Cattle	4,500,000
Buffalo	815,000
Pigs	400,000
Goats	175,000
Sheep	25,000
Elephants	6,000

Index of Agricultural Production (1935–1939 is 100) 1951 was 73.

Fisheries: 1950

	Estimates
Fishermen	100,000
Catch	330,000 tons

Mineral Production: 1951

Petroleum	708,000 bbl
Lead	6,000 tons
Tin	1,600 tons

Communications: 1950

Railways	1,777
Roads	12,500
Motor vehicles	30,000
Telegraph lines	?
Telephones	7,000
Post offices	378

Industrial Production: 1951

Electric power　　　35,000,000 kwhr

Foreign Trade: 1950–1951

Total imports　U.S. $139,100,000
Total exports　U.S. $206,000,000

Banking: Currency: Kyat, value in U.S. $0.21 in 1953
　　　　　Banks: 22

Population: Total, estimated 1952, 18,500,000.

Ethnic groups:

Burmese	13,650,000
Karen	1,500,000
Shan	1,200,000
Kachin	450,000
Chin	400,000
Wa-Palaung	275,000
Indians	600,000
Chinese	200,000

Cities: 1952

	Estimates
Rangoon	710,000
Mandalay	180,000
Moulmein	95,000

Religions: 1952

	Estimates
Buddhist	15,000,000
Animist	850,000
Moslem	650,000
Hindu	500,000
Christian	500,000

Schools: 1953

Primary schools	5,528	636,000 pupils
Secondary schools	390	72,500 pupils
Colleges and universities	3	3,650 students

Political: The Union of Burma became fully independent on January 4, 1948. Though continuing close economic relations with Great Britain it is not a part of the British Commonwealth in any way.

Divisional Burma comprises 7 administrative divisions, chiefly forming lowland Burma.

There are 3 special states and one special administrative division.

Capital: Rangoon.

THAILAND

Physical Data:

Area in square miles: 200,148.
Dimensions: 745 miles north-south, 485 miles east-west.
Length of coastline: 1,700 miles.
Rivers: Menam, 620 miles long, drainage basin 61,800 square miles. The proper name is Chao Phraya, though no one term is applied to the stream throughout its length.
Highest mountain: Doi Inthanon, 8,468 ft.

Acreage Data:

Total area in acres: 128,000,000
Forest　　　　　　　80,000,000
Area in farms, about　19,000,000

Chief Crops: 1950–1951

	Acres
Rice	14,500,000
Rubber	680,000
Peanuts	175,000
Coconut	150,000
Sugar cane	135,000
Beans	130,000
Tobacco	75,000
Sesamum	50,000

Animal Population: 1948

Buffalo	5,140,000
Cattle	4,800,000
Pigs	2,000,000

Index of Agricultural Production (1935–1939 is 100) 1951–1952 was 164.

Fisheries:

	Estimated average
Fishermen	80,000
Catch	200,000 tons

Mineral Production: 1950–1951

	Tons
Tin	10,300
Iron ore	7,000
Antimony	450

Communications: 1951

Railways	1,926 miles
Roads	3,600 miles
Motor vehicles	14,500
Telegraph lines	?
Navigable waterways	2,300 miles
Telephones	6,100
Post offices	770

Industrial Production: 1951

Cement	228,000 tons
Electric power	56,500,000 kwhr

Foreign Trade: 1951

Total imports　U.S. $166,400,000
Total exports　U.S. $228,400,000

Banking: Currency: Baht, value in U.S. $0.044 in 1950
　　　　　Banks, 25, with 67 offices in 1951

Population: Total, estimated 1952, 18,900,000.

Ethnic groups:

Thais	14,000,000
Chinese	2,700,000
Malays	350,000

Cities: Bangkok, 1,178,000 in 1952.

Schools: 1951

Primary schools	20,229	3,012,000 pupils
Secondary schools	1,240	105,000 pupils
Colleges and universities	5	31,600 students
Technical schools	207	18,200 students

Political: In 1939 the official name of the country was changed from Siam to Thailand. In 1945 Siam again was made the official name, but in 1949 the name Thailand became official. In the Tai language the official name is Prathet Thai.

The country in 1952 was divided into 71 provinces, or *changvads*.

Capital: Bangkok, known in Tai as Krung Thep.

INDOCHINA

Physical Data:

Area in square miles: 285,640.
Dimensions: 900 miles north-south, 465 miles east-west.
Length of coastline: 1,560 miles.
Rivers: Mekong, 2,600 miles long, drainage basin 307,000 square miles.
Song Koi (Red), 750 miles long, drainage basin 46,000 square miles.
Highest mountain: Fan Si Pan, 10,308 ft.

	Square miles
Subdivisions: Vietnam area	127,380
Laos	88,780
Cambodia	69,480

Acreage Data:

Total area in acres	182,800,000
Forest	77,000,000
Area in farms	18,000,000

Chief Crops: 1950–1952

	Acres
Rice	12,600,000
Maize	1,300,000
Rubber	325,000
Potatoes, white and sweet	305,000
Beans	200,000
Sugar cane	110,000
Coconut	75,000

Animal Population: 1951

	Estimates
Cattle	2,000,000
Buffalo	1,400,000
Pigs	4,000,000

Index of Agricultural Production (1935–1939 is 100) 1951–1952 was 80.

Fisheries: 1951

	Estimates
Fishermen	85,000
Catch	175,000 tons

Mineral Production: 1952

Coal	800,000 tons
Tin	950 tons

Communications: 1950

Railways	2,028 miles
Roads	19,840 miles
Motor vehicles	31,500
Telegraph lines	?
Telephones	11,500 sets
Navigable waterways	3,100 miles
Post offices	?

Industrial Production: 1951

Cement	204,000 tons
Electric power	265,000,000 kwhr

Foreign Trade: 1951

Total imports	U.S. $304,700,000
Total exports	U.S. $134,900,000

Banking: Currency: Piastre, value in U.S. $0.48.

Population: Total estimated 1952, 28,000,000.

Vietnam	23,000,000
Laos	1,400,000
Cambodia	3,500,000

Ethnic groups: 1952

	Estimates
Annamese	20,000,000
Cambodians	3,200,000
Thais	3,500,000
Chinese	850,000

Cities: 1952

	Estimates
Saigon-Cholon	1,400,000
Hanoi	260,000
Haiphong	200,000
Pnompenh	110,000

Schools: No satisfactory data.

Political: Indochina now is made up of the three Associated States of Indochina, which are members of the French Union, present arrangements dating from 1949.

Vietnam was set up under Emperor Bao Dai, with three administrative divisions, North, Central, and South, with its capital at Saigon.

Laos is a kingdom under King Sisavang Vong, with Ventiane the capital.

Cambodia is a kingdom under King Norodom Sihanouk Varman, with Pnompenh the capital.

MALAYA

Physical Data:

Area in square miles: 50,850.
Dimensions: 480 miles north-south, 195 miles east-west.
Length of coastline: 1,100 miles.
Rivers: Pahang, 285 miles long.
Highest mountain: Gunong Tahan, 7,186 ft.

Acreage Data:

Total area in acres: 32,500,000
Forest   23,000,000
Area in farms   6,000,000

Chief Crops: 1951

	Acres
Rubber	3,360,000
Rice	925,000
Coconut	520,000
Palm oil	98,000
Bananas	60,000
Areca nut	50,000
Manioc	42,000
Nipa	34,000
Pineapple	25,000

Animal Population: 1951

Cattle	248,000
Buffalo	228,000
Pigs	281,000
Goats	250,000
Sheep	22,000

Index of Agricultural Production (1935–1939 is 100) 1951 was 161.

Fisheries: 1951

Fishermen	70,000
Catch	173,000 tons

Mineral Production: 1951

Iron ore	846,000 tons
Coal	382,000 tons
Tin concentrates	57,167 tons
Ilmenite	43,500 tons
Tungsten	40 tons
Gold	17,000 ounces

Communications: 1951

Railways	1,116 miles
Roads	5,500 miles
Motor vehicles	48,500
Telegraph lines	?
Telephones	28,000 sets
Post offices	186

Industrial Production: 1951

Electric power   790,000,000 kwhr

Foreign Trade: 1951

Total imports   U.S. $377,000,000
Total exports   U.S. $659,300,000

Banking: Currency: Malayan dollar, value in U.S. $0.33.

Schools: 1951

Government primary schools:

Malay language	1,704	285,800 pupils
Chinese language	1,171	206,300 pupils
Indian language	881	37,100 pupils

English language primary and secondary schools	—	111,300 pupils

Technical schools and colleges	7	?
Universities	1	850 students

Population: Total estimated in 1952, 5,500,000.

Ethnic groups: 1952

	Estimates
Malays	2,750,000
Chinese	2,150,000
Indians	590,000

Cities: 1952

	Estimates
Penang	190,000
Kuala Lumpur	175,000

Political: Malaya is a Federation of nine native states and two settlements. This excludes Singapore Island. The Federation came into being in February 1948, as a Protectorate of the British Commonwealth.

Capital: Kuala Lumpur.

SINGAPORE

Area in square miles:

Crown Colony	286
Singapore	224
Christmas Island	62

Population: 1,100,000 in 1952.

Malays	150,000
Chinese	800,000
Indians	80,000

Singapore became a Crown Colony in 1946.

THE INDIES AS A WHOLE

Total area in square miles: 821,202.

Dimensions: 3,850 miles east-west, 1,250 miles north-south.

Islands: Well over 3,000.

Chief Islands:

	Square-mile area
New Guinea	304,000
Borneo	286,969
Sumatra	163,557
Celebes	69,277
Java	48,842
Timor	13,071
Halmahera	6,870
Ceram	6,622
Sumbawa	5,965
Flores	5,511
Bangka	4,611
Sumba	4,306
Buru	3,668
Bali	2,243
Billiton	1,866
Lombok	1,826
Madura	1,762

Total Population: estimated 1952, 80,550,000.

INDONESIA

Physical Data:

Area in square miles: 575,895 without disputed W. New Guinea.

Dimensions: About 2,500 miles east-west, Sumatra-Moluccas, 1,000 miles north-south.

Length of coastlines: undetermined for all the islands.

Rivers: Barito (Borneo), 550 miles long, 38,000 square miles in drainage basin.

Kapuas (Borneo), 710 miles long.

Solo (Java), 335 miles long.

Musi (Sumatra), 325 miles long.

Highest mountains: Bukit-Raja (Borneo), 7,474 ft.

Kerinchi (Sumatra), 12,487 ft.

Mahameru (Java), 12,060 ft.

Rantemario (Celebes), 11,286 ft.

Acreage Data:

Total area in acres: 368,570,000
Area in farms (est.)   43,000,000

Chief Crops: 1951

	Estimates in acres
Wet-field rice	11,500,000
Upland rice	3,400,000
Maize	7,500,000
Rubber	4,300,000
Manioc	3,000,000
Coconut	2,000,000
Sweet potatoes-yams	1,000,000
Soybeans	900,000
Peanuts	600,000
Taro	500,000
Sugar cane	350,000
Coffee	350,000
Tea	350,000
Tobacco	250,000
Palm oil	150,000
Cinchona	25,000
Cacao	25,000

Animal Population: 1950

	Estimates
Cattle	3,700,000
Buffalo	2,800,000
Horses	650,000
Goats	7,000,000
Sheep	1,750,000
Pigs	1,400,000
Chickens	35,000,000
Ducks	9,000,000

Index of Agricultural Production (1935–1939 is 100) 1951 was 101.

Fisheries: 1950

	Estimates
Fishermen	no reliable data
Catch	500,000 tons

Mineral Production: 1950

Petroleum	50,150,000 bbl
Coal	800,000 tons
Bauxite	535,000 tons
Tin	35,000 tons
Other minerals	no satisfactory data

Communications: 1950–1951

Railways	4,100 miles
Roads	43,000 miles
Motor vehicles	65,000
Navigable waterways	2,700 miles
Telegraph	?
Telephones	43,000 sets
Post offices	650

Industrial Production: No satisfactory data.

Foreign Trade: 1951

Total imports   U.S. $806,100,000
Total exports   U.S. $230,700,000

Banking: Currency: Rupiah, value in U.S. $0.087.

Population: Total, 1952 estimate, 78,500,000.

Religions:

	Estimates
Moslems	70,000,000
Animists	4,500,000
Christians	2,500,000
Hindu-Buddhists	1,500,000

Cities: 1952

	Estimates
Djakarta (Jakarta, Batavia)	2,250,000
Surabaja	1,500,000
Djokjakarta	1,500,000
Bandung	600,000
Semarang	250,000
Surakarta	200,000
Palembang	150,000
Bogor	125,000
Medan	105,000
Bandjarmassin	100,000
Makassar	100,000

Schools: 1951

Primary schools	30,650	5,860,000 pupils
Secondary schools	850	?
Chinese schools	681	162,000 pupils
Colleges and universities	11	?
Technical schools	204	?

A large-scale mass education movement has been under way for several years that is not amenable to statistical tabulation.

Political: Republic of Indonesia was formed in August, 1950. It is linked to the Netherlands through a loose connection under the Dutch Crown.

Provinces: 10 regular provinces, in addition to W. New Guinea which still is in dispute between the Republic and the Netherlands.

Capital: Djakarta (Batavia).

WEST NEW GUINEA

Area in square miles: 159,375.

Population: About 350,000.

Rivers: Mamberamo, 500 miles long.

Highest mountain: Carstenz, 16,400 ft.

West New Guinea is now often termed Irian, and has been in dispute between the Republic and the Netherlands since the first independence of the Indies after World War II. It is lightly populated and but slightly developed agriculturally.

SARAWAK

Physical Data:

Area in square miles: 47,071.
Dimensions: 455 miles north-south, 150 miles east-west.
Length of coastline: 450 miles.
Rivers: Rajang, 350 miles long.
Highest mountain: Mt. Mulu, 7,798 ft.

Acreage Data:

	Estimates in acres
Total area	30,125,000
Forest	8,000,000
Area in farms	3,200,000

Chief Crops: 1950

	Acres
Rice	250,000
Rubber	240,000
Sago palm	150,000
Coconut	21,000

Animal Population: No satisfactory data.

Fisheries: 1950

Fishermen	?
Catch	3,500 tons

Mineral Production: 1951

Petroleum	353,000 bbl

Communications: 1950

Railways	10 miles
Roads	460 miles
Motor vehicles	?
Navigable waterways	230 miles
Telegraph lines	?
Telephones	?
Post offices	?

Industrial Production: No satisfactory data.

Foreign Trade:

Total imports	?
Total exports	?

Banking: Currency: Malayan dollar, value in U.S. $0.33.

Population: Total in 1952 estimated at 565,000.

Ethnic groups:

Dyaks	235,000
Chinese	150,000
Malays	100,000

Cities: Kuching in 1951 was about 40,000.

Schools: 1950

Primary schools	380	41,000 pupils
Secondary schools	18	1,260 pupils
Higher schools	none	

Political: A British protectorate before World War II, Sarawak became a British Crown Colony in July, 1946.

Capital: Kuching.

BRUNEI

Physical Data:

Area in square miles: 2,226.
Irregularly shaped area on west coast of Borneo, divided into two parts by an extension of Sarawak.

Acreage Data: 1950

Total area in acres: 1,425,000.

Chief crops:

	Acres
Rubber	20,700
Rice	9,000
Sago palm	2,100
Coconut	500

Animal Population: 1950

Buffalo	7,700
Cattle	950
Pigs	4,000

Mineral Production: 1951

Petroleum   36,320,000 bbl

Communications: 1950

Railways	8 miles
Roads	137 miles
Motor vehicles	627
Telegraph lines	?
Telephones	50 sets
Post offices	?

Industrial Production: No satisfactory data.

Foreign Trade: Very slight volume beyond the movement of petroleum.

Banking: Currency: Malayan dollar, value in U.S. $0.33.

Population: Total in 1952 estimated at 46,000.

Ethnic groups:

Malays	22,000
Chinese	10,000
Dyaks	8,500

Cities: Brunei, in 1952 estimated at 11,000.

Schools: 1950 data indicated 37 primary schools with 4,500 pupils, but early in 1953 a material expansion of the program of education began.

Political: British protectorate under a Native Sultan, Omar Ali Saifuddin.

Capital: Brunei.

N O R T H   B O R N E O

Physical Data:

Area in square miles: 29,387.
Dimensions: A roughly regular block at the north end of Borneo about 275 miles north-south and east-west.
Length of coastline: About 900 miles.
Rivers: Kinabatangan, 350 miles long, 4,000 square miles in drainage basin.
Highest mountain: Kinibalu, 13,455 ft.

Acreage Data:

	Estimates in acres
Total area	18,800,000
Forest	9,000,000
Area in farms	500,000

Chief Crops: 1949–1950

	Acres
Rubber	132,000
Rice	90,000
Coconut	40,000
Manioc	20,000
Abaca and sisal	18,000
Sago palm	14,000
Tobacco	12,000

Animal Population: No satisfactory data.

Fisheries: No satisfactory data.

Mineral Production: No satisfactory data.

Communications: 1949

Railways	116 miles
Roads	380 miles
Motor vehicles	no data
Navigable waterways	about 75 miles
Telegraph lines	no data
Telephones	480 sets
Post offices	8

Industrial Production: No satisfactory data.

Foreign Trade: 1950

Total imports	U.S. $15,180,000
Total exports	U.S. $30,000,000

Banking: Currency: Malayan dollar, value in U.S. $0.33.
Banks: 8, with 17 offices.

Population: Total by census of 1951, 331,000.

Cities:

Sandakan	14,000
Jesselton	11,000

Schools: 1950

Primary schools	186	19,100 pupils
Secondary schools	10	484 pupils
Higher schools	none	

Political: Until World War II British North Borneo was held and administered by the British North Borneo Company. In 1946 the whole of North Borneo, including Labuan Island, became a British Crown Colony.

Divisions: Four administrative divisions, West Coast, East Coast, Interior, Labuan Island.

Capital: Jesselton.

B R I T I S H   N E W   G U I N E A

Physical Data:

Area in square miles: 160,240 for the main island alone.
Dimensions: About 700 miles east-west by 420 miles north-south.
Length of coastline: ?
Rivers:

Sepik	700 miles long
Fly	650 miles long

Highest mountain: Mt. Wilhelm, 14,190 ft.

Acreage Data: 1950

Total area in acres: 102,553,000.
Native agricultural acreage: no estimate available.

Chief Crops under Occidental management:

	Estimates in acres
Coconut	310,000
Rubber	26,500
Coffee	2,700
Cacao	2,000

Mineral Production: 1951

Gold   U.S. $3,300,000

Communications: 1951

Roads	620 miles
Motor vehicles	no data
Telegraph lines	1,700 miles
Telephones	500 sets
Navigable waterways	850 miles

Population: 1951 total estimated at 1,150,000.

Political: Territory of New Guinea, occupying the northeastern part of the island, is a U.N. Trusteeship under

Australia. The political unit includes territory off the main island of New Guinea. Papua is Australian territory, and also includes territory off the main island. Since 1950 both units have been united in political administration. Lae is a local political capital of the Territory of New Guinea, but Port Moresby now functions as the political capital of both regions under the new unified administration.

PORTUGUESE TIMOR

Total area: 7,383 square miles.

Population estimated at 460,000 in 1952.

Dili is the political capital, population 7,000.

PHILIPPINES

Physical Data:

Area in square miles: 115,600.
Dimensions: Archipelago 1,150 miles north-south, 680 miles east-west.
Length of coastline: About 14,400 miles.
Rivers:

Mindanao	330 miles long
Cagayan	220 miles long

Highest mountains:

Apo (Mindanao)	9,690 ft.
Pulog (Luzon)	9,593 ft.

Chief Islands:

	Areas in square miles
Luzon	40,420
Mindanao	36,527
Samar	5,049
Negros	4,904
Palawan	4,549
Panay	4,445
Mindoro	3,757
Leyte	2,785
Cebu	1,702
Bohol	1,492
Masbate	1,262

Lakes:

	Areas in square miles
Laguna de Bay, southern Luzon	344
Lanao, Mindanao	131

Acreage Data:

Total area in acres:	74,000,000
Forest	47,000,000
Area in farms	15,000,000

Chief Crops: 1952

	Estimates in acres
Rice	5,060,000
Maize	2,640,000
Coconut	2,605,000
Abaca	630,000
Sugar cane	500,000
Sweet potatoes	440,000
Manioc	175,000
Tobacco	144,000

Animal Population: 1952

Buffalo	2,400,000
Cattle	800,000
Horses	225,000
Goats	350,000
Sheep	30,000
Pigs	4,600,000
Chickens	37,000,000
Ducks	1,000,000

Index of Agricultural Production (1935–1939 is 100) 1951–1952 was 116.

Fisheries: 1952

Fishermen	?
Catch	250,000 tons

Mineral Production: 1952

Iron ore	1,170,000 tons
Chromite	54,500 tons
Manganese	20,600 tons
Coal	140,000 tons
Copper	13,200 tons
Lead	1,300 tons
Gold	469,200 oz
Silver	693,000 oz

Mining Production Index (1937 is 100) 1951–1952 was 68.

Communications: 1952

Railways	657 miles
Roads	18,200 miles
Motor vehicles	107,100
Telegraph lines	4,000 miles
Telephones	38,000 sets
Post offices	1,050

Industrial Production: 1952

Cement	260,000 tons
Cotton cloth	6,350,000 yards
Electric power	557,250,000 kwhr

Industrial Production Index (1937 is 100) 1951–1952 was 120.

Foreign Trade: 1952

Total imports	U.S. $420,613,000
Total exports	U.S. $352,000,000

Banking: Currency: Peso, value in U.S. $0.498.
Banks: 1951, 14 banks, 112 offices.

Population: estimated total, 1952, 20,800,000.

Religions:

	Estimates
Catholic Christians	18,750,000
Protestant Christians	400,000
Moslems	700,000
Animists	650,000

Cities:

Manila	1,100,000
Cebu	180,000
Iloilo	115,000
Quezon City	110,000
Davao	85,000

Schools: 1951

Primary schools	21,900	4,300,000 pupils
Secondary schools	1,350	600,000 pupils
Colleges and universities	15	?
Technical schools	290	?

English is the language of instruction throughout the whole school system.

Political: Independent country since July 4, 1946.

Divisions:

50 provinces
21 chartered cities directly under National Government
983 municipalities (counties)
18,859 barrios (wards or districts)

Capital: Manila functions as the capital pending completion of new facilities in near-by Quezon City, which is officially designated as the capital.

Tagalog, the speech of the region around Manila, is the official national language of the Philippines.

CHINA

Physical Data:

Area in square miles: 3,643,000.
Dimensions: 2,600 miles north-south, 2,850 miles east-west.
Length of coastline: 5,360 miles.
Rivers:

Yangtze, 3,470 miles long, 706,000 square miles in drainage basin.
Hwang, 2,897 miles long, 287,000 square miles in drainage basin.
Amur, 2,703 miles long, 709,000 square miles in drainage basin.
Si (West), 1,224 miles long, 168,000 square miles in drainage basin.
Tarim, 1,300 miles long.
Liao, 814 miles long.
Hwai, 620 miles long, 78,000 square miles in drainage basin.

Lakes:

Tungting, Hunan Province, varies from 1,400 to 3,200 square miles in area.
Poyang, Kiangsi Province, varies from 1,000 to 3,000 square miles in area.
Koko Nor, Chinghai Province, 2,300 square miles, 10,115 ft elevation.
Khanka, northeastern Manchuria, 1,700 square miles.
Tai, Kiangsu Province, 1,400 square miles.
Nam Tso, Southern Tibet, 950 square miles, 15,180 ft elevation.
Hungtze, Kiangsu Province, varies from 300 to 600 square miles in area.

Islands: Hainan, 13,700 square miles in area.
Highest mountain: Minya Gonka, 24,900 ft.

Acreage Data:

	Estimates in acres
Total area	2,231,500,000
Forest	200,000,000
Area in farms	290,000,000

Chief Crops: 1950–1952

	Estimates in acres
Wheat	55,000,000
Rice	48,000,000
Millets	23,000,000
Barley	18,000,000
Sorghums	18,000,000
Soybeans	17,000,000
Sesamum and rape	15,000,000
Maize	14,500,000
Cotton	9,000,000
Sweet potatoes	8,000,000
Peanuts	5,000,000
Oats	4,000,000
White potatoes	3,000,000

Animal Population: 1950–1952

	Estimates
Cattle	28,000,000
Buffalo	12,000,000
Donkeys-mules	14,000,000
Horses	5,000,000
Camels	400,000
Goats	22,000,000
Sheep	18,000,000
Pigs	70,000,000
Chickens	250,000,000
Ducks	7,000,000
Geese	10,000,000

Fisheries: 1950–1952

	Estimates
Fishermen	600,000
Catch	1,700,000 tons

Mineral Production: Rough averages for years 1930–1950

Coal	15,000,000–40,000,000 tons
Iron ore	1,000,000–10,000,000 tons
Petroleum	1,000,000–8,000,000 bbl
Tungsten	15,000–40,000 tons
Antimony	5,000–20,000 tons
Manganese	10,000–25,000 tons
Tin	3,000–10,000 tons
Mercury	50–400 tons

Communications: 1950–1952 estimates and calculations

Railways	17,500 miles
Roads	145,000 miles
Motor vehicles	?

Navigable waterways 50,000 miles, of which about 20,000 miles are open to small ships and power launches, and some 30,000 additional miles are open to small native craft.

Telegraph lines	150,000 miles
Telephones	360,000 sets
Post offices	10,000

Industrial Production: No satisfactory data.

Foreign Trade: No satisfactory data.

Banking: No satisfactory current data.

Population: Estimated current total about 500,000,000.

Religions: Rough estimates only

Buddhists, nominally	250,000,000
Taoists, nominally	150,000,000
Moslems	55,000,000
Christians, undeclared	6,000,000
Lamaists	2,500,000

Cities: rough estimates only as current figures

Shanghai	4,500,000
Peiping	1,600,000
Tientsin	1,700,000
Wuhan cities	1,400,000
Nanking	1,100,000
Chungking	1,050,000
Ch'ingtao	750,000
Mukden (Shenyang)	850,000
Harbin (Pinkiang)	650,000
Chengtu	625,000
Changch'un	600,000
Changsha	600,000
Dairen	600,000
Hangchow	610,000
Chinan	590,000
Hsian (Sian)	510,000

Schools: Communist government assertion, 1951

Primary schools	541,000	43,000,000 pupils
Secondary schools	5,400	2,100,000 pupils
Colleges and universities	275	175,000 students
Technical schools	800	175,000 students

Political:

Regional administrative zones	6
Provinces	30
Municipalities (under national control)	12

Counties
Administrative districts
National capital: Peiping.

HONGKONG

Physical Data:

Area in square miles: 391.

Hongkong Island	32
Kowloon Peninsula and Stonecutter's Island	3.5
New Territories	355.5

Acreage Data:

Total area: 250,000.
In farms, about 60,000 acres in the New Territories.

Rice	40,000
Vegetables	12,000

Fisheries: 1951

Fishermen	?
Catch	30,000 tons

Mineral Production: 1951

Iron ore	82,000 tons

Industrial Production: 1951

Cement	71,600 tons
Cotton cloth	29,000 tons
Electric power	344,000,000 kwhr

Foreign Trade: 1951

Total imports	U.S. $852,300,000
Total exports	U.S. $775,700,000

Banking: Currency: Hongkong dollar, value in U.S. $0.175.

Banks: 125 in 1951.

Population: Total in 1952 estimated at 2,300,000.

Cities:

Victoria	880,000
Kowloon	700,000

Schools: 1951

Primary schools	695	135,000 pupils
Secondary schools	?	21,000 pupils
Colleges and universities	3	5,200 students
Technical schools	4	2,070 students

Political: Hongkong is a Crown Colony of the British Empire.

The New Territories is leased from China, with the lease terminating in 1997.

Capital: Victoria.

FORMOSA

Physical Data:

Area in square miles:

Main Island	13,808
Pescadores and other islets	78
Total	13,886

Dimensions: 250 miles north-south, 93 miles east-west.
Length of coastline: main island, 708 miles.
Rivers: Choshui, 102 miles long.
Highest mountain: Hsin Kao Shan (Mt. Morrison), 13,145 ft.

Acreage Data:

	Estimates in acres
Total	8,877,000
Forest	4,150,000
Area in farms	2,200,000

Chief Crops: 1951 in acres

Rice	1,950,000
Sweet potatoes	575,000
Sugar cane	200,000
Sesamum	170,000
Tea	90,000
Bananas	45,000
Wheat	38,000
Manioc	30,000
Tobacco	25,000

Animal Population: 1951

Buffalo	280,000
Cattle	120,000
Goats	190,000
Pigs	2,200,000
Chickens	5,100,000
Ducks	3,000,000
Geese	395,000

Fisheries: 1951

Fishermen	?
Catch	104,000 tons

Mineral Production: 1951

Coal	1,650,000 tons
Petroleum	42,000 bbl
Copper	1,100 tons
Gold	U.S.$1,070,000

Communications: 1951

Railways	2,462 miles
Roads	10,800 miles

Industrial Production: 1951

Cement	389,000 tons
Cotton cloth	56,000,000 yards
Electric power	1,280,000,000 kwhr

Foreign Trade: 1952

Total imports	U.S. $115,200,000
Total exports	U.S. $119,500,000

Banking: Currency: Taiwan dollar, value in U.S. $0.20.

Population: Total in 1953 estimated at 9,500,000.

Ethnic groups:

Fukienese Chinese	4,800,000
Kwangtung Hakka Chinese	2,100,000
Post-war Chinese immigrants	2,400,000
Aborigines	150,000

Cities:

Taipei	503,000
Kaohsing	290,000
Tainan	240,000
Taichung	210,000

Schools: 1949

Primary schools	1,200	892,000 pupils
Secondary schools	170	76,000 pupils
Colleges and universities	6	5,415 students
Technical schools	117	39,000 students

Political: Formosa (Taiwan) is the seat of the exiled Chinese National Government.

Divisions:

16 counties.
5 cities under National Government direct administration.

Capital: Taipei.

KOREA

Physical Data:

Area in square miles: 85,228.

North Korea	48,528
South Korea	36,700

Dimensions: 627 miles north-south, 375 miles east-west.
Length of coastline: About 11,000 miles for mainland and islands.
Rivers:

	Length, miles	Drainage Basin, square miles
Yalu	493	24,200
Naktong	326	9,250
Tumen	324	15,200
Han	292	12,870

Highest mountain: Kwanmo, 8,337 ft.
Islands: There are many islands along the west coast. Cheju Island in the Yellow Sea is 713 square miles in area.

Acreage Data:

	Estimates in acres
Total area	54,545,000
Forest	38,000,000
Area in farms	12,500,000
Area in farms in South Korea	7,000,000

Chief Crops: Over-all estimate is based on 1949 data; estimate for South Korea is composite data of 1950–1952.

	All of Korea	South Korea
Rice	4,100,000	2,850,000
Barleys	2,200,000	1,550,000
Millets	2,100,000	450,000
Wheat	800,000	275,000
Soybeans	2,000,000	660,000
Cotton	625,000	430,000
Potatoes, white and sweet	600,000	225,000
Tobacco	—	50,000

Animal Population: 1950–1952 for South Korea only

Cattle	600,000
Pigs	400,000
Goats	50,000
Horses	35,000

Fisheries: Under Japanese control Korea ranked second in the total world catch of fish. Currently the South Korean catch is only about 300,000 tons.

Mineral Production: 1951 for South Korea only

Coal	112,000 tons
Tungsten	4,500 tons
Graphite	?
Gold	U.S. $800,000

Communications: no satisfactory data.

Industrial Production: 1951 for South Korea only

Cement	7,000 tons
Cotton yarn	5,600 tons
Cotton cloth	30,000,000 yards
Electric power	314,000,000 kwhr

Foreign Trade: no satisfactory data.

Banking: Currency: Whan, value in U.S. $0.016. The whan represents a new currency created and stabilized as of February, 1953.

Banks: 7, with 138 offices actually open in 1951.

Population: Total estimated in 1952 at 29,300,000. South Korean total estimated in 1952 at 22,000,000.

Cities:

Seoul	1,500,000
Pusan	450,000

Schools: 1951 data for South Korea only

Primary schools	3,921	2,525,000 pupils
Secondary schools	884	440,000 pupils
Colleges and universities	49	27,500 students
Technical schools and Teachers colleges	38	25,270 students

Political: Korea was to have been freed from Japanese domination and made independent after World War II. The post-war division of Korea into two parts resulted from military expediency.

Divisions of South Korea: 9 provinces and a federal capital area.

Capitals: Seoul for South Korea. Pyongyang for North Korea.

JAPAN

Physical Data:

Area in square miles: 147,690.

Dimensions: 1,150 miles northeast-southeast, 180 miles in width.

Length of coastline: 17,150 miles.

Rivers:

	Length, miles	Drainage Basin, square miles
Shinano	229	4,700
Ishikari	227	5,500

Islands: Areas in square miles for the main islands only

Honshu	87,426
Hokkaido	29,600
Kyushu	13,770
Shikoku	6,860
Sado	330
Tsushima	271
Fukae	129

Lakes: Biwa, in southern Honshu, 261 square miles.

Highest mountain: Fuji, Honshu, 12,395 ft.

Acreage Data:

	Estimates in acres
Total area	94,250,000
Forest	51,000,000
Area in farms	17,000,000

Chief Crops: 1950

	Estimates in acres
Rice	7,440,000
Barleys	2,520,000
Wheat	1,900,000
Sweet potatoes	985,000
Soybeans	750,000
White potatoes	480,000
Other beans	340,000
Oats	215,000
Flax	170,000
Buckwheat	145,000
Tobacco	125,000

Animal Population: 1950

Cattle	2,460,000
Horses	1,095,000
Goats	418,000
Sheep	364,000
Pigs	625,000
Rabbits	3,315,000
Chickens	22,000,000

Fisheries: 1951

Fishermen	900,000
Catch	4,450,000 tons

Mineral Production: 1950

Coal	39,750,000 tons
Iron ore	822,000 tons
Petroleum	2,000,000 bbl
Manganese	134,000 tons
Aluminum ores	28,300 tons
Copper	39,300 tons
Lead	10,850 tons
Zinc	52,000 tons
Graphite	7,000 tons
Asbestos	6,000 tons

Communications: 1950

Railways	17,000 miles
Roads, vehicular	515,000 miles
Roads, motorable	43,300 miles
Motor vehicles	165,000
Telegraph lines	120,000 miles
Telephones	1,800,000 sets
Post offices	14,100

Industrial Production: 1951

Finished steel	5,255,000 tons
Cement	6,548,000 tons
Cotton yarn	336,000 tons
Cotton cloth	1,822,000,000 yards
Electric power	41,110,000,000 kwhr

Foreign Trade: 1950

Total imports	U.S. $969,580,000
Total exports	U.S. $815,660,000

Banking: Currency: Yen, value in U.S. $0.00277 as of May, 1953.
Banks: 80, with 5,317 offices in 1951.

Population: Total estimated in 1951 at 84,300,000.

Cities: 1950

Tokyo	5,385,000
Osaka	1,956,000
Kyoto	1,101,000
Nagoya	1,030,000
Yokohama	951,000
Kobe	765,000
Fukuoka	392,000
Sendai	341,000
Kawasaki	319,000
Sapporo	313,000

Schools: 1951

Primary schools	22,000	11,400,000 pupils
Secondary schools	14,300	7,300,000 pupils
Colleges and universities and Technical schools	422	420,000 students

Press: 1951

Daily newspapers, 180; 27,780,000 circulation.

Political:

Prefectures (Ken), 47.
Cities, towns, and townships are the local divisions.
Townships (gun) are not now legal civil divisions, but are shown on most maps and are used in many ways.

Capital: Tokyo.

RYUKYU ISLANDS

Physical Data:

Area in square miles: 1,803.
Dimensions: A scattered archipelago some 775 miles long, made up of 140 islands and islets, 30 being inhabited.

Islands:

	Area in square miles
Okinawa	485
Amami	333
Yaku	208
Tanega	176
Iriomote	144
Tokuno	98
Ishigaki	83
Miyako	70

Acreage Data:

	Estimates in acres
Total area	1,254,000
Forest	510,000
Area in farms	200,000

Chief Crops: 1950

	Estimates in acres
Sweet potatoes	96,000
Rice	35,000
Soybeans	12,400
Wheat	12,350
Barley	9,900
Sugar cane	7,400

Population: Total estimated in 1952 at 950,000.

Cities: 1950

Naha   45,000

Schools: 1949

Primary schools	439	201,000 pupils
Secondary schools	21	9,000 pupils
Colleges	1	285 students
Technical schools	35	5,000 students

Political:

The Ryukyu Islands are under the supervision of the United States pending permanent settlement of political status.

Capital: Naha.

A Selected Bibliography

COMMENTARY OF WARNING

The total bibliography on the Orient today must exceed 50,000 entries in occidental languages alone, so that any short bibliography must be highly selective. The following list of slightly over 800 titles was chosen with two criteria in mind —though these could not always be followed—to select a list of recent materials relatively easily available to American readers. Only occasionally is there a date earlier than 1940, and many excellent studies published in new oriental periodicals were purposely omitted. Many good studies published in Dutch, German, and French were omitted, though there is a sprinkling of each. Also omitted were most government and military government reports, some far more useful than privately published studies, since their availability is quite limited. Only a few mimeographed items were included, since these are published in very limited editions and have a small distribution.

My own card files today contain over 12,000 entries, but every specialist will easily determine unforgivable omissions— I make no claim as an exhaustive bibliographer. Under the systematic chapters are listed both those materials that are general in nature and those chiefly illustrative of the discussion, though they may be concerned with restricted regions only. Similarly, both kinds of materials are included in the regional list. For any reader desiring a bibliography either on one topic or one country it will be necessary to scan the whole list.

BIBLIOGRAPHIES

Baqai, I. H., *Books on Asia,* Indian Council of World Affairs, New Delhi, 1947.

Barquissau, R. (Ed.), *L'Asie française et ses écrivains,* Vigneau, Paris, 1947.

Berton, P. A., *Manchuria; An Annotated Bibliography,* Library of Congress, Washington, 1951.

Borton, H., S. Elisseeff, and E. O. Reishauer, *A Selected List of Books and Articles on Japan in English, French, and German,* Amer. Council Learned Soc., Washington, 1940.

Bulletin of Far Eastern Bibliography, Library of Congress, Washington, 1936–1951.

Chih-yi, M. C., "A Bibliography of Books and Articles on Mongolia," *J. Roy. Cent. Asian Soc., 37,* 1950.

Current Geographical Publications, American Geographical Society, New York, ten issues per year.

"Far Eastern Bibliography," a section of the *Far Eastern Quarterly,* Far Eastern Association, annual inclusion.

Gardner, C. S., *A Union List of Selected Western Books on China in American Libraries,* Amer. Council Learned Soc., Washington, 1938.

Ghani, A. R., *Pakistan, A Selected Bibliography,* Pakistan Assoc. for the Advancement of Science, Lahore, 1951.

Hobbs, C., *Southeast Asia, 1935–1945, A Selected List of Reference Books,* Library of Congress, Washington, 1946.

Indochina, A Bibliography of the Land and the People, Library of Congress, Washington, 1950.

Jones, H. B., and R. L. Winkler, *Korea, an Annotated Bibliography of Publications in Western Languages,* Library of Congress, Washington, 1950.

Kennedy, R., *Bibliography of Indonesian Peoples and Cultures,* Yale Univ. Press, New Haven, 1945.

Pelzer, K. J., *Selected Bibliography on the Geography of Southeast Asia,* Part 1, Mimeo, Yale Univ. Press, New Haven, 1949.

Southern Asia Publications in Western Languages, Library of Congress, Division of Orientalia, *Quarterly,* vol. 1, 1951.

MATERIALS OF GENERAL REFERENCE

Bishop, C. W., "Origin of the Far Eastern Civilizations," *Smithsonian Inst. Publs. 3681,* Washington, 1942.

Cherian, T. O., *Handbook of Asian Statistics,* New Delhi, circa 1947, contains statistics of the 1930's and as late as 1944.

Cressey, G. B., *Asia's Lands and Peoples,* McGraw-Hill, New York, 2nd ed., 1951.

Dobby, E. H. G., *Southeast Asia,* John Wiley & Sons, New York, 1951.

East, W. G., and O. H. K. Spate, *The Changing Map of Asia, A Political Geography,* Dutton, New York, 1950.

Ghatz, B. G., *Asia's Trade,* Oxford Univ. Press, New York, 1949.

Freeman, O. W. (Ed), *Geography of the Pacific,* John Wiley & Sons, New York, 1951.

Helbig, K., *Die südostasiatische Inselwelt,* Kosmos Verlag, Stuttgart, 1949.

Helbig, K., *Am Rande des Pazifik,* Kohlhammer, Stuttgart, 1949.

Levy, R., *Extrême Orient et Pacifique,* Colin, Paris, 1948.

Mills, L. A., and Associates, *The New World of Southeast Asia,* Univ. of Minn. Press, Minneapolis, 1949.

Mitchell, K. L., *Industrialization in the Western Pacific,* Inst. Pac. Rel., New York, 1942.

Murray, J., *A Handbook for Travellers in India, Pakistan, Burma, and Ceylon,* Murray, London, 1949.

Osborn, F., *The Pacific World,* Norton, New York, 1944.

Panikkar, K., *The Future of Southeast Asia, An Indian View,* Macmillan, New York, 1943.

Pelzer, K. J., *Pioneer Settlement in the Asiatic Tropics,* American Geog. Soc., New York, 1945.

Peterson, A. D. C., *The Far East, A Social Geography*, Duckworth, London, 1949.

Robequain, C., *Le Monde Malais*, Payot, Paris, 1946.

Rosinger, L. K., and Associates, *The State of Asia, a Contemporary Survey*, Knopf, New York, 1951.

Shepherd, J., *Industry in Southeast Asia*, Inst. Pac. Rel., New York, 1942.

Shultz, A., *Der Erteil Asien*, Kosmos Verlag, Stuttgart, 1951.

Stamp, L. D., *Asia, A Regional and Economic Geography*, Dutton, London, 8th ed., 1950.

Steiger, G. N., H. O. Beyer, and C. Benitez, *A History of the Orient*, Ginn, Boston, 1929.

Talbot, P. (Ed.), *South Asia in the World Today*, Univ. of Chicago Press, 1950.

Turner, R., *The Great Cultural Traditions*, McGraw-Hill, New York, 1941, 2 vols.

Van Valkenburg, S., *Pacific Asia, A Political Atlas*, For. Policy Assoc., New York, 1947.

Wood, G. L., and P. R. Mc Bride, *The Pacific Basin, A Human and Economic Geography*, Oxford Univ. Press, Melbourne, rev. ed., 1946.

Wyatt, W., *Southward from China, A Survey of Southeast Asia Since 1945*, Hodder and Stoughton, London, 1952.

CHAPTERS 1 AND 2, GEOMORPHOLOGY AND THE BARE LANDSCAPE

Bemmelen, R. W. van, *The Geology of Indonesia*, Govt. Print. Office, The Hague, 1949, 2 vols.

Bemmelen, R. W. van, "The Geotectonic Structure of New Guinea," *De Ingenieur in Nederlandsch Indië*, 6 (1939), 17–27.

Burrard, S., and A. M. Heron, *A Sketch of the Geography and Geology of the Himalaya Mountains and Tibet*, Govt. Printer, New Delhi, rev. ed., 1933.

Chhibber, H. L., *India, Part 1, Physical Basis of Geography of India*, Nand Kishore, Benares, 1945.

Fromaget, J., "L'Indochine française; sa structure géologique, ses roches, ses mines, et leurs relations possibles avec la tectonique," *Bull. du service géologique de l'Indochine*, 26 (1941), 1–140.

Hall, R. B., and A. Watanabe, "Landforms of Japan," *Papers Mich. Acad. Sci.*, 18 (1932), 157–207.

Hanson-Lowe, J., "Notes on the Pleistocene Glaciation of the South Chinese-Tibetan Borderland," *Geog. Rev.*, 37 (1947), 70–87.

Hess, H. H., "Major Structural Features of the Western Pacific, Korea to New Guinea," *Bull. Geol. Soc. Amer.*, 59 (1948), 417–445.

Hobbs, W. H., "Mountain Growth, A Study of the Southwestern Pacific Region," *Proc. Am. Phil. Soc.*, 88 (1944), 221–268.

Hobbs, W. H., *Fortress Islands of the Pacific*, Edwards Bros., Ann Arbor, Mich., 1945.

Huang, T. K., *On the Major Tectonic Forms of China*, Geol. Mem., Geol. Survey China, Series A, No. 20, 1945.

Krishnan, M. S., *Geology of India and Burma*, Madras, 1943.

Lanoue, H., "The Structure of Indo-China," *Science and Society*, 15 (1951), 1–16.

Lee, J. S., *The Geology of China*, Murby, London, 1939.

Leuchs, K., *Geologie von Asien*, Borntraeger, Berlin, 1935.

McCune, S., "The Diversity of Indochina's Physical Geography," *Far Eastern Quarterly*, 6 (1947), 335–344.

Misch, P., "Remarks on the Tectonic History of Yunnan, with Special Reference to its Relations to the Young Type of Orogenic Deformation," *Bull. Geol. Soc. China*, 25 (1945), 47–155.

Pannekboek, A. J., "Outline of the Geomorphology of Java," *Tijdschr. Konink. Ned. Aardrijksk. Genootschap*, 66 (1949), 270–326.

Pithawala, M. B., "A Geographical Analysis of the Lower Indus Basin," *Proc. Indian Acad. Sci., B.*, 4 (1936), 283–355.

Richardson, J. A., "An Outline of the Geomorphical Evolution of British Malaya," *Geol. Mag.*, 84 (1947), 129–144.

Schuppli, H. M., "Geology of the Oil Basins of the East Indian Archipelago," *Bull. Am. Assoc. Petroleum Geol.*, 30 (1946), 1–22.

Smit Sibinga, G. L., "Pleistocene Eustasy and Glacial Chronology in Java and Sumatra," *Verhandel. Ned. Geol.-Mijnbouwkund. Genoot., Geol. Ser.*, 15 (1950), 1–31.

Umbgrove, J. H. F., "Geological History of the East Indies," *Bull. Am. Assoc. Petroleum Geol.*, 22 (1938), 1–70.

Umbgrove, J. H. F., "Coral Reefs of the East Indies," *Bull. Geol. Soc. Amer.*, 58 (1947), 730–777.

Wager, L. R., "The Arun River Drainage Pattern and the Rise of the Himalayas," *Geog. J.*, 89 (1937), 229–250.

Ward, F. K., "A Sketch of the Geography and Botany of Tibet," *Linnean Soc. London*, 50 (1935–37), 239–265.

Ward, F. K., "The Irrawaddy Plateau," *Geog. J.*, 94 (1939), 293–308.

Wissmann, H. von, "Die Klimate Chinas im Quartär," *Geog. Zeit.*, 44 (1938), 321–340.

Wissmann, H. von, "The Pleistocene Glaciation in China," *Bull. Geol. Soc. China*, 17 (1937), 145–168.

Wissmann, H. von, "Über Lössbildung und Würmeiszeit in China," *Geog. Zeit.*, 44 (1938), 201–220.

CHAPTER 3, CLIMATOLOGY AND SENSIBLE CLIMATE

Bannerji, S. K., "The Climate of India," *J. Bombay Nat. Hist. Soc.*, 50 (1952), 718–733.

Borchert, J. R., "A New Map of the Climates of China," *Annals, Assoc. Amer. Geog.*, 37 (1947), 168–176.

Climatographic Atlas of Japan, Cent. Met. Observ. Tokyo, 1948–1949, 2 vols.

Crowe, P. R., "Seasonal Variation of the Strength of the Monsoons," *Indian Geog. Soc. Silver Jubilee Souvenir*, 1952, 168–188.

Desai, B. N., and P. Koteswaram, "Air Masses and Fronts in the Monsoon Depressions in India," *Indian J. Meteorol. and Geophys.*, 2 (1951), 250–265.

Dobby, E. H. G., "Winds and Fronts over Southeast Asia," *Geog. Rev.*, 35 (1945), 204–218.

Garbell, M. A., *Tropical and Equatorial Meteorology*, Pitman, New York, 1947.

Glenn, A. H., "Examples of Topographic Convergence in the Equatorial Zone between 90' East and 160' East," *Bull. Am. Meteorol. Soc.*, 30 (1949), 50–55.

Hanson-Lowe, J., "Notes on the Climate of the South Chinese-Tibetan Borderland," *Geog. Rev.*, 31 (1941), 444–453.

Kimble, G. H. T., et al., "Tropical Land and Sea Breezes with Special Reference to the East Indies," *Bull. Am. Meteorol. Soc., 27* (1946), 99–113.

Malurkar, S. L., "Notes on Analysis of Weather of India and Neighborhood," *Mem. Indian Meteorol. Dept., 28* (1950), 139–215.

Sawyer, J. S., "The Structure of the Intertropical Front over NW India during the Monsoon," *Quart. J. Roy. Meteorol. Soc., 73* (1947), 346–370.

Stein, A., "Desiccation in Asia," *Hungarian Quarterly, 4* (1938), 642–654.

Thompson, B. W., "An Essay on the General Circulation of the Atmosphere over Southeast Asia and West Pacific," *Quart. J. Roy. Meteorol. Soc. 77* (1951), 569–579.

T'u, C. W., and S. S. Hwang, "The Advance and Retreat of the Summer Monsoon in China," *Bull. Am. Meteorol. Soc., 26* (1945), 9–22.

CHAPTER 4, MINERAL GEOGRAPHY

Braake, A. L. Ter, *Mining in the Netherlands East Indies,* Inst. Pac. Rel., New York, 1944.

Bromehead, C. N., "Ancient Mining Processes," *Antiquity, 16* (1942), 193–207.

Brown, G. F., et al., *Geologic Reconnaissance of the Mineral Deposits of Thailand, U. S. Geol. Survey Bull. 894,* Washington, 1951.

Chhibber, H. L., *Mineral Resources of Burma,* Macmillan, London, 1934.

Clegg, E. L. G., *The Mineral Deposits of Burma,* Times of India Press, Bombay, 1944.

Fermor, L. L., "Mineral Resources of Malaya," *Bull. Imp. Inst.,* 1940.

Gordon, D. H., "Early Use of Metals in India and Pakistan," *J. Roy. Inst. Gt. Brit. & Ireland, 80* (1950), 55–78.

Mineral Resources of China, Bureau of Mines, Washington, 1948.

Mining Industry in the Philippines, Bureau of Mines, Manila, 1947.

Read, T. T., "Chinese Iron—A Puzzle," *Harvard J. Asiatic Studies, 2* (1937), 398–407.

"Sources of Iron Ore in Asia," *U. S. Bur. Mines, Mineral Trade Notes, Supp. 38, 34,* 1952.

Terra, G. J. A., *De Tuinbouw in Indonesië,* Van Hoeve, The Hague, 1949.

Van Royen, W., and O. Bowles, *The Mineral Resources of the World,* Prentice-Hall, New York, 1952.

Wang, K. P., "Mineral Resources of China with Special Reference to the Nonferrous Metals," *Geog. Rev., 34* (1944), 621–635.

CHAPTER 5, SOILS, PLANTS, AND PLANT CULTURES

Alicante, M. M., "The Fertilizer Problem in the Ecafe Region," *J. Soil Sci. Soc. Philippines, 1* (1949), 18–30.

Anderson, E., "Millet Provides Food for Millions," *Foreign Agr., 12* (1948), 235–239.

Bohlin, B., *A Contribution to our Knowledge of the Distribution of Vegetation in Inner Mongolia, Kansu, and Chinghai,* Stockholm, 1949, Sino-Swedish Exped., Public 33.

Brass, L. J., "Stone Age Agriculture in New Guinea," *Geog. Rev., 31* (1941), 555–569.

Burkill, I. H., *A Dictionary of the Economic Products of the Malay Peninsula,* Crown Agents for the Colonies, London, 1935.

Chevalier, A., "Notes sur les conifers de l'Indochine," *Rev. Botan. appl. et d'agr. trop., 24* (1944), 7–34.

Grant, J. W., and A. N. P. Williams, "Burma Fruits and Their Cultivation," *Dept. Agr., Rangoon, Bull. 30,* 1949.

Hagerty, M. J., "Comments on Writings concerning Chinese Sorghums," *Harvard J. Asiatic Studies, 5* (1940), 234–260.

Hayes, W. B., *Fruit Growing in India,* Kitabistan, Allahabad, 1945.

Kraemer, J. H., *Trees of the Western Pacific Region,* pub. by author, West Lafayette, Indiana, 1951.

Lam, H. J., "Notes on the Historical Phytogeography of Celebes," *Blumea, 5* (1942), 600–640.

Merrill, E. D., *Plant Life of the Pacific World,* Macmillan, New York, 1945.

Mohr, E. C. J. (R. L. Pendleton, trans.), *The Soils of Equatorial Regions, with Special Reference to the Netherlands East Indies,* Edwards Bros., Ann Arbor, 1944.

Morse, W. J., "Soybeans Yesterday and Today," *Foreign Agr., 12* (1948), 91–95.

Naik, K. C., *South Indian Fruits and Their Culture,* Varadachary, Madras, 1947.

Owen, G., "A Provisional Classification of Malayan Soils," *J. Soil Sci., 2* (1951), 20–42.

Pendleton, R. L., "On the Use of the Term Laterite," *Bull. Am. Soil Survey Assoc., 17* (1936).

Pendleton, R. L., "Soils of Thailand," *J. Thailand Research Soc., Nat. Hist. Supp. 1 to Vol. 12* (1940), 235–260.

Pendleton, R. W., "Further Notes on Laterite," *Proc. Sixth Pac. Sci. Congr. Pacific Sci. Assoc., 1939, 4* (1940), 973–981.

Pendleton, R. W., "Laterite and Its Structural Uses in Thailand and Cambodia," *Geog. Rev., 31* (1941), 177–202.

Pendleton, R. W., "Formation, Development and Utilization of the Soils of Bangkok Plain," *Thailand Nat. Hist. Bull., 14* (1947).

Pendleton, R. W., "Land Use in South East Asia," *Far Eastern Survey, 16* (1947), 25–29.

Pendleton, R. W., "Soils of India: Four Surveys in Gwalior State," *Soil Sci., 63* (1947), 421–435.

Reynolds, P. K., "Earliest Evidence of Banana Culture," *J. Am. Oriental Soc., Suppl. 12 to Vol. 71* (1951), 1–28.

Reynolds, P. K., and C. Y. Fang, "The Banana in Chinese Literature," *Harvard J. Asiatic Studies, 5* (1940), 165–181.

Sauer, C. O., *Agricultural Origins and Dispersals,* American Geog. Soc., New York, 1952.

Smith, J. R., "Grassland and Farmland as Factors in the Cyclical Development of Eurasian History," *Annals, Assoc. Amer. Geog., 33* (1943), 135–161.

Steenis, C. G. G. J. van, "On the Origin of the Malaysian Mountain Flora," *Bull. jardin Botan. Buitenzorg, Serie 3, 13* (1934), 135–262 and 289–417.

Tardieu-Blot, M. L., "Étude phytogéographique des fougères d' Indochine," *Proc. Sixth Pacific Sci. Congr. Pacific Sci. Assoc., 1939, 4* (1940), 579–593.

Thorp, J., *Geography of the Soils of China,* Nat. Geol. Survey, Nanking, 1936.

Walker, E. H., "The Plants of China and Their Usefulness to Man," *Annual Repts. Smithsonian Inst. for 1943, Publ. 3741* (1944), 325–361.

Wickizer, V. D., and M. K. Bennett, *The Rice Economy of Monsoon Asia,* Food Research Inst., Stanford Univ., 1941.

Willahan, L. T., "Rice, A World Food Crop," *Foreign Agr., 12* (1948), 115–120.

CHAPTER 6, MARINE LIFE AND ANIMALS IN ORIENTAL ECONOMY

Burkenroad, M. D., "The Development of Marine Resources in Indonesia," *Far Eastern Quart., 5* (1946), 189–199.

Carter, T. D., J. E. Hill, and G. H. Tate, *Mammals of the Pacific World,* Macmillan, New York, 1945.

Deignan, H. G., "The Birds of Northern Thailand," *U. S. Natl. Museum Bull. 186,* 1945.

Delacour, J., *Birds of Malaysia,* Macmillan, 1947, New York.

Delacour, J., and E. Mayr, *Birds of the Philippines,* Macmillan, New York, 1946.

Delsman, H. C., "Fishing and Fish Culture in the Netherlands Indies," *Bull. Col. Inst. Amsterdam, 2* (1939), 92–105.

Ekman, S., *Tiergeographie des Meeres,* Akad. Verlags, Leipzig, 1935.

Espenshade, A., "A Program for Japanese Fisheries," *Geog. Rev., 39* (1949), 76–85.

Hardy, A. C., *Sea Food Ships,* Lockwood, London, 1947.

Herre, A. W., "Philippine Fisheries and Their Possibilities," *Far Eastern Quart., 4* (1945), 158–162.

Hermanns, M., *Die Nomaden von Tibet, Die sozial-wirtschaftlichen Grundlagen der Hirtenkulturen im Amdo und von Innerasien,* Vienna, Herold Verlag, 1949.

Hickling, C. F., "Fish Farming in the Middle and Far East," *Nature, 161* (1948), 748–751.

Hora, S. L., "Fisheries Resources of Western Bengal and Their Utilization," *Science and Culture (India), 15* (1949), 176–180.

Hornell, J., "The Chank Shell Cult of India," *Antiquity, 16* (1942), 113–133.

Hornell, J., *Water Transport, Origins and Early Evolution,* Cambridge Univ. Press, 1946.

Hornell, J., *Fishing in Many Waters,* Cambridge University Press, London, 1950.

Hutchinson, G. E., "Biochemistry of Vertebrate Excretion," *Bull. Am. Museum Nat. Hist., 96,* 1950.

Kesteven, G. L., "Fisheries of Southeast Asia," *Science and Culture (India), 17* (1952), 353–360.

Khin, U., *Fisheries of Burma,* Gov't Printer, Rangoon, 1948.

Le Souef, A. S., and H. Burrell, *The Wild Animals of Australasia,* Harap, London, 1926.

Mayr, E., "Wallace's Line in the Light of Recent Zoogeographic Studies," *Quart. Rev. Biol., 19* (1944), 1–14.

Myers, G. S., "The Fish Fauna of the Pacific Ocean," *Proc. Sixth Pacific Sci. Congr. Pacific Sci. Assoc., 1939, 3* (1940), 201–211.

Nichols, J. T., *The Fresh Water Fishes of China,* vol. 9 of *Natural History of Central Asia,* Amer. Museum Nat. Hist., New York, 1943.

Nichols, J. T., and P. Bartsch, *Fishes and Shells of the Pacific World,* Macmillan, New York, 1945.

Phillips, R. W., R. G. Johnson, and R. T. Moyer, *The Livestock of China,* U. S. Dept. State, Publ. 2249 (1945).

Pocock, R. I., *The Fauna of British India, Mammalia,* Taylor & Francis, London, 2 vols., 1939–1941.

Randhawa, M. S., "Role of Domesticated Animals in Indian History," *Science and Culture (India), 12* (1946), 5–14.

Raven, H. C., "Wallace's Line and the Distribution of Indo-Australian Mammals," *Bull. Am. Museum Nat. Hist., 48* (1935), 179–293.

Schafer, E. H., "The Camel in China down to the Mongol Dynasty," *Sinologica, 2* (1950), 165–194.

Scrivenor, J. B. (Ed.), "A Discussion on the Biogeographic Division of the Indo-Australian Archipelago," *Proc. Linnean Soc. London, 154* (1941), 120–165.

Smith, H. M., *The Fresh Water Fishes of Siam, or Thailand, U. S. Natl. Museum Bull. 188,* 1945.

Tate, G. H. H., *Mammals of Eastern Asia,* Macmillan, New York, 1947.

Villadolid, J., "Philippine Fisheries and Problems of Their Conservation," *Proc. Sixth Pacific Sci. Congr. Pacific Sci. Assoc., 1939, 3* (1940), 369–389.

CHAPTER 7, THE GEOGRAPHY OF HEALTH AND DISEASE

Bates, M., *The Natural History of Mosquitoes,* Macmillan, New York, 1949.

Balfour, M. C., *Public Health and Demography in the Far East,* Rockefeller Foundation, New York, 1950.

Covell, G., "Notes on the Distribution, Breeding Places, Adult Habits and Relation to Malaria of the Anopheline Mosquitoes of India and the Far East," *J. Malaria Inst. India, 5* (1944), 399–434.

Feng, L. C., The Anopheline Mosquitoes and the Epidemiology of Malaria in China," *Chinese Med. J., 51* (1937), 1005–1020.

Hume, E. H., *The Chinese Way in Medicine,* Johns Hopkins Press, Baltimore, 1940.

McArthur, J., "The Transmission of Malaria in Borneo," *Trans. Roy. Soc. Trop. Med. Hyg., 40* (1947), 537–558.

Megaw, J., "The Health of India," *J. Roy. Soc. Arts, 94* (1946), 242–257.

Postmus, S., "Dietary Surveys in Java and East Indonesia," *Chronica Naturae, 105* (1949), 229–236, 261–268, 316–323.

Reed, A. C., "The Curse of Angkor; Death Comes Quickly in the Tropics," *Sci. Monthly, 48* (1939), 210–231.

Rogers, L., "Cholera Incidence in India in Relation to Rainfall, Absolute Humidity, and Pilgrimages," *Trans. Roy. Soc. Trop. Med. Hyg., 38* (1944), 73–89.

Simmons, J. S., et al., *Global Epidemiology,* Lippincott, Philadelphia, 1944.

Sinton, J. A., *What Malaria Costs India,* Gov't of India Press, Simla, 1939.

Snapper, I., *Chinese Lessons to Western Medicine,* Interscience Publishers, New York, 1941.

Spencer, J. E., and W. L. Thomas, Jr., "The Hill Stations and Summer Resorts of the Orient," *Geog. Rev., 38* (1948), 635–651.

Watson, M., "The Geographical Aspects of Malaria," *Geog. J., 99* (1942), 161–172.

CHAPTER 8, PEOPLES AND THEIR LANGUAGES

Alisjahbana, T., "The Indonesian Language—a By-Product of Nationalism," *Pacific Affairs, 22* (1949), 388–391.

Andersson, J. G., "Topographic and Archaeologic Studies in the Far East," *Mus. Far East Antiq. Bull., 11* (1939), 75–109. Concerned with Indochina.

Baradat, R., "Les Samre ou Pear," *Bull. école fran. d'Extrême Orient, 41* (1941), 1–151. Concerned with Indochina.

Bell, C., *The People of Tibet,* Clarendon Press, Oxford, 1928.

Benedict, P. K., "A Cham Colony on the Island of Hainan," *Harvard J. Asiatic Studies, 6* (1941), 129–134.

Benedict, P. K., "Thai, Kadai, and Indonesia; A New Alignment in Southeast Asia," *Amer. Anthrop., 44* (1942), 576–601.

Benedict, P. K., "Languages and Literatures of Indochina," *Far Eastern Quart., 6* (1947), 379–389.

Bernatzik, H., *Akha und Meau, Probleme der angewandten Völkerkunde in Hinterindien,* Wagnerische Univ. Buchdr., Innsbruck, 1947, 2 vols.

Beyer, H. O., *Philippine and East Asia Archaeology and Its Relation to the Origin of the Pacific Islands Population,* Natl. Research Council (*U. S.*), *Bull. 29,* 1948, Manila.

Briggs, L. P., "The Appearance and Historical Usage of the Terms Tai, Thai, Siamese, and Lao," *J. Am. Or. Soc., 69* (1949), 60–73.

Brodrick, A. H., *Early Man, A Survey of Human Origins,* Hutchinson, London, 1948.

Buxton, L. H. D., *Peoples of Asia,* Knopf, New York, 1925.

Capell, A., "Peoples and Languages of Timor," *Oceania, 14* (1943–1944), 191–219, 311–317; *15* (1944–1945), 19–48.

Capell, A., "Distribution of Languages in the Central Highlands, New Guinea," *Oceania, 19* (1948–1949), 104–129, 234–254, 349–377.

Chang, Y. T., "Anthropological Features of the Shan and Their Geographical Environment in Southwest Yunnan," *Man, 44* (1944), 61–68.

Cole, F. C., *The Peoples of Malaysia,* Van Nostrand, New York, 1945.

Cuisiner, J., *Monographie des Muong, géographie humaine et sociologie,* Musée de l'Homme, Paris, 1948. On Indochina.

Doumes, J., *Les Populations Montagnardes du sud-Indochinois,* Derain, Lyons, 1950.

Eberhard, W., "Kultur und Siedlung der Randvölker Chinas," *T'oung Pao, 36, Supp.* (1942).

Eichstedt, E. F. von, "The Position of Mysore in India's Racial History," in L. K. A. Iyer, *The Mysore Tribes and Castes,* Mysore Univ. Press, 1935, 4 vols., pages 1–8 of vol. 1.

Eichstedt, E. F. von, *Rassendynamik von Ostasien,* DeGruyter, Berlin, 1944.

Embree, J. F., and W. L. Thomas, Jr., *Ethnic Groups of Northern Southeast Asia,* Yale Univ. Press, New Haven, 1950, mimeo.

Emory, K. P., "The Native Peoples of the Pacific," in O. W. Freeman, (Ed.) *Geography of the Pacific,* John Wiley & Sons, New York, 1951.

"Ethnological Reconnaissance in New Guinea," *Bull. Univ. Penna. Museum, 17* (1952), 5–37.

Feng, H. Y., and J. K. Shryock, "The Historical Origins of the Lolo," *Harvard J. Asiatic Studies, 3* (1938), 103–127.

Fürer-Haimendorf, C. von, "The Aboriginal Tribes of India," *J. Roy. Soc. Arts, 98* (1950), 997–1011.

Grierson, G. A., *Linguistic Survey of India,* Gov't of India, Calcutta, 1927, vol. 1.

Howells, W. W. (Ed.), *Early Man in the Far East,* Amer. Assoc. Phys. Anthropologists, Philadelphia, 1949.

Iyer, L. K. A., *The Mysore Tribes and Castes,* Mysore Univ. Press, 1935, 4 vols.

Izikowitz, K. G., "Lamet, Hill Peasants of French Indochina," *Etnologiska Studier, 17* (1951).

Keers, W., "An Anthropological Survey of the Eastern Little Sunda Islands," *Koninkl. Ver. Indisch Inst., Amsterdam, Mededeel. 74, Afdeel. 26,* 1948.

Keesing, F. M., *Native Peoples of the Pacific World,* Macmillan, New York, 1945.

Kuder, E. M., "The Moros in the Philippines," *Far Eastern Quart., 4* (1945), 119–126.

Kunst, J., *The Peoples of the Indian Archipelago,* Brill, Leiden, 1946.

Lasker, B., *Peoples of Southeast Asia,* Knopf, 1944, New York.

Lasker, B., *Asia on the Move,* Holt, New York, 1945.

Lasker, B., "The Role of the Chinese in the Netherlands Indies," *Far Eastern Quart., 5* (1946), 162–171.

Lin, Y. H., "The Miao-Man Peoples of Kweichow," *Harvard J. Asiatic Studies, 5* (1941), 261–345.

Linton, R. (Ed.), *Most of the World,* Columbia Univ. Press, New York, 1949.

Liu, C. S. H., "A Tentative Classification of the Races of China," *Z. für Rassenkunde, 6* (1937), 129–150.

Mahony, D. J., "The Problem of Antiquity of Man in Australia," *Mem. Natl. Museum (Australia),* Melbourne, *13* (1943), 7–56. Includes New Guinea.

Majumdar, D. N., *The Fortunes of Primitive Tribes,* Lucknow Univ. Press, Lucknow, 1944.

Manuel, A., *Chinese Elements in the Tagalog Language,* Manila, 1948.

Marshall, H. I., *The Karens of Burma,* Longmans, Green, Calcutta, 1945.

Movius, H. L., Jr., "Early Man and Pleistocene Stratigraphy in Southern and Eastern Asia," *Peabody Museum Amer. Archaeol. Ethnol., 19* (1944).

Movius, H. L., Jr., "The Lower Paleolithic Cultures of Southern and Eastern Asia," *Trans. Am. Phil. Soc., 38* (1949), Part 4.

Purcell, V., *The Chinese in Southeast Asia,* Oxford Univ. Press, London, 1951.

Schechtman, J. B., *Population Transfers in Asia,* Hallsby, New York, 1949.

Sebeok, T. A., "An Examination of the Austroasiatic Family of Languages," *Language, 18* (1942), 206–217.

Sebeok, T. A., "The Languages of Southeastern Asia," *Far Eastern Quart., 2* (1943), 349–356.

Sebeok, T. A., "Finno-Ugric and the Languages of India," *J. Am. Or. Soc., 65* (1945), 45–62.

Sutherland, I. L. G., "The Ainu People of Northern Japan," *J. Polynesian Soc., 57* (1948), 203–226.

Taeuber, I. B., "The Demographic Statistics of Southern and Eastern Asia," *J. Am. Stat. Assoc., 40* (1945), 29–37.

Taeuber, I. B., "Migration and the Population Potential of Monsoon Asia," *Milbank Mem. Fund Quart., 25* (1947), 25–43.

Terra, H. de, "The Quarternary Terrace System of Southern Asia and the Age of Man," *Geog. Rev., 29* (1939), 101–118.

Terra, H. de, and H. L. Movius, Jr., "Research on Early Man in Burma," *Trans. Am. Phil. Soc., 32* (1943), 263–436.

Thompson, W. S., *Population and Peace in the Pacific,* Univ. of Chicago Press, 1946.

Unger, L., "The Chinese in Southeast Asia," *Geog. Rev., 34* (1944), 196–217.

Vogel, A. A., *Papuaner och Pygmeer*, Natur och Cultur, Stockholm, 1951.

Ward, F. K., "Yunnan and the Tai Peoples," *J. Roy. Cent. Asian Soc.*, 24 (1937), 624–637.

Yuen, R. C., "Languages and Dialects of China," *Geog. J.*, 102 (1943), 63–67.

Zelinsky, W., "The Indochinese Peninsula, a Demographic Anomaly," *Far Eastern Quart.*, 9 (1950), 115–145.

CHAPTER 9, RELIGION, LAW, AND THE SOCIAL ORDERS

Archer, J. C., *The Sikhs*, Princeton Univ. Press, 1946.

Ball, W. M., *Nationalism and Communism in East Asia*, Melbourne Univ. Press, Melbourne, 1952.

Blakemore, R. L., "Postwar Development in Japanese Law," *Wisconsin Law Review*, July, 1947, 632–653.

Blasdell, R. A., "Islam in Malaya," *Intern. Rev. Missions, 34* (1945), 165–172.

Bouquet, A. C., *Hinduism*, Longmans, Green, New York, 1950.

Brush, J. E., "The Distribution of Religious Communities in India," *Annals Assoc. Amer. Geog.*, 39 (1949), 81–98.

Dobby, E. H. G., "Some Aspects of the Human Ecology of Southeast Asia," *Geog. J.*, 108 (1946), 40–51.

Embree, J. F., "Thailand—A Loosely Structured Social System," *Amer. Anthrop.*, 52 (1950), 181–193.

Fei, H. T., "Peasantry and Gentry, an Interpretation of Chinese Social Structure and Its Changes," *Am. J. Sociol., 52* (1946), 1–17.

Firth, Raymond, "The Peasantry of Southeast Asia," *Intern. Affairs, 26* (1950), 503–514.

Freytag, W., *Spiritual Revolution in the East*, Butterworth, London, 1940.

Furnivall, J. S., "Political Education in the Tropical Far East," *Polit. Quart.*, 17 (1946), 123–133.

Hazard, H., *Atlas of Islamic History*, Princeton Univ. Press, 1951.

Heine-Geldern, R., "Concepts of State and Kingship in Southeast Asia," *Far Eastern Quart.*, 2 (1942), 15–30.

Holtom, D. C., *The National Faith of Japan*, Kegan Paul Trench Trubner, London, 1938.

Hornell, J., "The Ancient Village Gods of South India," *Antiquity, 18* (1944), 78–87.

Hutton, J. N., *Caste in India*, Macmillan, New York, 1946.

Iwamura, S., "The Structure of Moslem Society in Inner Mongolia," *Far Eastern Quart.*, 8 (1948), 34–44.

Jacoby, E. H., *Agrarian Unrest in Southeast Asia*, Columbia Univ. Press, New York, 1949.

Jurji, E. J. (Ed.), *The Great Religions of the Modern World*, Princeton Univ. Press, 1946.

Landon, K. P., "Nationalism in Southeastern Asia," *Far Eastern Quart.*, 2 (1943), 139–152.

Landon, K. P., *Southeast Asia, Crossroads of Religion*, Univ. of Chicago Press, 1949.

Lasswell, H. D., et al, "Religion and Modernization in the Far East: A Symposium," *Far Eastern Quart.*, 12 (1953), 123–202.

Latourette, K. S., *A History of the Expansion of Christianity*, Harpers, New York, 7 volumes, varied dates. Vol. 6 (1944) deals with the nineteenth century in Asia.

Lin, M. S., *Men and Ideas, an Informal History of Chinese Political Thought*, John Day, New York, 1942.

Mandelbaum, D. G., "The Family in India," *S. W. J. Anthrop., 4* (1948), 123–139.

Mathews, B., *Unfolding Drama in Southeast Asia*, Friendship Press, New York, 1944. On the subject of religious change.

Morrison, G. E., "The Coming of Islam to the East Indies," *J. Malayan Branch Roy. Asian Soc.*, 24 (1951), 28–37.

Needham, J., "Human Laws and Laws of Nature in China and the West," *J. History Ideas, 12* (1951), 194–230.

Ner, M., "Les Musulmans de l'Indochine française," *Bull. école fran. d'Extrême Orient, 41* (1941), 151–201.

Northrop, F. S. C., *The Meeting of East and West*, Macmillan, New York, 1946.

Rankin, G. C., *Background to the Indian Law*, Cambridge Univ. Press, 1946.

Rice, S., *Hindu Customs and Their Origins*, Allen & Unwin, London, 1937.

Roy, N. R., "Early Traces of Buddhism in Burma," *J. Greater India Soc.*, 6 (1939), 1–80, 99–123.

Sharma, R. S., "Role of ·Property, Family, and Caste in the Origin of the State in Ancient India," *J. Bihar Research Soc., 38* (1952), 117–134.

Smith, W. C., *Modern Islam in India*, Minerva Book Shop, Lahore, 1943.

Soothill, W. E., *The Hall of Light, A Study of Early Chinese Kingship*, Butterworth, London, 1951.

Wales, H. G. Q., *Ancient Southeast Asian Warfare*, Quartich, London, 1952.

Ward, R. E., "The Socio-Political Role of the Buraku (Hamlet) in Japan," *Am. Pol. Sci. Rev., 45* (1951), 1025–1040.

CHAPTER 10, SETTLEMENTS AND THEIR ARCHITECTURE

Acharya, P. K., *Indian Architecture*, Oxford Univ. Press, Allahabad, 1927.

Ahmad, E., "Rural Settlement Types in the Uttar Pradesh (United Provinces of Agra and Oudh)," *Annals, Assoc. Amer. Geog.*, 42 (1952), 223–246. Deals with Ganges Valley, India.

Bishop, C. W., "Long Houses and Dragon Boats," *Antiquity, 12* (1938), 411–424.

Brown, P., *Indian Architecture, Islamic Period*, Taraporevala, Bombay, 1942.

Chesneaux, J., "Notes sur l'évolution recente de l'habitat urbain en Asie," *L'Information géographique, 13* (1949), 169–175, *14* (1950), 1–8.

Cooper, E., "Urbanization in Malaya," *Population Studies, 5* (1951), 117–131.

Davis, S. G., *Hongkong in Its Geographic Setting*, Collins, London, 1949.

Dobby, E. H. G., "Singapore, Town and Country," *Geog. Rev.*, 30 (1940), 84–109.

Dobby, E. H. G., "Settlement Patterns in Malaya," *Geog. Rev., 32* (1942), 211–232.

Ginsburg, N. S., "Ch'ang-ch'un," *Econ. Geog., 23* (1947), 290–307.

Gosh, S., "The Urban Pattern of Calcutta, India," *Econ. Geog., 26* (1950), 51–58.

Griffiths, P. J., *Better Towns; A Study of Urban Reconstruction in India*. Kitabistan, Allahabad, 1945.

Hughes, R. H., "Hongkong, an Urban Study," *Geog. J., 117* (1951), 1–23.

Izikowitz, K. G., "The Community House of the Lamet," *Ethnos, 8* (1943), 10–60.

Loeb, E. M., and J. O. M. Broek, "Social Organization and the Long House in Southeast Asia," *Amer. Anthrop., 49* (1947), 414–425.

Marchal, H., *L'Architecture comparée dans l'Inde et L'Extrême Orient,* Les édit. d'art et d'hist., Paris, 1944.

Mukerjee, R., *Man and His Habitation,* Longmans, Green, London, 1940.

Mukerjee, R., "La Structure économique de six villages du Bengale," *Ann. géographie, 58* (1949), 313–324.

Pithawalla, M. B., "Settlements in the Lower Indus Basin," *J. Madras Geog.* Soc., 13 (1938), 323–357.

Spate, O. H. K., "The Burmese Village," *Geog. Rev., 35* (1945), 523–543.

Spate, O. H. K., "The Indian Village," *Geography, 37* (1952), 142–152.

Spate, O. H. K., and E. Ahmad, "Five Cities of the Gangetic Plain, a Cross Section of Indian Culture History," *Geog. Rev., 40* (1950), 260–278.

Spate, O. H. K., and L. W. Trueblood, "Rangoon; a Study in Urban Geography," *Geog. Rev., 32* (1942), 56–73.

Spencer, J. E., "Changing Chungking: the Rebuilding of an Old Chinese City," *Geog. Rev., 29* (1939), 46–60.

Spencer, J. E., "The Houses of the Chinese," *Geog. Rev., 37* (1947), 254–273.

Trewartha, G. T., "Chinese Cities, Numbers and Distribution," *Annals, Assoc. Amer. Geog., 41* (1951), 331–347.

Trewartha, G. T., "Chinese Cities, Origins and Functions," *Annals, Assoc. Amer. Geog., 42* (1952), 69–93.

Yang, M. C., *A Chinese Village, Taitou, Shantung Province,* Columbia Univ. Press, New York, 1945.

CHAPTER 11, THE PATTERNS OF HISTORICAL CONTACT

Briggs, L. P., "The Hinduized States of Southeast Asia, a Review," *Far Eastern Quart., 7* (1948), 376–393.

Cameron, M. E., *China, Japan, and the Powers,* Ronald, New York, 1952.

Christian, J. L., "Anglo-French Rivalry in Southeast Asia, Its Historical Geography and Diplomatic Climate," *Geog. Rev., 31* (1941), 272–282.

Coedes, G., *Les États Hindouises d'Indochine et Indonesie,* Boccard, Paris, 1948.

Eckel, P. E., *The Far East Since 1500,* Harcourt, Brace, New York, 1947.

Eldridge, F. B., *The Background of Eastern Sea Power,* Georgian House, Melbourne, 1945. Covers period to mid-eighteenth century.

Fairbank, J. K., "Tributary Trade and China's Relations with the West," *Far Eastern Quart., 1* (1942), 130–149.

Goncalves, J., *Os Portugueses e o Mar das Indias—da India Antiga e sua historia,* Luso-Espanhola, Lisbon, 1947.

Hornell, J., "Sea Trade in Early Times," *Antiquity, 15* (1941), 233–256.

Huzayyin, S. A., *Arabia and the Far East, Their Commercial and Cultural Relations in Graeco-Roman and Irano-Arabian Times,* Roy. Soc. of Geog., Cairo, 1942.

Hyma, A., *The Dutch in the Far East, a History of the Dutch Commercial and Colonial Empire,* Wahr, Ann Arbor, 1942.

Latourette, K. S., *A Short History of the Far East,* Macmillan, New York, rev. ed., 1951.

Majumdar, R. C., *Hindu Colonies in the Far East,* General Printers, Calcutta, 1944.

Manchester, C. A., Jr., "Exploration and Mapping of the Pacific," in O. W. Freeman, *Geography of the Pacific,* John Wiley & Sons, New York, 1951, pp. 61–88.

Morley, J. A. E., "The Arabs and the Eastern Trade," *Journal Malayan Branch Roy. Asiatic Soc., 22* (1949), 143–175.

Rowbotham, A. H., *Missionary and Mandarin: The Jesuits at the Court of China,* Univ. of Calif. Press, Berkeley, 1942.

Sastri, K. A. N., *South Indian Influences in the Far East,* Hind Kitabs, Bombay, 1949.

Villiers, A., *Monsoon Seas,* McGraw-Hill, New York, 1952.

Vinacke, H. M., *A History of the Far East in Modern Times,* Crofts, New York, rev. ed., 1950.

Wilbur, M. E., *The East India Company,* Smith, New York, 1945.

CHAPTER 12, THE PROCESSES OF MODERNIZATION

Bekker, C., J. M. van der Kroef, and C. DuBois, "Culture Contact and Cultural Change in Southeast Asia; a Symposium," *Far Eastern Quart., 11* (1951), 3–34.

Brandt, W., "Institutions and Ideologies, American and Asiatic," *Pacific Affairs 15* (1942), 61–76.

Clyde, P. H., *The Far East, a History of the Impact of the West on Eastern Asia,* Prentice-Hall, New York, 1948.

Emerson, R., L. A. Mills, and V. Thompson, *Government and Nationalism in Southeast Asia,* Inst. Pac. Rel., New York, 1942.

Furnivall, J. S., "Colonial Southeast Asia—Instruction or Education," *Pacific Affairs, 15* (1942), 77–89.

Harper, N. D., "Some Historical Aspects of Race and Culture Contact," *Hist. Stud., Australia and New Zealand, 3* (1944), 35–57.

Hsu, F. L. K., "Influence of South Seas Emigration on Certain Chinese Provinces," *Far Eastern Quart., 5* (1945), 47–59.

Hubbard, G. E., *Eastern Industrialization and its Effect on the West,* Oxford Univ. Press, London, 1938.

Hughes, E. R., *The Invasion of China by the Western World,* Macmillan, New York, 1938.

Hughes, T. L., "British Contributions to the Industrial Development of Burma," *J. Roy. Soc. Arts, 98* (1949), 121–136.

Ike, N., "Taxation and Land Ownership in the Westernization of Japan," *J. Econ. Hist., 7* (1947), 160–182.

Ike, N., "Western Influences on the Meiji Restoration," *Pacific Hist. Rev., 17* (1948), 1–10.

Keesing, F. M., *The South Seas in the Modern World,* John Day, New York, 1941.

O'Malley, L. S. S. (Ed.), *Modern India and the West,* Roy. Inst. Intern. Affairs, London, 1941.

Pratt, J. T., *The Expansion of Europe into the Far East,* Sylvan Press, London, 1947.

Ruthnaswamy, M., *Some Influences That Made the British Administrative System in India,* Luzac, London, 1939.

Sansom, G. B., *The Western World and Japan, A Study in the Interaction of European and Asiatic Cultures,* Knopf, New York, 1950.

Spear, P., *India, Pakistan, and the West,* Oxford Univ. Press, New York, 1949.

Taylor, E., *Richer by Asia,* Houghton Mifflin, Boston, 1947.

Wales, H. G. Q., *The Making of Greater India, a Study in Southeast Asian Culture Change,* Quartich, London, 1951.

CHAPTER 13, REGIONS: PHYSICAL, CULTURAL, OR GEOGRAPHIC. AN INCOMPLETE LIST ON GENERAL CULTURAL REGIONALISM

Bacon, E., "A Preliminary Attempt to Determine the Culture Areas of Asia," *S. W. J. Anthrop., 2* (1946), 117–132.

Bacon, E., "Problems Related to Delimiting the Culture Areas of Asia," *Amer. Antiquity, 18* (1953), 17–23.

Broek, J. O. M., "Diversity and Unity in Southeast Asia," *Geog. Rev., 34* (1944), 175–195.

Kroeber, A. L., "Culture Groupings in Southeast Asia," *S. W. J. Anthrop., 3* (1947), 322–330.

Naroll, R. S., "A Draft Map of the Culture Areas of Asia," *S. W. J. Anthrop., 6* (1950), 183–187.

Vandenbosch, A., "Regionalism in Southeast Asia," *Far Eastern Quart., 5* (1946), 427–438.

Cressey, Dobby, and Stamp also have each dealt with this problem and have discussions on the subject from the more normal "geographic" points of view.

CHAPTERS 14 AND 15, MOTHER INDIA: IN THE BEGINNING AND IN THE MODERN WORLD

Ahmad, M. R., *Pakistan, an Economic Proposition,* Kitabistan, Allahabad, 1948.

Ahmad, N., *The Basis of Pakistan,* Thacker Spink, Calcutta, 1947.

Bagchi, K., *The Ganges Delta,* Univ. of Calcutta Press, 1944.

Barton, W., "Postwar Development Schemes in the States of Southern India,," *J. Roy. Soc. Arts, 93* (1945), 477–488.

Barton, W., "Postwar Development Schemes in the Northern and Central Indian States," *J. Roy. Soc. Arts, 94* (1946), 90–100.

Bose, A., *Social and Rural Economy of Northern India,* Univ. of Calcutta Press, 1942.

Brown, W. N. (Ed.), *India, Pakistan, and Ceylon,* Cornell Univ. Press, Ithaca, 1951.

Brush, J. E., "The Iron and Steel Industry in India," *Geog. Rev., 42* (1952), 37–55.

Burns, W., *Technological Possibilities of Agricultural Development in India,* Gov't Printer, Lahore, 1944.

Chand, G., *India's Teeming Millions,* George Allen & Unwin, London, 1939.

Chandrasekhar, S., *India's Population; Fact and Policy,* John Day, New York, 1946.

Chatterjee, S. P., *Bengal in Maps,* Orient Longmans, Calcutta, 1949.

Chaudhury, T. C. R., "The Racial Problem in Bengal," *Man in India, 32* (1952), 52–63.

Chhibber, H. L., *India, Part 1, Physical Basis of Geography of India,* Nand Kishore, Benares, 1945.

Chhibber, H. L., *Advanced Economic Geography of India and Pakistan,* Nand Kishore, Benares, 1949.

Codrington, H. W., *A Short History of Ceylon,* Macmillan, London, 1939.

Cook, R. C., "India's Basic Need: Population Control," *Pop. Bull., 8* (1952), 37–46.

Crop Atlas of India, Gov't Printer, New Delhi, 1939.

Cumming, J. G. (Ed.), *Revealing India's Past,* Indian Soc., London, 1939. Review of archaeological studies.

Dantwala, M. L., "Land Reforms in India," *Intern. Labor Rev., 66* (1952), 419–443.

Das Gupta, B. B., *A Short Economic Survey of Ceylon,* Assoc. Newspapers, Colombo, 1949.

Das Gupta, P. C., "Some Glimpses of Ancient Indian Shipping," *Calcutta Rev., 121* (1951), 95–104.

Davies, C. C., *An Historical Atlas of the Indian Peninsula,* Oxford Univ. Press, Calcutta, 1949.

Davis, K., *The Population of India and Pakistan,* Princeton Univ. Press, 1951.

Day, W. M., "Relative Permanence of Former Boundaries of India," *Scottish Geog. Mag., 65* (1949), 113–122.

Diver, K. H. M., *Royal India, a Descriptive and Historical Study of India's Fifteen Principal States and Their Rulers,* Appleton-Century, New York, 1942.

Dubey, R. N., *Economic Geography of India,* Kitab-Mahal, Allahabad, 1943.

Dutt, C. P., *Farm Science and Crop Production in India,* Kitabistan, Allahabad, 2nd ed., 1947.

Engebretson, T. O., "Agriculture and Land Tenure in India," *Foreign Agr., 15* (1952), 262–267.

Farmer, B. H., "Agriculture in Ceylon," *Geog. Rev., 40* (1950), 42–66.

Fowler, F. J., "Some Problems of Water Distribution between East and West Punjab," *Geog. Rev., 40* (1950), 583–589.

Fürer-Haimendorf, C. von, "The Problem of Megalithic Cultures in Middle India," *Man in India, 25* (1945), 73–86.

Geddes, A., "The Population of India; Variability of Change as a Regional Demographic Index," *Geog. Rev., 32* (1942), 562–573.

Ghosh, B. B., *Indian Economics and Pakistani Economics,* Mukkerjee, Calcutta, 1949.

Ghosh, D., *Pressure of Population and Economic Efficiency in India,* Oxford Univ. Press, New Delhi, 1946.

Gilbert, W. H., "Peoples of India," *Smithsonian Inst. Publ. 3767,* Washington, 1944.

Gorrie, R. M., "Countering Desiccation in the Punjab," *Geog. Rev., 38* (1948), 30–40.

Jayasuriya, C. E. P., "A Historical Survey of Ceylon Trade," *J. Roy. Soc. Arts, 97* (1949), 757–768.

Jennings, W. I., *The Economy of Ceylon,* Oxford Univ. Press, Madras, 2nd ed., 1951.

Kantawala, M. H., *The Food Grains,* Lotus Trust, Bombay, 1945.

Karan, P. P., "Economic Regions of Chota Nagpur, Bihar, India," *Econ. Geog., 29* (1953), 216–250.

Kini, K. S., and U. B. S. Rao, *Oxford Pictorial Atlas of Indian History,* Oxford Univ. Press, London, 4th ed., 1942.

Kirk, W., "The Damodar Valley—'Valles Opima,' " *Geog. Rev., 40* (1950), 415–443. The growth of a little TVA.

Krishnaswami, V. D., "Stone Age of India," *Ancient India, 3* (1947), 11–57.

Kuriyan, G., *Hydro-Electric Power in India—A Geographical Analysis,* Indian Geog. Soc. Monog. No. 1, Madras, 1945.

McCune, S., "The Land of Ceylon," *J. Geog., 46* (1947), 83–91.

McCune, S., "Man's Activities in Ceylon, *J. Geog., 46* (1947), 148–159.

McCune, S., "Sequence of Plantation Agriculture in Ceylon," *Econ. Geog., 25* (1949), 226–235.

Mahalingham, T. V., *Administration and Social Life under Vijayanagar,* Univ. of Madras Press, 1940.

Mahalingham, T. V., *Economic Life in the Vijayanagar Empire,* Univ. of Madras Press, 1951.

Majumdar, D. N., *Races and Cultures of India,* Allahabad, n.d.

Majumdar, R. C. (Ed.), *The Vedic Age,* George Allen & Unwin, London, 1951.

Mayer, A. C., *Land and Society in Malabar,* Oxford Univ. Press, London, 1952.

Mills, L. A., *Britain and Ceylon,* Longmans, Green, London, 1945.

Mitchell, K., "Roads and Road Transport in India," *J. Roy. Soc. Arts,* 95 (1947), 592–610.

Moreland, W. H., and A. C. Chatterjee, *A Short History of India,* Longmans, Green, London, 2nd ed., 1944.

Muranjan, S. K., *Economics of Postwar India,* Hind-Kitabs, Bombay, 2nd ed., 1946.

Nag, N. S., *A Study of Economic Plans for India,* Hind-Kitabs, Bombay, 1949.

Nanavati, M. B., and J. J. Anjaria, *The Indian Rural Problem,* Indian Soc. Agr. Econ., Bombay, 1944.

Northey, W. B., *The Land of the Ghurkas, or the Himalayan Kingdom of Nepal,* Heffer, Cambridge, 1937.

Panikkar, K. M., *India and the Indian Ocean, an Essay on the Influence of Sea Power on Indian History,* George Allen & Unwin, London, 1945.

Parthasarathy, C., "Major Ports in India and Their Future Development," *Trans. & Communic. Rev.,* 4 (1951), 23–35.

Piggott, S., *Some Ancient Cities of India,* Oxford Univ. Press, Bombay, 1945.

Piggott, S., *Prehistoric India to 1,000 B.C.,* Penguin Books, Baltimore, 1950.

Pithawalla, M. B., *An Introduction to Pakistan: Its Resources and Potentialities,* Karachi, 1948.

"Present Situation and Plans for Development of Roads in India," *Trans. & Communic. Rev.,* 2 (1949), 25–35.

Russell, E. J., "India's Peoples and Their Food," *Geography,* 37 (1952), 125–141.

Ryan, B., "Socio-Cultural Regions of Ceylon," *Rural Sociol.,* 15 (1950), 3–19.

Saletore, R. N., *Life in the Gupta Age,* Popular Book Depot, Bombay, 1943.

Sastri, K. A. N., *The Colas,* Univ. of Madras Press, 1935. A south Indian people and empire of the first millennium A.D.

Sharma, T. R., *Location of Industries in India,* Hind-Kitabs, Bombay, 2nd ed., 1948.

Silva, S. F. de, *The New Geography of Ceylon,* Colombo Apothecaries, Colombo, rev. ed., 1947.

Smith, R. A., *Divided India,* McGraw-Hill, New York, 1947.

Sovani, N. V., *Economic Relations of India with Southeast Asia and the Far East,* Oxford Univ. Press, New York, 1951.

Spate, O. H. K., "Geographical Aspects of the Pakistan Scheme," *Geog. J.,* 102 (1943), 125–136.

Spate, O. H. K., "The Partition of India and the Prospects of Pakistan," *Geog. Rev.,* 38 (1948), 5–29.

Statistical Atlas of Bombay State, Bur. Econ. and Stat., Bombay, 1950.

"Survey of Indian Ports," *Dock and Harbour Authority,* 28 (1947), continued paging.

Taeuber, I. B., "Ceylon as a Demographic Laboratory," *Pop. Index,* 15 (1949), 293–304.

Terra, H. de, and T. T. Paterson, "Studies on the Ice Age of India and Associated Human Cultures," *Carnegie Inst. Publ. 493,* Washington, 1939.

Thomas, P. J., *India's Basic Industries,* Orient Longmans, Calcutta, 1948.

Tiwari, R. D., *Indian Agriculture,* New Book Co., Bombay, 1943.

"Transport and Communication in Pakistan," *Trans. & Communic. Rev.,* 4 (1951), 19–33.

Trivedi, A. B., *The Wealth of Gujarat,* published by author, sold by Dave, Bombay, 1943.

Trotter, H., *Manual of Indian Forest Utilization,* Oxford Univ. Press, London, 1940.

Vakil, C. N., *Economic Consequences of Divided India,* Vora, Bombay, 1950.

Venkatasubbiah, H., *The Structural Basis of Indian Economy,* George Allen & Unwin, London, 1940.

Vidyarthi, M. L., *India's Culture through the Ages,* Mandir, Kanpur, 2nd ed., 1952.

Wheeler, R. E. M., *Five Thousand Years of Pakistan,* Johnson, London, 1950.

Wijesekera, N. D., *The People of Ceylon,* Gunasena, Colombo, 1950.

Wikhramatileke, R., "Ella Village—an Example of Rural Settlement and Agricultural Trends in Highland Ceylon," *Econ. Geog.,* 28 (1952), 355–363.

Worman, E. C., "The Neolithic Problem in the Prehistory of India," *J. Wash. Acad. Sci.,* 39 (1949), 181–201.

CHAPTER 16, THE IRRAWADDY VALLEY BECOMES BURMA

Andrus, J. R., *Burmese Economic Life,* Stanford Univ. Press, 1947.

Appleton, G., *Buddhism in Burma,* Longmans, Green, Calcutta, 1943.

Atkinson, D. J., "Forests and Forestry in Burma," *J. Roy. Soc. Arts,* 94 (1948), 478–491.

Binns, B. O., *Agricultural Economy in Burma,* Gov't Printer, Rangoon, 1948, but written in 1943.

Burma Petroleum Industry, Longmans, Green, Calcutta, 1946.

Burma Rice, Longmans, Green, Calcutta, 1944.

Chhibber, H. L., *Geology of Burma,* Macmillan, London, 1934.

Chhibber, H. L., *Mineral Resources of Burma,* Macmillan, London, 1934.

Christian, J. L., *Modern Burma, a Survey of Political and Economic Development,* Univ. of Calif. Press, Berkeley, 1942.

Deignan, H. L., "Burma—Gateway to China," *Smithsonian Inst. Publ. 3738,* Washington, 1943.

Furnivall, J. S., *Colonial Policy and Practice, a Comparative Study of Burma and Netherlands India,* Cambridge Univ. Press, 1948.

Hall, D. G. E., *Europe and Burma,* Oxford Univ. Press, London, 1945.

Harvey, G. E., *British Rule in Burma, 1824–1942,* Faber & Faber, London, 1946.

Morehead, F. T., *The Forests of Burma,* Longmans, Green, Calcutta, 1944.

Pearn, B. R., *Burma Background,* Longmans, Green, Calcutta, 1943.

Pearn, B. R., *The Indian in Burma,* LePlay House, Ledbury, England, 1946.

Richards, C. J., *The Burman, an Appreciation*, Longmans, Green, Calcutta, 1945.

Spate, O. H. K., *Burma Setting*, Longmans, Green, Calcutta, 1943.

Stevenson, H. N. C., *Economics of the Central Chin Tribes*, Times of India, Bombay, 1944.

Stevenson, H. N. C., *The Hill Peoples of Burma*, Longmans, Green, Calcutta, 1946.

Terra, H. de, "Component Geographic Factors of the Natural Regions of Burma," *Annals, Assoc. Amer. Geog.*, 34 (1944), 67–96.

CHAPTER 17, THE EVOLUTION OF THAILAND

Briggs, L. P., "A Sketch of Cambodian History," *Far Eastern Quart.*, 6 (1947), 345–363.

Briggs, L. P., "Siamese Attacks on Angkor before 1430," *Far Eastern Quart.*, 8 (1948), 3–33.

Briggs, L. P., "The Ancient Khmer Empire," *Trans. Am. Phil. Soc.*, 41 (1951), 1–295.

Christian, J. L., and N. Ike, "Thailand in Japan's Foreign Relations," *Pacific Affairs*, 15 (1942), 195–221.

Coedes, G., *Pour mieux comprendre Angkor*, Librarie d'Amérique et d'Orient, Paris, 1947.

Credner, W., *Siam, das Land der Tai*, Englehorn, Stuttgart, 1935.

Crosby, J., *Siam, the Crossroads*, Hollis & Carter, London, 1945.

Deignan, H. G., "Siam, Land of Free Men," *Smithsonian Inst. Publ. 3703*, Washington, 1943.

Landon, K. P., *Siam in Transition*, Univ. of Chicago Press, 1939.

Landon, K. P., *The Chinese in Thailand*, Oxford Univ. Press, New York, 1941.

Majumdar, R. C., *Kambuja-Desa, or An Ancient Hindu Colony in Cambodia*, Univ. of Madras Press, 1944.

Pendleton, R. L., "Land Use in Northeastern Thailand," *Geog. Rev.*, 33 (1943), 15–41.

Pendleton, R. L., "The Agriculture of Siam," *Foreign Agr.*, 10 (1946), 154–167.

Ponder, H. W., *Cambodian Glory*, Butterworth, London, 1936.

Reeve, W. D., *Public Administration in Siam*, Roy. Inst. Intern. Affairs, London, 1951.

"Study on Highways in Thailand," *Trans. & Communic. Rev.*, 5 (1952), 49–62.

Sarasas, P., *My Country Thailand, Its History, Geography, and Civilization*, Maruzen, Tokyo, 1942.

Thompson, V., *Thailand, the New Siam*, Macmillan, New York, 1941.

Wales, H. G. Q., *Ancient Siamese Government and Administration*, Quartich, London, 1934.

Wales, H. G. Q., "The Exploration of Sri-Deva, an Ancient Indian City in Indochina," *Indian Arts and Letters*, 10 (1936), 61–100.

Zimmerman, C. C., "Some Phases of Land Utilization in Siam," *Geog. Rev.*, 27 (1937), 378–393.

CHAPTER 18, INDOCHINA, A STATE OF MIXED CULTURES

Barquissau, R. (Ed.), *L'Asie française et ses écrivains*, Vigneau, Paris, 1947. Contains a long bibliography.

Birnbaum, M., *Angkor and the Mandarin Road*, Vantage Press, New York, 1952.

Brodrick, A. H., *Little China, the Annamese Lands*, Oxford Univ. Press, London, 1942.

Deveze, M., *La France d'outre mer de l'empire colonial*, Hachette, Paris, 1948.

"French Indochina; Demographic Imbalance and Colonial Policy," *Pop. Index*, 11 (1945), 68–81.

Gourou, P., *Archaeological Research in Indo-China*, Harvard Univ. Press, Cambridge, 2 vols., 1947–1949.

Gourou, P., "Land Utilization in Upland Areas of Indochina," in *Development of Upland Areas of the Far East*, vol. 2, pp. 24–42, Inst. Pac. Rel., New York, 1951, mimeo.

Gourou, P., *Les Paysans du delta Tonkinois, étude de géographie humaine*, Les édit. d'art et d'histoire, Paris, 1936.

Gourou, P., *L'utilization du sol en Indochine française*, Hartmann, Paris, 1940.

Janse, O. R. T., "The Peoples of Indochina," *Smithsonian Inst., Publ. 3768*, Washington, 1944

Lartillaeux, H., *Géographie des chemins de fer français*, Paris, 1950. Pages 89–162 are on Indochina.

Miller, E. W., "Industrial Resources of Indochina," *Far Eastern Quart.*, 6 (1947), 396–408.

Robequain, C., *Economic Development of French Indo-China*, Oxford Univ. Press, New York, 1944.

Renouvin, P., *La question d'Extrême Orient, 1840–1940*, Hachette, Paris, 1946.

Thompson, V., *French Indo-China*, Macmillan, 1937.

CHAPTER 19, MALAYA: MALAY, BRITISH, AND CHINESE

Braddell, R., "Notes on Ancient Times in Malaya," *J. Malayan Branch Roy. Asiatic Soc.*, 20 (1947), 161–186.

Briggs, L. P., "The Khmer Empire and the Malay Peninsula," *Far Eastern Quart.*, 9 (1950), 256–305.

Desch, H. E., "Malayan Forests and their Utilization," *Asiatic Rev.*, 34 (1938), 719–728.

Dobby, E. H. G., "Settlement and Land Utilization, Malacca," *Geog. J.*, 94 (1939), 466–478.

Dobby, E. H. G., "The Development of Malaya's Uplands," in *The Development of the Upland Areas of the Far East*, vol. 2, pp. 1–23, Inst. Pac. Rel., New York, 1951, mimeo.

Dobby, E. H. G., "The Kelantan Delta," *Geog. Rev.*, 41 (1951), 226–255.

Dobby, E. H. G., "The North Kedah Plain, a study in the Environment of Pioneering for Rice Cultivation," *Econ. Geog.*, 27 (1951), 287–315.

Finkelstein, L. S., "Prospects for Self Government in Malaya," *Far Eastern Survey*, 21 (Jan. 30, 1952), 9–17.

Firth, Raymond, *Malay Fishermen: Their Peasant Economy*, Kegan Paul, London, 1946.

Firth, Rosemary, "Housekeeping among Malay Peasants," *London School of Econ. & Pol. Sci. Monograph on Social Anthropology*, 7, 1943.

Fisher, C. A., "The Railway Geography of British Malaya," *Scottish Geog. Mag.*, 64 (1948), 123–136.

Gibson-Hill, C. A., "A Note on the Cocos-Keeling Islands," *Bull. Raffles Museum*, 22 (1950), 11–28.

Grist, D. H., *An Outline of Malayan Agriculture*, Dept. of Agr., Kuala Lumpur, 1936.

King, A. W., "Plantations and Agriculture in Malaya, with Notes on the Trade of Singapore," *Geog. J., 93* (1939), 137–148.

Kunst, J., "New Light on the Early History of the Malay Archipelago," *Indian Art and Letters, 12* (1938), 99–106.

Marsh, T. D., and V. Dawson, "Animal Husbandry in Malaya," *Malayan Agr. J., 30* (1947), 133–142.

Morrison, I., "Aspects of the Racial Problem in Malaya," *Pacific Affairs, 22* (1949), 239–253.

Purcell, V., *The Chinese in Malaya,* Oxford Univ. Press, London, 1948.

Smith, T. E., *Population Growth in Malay, an Analysis of Recent Trends,* Roy. Inst. Intern. Affairs, London, 1952.

Tweedie, M. W. F., "Prehistory in Malaya," *J. Roy. Asiatic Soc.,* 1942, 1–13.

Wales, H. G. Q., "Archaeological Researches on Ancient Indian Colonization in Malaya," *J. Malayan Branch Roy. Asiatic Soc., 18* (1950), 1–85.

Winstedt, R., *Britain and Malaya, 1786–1941,* Longmans, Green, London, 1941.

Winstedt, R., *The Malays, a Cultural History,* Philosophical Library, New York, 1950.

CHAPTER 20, THE SEVERAL INDIES

Atlas van Tropisch Nederland, Nijhoff, The Hague, 1938.

Blackwood, B., "Life on the Upper Watut, New Guinea," *Geog. J., 94* (1939), 11–28.

Boeke, J. H., *The Structure of Netherland Indian Economy,* Inst. Pac. Rel., New York, 1942.

Boeke, J. H., *The Evolution of the Netherlands Indies Economy,* Inst. Pac. Rel., New York, 1946.

Boeke, J. H., *Economie van Indonesie,* Willink & Zoon, Haarlem, 1951.

Bowman, R. G., "Prospects for Settlement in Northeastern New Guinea," *State Univ. Iowa Stud. Nat. Hist., 19* (1948), No. 1, 120 pages.

Bowman, R. G., "Northern Melanesia, New Guinea, and the Bismarck Archipelago," in O. W. Freeman, *Geography of the Pacific,* John Wiley & Sons, New York, 1951, pp. 157–172.

Briggs, L. P., "The Origin of the Sailendra Dynasty," *J. Am. Or. Soc., 72* (1952), 37–39.

Broek, J. O. M., "The Economic Development of the Outer Provinces of the Netherlands Indies," *Geog. Rev., 30* (1940), 187–200.

Broek, J. O. M., *Economic Development of the Netherlands Indies,* Inst. Pac. Rel., New York, 1942.

Broek, J. O. M., "Man and Resources in the Netherlands Indies," *Far Eastern Quart., 5* (1946), 121–132.

Cator, W. J., *The Economic Position of the Chinese in the Netherlands Indies,* Univ. of Chicago Press, 1936.

Cator, G., "Labuan," *Asiatic Rev., 43* (1947), 84–88.

Daniel, H., *Islands of the East Indies,* Putnam, New York, 1944.

Dekker, N. A. D., *Tanah Air Kita, a Book on the Country and People of Indonesia,* Van Hoeve, The Hague, 2nd ed., 1951.

DeKlerck, E. S., *History of the Netherlands East Indies,* Brusse, Rotterdam, 1938, 2 vols.

De Meel, H., "Demographic Dilemma In Indonesia," *Pacific Affairs, 24* (1951), 266–283.

Devries, E., "Problems of Agriculture in Indonesia," *Pacific Affairs, 22* (1949), 120–143.

DuBois, C., *The People of Alor, a Socio-Psychological Study of an East Indian Island,* Univ. of Minn. Press, Minneapolis, 1944.

Finkelstein, L. J., "Iran in Indonesian Politics," *Far Eastern Survey, 20* (April 18, 1951), 76–80.

Furnivall, J. S., *Netherlands India, a Study in Plural Economy,* Cambridge Univ. Press, 1939.

Furnivall, J. S., *Colonial Policy and Practice, a Comparative Study of Burma and the Netherlands India,* Cambridge Univ. Press, 1948.

Helbig, K., *Indonesiens Tropenwelt,* Kosmos Verlag, Stuttgart, 1947.

Honig, P., and F. Verdoorn (Eds.), *Science and Scientists in the Netherlands Indies,* Board for Neth. Indies, New York, 1945.

Kahin, G. McT., "The State of North Borneo, 1881–1946," *Far Eastern Quart., 7* (1947), 43–65.

Kahin, G. McT., *Nationalism and Revolution in Indonesia,* Cornell Univ. Press, Ithaca, 1952.

Kennedy, R., *The Ageless Indies,* John Day, New York, 1942.

Kennedy, R., "Islands and Peoples of the Indies," *Smithsonian Inst. Publ. 3734,* Washington, 1943.

Krieger, H. W., "Island Peoples of the Western Pacific," *Smithsonian Inst. Publ. 3737,* Washington, 1943.

Loeb, E. M., and R. Heine-Geldern, *Sumatra, Its History and People,* Univ. of Vienna, Vienna, 1935.

Lett, L., *Papua: Its People and Its Promise,* Cheshire, Melbourne, 1944.

Mair, L. P., *Australia in New Guinea,* Christophers, London, 1948.

Mendez-Correa, A. A., *Timor Portugues, Contribucoes para o seu Estudo Anthropologico,* Imprensa Nacional, Lisbon, 1944. Has an English summary, pp. 197–215.

Metcalf, J. E., *The Agricultural Economy of Indonesia,* Dept. of Agriculture, Washington, 1952.

Moens, J. L., "Crivijaya, Yava en Kataka," *Tijdschrift voor Indische Taal-Land—en Volkenkunde, 77* (1937), 317–488. On the history and location of Sri Vijaya.

Nilles, J., "Natives of the Bismarck Mountain, New Guinea," *Oceania, 14* (1943–1944), 104–123; *15* (1944–1945), 1–18.

Noakes, J. L., *A Report on the 1947 Population Census, Sarawak and Brunei,* Gov't Printer, Kuching, 1948.

Pelzer, K. J., "Tanah Sabrang and Java's Population Problem," *Far Eastern Quart., 5* (1946), 133–142.

Reed, S. W., *The Making of Modern New Guinea,* Amer. Philosoph. Soc., Philadelphia, 1943.

Sastri, K. A. N., "Sri Vijaya," *Bull. école fran. d'Extrême Orient, 40* (1940), 239–313.

Schafer, A., "Haus und Siedlung in Zentral Neuguinea," *Ethnos, 10* (1943), 97–114.

Schneeberger, W. F., "The Kerayan-Kalabit Highland of Central Northeast Borneo," *Geog. Rev., 35* (1945), 544–562.

Schnitger, F. M., *Forgotten Kingdoms in Sumatra,* Brill, Leiden, 1939.

Sokol, A. E., "Communication and Production in Indonesian History," *Far Eastern Quart., 7* (1948), 339–353.

Sokol, A. E., "Indonesia," in O. W. Freeman (Ed.), *Geography of the Pacific,* John Wiley & Sons, New York, 1951, pp. 460–494.

Sowash, W. B., "Colonial Rivalries in Timor," *Far Eastern Quart., 7* (1948), 227–235.

Spate, O. H. K., "Changing Native Agriculture in New Guinea," *Geog. Rev., 43* (1953), 151–172.

Stikker, A. H., *Leerboek der economie voor Indonesie,* Wolters, Groningen, 1949.

Stirling, M. A., "The Native Peoples of New Guinea," *Smithsonian Inst. Publ. 3726,* Washington, 1943.

Taylor, N., *Cinchona in Java,* Greenberg, New York, 1945.

Ter Braake, A. L., *Mining in the Netherlands East Indies,* Inst. Pac. Rel., New York, 1944.

Tergast, G. C. W. Ch., and E. DeVries, "Utilization of Upland Areas in Indonesia and Western New Guinea," in vol. 2 of *The Development of Upland Areas of the Far East,* Inst. Pac. Rel., New York, 1951, mimeo. pp. 43–102.

Ter Haar, B., *Adat Law in Indonesia,* Inst. Pac. Rel., New York, 1948.

The Republic of Indonesia, the Country, the People, the History, Embassy of Indonesia, Washington, 1951.

"Transportation and Communications in the U. N. Trust Territories," *Trans. & Communic. Rev., 2* (1949), 44–71.

Vandenbosch, A., *The Dutch East Indies, Its Government, Problems, and Politics,* Univ. of Calif. Press, Berkeley, 1942.

Van der Kroef, J. M., "The Term Indonesia: Its Origin and Usage," *J. Am. Or. Soc., 71* (1951), 166–171.

Vlekke, B. H. M., *Nusantara, a History of the East Indian Archipelago,* Harvard Univ. Press, Cambridge, 1945.

Wolf, C., Jr., *The Indonesian Story, the Birth, Growth, and Structure of the Indonesian Republic,* John Day, New York, 1948.

CHAPTER 21, THE PHILIPPINES: AN ISLAND BORDERLAND

Alip, E. M., *Philippine History,* Alip & Brion, Manila, 1948.

Alip, E. M., *Philippine Government, Origins, Development, Organization and Functions,* Alip & Brion, Manila, 1948.

Benitez, C., *History of the Philippines,* Ginn, Boston, 1940.

Beyer, H. O., "Philippine and East Asian Archaeology, and Its Relation to the Origin of the Pacific Island Population," *Natl. Research Council, Manila, Bull. 29,* 1949.

Beyer, H. O., "Outline Review of Philippine Archaeology by Islands and Provinces," *Philippine J. Sci., 77* (1947).

Castillo, A. V., *Philippine Economics,* privately published, Manila, 1949.

Cutshall, A., "Problems of Land Ownership in the Philippine Islands," *Econ. Geog., 28* (1952), 31–36.

Hainsworth, R. G., and R. T. Moyer, *Agricultural Geography of the Philippine Islands, a Graphic Summary,* Office Foreign Agr. Rel., Washington, 1945.

Hayden, J. R., *The Philippines, a Study in National Development,* Macmillan, New York, 1942.

Kolb, A., *Die Philippinen,* Koehler, Leipzig, 1942.

Krieger, H. W., "Peoples of the Philippines," *Smithsonian Inst. Publ. 3694,* Washington, 1942.

Pelzer, K. J., *Pioneer Settlement in the Asiatic Tropics,* Amer. Geog. Soc., New York, 1945.

Pendleton, R. L., "Land Utilization and Agriculture of Mindanao, Philippines," *Geog. Rev., 32* (1942), 180–210.

Report of the Philippine-United States Agricultural Mission, Office of Foreign Agr. Rel., Washington, 1947.

Spencer, J. E., "Land Use in the Upland Philippines," in vol. 1 of *The Development of Upland Areas in the Far East,* Inst. Pac. Rel., New York, 1949, pp. 26–58, mimeo.

Spencer, J. E., "The Philippine Islands," in O. W. Freeman, *The Geography of the Pacific,* John Wiley & Sons, New York, 1951, 298–327.

Spencer, J. E., *Land and People in the Philippines,* Univ. of Calif. Press, Berkeley, 1952.

Stephens, R. P., "The Prospect for Social Progress in the Philippines," *Pacific Affairs, 23* (1950), 139–152.

CHAPTERS 22 AND 23, CHINA DURING FIFTY CENTURIES

Alexander, J. W., "The Prewar Population of China, Distribution and Density," *Annals, Assoc. Amer. Geog., 38* (1948), 1–5.

Andersson, J. G., "Researches into the Prehistory of the Chinese," *Bull. Museum Far East Antiq., 15* (1943), 1–304.

Andersson, J. G., "Prehistoric Sites in Honan," *Bull. Museum Far East Antiq., 19* (1947), 1–124.

Bielenstein, H., "The Census of China during the Period 2–742 A.D.," *Bull. Museum Far East Antiq., 19* (1947), 125–163.

Bodde, D., *China's First Unifier, a Study of the Ch'in Dynasty as Seen in the Life of Li Ssu, 280–208 B.C.,* Brill, Leiden, 1938.

Borchert, J. R., "A New Map of the Climates of China," *Annals, Assoc. Amer. Geog., 37* (1947), 169–176.

Buck, J. L., *Land Utilization in China,* Commercial Press, Shanghai, and Univ. of Chicago Press, 1937, 3 vols.

Chang, C. V., "Climate and Man in China," *Annals, Assoc. Amer. Geog., 26* (1936), 44–73.

Chang, C. V., *The Natural Resources of China,* Sino-Intern. Econ. Research Center, New York, 1945.

Chang, K. N., *China's Struggle for Railroad Development,* John Day, New York, 1943.

Chang, T. T., "Land Utilization in Taiwan," *Land Econ., 28* (1952), 362–368.

Chao, K. C., "Current Agrarian Reform Policies in Communist China," *Ann. Am. Acad. Pol. Soc. Sci., 277* (1951), 113–123.

Chen, C. S., "Land Utilization in Formosa," *Geog. Rev., 41* (1951), 438–456.

Chen, C. S., "The Pescadores," *Geog. Rev., 43* (1953), 77–88.

Chen, H. S., *Frontier Land Systems in Southernmost China,* Inst. Pac. Rel., New York, 1949, mimeo. Areas really located in west China.

Chi, C. T., *Key Economic Areas in Chinese History as Revealed in the Development of Public Works for Water Control,* Allen & Unwin, London, 1936.

Ch'ien, T. S., "The Role of the Military in Chinese Government," *Pacific Affairs, 21* (1948), 239–251.

Ch'ien, T. S., *The Government and Politics of China,* Harvard Univ. Press, Cambridge, 1950.

Christian, J. L., "Trans Burma Trade Routes to China," *Pacific Affairs, 13* (1940), 173–191.

"Colonial Demography, Formosa," *Population Index, 10* (1944), 147–157.

Creel, H. G., *The Birth of China,* Reynal & Hitchcock, New York, 1937.

Creel, H. G., *Studies in Early Chinese Culture,* Waverly Press, Baltimore, 1937.

Cressey, G. B., *China's Geographic Foundations,* McGraw-Hill, New York, 1934.

Dubs, H. H., "The Date of the Shang Period," *T'oung Pao, 40* (1951), 322–335.

Eberhard, W., "Lokalkulturen im Alten China," *Monumenta Serica*, Monograph No. 3, 1942, Peiping.

Eberhard, W., *A History of China*, Univ. of Calif. Press, Berkeley, 1950.

Eberhard, W., *Conquerors and Rulers, Social Forces in Medieval China*, Brill, Leiden, 1952.

Fairbank, J. K., *The United States and China*, Harvard Univ. Press, Cambridge, 1949.

Fairbank, J. K., and S. Y. Teng, "On the Ch'ing Tributary System," *Harvard J. Asiatic Studies, 6* (1941), 135–246.

Fei, H. T., and C. I. Chang, *Earthbound China, a Study of Rural Economy in Yunnan*, Univ. of Chicago Press, 1945.

Fitzgerald, C. P., *The Tower of Five Glories, a Study of the Min-Chia of Tali, Yunnan*, Cresset Press, London, 1941.

Fitzgerald, C. P., *China, A Short Cultural History*, Cresset Press, London, 1950.

Fitzgerald, C. P., *Revolution in China*, Praeger, New York, 1952.

Freyn, H., *Free China's New Deal*, Macmillan, 1943.

Ginsburg, N. S., "Ch'ing-tao; Development and Land Utilization," *Econ. Geog., 24* (1948), 181–200.

Ginsburg, N. S., "China's Railroad Network," *Geog. Rev., 41* (1951), 470–474.

Ginsburg, N. S., "China's Changing Political Geography," *Geog. Rev., 42* (1952), 102–107.

Goodrich, L. C., *A Short History of the Chinese People*, Harper, New York, 1943.

Goodrich, L. C., and C. S. Feng, "The Early Development of Firearms in China," *Isis, 36* (1946), 114–123.

Gourou, P., "The Development of Upland Areas in China," in *The Development of Upland Areas in the Far East*, vol. 1, 1949, Inst. Pac. Rel., New York, mimeo., pp. 1–25.

Grajdanzev, A. J., *Formosa Today*, Inst. Pac. Rel., New York, 1942.

Hermann, A., *Historical and Commercial Atlas of China*, Harvard Univ. Press, Cambridge, 1935.

Hermann, A., *Das Land Der Seide und Tibet im licht der Antike*, Koehler, Leipzig, 1939.

Hsiang, C. Y., "Mountain Economy in Szechuan," *Pacific Affairs, 14* (1941), 448–462.

Hu, H. Y., "A Geographical Sketch of Kiangsu Province," *Geog. Rev., 37* (1947), 609–617.

Jaffe, A. J., "A Review of the Censuses and Demographic Statistics of China," *Population Studies, 1* (1947), 308–337.

Jen, M. N., "Agricultural Landscape of Southwest China, a Study in Land Utilization," *Econ. Geog., 24* (1948), 157–169.

Keyes, F., "Urbanism and Population Distribution in China," *Am. J. Sociol., 56* (1951), 519–527.

Kracke, E. A., Jr., "Family vs. Merit in Chinese Civil Service Examinations under the Empire," *Harvard J. Asiatic Studies, 10* (1947), 103–123.

Lang, O., *Chinese Family and Society*, Yale Univ. Press, New Haven, 1946.

Latourette, K. S., *The Chinese, Their History and Culture*, Macmillan, New York, 1934, 2nd ed.

Lattimore, O., "Origins of the Great Wall of China; a Frontier Concept in Theory and Practice," *Geog. Rev., 27* (1937), 529–549.

Lattimore, O., "The Mainsprings of Asiatic Migration," in I. Bowman, *Limits of Land Settlement*, Council of Foreign Rel., New York, 1937, 119–136.

Lattimore, O., *Inner Asian Frontiers of China*, American Geog. Soc., New York, 1940.

Lattimore, O., "An Inner Asian Approach to the Historical Geography of China," *Geog. J. 110* (1948), 180–188.

Lattimore, O. and E., *China, a Short History*, Norton, New York, 1947.

Lee, S. C., "Pattern of Land Utilization and Possible Expansion of Cultivated Land in China," *J. Land Pub. Util. Econ., 23* (1947), 142–157.

Lee, S. T., "Delimitation of the Geographic Regions of China," *Annals, Assoc. Amer. Geog., 37* (1947), 155–168.

Levy, M. J., Jr., *The Family Revolution in Modern China*, Harvard Univ. Press, Cambridge, 1949.

Liang, S. Y., "The Lungshan Culture: a Prehistoric Phase of Chinese Civilization," *Proc. Sixth Pacific Sci. Congr. Pacific Sci. Assoc., 4* (1940), 69–79.

Liu, E. L., "The Ho-si Corridor," *Econ. Geog., 28* (1952), 51–56. On the piedmont oasis strip leading to central Asia.

MacNair, F. F. (Ed.), *China*, Univ. of Calif. Press, Berkeley, 1946.

Mendiola, J., "Rice Culture in Taiwan," *Philippine J. Agr., 14* (1949), 41–83.

Michael, F., *The Origin of Manchu Rule in China*, Johns Hopkins Press, Baltimore, 1942.

Moyer, R. T., "Agricultural Practices in Semi-Arid North China," *Sci. Monthly, 55* (1942), 301–316.

Moyer, R. T., "Agriculture and Foodstuffs in Taiwan," *Foreign Agr., 9* (1945), 2–12.

Pratt, J. T., *Britain and China*, Collins, London, 1944.

Read, T. T., "Economic-Geographic Aspects of China's Iron Industry," *Geog. Rev., 33* (1943), 42–55.

Report of the China-United States Agricultural Mission, Office of Foreign Agr. Rel., Washington, 1947.

Reischauer, E. O., "Notes on T'ang Dynasty Sea Routes," *Harvard J. Asiatic Studies, 5* (1940), 142–164.

Riggs, F. W., *Formosa under Chinese Nationalist Rule*, Macmillan, New York, 1952.

Rock, J. F., *The Ancient NaKhi Kingdoms of Southwest China*, Harvard Univ. Press, Cambridge, 1947, 2 vols.

Rowe, D. N., *China among the Powers*, Harcourt, Brace, New York, 1945.

Sargent, C. B., "Subsidized History, Pan Ku and the Historical Records of the Former Han Dynasty," *Far Eastern Quart., 3* (1944), 119–143. How Chinese history got written.

Scholz, H., "The Rural Settlements in the Eighteen Provinces of China," *Sinologica, 3* (1951), 37–49.

Shen, T. H., *Agricultural Resources of China*, Cornell Univ. Press, Ithaca, 1951.

Shindman, B., *Taiwan, a Geographical Appreciation*, Dept. Mines & Tech. Surveys, Ottawa, 1952.

Siguret, J., *Territoires et populations des confins du Yunnan*, Vetch, Peiping, 1937–1940, 2 vols.

Siren, O., *Gardens of China*, Ronald Press, New York, 1951.

Spencer, J. E., "Trade and Transshipment in the Yangtze Valley," *Geog. Rev., 28* (1938), 112–123.

Spencer, J. E., "Kueichow: an Internal Chinese Colony," *Pacific Affairs, 13* (1940), 162–172.

Steiner, H. A., "The Role of the Chinese Communist Party," *Ann. Am. Acad. Pol. Soc. Sci., 277* (1951), 56–66.

Swann, N. L., *Food and Money in Ancient China*, Princeton Univ. Press, 1950.

Ta Chen, *The Population of Modern China*, Univ. of Chicago Press, 1946.

Trewartha, G. T., and S. J. Yang, "Notes on Rice Growing in China," *Annals, Assoc. Amer. Geog.*, 38 (1948), 277–281.

Wang, K. P., *Controlling Factors in the Future Development of the Chinese Coal Industry*, King's Crown Press, New York, 1947.

Wang, Y. C., *Early Chinese Coinage*, Amer. Numis. Soc., New York, 1951.

Wenley, A. G., and J. A. Pope, "China," *Smithsonian Inst. Publ. 3770*, Washington, 1944.

Wiens, H. J., "The Shu Tao, or Road to Szechwan," *Geog. Rev.*, 39 (1949), 584–604.

Wilbur, C. M., "Slavery in China during the Former Han Dynasty, 206 B.C.–A.D. 25," *Field Museum Nat. History, Chicago, Anthrop. Ser.*, 34 (1943).

Winfield, G. F., *China, the Land and the People*, Sloane, New York, 1948.

Wittfogel, K. A., and C. S. Feng, *History of Chinese Society, Liao*, Macmillan, New York, 1949.

Yao, S. Y., "The Chronological and Seasonal Distribution of Floods and Droughts in Chinese History, 206 B.C.–1911 A.D.," *Harvard J. Asiatic Studies*, 6 (1941), 273–312.

Yao, S. Y., "The Geographical Distribution of Floods and Droughts in Chinese History," *Far Eastern Quart.*, 2 (1943), 357–378.

CHAPTER 24, THE INNER ASIAN FRINGE

Chang, C. Y., "Land Utilization and Settlement Possibilities in Sinkiang," *Geog. Rev.*, 39 (1949), 57–75.

Friters, G., *Outer Mongolia and Its International Position*, Johns Hopkins Press, Baltimore, 1949.

Hazard, J. W., "The Constitution of the Mongol People's Republic and Soviet Influences," *Pacific Affairs*, 21 (1948), 162–170.

Iwamura, S., "The Structure of Moslem Society in Inner Mongolia," *Far Eastern Quart.*, 8 (1948), 34–44.

Lattimore, O., "The Geographical Factor in Mongol History," *Geog. Journal*, 91 (1938), 1–20.

Lattimore, O. (Ed.), "Sinkiang Survey," *Far Eastern Survey*, 17 (March 10, 1949).

Lattimore O., and Associates, *Pivot of Asia, Sinkiang and the Inner Asian Frontiers of China and Russia*, Little Brown, Boston, 1950.

McGovern, W. M., *The Early Empires of Central Asia*, Univ. of N. Carolina Press, Chapel Hill, 1939.

McLean, N. L. D., "The New Dominion," *J. Roy. Cent. Asian Soc.*, 35 (1948), 131–143. Concerning Sinkiang.

Martin, H. D., "The Mongol Army," *J. Roy. Cent. Asian Soc.*, 33 (1943), 46–85. Organization and tactics in earlier times.

Martin, H. D., "Chenghiz Khan's First Invasion of the Chinese Empire," *J. Roy. Cent. Asian Soc.*, 33 (1943), 182–216.

Norins, M. R., *Gateway to China; Sinkiang, Frontier of the Chinese Far West*, John Day, New York, 1944.

Petech, L., *China and Tibet in the Early 18th Century; History of the Establishment of the Chinese Protectorate in Tibet*, Brill, Leiden, 1950.

Prawdin, M., *The Mongol Empire, Its Rise and Legacy*, Macmillan, New York, 1940.

Riencourt, A. de, *Roof of the World, Tibet, Key to Asia*, Rinehart, New York, 1951.

Vladimirtsov, B., *Le régime social des Mongols: le Féodalisme nomade*, Maisonneuve, Paris, 1948.

Ward, F. K., "Tibet as a Grazing Land," *Geog. J.*, 110 (1947), 60–75.

Wiens, H. J., "Geographical Limitations to Food Production in the Mongolian People's Republic," *Annals, Assoc. Amer. Geog.*, 41 (1951), 348–369.

Wu, A. K., *Turkestan Tumult*, London, Methuen, 1940.

CHAPTER 25, THE NORTH-EASTERN FRONTIER: MANCHURIA

Beal, E. G., Jr., "The 1940 Census of Manchuria," *Far Eastern Quart.*, 4 (1945), 243–262.

Ginsburg, N. S., "Manchurian Railway Development," *Far Eastern Quart.*, 8 (1949), 398–411.

Grajdanzev, A. J., "Manchuria as a Region of Colonization," *Pacific Affairs*, 19 (1946), 5–19.

Ladejinsky, W., "Agriculture in Manchuria," *Foreign Agr.*, 1 (1937), 157–182.

Lattimore, O., *The Mongols of Manchuria*, John Day, New York, 1934.

"Manchuria as a Demographic Frontier," *Pop. Index*, 11 (1945), 260–274.

Moyer, R. T., "The Agricultural Potentialities of Manchuria," *Foreign Agr.*, 8 (1944), 171–191.

Rodgers, A., "The Manchurian Iron and Steel Industry and Its Resource Base," *Geog. Rev.*, 38 (1948), 41–54.

CHAPTER 26, KOREA, THE LAND BETWEEN

Butler, P., "A Korean Survey," *Intern. Affairs*, 22 (1946), 361–375.

Grajdanzev, A. J., *Modern Korea*, John Day, 1944.

Keith, E., and E. K. R. Scott, *Old Korea*, Philosophical Library, New York, 1947.

"Korea in Transition, Demographic Aspects," *Pop. Index*, 10 (1944), 230–255.

Ladejinsky, W., "Chosen's Agriculture and Its Problems," *Foreign Agr.*, 4 (1940), 95–122.

Lautensach, H., *Korea: Eine Landeskunde auf Grund eigener Reisen und der Literatur*, Koehler, Leipzig, 1945.

Lautensach, H., *Korea, Land, Volk, Schicksal*, Koehler, Stuttgart, 1950.

Lee, H. K., *Land Utilization and Rural Economy in Korea*, Univ. of Chicago Press, 1936.

McCune, G. M., *Korea Today*, Harvard Univ. Press, Cambridge, 1950.

McCune, S., "Climatic Regions of Korea and Their Economy," *Geog. Rev.*, 31 (1941), 95–99.

McCune, S., "Physical Basis for Korean Boundaries," *Far Eastern Quart.*, 5 (1946), 272–288.

McCune, S., "Geographic Regions in Korea," *Geog. Rev.*, 39 (1949), 658–660.

McCune, S., "Utilization of Upland Areas in Korea," in vol. 2 of *The Development of Upland Areas of the Far East*, Inst. Pac. Rel., New York, 1951, mimeo., pp. 103–121.

Meade, E. G., *American Military Government in Korea*, King's Crown Press, New York, 1951.

Nelson, M. F., *Korea and the Old Orders in Eastern Asia*, Louisiana State Univ. Press, Baton Rouge, 1945.

Osgood, C., *The Koreans and Their Culture*, Ronald, New York, 1951.

Robinson, A. H., and S. McCune, "Notes on a Physiographic Diagram of Tyosen (Korea)," *Geog. Rev.*, 31 (1941), 653–658.

Taylor, G. D., *Korea, a Geographical Appreciation,* Dept. Mines & Tech. Surveys, Ottawa, 1951.

Taeuber, I. B., "The Population Potential of Postwar Korea," *Far Eastern Quart., 5* (1946), 289–307.

Zaichikov, V. T., *Geography of Korea,* translated-mimeo version without maps and other material, Inst. Pac. Rel., New York, 1952.

CHAPTERS 27 AND 28, JAPAN
AND JAPAN OF YESTERDAY,
TODAY, AND TOMORROW

Allen, G. C., *A Short Economic History of Modern Japan,* Allen & Unwin, London, 1946.

Beal, E. G., Jr., "The Population of the Prefectures and Cities of Japan in Most Recent Times," *Far Eastern Quart., 3* (1944), 313–361.

Benedict, R., *The Chrysanthemum and the Sword: Patterns of Japanese Culture,* Houghton Mifflin, Boston, 1946.

Borton, H. (Ed.), *Japan,* Cornell Univ. Press, Ithaca, 1951. Book publication of articles on Japan from 1950 *Encyclopedia Americana.*

Carus, C. D., and C. L. McNichols, *Japan, Its Resources and Industries,* Harper, New York, 1944.

Cohen, J. B., *Japan's Economy in War and Reconstruction,* Univ. of Minn. Press, Minneapolis, 1949.

Cohen, J. B., *Economic Problems of Free Japan,* Center for Intern. Studies, Princeton, 1952.

Daikufu, H., "The Early Cultures of the Island of Kyushu," *S. W. J. Anthrop., 5* (1949), 253–271.

Embree, J. F., "The Japanese," *Smithsonian Inst. Publ. 3702,* Washington, 1943.

Eyre, J. D., "Elements of Instability in the Current Japanese Land Tenure System," *Land Econ., 28* (1952), 193–202.

Feary, R. A., *The Occupation of Japan, Second Phase, 1948–1950,* Macmillan, New York, 1950.

Fisher, C. A., "The Expansion of Japan, a Study in Oriental Geopolitics," *Geog. J., 115* (1950), 1–19, 179–193.

Fisher, G. M., "Main Drives behind Japanese National Policies," *Pacific Affairs, 13* (1940), 381–392.

Grad, A. J., "Land Reform in Japan," *Pacific Affairs, 21* (1948), 115–135.

Grad, A. J., *Land and Peasant in Japan,* Inst. Pac. Rel., New York, 1952, mimeo.

Groot, G. J., *The Prehistory of Japan,* Columbia Univ. Press, New York, 1951.

Hacker, W. R., "The Kuril and Ryukyu Islands," in O. W. Freeman, *Geography of the Pacific,* John Wiley & Sons, New York, 1951, pp. 495–521.

Hall, R. B., "Tokaido, Road and Region," *Geog. Rev., 27* (1937), 353–377.

Haring, D. G., (Ed.) *Japan's Prospect,* Harvard Univ. Press, Cambridge, 1946.

Hewes, L. I., Jr., "On the Current Readjustment in Japanese Land Tenure," *Land Econ., 25* (1949), 246–259.

James, D. H., *The Rise and Fall of the Japanese Empire,* Allen & Unwin, London; Macmillan, New York, 1951.

Johnson, B. F., "Agricultural Productivity and Economic Development in Japan," *J. Pol. Econ., 59* (1951), 498–513.

Kraus, B. S., "An Outline of Japan's Prehistoric Cultures," *Am. Antiq., 18* (1953), 12–16.

Kuno, Y. S., *Japanese Expansion on the Asiatic Continent,* Univ. of Calif. Press, Berkeley, 2 vols., 1937–1940.

Ladejinsky, W., "Land Reform Progress in Japan," *Foreign Agr., 13* (1949), 38–41.

Leggett, T. P., "Tokaido—Japan's Ancient Highway," *Geog. Mag., 23* (1950), 181–188.

Leonard, W. H., "Principal Field Crops in Japan," *Foreign Agr., 12* (1948), 174–180.

Martin, E. M., *The Allied Occupation of Japan,* Inst. Pac. Rel., New York, 1948.

Mecking, L., *Japan, Meerbestimmtes Land,* Kosmos Verlag, Stuttgart, 1951.

Newman, M. T., and R. L. Eng, "The Ryukyu People, a Cultural Appraisal," *Ann. Rep. Smithsonian Inst. for 1947,* 379–405.

Norman, E. H., *Japan's Emergence as a Modern State,* Inst. Pac. Rel., New York, 1940.

Norman, E. H., "Soldier and Peasant in Japan: The Origins of Conscription," *Pacific Affairs, 16* (1943), 47–64, 149–165.

Pelzer, K. J., "Japanese Migration and Colonization," in I. Bowman, *Limits of Land Settlement,* Council on Foreign Relations, New York, 1937, pp. 155–194.

Rager, F. A., "Japanese Emigration and Japan's 'Population Pressure'," *Pacific Affairs, 14* (1941), 300–321.

Raper, A. F., "Some Recent Changes in Japanese Village Life," *Rural Sociol., 16* (1951), 3–16.

Reischauer, E. O., *Japan, Past and Present,* Knopf, New York, 1947.

Reischauer, R. K., *Early Japanese History,* Princeton Univ. Press, 1937.

Sansom, G. B., *Japan, a Short Cultural History,* Appleton-Century, New York, 1943.

Schumpeter, E. B., et al., *The Industrialization of Japan and Manchukuo,* 1930–1940, Macmillan, New York, 1940.

Smith, H. F., "Food Controls in Occupied Japan," *Agr. Hist., 23* (1949), 220–223.

Smith, G. H., D. Good, and S. McCune, *Japan, a Geographical Review,* Amer. Geog. Soc., New York, 1943.

Steiner, J. F., "Social Change in Japan," *Sociol. & Social Research, 31* (1946), 3–8.

Steiner, P. E., "Okinawa and Its People," *Sci. Monthly, 24* (1947), 233–241, 306–312.

Stewart, J. R., *Japan's Textile Industry,* Inst. Pac. Rel., New York, 1949.

Taeuber, I. B., "Japan's Increasing People: Facts, Problems, and Policies," *Pacific Affairs, 23* (1950), 271–293.

Taeuber, I. B., "Family, Migration, and Industrialization in Japan," *Am. Sociol. Rev., 16* (1951), 149–157.

Taeuber, I. B., "Population Growth and Economic Development in Japan," *J. Econ. Hist., 11* (1951), 417–428.

Taeuber, I. B., and F. W. Notestein, "The Changing Fertility of the Japanese," *Pop. Studies, 1* (1947), 2–28.

Thompson, W. S., "Future Readjustments of Population to Resources in Japan," *Milbank Mem. Fund Quart., 28* (1950), 191–202.

Trewartha, G. T., *Japan, a Physical, Cultural, and Regional Geography,* Univ. of Wisconsin Press, Madison, 1945.

Trewartha, G. T., "Utilization of Upland Areas of Japan," in vol. 1 of *The Development of Upland Areas of the Far East,* Inst. Pac. Rel., New York, 1949, mimeo., pp. 59–82.

Trewartha, G. T., "Land Reform and Land Reclamation in Japan," *Geog. Rev., 40* (1950), 376–396.

Williamson, M. B., "Land Reform in Japan," *J. Farm Econ., 33* (1951), 169–176.

Yanaga, C., *Japan Since Perry,* McGraw-Hill, New York, 1949.

Place Name Index

Subject Index

The statistical appendix has not been indexed except as to paging of the abstract for each political unit.

1

2

3

4

5

1. Hindu Indian woman of northern India
2. Moslem Indian (Borah) man of Bombay
3. Tibetan man of southern Tibet
4. Karen hillman of southern, eastern Burma
5. White Miao woman of Tonking hill country, Indochina